Global Health Law & Policy

Global Health Law & Policy

Ensuring Justice for a Healthier World

Edited by

LAWRENCE O. GOSTIN

and

BENJAMIN MASON MEIER

Oxford University Press is a department of the University of Oxford. It furthers the University's objective of excellence in research, scholarship, and education by publishing worldwide. Oxford is a registered trade mark of Oxford University Press in the UK and certain other countries.

Published in the United States of America by Oxford University Press
198 Madison Avenue, New York, NY 10016, United States of America.

© Oxford University Press 2023

All rights reserved. No part of this publication may be reproduced, stored in a retrieval system, or transmitted, in any form or by any means, without the prior permission in writing of Oxford University Press, or as expressly permitted by law, by license, or under terms agreed with the appropriate reproduction rights organization. Inquiries concerning reproduction outside the scope of the above should be sent to the Rights Department, Oxford University Press, at the address above.

You must not circulate this work in any other form
and you must impose this same condition on any acquirer.

Library of Congress Cataloging-in-Publication Data
Names: Gostin, Lawrence O. (Lawrence Ogalthorpe), editor. |
Meier, Benjamin Mason, editor.
Title: Global health law and policy : ensuring justice for a healthier world /
Lawrence O. Gostin, Benjamin Mason Meier.
Description: New York : Oxford University Press, 2023. |
Includes bibliographical references and index.
Identifiers: LCCN 2023033259 | ISBN 9780197687710 (hardback) |
ISBN 9780197687734 (epub) | ISBN 9780197687727 (updf) |
ISBN 9780197687741 (online)
Subjects: LCSH: Public health laws. | Right to health.
Classification: LCC K3570.G53 2023 | DDC 344.03/21—dc23/eng/20230802
LC record available at https://lccn.loc.gov/2023033259

DOI: 10.1093/law/9780197687710.001.0001

Printed by Integrated Books International, United States of America

Note to Readers
This publication is designed to provide accurate and authoritative information in regard to the subject matter covered. It is based upon sources believed to be accurate and reliable and is intended to be current as of the time it was written. It is sold with the understanding that the publisher is not engaged in rendering legal, accounting, or other professional services. If legal advice or other expert assistance is required, the services of a competent professional person should be sought. Also, to confirm that the information has not been affected or changed by recent developments, traditional legal research techniques should be used, including checking primary sources where appropriate.

(Based on the Declaration of Principles jointly adopted by a Committee of the American Bar Association and a Committee of Publishers and Associations.)

You may order this or any other Oxford University Press publication
by visiting the Oxford University Press website at www.oup.com.

For those we lost in the COVID-19 pandemic

May their memories inspire the next generation to build a healthier world . . .

Contents

Foreword: *The Law as a Fundamental Determinant of Global Health*   xi
   Dr. Tedros Adhanom Ghebreyesus
Preface: *A Field Born of Trying Times*   xv
List of Contributors   xix

Introduction: Foundations of Global Health Law & Policy   1
   Lawrence O. Gostin and Benjamin Mason Meier

I. FRAMEWORKS & INSTITUTIONS OF GLOBAL HEALTH: SHIFTING ACTORS & NORMS IN A GLOBALIZING WORLD

1. Global Health: Global Determinants, Global Governance, and Global Law   15
   Lawrence O. Gostin and Alexandra Finch

2. Global Health Law: Legal Frameworks to Advance Global Health   39
   Sharifah Sekalala and Roojin Habibi

3. Global Health Landscape: The Proliferating Actors Influencing Global Health Governance   65
   Benjamin Mason Meier and Matiangai Sirleaf

4. Global Health Norms: Human Rights, Equity, and Social Justice in Global Health   91
   Judith Bueno de Mesquita and Lisa Forman

5. Global Health Diplomacy: The Process of Developing Global Health Law and Policy   119
   Gian Luca Burci and Björn Kümmel

II. GLOBAL HEALTH GOVERNANCE FOR DISEASE PREVENTION & HEALTH PROMOTION

6. Infectious Disease: Preventing, Detecting, and Responding to Pandemic Threats under International Law   147
   Pedro A. Villarreal and Lauren Tonti

7. Non-Communicable Disease: Regulating Commercial
   Determinants Underlying Health   175
   Roger Magnusson and Lawrence O. Gostin

8. Mental Health: From Institutions to Community Inclusion   205
   Priscila Rodríguez and Eric Rosenthal

9. Environmental Health: Regulating Clean Air and Water as
   Underlying Determinants of Health   231
   Marlies Hesselman and Benjamin Mason Meier

III. ECONOMIC INSTITUTIONS, CORPORATE REGULATION & GLOBAL HEALTH FUNDING

10. Sustainable Development: The 2030 Agenda and Its
    Implications for Global Health Law   259
    Stéphanie Dagron and Jennifer Hasselgård-Rowe

11. Economic Development Policy: Poverty Alleviation for
    Public Health Advancement   285
    Diane A. Desierto and Erica Patterson

12. International Trade Governance: Free Trade and Intellectual
    Property Threaten Public Health   311
    Lisa Forman, Katrina Perehudoff, and Chuan-Feng Wu

13. Commercial Determinants of Health: Corporate Social
    Responsibility as Smokescreen or Global Health Policy?   339
    Roojin Habibi and Thana C. de Campos-Rudinsky

14. Global Health Funding Agencies: Developing
    New Institutions to Finance Health Needs   365
    Sam Halabi and Lawrence O. Gostin

IV. INTERNATIONAL LEGAL EFFORTS TO ADDRESS RISING HEALTH THREATS

15. Antimicrobial Resistance: Collective Action to Support
    Shared Global Resources   395
    Isaac Weldon and Steven J. Hoffman

16. Pathogen Sharing: Balancing Access to Pathogen
    Samples with Equitable Access to Medicines   423
    Mark Eccleston-Turner and Michelle Rourke

17. Sexual and Reproductive Health and Rights: Advancing Human
    Rights to Protect Bodily Autonomy and Sexuality   447
    Aziza Ahmed and Terry McGovern

18. Health in Conflict: International Humanitarian Law as Global
    Health Policy   473
    Jocelyn Getgen Kestenbaum and Benjamin Mason Meier

19. Climate Change: A Cataclysmic Health Threat Requiring
    Global Action   501
    Alexandra Phelan and Kim van Daalen

20. Universal Health Coverage: Whole of Government Approaches
    to Determinants of Health   525
    Lawrence O. Gostin and Benjamin Mason Meier

Afterword: Foundational Information for a New Generation   551
    Steven Solomon
Index   555

Foreword: The Law as a Fundamental Determinant of Global Health

Dr. Tedros Adhanom Ghebreyesus

In 1948, as nations sought to build a new world order in the aftermath of World War II, they adopted a foundational instrument of global health law: the Constitution of the World Health Organization. In its unprecedented preambular declaration, the Constitution affirmed that "the enjoyment of the highest attainable standard of health is one of the fundamental rights of every human being without distinction of race, religion, political belief, economic or social condition." In the decades since, global health law and policy have become crucial to addressing major health threats in a rapidly globalizing world, including infectious diseases, non-communicable diseases, injuries, and mental health.

Having long championed the importance of law in global health, I congratulate Professors Lawrence Gostin and Benjamin Meier for this groundbreaking book on *Global Health Law & Policy*, bringing together leading scholars in the Global Health Law Consortium to provide an academic foundation for the next generation of global health leaders.

Global health law, based on the best available evidence, can promote healthy behaviors, regulate hazardous activities, and assure the safety and effectiveness of vaccines, pharmaceuticals, and other medical products. These legal instruments can also shape the underlying social, behavioral, and economic determinants of health. Appropriate law reforms can structure affordable, accessible, and equitable health systems that promote universal health coverage (UHC), providing access to high-quality, affordable health services while ensuring financial protection against potentially impoverishing out-of-pocket expenses.

During my time as Minister of Health in Ethiopia, we made significant changes to laws that increased access to health services and underlying determinants of health for millions of people. These domestic reforms gave me a deep understanding of the importance of global health governance in supporting national health policy—and have informed my work in the World Health Organization (WHO) to advance global health law and policy with WHO's Member States in the World Health Assembly.

Global health law and policy have always been central to WHO's mission and mandate. The WHO Constitution provides the organization with expansive authority to negotiate and codify international treaties, regulations, and recommendations, which WHO has used to develop international instruments to encourage, and at times to bind, states to take action to reduce threats common to all.

WHO's first legal instrument was the International Health Regulations (IHR), which provide the legal foundation for international efforts to prevent, detect, and respond to potential public health emergencies of international concern. Under the IHR, WHO has maintained its principal role in coordinating international cooperation in infectious disease control. Last revised in 2005, the IHR have established a global surveillance and reporting system for infectious disease control and set national minimum standards to prepare for, and respond to, infectious disease outbreaks—balancing health with international travel, trade, and human rights.

Beyond the IHR, WHO Member States have long been reluctant to use WHO's legal authority to adopt conventions or agreements. The most notable exception is the adoption in 2003 of the Framework Convention on Tobacco Control (FCTC), with WHO Member States developing a coordinated response to tobacco under international law. The FCTC sets out specific legal obligations in reducing the supply of and demand for tobacco, providing a crucial model for employing global health law to respond to new health threats.

The COVID-19 pandemic has revealed limitations in the global health architecture. Despite an imperative to come together in facing a common threat, including under the IHR, compliance with a range of global health obligations remains a challenge. International assistance and genuine collaboration to build resilient public health capacities and ensure equity continue to be lacking. The pandemic has served as a stark reminder of the importance of global law for global solidarity.

The international community must learn crucial lessons from the COVID-19 response to reform and rebuild key global norms and institutions. In providing a new legal foundation for global health governance, the World Health Assembly has initiated a process for global health law reforms—through both amendments of the IHR and a new, legally binding WHO convention or agreement on pandemic preparedness and response. The outcome of these international negotiations will have significant implications for the future of global health.

Global health challenges have changed drastically since WHO's founding, from rapid travel and mass migrations to zoonotic spillovers and climate change. Yet, if globalization has presented challenges to disease prevention and health promotion, global law and good governance offer the promise of bridging national boundaries to advance global norms and alleviate health inequities. Safeguarding public health requires cooperation and shared responsibilities among state and non-state actors, which can only be fostered through global health law.

Still, there remain formidable challenges facing global health law. Financial constraints and unsustainable debt threaten gains in health, with funding cuts affecting domestic health systems, international organizations, and key populations. Skepticism toward science and loss of public trust are undermining crucial public health interventions such as vaccinations. Restrictions on civil society and political freedoms are subverting social participation and universal rights. Global threats such as environmental degradation, antimicrobial resistance, and armed conflict are exacerbating divisions within and across nations.

In preparing the next generation to respond to these challenges, *Global Health Law & Policy* draws from the history of the field to examine how the law can be an effective tool to advance global health. Looking beyond the health sector, this foundational text explains how we must meet new health challenges through governance across a range of sectors. Such a comprehensive view of global governance for health will be necessary to prepare today's students for tomorrow's challenges.

I am confident this text will serve as an essential foundation for these students—our future leaders—to make the right to health a reality and advance global health with justice.

Dr. Tedros Adhanom Ghebreyesus
Director-General, World Health Organization

Preface: A Field Born of Trying Times

Global health faces an existential crisis. The COVID-19 pandemic has shaken the foundations of public health and revealed the importance of global governance. Where no country acting alone can respond effectively to the health threats of a globalizing world, global governance has become necessary to coordinate the global health response. Yet, amid unprecedented global health challenges, national governments have rejected public health science, violated human rights, and undermined global solidarity. It will be crucial to reform global health governance to prepare for future global health threats, but the world remains divided in confronting common threats through global action. These uncertain times for global health call for the advancement of global health law.

Global health law encompasses the law and policy frameworks that apply to the new public health threats, non-state actors, and regulatory instruments that structure global health. These legal frameworks, placing public health obligations on the global community of state and non-state actors, facilitate social justice in global health through global institutions. Looking beyond the scope of international legal instruments between national governments, global health law extends to an encompassing set of global health determinants through the obligations of state and non-state actors, structuring new forms of global governance responsive to the major health threats of a globalizing world and establishing the normative frameworks necessary to realize global health with justice.

The modern foundations of global health arose from the ashes of crisis. The United Nations (UN) was formed out of the ruins of World War II, bringing nations together to address collective threats through international action. Giving rise to a new system of international governance, the UN Charter called for the establishment of an international health organization, the World Health Organization (WHO), which has evolved alongside other UN institutions to shape global health law and policy over the past 75 years. The COVID-19 pandemic has challenged this international system, threatening the global solidarity necessary to establish global governance for health. The world now approaches a pivotal crossroads in the global governance response, with crucial global health law reforms being undertaken simultaneously amid this ongoing crisis.

Following from these sweeping reforms, there is a need to prepare a new generation to ensure justice for a healthier world, raising an imperative for a foundational text to support students and scholars to address the global health challenges of the future through global health law and policy.

Global health law offers the promise of bridging national boundaries to alleviate global inequities. Arising out of international health law—which narrowly focuses on obligations among states—the academic field of global health law seeks to address a new landscape for global health in a rapidly globalizing world, including the rise of new actors in the global health landscape and new threats beyond the reach of the state. Global health law and policy thus encompass the changing global landscape, norms, and governance necessary to respond to the health challenges of the 21st century. The rapidly expanding literature in the field has fostered a generation of thought leaders in global health law, and the collaborative efforts of these scholars come together in this volume.

Recognizing limitations in legal authority for global health, twenty faculty came together in April 2019 to form the Global Health Law Consortium, bringing together their collective expertise to advance the academic field of global health law; provide authoritative interpretations of legal instruments in global health; and facilitate collaborative global health law research projects. The work of the Consortium would become crucial as the world sought to come together in an unprecedented pandemic response. Through these challenging years, policymakers have looked to the Consortium's academic research to structure the response to COVID-19—and to consider future legal standards in global health governance. We now look to the future of our field. To support the next generation of the field, scholars in the Consortium saw the need to develop this foundational text.

Given the expansive growth of the field, it was necessary to bring together a wide range of the field's leading scholars to develop its seminal text, working across the Global Health Law Consortium and complemented by a larger set of global health scholars throughout the world. The authors who contributed to this edited volume represent the academic leaders in their respective sub-fields, with this volume drawing on their combined expertise to provide a holistic survey of the field. As scholarship on global health law and policy has expanded, over the past decade and especially through the COVID-19 response, these contributors provide a comprehensive introduction to global health law—working together to advance law and policy to realize the highest attainable standard of health.

Global Health Law & Policy seeks to define the academic field of global health law, explore its major doctrinal boundaries, establish its relationship with global health governance, and look into some of its enduring controversies. This volume is organized in four main sections, devoted to:

I. Explaining the conceptual frameworks and governance institutions that define the field—introducing the reader to: the evolving nature of global health and global governance, the encompassing scope of global health law, the expanding actors in the global health landscape, the norms that structure global health efforts, and the diplomatic processes by which global health law and policy are developed.
II. Applying global health governance to disease prevention and health promotion—providing an understanding of the divergent law and policy approaches taken in global health governance to respond to threats from: the spread of infectious disease, the commercial products that underlie non-communicable disease, the human rights violations undermining mental health policy, and the environmental health challenges that have structured a "One Health" approach.
III. Examining economic institutions that influence global health—exploring poverty as a fundamental underlying determinant of health and looking to development as a means to improve public health through: the adoption of the Sustainable Development Goals, the evolution of economic development policy, the responses to international trade law, the advancement of corporate social responsibility, and the establishment of global health funding agencies.
IV. Analyzing international legal efforts to address the rising health threats of a rapidly globalizing world—recognizing efforts in global governance to: frame collective action to address antimicrobial resistance, ensure pathogen sharing in exchange for access to medicines, safeguard sexual and reproductive health and rights, implement international humanitarian law in conflicts and emergencies, mitigate and adapt to the health threats of climate change, and promote universal health coverage.

These sections are intended to be read sequentially, with each chapter building from the one before it while adding new understanding of the field. This volume is thus intended to be read as a single text, rather than a series of independent chapters, providing a complete foundational education across the field of global health law. As an educational text, the contributing authors have followed a consistent structure for their respective chapters to ensure coherence across the volume. With each chapter reviewing the historical evolution, current state, and the forward-looking areas of a distinct sub-field, every chapter includes three case studies—to complement the theoretical analysis of the chapters by highlighting the practical application of global health law. This volume can thus provide a basis for teaching, and to facilitate this pedagogical use, each chapter is followed by questions for consideration, prompting areas for further study or classroom discussion. Upon completion of this theoretical and practical examination of global health law and policy, it is our hope that readers will have acquired a thorough understanding of the social, economic, cultural, legal, and political processes by which global health law and policy frame efforts to realize global health objectives.

We remain immensely thankful for those who supported the development of this foundational text for the field. As editors, we greatly appreciate the groundbreaking contributors to this volume, who recognized the need for a foundational text and employed their interdisciplinary expertise to explain the areas of the field they know best. Developing this volume has required not only the substantive expertise of scholars in the field but also the administrative assistance of students at our respective universities. We remain inspired by the dedicated efforts of Mercy Adekola, Chris Burch, Taylor Corpening, Ryan Doerzbacher, Eric Friedman, Quintin Gay, Hanna Huffstetler, Erin Jones, Ashley Lim, Kerstan Nealy, Neha Saggi, Sonam Shah, Rishabh Sud, and Sarah Wetter, whose work was crucial to developing our own research, reviewing the contributing chapters, and compiling the complete volume. It is our hope that these early experiences in the field will provide a foundation for their promising careers. Finally, we are grateful to Oxford University Press, who have now worked with us on three separate volumes to frame three distinct fields at the intersection of international law and global health. Our publishers have long seen the value of this interdisciplinary scholarship, and we continue to appreciate their faith in our vision for new fields of study to advance health in a globalizing world.

Drawing from the steadfast efforts of our contributing authors throughout the world, research assistants at Georgetown University and the University of North Carolina at Chapel Hill, and editors at Oxford University Press, *Global Health Law & Policy* reflects the dramatic development of the field—highlighting the successes of legal advancements, the challenges of the 21st century, and the resilience of global governance. We look to this book in providing a foundation for students of global health law and policy. *Global Health Law & Policy* will be widely used in policy contexts, health advocacy, and classroom teaching across schools of law, public health, global studies, and public policy, laying an academic foundation for the future of the field. In supporting the continuing struggle to uphold law in global health in these trying times, we hope that this academic text for the field will prove essential for this next generation—who hold the power to build a healthier world.

List of Contributors

Aziza Ahmed is the R. Gordon Butler Scholar in International Law at the Boston University School of Law and the Co-Director of the BU Law Program in Reproductive Justice. Her scholarship examines the intersection of law, politics, and science in the fields of constitutional law, criminal law, health law, and family law.

Judith Bueno de Mesquita is the Co-Deputy Director of the Human Rights Centre and a Senior Lecturer in International Human Rights Law at Essex Law School and Human Rights Centre at the University of Essex, United Kingdom. Her research and teaching focus on global health, development, and human rights.

Gian Luca Burci is an Adjunct Professor of International Law at the Geneva Graduate Institute of International and Development Studies and an Academic Advisor of the Global Health Centre of the Institute. As the former Legal Counsel of the World Health Organization, his research focuses on global health law and governance as well as the law and practice of international organizations.

Stéphanie Dagron is a professor of international law at the medical and the law faculties of the University of Geneva. She additionally practices international law in her work as a member of the WHO Research Ethics Committee and of the Swiss National Advisory Commission on Biomedical Ethics.

Thana C. de Campos-Rudinsky is an Associate Professor at Pontifical Catholic University of Chile and a research associate at the Von Huguel Institute, University of Cambridge. She is the author of *Global Health Crisis: Ethical Responsibilities* (Cambridge 2017) and directs the research program on Dignity and Equity in Women's Health at the UNESCO Chair in Bioethics and Human Rights.

Diane A. Desierto is a tenured Professor of Law and Global Affairs at both the Notre Dame Law School and the Keough School of Global Affairs, University of Notre Dame. She serves as the Notre Dame Law School's Faculty Director for the LLM in International Human Rights Law and the Founding Director of its Global Human Rights Clinic.

Mark Eccleston-Turner is a Senior Lecturer in Global Health Law at King's College London, and an Academic Fellow at the Honourable Society of the Middle Temple. His research addresses the field of international law and infectious diseases. He is a Fellow of the Royal Society of the Arts in recognition of his work on access to vaccines.

Alexandra Finch is an Associate at the O'Neill Institute for National and Global Health Law and an Adjunct Professor of Law at Georgetown University Law Center. She has degrees from the University of Sydney and previously worked as a solicitor advising on the regulation of therapeutic goods in Australia. Her research and teaching focuses on global health law and policy.

Lisa Forman is an Associate Professor and Canada Research Chair in Human Rights and Global Health Equity at the Dalla Lana School of Public Health at the University of Toronto. Her work focuses on the right to health in international law and its contributions to advancing health equity, including in relation to access to medicines, universal health coverage, and pandemic responses.

Jocelyn Getgen Kestenbaum is a Professor of Law at the Benjamin N. Cardozo School of Law, where she directs the Benjamin B. Ferencz Human Rights and Atrocity Prevention Clinic and the Cardozo Law Institute in Holocaust and Human Rights. Her scholarship, teaching, and practice focuses on international law and atrocity prevention.

Lawrence O. Gostin is a University Professor (Georgetown University's highest academic rank), Founding O'Neill Chair in Global Health Law, and Director of the O'Neill Institute for National and Global Health Law. In supporting global health law, he is the Director of the World Health Organization Collaborating Center on Public Health Law & Human Rights and serves on expert WHO advisory committees.

Roojin Habibi is an Assistant Professor at the Faculty of Law, University of Ottawa, and a Research Fellow of the Global Strategy Lab in Canada. Her research and teaching focus on health law (including global health law), international law, and human rights. In 2022, she was appointed to WHO's Review Committee on amendments to the International Health Regulations (2005).

Sam Halabi is the Co-Director of the Center for Transformational Health Law at the O'Neill Institute for National and Global Health Law and a Professor at the Georgetown University School of Health. His most recent volume, *Borders, Boundaries, and Pandemics*, is forthcoming from Routledge.

Jennifer Hasselgård-Rowe is a lecturer and researcher at the Institute of Global Health at the Faculty of Medicine of the University of Geneva and a Policy Analyst at the Global Commission on Drug Policy. Her research focuses on human rights law, drug policy, and global health.

Marlies Hesselman is an Assistant Professor in Public International Law at the Faculty of Law, University of Groningen and the current Chair of the Groningen Center for Health Law. Her teaching and publications intersect at the areas of environmental health and international human rights law, international environmental law, international climate law, access to energy, and just transition.

Steven J. Hoffman is the Director of the Global Strategy Lab, Dahdaleh Distinguished Chair in Global Governance & Legal Epidemiology, and Professor of Global Health, Law, and Political Science, York University. His research leverages various methodological approaches to craft global strategies that better address transnational health threats and social inequalities.

Björn Kümmel is the Deputy Head of Unit for Global Health in the German Federal Ministry of Health. He covers the World Health Organization (WHO) with a specific focus on strengthening WHO's role in global health governance. He has served as the German representative to the Executive Board of WHO; Chair of the Programme, Budget and Administration Committee of WHO; and Vice-Chair of the WHO Executive Board—and led the work on WHO financing as Chair of the WHO Working Group on Sustainable Financing.

Roger Magnusson is a Professor of Health Law & Governance at Sydney Law School, The University of Sydney. He was Co-Chair of the Working Group on Implementation, Monitoring and Accountability for WHO's Commission on Ending Childhood Obesity and was principal author of the WHO report *Advancing the Right to Health: The Vital Role of Law* (2017).

Terry McGovern is a Professor and Senior Associate Dean for Academic and Student Affairs at the City University of New York Graduate School of Public Health and Health Policy. Previously, she served as Chair of the Heilbrunn Department of Population and Family Health at the Columbia University Mailman School of Public Health. Her research focuses on health and human rights, sexual and reproductive health and rights, and gender and environmental justice.

Benjamin Mason Meier is a Professor of Global Health Policy at the University of North Carolina at Chapel Hill, a Senior Scholar at Georgetown University's O'Neill Institute for National and Global Health Law, and the Chair of the Global Health Law Consortium. His interdisciplinary research—at the intersection global health, international law, and public policy—examines rights-based approaches to health.

Erica M. Patterson is a 2024 Georgetown University Law Center National and Global Health Law LLM candidate and a Georgetown University Law Center Global Health Law Scholar. She recently graduated from Notre Dame Law School with a Juris Doctorate in May 2023.

Katrina Perehudoff is a health scientist and legal scholar with over a decade of experience in pharmaceutical policy, intellectual property, human rights, and drug regulation. She is an assistant professor and Co-Director of the University of Amsterdam's Law Centre for Health and Life. Her research focuses on global and European aspects of pharmaceutical law and access to medicines policy.

Alexandra Phelan is an Associate Professor at the Bloomberg School of Public Health at Johns Hopkins University and a Senior Scholar at the Johns Hopkins Center for Health Security. Her work focuses on international health law at the intersection of infectious diseases and global impact events, advising numerous international organizations in responses to infectious diseases and potential pandemic threats.

Priscila Rodríguez is the Associate Director for Disability Rights International (DRI), where she has led DRI's investigations, published reports, and filed cases at the regional and international level to advance the rights of persons with disabilities. She previously served as a mental health specialist for the United Nations High Commissioner for Human Rights.

Eric Rosenthal is the founder and Executive Director of Disability Rights International. Since 1993, he has conducted human rights investigations and trained disability rights activists in more than forty countries, participated in drafting the UN Convention on the Rights of Persons with Disabilities, and held the Father Robert Drinan Chair in International Human Rights Law at Georgetown University Law Center.

Michelle Rourke is a Griffith University Postdoctoral Research Fellow at the Law Futures Centre in Brisbane, Australia. She researches international Access and Benefit Sharing laws with a focus on pathogens, genetic sequence data, and synthetic biology.

Sharifah Sekalala is a Professor of Global Health Law at the University of Warwick. Addressing global health crises and the impact of law in curbing inequalities, her research is focused primarily on Sub Saharan Africa. She is currently the Principal Investigator on a Wellcome-Trust-funded project on digital health apps in Sub-Saharan Africa.

Matiangai Sirleaf is the Nathan Patz Professor of Law at the University of Maryland School of Law and a professor in the Department of Epidemiology and Public Health at the University of Maryland School of Medicine. She serves as executive editor at *Just Security* and is a member of the board of editors for the *American Journal of International Law*.

Steven Solomon is the Principal Legal Officer at the World Health Organization in Geneva, Switzerland, where he leads the Legal Office's team on International, Constitutional and Global Health Law matters. His work focuses on governance, and international and global health law matters, with a particular emphasis recently on matters related to international and institutional aspects of the COVID-19 response.

Lauren Tonti is a researcher and doctoral candidate at the Max Planck Institute for Social Law & Social Policy. Having earned degrees in both law and public health, her research focuses on a variety of topics in the fields of public health law, legal epidemiology, global health law, and the social determinants of health.

Pedro A. Villarreal is a researcher at both the German Institute for International and Security Affairs and the Max Planck Institute for Comparative Public Law and International Law in Germany. He has a PhD in Law from the National Autonomous University of Mexico.

Isaac Weldon is a PhD Candidate in the Department of Politics and a Dahdaleh Research Fellow at the Global Strategy Lab, York University, Toronto, Canada. His research explores novel ideas, innovative strategies, and transformative approaches for addressing global and planetary health challenges.

Chuan-Feng Wu is an associate research professor at Institutum Iurisprudentiae, Academia Sinica and the director of the Information Law Center. He also serves as a joint appointment assistant professor at the College of Public Health, National Taiwan University. His specialty fields of study include public health law and ethics, healthcare distributive justice, international human rights law, and information law.

Introduction

Foundations of Global Health Law & Policy

Lawrence O. Gostin and Benjamin Mason Meier

Globalization has unleashed new health threats, connecting societies in shared vulnerability to common challenges, including infectious disease, non-communicable disease, environmental pollution, injuries, and inequitable poverty. The COVID-19 pandemic has made clear the cataclysmic health threats of a rapidly globalizing world and the limitations of domestic law and policy in addressing economic, social, and political determinants of health. No country acting on its own can stem major health hazards that go well beyond national borders. Where national laws cannot reach threats beyond national borders, global law is necessary to promote health and justice. If globalization has presented global challenges to disease prevention and health promotion, global health law offers the promise of bridging national boundaries to promote public health and reduce health inequities.

Global health law seeks to establish strong and innovative governance to respond to the major health challenges of the 21st century. Law and policy have become crucial to the advancement of global health. Global health law encompasses the study and practice of international law—both "hard" law treaties that bind states and "soft" law instruments that shape norms, processes, and institutions to realize the highest attainable standard of physical and mental health throughout the world. As an academic field of study, global health law has become a basis to describe new legal and policy frameworks that apply to the new set of public health threats, non-state actors, and regulatory instruments that structure global health. Ensuring justice in global health, the field of global health law is infused with norms of equity, social justice, and human rights, striving for collective action and mutual solidarity throughout the world, with particular concern for the world's most disadvantaged people. This burgeoning field requires a foundational text.

This chapter introduces the central importance of global health law to advance global health with justice, providing a foundation for this book by laying out the role of law and policy in global health. Framing the need for law in global health, Part I examines public health at the global level, raising an imperative for global health law. Part II defines global health law as encompassing binding international law, "soft" law, and global health policy. These law and policy efforts have evolved rapidly in the 21st century, with Part III examining how contemporary challenges in a globalizing world have given rise to the academic field of global health law. Part IV describes the academic basis for the field and outlines the structure of this foundational text, delineating the chapters that describe the institutions of global health law, the role of global health governance, the influence of global economic governance, and the challenges amid rising health threats. This introduction concludes that despite the dramatic development of the field of global health law, the world faces new challenges that threaten to divide the world when solidarity is needed most, with ongoing reforms that will shape global health for generations to come.

I. Law as a Foundation of Global Health

Globalization has tightened connections between nations and peoples, giving rise to shared health threats across the world. These common challenges call for collective action from the global community (Frenk and Moon 2013). In responding to these threats, the modern public health order embraces a more holistic approach to health, now considering socioeconomic conditions, social justice, and preventative measures for health promotion. This framing requires an examination of "the way society organizes itself, produces and distributes wealth, and interacts with the natural environment"—implicating "collective responsibility for unhealthy behavior" (Gostin, Burris, and Lazzarini 1999, 64). Such an expansive focus on the public health threats of a globalizing world allows for consideration of an encompassing set of global health challenges, including ecosystem threats, food availability, democratic governance, and realization of human rights. Shifting away from "international health," a colonial practice that historically focused on controlling infectious disease across national borders, global health looks across health threats to focus on achieving equity in health worldwide (Koplan et al. 2009).

The field of global health has come to encompass the study, research, and practice of public health across the globe. Elevating the central importance of public health, global health examines global determinants of health, recognizing the interconnections between global contexts and local conditions. In the practice of global health, however, a debate has endured on the importance and relative priority of vertical and horizontal interventions:

- Vertical health interventions often look to narrow, disease specific, and specialized approaches to individual health threats (Frenk and Gómez-Dantes 2017).

- Horizontal approaches look across health threats to implement health system interventions that address a wide range of determinants of health (Kickbusch and Buckett 2010).

Vertical health approaches have long faced critiques in public health for seeking to address health threats in isolation, neglecting to address the underlying determinants that lead to the spread of disease and the impediments to well-being across populations (Frenk, Gómez-Dantés, and Moon 2014). Looking to horizontal approaches to address public health, global health has come to span a broad approach to determinants of health across sectors—from education, employment, and income to behaviors related to infectious and non-communicable diseases. As an interdisciplinary field, global health now examines the systemic determinants that underlie global health (Lomazzi, Jenkins, and Borisch 2016). To address these determinants of public health at a global level, global health brings together actors to improve underlying determinants of health throughout the world, looking to global governance in structuring these global determinants (Fried et al. 2010). In seeking to achieve this global health governance, state and non-state actors have joined together in a collective effort under global law.

The promotion of global health necessitates global governance beyond the reach of national governments, requiring international organizations, national governments, and non-governmental actors to come together under law to respond to globalized health threats. Global health thus looks beyond the individual state to encompass a diverse array of non-state actors—including organizations, foundations, and corporations—in understanding and developing collaborative solutions to today's public health challenges. To bring together the work of these state and non-state actors, global health actors engage in varying functions, all with the goal of improving health across borders and throughout the world. Global health looks to address interconnected determinants of health through global collaboration, with local, national, and international actors partnering and integrating their actions to form a global governance structure that seeks to mitigate global threats that undermine public health.

Where global health has come to frame efforts to advance public health across actors, law has become crucial to address the global health governance challenges that have arisen in a rapidly globalizing world. Law directly and indirectly impacts health determinants and outcomes across local, national, and global contexts (Gostin et al. 2019). Structuring health outcomes through law, legal instruments shape underlying determinants of health. These "legal determinants of health" thus influence societal interactions that structure, perpetuate, and mediate underlying determinants of health, establishing standards and norms that guide conduct (e.g., tobacco taxes), resolve disputes (e.g., via courts of law), and govern institutions (e.g., public and private health systems) (Gostin and Wiley 2016). While laws are developed and operationalized across different levels of governance (locally, nationally, globally), each have "downstream" influence on the lives of individuals and shape the conditions for people to live healthy lives (Gostin, Cohen, and Phelan *forthcoming*). If well designed, law can be a powerful tool for advancing justice in health—from protecting standards for health promotion, to strengthening health systems, to holding institutions accountable for health harms (Magnusson 2017). Operating at the global level to address global determinants of public health through global action, global health law presents a legal framework to structure new efforts by the global community to advance global health.

II. Defining Global Health Law

Global health law encompasses the legal and policy frameworks—both binding and non-binding—that structure public health in a globalizing world. With globalization giving rise to global health threats, global health law has become necessary to address these common threats and shared burdens across nations and sectors. Connecting societies in shared vulnerability, these globalizing forces have exposed the limitations of domestic law in addressing global determinants of health. Laws at the national level are not sufficient to address these global threats because such domestic laws cannot reach beyond national borders, and therefore, global health law is necessary to bridge the gap between global norms and national laws to promote global health (Gostin and Meier 2019). Arising out of international law, which focuses on multilateral cooperation among states, the focus of global health has necessitated action beyond national governments. In bringing together state and non-state actors, global health law seeks to respond to major health challenges in a rapidly globalizing world while improving the health and well-being of the world's people through the establishment of global governance for health.

Global governance has become crucial in developing legal norms and implementing those norms through global institutions. Global health law recognizes that all nations face interconnected public health threats, requiring collective global action to realize global health equity (Gostin 2014). Operationalized through common norms, global health law is guided by values of social justice, mutual solidarity, and human rights (Meier and Gostin 2018). Governance institutions can set norms for global action, form partnerships with key stakeholders, and develop consensus on shared goals for global health (Toebes 2018) under global health law. In uniting states under binding legal obligations and bringing together state and non-state actors under "soft law" commitments, global health law could not exist without global health governance (Gostin, Cohen, and Phelan *forthcoming*).

Through an extensive body of governance institutions, actors have come together to respond to global challenges, working to create coordinated responses to rising threats. International organizations serve as the primary governance institutions for the creation of this legal framework across states—including both binding and non-binding agreements—which, in turn, shapes national responses as states implement international legal obligations. Through the development of international law, these global governance institutions can develop global health law to frame the legal obligations of states, with international organizations providing a basis for member states to negotiate international legal agreements, facilitate international accountability, and shape global health norms (Meier et al. 2020). Yet numerous international organizations and legal regimes now impact health through state and non-state actors, and global health governance requires global health law to encompass multiple sectors and multiple actors—to coordinate actions between these actors and sectors to enhance global health (Gostin and Sridhar 2014). With globalization exacerbating the risks of disease and increasing the need for global cooperation, global health governance grows increasingly crucial in developing international law and global policy to unite state and non-state actors against global threats.

Global health law can thus shape this expanding law and policy landscape for global health, coordinating the global community through institutions of global governance. Law has become a central aspect of governance, with global health governance often taking the form of laws through constitutions, regulations, and bylaws (Gostin 2014). Global health law presents a legal framework to structure coordinated efforts by the global community to advance global health (Toebes 2018). Providing an international legal foundation for global health governance, global health law supports global institutions to negotiate a shared vision of global health, coordinate with organizations across sectors, and align national laws to advance public health in a globalizing world (Gostin and Meier 2019). Global health law thereby sets the global goals necessary to structure global health governance. Facilitating accountability for these shared global health goals, global health law can provide an institutional basis for developing benchmarks, monitoring progress, and enhancing compliance for achieving global health with justice (Gostin 2014).

III. An Evolving Field

The expansion of health law scholarship to encompass global health law has laid out a law and policy framework to structure efforts by the global community to advance global health. The need for law in global health has been in motion for centuries, as populations came to recognize the importance of cooperation across nations to protect public health. A variety of sanitary conventions in the mid-to-late 19th century began to shape the field (Gross 2021). Arising out of efforts to control infectious threats along international trade routes, these legal efforts soon moved beyond infectious diseases to include aspects of environmental health, non-communicable threats of alcohol and tobacco, and occupational health across the globe (Fidler 2001). Some of the first international health organizations, developed in the years leading up to World War II, laid a path for international governance to establish international law to protect public health.

Following World War II, the birth of the United Nations (UN) and World Health Organization (WHO) would provide a permanent foundation for global health governance. These governing institutions, which remain the core of law and policy in the international community, have solidified the focus on law to advance global health (Meier et al. 2020). Amid rising tensions in a globalizing world—through the Cold War, pandemic threats, and inequitable development—global health law would rise in importance (Bélanger 1989). Beyond WHO, global institutions formed rapidly to address global determinants of health, establishing a complex landscape that serves to frame health policies, programs, and practices in the global sphere (Moon et al. 2010). In facing new health challenges, global health law now encompasses binding and non-binding instruments of health law, human rights law, environmental law, trade law, and other law and policy instruments developed across sectors. The interconnections between these areas of global health law have been revealed amid the challenges of the COVID-19 response (Gostin 2021). As the importance of law and policy in global health became more evident, the field of global health law emerged.

The field of global health law has expanded rapidly in the 21st century. Arising out of international health law—which focuses narrowly on international legal relationships among states—global health law has a vast scope, including cooperative partnerships among state and non-state actors and soft law approaches to global health policy. Looking beyond the regulation of states through international treaty law, global health law can apply new global policies to facilitate cooperation across state and non-state actors, frame institutions of global governance, and realize global health with justice. Where once international health law was the only option for states to address issues of international health, contemporary soft law policy instruments (including non-binding international resolutions, global strategies, and codes of practice) have proven far easier to negotiate and adopt—without the need for formal ratification by states (Sekalala 2017). While lacking the formal legal enforceability of international law, these global health policies nevertheless codify consensus across the global community, providing a foundation under global health law to set priorities, mobilize constituencies, create incentives, coordinate actors, and facilitate accountability in global health. Through hard and soft law norm-setting, global health law seeks to create new policy institutions to alter behaviors, sustain funding, and coordinate partnerships (Gostin 2014). Without the practical need to develop international law, global health law and policy seeks to bind all the actors that influence public health in a globalizing world. Shifting from international health law (with treaties applicable to states) to global health law (with law and policy applied to both state and non-state actors), a proliferation of international, national, non-governmental, and corporate actors has organized to address a multisectoral array of determinants of health (Szlezák et al. 2010). Global health law thus encompasses the changing global landscape and governance necessary to respond to the health challenges of the 21st century.

As an academic discipline, global health law describes the legal and policy frameworks that apply to the expanding set of public health threats, non-state actors, and regulatory instruments that structure global health. Evolving beyond the traditional confines of formal sources and subjects of international law, global health law seeks to describe legal institutions that speak to:

- Rising health threats—including communicable and non-communicable diseases, injuries, mental health, dangerous products, and other globalized health threats;
- Proliferating health actors—including transnational corporations, private philanthropists, civil society, and other non-state actors; and
- Expanding health regulations—including "soft law" instruments, strategy documents, and other norms of global health policy (Gostin 2014).

As the limitations of international law led to the establishment of global health law, stakeholders have engaged a diverse array of actors through the rise of new policy institutions—institutions developed through their normative foundations in justice (Ruger 2018). These law and policy frameworks, placing public health obligations on the global community of state and non-state actors, facilitate justice in global health through global institutions that are governed well, embracing values of transparency, monitoring, multisectoral engagement, and accountability (Gostin, Cohen, and Phelan *forthcoming*).

IV. Structure of the Volume

Where law and policy are complementary approaches to global health law, this foundational text looks to global standards by which to frame government responsibilities and establish global governance. This volume is organized in four main sections: (1) explaining the conceptual frameworks and governance institutions that define the field, (2) applying global health governance to disease prevention and health promotion, (3) examining economic institutions that influence global health, and (4) analyzing international legal efforts to address the rising health threats of a rapidly globalizing world. These sections are intended to be read sequentially, with each chapter building from the one before it while adding new information to the reader's understanding of the field. To complement the theoretical foundations of the text, each chapter includes brief case studies to highlight the practical application of law and policy in global health.

Section I introduces the reader to the conceptual frameworks and institutional foundations necessary to understand the role of law and policy in protecting and promoting public health in a globalizing world. The first chapter provides an understanding of the evolving meaning of global health, examining the modern birth of global governance under the UN and establishment of international legal authorities under WHO. Given the limitations of international health law in a globalizing world, Chapter 2 introduces the legal foundations for the book by defining global health law, conceptualizing the hard and soft law authorities necessary to bind together the state and non-state actors that make up the expanding global health landscape. This landscape is the focus of Chapter 3, which explores the proliferating actors and partnerships in the global health architecture, analyzing the role of global health law as a foundation of global health governance. Binding these actors together, Chapter 4 considers the normative frameworks that structure global health efforts, considering equity and social justice in global health and human rights under international law. Chapter 5 concludes Section I by looking to the diplomatic process by which global health law and policy are developed, considering the politics of negotiating global health law through global health governance.

This conceptual framework for global health law and policy in Section I establishes a foundation for a closer examination of some of the most pressing legal issues in global health in Sections II through IV.

Shifting to the application of global health law and policy in global health governance, Section II provides the reader with an understanding of the divergent approaches taken in global health governance to respond to leading global health threats. Chapter 6 chronicles how global health law has evolved to combat the spread of infectious diseases, tracing the evolution of the WHO International Health Regulations, examining contemporary responses from HIV/AIDS to COVID-19, and considering the importance of ongoing law reforms to face future threats to global health security. This infectious disease response is distinct from policy approaches to addressing non-communicable disease, with the global trade of unhealthy products leading to a series of hard and soft law approaches to the regulation of commercial determinants of health, and Chapter 7 examines policies to shape smoking, eating, and drinking behaviors throughout the world. Recognizing the underlying conditions that contribute to physical, mental, and social well-being, Chapter 8 explores changing approaches to mental health under global health policy, analyzing how global health governance has shifted from institutionalization to medicalization to community-based rehabilitation. In focusing on the environmental threats of an industrializing world, Chapter 9 investigates policy frameworks to support environmental health through the regulation of environmental pollutants and the establishment of a "One Health" approach to global health governance.

Section III considers the influence of economic governance on the public's health, examining the role of global health law in shaping economic development, international trade, corporate regulation, and health funding for the realization of a healthier world. Where economic development underlies public health, the Sustainable Development Goals provide a foundation for all global efforts to ensure sustainable development, with Chapter 10 delineating the wide range of health-related goals and targets. This focus on economic development is extended through international economic governance under the International Monetary Fund and World Bank, and Chapter 11 analyzes the evolving influence of these development institutions in alleviating poverty to promote global health. Expanding to international trade governance, Chapter 12 looks to efforts to liberalize international trade through the World Trade Organization, considering the harmful consequences of trade agreements and examining rising efforts to challenge intellectual property protections to ensure access to essential medicines. This focus on essential medicines requires transnational corporations, and Chapter 13 looks to the rising influence of transnational corporations on commercial determinants of health, analyzing models for regulating harmful corporate actions and considering whether corporate social responsibility doctrines can support corporate engagement in global health governance. In bringing these economic actors together to support global health, Section III ends by focusing on international assistance and cooperation in health, with Chapter 14 examining the establishment of new global health funding agencies, bringing state and non-state actors together to pool resources to meet basic needs and distribute essential medicines.

Globalization has fundamentally altered public health, raising an imperative for international law to address rising health threats, and Section IV analyzes these issues at the leading edge of global governance. Recognizing the importance of anti-microbials to the treatment of infectious disease, Chapter 15 confronts the rising challenge of anti-microbial resistance and the need for collective action through international law to prevent and respond to resistant strains. This focus on the infectious disease response is extended in Chapter 16, considering the rise of international agreements to ensure pathogen sharing as a basis for both responding promptly to disease threats and ensuring access to medicines and vaccines. Chapter 17 looks to the evolution of international law to safeguard sexual and reproductive health and rights, exploring how human rights advocacy has reframed health policy and transformed health institutions. Framing international humanitarian law as global health policy, Chapter 18 examines international efforts to protect public health and human rights in the context of armed conflict and humanitarian emergencies, looking to health protections for refugees and ethical responsibilities of health professionals in avoiding harm and upholding human rights. Climate change is affecting the health of the entire planet, and given the cataclysmic threat to planetary health, Chapter 19 considers climate change mitigation and adaptation under the UN Framework Convention on Climate Change. Bringing together efforts across sectors to advance public health through global health law, Chapter 20 concludes Section IV by examining evolving policies to promote Universal Health Coverage, seeking a multisectoral approach to addressing health in all policies.

Conclusion

Global health law is rapidly expanding, creating new governance institutions to alter behaviors, sustain funding, and coordinate partnerships for justice in global health. This foundational text reflects on the dramatic development of the field of global health law, highlighting the advancements of law and policy in promoting health equity, the challenges exposed by the COVID-19 pandemic, and the need for new legal and governance frameworks in responding to the threats of the 21st century.

Out of the ashes of World War II, institutions of global health have brought the world together in unprecedented cooperation through global health law, giving rise to the successes and opportunities detailed throughout this text. This expansion of international law to encompass global health law has laid out a legal framework to structure efforts by the global community to advance global health. However, the current age of rising nationalism amid emerging threats has cast doubt on many of these successes and raised obstacles to future progress. In violent contrast with the shared goals of a globalizing world, populist nationalism seeks to retrench nations inward, with rising nationalist movements directly challenging norms of human rights, violating tenets of international law, and spurring isolationism in global affairs. These challenges to global health law have coincided with sweeping new global health threats, as nationalist retrenchment has led to a rejection of global health law as a basis for global health solidarity. Such compounding crises offer a unique opportunity to reform global health law to effectively coordinate pandemic preparedness and strengthen legal authorities to advance global health.

Global health law remains necessary—now more than ever before. As infectious disease threats expand, the global climate changes, and humans, animals, and environments are increasingly interconnected, bold law and governance have become vital to a world that is safer and fairer. Global governance provides hope for the future, with these governance institutions facilitating the durability of global health law through the unprecedented challenges ahead. In preparing for future threats, a wide range of crucial global health law reforms are being undertaken simultaneously in the coming years, with the chapters of this book grappling with these ongoing reforms. These reforms of global health law, while each responding to distinct concerns, must be considered as interrelated instruments across an interconnected legal landscape, with the reforms undertaken in the coming years shaping the next generation of the field.

References

Bélanger, Michael. 1989. "The Future of International Health Law: A Round Table." *International Digest of Health Legislation* 40(1): 1–29.

Fidler, David P. 2001. "The Globalization of Public Health: The First 100 Years of International Health Diplomacy." *Bulletin of the World Health Organization* 79(9): 842–849.

Frenk, Julio and Octavio Gómez-Dantés. 2017. "False Dichotomies in Global Health: The Need for Integrative Thinking." *The Lancet* 389(10069): 667–670.

Frenk, Julio, Octavio Gómez-Dantés, and Suerie Moon. 2014. "From Sovereignty to Solidarity: A Renewed Concept of Global Health for an Era of Complex Interdependence." *Lancet* 383 (9911): 94–97.

Frenk, Julio and Suerie Moon. 2013. "Governance Challenges in Global Health." *The New England Journal of Medicine* 368: 936–942.

Fried, Linda P., Margaret E. Bentley, Pierre Buekens, Donald S. Burke, Julio J. Frenk, Michael J. Klag, and Harrison C. Spencer. 2010. "Global Health is Public Health." *The Lancet* 375(9714): 535–537.

Gostin, Lawrence O. 2021. *Global Health Security: A Blueprint for the Future*. Cambridge: Harvard University Press.

Gostin, Lawrence O. 2014. *Global Health Law*. Cambridge: Harvard University Press.

Gostin, Lawrence O., Glenn Cohen, and Alexandra Phelan. Forthcoming. *Global Health Law*. Cambridge: Cambridge University Press.

Gostin, Lawrence O., Scott Burris, and Zita Lazzarini. 1999. "The Law and the Public's Health: A Study of Infectious Disease Law in the United States." *Columbia Law Review* 99(59): 64.

Gostin, Lawrence O. and Benjamin Mason Meier. 2019. "Introducing Global Health Law." *Journal of Law, Medicine & Ethics* 47(4): 788–793.

Gostin, Lawrence O., John T. Monahan, Jenny Kaldor, Mary DeBartolo, Eric Friedman et al. 2019. "The Legal Determinants of Health: Harnessing the Power of Law for Global Health and Sustainable Development." *The Lancet* 393(10183): 1857–1910.

Gostin, Lawrence O. and Devi Sridhar. 2014. "Global Health and the Law." *New England Journal of Medicine* 370: 1732–1740.

Gostin, Lawrence O. and Lindsay F. Wiley. 2016. *Public Health Law: Power, Duty, Restraint.* 3rd ed. Oakland: University of California Press.

Gross, Aeyal. 2021. "The Past, Present, and Future of Global Health Law Beyond Crisis." *American Journal of International Law* 115(4): 754–771.

Kickbusch, Ilona, Kevin Buckett, South Australia, Department of Health, and Health in All Policies Unit. 2010. *Implementing Health in All Policies: Adelaide 2010.* Australia: SA Department of Health.

Koplan, Jeffrey P., T. Christopher Bond, Michael H. Merson, K. Sirnath Reddy, Mario Henry Rodriguez, Nelson K. Sewankombo, and Judith N. Wasserheit. 2009. "Towards a Common Definition of Global Health." *The Lancet* 373: 1993–1995.

Lomazzi, Marta, Christopher Jenkins, and Bettina, Borisch. 2016. "Global Public Health Today: Connecting the Dots." *Global Health Action* 9(1): 28772.

Magnusson, Roger. 2017. *Advancing the Right to Health: The Vital Role of Law.* Sydney Law School Research Paper No 17(43).

Meier, Benjamin Mason and Lawrence O. Gostin. 2018. "Framing Human Rights in Global Health Governance." In *Human Rights in Global Health: Rights-Based Governance for a Globalizing World*, edited by Benjamin Mason Meier and Lawrence O. Gostin, 63–86. New York: Oxford University Press.

Meier, Benjamin Mason, Allyn Taylor, Mark Eccleston-Turner, Roojin Habibi, Sharifah Sekalala, and Lawrence O. Gostin. 2020. The World Health Organization in Global Health Law. *Journal of Law, Medicine & Ethics* 48(4): 796–799.

Moon, Suerie, Nicole A. Szlezák, Catherine M. Michaud, Dean T. Jamison, Gerald T. Keusch, William C. Clark, and Barry R. Bloom. 2010. "The Global Health System: Lessons for a Stronger Institutional Framework." *PLoS Medicine* 7(1): e1000193.

Ruger, Jennifer Prah. 2018. *Global Health Justice and Governance.* New York: Oxford University Press.

Sekalala, Sharifah. 2017. *Soft Law and Global Health Problems Lessons from Responses to HIV/AIDS, Malaria and Tuberculosis.* Cambridge: Cambridge University Press.

Szlezák, Nicole, Barry R. Bloom, Dean T. Jamison, Gerald T. Keusch, Catherine M. Michaud, Suerie Moon, and William C. Clark. 2010. "The Global Health System: Actors, Norms, and Expectations in Transition." *PLoS Medicine* 7(1): e1000183.

Toebes, Brigit. 2018. "Global Health Law: Defining the Field." In *Research Handbook on Global Health Law*, edited by Gian Luca Burci and Brigit Toebes, 2–23. Northampton: Edgar.

I
FRAMEWORKS & INSTITUTIONS OF GLOBAL HEALTH

Shifting Actors & Norms in a Globalizing World

1
Global Health

Global Determinants, Global Governance, and Global Law

Lawrence O. Gostin and Alexandra Finch

Introduction

Global health reflects efforts to achieve population health throughout the world. Looking to public health principles as a basis for global health, the advancement of health has shifted from a focus on individual medical care to approaches that address broad underlying determinants of health for entire populations. In an increasingly globalized world, national responses are no longer sufficient to address these determinants of health. Globalization has enabled the spread of disease and proliferation of a vast range of health hazards, from unhealthy foods and unsafe products to global poverty and environmental degradation, highlighting the limitations of domestic public health interventions. Responding to these global threats requires global efforts to address global determinants of health. These global efforts rely upon global governance, bringing together actors throughout the world to address health threats that transcend national boundaries, and states have come to look to the United Nations (UN) system as a central pillar of global governance.

Where advancing public health in a globalizing world requires global governance, global health governance has sought to address political, social, commercial, and behavioral determinants of health through global health law. Drawing from a long history of international cooperation to address infectious disease, states worked through the UN after World War II to develop international health governance under the World Health Organization (WHO). In establishing WHO as the first UN specialized agency, states envisioned it as the world's health champion, granting it sweeping authority to bind states together through international law to coordinate national governments to prevent disease and promote health. WHO emerged as the early leader of global health governance. This system of global health governance has evolved to encourage global coordination to promote public health and mitigate health threats, codifying these efforts in global health law and policy. Law and policy have thus become a foundation of good governance for health.

This chapter examines the contested meaning of global health, the health implications of a globalizing world, and the importance of global governance for health. Part I describes how global health reflects the practice of public health, examining the progression of the field of public health and government efforts to promote public health through public policy. In a globalizing world, such public policy to address global threats would require global governance. Examining the shift from international health to global health, Part II traces the evolving field of global health, the rise of international health governance, and the birth of global governance for health after World War II. Part III analyzes global health governance under the UN, with the establishment of WHO giving rise to the contemporary system of global health law. This chapter concludes that global health governance has become the foundation for advancing global health law in a globalizing world, bringing together state and non-state actors to realize the highest attainable standard of health for all.

I. Global Health Is Public Health

As populations first came into contact with each other, public health practice came to be seen as critical in preventing disease and promoting health. Rising public health movements for social medicine in the progressive era of the 19th century would focus both on prevention of injury and disease and on a broad population-based understanding of health. Governments, in recognizing their central responsibility to secure health and safety, evolved their governance to develop policies to protect public health. These policies would look to address underlying determinants of health, shaping the living conditions that ultimately determine the health of populations.

A. From Individual Health to Public Health

Health entails a state of complete physical, mental, and social well-being. This standard of health is not inherent in the individual but is derived from interpersonal, community, and institutional factors that interact with local, national, and global environments. Reflecting determinants of the public's health, health is strongly influenced by underlying social, political, and economic conditions at the population level (Birn, Pillay, and Holtz 2017). Public health is thus focused on the health of entire populations, reflecting societal actions that promote health and prevent disease by focusing on the improvement of underlying determinants of health. These determinants—across a range of social, economic, and political factors—encompass an expansive array of sectors and conditions in both the natural and built environments.

From the earliest civilizations, humans have faced a myriad of determinants that impacted the health of the public. As early civilizations looked from divine forces to natural forces as the cause of disease, rulers sought to monitor potential physical and environmental factors that influence health, with Greco-Roman philosophers theorizing that poor health and disease were the result of an "imbalance between man and his environment" (Rosen 1958, 33). As science advanced, thinkers of the Middle Ages (from the late 5th century through the 15th century) began to theorize that disease could spread between individuals, giving rise to concerns around infectious disease. These infectious diseases repeatedly threatened populations in the Middle Ages, as rapid population growth left cities overcrowded and unhygienic. Following the fall of the Roman Empire, municipalities across Europe moved to introduce some of the first public health measures. Municipalities sought to prohibit dead animals and other waste from being dumped in rivers and streams, placing restrictions on manufacturing to protect the water supply. By the late Middle Ages, cities introduced policies for street cleaning and refuse pickup. With the Bubonic Plague ravaging much of Europe in the 14th century, governmental entities moved to combat this deadly infectious disease threat, implementing the first quarantine and isolation strategies to prevent the spread of disease (Porter 1999). The rise of educational systems during the Middle Ages established the knowledge base to promote individual and societal medicine during the Enlightenment era.

Scientific advancements during the Enlightenment (from the late 17th century through the 18th century) would set the stage for health advancements—transitioning from individual medicine for specific ailments to societal efforts to promote public health. As industrial and urban population centers rapidly grew, so did the threat of dangerous living conditions and poor health outcomes (Tulchinsky and Varavikova 2014). This recognition of disease threats would give rise to the field of epidemiology, the study of the determinants and distribution of health and disease across populations. Yet, to curb disease, societal efforts would require policy reforms. Early public health was centralized and focused on bettering health among the upper levels of the social and economic hierarchy. However, this focus would shift as the wealthy realized they could no longer ignore the impoverished in neighboring districts (Goudsblom 1986). Public health movements looked across social hierarchies to address the plight of the impoverished, establishing the modern elements of public health through the fight for "social medicine" (Mackenbach 2009).

Case Study: Social Medicine and 1848 Revolutions: From Medicine to Public Health

Born out of the Industrial Revolution and working class movements across Europe, the rise of social medicine examined how economic inequalities shape the rise and experience of disease. Prussian researcher Rudolf Virchow gave rise to this movement in analyzing the socioeconomic causes of a typhus epidemic in Upper Silesia, concluding that "the government has rendered impossible the mental and material development of these people through the most preposterous neglect of this country, and by its equally dilatory internal and external politics." With Virchow holding that "medicine is a social science, and politics is nothing more than medicine on a grand scale," this focus on health inequities would shape revolutionary movements across Europe, with the summer of 1848 bringing armed revolts, calling on governments to guarantee safe water and health standards amidst cholera and other infectious disease outbreaks. While these 1848 revolutions failed to overthrow the political order, they would lead to new social policies to institute public health governance. Laying the groundwork for these policies, Friedrich Engels would consider the inequalities of Industrialization in England, posing the question: "How is it possible, under such conditions, for the lower class to be healthy and long lived?" These inequitable determinants of health would become a focus of government responsibility and public policy—beginning in Europe and spreading well beyond—to address economic development as a basis for health promotion. Even as some policymakers argued that central governments could not guarantee health, others looked to governments to establish policies that could, through financial and legal standards, create a social medicine system for reforming conditions to improve underlying determinants of health.

Building from the early days of social medicine, scientific discoveries in the late 19th century supported the identification of disease-causing agents, allowing for the realization of societal goals to prevent disease.

In drawing from epidemiology, government record keeping led to statistical analysis that would provide insights on health at the population level. Disease surveillance could trace diseases back to their initial source, with epidemiology seeking to reveal the causal connections between environmental conditions, disease outbreaks, and individual morbidity. Epidemiologists began to study the influence of societal ills, including poverty and malnutrition, on mortality and morbidity (Sand 1934).[1] The 20th century began with efforts to preserve and promote the well-being of populations, spawning the modern field of public health. Even as modern medicine rose alongside public health, epidemiological data undercut the "triumphalist myths of clinical medicine" (Porter 1997, 102), highlighting the overwhelming role of public health measures in driving health improvements. Governments recognized that medical interventions alone could not sufficiently promote health, with public health improvements occurring largely as a result of the "modification of the conditions which led to disease, rather than from intervention in the mechanism of disease after it occurred" (McKeown 1979, 198). This holistic approach to disease prevention—looking at improvements in nutrition, education, and living conditions—would seek to address underlying determinants of public health.

Public health has come to take a broader view of the conditions for health and well-being, focusing on underlying determinants of health and the policy interventions necessary to improve them. From the birth of early reforms to the seeds of modern-day public health, it has been clear that government efforts are necessary to address underlying determinants of health. By addressing these underlying determinants, health is shaped across government sectors, and at all levels of society, through various laws and policies. Through public health law and policy, governments authority is central in structuring public health.

B. Government Authority for Public Health

Governments have come to accept responsibility to address the underlying conditions that affect public health. Public health is integral to government functioning, making promoting public health and well-being a significant government interest (Gostin and Wiley 2016). Government authority is seen as necessary to propel the collective action required to protect and promote public health. To operationalize this societal goal, governments develop public policy to prevent disease and promote health, taking on responsibilities that individuals alone cannot (Carey 1970). Collective action through public policy is necessary

---

[1] This new study would eventually give rise to the field of social epidemiology, utilizing statistical evidence to display health inequities and examine disproportionate harms impacting those living in poverty. Through this focus on underlying social determinants of health, it became apparent that public health cannot be dissociated from socioeconomic factors, with poverty serving as a fundamental underlying determinant of health and well-being, and thus—no matter the disease or its origin—health threats will inevitably descend the social gradient to disproportionately threaten the poor (Marmot, Kogevinas, and Elston 1987).

to secure public health and general welfare. Government entities dedicated to promoting public health have accordingly arisen through public policy and play a central role in developing and implementing standards for health and well-being.

The development of public policy in public health evolved slowly, with government concern for population health largely ignored for centuries. Amid the sanitary movements of the 19th century, many governments for the first time looked to public policy to advance public health, with rapid population growth and unprecedented levels of disease leading to popular calls for clean water systems, refuse removal, and hygiene protocols (Porter 1999). As seen in France, which first operationalized health councils, the formalization of health institutions would address hygiene and sanitation through public policy to prevent disease across populations—as a government responsibility (De Feo et al. 2014).[2] However, these health councils operated at a local level, and it would take until the turn of the 20th century for governments to advance public health through national policy.

As national governments across the globe began to embrace an obligation to prevent disease and promote health, they enacted national policies across sectors to protect public health. The United States implemented some of the strongest early examples of national policy to promote public health. The 1911 Triangle Shirtwaist Factory fire would result in the death of 146 people (largely immigrant women and girls), as the factory had locked exit doors to prevent workers from taking breaks and leaving their workstations. Following from this preventable tragedy, the U.S. government strengthened labor laws to protect public health.[3] Such responsive government actions across countries would solidify national authority in central aspects of public health policy. The continuing need for government action would lead to the establishment of the first health departments, tasked with overseeing public health policy on a continuing basis (Winslow 1923). By instituting these public health departments, national health systems moved toward a focus on permanent health institutions, capable of adapting to changing policy needs and providing for rapid policy responses.

---

[2] These French health councils maintained some of the first modern-day sewage systems. Centralized in Paris, these reforms shifted populations from open air waste disposal to closed, underground sewage systems. Under Napoleon III, Paris in the 1830s underwent major city developments to lay these underground sewage pipes and ducts. By ensuring proper methods of both cleaning the sewage system and disposal of waste products, Parisian infrastructures achieved drastic decreases in cholera and other waste-borne diseases (De Feo et al. 2014).

[3] Similarly, the public recognition of unsanitary food conditions reached public consciousness in the United States through the writings of Upton Sinclair in *The Jungle*, leading to the Meat Inspection Act of 1906. The United States would go on in the decades that followed, and amid the Great Depression in the West, to create sweeping public policies that brought about new regulations in daily lives and commercial industries to promote public health and well-being (McEvoy 1995).

As national governments came to recognize an imperative to develop governing institutions to protect and promote the health and well-being of people within their borders, it became increasingly important to apply this focus to public health across nations. With the rise of globalized trade and international relations, governments came to see the rise of health threats and destructive behaviors abroad as a threat to domestic prosperity (Fidler 2001). Diseases and disease vectors once relegated to specific nations and continents now spread rapidly across national borders. This rapid change in human interaction necessitated the adoption of health governance across nations. Developments in international affairs led to the birth of "international health," which framed early efforts to prevent the spread of disease across national borders, with governments recognizing a corollary need for international governance to establish laws that would protect public health throughout the world.

II. Global Health Requires Global Governance

To advance public health in a globalizing world, health institutions and instruments must look beyond the actions of singular nations to address a larger set of global health determinants. Rising from international principles drawn up to prevent the spread of epidemic disease, the evolution of international sanitary regulations led to a series of early treaties that served as the foundation of the modern global health order. Early institutions of international health governance soon followed. Yet these institutions were unable to bring the world together to address public health challenges, and as the bloodshed of two world wars left nations and their populations decimated, states sought to lay a new foundation for global health governance. Seeking to overcome the limitations of international health governance, global health governance brought states together following the atrocities of World War II to take collective action to build a healthier world under the UN.

A. Origins of International Health

National governments first came together formally to address international health in the 19th century, looking across nations to understand international determinants of public health and develop common regulations to protect populations. The earliest measures to limit the spread of disease had relied on isolating populations through the formation of a "cordon sanitaire," where armed guards surrounded towns stricken by illness, but it was not until the 14th century that measures were introduced to prevent the introduction of disease into a population (Goodman 1952). These measures required those entering a community to isolate for a period of time in order to observe whether the visitor developed signs of illness. (Such requirements came to be known as "quarantine" based on the forty-day "*quarantino*" isolation period required by Venice.) The Venetian quarantine practice served as a model for other European governments over the course of the next two centuries (Goodman 1952). Governments came to understand that preventing infectious disease outbreaks would require international cooperation, but they long failed to work together to advance their common needs. Yet, with an increase in disease outbreaks driven by international commerce amid industrialized production in the mid-1800s, states looked to "international health" partnerships to protect their own self-interests (Goodman 1952). Recognizing the cross-border threat of disease, the European trading powers began efforts to standardize international health cooperation to prevent the spread of epidemics across national borders and throughout their colonies. Creating new avenues to report disease outbreaks and secure cross-border traffic, cooperative efforts to ensure mutual self-interest would lead to the first international health agreements to prevent the spread of disease (Kelley 2011).

However, with powerful nations basing these early international health agreements on exploitative colonial systems and economic self-interest, governments failed to ensure cooperation across nations and overlooked rising threats in the environmental, physical, social, and cultural space. Agreements among European powers often excluded the lands and peoples they had colonized, which were governed instead through a focus on "tropical disease"— encompassing diseases that originate from temperate or tropical areas with no previous origin point within Europe and the Western world (Hewa 1995). Leading to the development of the field of "tropical medicine," this focus on disease in colonized lands in Africa, Asia, and the Middle East sought to keep European colonizers free of diseases that they had not faced previously (Coghe 2020).[4] Notwithstanding these imperialistic motives, efforts to prevent, control, and treat "tropical disease" were framed as humanitarian efforts, which helped to justify colonial oppression while furthering colonial expansion (Bump and Aniebo 2022). Yet this narrow focus on tropical diseases and tropical medicine neglected to address the broader set of health concerns that continued to plague the colonies and beyond, including non-communicable diseases and wider determinants of health such as basic sanitation, nutrition, and housing.

Despite an imperative for greater cooperation across nations, national governments were slow to adapt to public health conditions that demanded

---

[4] This understanding of "tropical medicine" arises out of the colonial history of health, and these colonial legacies of global health have persisted in global health practice to this day. Where major Western organizations still embrace a focus on "tropical diseases," offering "innovative" solutions to the lands they once colonized, this anachronistic term reflects the continuing influence of colonial power dynamics in global health (Lang 2001).

international cooperation to address health threats across all nations, rather than to protect the economic interests of wealthy nations (Fidler 2001). These international health threats were increasing, exacerbated by increasing interconnections in a rapidly globalizing world, bringing nations together in shared vulnerability (Birn, Pillay, and Holtz 2017). Globalizing forces fueled the spread of infectious diseases and disease vectors, transborder trade of harmful products, environmental degradation, and economic shocks, resulting in sweeping health consequences across the world. These threats would challenge all nations, and no single nation could respond to them alone. States began to look to new health frameworks to bolster cooperation—in a shift toward international health (McMichael and Beaglehole 2009). This focus on international health encompassed broad notions of collective action and underlying determinants of health for all (Brown, Cueto, and Fee 2006). To coordinate national health interventions at the international level, a new international governance landscape arose for public health advancement throughout the world.

B. Rise of an International Health Order

Drawing from increasing attention to international health, an international health order arose, looking to international law to drive collective action and harmonize national public health measures. International cooperation was becoming essential to coordinate national policies across states—to prevent the spread of disease without undermining economic and security interests (Aginam 2005). The Industrial Revolution had propelled international trade, and with it, the spread of disease across borders. The development of the steamship and the railway in the early 19th century hastened travel, which led to a growing frustration over quarantine measures. In an effort to reduce the spread of disease, travelers were held for inspection at borders and goods were regularly destroyed, slowing the movement of people and goods. Powerful economic interests began to grow weary of trade delays incurred by distinct health policies at each port of entry. Governments faced pressure to establish reformed quarantine laws that were less burdensome on tradespeople and private interests. By the late 1840s, governments in Europe began to organize international conferences in an effort to establish international cooperation for resolving technical questions on quarantine methods and other public health measures (Goodman 1952).

The first International Sanitary Conference, held in Paris in 1851, sought to bring together physicians and diplomats to reach consensus among those states with trade interests in the Mediterranean region. Additional conferences would be held over the next fifty years, and this rising international health order would ultimately establish the international legal foundation upon which permanent international health institutions could be constructed (Gostin and Meier 2019).

Case Study: International Governance: From Sanitary Conferences to Permanent Institutions

With national governments recognizing the nature of disease and spread of infection across populations, states saw that disease prevention could not be undertaken only at the domestic level, raising an imperative to coordinate responses internationally. European trading powers gathered for the first International Sanitary Conference in 1851, and this groundbreaking meeting would establish a cooperative architecture to address the threat of infectious disease, seeking to harmonize quarantine regulations across nations without causing undue interference with international travel or trade. However, state agreements could not garner the widespread national ratification necessary for adoption of a binding convention. It would take until the end of the 19th century for states to reach sufficient consensus on epidemiological methods and public health practice to work together to prevent the spread of infectious disease. The preamble of the first International Sanitary Convention of 1892, establishing quarantine requirements for ships traveling along the Suez Canal, recognized that national governments must gather regularly "to establish common measures for protecting public health during cholera epidemics without uselessly obstructing commercial transactions and passenger traffic." Subsequent conventions would seek to require states to notify other states of potential outbreaks of diseases, outlining public health measures at national borders to identify diseases at points of entry. Subsequent international sanitary conventions at the start of the 20th century would establish binding provisions to ensure the practice of public health and safety from infectious disease. At the eleventh International Sanitary Conference in Paris in 1903, delegates drafted the first International Sanitary Convention of widespread applicability. This Convention not only established international obligations but also laid the foundations for permanent international health institutions—calling for the creation of an international health office.

These international sanitary conventions during the first decades of the 20th century, focusing on specific infectious diseases,[5] provided

---

[5] Early sanitary conventions had concerned cholera, plague, and yellow fever—diseases not considered endemic to Europe and North America but whose spread from Asia and the Middle East was of deep concern to the trade and colonial powers. The International Sanitary Convention of 1926 added notification requirements for typhus and smallpox—diseases endemic to Europe.

opportunities for states to develop governance institutions to ensure permanent public health leadership across nations. Given the recurring threat of infectious diseases—as trade, travel, and industrialization continued to expand—such permanent institutions would allow for monitoring and surveillance across the world to prevent the spread of disease at the earliest possible time. Building from early sanitary conventions and moving toward permanent international bodies, collaborative frameworks were formed to establish communication between nations and give rise to international public health bureaucracies.

C. New Governance Institutions

Public health was among the earliest fields to seek international cooperation through international institutions, born out of an understanding that disease transmission required states to collaborate—for the health of their populations and advancement of their economic interests. To protect public health as a foundation of national security, early international health councils and meetings concerning infectious diseases would soon evolve into standing health bureaucracies, guided by multilateral treaties and seeking to maintain the public health order (Jacobson 1979). During the fifth International Sanitary Conference in 1881, states recommended improvements in disease notification procedures—through weekly epidemiological bulletins—providing a foundation for sanitary authorities from different countries to communicate (Goodman 1952). By the end of the 19th century, health professionals began to appreciate the need for permanent international governance to coordinate disease control measures across countries, recognizing the recurring disease threats that faced increasingly interconnected states (Pannenborg 1979).

The first permanent institutions emerged in the early 20th century. In the Americas, states in 1902 would form the Pan American Sanitary Bureau, seeking to standardize national regulations in the Western Hemisphere and control infectious disease at regional ports (Meier and Ayala 2015). European states thereafter established the *Office International d'Hygiène Publique* (OIHP) in 1907, building from commitments in the 1903 International Sanitary Convention. The OIHP soon expanded across regions to encompass nearly sixty nations, as member states sent representatives to Paris to discuss and circulate key epidemiological information and coordinate international sanitary conferences (WHO 1958). Yet, these nascent governing bodies would soon be challenged by unprecedented public health threats, as the "Great War" caused suffering unlike any the world had ever seen, giving rise to new international institutions of public health.

26 GLOBAL HEALTH LAW & POLICY

Figure 1.1 LNHO Members Meet in 1925 to Address Malaria (United Nations Archives at Geneva)

World War I brought about numerous new public health challenges—widespread famine, refugee crises, and pandemic threats[6]—and the aftermath of the war would give rise to new institutions of international governance. In a postwar effort to maintain and promote peace and security throughout the world, the League of Nations was founded in 1920, with founding states seeking to establish a stable political order governed under international laws and institutions (Borowy 2009). These states understood that addressing the world's growing public health challenges would be central to their international efforts. Going beyond OIHP's mandate to collect, validate, and publish epidemiological data, the League of Nations would also address health conditions within countries and across regions, as seen in Figure 1.1, through the establishment of a health-specific agency under the League's umbrella: the League of Nations Health Organization (LNHO) (Cueto, Brown, and Fee 2019).

Despite an already crowded landscape of international health organizations, the LNHO became the preeminent hub for public health, cooperating

---

[6] These wartime challenges were exacerbated by the 1918 influenza pandemic, which would kill over fifty million people—more than the war itself. In the face of one of the worst pandemics in human history, governments employed public health strategies developed over the centuries, implementing measures such as isolation, quarantine, and suspension of mass gatherings, but without international institutions in place to coordinate these national measures (Bootsma and Ferguson 2007).

with high-level health officials in virtually every member country, convening panels of experts, and even leveraging new communications technologies (i.e., telephone and telegraph) to rapidly transmit epidemiological data to member states around the world. The LNHO developed international commissions on diseases, shared epidemiological surveillance, and published technical health reports. However, the LNHO was constrained by its narrow disease-centered mandate, lack of funding and membership, and mounting geopolitical pressures (Borowy 2009). Just as new sweeping threats to underlying determinants of health were emerging, requiring LNHO leadership amid a "Great Depression" in the West,[7] the League of Nations was collapsing amid a deterioration in the international order. By the late 1930s, the rise of fascist regimes and a wave of imperialistic repression had brought nations once again to the edge of war. The spirit of multilateral cooperation that had led to the League's creation would yield to these divisive ideologies. As armies mobilized across Europe and Asia, states rapidly withdrew from the League of Nations, with international health and international institutions hanging in the balance of another world war.

D. World War II Challenges Governance Regimes

World War II saw renewed atrocities throughout the world, and new international governance institutions would be formed in response to this cataclysmic suffering. As the German army marched through European nations, the Nazi regime's genocidal plans became a horrific reality. The Nazi regime carried out mass extermination of entire populations—including millions of Jews, Roma, homosexuals, and people with disabilities—with millions of others imprisoned and forced into concentration camps. This complete Nazi disregard for the value of human life arose out of the German medical field's widespread promotion of "eugenics," a distortion of public health principles that posited the genetic inferiority of entire peoples, with physicians voluntarily aiding in theorizing, planning, and operating death camps that would slaughter all those deemed "unworthy of life" (Bachrach and Kuntz 2004).[8] War simultaneously spread across eastern Asia, as the Japanese Empire sought colonial domination

---

[7] The Great Depression was a long and pronounced economic downturn in the 1930s that led to rising unemployment, food insecurity, and widespread immiseration in the industrialized world—and required novel government programs to provide labor rights and public assistance to millions facing poverty.

[8] Beyond this genocidal horror, Nazi doctors furthered their disregard for the value of human life by conducting medical experiments on healthy individuals in countries under German occupation. These experiments occurred without consent and led to murder, brutality, cruelty, torture, and other atrocities that would come to be seen as "crimes against humanity" (Constantin and Andorno 2020).

over the region, subjugating peoples across Korea, Manchukuo, southeast Asia, and Micronesia. The world was again at war, touching almost every nation, with this unprecedented violence threatening international governance and health advancements.

As war raged unchecked, international governance was unable to respond to the escalating slaughter and suffering, leading to the rise of new wartime health institutions. The League of Nations had collapsed, and OIHP was unable to operate effectively as the Nazi army descended upon its headquarters in Paris (Cueto, Brown, and Fee 2019). Amid this absence of international health governance, forty-four nations came together in 1943 to form the United Nations Relief and Rehabilitation Administration (UNRRA). UNRRA rapidly assumed wartime responsibility for public health, establishing offices across the world that would provide technical assistance to prevent disease outbreaks, rebuild national health agencies, and assist with the procurement of medical supplies (Sawyer 1947). Although UNRRA was only intended to be a temporary governance body, it provided essential public health coordination during a time of international crisis, developing flexible local responses during one of the most difficult times in humanity's history and creating a model for a new permanent international governance body.

It was out of the destruction of World War II that the current global governance structures would arise. From these atrocities, states sought a path forward to create a healthier world. In the autumn of 1944, state delegations (led by the United States, the United Kingdom, the Soviet Union, and the Republic of China) held a series of meetings at the Dumbarton Oaks Estate in Washington, D.C. to begin planning for the postwar period. These allied states sought to provide a framework for a new international organization to replace the League of Nations. This new organization, as they envisioned it, would maintain peace and stability by safeguarding human rights and facilitating collective governance over the world's most pressing challenges (Meier 2010). Less than a year later, their vision would come to fruition with the birth of the UN. States looked to the UN as a renewed institutional basis for global governance, with the 1945 Charter of the United Nations (UN Charter) bringing nations together to develop international laws to ensure global cooperation. New institutions of public health would be developed under the UN, establishing a global governance foundation for the development of global health law.

III. Global Governance Requires Global Law

The UN system of global governance plays a crucial role in coordinating the activities and defining the objectives of global actors to promote global health.

At the end of World War II, the international community was more interconnected than ever before—and more vulnerable to international health threats. States recognized that a more robust international law framework would be necessary for international health governance. International health law under the UN would seek to codify common values across states, binding them to mutual obligations and providing an international legal foundation for national law reforms to address public health challenges of global significance (Meier and Gostin 2018). With public health increasingly impacted by a range of global determinants and international bodies, global health law would become necessary for collective governance throughout the world, with the establishment of WHO providing new centralized legal authorities to advance global health and unite state and non-state actors in common cause.

A. Birth of the UN and Governance under International Law

The 1945 UN Charter would frame the global governance landscape for health. This constitutional framework for UN governance was the culmination of two months of deliberations at the San Francisco Conference, where representatives from fifty countries defined the structure and powers of a new international organization. The UN's framers built on the proposals from the Dumbarton Oaks Conference, entrusting the UN with legal authorities and funding support that far surpassed the League of Nations. The resulting UN Charter provided an institutional foundation to develop international law, representing necessary and unprecedented cooperation to further global solidarity in the postwar world (Gostin, Moon, and Meier 2020). This cooperation would allow for the implementation of a broad range of collective health responses by states in accordance with international law (Bélanger 1989).

In drafting the UN Charter, states did not initially address health; however, late-breaking additions at the San Francisco Conference would mainstream health authorities across the text of the UN Charter (Lancet 1945).[9] These diplomatic efforts to incorporate health authorities under UN governance would form the legal foundation for the world's governance architecture for health. Yet, notwithstanding this invocation of international health in the UN Charter, it would fall to subsequent international negotiations to frame the international governance regime for health, with the UN proposing an International Health

---

[9] These initiatives to incorporate health in the UN Charter arose out of collaborative efforts between physicians in the Brazilian and Chinese delegations to the 1945 San Francisco Conference on International Organization, who worked to establish the word "health" as a matter of international cooperation through the UN General Assembly, mandate the UN to promote solutions to international health problems, and propose a UN specialized agency to govern health (Sze 1988).

Conference that would give rise to WHO as the first UN specialized agency (Doull 1949).

B. Establishment of WHO

This International Health Conference brought together technical experts from around the world to develop the Constitution of the World Health Organization (WHO Constitution). In late 1945, the U.S. government worked with public health scholars to create a draft constitution, with that early draft serving as an outline for the UN's Technical Preparatory Committee. The Preparatory Committee's work in Paris, in turn, served as the foundation for the 1946 International Health Conference in New York, where state delegates deliberated for four and a half weeks before officially adopting the WHO Constitution pursuant to the UN Charter (Sharp 1947). In establishing WHO, the delegates agreed that this new international organization would assume the responsibilities of all the leading international health organizations—OIHP, LNHO, and UNRRA's Health Division—positioning WHO alone at the center of the global health landscape. Under this expansive global health mandate, states inaugurated WHO in 1948, launching its operations as the leading institution of global health governance.

1. Governing Structure

In facilitating this governance, states developed WHO's governing structure under the three organs diagrammed in Figure 1.2: an Assembly of member states to serve as the principal legislative and policy-making body of the organization; an Executive Board to set the agenda of the Assembly and implement its decisions; and a Secretariat made up of appointed professional staff and led by the elected Director-General (Cueto, Brown, and Fee 2019).

The World Health Assembly is WHO's ultimate policy-making body. Made up of all WHO member states, the Assembly has the authority to set WHO's agenda, approve its budget, and instruct the Executive Board and Director-General. It thus has wide-ranging authority to respond to global health concerns. Assembly resolutions, while not legally binding, reflect the will of WHO member states and have the potential to be effective tools in spurring action across nations. Most resolutions and decisions of the World Health Assembly can be adopted by a

Figure 1.2 WHO's Governing Structure (Gostin and Finch)

majority vote during annual plenary sessions, with each member state having an equal vote in all Assembly decision-making.[10]

Operating as a subset of the World Health Assembly, the WHO Constitution stipulates that WHO's Executive Board implements the decisions and policies set forth by the Assembly. Executive Board members are elected by the Assembly, taking into consideration an equitable geographic distribution, with members serving a term of three years. The Executive Board meets twice each year to guide the Assembly agenda, submit WHO's general program of work, and carry out decisions by the Assembly. Where immediate action is required, including in efforts to combat epidemics, the Constitution provides Executive Board authority to take emergency measures.

The WHO Secretariat, comprised of appointed technical staff and an elected Director-General, plays a crucial administrative role in coordinating the agency's day-to-day activities—convening technical experts, setting global standards, and supporting member states. The Secretariat is led by the Director-General, elected to a five-year term by the World Health Assembly and responsible for raising funds; coordinating with member states, partners, and other actors; and maintaining the credibility of the Organization. Serving as the public face of WHO, the Director-General is called upon to play a diplomatic role, balancing the interests of WHO's member states, mediating disputes in global health, and carrying out WHO's mission and core functions.

2. Mission and Core Functions

The WHO Constitution has provided WHO with an unprecedented mandate: "the attainment by all peoples of the highest possible level of health"—a lofty, if not unattainable, goal that seeks to achieve for every person "a state of complete physical, mental and social well-being and not merely the absence of disease or infirmity" (WHO 1946, preamble). This sweeping mission represented a significant expansion from the limited scope of authority held by previous international health governance bodies (Gostin and Meier 2020), entrusting WHO not just with controlling the spread of disease but also achieving a state of global well-being—and, in the process, safeguarding health as a "one of the fundamental rights of every human being" (WHO 1946, preamble).[11]

---

[10] While a majority vote is sufficient for most Assembly resolutions, the WHO Constitution provides that more consequential decisions—including those proposing amendments to the WHO Constitution, suspending a member's voting privileges, or adopting conventions or agreements—have a higher voting threshold of two-thirds for adoption. In practice, however, virtually all decisions by the Assembly are adopted on a consensus basis without a formal vote (OECD 2014).

[11] This right to health, first declared in the WHO Constitution, was later echoed across international human rights treaties, as discussed in Chapter 4, laying a foundation for the field of health and human rights (Gostin and Meier 2020).

The WHO Constitution positioned WHO as the world's leader in international health governance, stating that, among other functions, it is to "act as the directing and co-ordinating authority on international health work" (WHO 1946, art. 2). Drawing from this expansive authority to govern public health across nations, the WHO Constitution provided specific authority for a wide range of technical functions, tasking WHO with furnishing technical assistance and emergency aid, eradicating disease, promoting the prevention of injury, improvement of nutrition, and cooperation among scientific and professional groups (Gutteridge 1963). Beyond these technical functions, WHO was endowed with expansive normative functions, unique among global governance institutions, that provide WHO with extensive lawmaking authority.

3. Legal Authorities: Conventions, Regulations, and Recommendations
To enable WHO to carry out its wide-ranging mandate, drafters of the WHO Constitution granted the agency unprecedented legal authority in international health. WHO's quasi-legislative powers were a key innovation in international governance, allowing the World Health Assembly to adopt different types of legal instruments and thereby offering WHO flexibility in addressing distinct public health challenges with varying degrees of legal authority (Sharp 1947).

Case Study: Legal Authorities of the World Health Organization

The WHO Constitution confers legal authorities that are both robust and varied, delineating separate authorities to develop conventions, regulations, and recommendations. The World Health Assembly, under Article 19 of the WHO Constitution, has broad authority to adopt conventions or agreements with respect to "any matter within the competence of the Organization"—a major departure from predecessor organizations. A rare feature in international law, the WHO Constitution thus allows for the development of binding obligations, with the Assembly authorized to adopt legally binding treaties and agreements that set standards to promote public health and provide paths for state ratification. Similarly providing means to bind all WHO member states, Article 21 of the WHO Constitution empowers the Assembly to adopt regulations in specific areas of global health: the international spread of disease, public health nomenclature, and standards for diagnostic procedures and the international trade and advertising of biological and pharmaceutical products. In these specific areas, regulations promulgated by the World Health Assembly automatically bind WHO member states unless they specifically opt out, with this "contracting out" approach requiring member states to either accept or reject a regulation. Yet, not all health threats require binding obligations. For areas where non-binding obligations are sufficient (or at least politically expedient) to support global action, Article 23 of the Constitution confers authority on the World Health Assembly to develop non-binding recommendations, with these recommendations offering guidance to member states on any matter within the competence of WHO. These three distinct lawmaking authorities under Articles 19, 21, and 23 of the WHO Constitution put WHO in a position to achieve maximum possible adherence from WHO member states, with varied legal authorities providing the flexibility to pursue the most expedient legal path to advance global health.

The drafters of the WHO Constitution expected that this lawmaking authority would enable WHO to develop international health law across various global health threats, creating binding public health obligations for states and more effectively aligning national public health actions with international public health strategies—providing the uniformity under international law that had been missing in the work of previous organizations (Bélanger 1989). However, this hope that international health law would bind the world came to be challenged by the rapid rise of non-state actors in global health governance, raising an imperative to look beyond international law for lawmaking authority in global health (Gostin 2014).

C. Norm Setting Beyond Treaty Law: An Imperative for Global Health Law

Building from the development of international law to bind WHO member states in the prevention, control, and response to diseases, global health law has come to address a larger set of global health determinants that require globally coordinated action. Global health law supports WHO in binding states to shared commitments under "hard law" instruments, but also provides a path under "soft law" to unite state and non-state actors in the pursuit of global health goals (Meier et al. 2020). These non-binding soft law instruments—including resolutions, guidelines, protocols, global strategies, declarations, and recommendations—do not offer the enforceability of binding international law but are nonetheless authoritative, providing a path to incorporate non-state actors (from non-governmental organizations to private sector organizations) in global health governance (Fidler 1999).

Expanding the range of law and policy instruments in responding to global health crises, soft law norms have offered flexibility in structuring responsibilities for the full range of state and non-state actors in global health. The increasing health threats of a globalizing world have required global governance institutions to look beyond international treaties, utilizing soft law frameworks and innovative policy partnerships to enable the attainment by all peoples of the highest possible level of health (Gostin 2014). WHO has come to look largely to soft law approaches in establishing its policy agenda, regulating issues as broad as unhealthy diets, breastmilk substitutes, and environmental health. Soft law instruments dominate WHO governance because they are faster and easier to adopt than treaties and their non-binding nature may encourage actors to accept them more readily—precisely because they are not legally bound (Sekalala and Masud 2021). This advantage in developing soft law has thus served as an important building block for more ambitious instruments in global health law and policy—beyond international law and across the global health landscape.

Conclusion

The advancement of public health has changed dramatically over the centuries. Globalization has woven together the fates of people from different countries and the health challenges they face. The world must act together to address common threats. Addressing public health in a globalizing world requires efforts to understand global governance. Global governance for health is essential to coordinate actors throughout the world, with the end of World War II and establishment of the UN giving rise to WHO as the world's directing and coordinating authority on health. The WHO Constitution reflected a groundbreaking effort to establish international health governance in a world torn apart by war. Under WHO governance, the global community recognized that the most pressing health threats require international responses, and that belief is reflected in the development of international health law—from the first sanitary conventions to the postwar birth of WHO's legal authorities.

While the WHO Constitution would provide the organization with sweeping legal authorities to shape norms and address global health under a range of law and policy approaches, threats to global health have continued to evolve, requiring new legal authorities to promote public health. Under WHO governance, the application of law to global health has grown from a narrow set of international legal obligations for responding to specific infectious diseases to a wide-ranging field of practice that strives to prevent disease and promote health and well-being. These responses to global health challenges implicate a vast number of sectors and actors, and are influenced by developments in science and underlying social environments, requiring global health law to encompass both binding "hard" and non-binding "soft" law instruments. Global health law now seeks to establish mutual obligations across state and non-state actors to face new threats—looking beyond the spread of infectious disease and recognizing our common humanity and shared vulnerability.

The history of global health law provides a path to understand the importance of law and policy as a foundation of global health governance. As in the past, global health threats can only be solved through global health cooperation, and that cooperation can only be achieved through global health law. Global health law, like the public health science that underpins it, has evolved through iterative processes. Only by reflecting on the past successes and failures of legal responses to public health challenges is it possible to understand how global health law has come to shape global health governance. Law has provided a path for populations to claim entitlements to health services and systems, with corresponding obligations developed, implemented, and enforced. These obligations provide a foundation for fragmented national responses to be harmonized, looking to global health governance to bring the world together to respond to global health challenges under global health law.

Questions for Consideration

1. How does public health differ from the practice of medicine? How did social medicine expand the definition of public health?
2. Why do governments bear responsibility for addressing public health? How do governments meet this responsibility through public policy?
3. How did states first come to see the need for international cooperation to address public health threats? Why did these early international efforts fail to achieve true cooperation?
4. What did early institutions of international health governance provide that was lacking in international sanitary conferences? Why did nations develop competing institutions across the Pan American Sanitary Bureau, *Office International d'Hygiène Publique* (OIHP), and League of Nations Health Office (LNHO)?
5. How did the United Nations Relief and Rehabilitation Administration (UNRRA) succeed in providing international health governance amid the challenges of World War II?
6. How did the horrors of World War II shape the development of the United Nations (UN) as a new system of global health governance? Why

did states see the UN as necessary to the postwar development of international law?
7. Given the establishment of the UN, why was it necessary to develop the World Health Organization (WHO) as a separate organization? How did WHO governance draw from previous institutions of international health governance?
8. Why was WHO's mandate so much broader than that of previous institutions? Was this mandate realistic, encompassing WHO efforts to realize for all people "a state of complete physical, mental and social well-being and not merely the absence of disease or infirmity"?
9. Why was it necessary to endow WHO with expansive normative functions to develop global health law? Why did states delineate multiple types of legal authorities (binding and non-binding) for multiple types of global health challenges?
10. Why does global health law need to look beyond international treaty law (applicable to states) to encompass global health law (over a larger set of state and non-state actors)?

Acknowledgments

The authors are grateful for the research assistance of Chris Burch in defining the encompassing field of global health, Erin Jones in examining the rise of international governance to protect public health, Karina Shaw in describing WHO's governing bodies and constitutional functions, Oliver Redsten for his thorough description of the history of WHO's normative authorities, and Sonam Shah for her analysis of the WHO Constitution.

References

Aginam, Obijiofor. 2005. *Global Health Governance: International Law and Public Health in a Divided World*. Toronto: University of Toronto Press.
Bachrach, Susan and Dieter Kuntz. 2004. *Deadly Medicine: Creating the Master Race*. Washington, D.C.: United States Holocaust Memorial Museum.
Bélanger, Michel. 1989. "The Future of International Health Law: A Round Table." *International Digest of Health Legislation* 40(1): 1–29.
Birn, Anne-Emanuelle, Yogan Pillay, and Timothy H. Holtz. 2017. *Textbook of Global Health*. Fourth edition. New York: Oxford University Press.
Borowy, Iris. 2009. *Coming to Terms with World Health: The League of Nations Health Organization 1921–1946*. Bern: Peter Lang.
Bootsma, Martin C. J., and Neil M. Ferguson. 2007. "The Effect of Public Health Measures on the 1918 Influenza Pandemic in U.S. Cities." *Proceedings of the National Academy of Sciences* 104(18): 7588–7593.

Brown, Theodore M., Marcos Cueto, and Elizabeth Fee. 2006. "The World Health Organization and the Transition from 'International' to 'Global' Public Health." *American Journal of Public Health* 96(1): 62-72.

Bump, Jesse B. and Ifeyinwa Aniebo. 2022. "Colonialism, Malaria, and the Decolonization of Global Health." *PLOS Global Public Health* 2(9): e0000936.

Carey, H. L. 1970. "A War We Can Win. Health as a Vector of Foreign Policy." *Bulletin of the New York Academy of Medicine* 46(5): 334-50.

Coghe, Samuël. 2020. "Disease Control and Public Health in Colonial Africa." In *Oxford Research Encyclopedia of African History*. New York: Oxford University Press.

Constantin, Andrés and Roberto Andorno. 2020. "Human Subjects in Globalized Health Research." In *Foundations of Global Health & Human Rights*, edited by Lawrence O. Gostin and Benjamin Mason Meier. New York: Oxford University Press, 395-416.

Cueto, Marcos, Theodore M. Brown, and Elizabeth Fee. 2019. *The World Health Organization: A History*. Cambridge: Cambridge University Press.

De Feo, Giovanni, George Antoniou, Hilal Fardin, Fatma El-Gohary, Xiao Zheng, Ieva Reklaityte, David Butler, Stavros Yannopoulos, and Andreas Angelakis. 2014. "The Historical Development of Sewers Worldwide." *Sustainability* 6(6): 3936-3974.

Doull J. A. 1949. "Nations United for Health." In *Public Health in the World Today*, edited by James S. Simmons, 317-332. Cambridge: Harvard University Press.

Fidler, David P. 1999. *International Law and Infectious Diseases*. New York: Oxford University Press.

Fidler, David P. 2001. "The Globalization of Public Health: The First 100 Years of International Health Diplomacy." *Bulletin of the World Health Organization* 79(9): 842-849.

Goodman, Neville M. 1952. *International Health Organizations*. Philadelphia: Blakiston.

Gostin, Lawrence O. 2014. *Global Health Law*. Cambridge: Harvard University Press.

Gostin, Lawrence O. and Benjamin Mason Meier. 2019. "Introducing Global Health Law." *Journal of Law, Medicine & Ethics* 47(4): 788-793.

Gostin, Lawrence O. and Benjamin Mason Meier. 2020. *Foundations of Global Health & Human Rights*. New York: Oxford University Press.

Gostin, Lawrence O. and Lindsay F. Wiley. 2016. *Public Health Law: Power, Duty, Restraint*. Third edition. Oakland: University of California Press.

Gostin, Lawrence O., Suerie Moon, and Benjamin Mason Meier. 2020. "Reimagining Global Health Governance in the Age of COVID-19." *American Journal of Public Health* 110(11): 1615-1619.

Goudsblom, Johan. 1986. "Public Health and the Civilizing Process." *The Milbank Quarterly* 64(2): 161-88.

Gutteridge, Frank. 1963. "The World Health Organization: Its Scope and Achievements." *Temple Law Quarterly* 37(1): 1-14.

Hewa, Soma. 1995. *Colonialism, Tropical Disease, and Imperial Medicine: Rockefeller Philanthropy in Sri Lanka*. Lanham: University Press of America.

Jacobson, Harold K. 1979. *Networks of Interdependence*. New York: Alfred L. Knopf.

Kelley, Patrick W. 2011. "Global Health: Governance and Policy Development." *Infectious Disease Clinics of North America* 25(2): 435-453.

Lancet. 1945. "Health and the Nations." *Lancet* 246(6363): 177.

Lang, T. 2001. "Public Health and Colonialism: A New or Old Problem?" *Journal of Epidemiology & Community Health* 55(3): 162-163.

Mackenbach, J P. 2009. "Politics Is Nothing but Medicine at a Larger Scale: Reflections on Public Health's Biggest Idea." *Journal of Epidemiology & Community Health* 63(3): 181-184.

Marmot, Michael G., M. Kogevinas, and M.A. Elston. 1987. "Social/Economic Status and Disease." *Annual Review of Public Health* 8(111): 112-115.

McEvoy, Arthur F. 1995. "The Triangle Shirtwaist Factory Fire of 1911: Social Change, Industrial Accidents, and the Evolution of Common-Sense Causality." *Law & Social Inquiry* 20(1995): 621–651.
McKeown, Thomas. 1979. *The Role of Medicine: Dream, Mirage, or Nemesis?* Princeton: Princeton University Press.
McMichael, Anthony and Robert Beaglehole. 2009. "The Global Context for Public Health." In *Global Public Health: A New Era*, 2nd Edition, edited by Robert Beaglehole and Ruth Bonita. Oxford: Oxford University Press, 1–22.
Meier, Benjamin Mason. 2010. "Global Health Governance and the Contentious Politics of Human Rights: Mainstreaming the Right to Health for Public Health Advancement." *Stanford Journal of International Law* 46: 1–50.
Meier, Benjamin Mason and Ana S. Ayala. 2015. "The Pan American Health Organization and the Mainstreaming of Human Rights in Regional Health Governance." *Journal of Law, Medicine & Ethics* 42(3): 356–374.
Meier, Benjamin Mason and Lawrence O. Gostin. 2018. *Human Rights in Global Health: Rights-Based Governance for a Globalizing World*. New York: Oxford University Press.
Meier, Benjamin Mason, Allyn Taylor, Mark Eccleston-Turner, Roojin Habibi, Sharifah Sekalala, and Lawrence O. Gostin. 2020. "The World Health Organization in Global Health Law." *The Journal of Law, Medicine & Ethics* 48(4): 796–799.
OECD (Organization for Economic Co-operation and Development). 2014. International Regulatory Co-Operation and International Organisations: The Case of the World Health Organization (WHO). OECD.
Pannenborg, Charles O. 1979. *A New International Health Order: An Inquiry into the International Relations of World Health and Medical Care*. Alphen aan den Rijn: Sijthoff and Noordhoff.
Porter, Dorothy. 1997. *Social Medicine and Medical Sociology in the Twentieth Century*. Amsterdam: Clio Medica.
Porter, Dorothy. 1999. *Health, Civilization, and the State: A History of Public Health from Ancient to Modern Times*. London: Routledge.
Rosen, George. 1958. *A History of Public Health*. New York: MD Publications.
Sand, René. 1934. *L'Économie Humaine par la Médicine Sociale*. Paris: Éd. Rieder.
Sawyer Wilbur A. 1947. "Achievements of UNRRA as an International Health Organization." *American Journal of Public Health* 37(1): 41–58.
Sekalala, Sharifah and Haleema Masud. 2021. "Soft Law Possibilities in Global Health Law." *Journal of Law, Medicine & Ethics* 49(1): 152–155.
Sharp, Walter R. 1947. "The New World Health Organization." *American Journal of International Law* 41: 509–530.
Sze, Szeming. 1988. "WHO: From Small Beginnings." *World Health Forum* 9(1): 29–34.
Tulchinsky, Theodore H. and Elena A. Varavikova. 2014. "A History of Public Health." *The New Public Health*, 1–42. Amsterdam: Elsevier. https://doi.org/10.1016/B978-0-12-415 766-8.00001-X.
WHO (World Health Organization). 1946. *The Constitution of the World Health Organization*. New York: World Health Organization.
WHO. 1958. *The First Ten Years of the World Health Organization*. Geneva: World Health Organization.
Winslow, C.E.A. 1923. The Evolution and Significance of the Modern Public Health Campaign. New Haven: Yale University Press.

2
Global Health Law
Legal Frameworks to Advance Global Health

Sharifah Sekalala and Roojin Habibi

Introduction

In a globalizing world, threats to public health increasingly transcend national frontiers and require coordination and cooperation within and across countries. This imperative for cooperation has been coupled with an expanding number of non-state actors, who are increasingly involved in responding to global health threats. These new threats and actors have shifted the traditional forms of collaboration through new forms of legal and policy frameworks. International law lies at the heart of such cooperation, offering actors in the international community a platform to set common rules toward the common interest of a healthier world for all. State and non-state actors have come to use diverse instruments of international law to respond to global health threats. Encompassing the legal and policy frameworks that structure global health, global health law seeks to bring together these frameworks with the aim of bridging national boundaries and alleviating inequities in global health.

Global health law is shaped by laws that are both "hard" and "soft," with a range of international legal instruments that determine how a vast landscape of state and non-state actors engage in disease prevention and health promotion. Hard international law presents binding obligations on states, which incur sanctions if these obligations are breached. Legal scholars that ascribe to a positivist school of thought find that international law should include only law that is binding on states. Constructivist legal scholars, on the other hand, look to a sliding scale of obligations, which range from binding to non-binding. These constructivists thus look to soft law, which encompasses quasi-legal instruments, whose binding force is weaker than that of recognized international law. Complementing hard law, soft law policies have served to advance global health by providing normative clarification of treaties, setting standards, ensuring monitoring and accountability, and serving as precursors to hard law. Under this larger constructivist framing, both hard law and soft law are necessary to the advancement of global health through global health law and policy.

This chapter introduces the international law and global policy structures that make up global health law. Part I examines initial efforts to harness international law to promote public health while protecting rapidly expanding trade relations. Following from the development of the contemporary system of global health governance under the United Nations (UN), Part II examines the contribution of soft law to global health law and policy, exploring the deployment of soft laws under the auspices of the World Health Organization (WHO) and other institutions of global health governance. Part III looks to the combined application of soft and hard law in the COVID-19 pandemic response, discussing how these responses complemented each other in the larger global health governance response. Moving beyond the distinct application of soft law and hard law in global health governance, the chapter concludes that the future of global health law and policy lies in the complementarity of hard and soft laws and their strategic and holistic contributions to the ultimate aim of promoting global health with justice.

I. Birth of Law across Nations to Prevent Disease and Promote Health

Governments have sought for centuries to mitigate cross-border threats to public health through instruments of international law—that is, law that emanates from the will of states and follows from predefined legal sources and procedures.[1] Traditionally, states relied on hard international law to protect public health through written agreements between two or more states, referred to variously as "treaties," "conventions," or "accords." While the progression of binding international health law remained hampered by piecemeal lawmaking, unequal power relations, and narrow understandings of health, the policy experimentation that took place during these early years laid the foundation for the development of international health law under the UN and the evolution of a far more complex field of global health law through WHO.

A. Origins of International Health Law

It has long been understood that diseases in one part of the world may quickly reach people elsewhere. By the middle of the 19th century, with the

---

[1] International law is often delineated into two overarching branches—public international law (dealing primarily with matters between states; or between states and other entities, such as international organizations) and private international law (governing international relations between private entities)—with this chapter focusing on the role of public international law.

intensification of international trade, this "unification of the globe by disease" gave rise to an impetus for nations—concentrated primarily among the trading powers in Europe—to control external threats to public health through international cooperation and common standards (Huber 2006, 476). These early international health negotiations, first introduced in Chapter 1, emphasized the need for cooperation across nations to prevent the spread of specific infectious diseases, leading to the first International Sanitary Convention (Carvalho and Zacher 2001).

Case Study: The First International Sanitary Convention

As the forces of industrialization and globalization intensified the spread of cholera across Europe and undermined national policies on infectious disease control, it became evident in the 19th century that the threat of infectious disease spread would demand international cooperation. Recognizing the impact of infectious disease outbreaks on international trade and the flow of capital, major European nations convened the first International Sanitary Conference in 1851. This meeting culminated in a convention, but a lack of consensus around the use of quarantine measures led only three states to ratify it, and as such, the convention failed to come into force. Despite the failure to establish international law, these early conferences were fruitful in developing important guidelines that influenced the way states dealt with issues of sanitation standards for ships, port inspections, mandatory quarantine periods, and public health surveillance. In 1892, the first International Sanitary Convention was adopted, aimed at "protecting" Europe from the threat of infectious diseases spreading from Asia and the Middle East through pilgrimages. Scientific advances in the years that followed (particularly in relation to cholera, plague, and yellow fever) would see increased coordination in subsequent conferences, as states reconvened to strengthen international rules on public health. Through the 1903 International Sanitary Conference in Paris, states agreed on the need to codify all the previous agreements into a single instrument and to establish an international health organization. The agreement reached in 1903 established the core structure of the International Sanitary Convention, which would be revised repeatedly in the decades that followed, and led to the creation of the *Office International d'Hygiène Publique* (OIHP), which was charged with overseeing this international health agreement.

Beyond infectious disease, these early negotiations also sought to regulate activities that posed non-communicable disease threats, such as the international trade of narcotic drugs and alcohol, transboundary air and water pollution, and occupational safety and health (Fidler 2001).

However, these initial efforts to develop international health law, balancing efforts to protect public health and preserve lucrative transcontinental trade relations, remained grossly inadequate in achieving equitable health improvements throughout the world. Reflecting the injustice of international cooperation at this time, the vast majority of nations, representing most of the world's population, were absent from this fragmented landscape of lawmaking under international health law in the late 19th and early 20th centuries. Compounding the limitations of these international inequities and patchwork institutions, early diplomatic efforts coalesced around a narrow, biomedical conception of health, which focused primarily on technical aspects of disease prevention such as containment measures for people and products at national borders. Where these biomedical models of disease prevention overlooked underlying social and economic determinants of the spread of infectious disease, international health law would soon expand in scope and breadth through the radical transformation of international health governance under the UN, with the establishment of WHO providing new legal authorities to advance public health throughout the world.

B. International Lawmaking under the UN

The birth of the UN in the aftermath of World War II marked the beginning of a new era of multilateral lawmaking in the pursuit of international peace, security, and development, vastly expanding the scope of international authority. The role of the UN in developing international law would feature in debates leading up to the 1945 San Francisco Conference on International Organization and subsequent adoption of the Charter of the United Nations (UN Charter) (Kreuder-Sonnen and Zurn 2020). The UN and its specialized agencies would reflect a marked departure from the international community's weak lawmaking authorities under the League of Nations, with the UN Charter seeking to create "conditions under which justice and respect for the obligations arising from treaties and other sources of international law can be maintained" (UN 1945, preamble).

However, the UN Charter did not provide further guidance on what such "other sources of international law" may include. To interpret the substantive content of international law, the UN Charter established a new international judicial institution, the International Court of Justice,[2] with the Statute of the International Court of Justice delineating the following sources of international law:

---

[2] The International Court of Justice, one of the principal organs established by the UN Charter, is mandated to oversee the peaceful settlement of disputes of international law between states and issue advisory opinions on legal questions referred to it by UN organs and specialized agencies (UN Charter 1945).

(a) international conventions which establish rules expressly recognized by states;
(b) international custom, as evidence of a general practice accepted as law;
(c) the general principles of law recognized by all nations; and
(d) judicial decisions and the teachings of the most highly qualified publicists of the various nations, as subsidiary means for the determination of rules of law (UN, 1946, Article 38).

Despite these wide-ranging sources of law—seeking to allow legal practitioners to ascertain the specific content of international law—it has long remained unclear which other sources of law count as the most authentic representations of international legal obligations, with much of what is known as hard international law focused on international legal conventions—written agreements that states directly and voluntarily adopt.

While the Charter remains vague on procedures for developing and adopting international legal conventions to bind states, it does establish key structures and platforms of interstate lawmaking, including the UN General Assembly, bringing together all UN Member States and mandated with the task of "encouraging the progressive development of international law and its codification"; and the Economic and Social Council, which is empowered to draft conventions and other hard law instruments. The UN Charter also provides authority under the UN for the establishment of a specialized agency with "wide international responsibilities" in health. With the 1946 adoption of the Constitution of the World Health Organization, states established WHO, as reflected in Figure 2.1, as this new international health body under the UN.

WHO transformed the landscape of international health law—not only by centralizing normative authority in the field, but also by expansively defining health within the Preamble of its Constitution as "a state of complete physical, mental and social well-being and not merely the absence of disease or infirmity" and articulating the first international expression of the human right to health (WHO 1946, preamble). This conceptualization of health paved the way for WHO's vision to "act as the directing and co-ordinating authority on international health work" (ibid., art. 2). To this end, significant lawmaking authorities would be entrusted to WHO and its plenary body of Member States, the World Health Assembly, including the authority, as introduced in Chapter 1, to:

- Adopt conventions or agreements that touch on any matter within the competence of the Organization (Article 19);
- Adopt legally binding regulations that enter into force for all parties after a specified period of time (Articles 21 and 22);[3] and

---

[3] Under the WHO Constitution, the World Health Assembly may adopt regulations concerning a subset of issues, including with respect to "sanitary and quarantine requirements and

Figure 2.1 WHO accession to the UN, with signing by UN Secretary General Trygvie Lie and WHO Director-General Brock Chisholm, 1948 (UN)

- Issue recommendations with respect to any matter within the competence of the Organization (Article 23).

The WHO Constitution would thus provide WHO legal authority to engage in a wide range of health-promoting agendas, including those shaped by the social, commercial, and environmental determinants of health.

In an early effort to exercise these legal authorities, WHO Member States worked to transition the prewar patchwork of rules governing international cooperation on infectious disease control into a single legal instrument under the auspices of WHO. Consolidating the multilateral conventions on infectious diseases that had been adopted in a piecemeal fashion over the previous

---

other procedures designed to prevent the international spread of disease" (WHO 1946, art. 21). Importantly, regulations adopted under Article 21 are opt-out instruments, requiring WHO Member States to notify the Director-General of their wish not to be bound by the instrument within a stipulated period of time. In the absence of such notification, regulations will be automatically binding.

century, a Special Committee on International Sanitary Regulations met in Geneva with all WHO Member States, with more than sixty nations deliberating for five weeks on these regulations. These inclusive deliberations concluded at the World Health Assembly, which unanimously adopted the International Sanitary Regulations in May 1951, thus harmonizing a global surveillance and reporting system for infectious disease control at the international level. Under the governance of WHO, the International Sanitary Regulations combined substantive legal approaches to infectious disease control that had been developed since the first International Sanitary Convention in 1851—alongside procedural mechanisms to help states address infectious disease threats. In 1969, the International Sanitary Regulations would be renamed the International Health Regulations (Fidler 1998).

C. WHO and the Fragmentation of International Law in Global Health

Despite these expansive legal authorities, WHO has little power to act in the absence of state consent and, as a consequence, has developed only two treaties since its inception: the International Health Regulations and the Framework Convention on Tobacco Control. Multiple reasons underpin WHO's historical reluctance to wield international law to advance its constitutional, technical, and operational objectives. First, as with any regime of international law, the development of international law does not guarantee its implementation, and in the absence of effective mechanisms of enforcement, the impact of international treaties may prove elusive (Hoffman et al. 2022). More fundamentally, the highly complex and interdependent nature of global health issues implies their interaction with other international law regimes (such as trade law and environmental law). With a diverse range of intergovernmental organizations and legal instruments bearing on global health, it has historically been difficult for the World Health Assembly to reach multilateral agreement on the development of international law, with WHO often looking outside its legal authorities to realize its constitutional mandate (Taylor 1992).

Notwithstanding this WHO reluctance, other UN specialized agencies have developed international legal standards to realize their institutional mandates—developing robust legal instruments that impact upon global health. The International Labor Organization, for instance, has adopted over forty standards on occupational health and safety at work (Wilson et al. 2006). These standards have dealt with a variety of issues that have vast implications for health, including instruments that address the provision of healthcare for migrant workers; occupational diseases; standards of health and safety in workplaces; as well as broader provisions such as social security, thereby addressing underlying determinants of public health (Swepston 2018).

Beyond other intergovernmental bodies, an array of non-state actors have emerged in the global health landscape. These non-state institutions—including transnational corporations, individual philanthropists, and civil society—hold growing influence over global health outcomes—even though they are outside the direct scope of WHO's governance (Gostin 2014). Because these non-state actors are not bound by hard law, WHO has sought to rely on "softer" forms of normative authority (including recommendations under article 23 of its Constitution) in efforts to structure the behaviors of these varied non-state actors. The reliance on these non-legally binding norms has hastened the transformation of international health law, made primarily between states and international organizations, into global health law, which looks to both state and non-state actors (Gostin and Meier 2019). Confronted by proliferating non-state actors in the global health governance landscape, the development of soft law has become central to dialogue, deliberation, and politics under global health law.

II. Contributions of Soft Law to Global Health Law

Global health law ranges from binding treaties and norms (those codified under international law) to authoritative yet non-binding normative instruments (such as resolutions, declarations, guidelines, protocols, and recommendations). These latter instruments reflect soft law norms, framing standards of legal behavior, and include a series of quasi-legal instruments that do not have binding force—or whose binding force is weaker than that of recognized international law (Trubek, Cottrell, and Nance 2005). Soft law can thus be categorized as any (1) agreement by states and/or international organizations vested with authority; (2) which has normative character; and (3) is technically non-binding, but some scope exists for consequences where noncompliance occurs (Sekalala 2017). The expansion of global health law to encompass soft law preserves the doctrinal distinction between binding and non-binding norms, tracking an intuitive difference between quasi-legal policy norms and merely political statements, with soft law policies forming a central basis of global health law—under WHO governance and across the global health landscape.

A. Soft Law as a Basis of Global Health Policy

Although hard law is binding and soft law is not, the distinction between the two is far more nuanced. Constructivist legal theories find that legal norms are not binary but are based on graduated normativity: from binding to non-binding (Chinkin 2000). For constructivists, the distinction between law and policy lies in the degree of normativity, which gives law its legal character. For instance, a resolution of the World Health Assembly, which is considered a form of soft law, may provide policy guidance to health practitioners about its implementation. Although this broad approach to soft law may raise alarm for positivists, who find that such "soft" definitions run the risk of weakening international law (Klabbers 1998), this is not necessarily true—as soft law still remains law because it contains three normative aspects: obligation, precision, and delegation (Abbott et al. 2000). These three characteristics are important as they ensure that soft law presents a precise obligation that parties are bound by and a mechanism of ensuring that parties comply with it. Given the increasing number of non-state actors in the global health governance landscape, soft law can effectively coordinate behavior across a varied range of actors while still framing obligations in global health (Sekalala 2017).

While such soft law norms lack the legal enforcement of hard law (Goldsmith and Posner 2004), they can provide other mechanisms of accountability—as seen through risk of reputational loss or through softer mechanisms of compliance. Rather than formal legal enforcement, states often comply with international law norms due to persuasion, congruence, and habit, rather than through the threat of legal sanctions (Abbott and Snidal 2000). Compliance can be equally effective whether for binding or non-binding reasons. This accountability process is strengthened by the role of non-state actors, who can become a constitutive part of the lawmaking process. Given unequal power dynamics, non-state actors and weaker states can use persuasion to encourage stronger states to develop laws and policies that may go against their vested self-interest, engendering compliance through mechanisms such as "naming and shaming" (Abbott and Snidal 2000).[4]

Using soft law to shape the behaviors of state and non-state actors can enable soft law to "harden" over time into binding international law. This behavioral aspect of soft law allows states, which may be unable to reach agreement on a binding obligation with each other, to achieve consensus incrementally over time. In building toward hard law, states may use the negotiation of soft

---

[4] "Naming and shaming" tactics are considered an important primary step in facilitating accountability. Through the identification of evidence of violations (naming), advocates aim to apply pressure on violators (shaming)—with documentation to denounce violators' actions (Meernik et al. 2012).

law standards to persuade their people about the necessity of binding law in the future, to allow scientific understanding to evolve, or to build infrastructure or technical competence before agreeing to newer standards (Chayes and Chayes 1995). Constructivists conclude that this hardening of legal obligations illustrates the role of international law as an organic process, by which parties can gradually harmonize existing rules within a legal system that is flexible and adaptable (Guzman and Meyer 2009). This process can allow global health law to develop in a gradual and dynamic manner and avoid the divisive dangers of legal codification that have long limited international health law in global health governance.

B. Necessity of Soft Law in Global Health Governance

As global health governance has expanded, soft law has strengthened global health law. While traditional international lawmaking invariably involves state parties, increasingly non-state actors engage in developing and implementing global health law—thereby changing the scope of obligations, precision, and application (Sekalala 2017). The global health governance landscape has seen a proliferation of non-state actors, as will be elaborated in Chapter 3, ranging from international financial institutions, public-private partnerships such as Gavi, the Vaccine Alliance, bilateral donor agencies such as the US President's Emergency Plan for AIDS Relief (PEPFAR), and non-governmental organizations (NGOs) that deal primarily with health such as Médecins Sans Frontières. These new non-state actors in the global health landscape do not have the legal personality or capacity to enter into legally binding agreements adopted by states. Providing new opportunities in global health governance, soft law has been used to create clearer legal obligations, balance competing treaty obligations, fill gaps in hard law instruments, and even establish new organizations to respond to specific health problems.

Soft law has proven particularly important in global governance for health, where speed is essential in responding quickly to emerging threats. When faced with new global health threats, the science is often uncertain, as seen in emerging infectious diseases, where mitigation measures may be implemented without complete understanding of how a disease spreads or who is at greatest risk (Sekalala 2017). In these global health contexts, soft law can serve a crucial role in developing obligations amid uncertainties, with the development of soft law instruments helping to create awareness of the crisis, develop guidelines as scientific knowledge evolves, and lay the foundation for future hard law norms. Where states may be unwilling to yield sovereignty to global governance, they may be more willing to cede authority through non-binding agreements.

This need for soft law is additionally imperative because global health threats are often complex, falling at the intersection of multiple treaty regimes. While infectious disease threats are governed through WHO by the International Health Regulations, other treaty regimes can become relevant in a public health emergency—as seen where human rights, international trade, or medical supplies are affected.[5] Networked global health problems require networked responses that bring together a wide range of institutions (Slaughter 2004). Global governance in health reflects this changing state of affairs, bringing together organizations representing a diversity of interests. For these inter-organizational collaborations, soft law provides much better prospects of circumventing the predilections of existing legal structures and focusing on the main concern: solving global health problems (Sekalala 2017). By creating greater awareness of the inter-sectoral nature of health threats, coordination across sectors can best be achieved through standard setting under soft law, as it is relatively easy and quick to develop and entails low "contracting costs"— as states are not enforceably bound under international law. This efficiency in policymaking has become a principal reason why WHO has looked to soft law as a central approach to the development of global health policy.

C. WHO's Use of Soft Law

Since its inception, WHO has predominantly used soft law to guide its leadership in global health governance: to regulate underlying determinants of health, give normative clarification to treaties, set standards in global health, ensure monitoring and accountability, and lay a foundation for hard law. As the "directing and co-ordinating authority on international health work" (WHO 1946, art. 2), WHO holds an explicit function under the WHO Constitution to adopt normative instruments to advance global health. WHO was endowed with unprecedented norm-making power under its Constitution, but its "most salient normative activity has been to create 'soft' standards underpinned by science, ethics, and human rights" (Gostin, Sridhar, and Hougendobler 2015, 855). WHO's core normative functions can be divided into three categories: constitutional standards, scientific and technical standards, and health trend assessments.

---

[5] For example, the movement for access to medicines, as discussed in Chapter 12, is widely seen as a public health issue, but it also involves challenges to intellectual property laws such as the World Trade Organization Agreement on Trade-Related Aspects of Intellectual Property Rights (TRIPS Agreement).

- Constitutional standards are those norms that are approved by the World Health Assembly or an equivalent state legislative body. While not necessarily binding under international law, an agreement or resolution adopted by the Assembly is normatively stronger than other WHO standards, as they often draw from regional and national-level efforts in the preparation, implementation, and compliance of these normative standards, as seen in the International Code of Marketing of Breast-milk Substitutes.[6]
- Scientific and technical standards are norms that are set by the WHO Secretariat and cover a broad range of thematic areas, based on scientific evidence brought together by WHO technical experts, as seen in WHO's development of an Essential Medicines List, which has been a critical tool in promoting the use of generic medicines over branded alternatives—and thereby ensuring greater access to high-quality medicines through global health policy.
- Health trend assessments create core standards over time and enable countries both to make comparisons on their health burdens and also to guide improvements to reflect national "best practices," as exemplified by WHO's annual World Health Statistics, Global Burden of Disease, Risk and Injury, World Malaria Report, and Maternal Mortality Report (WHO 2017). Over time, states use these WHO standards to benchmark their progress against other states, which entrenches the development of norms in these areas and enables states to create national plans—and thereby raise standards globally.

As WHO has the capacity to set norms using a range of different legal and policy tools, these soft law approaches are most influential where the World Health Assembly passes a resolution expressing the will of WHO Member States, "representing the highest level of commitment" by states in global health (Gostin, Sridhar, and Hougendobler 2015, 855). However, regulatory and technical guidance, as well as codes of practice, also help states to make policy decisions based on expert advice.

Soft law has thus grown under WHO governance, as soft law standards can be adopted relatively quickly and easily, especially when the science is still uncertain or there is a lack of political consensus. WHO itself has acknowledged speed as one of the reasons why it often engages with soft law in rapidly unfolding global health responses. In the early days of the HIV/AIDS response, WHO looked to soft law to enact global surveillance programs in order to understand the magnitude of the global threat (Sekalala 2017). WHO's legal counsel at the time used

---

[6] As discussed in detail in Chapter 13, the World Health Assembly adopted the 1981 International Code of Marketing of Breast-milk Substitutes to promote breastfeeding and enshrine restrictions on the marketing of breast milk substitutes, such as infant formula, and since then, a number of subsequent World Health Assembly resolutions have further clarified or extended certain provisions of the Code, leading to national legislative reforms across WHO Member States.

the HIV/AIDS response to illustrate the problems that WHO would face if it tried to use binding international law to address a rapidly escalating crisis:

> The use of binding mechanisms would seem unrealistic. Leaving aside conventions, for which the future promises no more than the past to resort to regulations, appears a very doubtful undertaking... The real difficulty is that the measures cannot be adopted quickly enough to meet the health requirements of the moment (Vignes 1989, 18).

WHO additionally looks to non-binding soft law to achieve consensus in politically challenging areas where Member States have divergent interests, as seen where access to medicines in the emergency context of HIV would require prioritizing public health over international trade and intellectual property concerns, limiting the profits of transnational pharmaceutical corporations in the response to a public health emergency.

Working closely with WHO to set normative standards in the HIV/AIDS response, the Joint United Nations Programme on HIV/AIDS (UNAIDS) has been revolutionary in setting soft law standards through the adoption of performance and achievement indicators. Through health trends assessments, UNAIDS measures the number of adults and children receiving HIV treatment, in accordance with the nationally approved treatment protocols (or with WHO standards) at the end of the reporting period.[7] Soft law thereby brokers compliance through monitoring and review mechanisms to facilitate accountability for compliance with international agreements. Despite being soft commitments, the institutionalization of these norms has led to the creation of indicators to measure progress at both the national and the international levels, thus allowing soft law to serve as a basis for collaboration across UN agencies—in the HIV/AIDS response and beyond.

D. Harnessing Soft Law beyond WHO

In global health crises, soft law can be used to create greater awareness about the nature of health threats across the global health governance landscape. Bringing together actors in the HIV/AIDS response, the UN General Assembly's 2001 Declaration of Commitment on HIV/AIDS and two subsequent General

---

[7] Similarly developing technical standards, WHO has been at the forefront of setting food standards with the Food and Agriculture Organization of the United Nations (FAO) in order to prevent, detect, and respond to public health threats that may arise from unsafe food. WHO has thus worked to devise the Codex Alimentarus, which provides guidelines and recommendations for independent scientific assessments on microbiological and chemical hazards that form the basis for international food standards.

Assembly resolutions led to the Global AIDS Reporting Mechanism (UNAIDS 2001). UNAIDS has sought to implement this non-binding soft law framework, which provided specific commitments and targets that states must reach. The non-binding nature of the Declaration was essential in helping countries to reach agreement to create accountability mechanisms, and this flexibility enabled the international community to make subsequent changes to the Declaration in ways that would seek to ensure human rights in the HIV/AIDS response (Murthy 2018).

Case Study: HIV/AIDS and the Soft Law Response

Due to the sexually transmitted nature of HIV/AIDS, and its rapid transmission across national borders, there has long been a danger that national public health responses would be inherently discriminatory toward the most vulnerable people, such as women, children, and gay people, with these public health responses violating human rights. Soft law has helped to raise awareness of the threat of discriminatory approaches to curbing the disease, allowing states to achieve consensus quickly and easily due to low contracting costs that ensured that countries retained their sovereignty. This reflection of the importance of human rights to public health, which started with World Health Assembly resolutions and then moved to the UN General Assembly and across the UN system, supported efforts to translate scientific knowledge into global health norms. By reinforcing state commitments to hard law obligations under international human rights treaties, soft law would become crucial in ongoing global efforts, building from efforts to prevent discrimination toward affected populations to frame subsequent efforts to ensure universal access to essential medicines. The AIDS pandemic has illustrated the inequity of expensive medications in ways that have revealed continuing threats to human rights. Despite the development of effective HIV treatments, many people in the Global South found themselves unable to afford these essential medicines. In bringing together a wide range of actors, WHO, UNAIDS, and the entire UN system have drawn on soft law to raise awareness about the links between the right to health and access to essential medicines. These policies across international organizations culminated in soft law efforts to reaffirm state commitments to human rights in the context of access to essential medicines.[a]

[a] The Doha Declaration on the TRIPS Agreement and Public Health, as discussed in detail in Chapter 12, looked to soft law to clarify which international legal obligations take precedence when there is a clash across competing regimes, as seen between the health and trade regimes. This soft law consensus enabled countries to agree that intellectual property rights should be implemented in ways that protect public health in situations of extreme emergency, thereby giving countries the right to use flexibilities within the TRIPS Agreement to create cheaper generic versions of essential medicines in the HIV/AIDS response.

Drawing from these soft law accountability mechanisms across institutions, the UN's 2002 establishment of the Global Fund to Fight AIDS, Tuberculosis and Malaria (the Global Fund) has led to the development of core indicators to assess the impact of funding for HIV/AIDS, tuberculosis, and malaria. Robust assessments under soft law are essential in holding governments accountable for global commitments. Looking beyond the number of people who have access to medicines, these Global Fund indicators provide a basis to assess laws on criminalizing vulnerable groups, such as homosexuals and women, which, while not directly concerning HIV/AIDS, may be an underlying factor impeding access to determinants of health. Such indicators allow for the measurement of public health progress to be quantified, taking into account how countries are progressing rather than simply focusing on evidence of violations (Beco 2008). In facilitating accountability, non-state actors have used these indicators to name and shame countries that are not making sufficient progress and to mobilize the international community in sustaining funding momentum to address HIV/AIDS, tuberculosis, and malaria (Taylor et al. 2014). Despite the soft law nature of indicators, compliance with these indicators is extremely high, with almost all countries submitting reports to the UNAIDS Global Progress Report and providing hope for the future of soft law in global health law and policy.

III. A Holistic Future of Global Health Law and Policy

Soft law supports global health law in a global health crisis to raise awareness about the severity of the health threat and respond quickly as events unfold. In the COVID-19 pandemic response, global governance has looked to bring together soft law and hard law to respond to a rapidly unfolding crisis that threatened the entire world.

A. Soft Law in the COVID-19 Response

Soft law has played a central role in the global health governance response to COVID-19. Where soft law is flexible, and generally developed and adopted more quickly than hard law, soft law standards have proven effective within the WHO framework of global health law (Sekalala and Masud 2021). These instruments of soft law, such as resolutions and decisions of the World Health Assembly, have been particularly important in managing a common response to this global threat (Bosi 2021). Drawing from the model set in the early HIV/AIDS response, WHO and other global institutions have looked to soft law in the COVID-19 response to create greater coordination and preparedness, shore up the supply of medical resources, protect vulnerable groups from discrimination, and seek global solidarity in ensuring support for states that have less resources.

In the initial stages of the global response through WHO, the World Health Assembly adopted a resolution on the "COVID-19 Response," which called on WHO Member States to develop national COVID-19 preparedness and response plans, in coordination with relevant international organizations and stakeholders as well as local communities (WHO 2020a). Simultaneously, the Assembly adopted a resolution on "strengthening preparedness for health emergencies," calling on Member States to comply with international legal obligations under the IHR (WHO 2020b). Supported by the UN General Assembly, early UN resolutions reinforced WHO leadership, recognizing that WHO had the constitutional authority and technical legitimacy to oversee global health crises under international law. In looking to law as the foundation of the global response, the UN General Assembly reinforced the need for multilateralism amid increasing isolationism by states—calling for greater collaboration, information sharing, scientific knowledge, and best practices. With this support for global action under WHO legal authority, WHO and UN resolutions reinforced state obligations to share information and coordinate responses with WHO in order to ensure collective action in response to the global crisis.[8]

Given the disproportionate impact of COVID on vulnerable groups, resolutions from organizations across global health governance called for the protection of vulnerable or at-risk groups such as health workers, women, racial minorities, older persons, children, young people, and people with disabilities. For instance, the disproportionate impact of the pandemic on women and girls led to calls in the UN General Assembly for a "gender responsive COVID-19 recovery and response" (UN General Assembly 2020). The impact of lockdowns on mental and social well-being renewed World Health Assembly calls to ensure the availability of mental health support, recognizing that adversities such as isolation and unemployment must be addressed in order to alleviate their mental health impacts (WHO 2020a).

As the pandemic response evolved and vaccines were developed, governance institutions developed additional resolutions to support access to this essential pharmaceutical intervention, ensuring greater vaccine equity

---

[8] Increased information was important to ensure that all countries had a greater awareness of the epidemiological patterns in which COVID was spreading – as a basis to inform their country responses. Thus, WHO resolutions also called on states to leverage digital technology for the COVID response in order to produce more accurate health data.

in order to hasten the end of the crisis. World Health Assembly resolutions have remained clear and consistent on the necessity of greater equity to pharmaceutical interventions such as vaccines. Through a 2021 resolution on "Strengthening local production of medicines and other health technologies to improve access," the World Health Assembly recognized inequities in access to vaccines, medicines, and other health technologies in the context of the COVID-19 pandemic, calling for the enhancement of production capacities in low- and middle-income countries. The UN General Assembly has supported these WHO efforts by repeatedly calling for greater international cooperation to ensure access to vaccines (UN General Assembly 2020). Additionally, the UN Human Rights Council called on states to ensure equitable, affordable, timely, and universal access to vaccines, urging national governments to increase the exports of vaccine stocks as a basis to avoid stockpiling and reduce costs (UN HRC 2021). However, despite this persuasive body of soft law—which made it clear that the COVID-19 vaccine must be recognized as "a global public good" and a human right for all—global solidarity nevertheless faltered once viable vaccines entered the market, as countries began hoarding scarce vaccines in violation of WHO and UN resolutions (Sekalala et al. 2021). Given these limitations of soft law in the COVID-19 pandemic, states have turned their focus to hard law in order to avert some of the perceived failures of the existing global health regime, proposing hard law reforms to strengthen global health law and WHO governance.

B. Hard Law in the COVID-19 Response

The IHR provide hard law obligations under international law to frame the global health response to a public health emergency of international concern (PHEIC);[9] yet, WHO has repeatedly faced challenges from state violations of IHR obligations. When the World Health Assembly revised the IHR in 2005, as addressed in detail in Chapter 6, the international community had just emerged from the grip of the 2003 SARS outbreak. In a series of events not unlike the early response to COVID-19, SARS impacted every region of the world, as isolated cases of pneumonia of unknown origin in China rapidly progressed into

---

[9] As further elaborated in Chapter 6, the 2005 revision of the IHR enabled the WHO Director-General to determine events that may constitute a "public health emergency of international concern," a determination that has effectively served as the world's premier alert mechanism to global health threats.

a localized outbreak that within weeks became a cross-border public health emergency (Burci 2020). Although short-lived, the SARS outbreak spurred a recalibration of acceptable obligations to ensure international cooperation for infectious disease control and catalyzed efforts to revise the IHR to respond to the rising public health threats of a globalizing world (Davies, Kamradt-Scott, and Rushton 2015). In a press release announcing the revised IHR's entry into force, WHO Director-General Margaret Chan called SARS a "wake-up call" and affirmed that the revised IHR would help prepare the world for the next pandemic (WHO 2007).

The IHR (2005) provide a range of legally binding obligations, including state obligations to build "core capacities" for public health risk surveillance and response, to notify WHO of events that may constitute a PHEIC, and to avoid taking measures in response to public health risks that disproportionately limit travel or trade. Recognizing rising public health threats beyond infectious disease, the IHR adopt an "all-hazards" approach to a broad range of public health risks (including novel pathogens), irrespective of source or origin (Fidler 2005). Yet in spite of these legal innovations in the IHR revisions, this hard law instrument remains largely "technical" in nature and has found itself silent on many of the deep fractures in the international public health emergency response to the COVID-19 pandemic (Gostin, Habibi, and Meier 2020).

The record of state compliance with the legally binding obligations codified within the IHR (2005) has remained poor in the COVID-19 pandemic, especially during periods when a coordinated global health emergency response was needed. For instance, although China officially notified WHO of the novel coronavirus outbreak in Wuhan on December 31, 2019, reports suggest that the virus had likely been circulating in the city for several weeks prior, with evidence of human-to-human transmission, and had been brought to the attention of authorities in Wuhan through various channels without triggering timely information sharing in accordance with IHR obligations (Singh et al. 2021). This reluctance to share information led WHO leaders, as seen in Figure 2.2, to meet directly with Chinese officials to encourage compliance with IHR obligations and offer WHO support.

Even after the COVID-19 outbreak was declared a PHEIC under the IHR, legal regulations continued to be neglected by states—as governments mounted national responses to combat the virus in violation of IHR obligations (Gostin, Habibi, and Meier 2020). While SARS provided a wake-up call to establish IHR obligations on information sharing, public health capacity building, and coordination in implementing additional health measures, COVID-19 has dramatically underscored the need for states to operationalize global solidarity in pandemic prevention, preparedness, and

Figure 2.2 WHO Director-General Tedros Meets with Chinese General Secretary Xi, January 2020 (AP/Anna Ratkoglo)

response, including in global access to, and distribution of, urgently needed medical countermeasures such as diagnostics, personal protective equipment, vaccines, and therapeutics (Meier et al. 2020). The challenges faced by the IHR have led WHO to look to soft law policies to complement hard law obligations in the pandemic response.

Case Study: Hard and Soft Law in the COVID-19 Response

In the context of the COVID-19 pandemic, WHO has used hard and soft law together to develop global health law and policy to prevent, detect, and respond to COVID-19. WHO has drawn on the IHR to hold countries accountable to their global health obligations, but taking account of the insufficiency of the IHR, it has also favored using soft law approaches, which have been more quickly developed and accepted by Member States. The World Health Assembly has sought to support the WHO Secretariat through resolutions that attempted to reaffirm IHR obligations and shore up international solidarity, reminding countries of the dangers of border closures on the free flow of international traffic and calling for Member States to support vulnerable and at-risk countries through increased political, technical, and financial support. Beyond the scope of IHR obligations, these Assembly resolutions also addressed the need for greater transparency around purchasing and supplying health products in order to avoid shortages of essential products such as medicines, personal protective equipment, and emergency health supplies such as ventilators. WHO has thus been successful in using soft law to provide clarification of treaty requirements, regulate specific issues beyond the IHR, and set standards for monitoring and accountability. As a basis to extend the influence of hard law, WHO has used soft law to interpret state obligations in addressing the pandemic, provide normative guidance to states amid a rapidly escalating threat, and lay the foundation for future amendments of the IHR, looking to hard law reforms as a stronger foundation to advance global health law to prepare for future pandemics.

The scale, intensity, and endurance of the COVID-19 health threat have once again created a window of opportunity for international law reforms to strengthen public health emergency preparedness and response. Whether such lawmaking opportunities will lead to improved preparedness and response under hard law will depend on the degree to which states are willing to negotiate in good faith on the basis of solidarity—inside WHO and across global governance—to advance soft and hard law obligations in global health law.

C. Bringing Together Soft and Hard Law across Global Governance

The COVID-19 pandemic underscores not only the essential contribution of both binding and non-binding normative instruments emanating from WHO, but it also reveals that this mosaic of WHO instruments operates not in a vacuum, but alongside multiple other regimes, instruments, and actors of international law (both state and non-state), each advancing mandates unique to their constitutive instruments and/or organizational composition. At times at odds with WHO lawmaking, the pandemic response saw multiple intergovernmental organizations—including the Human Rights Council, the International Civil Aviation Organization, the International Organization for Migration, UNAIDS, the World Bank, and the World Trade Organization—develop soft law instruments such as recommendations and guidelines. These soft law advancements across global governance sought to guide states in their response to the prolonged pandemic. However, in some institutions, these parallel processes contradicted the mandate of WHO and resolutions adopted by the World Health Assembly (Sekalala and Masud 2021).[10]

Given the inherently divided architecture in global health governance, global health law reforms must contend with the need for harmonization across this fragmented proliferation of actors that make up the global health landscape. The World Health Assembly has embarked upon crucial law reform initiatives, as introduced in the Foreword, including potential amendments to the IHR and an entirely new pandemic convention, accord, or other instrument. In clarifying multiple legal regimes, it will be necessary for these global health law reforms to provide normative guidance to states regarding the primacy of some regimes over others, particularly during a state of emergency, with complementary reforms to align global health law across multiple institutions of global health governance.

Conclusion

Global health law encompasses the multifaceted law and policy structures that constitute and constrain global health. Threats to public health in a globalizing world can now rarely be addressed within narrow national boundaries, and international legal frameworks encompassing institutions, processes, and instruments are vital. A multitude of state and non-state actors now impact the course of global health in this modern and interconnected world. The governance of global health, coordinating the actions of institutions in the promotion of global health, will require a joined-up solution—consisting of hard, legally binding laws and soft laws of graduated normativity but greater dexterity.

In order to advance global health law and policy, hard law and soft law must no longer be seen as distinct approaches or in competition with one another, moving global health governance beyond futile debates about which is better suited to addressing global health threats. Hard law, with its binding obligations on states, is frequently necessary to compel state behavior that will prevent disease and promote health. Treaties, both bilateral and multinational, along with regional agreements and customary international law can provide powerful ways to address public health challenges, and these are an important part of the global health response. However, hard law is not always necessary, and, indeed, it is not always the most timely or productive approach to a rapidly moving crisis. Soft law, while not legally binding, can provide highly effective measures, including

---

[10] These conflicting legal regimes in the pandemic response include deliberations on a proposed waiver of intellectual property rules governing vaccines, therapeutics, and other medical countermeasures under the auspices of the World Trade Organization, which were seen to undermine WHO efforts to treat vaccination as a global public good (Sekalala et al. 2021).

policy instruments such as resolutions, declarations, guidelines, protocols, and recommendations. Soft law can provide normative clarification of treaties, and it can set standards to ensure positive change to improve global health. A more expansive soft law framework can work quickly and motivate both state and non-state actors to address global health issues in a timely fashion. To be effective, global health governance will need to harness the promise of both hard and soft law, holistically and in equal measure, to guide actions taken by all stakeholders, bringing together global health law and policy.

Global health law comprises an ever-diversifying array of institutions as well as hard and soft norms, with the ability to influence how global health is promoted in practice. In responding to the threat of COVID-19 and preparing for future threats, the landscape of hard and soft law will continue to evolve—with proposals of new treaties to cover pandemics, revisions of existing ones such as the IHR, and the proliferation of even more soft law standards to cover emerging areas and new technologies. Scholars and practitioners of global health law and policy must critically reflect on the successes and obstacles of past efforts in soft and hard law and build upon these legal efforts in global health to develop the future landscape of global health governance.

Questions for Consideration

1. How did states come together to develop the first International Sanitary Convention? Why were these 19th-century international legal negotiations insufficient in protecting public health throughout the world?
2. Why did the UN Charter seek to centralize lawmaking under the UN and its specialized agencies? Why did the WHO Constitution provide authority to develop different types of legal instruments?
3. What has led to WHO reluctance to exercise its legal authorities? How have other international organizations sought to meet the need for international law to shape global health?
4. How does soft law complement hard law in the development of obligations in global health?
5. Why does global health law rely heavily on soft law to shape public health throughout the world? What are the advantages of this soft law approach in global health governance—within WHO, across organizations, and with state and non-state actors?
6. When does WHO look to soft law to structure global health standards? How does WHO exercise its normative functions—through constitutional standards, scientific and technical standards, and health trend assessments—to establish soft law in global health policy?

7. Why was soft law crucial in bringing together global governance institutions in the HIV/AIDS response?
8. How did World Health Assembly resolutions seek to frame the COVID-19 response through soft law? Why did UN General Assembly resolutions seek to support WHO leadership in the response? Why did states neglect to follow these WHO and UN resolutions?
9. What distinguishes IHR obligations from World Health Assembly resolutions? Why did states neglect their international legal obligations under the IHR? How did WHO seek to coordinate the application of both hard and soft law in the COVID-19 response?
10. Why must future reforms of global health law include both binding and non-binding components under hard and soft law? How can states align global health law reforms across distinct legal regimes and global governance institutions?

Acknowledgments

The authors would like to acknowledge Belinda Rawson, Harshit Rai, and Sonam Shah for their research assistance.

References

Abbott, Kenneth W., and Duncan Snidal. 2000. "Hard and Soft Law in International Governance." *International Organization* 54(3): 421–456.
Abbott, Kenneth W., Robert O. Keohane, Andrew Moravcsik, Anne-Marie Slaughter, and Duncan Snidal. 2000. "The Concept of Legalization." *International Organization* 54(3): 401–419.
Bosi, Giulia. 2021. "Overcoming the 'Soft vs Hard Law' Debate in the Development of New Global Health Instruments." *Opinio Juris*. November 11.
Burci, Gian Luca. 2020. "The Legal Response to Pandemics." *Journal of International Humanitarian Legal Studies* 11(2): 204–217.
Carvalho, Simon, and Mark Zacher. 2001. "The International Health Regulations in Historical Perspective." In *Plagues and Politics: Infectious Disease and International Policy*, edited by Andrew T. Price-Smith, 235–261. London: Palgrave Macmillan.
Chayes, Abram, and Antonia Handler Chayes. 1995. *The New Sovereignty: Compliance with International Regulatory Agreements*. Cambridge: Harvard University Press.
Chinkin, Christine. 2000. "Normative Development in the International Legal System." In *Commitment and Compliance: The Role of Non-Binding Norms in the International Legal System*, edited by Dinah Shelton, 21–42. Oxford: Oxford University Press.
Davies, Sara E., Adam Kamradt-Scott, and Simon Rushton. 2015. *Disease Diplomacy: International Norms and Global Health Security*. Baltimore: Johns Hopkins University Press.
de Beco, Gauthier. 2008. "Human Rights Indicators for Assessing State Compliance with International Human Rights." *Nordic Journal of International Law* 77(31): 23–49.

Fidler, David P. 1998. "The Future of the World Health Organization: What Role for International Law?" *Vanderbilt Journal of Transnational Law* 31(5): 1079–1126.

Fidler, David P. 2001. "The Globalization of Public Health: The First 100 Years of International Health Diplomacy." *Bulletin of the World Health Organization* 79(9): 842–849.

Fidler, David P. 2005. "From International Sanitary Conventions to Global Health Security: The New International Health Regulations." *Chinese Journal of International Law* 4(2): 325–392.

Goldsmith, Jack L., and Eric A. Posner. 2004. *The Limits of International Law.* Oxford: Oxford University Press.

Gostin, Lawrence O. 2014. *Global Health Law.* Cambridge: Harvard University Press.

Gostin, Lawrence O., Roojin Habibi, and Benjamin Mason Meier. 2020. "Has Global Health Law Risen to Meet the COVID-19 Challenge? Revisiting the International Health Regulations to Prepare for Future Threats." *Journal of Law, Medicine & Ethics* 48(2): 376–381.

Gostin, Lawrence O., and Benjamin Mason Meier. 2019. "Introducing Global Health Law." *Journal of Law, Medicine & Ethics* 47(4): 788–793.

Gostin, Lawrence O., Devi Sridhar, and Daniel Hougendobler. 2015. "The Normative Authority of the World Health Organization." *Public Health* 129: 854–863.

Guzman, Andrew T., and Timothy L. Meyer. 2009. "Explaining Soft Law." *Journal of Legal Analysis* 2(1): 1–45.

Hoffman, Steven J., Prativa Baral, Susan Rogers Van Katwyk, Lathika Sritharan, Matthew Hughsam, Harkanwal Randhawa, Gigi Lin et al. 2022. "International Treaties Have Mostly Failed to Produce Their Intended Effects." *Proceedings of the National Academy of Sciences* 119(32):1–9.

Huber, Valeska. 2006. "The Unification of the Globe by Disease? The International Sanitary Conferences on Cholera, 1851–1894." *The Historical Journal* 49(2): 453–476.

Klabbers, Jan. 1998. "The Undesirability of 'Soft Law.'" *Nordic Journal of International Law* 67: 381–391.

Kreuder-Sonnen, Christian, and Michael Zürn. 2020. "After Fragmentation: Norm Collisions, Interface Conflicts, and Conflict Management." *Global Constitutionalism* 9(2): 241–267.

Meernik, James, Rosa Aloisi, Marsha Sowell, and Angela Nichols. 2012. "The Impact of Human Rights Organizations on Naming and Shaming Campaigns." *Journal of Conflict Resolution* 56(2): 233–256.

Meier, Benjamin Mason, Allyn Taylor, Mark Eccleston-Turner, Roojin Habibi, Sharifah Sekalala, and Lawrence O. Gostin. 2020. "The World Health Organization in Global Health Law." *Journal of Law, Medicine & Ethics* 48(4): 796–799.

Murthy, Sharmila L. 2018. "Translating Legal Norms into Quantitative Indicators: Lessons from the Global Water, Sanitation, and Hygiene Sector." *William & Mary Environmental Law and Policy Review* 42(2): 385–446.

Sekalala, Sharifah. 2017. *Soft Law and Global Health Problems: Lessons from Responses to HIV/AIDS, Malaria and Tuberculosis.* Cambridge: Cambridge University Press.

Sekalala, Sharifah, and Haleema Masud. 2021. "Soft Law Possibilities in Global Health Law." *Journal of Law, Medicine & Ethics* 49: 152–155.

Sekalala, Sharifah, Lisa Forman, Timothy Hodgson, Moses Mulumba, Hadijah Namyalo-Ganafa, and Benjamin Mason Meier. 2021. "Decolonising Human Rights: How Intellectual Property Laws Result in Unequal Access to the COVID-19 Vaccine." *BMJ Global Health* 6(7): 1–9.

Slaughter, Anne-Marie. 2004. *A New World Order*. Princeton: Princeton University Press.
Singh, Sudhvir, Christine McNab, Rose McKeon Olson, Nellie Bristol, Cody Nolan, Elin Bergstrøm, Michael Bartos et al. 2021. "How an Outbreak Became a Pandemic: A Chronological Analysis of Crucial Junctures and International Obligations in the Early Months of the COVID-19 Pandemic." *Lancet* 398(10316): 2109–2124.
Swepston, Lee. 2018. "The International Labor Organization: Human Rights to Health and Safety at Work." In *Human Rights in Global Health*, edited by Benjamin Mason Meier and Lawrence O. Gostin. Oxford University Press, 201–220.
Taylor, Allyn Lise. 1992. "Making the World Health Organization Work: A Legal Framework for Universal Access to the Conditions for Health." *American Journal of Law & Medicine* 18(4): 301–346.
Taylor, Allyn, Tobias Alfvén, Daniel Hougendobler, and Kent Buse. 2014. "Nonbinding Legal Instruments in Governance for Global Health: Lessons from the Global AIDS Reporting Mechanism." *Journal of Law, Medicine & Ethics* 42(1): 72–87.
Trubek, David M., Patrick Cottrell, and Mark Nance, 2005, "'Soft Law,' 'Hard Law,' and European Integration: Toward a Theory of Hybridity." *Univ. of Wisconsin Legal Studies Research Paper No. 1002*, 1–42.
UNAIDS (The Joint United Nations Programme on HIV/AIDS). 2001. "Declaration of Commitment on HIV/AIDS." June 25–27. A/Res/S-26/2.
UN (United Nations). 1945. Charter of the United Nations.
UN General Assembly. 2020. "International Cooperation to Ensure Global Access to Medicines, Vaccines and Medical Equipment to Face COVID-19." April 21. A/RES/74/274.
UN General Assembly. 2020. "Women and Girls and the Response to the Coronavirus Disease (COVID-19)." December 16. A/RES/75/157.
UN HRC (UN Human Rights Council). 2021. "Ensuring Equitable, Affordable, Timely and Universal Access for all Countries to Vaccines in Response to the Coronavirus Disease (COVID-19) Pandemic." March 29. A/HRC/RES/46/14.
United Nations. 1946. Statute of the International Court of Justice.
Vignes, Claude-Henri. 1989. "The Future of International Health Law: WHO Perspectives." *International Digest of Health Legislation* 40(1): 16–19.
WHO (World Health Organization). 1946. *Constitution of the World Health Organization*. New York: WHO.
WHO. 2007. "International Health Regulations Enter into Force: New Opportunity to Respond to International Public Health Threats." Geneva: WHO.
WHO. 2017. "Evaluation of WHO's Normative Function (Volume 1: Evaluation Report)." Corporate evaluation commissioned by the WHO Evaluation Office. Oslo: Nordic Consulting Grou.
WHO. 2020a. "Coronavirus Disease (COVID-19)." Geneva: WHO.
WHO. 2020b. "Resolution EB146.R10 on Strengthening Preparedness for Health Emergencies: Implementation of the International Health Regulations (2005)." Geneva: WHO.
Wilson, Donald J., Ken Takahashi, Derek R. Smith, Masako Yoshino, Chieko Tanaka, and Jukka Takala. 2006. "Recent Trends in ILO Conventions Related to Occupational Safety and Health." *International Journal of Occupational Safety and Ergonomics* 12(3): 255–266.

3

Global Health Landscape

The Proliferating Actors Influencing Global Health Governance

Benjamin Mason Meier and Matiangai Sirleaf

Introduction

Global health law is shaped by the actors that develop and implement law and policy in global governance. While international law looks to states and international organizations under the United Nations (UN), these traditional actors are now being joined (and in many ways challenged) by a far larger set of state and non-state actors in disparate global health policy efforts. Where once the World Health Organization (WHO) held central leadership in global health governance, the new architecture of global health lacks both centralization and leadership. This new global governance architecture has presented challenges to the development of global health law. Yet, even as the global health landscape has presented challenges in applying law to state and non-state actors, the broader focus on global health law and policy has presented opportunities for novel partnerships to advance global health.

This expanding global health landscape now encompasses the proliferating initiatives of individual governments, international organizations, non-governmental organizations (NGOs), philanthropic foundations, and transnational corporations, all seeking to address select global health concerns through global health governance. Yet with so many new actors joining in global health governance, concerns of duplicative initiatives, unsustainable programs, and inefficient efforts have raised an imperative for partnerships across actors—to coordinate action across the global health landscape. These partnerships have been established to bring actors together in policy initiatives, and ensuring cooperation among these diverse actors will be crucially important to the success of global health governance. With more public and private actors joining in global health governance, aligning these actors under global health law and policy will be more important than ever to achieve the highest attainable standard of health.

This chapter examines the actors that influence global health governance. Beginning in the centralized early leadership of WHO, Part I traces WHO leadership through the political challenges of the Cold War and the birth of newly decolonized states, with WHO bringing nations together to develop a global policy agenda to achieve primary health care. Yet amid the challenges of neoliberal globalization, WHO lost its role as the unquestioned leader in international health governance, with WHO left fighting for relevance among rising new actors across the global health landscape. Part II describes this contemporary landscape of global health governance, encompassing national governments, international organizations, NGOs, and private sector actors, with these state and non-state actors coming together in discrete partnerships to coordinate their efforts under global health law and policy. In seeking to bind together the global governance landscape, the UN has sought to develop new goals for development and health, with Part III discussing the rise of a common governance agenda under the 2030 Agenda for Sustainable Development and continuing efforts to build a more just global order by decolonizing global health. The chapter concludes that the rise of new actors presents opportunities and challenges in global health governance, requiring global health law and policy to align actors across the global health landscape.

I. An Expanding Global Health Landscape: From the World Health Organization to the World

The 1948 inauguration of WHO brought national governments together into a centralized institution with global authority. WHO rapidly established its leadership over the entire international health governance system, with the unification of all aspects of public health under its constitutional mandate. However, this leadership was challenged by the geopolitical rifts of the Cold War and the neoliberal agenda of economic institutions. Limiting WHO's authority in the global health landscape, this leadership vacuum would give rise to new global health actors to address specific health issues.

A. Cold War Health Debates Challenge WHO

The Cold War was beginning just as World War II was ending, with ideological, political, and economic tensions dividing the world and shaping international health governance. WHO struggled to unify Member States in the face of these geopolitical hostilities, as efforts to secure a shared vision for public health were undermined by intractable conflicts on international health policies. Yet even as the Cold War burned, a new international order would rise amid decolonization, with the end of colonial rule bringing new voices and priorities into the international health landscape. In prioritizing economic development and health equity in international health governance, WHO would seek to reassert its leadership in advancing primary health care.

1. Superpower Rivalry in Global Health

States looked to WHO to coordinate public health efforts, but almost immediately after its inception, the UN saw geopolitical divisions rise between states, as the birth of WHO coincided with the start of the Cold War. New tensions intensified between the United States and Soviet Union, as the two nuclear-armed "Superpowers" clashed over ideals about government authorities, economic production, and public health (Evang 1967). This division of the world would impact WHO's public health leadership, with WHO caught between two opposing ideological camps—Western capitalist democracies and Soviet communist regimes (Meier 2010). The Soviet-led communist bloc maintained that it was essential for WHO to address underlying determinants of health, which would be impossible without acknowledging social and economic conditions. For communist governments, capitalist approaches to health failed to address these determinants of health, leaving WHO "superficial because it had neglected the root causes of disease"—poverty and inequality (Allen 1950, 41).

This growing divide in public health ideology between communism and capitalism could not be reconciled within WHO, as the Soviet bloc argued that WHO's domination by Western states (especially the United States) left it unable to lead international health efforts. Hobbling WHO leadership to unite the world under shared health goals, these Cold War tensions would result in the withdrawal of the Soviet Union and its satellite states from WHO. In February 1949, the Soviet Union, Ukrainian Soviet Republic, and Byelorussian Soviet Republic informed the Geneva Secretariat of their withdrawal—followed in short order by fellow communist states, including Bulgaria, Romania, and Poland (Pethybridge 1965).[1] Leaving WHO reliant on the West, U.S. policymakers looked to WHO's disease prevention efforts as central to Cold War objectives to prevent the spread of communism, seeking a medicalization of disease eradication efforts in WHO policy while keeping WHO from examining underlying economic determinants of health (Jacobson and Cox 1974).

---

[1] As the WHO Constitution includes no provisions for the withdrawal of a Member State, the WHO Secretariat simply referred to these communist states as "inactive," making it easier in subsequent years to bring these states back into WHO membership. This situation would reoccur in 2020, when the United States sought to withdraw from WHO, purportedly due to biases toward China in the COVID-19 response; however, changes in U.S. leadership halted this withdrawal, allowing the United States to remain a WHO Member State.

However, the death of Soviet leader Joseph Stalin ushered in a new era of Soviet engagement with the UN system, as communist states returned to WHO in 1955 and 1956, pressing once again for the advancement of socialist health systems in international health policy. These communist states advocated anew for health policies to achieve the universal protection of health and provision of care (Osakwe 1972). Within the World Health Assembly, they advanced this socialist health paradigm in meeting the health needs of "developing" states in the Global South (Farley 2008). The Soviet Union thereby sought to shift the focus of international health governance—from the establishment of medical care services to the development of public health systems that addressed underlying determinants of health—and this focus on health systems would continue to grow as WHO Member States expanded.

2. Decolonization and Rise of Non-Aligned Movement

The end of colonial rule would reshape the world order in ways that would challenge international health governance, with decolonization opening space for new nations and leading WHO to new health priorities. Where imperial powers had long pursued health in colonized nations under the guise of "tropical medicine," as introduced in Chapter 1, these colonial efforts looked to medicalized health systems that disregarded and subverted indigenous health systems (Greene et al. 2013).[2] Tropical medicine thus grew to focus specifically on vector-borne diseases and infectious disease control, as preventing these diseases had the greatest implications for the expansion of colonial empires—enabling colonial troops to better cope with unfamiliar diseases and fight Indigenous populations resisting colonial subjugation (Sirleaf 2022).

As nations freed themselves from colonial domination, these newly independent states would take their place among the community of nations in international affairs, bringing their voices into global governance and leading to the emergence of a new world order. While many of these nations would align with one of the Superpowers, some sought to avoid the Cold War rivalry altogether, banding together under the "Non-Aligned Movement" (Cueto, Brown, and Fee 2019). Bringing together states in Asia, Africa, the Americas, and the Middle East, this Non-Aligned Movement of "developing" states worked together to advance their own interests—rather than those of the dominant Cold

---

[2] Early efforts to support international health cooperation by European powers were premised on containing racialized threats of disease contagion from colonized peoples (Sirleaf 2020). Where colonization was largely motivated by economic exploitation, the transition away from systems of colonization shifted the makeup of "the world," allowing states in Asia, Africa, and the Americas to assume new roles in the international order (Pannenborg 1979).

War powers. This movement would look to equitable economic development policies as a foundation of public health, bringing health equity to the center of international health (Meier 2010). From this focus on health equity to address systemic health disparities, the concept of "primary health care" arose, recognizing the need to address the structures, systems, and determinants affecting health.

This emergence of primary health care in global health governance was reflected in WHO's "Health for All" program. WHO would launch initiatives in the early 1970s to improve basic health services in new nations—including water and sanitation systems—and this prioritization of health infrastructure demonstrated a widespread recognition that improving global health required robust horizontal health systems and an understanding that all people, regardless of their wealth or nationality, have a right to be healthy. This focus on primary health care would directly contrast with the vertical nature of disease-specific programs that had predominated in WHO policy through the 1950s and 1960s (Brown, Cueto, and Fee 2006). WHO published reports throughout the 1970s on horizontal systems for primary health care, including a series of reports with the United Nations Children's Fund (UNICEF). These collaborative efforts to advance primary health care culminated, as seen in Figure 3.1, in the 1978 International Conference on Primary Health Care in Alma-Ata, USSR.

Figure 3.1 International Conference on Primary Health Care, 1978 (WHO)

Case Study: WHO as a Global Health Leader: The Declaration of Alma-Ata

The International Conference on Primary Health Care brought together representatives from 134 countries to advance international policy for primary health care. WHO and UNICEF were the major organizing leaders, and this conference followed from their joint 1975 report, "Alternative Methods to Meeting Basic Health Needs in Developing Countries." This collaborative inter-organizational work began to build consensus among leading "developing" and "developed" states on the fundamental importance and potential benefits of primary health care. Notwithstanding Cold War divisions, both the United States and Soviet Union came to support this approach to advancing primary health care under WHO governance. As representatives arrived in Alma-Ata, many of the conference delegates already had a detailed understanding of primary health care, leading them to find sweeping international agreement in the resulting Declaration of Alma-Ata. This 1978 Declaration reaffirmed the principles of the 1948 WHO Constitution, with Article I proclaiming that:

> health, which is a state of complete physical, mental and social well-being, and not merely the absence of disease or infirmity, is a fundamental human right [and] the attainment of the highest level of health is a most important world-wide social goal whose realization requires the action of many other social and economic sectors in addition to the health sector.

The Declaration clearly stated the need for primary health care as a basis to reach the goal of "Health for All by the Year 2000," recognizing the link between health systems and socioeconomic development. Bringing together the world to strengthen public health policy, the Declaration of Alma-Ata continues to be seen as a foundational statement of public health priorities.

Yet despite rising international momentum to support primary health care, the Declaration of Alma-Ata came to be abandoned in international health governance in the years that followed, as the socioeconomic context changed, WHO lost its international influence, and new actors proliferated across the global health landscape.

B. WHO Seeks to Maintain Leadership over a Fragmented Global Health Landscape

As political and economic circumstances shifted in the 1980s, WHO would struggle to maintain its authority, influence, and leadership. International cooperation for primary health care was rapidly waning, as conservative donor states sought to narrow international health funding toward vertical initiatives that were thought to be more economically efficient. Drawing from this "neoliberal" ethos, the World Bank and Rockefeller Foundation sponsored a 1979 conference to advance "selective" primary health care—selectively focusing on low-cost, disease-specific technological interventions (Brown, Cueto, and Fee 2019). While recognizing that selective primary health care was a step back from the comprehensive vision of primary health care, this narrow approach was more appealing to wealthy donor countries, which saw these projects as shorter in duration and easier to accomplish—without the need for policy reforms that would challenge entrenched financial interests.

WHO maintained its support for primary health care as the principal focus of international health governance, but other actors increasingly endorsed selective primary health care, dividing the global health landscape. As WHO's authority declined, governance began to shift toward financial actors. The World Bank was growing in power and influence, and its promotion of vertical health programs further destabilized WHO's public health authority (Shawar and Prah Ruger 2018). With neoliberal reforms imposed by international financial institutions, many nations in the Global South were pressed to undertake austerity measures and structural adjustments, which limited horizontal investment in the health sector (Sirleaf 2022).[3] The complexities of implementing primary health care, combined with the political and economic challenges of a neoliberal world order, shifted global health priorities as WHO lost support as the central leader in international health governance.

WHO continued to lose authority as Member States—seeing WHO as inefficient and corrupt—lessened their financial support. Reflecting this decreasing support from conservative donor governments, WHO's dwindling funding shifted from the assessed contributions of its Member States to a larger reliance on "extrabudgetary" funding, taking contributions from wealthy donors tied to

---

[3] As elaborated in Chapter 10, neoliberalism, a political and economic ideology centered around deregulation and free-market capitalism, came to the forefront of global governance in the 1980s. Advanced by conservative governments, neoliberal economic policies—including initiatives to promote widespread privatization, decrease taxes, and limit government spending—led to a decrease in support for primary health care (Brown, Cueto, and Fee 2019).

specific programs. This reliance on extrabudgetary funding, which would rise to constitute more than half of WHO's overall budget, highlighted the disconnect between the priorities of the World Health Assembly, with each state having one vote, and the priorities of donor nations and agencies—favoring discrete programs without having to answer to WHO's legislative bodies (Brown, Cueto, and Fee 2006). WHO programming thus became more fragmented and its policies became less impactful, as a proliferation of new actors weakened WHO's global health leadership.

Seeing WHO as unable to address major health challenges, donors shifted support to new global initiatives, recognizing the advantages of their:

- Governing Structures—New initiatives had governing structures that were not only controlled by states, but included representatives from civil society, philanthropic organizations, and the private sector.
- Narrow Mandates—These initiatives had narrow mandates, often focusing vertically on one disease or intervention, which allowed for targeted programs to meet narrow goals that could show rapid results.
- Funding Mechanisms—Funding mechanisms were based entirely on voluntary contributions, allowing wealthy donors to play an even greater role in controlling initiatives (Clinton and Sridhar 2017).

These disparate global health initiatives operated independent of each other, creating the appearance of "anarchy" in the global health landscape (Fidler 2007, 7). As WHO recognized its waning leadership in this expanding landscape, it sought ways to retain influence as a central coordinator in an increasingly fragmented architecture of global health governance.

II. Global Health Governance for a Globalizing World

Global health governance seeks to realize greater institutional coordination across a chaotic global health landscape. Where once WHO reigned supreme over global health, the contemporary era lacks a singular institutional authority to coordinate global initiatives to prevent disease and promote health (Moon et al. 2010). The expansion of global health governance has required measures beyond the purview of national governments and international organizations, allowing for both state and non-state actors to undertake varied functions to respond to threats of global concern (Meier and Gostin 2018). Global health governance institutions now encompass a wide range of intergovernmental organizations, funding agencies, and international bureaucracies that work across a range of economic, social, and cultural fields that underlie public health in a globalizing world (Youde 2013). In seeking to bring together this wide range of new actors without centralized WHO leadership, global health governance now seeks institutional coordination in a more fragmented landscape of organizations—through global health partnerships. Increasingly influential in global health governance, these governance partnerships are playing crucial roles in the development and implementation of global health law.

A. Contemporary Global Health Landscape

Global health law now works across an expanding landscape of proliferating actors. Given the rise of public health on the global governance agenda and the political spotlight on global health inequalities, national governments and international organizations are now being joined by non-state actors to address determinants of global health (Moon et al. 2010). These non-state institutions can provide expert policy guidance, financial and technical assistance, normative standards, and accountability mechanisms (Clinton and Sridhar 2017). Bringing together these state and non-state actors has required institutional partnerships across national governments, international organizations, non-governmental initiatives, and transnational corporations.

1. National Governments

Where once foreign policy was conceptualized exclusively through state power to advance national interests, some national governments are increasingly framing foreign policy to advance global health—whether acting alone through bilateral foreign assistance efforts or acting in concert with other donor countries. National interests are being transformed as public health is defined as a foreign policy issue, and foreign assistance, as discussed in greater detail in Chapter 14, is devoted to disease prevention and health promotion. Alongside other high-income nations, global health has become an explicit goal of U.S. foreign policy, and, as the largest donor to global health in absolute dollars (albeit less relative to GDP), "official development assistance" for health is fast becoming an anchor of U.S. "soft power." In shifting donor states from uncoordinated vertical approaches to address select high-profile diseases, with recipient states once selected solely on the basis of economic interests, several high-income states are increasingly joining together in moving toward coordinated foreign assistance. For some states, supporting horizontal health systems is viewed as a way to address specific "health threats" to promote "global health security" (Sirleaf 2018a). Within high-level multilateral forums, the G7 and G20 political agendas have shifted to place an explicit focus on global health (McBride, Hawkes, and Buse 2019).

Although states long neglected making global health a political priority, this tradition of neglect has begun to change across many nations, which have come together as a global community to advance health in the UN General Assembly. The political statements of the General Assembly, as introduced in Chapter 2, have achieved some of the goals of formal norm-setting without requiring the adoption of a treaty or the establishment of new institutions. Addressing global health for the first time in an unprecedented "high-level" special session, states met together in a June 2001 UN General Assembly Special Session (UNGASS) on HIV/AIDS, dealing belatedly with an issue then of primary concern to the Global South, in particular the most impoverished regions of Sub-Saharan Africa (Parker 2002).[4] In drawing from this initial HIV/AIDS initiative, global health justice has risen in prominence in UN policymaking in the 21st century, giving international political legitimacy to global health governance (Meier 2011). Through this advancement of global health in international policy, health has moved beyond soft power to become a basis for global political action through international organizations.

2. International Organizations

Within the UN system of international organizations, responsibility for specific health functions is decentralized across several UN specialized agencies, with overlapping organizational mandates across economic, social, cultural, education, health, and related fields. Where states delegate to these international organizations to coordinate their global health efforts, many long-standing international organizations have taken on a greater role in global health within the purview of their own institutional mandates. WHO has long served as the primary UN specialized agency for health, but many other international organizations hold authority to develop independent institutional policies and programs to address health within their respective spheres of influence, as seen in UNICEF work on child health, UN Development Program (UNDP) work on health in development, and UN Population Fund (UNFPA) work on reproductive health (Koivusalo and Ollila 1997). Such functional decentralization within the UN system has created a fragmented global governance system for public

---

[4] Although HIV/AIDS was initially framed by the UN Security Council in 2000 as a "threat to international peace and security," this security framing yielded in the UN General Assembly to a normative focus on public health, human rights, and international development (Rushton 2010). When the UN Security Council next faced a global health challenge in the 2014 Ebola epidemic in West Africa, it recognized that "the unprecedented extent of the Ebola outbreak in Africa constitutes a threat to international peace and security," but with states expressing varying rationales for their support: some explicitly linked the Ebola outbreak to the prospect of future violence; some addressed the economic and social instability engendered by the disease; and others emphasized how Ebola threatened "human security" (Sirleaf 2018a).

health, with international organizations operating independently to address select health concerns.

Beyond these long-standing organizations, states have also developed new international organizations to address global health. As the HIV/AIDS crisis grew to become a leading priority in global health governance, WHO was thought to be unable to lead the unprecedented global health response. States called for a new UN agency to focus specifically on the AIDS crisis while creating horizontal, multilevel programming that could address health determinants and structural issues beyond the medical aspects of HIV/AIDS (Knight, Clevees, and Davies 2008). States came together in 1996 to establish the Joint United Nations Programme on HIV/AIDS (UNAIDS), looking to the UNAIDS Secretariat leadership to coordinate eleven other agencies, including WHO, UNICEF, and the World Bank. In drawing from actors beyond the UN system, UNAIDS would also seek to unite a wide range of non-state actors, bringing together governmental and non-governmental initiatives to address this disease threat.

3. Non-Governmental Initiatives

Non-governmental initiatives have advanced rapidly in the global health landscape, whether established through civil society or individual philanthropists. However, the multitude of global health NGOs and their various initiatives have complicated the global health architecture amid overlapping organizational mandates in global health. These NGOs are frequently seen as narrow in focus— "indeed, the narrow (or more vertical) mandates were arguably the catalysts for their creation" (Clinton and Sridhar 2017, 52). Given the narrow focus of NGO initiatives, NGOs often compete with each other (and with governments) for attention and resources, creating an NGO funding landscape that results in programs that are inefficient, duplicative, and unsustainable (Szlezák et al. 2010). This "NGO-ization" of global health has thus faced criticisms for undermining the development of horizonal public health systems and the provision of primary health care.[5]

Beyond these organizational efforts, individual philanthropists and their foundations have long played a role in global health governance, but this charitable programming and influence has greatly increased in recent years. With an expanding set of private foundations now working in global health, these philanthropic initiatives have challenged state authorities and led to questions about

---

[5] The harm of this proliferation of NGO actors is seen in the fragmentation of health delivery prior to the 2014 Ebola epidemic in West Africa, where there was often a mismatch between national priorities for health development and donor funding stipulations. As donor governments and NGOs often directed aid to specific health projects and diseases, the more comprehensive, horizontal task of building up the capacity of the state health system and shoring up its ability to train, pay, and retain qualified health staff was not prioritized (Sirleaf 2018a).

their financial influence—no more so than the Bill & Melinda Gates Foundation. Founded in 2000 with proceeds from the Microsoft corporation, the Gates Foundation controls unprecedented wealth and provides unrivaled funding in the global health landscape. This level of financial control has left the financing of a wide range of organizations and initiatives in the hands of Foundation leaders—rather than government representatives. The Gates Foundation's unparalleled financing, largely supporting vertical initiatives, has given it a uniquely influential role that no other non-state actor possesses in global health governance (Clinton and Sridhar 2017). Yet despite this sweeping power, its role as a private nonprofit organization allows it to escape the transparency expected of other state and non-state actors, raising concerns about its rising influence without democratic legitimacy or clear accountability (McGoey 2021).

4. Transnational Corporations

Presenting similar legitimacy and accountability concerns, the global health landscape has seen rising involvement of corporate actors in global health governance. Governments have long sought corporate regulation to correct market failures and protect public health. Where governments have increasingly looked to global governance to regulate the harmful ramifications of corporate actions—regulating both unsafe products and harmful production processes—private sector influence in global health initiatives has grown, with regulated industries often seeking to influence global health policymaking to their benefit (Suzuki et al. 2021).[6] Industry representatives thus increasingly engage in the development of global health law and policy, but during negotiations, will often propose corporate self-regulation, as discussed in greater detail in Chapter 13, as opposed to legal regulations (McCambridge et al. 2020).

Pharmaceutical corporations specifically have embraced norms of corporate social responsibility to address a multitude of global health issues through the development and discovery of new drugs. These pharmaceutical corporations are the main manufacturers of medicines, and thus "hold the ball" in drug development—making themselves necessary actors in global health governance (Buse and Walt 2000). However, market-based patent incentives for pharmaceuticals have been shown to be ill-suited for addressing health needs (Sirleaf 2021). While often criticized for advancing technological and vertical approaches to global health and prioritizing corporate profits over public health (Ng and Ruger 2011), pharmaceutical companies benefit from tax breaks,

---

[6] The inclusion of transnational corporations in health policymaking has been found to weaken the regulation of commercial products that negatively impact public health, with both the alcohol and tobacco industries, introduced in Chapter 7, using similar tactics to undermine public health policy (McCambridge et al. 2020).

increased exposure to policymakers (to influence the regulatory process), and public relations (to improve their corporate image). This engagement has raised concerns about new global health partnerships.

B. Partnerships among State and Non-State Actors

Each of these actors influences global health, but given the fragmentation, duplication, and confusion resulting from their uncoordinated initiatives, policymakers have sought to coordinate actors through inter-institutional partnerships. Without centralized leadership in global health governance, health advocates have turned to global partnerships as a way of galvanizing disparate actors to embrace shared health goals through global health policy (Harmer and Buse 2009). Bringing together these distinct actors (each operating with different motivations), partnerships have become particularly relevant given scarce resources (and increased competition for those resources among an expanding set of actors), with partnerships for specific health priorities combining the efforts of inherently limited actors to achieve collective health goals (Szlezák et al. 2010).

These partnerships encompass collaborative relationships among diverse actors, working together to meet a common goal. Compared to traditional state governance, global partnerships provide an innovative method for "bridging multilateral norms and local action" and improving upon deficits in governance—creating predictable and sustained commitments across multiple partners (Bäckstrand 2006, 291). Such partnerships can coordinate distinct functions for each actor—including research and development, technical assistance/service support, advocacy, and financing—seeking to achieve a goal together that none could accomplish alone.[7] While these decentralized partnerships lack the centralized leadership and hierarchical structures of past efforts, the cooperation of actors allows for the combination of multiple institutions with distributed authorities, with each actor undertaking a coordinated aspect of a single global policy. These advantages in recruiting a coalition of diverse, specialized actors became the foundation for the 2002 creation of the Global Fund for AIDS, Tuberculosis, and Malaria (Global Fund) (Youde 2013).

---

[7] For example, following the failure of WHO's malaria eradication effort in the 1950s and 1960s, the current Roll Back Malaria Partnership has brought together over five hundred governmental, intergovernmental, and non-governmental partners to create a coordinated global response, developing shared goals to articulate, conduct, and sustain a global health policy effort to realize malaria eradication (Keusch et al. 2010).

Case Study: Global Health Partnerships: The Birth of the Global Fund

Amid the rising global focus on the HIV/AIDS pandemic, the development of antiretroviral therapy (ART) provided an effective HIV treatment that offered hope in the global response. However, donors determined that ART was financially and logistically "unsustainable" and remained reluctant to fund access to these essential medicines in the Global South. Yet, with a rising number of donor states focused on combating HIV/AIDS, the 2001 UNGASS on HIV/AIDS secured a new international commitment to create a new funding mechanism, leading to the January 2002 launch of the Global Fund. Developed principally as a funding agency, drawing on voluntary contributions to fund vertical programming for specific diseases, the Global Fund is a partnership among various public and private actors—all functioning together in a system of shared deliberative governance. This partnership has brought together international organizations such as WHO and UNAIDS, as well as NGOs, philanthropic organizations including the Gates Foundation, and, importantly, both donor and recipient nations. Nations are not only partners through their financial contributions; they hold decision-making powers as recipients. The Global Fund's organizational structure seeks to facilitate "country ownership" through its inclusion of a wide range of recipient state stakeholders in decision-making activities, including representatives from civil society, the private sector, and affected communities. Central to the Global Fund's grants are country coordination mechanisms (CCMs), which are national committees that coordinate applications for and oversee the implementation of Global Fund grants, giving recipient countries greater agency over where and how health assistance is operationalized within their countries. The Global Fund's coordinated funding system has increased efficiencies in providing aid to nations for the treatment of HIV, tuberculosis, and malaria, and its model seeks to ensure that this vertical assistance fills existing gaps rather than supplanting governmental and international aid initiatives.

In facilitating access to essential medicines, the Global Fund serves as a public-private partnership (PPP), a shared collaboration between public and private actors to improve health. While the early years of the UN saw limited collaborations between the public and private sectors in public health, the emergence of neoliberal ideologies in the early 1980s led to a shift toward global health partnerships with the private sector—with the assumption that free markets and corporate partners would prove more efficient (Reich 2000). This perception of private sector efficiency has propelled the rise of PPPs in global health governance, but rapacious corporate practices continue to necessitate public sector safeguards to ensure health equity, as seen where certain vaccines have been deprioritized by the pharmaceutical industry as insufficiently profitable (Sirleaf 2021). To create financial incentives and global oversight for the pharmaceutical industry, the Global Alliance on Vaccines and Immunizations (now Gavi, the Vaccine Alliance) has brought together industry actors with donor governments in a PPP to increase immunizations in the Global South, seeking to reduce bureaucracy and optimize efficiency to facilitate equitable global access to immunizations (Singh et al. 2022). While public health advocates remain wary of efforts to work with the private sector, global health partnerships have provided a path for collaborations between public and private institutions to achieve collective health goals, with each actor undertaking coordinated aspects of a single global policy.

C. Developing Partnerships under Global Health Law

Global health law is playing a vital role in structuring the interconnected goals of a wide range of decentralized actors in global health—and the partnerships among them. A proliferation of national, international, non-governmental, and corporate actors has arisen to address a multisectoral array of determinants of health; however, as introduced in Chapter 2, this expanding global health landscape has complicated initiatives to develop international law to promote global health. Where global health partnerships, especially PPPs, bring together state and non-state actors, these collaborations reside outside the traditional frameworks of international law, raising questions of legal responsibility and accountability.

Given the established need for global cooperation, global health law can serve an important role in holding together these partnerships, providing a path to ensure responsibility and facilitate accountability. Filling gaps in international legal regulation, global health law extends regulations and responsibilities to non-state actors involved in global health partnerships (Clarke 2011). Global health law provides non-binding "soft law" instruments that can influence global health actors, including codes of practice and international resolutions, to establish global consensus and create incentives that can influence non-state actors (Gostin and Meier 2019). Ensuring the implementation of these responsibilities, global health law can facilitate accountability through transparent information on processes and outcomes, strengthening the coalition among state and non-state actors.

Global health law can thus serve to maintain cooperation among diverse actors, with partnerships holding the potential to strengthen global health law. Partnerships provide the ability to exert greater control over non-state actors and bypass the traditional legal boundaries that inhibit rapid progress (Gostin et al. 2019). The scope of partnerships, encompassing both public and private partners, can seek to expand the boundaries of law. While traditional international legal frameworks are focused on regulating states and international organizations, their scope fails to provide obligations to regulate NGOs and corporate actors, limiting the influence of international law. The rise of partnerships of state and non-state actors can expand the scope of global health law norms and obligations across private and public actors (Gostin and Sridhar 2014). This expansion of collaborative partnerships can potentially strengthen the ability of global health law to frame the entire global health landscape, bringing the world together under a common agenda for global health.

III. A Common Agenda for Global Health

As parallel initiatives guide a range of discrete partnerships across the global health landscape, the UN has sought to bring all these partners together under singular overarching policy frameworks. Global health policies can seek to develop a voluntary compact among states and partners in business, philanthropy, and civil society to redress global health inequities, developing "common but differentiated" responsibilities in global health governance (Sirleaf 2018b). The international community has put forward sweeping global agendas to align the proliferating actors that shape global governance in meeting a singular goal, building from the limitations of the Millennium Development Goals (MDGs) (2000–2015) to structure the current Sustainable Development Goals (SDGs) (2015–2030) and providing a long-sought path to decolonize global health.

A. Establishing a Development Agenda for the New Millennium

At the end of the 20th century, the world was facing significant global health and development challenges. Concurrent with the rise in neoliberal globalization, many countries across the globe were confronting or recovering from economic crises, with disastrous public health impacts (Kim et al. 1999).[8] Neoliberal reforms

---

[8] Countries across Latin America faced cascading debt crises throughout the 1980s, former Soviet states faced economic crisis following the 1991 collapse of the Soviet Union, and countries across Asia encountered a widespread financial crisis in the late 1990s with the collapse of domestic and international investment markets.

in the Global South—led by the International Monetary Fund and the World Bank—had fomented deep-seated mistrust toward international development institutions. Compounded by rising global health challenges, the acceleration of the HIV/AIDS pandemic had left millions infected with HIV, as development inequities abandoned impoverished populations to die (Lidén 2014). These challenges made clear the need to establish a unified effort to address global development, with development policy serving as a foundation of global health.

The UN seized this opportunity to create a common platform to meet the evolving needs of the 21st century, culminating in 2000 in the UN Millennium Summit that led to the adoption of the UN Millennium Declaration. Through this Declaration, the UN General Assembly outlined eight goals, the MDGs, to structure global efforts over the next fifteen years (UN General Assembly 2000). While each of these goals had been areas of concern in prior UN initiatives, the MDGs reflected a contemporary commitment to place human needs—rather than economic growth—at the center of the global development agenda. The MDGs thereby created a common policy framework for an unprecedented global campaign to advance human development. Four of the eight MDGs explicitly focused on improvements in health, including the reduction of maternal and infant mortality, the prevention of HIV infection, and the eradication of poverty and hunger—with the MDGs seeking to bring the world together to address specific health conditions (Freedman 2005).

Where efforts to meet the MDGs were tied to the actions (or inactions) of a wide range of actors—including national governments, international organizations, NGOs, and transnational corporations—development cooperation would be a necessary prerequisite for global health advancement. To this end, the MDGs provided a policy framework for the alignment of global health initiatives, serving as a reference point for global health programs and a central catalyst for increased financial commitments (Lomazzi, Borisch, and Laaser 2014). Collaborative partnerships under the MDGs led to significant achievements across the eight goals; however, stakeholders were frustrated by the highly technocratic approach taken in implementing the MDGs, the failure to effectively address health determinants across countries, and the lack of grounding in fundamental principles of equity and human rights (Fukuda-Parr 2016). Many concluded that the MDGs were not nearly as transformative as they needed to be to address the needs of global development and global health in the 21st century. These shortcomings sparked debates in developing a "post-2015 agenda," which would seek to correct the limitations of the MDGs and lay a path forward for sustainable development.

B. A New Agenda for Sustainable Development

Facilitating new collaborations across institutions, the 2030 Agenda for Sustainable Development (2030 Agenda) has provided a renewed basis for

Figure 3.2 UN General Assembly Launch of the Sustainable Development Goals, 2015 (UN)

cooperative efforts to promote global health and development. Whereas the MDGs were largely driven by countries in the Global North, the SDGs were a product of more inclusive processes that included representation from both the Global North and Global South (Fukuda-Parr 2016). Convening in a 2012 UN Conference on Sustainable Development, states adopted "The Future We Want," resolving to establish a UN High-Level Political Forum on Sustainable Development (UN General Assembly 2012). The following year, the UN General Assembly established an Open Working Group that would develop proposals for the discrete SDGs. Deliberations on the post-2015 development agenda were finalized during the 2015 UN Sustainable Development Summit, as seen in Figure 3.2, at which the UN General Assembly adopted the 2030 Agenda. Under this new agenda for development cooperation, UN member states outlined seventeen interrelated SDGs, establishing interconnected goals that the global community would strive to reach over the next fifteen years.

These current goals reflect a universal call to action, looking to sustainable development to improve the prosperity and well-being of people across the globe. Compared to the MDGs, the SDGs encompass a more expansive vision of global development that draws from foundational principles of equity and human rights (Sidibé et al. 2018). The 2030 Agenda, as discussed in greater detail in Chapter 10, recognizes that sustainable development cannot be achieved without integrated strategies and global partnerships. These global ambitions set out a broad agenda under the SDGs to bring the world together to advance global health.

Case Study: Bringing the World Together under SDG 3

While many of the SDGs address underlying determinants of health—including poverty, hunger, and climate action—SDG 3 seeks specifically to "ensure healthy lives and promote well-being for all at all ages." To evaluate progress throughout the world in meeting this goal, the UN has established thirteen different targets and twenty-eight indicators, which address a range of health issues—from reducing infant and maternal mortality to improving access to essential medicines, vaccines, and health services. This standardized accountability framework has created opportunities to align health-related efforts across global governance institutions and support the adoption of coordinated reforms to ensure the promotion and protection of health for all. Such reforms seek to require the engagement of a wide range of actors and processes at all levels of governance—creating a unified global agenda to promote health. Achieving the SDGs has thus demanded new multisectoral and multilevel partnerships—between government sectors, international organizations, transnational corporations, and civil society—that operate globally, regionally, and within countries and communities. As institutions seek collaboratively to translate the SDGs from abstract goals to measurable realities, more than nine hundred voluntary commitments and multi-stakeholder partnerships have been developed across the globe in support of SDG 3. These partnerships include initiatives focused on strengthening food systems, access to clean drinking water, and distribution of essential medicines, as well as initiatives born in response to the COVID-19 pandemic – with these partnerships providing new momentum for investments in health systems and services under SDG 3.

As with the MDGs, the adoption of the SDGs has been followed by periodic assessments of progress across the different goals, targets, and indicators. These annual reports provide monitoring and assessment to facilitate shared accountability among stakeholders for the realization of the SDGs. Recognizing that multi-stakeholder partnerships are critical catalysts for the achievement of the SDGs, the UN has taken additional steps in supporting, facilitating, and monitoring partnerships and commitments towards the SDGs. However, the world is not on track to achieve many of the SDGs by 2030, with the SDGs facing continuing criticisms for not being sufficiently transformative in reshaping the global landscape

(Achiume 2022). As 2030 approaches, there is an urgent need to look beyond the SDGs in bringing the world together to meet a rising imperative to decolonize global health.

C. A Rising Imperative to Decolonize Global Health

Efforts to "decolonize" global health seek to give greater voice to actors in the Global South in global health governance. Colonial mentalities in global health continue to influence the underlying assumptions and structuring of global health law and policy, which assume the need for "white saviorism"—to save supposedly uncivilized, ignorant, and diseased natives from themselves. These neocolonial approaches to global health governance, a continuing legacy of tropical medicine, have exacerbated inequities in global health. Global health law cannot and should not be divorced, decontextualized, nor depoliticized from its colonial roots and governing logics.

The ongoing coloniality of global health governance continues to displace and supplant local systems of knowledge production and focus on one-off biomedical solutions. The contemporary global health landscape continues to reflect the top-down dynamics of colonial approaches to tropical medicine—with little to no consultation with local communities. Global health partnerships frequently involve relationships between countries and researchers in the Global North and Global South, wherein former colonial powers exercise the predominant influence, power, and control over resources (Denend et al. 2015).[9] The vertical approaches favored by donors are often quick-fixes—as opposed to more time-consuming horizontal approaches that would require addressing underlying determinants of health. Such neocolonial approaches continue to surface during contemporary global health challenges, including in the COVID-19 response. Even as pandemic threats have demanded global solidarity, global health governance actors blamed marginalized populations for being noncompliant and facilitating the spread of disease in a way that obscured geopolitical and structural factors that set the conditions for disease transmission.

In redressing the legacy of these continuing injustices, the imperative to decolonize global health governance is clear. Decolonization of the international order could be achieved by revisiting the redistributive and reparative project embodied in the Declaration of Alma-Ata—seeking health equity both within and between countries, emphasizing primary health care for all, and conceptualizing health

---

[9] Given these power imbalances in global health partnerships, such partnerships are often skewed in how the distribution of partnership benefits are allocated.

as more than the absence of infirmity or disease. This will require implementing global health policies and developing global health partnerships that explicitly redress and repair historical injustices against Indigenous communities and historically subordinated peoples as well as their contemporary manifestations (Richardson 2019).[10] The inequitable impact of the COVID-19 pandemic has reinforced the imperative for a new global health landscape, recentering the need to develop public health systems horizontally in ways that address underlying determinants of health. Recent initiatives to ensure the equitable distribution of COVID-19 vaccines, therapeutics, and diagnostics provide for immediate and near-term measures that could further decolonial efforts—drawing from transnational social movements born from the early years of the HIV/AIDS pandemic to provide access to essential medicines in the Global South (Sirleaf 2022). The disruption engendered by COVID-19 provides a path to potentially reshape the global health landscape and reform global health governance in ways that could create a more just world order.

Conclusion

Global health law is framed by the actors who exert influence over global health. Out of the horrors of World War II, states sought to establish new authority for international health cooperation, creating a new international organization to lead global efforts. However, WHO has faced limitations in responding to the health threats of a globalizing world, and a wide range of new actors have entered the global health landscape. The divergent efforts of these proliferating state and non-state actors have led to a fragmented landscape of vertical initiatives that compete for funding in unsustainable ways and further colonial power dynamics in global health. Global health partnerships have sought to coordinate these efforts and potentially provide new paths to advance global health governance. As the global health landscape expands further in response to new pandemic threats, the need has never been greater to rethink how global health governance can better meet global health challenges.

Despite the rise of partnerships, these governance systems are ill-equipped to respond to the wide-ranging global health challenges faced today. Overlapping mandates and competition for scarce resources and influence create confusion in a crowded global health landscape. State and non-state actors in the global health landscape have structured governance in ways that are fundamentally unjust and

---

[10] The calls for decolonization also necessitate transformation of the academic discipline of global public health, since both the study and practice of the field can inform what is on the global health agenda and the policies that are implemented.

unable to address today's pressing global health needs—dividing the world at a moment when common purpose is essential. At this crossroads in global health governance, it is critical that the global community take stock of the changing actors in global health and consider how governance approaches must be changed drastically to achieve sustainable development and redress the legacies of colonialism in global health law and policy.

Global health law aims to influence how actors behave, seeks to constrain their activities, and works to shape their expectations in global health governance. Correspondingly, such governance provides a means for actors to advance their interests and come together in partnerships to promote global health law. In developing these partnerships across the global health landscape, the SDGs have sought to bring the entire world together under a unified policy framework to achieve a common set of goals. Looking beyond the SDGs, it will be crucial for global health policy frameworks to provide state and non-state actors with new common norms—shared values to promote global health. These future norms will be essential to bind together actors across the global health landscape, framing universal values to realize the highest attainable standard of health.

Questions for Consideration

1. Why did the Cold War undermine WHO leadership in global health governance? How did the end of colonial rule and rise of decolonized nations alter global health priorities under WHO governance?
2. Why was the Declaration of Alma-Ata a seminal advancement in international health governance? How did WHO bring together states in Alma-Ata to reaffirm public health under WHO governance?
3. What led to the proliferation of new actors in the global health landscape? How have these new actors challenged WHO leadership and shifted agendas in global health governance?
4. Why has public health risen on the global policy agenda? For what reasons do states pursue bilateral assistance over global governance?
5. What are the sources of legitimacy and credibility of non-governmental initiatives in global health governance? How have philanthropists sought to shift the global health agenda?
6. How has the proliferation of actors in global health limited the efficiency and effectiveness of global health governance?
7. How do partnerships seek to support global health governance? How has the Global Fund brought together state and non-state actors to support shared health goals in the distribution of essential medicines?

8. What concerns arise from the involvement of the private sector in global health governance? Do PPPs alleviate or exacerbate these concerns?
9. How did the MDGs provide a common agenda across all the actors in the global health landscape? How does SDG 3 seek to overcome the challenges faced by the health-related goals of the MDGs—and advance partnerships under a common health agenda?
10. What do efforts to decolonize global health seek to change in global health governance? Why have these changes proven so difficult to realize?

Acknowledgments

The authors are grateful for the research assistance of Neha Saggi in chronicling the history of WHO governance, Erin Jones in examining public-private partnerships, Hanna Huffstetler in analyzing the influence of the SDGs on the global health landscape, and Alexis Lovings and Tamia Morris for their editorial support.

References

Achiume, Tendayi. 2022. 2030 Agenda for Sustainable Development, the Sustainable Development Goals and the Fight Against Racial Discrimination. A/HRC/50/60.

Allen, Charles E. 1950. "World Health and World Politics." *International Organization* 4(1): 27–43.

Bäckstrand, Karin. 2006. "Multi-stakeholder partnerships for sustainable development: Rethinking Legitimacy, Accountability and Effectiveness." *European Environment* 16(5): 290–306.

Brown, Theodore M., Marcos Cueto, and Elizabeth Fee. 2006. "The World Health Organization and the Transition from "International" to "Global" Public Health." *American Journal of Public Health* 96(1): 62–72.

Buse, Kent and Gill Walt. 2000. "Global Public-Private Partnerships: Part I—A new Development in Health?" *Bulletin of the World Health Organization* 78: 549–561.

Clarke, Lisa. 2011. "Responsibility of International Organizations under International Law for the Acts of Global Health Public-Private Partnerships." *Chicago Journal of International Law* 12(1): 55.

Clinton, Chelsea, and Devi Sridhar. 2017. *Governing Global Health: Who Runs the World and Why?* Oxford: Oxford University Press.

Cueto, Marcos, Theodore Brown, and Elizabeth Fee. 2019. *The World Health Organization: A History*. Cambridge: Cambridge University Press.

Denend, Lyn, Amy Lockwood, Michele Barry, and Stefanos Zenios. 2015. "Lessons for Creating Better Global Health Programs." *Stanford Social Innovation Review.* November 9.

Evang, K. 1967. *Health of Mankind*. Churchill, London.

Farley, John. 2008. *Brock Chisholm, the World Health Organization, and the Cold War*. Vancouver: University of British Columbia Press.

Fidler, David. 2007. "Architecture Amidst Anarchy: Global Health's Quest for Governance." In *Global Health Governance* 1(1): 1–17.

Freedman, Lynn P. 2005. "Achieving the MDGs: Health Systems as Core Social Institutions." *Development* 48(1): 19–24.

Fukuda Parr, Sakiko. 2016. "From the Millennium Development Goals to the Sustainable Development Goals: Shifts in Purpose, Concept, and Politics of Global Goal Setting for Development." *Gender and Development* 24(1): 43–52.

Gostin, Lawrence O. and Benjamin Mason Meier. 2019. "Introducing Global Health Law." *Journal of Law, Medicine & Ethics* 47(4): 788–793.

Gostin, Lawrence O. and Devi Sridhar. 2014. "Global Health and the Law." *New England Journal of Medicine* 370(18): 1732–1740.

Gostin, Lawrence O., John T. Monahan, Jenny Kaldor, Mary DeBartolo, Eric A. Friedman, Katie Gottschalk, Susan C. Kim et al. 2019. "The Legal Determinants of Health: Harnessing the Power of Law for Global Health and Sustainable Development." *Lancet* 393(10183): 1857–1910.

Greene, Jeremy, Marguerite Thorp Basilico, Heidi Kim, and Paul Farmer. 2013. "Colonial Medicine and Its Legacies." In *Reimagining Global Health: An Introduction*, edited by Paul Farmer, Jim Yong Kim, Arthur Kleinman, and Matthew Basilico, 33–73. Oakland: University of California Press.

Harmer, Andrew and Kent Buse. 2009. "Global Health Partnerships: The Mosh Pit of Global Health Governance." In *Making Sense of Global Health Governance: A Policy Perspective*, edited by Wolfgang Hein and Nick Drager. 63–86. London: Palgrave Macmillan.

Jacobson, Harold K. and Robert W. Cox. 1974. "WHO: Medicine, Regionalism, and Managed Politics." In *The Anatomy of Influence: Decision Making in International Organization*. 175–215. New Haven: Yale University Press.

Keusch, Gerald T., Wen Kilama, Suerie Moon, Nicole Szlezak, and Catherine Michaud. 2010. "The Global Health System: Linking Knowledge with Action—Learning from Malaria." *PLoS Medicine* 7(1).

Kim, Jim Yong, Joyce V. Milllen, Alec Irwin, and John Gershman. 1999. *Dying for Growth: Global Inequality and the Health of the Poor*. Monroe: Common Courage Press.

Knight, Lindsay, Julia Cleves, and Keith Davies. 2008. "UNAIDS: The First 10 Years, 1996–2006." *World Health Organization*.

Koivusalo, Meri and Eeva Ollila. 1997. *Making a Healthy World: Agencies, Actors and Policies in International Health*. New York: Zed.

Lidén, J. 2014. "The World Health Organization and Global Health Governance: Post-1990." *Public Health* 128(2): 141–147.

Lomazzi, Marta, Bettina Borisch and Ulrich Laaser. 2014. "The Millennium Development Goals: Experiences, Achievements and What's Next." *Global Health Action* 7(1): 23695.

McBride, Bronwyn, Sarah Hawkes, and Kent Buse. 2019. "Soft Power and Global Health: The Sustainable Development Goals (SDGs) Era Health Agendas of the G7, G20 and BRICS." *BMC Public Health* 19(1): 1–14.

McCambridge, Jim, Kypros Kypri, Trevor A Sheldon, Mary Madden, and Thomas F Babor. 2020. "Advancing Public Health Policy Making through Research on the Political Strategies of Alcohol Industry Actors." *Journal of Public Health* 42(2): 262–269.

McGoey, Linsey. 2021. "Philanthrocapitalism and the Separation of Powers." *Annual Review of Law and Social Science* 17(1): 391–409.
Meier, Benjamin Mason. 2010. "Global Health Governance and the Contentious Politics of Human Rights: Mainstreaming the Right to Health for Public Health Advancement." *Stanford Journal of International Law* 46(1):1–50.
Meier, Benjamin Mason. 2011. "Global Health Takes a Normative Turn: The Expanding Purview of International Health Law and Global Health Policy to Meet the Public Health Challenges of the 21st Century." *Global Community: Yearbook of International Law and Jurisprudence* 1: 69–108.
Meier, Benjamin Mason and Lawrence O. Gostin. 2018. "Introduction." In *Human Rights in Global Health: Rights-Based Governance for a Globalizing World*, edited by Benjamin Mason Meier and Lawrence O. Gostin, 2–18. New York: Oxford University Press.
Moon, Suerie, Nicole A. Szlezák, Catherine M. Michaud, Dean T. Jamison, Gerald T. Keusch, William C. Clark, and Barry R. Bloom. 2010. "The Global Health System: Lessons for a Stronger Institutional Framework." *PLoS Medicine* 7(1): e1000193.
Ng, Nora Y. and Jennifer Prah Ruger. 2011. "Global Health Governance at a Crossroads." *Global Health Governance* 3(2): 1.
Osakwe, Christopher Olomu. 1972. *Participation of the Soviet Union in Universal International Organizations: A Political and Legal Analysis of Soviet Strategies and Aspirations Inside ILO, UNESCO and WHO*. Leiden: Sijthoff.
Pannenborg, Charles O. 1979. *A New International Health Order: An Inquiry into the International Relations of World Health and Medical Care*. Alphen aan den Rijn: Sijthoff & Noordhoff.
Parker, Richard. 2002. "The Global HIV/AIDS Pandemic, Structural Inequalities, and the Politics of International Health." *American Journal of Public Health* 92(3): 343–347.
Pethybridge, Roger. 1965. "The Influence of InSternational Politics on the Activities of 'Non-Political' Specialized Agencies—a Case tudy." *Political Studies*. 3(2): 247–251.
Reich, Michael R. 2000. "Public–Private Partnerships for Public Health." *Nature Medicine* 6 (6): 617–620.
Richardson, Eugene T. 2019. "On the Coloniality of Global Public Health." *Medicine Anthropology Theory* 6(2019): 101–118.
Rushton, Simon. 2010. "AIDS and International Security in the United Nations System." *Health Policy and Planning* 25(6): 495–504.
Sidibé, Michel, Helena Nygren-Krug, Bronwyn McBride, and Kent Buse. 2018. "The Future of Global Governance for Health." In *Human Rights in Global Health: Rights-Based Governance for a Globalizing World*, edited by Benjamin Mason Meier and Lawrence O. Gostin, 87–108. New York: Oxford University Press.
Singh, Sandeep, Jagmeet Bawa, Bawa Singh, Balinder Singh, and Shankar Lal Bika. 2022. "Analyzing GAVI the Vaccine Alliance as a Global Health Partnership Model: A Constructivist Analysis of the Global Health Crisis." *Millennial Asia*.
Sirleaf Matiangai. 2018a. "Ebola Does Not Fall from the Sky: Global Structural Violence and International Responsibility." *Vanderbilt Journal of Transnational Law* 51: 477–554.
Sirleaf, Matiangai. 2018b. "Responsibility for Epidemics." *Texas Law Review* 285: 101–169.
Sirleaf, Matiangai. 2020. "Entry Denied: COVID-19, Race, Migration & Global Health." *Frontiers in Human Dynamics* 2: 599157.
Sirleaf, Matiangai. 2021. "Disposable Lives: COVID-19, Vaccines, and the Uprising." *Columbia Law Review* 121(5): 71–94.

Sirleaf, Matiangai. 2022. "COVID-19 and Cooperation in Times of Disaster." In *The Cambridge Handbook of Disaster Law and Policy*, edited by Susan S. Kuo, John Travis Marshall, and Ryan Rowberry, 221–228. New York: Cambridge University Press.

Shawar, Yusra Ribhi and Jennifer Prah Ruger. 2018. "The World Bank." In *Human Rights in Global Health: Rights-Based Governance for a Globalizing World*, edited by Benjamin Mason Meier and Lawrence O. Gostin, 353–373. New York: Oxford University Press.

Suzuki, Mao, Douglas Webb, and Roy Small. 2021. "Competing Frames in Global Health Governance: An Analysis of Stakeholder Influence on the Political Declaration on Non-Communicable Diseases." *International Journal of Health Policy and Management* 11(7): 1078–1089.

Szlezák, Nicole A., Barry Bloom, Dean Jamison, Gerald Keusch, Catherine M. Michaud, Suerie Moon, and William C. Clark. 2010. "The Global Health System: Actors, Norms, and Expectations in Transition." *PLoS Medicine* 7(1): e1000183.

UN General Assembly. 2000. "United Nations Millennium Declaration." September 18. A/RES/55/2.

UN General Assembly. 2012. "The Future We Want." September 11. A/RES/66/288.

UN General Assembly. 2015. "2030 Agenda for Sustainable Development." October 15. A/RES/70/1.

Youde, Jeremy. 2013. *Global Health Governance*. Oxford: Wiley.

4

Global Health Norms

Human Rights, Equity, and Social Justice in Global Health

Judith Bueno de Mesquita and Lisa Forman

Norms in global health—whether expressed implicitly or codified explicitly—reflect shared core values, standards, and expectations that guide behaviors and actions. Global health law and policy look predominantly to human rights, equity, and social justice to provide moral foundations in global health. With distinct origins in political and moral philosophy, these normative approaches have been shaped by struggles against oppression and inequality. Equity and social justice increasingly came to frame global health as the international community turned its attention to social and political determinants of health in the 1970s, and human rights came to the forefront of global health governance in the response to HIV/AIDS in the 1990s. These frameworks together now have a sweeping influence over global health, framing calls to reduce health inequalities within and between countries, centering public health practice in the equal worth of every human, and providing a normative lens to address structural and systemic determinants of health. These normative framings have much in common and are often applied alongside each other to advance global health.

These norms have come to be operationalized in global health governance, providing moral foundations for law and policy decisions to improve the health and well-being of individuals and groups. Normative standards can be utilized by global health institutions to achieve common understandings across disparate actors—to define expectations, reinforce principles, and realize justice. Framing the scope of acceptable action, they have been drawn on to promote, limit, and challenge policies. Laws, policies, and actions that follow these norms—whether termed equity, social justice, or human rights—are thus focused on benefiting those who experience disadvantage or discrimination to establish a just basis for a healthier world. These normative frameworks are increasingly applied in global health governance, including by international organizations under the United Nations (UN). However, they have not been mainstreamed across all state and non-state actors relevant to global health, with the World Trade Organization, international financial institutions, and transnational corporations drawing particular criticism for limited promotion and protection of human rights, equity, and social justice norms.

This chapter analyzes these norms that frame actions in global health law and policy, providing a foundation for structuring partnerships in global health governance. In defining norms in global health, Part I introduces the philosophical origins of human rights, equity, and social justice. Part II highlights milestones in the operationalization of these normative frameworks in global health law, describing how these norms have increasingly come to shape global health governance, even as there remain challenges to normative integration in some institutions. Examining contemporary challenges that are reshaping normative frameworks in global health, Part III highlights how the COVID-19 pandemic has revealed human rights limitations in public health emergencies; global crises have raised an imperative for extraterritorial obligations to promote global solidarity; and health inequities have exposed ongoing legacies of racism, slavery, and colonialism. This chapter concludes that human rights can provide a legal foundation for norms in global health governance, but these norms must evolve to address future challenges.

I. The Origins of Human Rights, Equity, and Social Justice in Global Health

Human rights, equity, and social justice have distinct origins in political and moral philosophy, coming to prominence in struggles against oppression and inequality. Under the UN, these norms have come to frame global health governance. The evolution of human rights under international law has provided a legal basis for global health governance, whereas public health research has shined a light on global health inequalities, galvanizing the rise of equity and social justice discourses in global health.

A. Philosophical Foundations

Norms of justice in health are embedded in a broader philosophical tradition and history of struggles against tyranny, oppression, and inequality. Principles associated with human rights—including religious tolerance, abolition of slavery, rule of law, promotion of education as well as health—have been promoted by societies throughout history (Freeman 2022). The concept of rights has been linked back to Greek and Roman philosophy. During the Middle Ages and Enlightenment periods in Europe, concepts of natural law and rights conferred by reason, nature, or divinity were developed as a basis to challenge the absolute authority of monarchs. These visions of rights—formalized in, among other documents, the 1215 Magna Carta, agreed to by King John of England, and the 1789 Declaration on the Rights of Man and the Citizen, promulgated during the French revolution—reconceptualized the relationship between the government and governed (Meier, Murphy, and Gostin 2020). Yet during the 19th century, with industrialization increasingly defining economic and social life across Europe, economic inequalities and political exclusion of working classes redefined struggles for rights to include not only individual freedoms but also socioeconomic emancipation and equality, laying the foundation for the development of the economic and social rights that underlie health (Freeman 2022).

The normative framing of public health as a social justice and equity imperative was similarly influenced, as introduced in Chapter 1, by the 19th century development of social medicine. This rising attention to equity in framing public health was advanced through: research pointing to health disparities between different socially, economically, and culturally constructed groups; redistribution policies, including welfare states, as a basis to improve population health outcomes; health inequalities in the context of economic globalization; and colonial regimes in shaping racial disparities within and between states (Büyüm et al. 2020). In focusing on efforts to reduce unnecessary and unjust differences in health, health equity is thus understood to refer to the absence of systematic disparities in health (or health determinants) between populations with different levels of underlying social advantage (Braveman and Gruskin 2003).

Social justice frameworks thus came to be rooted in distributive justice, recognizing that it is unjust if key social institutions seek to benefit best off groups at the expense of those who are worst off (Rawls 1993). This focus on social justice emerged during the 19th century with attempts to create more egalitarian societies and reduce economic exploitation. During the 20th century, the concept evolved as early economic focus on wealth and property redistribution broadened to other forms of inequality, including race and gender, and global inequalities between populations in the Global South and the Global North. Social justice has provided core values that drive public health (Beauchamp 1976). These philosophical foundations of justice in global health have influenced the development of human rights under international law.

B. Codifying Human Rights Norms under International Law

The UN has been foundational to the protection of human rights under international law, providing a basis for the progressive adoption of international treaties and soft law standards. Catalyzed by the devastation of World War II, human rights were propelled to the center of the international agenda through the 1945 UN Charter, which provided the first recognition of human rights under international law, establishing human rights as a normative, moral, and legally binding foundation for global governance under the UN.[1] Human rights instruments adopted under the auspices of the UN have since come to shape global health by establishing obligations to ensure state accountability, mainstreaming human rights norms across international organizations, and providing a universal legal basis for advancing social justice.

1. Human Rights under International Law as a Basis for Public Health

The UN's 1948 Universal Declaration of Human Rights (UDHR) has become the cornerstone of human rights protection under international law, setting out foundational norms and principles that are intrinsic to the international protection of human rights. In a direct liberal riposte to fascism and Nazi ideology (Morsink 1999), the UDHR established equal dignity and freedom as grounding principles for human rights, recognizing that human rights are to be enjoyed "without discrimination of any kind" (UN General Assembly 1948, art. 1). Declaring these universal rights to provide "a common standard of achievement for all peoples and all nations" (ibid., preamble), the UDHR recognized a right to an international order to realize the full spectrum of civil, political, economic, social, and cultural rights (ibid., art. 28), which would be detailed in binding international treaties in the years that followed.

With the universal view of rights in the UDHR giving way to Cold War rivalries, as first described in Chapter 3, political and ideological tensions shaped the framing of international human rights law in ways that limited the implementation of and accountability for economic, social, and cultural rights, including the right to health. Despite the original intent to develop a single international human rights treaty to protect all human rights, Cold War divisions resulted in a UN decision to adopt in 1966 two separate treaties, the International Covenant on Civil and Political Rights (ICCPR); and the International Covenant on Economic, Social and Cultural Rights (ICESCR) (Gostin, Sirleaf, and Friedman 2020). The ICESCR centrally codified a right to health under international law—alongside a wide range of rights that underlie public health (Meier 2010).

Case Study: Birth of a Right to Health

While health has long been valued as an intrinsic good, its casting as a human right has gained legal protection over the past seventy-five years. The idea of

---

[1] The notion of rights under international law, however, predates the UN, with the international community adopting international legal protections in the 19th century on issues related to human rights, including the abolition of the slave trade, humanitarian laws of war, and workers' rights (Meier, Murphy, and Gostin 2020).

health as a human right first entered the lexicon of international law in the 1946 Constitution of the World Health Organization (WHO), whose preamble proclaimed that "the enjoyment of the highest attainable standard of health is one of the fundamental rights of every human being." Two years later, the UDHR recognized a right to health by which "[e]veryone has the right to a standard of living adequate for the health and well-being of himself and of his family, including food, clothing, housing and medical care and necessary social services . . ." This broad vision of a right to health, embracing underlying determinants and medical care, was shaped by (i) the discourse of social medicine, which had highlighted the social causes of ill health and the promotion of public health through political reforms; and (ii) the rise of welfare states, encompassing national health systems under expanding notions of government responsibility for well-being. As the Cold War intensified, ideological disagreements led Western states to endorse the supremacy of "justiciable" civil and political rights under the ICCPR, with the Soviet Bloc promoting economic, social, and cultural rights, including the right to health, under the ICESCR. This right to health and other health-related human rights would subsequently gain further legal protection under core international human rights treaties and non-binding soft law instruments. This corpus of international human rights law has become the foundation of international accountability for health and human rights under UN oversight procedures.

Despite Cold War divisions in the conceptualization of human rights, states continued to develop core international treaties, reinforcing protections for groups experiencing systemic inequality and discrimination, many of which recognize, as outlined in Table 4.1, a wide spectrum of human rights underlying health.[2]

During the 1960s, states in the Global South drove an initiative to develop an oversight system for international human rights law, which would seek to hold states to account for human rights and support normative interpretation of legal obligations, placing UN treaty bodies and other human rights accountability mechanisms on the UN agenda (Jensen 2016). These states, among them newly decolonized states, would also lead efforts to develop soft law standards to advance human rights, including the 1986 Declaration on the Right to Development, under a broader campaign to create a more just world order. Supported by the evolution of global health law, as introduced in Chapter 2, these law and policy advancements provided new opportunities to extend protections

---

[2] Beyond the core UN human rights system, states adopted human rights treaties protecting the right to health under regional organizations, including the African (Banjul) Charter on Human and Peoples Rights, the American Convention on Human Rights, and the European Social Charter.

Table 4.1. Core International Human Rights Treaties: Selected Health-Related Human Rights Protections (Bueno de Mesquita and Forman)

International Convention on the Elimination of All Forms of Racial Discrimination (1965)	International Covenant on Economic, Social, and Cultural Rights (1966)	International Covenant on Civil and Political Rights (1966)	Convention on the Elimination of All Forms of Discrimination Against Women (1979)	Convention Against Torture and Other Cruel, Inhuman or Degrading Treatment and Punishment (1984)	Convention on the Rights of the Child (1989)	International Convention on the Protection of the Rights of Migrant Workers and Members of Their Families (1990)	Convention on the Rights of Persons with Disabilities (2006)
Non-discrimination Security of the person Participation in in political and public life	Self-determination Non-discrimination Equal protections for women	Self-determination Non-discrimination Life Freedom from torture or to cruel, inhuman or degrading treatment or punishment	Non-discrimination Equal protections for women Participation in political and public life Education	Freedom from torture or to cruel, inhuman or degrading treatment or punishment	Non-discrimination Best interests of the child Life Birth registration Freedom of expression Freedom of association Privacy Access to information Protection from violence	Non-discrimination Prohibition on torture Freedom of expression Privacy Liberty and security of the person Terms and conditions of work	Non-discrimination and equality Life Liberty and security of the person Freedom from torture or to cruel, inhuman or degrading treatment or punishment

Freedom of expression	Rights to and in work	Liberty and security of the person	Work and social security	Rights of children with disabilities to full and decent life	Social security	Freedom from exploitation, violence and abuse
Work	Social security	Privacy	Healthcare	Health	Emergency medical care	Live in the community
Housing	An adequate standard of living	Freedom of expression	Economic and social life	Social security	Birth registration	Expression
Public health, medical care, social security and social services	Health	Freedom of association	Rights of rural women to social development	Standard of living	Education for migrant children	Privacy
Education and training	Education	Participation in political and public life rights		Education		Education
Remedies	Cultural rights	Equality before the law		Rest and leisure		Health
	Benefits of science			Protection from economic exploitation		Habilitation and rehabilitation
				Protection from sexual/trafficking/other forms of exploitation		Work
				Prohibition of torture		Adequate standard of living and protection
				Physical and psychological recovery		Participation in political and public life

of human rights in global health law through institutions of global health governance.

2. Human Rights Mainstreaming in Global Health Governance

The end of the Cold War heralded a new era in promoting and protecting health-related human rights—across the UN and throughout the world. At the 1993 World Conference on Human Rights in Vienna, states committed to treating civil and political rights and economic, social, and cultural rights equally, recognizing that all human rights are interrelated and interdependent (World Conference on Human Rights 1993). With this post-Cold War support, the Vienna Declaration and Programme of Action called for increased coordination on human rights across the UN system (World Conference on Human Rights 1993). UN Secretary General Kofi Annan responded to this mandate by calling for all UN programs, funds, and specialized agencies to "mainstream" human rights across their global governance efforts (UN Secretary General 1997). Supported by the establishment of the Office of the UN High Commissioner for Human Rights, UN organizations began to integrate human rights into their programming, seeking to develop a common understanding of the "human rights-based approach" (Meier and Gostin 2018). WHO and other health-related UN agencies, as introduced in Chapter 3, would continue to develop and implement human rights norms in the decades that followed—in institutional policies, technical guidance, and country cooperation (Hunt 2017).

Amid these early advances of human rights mainstreaming, the UN human rights system began to clarify the content of the right to health and other rights underpinning health. The UN Committee on Economic, Social and Cultural Rights (CESCR), established in 1985 to oversee implementation of the ICESCR, adopted a General Comment in 2000 to interpret the normative content of the right to health under the ICESCR. Through the adoption of General Comment 14, the CESCR reaffirmed that the right to health encompasses rights to underlying determinants of public health, including water and sanitation, environmental conditions, and adequate housing. With the UN thereafter appointing a Special Rapporteur on the right to health, this UN mandate holder has applied the normative framework of the right to health to analyze specific health issues—including maternal health, neglected diseases, health systems, and social determinants of health—at the forefront of global health governance (Hunt and Leader 2010).

C. The Emergence of Equity and Social Justice in Global Health Governance

Whereas human rights entered global health governance from developments in international law and struggles against oppression, concern for equity arose from public health research on health inequalities. There was long an optimism that economic growth and social protection policies, including universal healthcare, would eliminate health inequalities; however, data in high-income countries continued to show persistent health inequalities despite equal healthcare access, reflecting social inequalities in income, housing, education, and conditions of work (Whitehead et al. 2001). This early social epidemiology research, first introduced in Chapter 1, countered a predominantly biomedical approach to health research that had long led to a neglect of health inequalities by policymakers (Ostlin, George, and Sen 2001). Drawing from this evolving research on social class, research into health inequalities rapidly increased in the 21st century (Sim and McKee 2011). This body of research highlighted that despite overall health gains, there have been widening health inequalities—and in some cases, worsening outcomes across income, gender, racial, and ethnic lines. This social science research has focused on the underlying causes of these disparities, including the unequal distribution of power, income, goods, and services—locally, nationally, and globally—and the bearing of these inequalities on proximate causes of ill health, such as access to health services, education, housing, and work.

These health inequalities came to be seen as an injustice, recognizing societal conditions as determining people's capabilities to flourish. Looking to health as fundamental—not simply to human life but to flourishing—health justice scholars examined duties at the national and global level to promote human capabilities, recognizing that every person has a moral entitlement to the capability to be healthy (Venkatapuram 2013).[3] Increasing efforts in the past twenty years have sought to address these inequities in the global health agenda (Prah Ruger 2018). Shifting health governance away from neoliberal policy, which had focused on cost–benefit analysis in global health policies and led to increasing health inequities, governance efforts came to reframe health policies to achieve equity. This renewed focus on equity and social justice emphasized the importance of addressing the health status of the worst off through global health law and policy.

II. Global Health Law and Policy as a Means to Advance Norms in Global Health

These normative frameworks have come to structure law and policy in global health, providing a foundation to promote and protect health and well-being for

---

[3] The capability approach has come to be applied to global health governance, advocating for voluntary cooperation from domestic and global health actors to realize global health equity as a basis for capabilities (Prah Ruger 2018).

all. International treaties and global policies are increasingly framed by human rights and equity and underpinned by notions of social justice, structuring partnerships and shared commitments among global health actors to ensure justice in global health. Through this normative framing of global health law and policy, human rights, equity, and social justice play an increasingly prominent role in global health governance.

A. Human Rights in Global Health Law

Human rights have become a central normative framework in global health governance, propelled by the emergence of a health and human rights movement; the growing legal, political, and social force of the right to health; and the commitment to mainstreaming human rights across the United Nations.

1. A "Health and Human Rights" Movement

The evolution of human rights under international law in global health governance has been matched by the growth of a health and human rights movement—focused on the realization of human rights in public health policies, programs, and practices. Activists and scholars from around the world have drawn on human rights norms and legal protections to analyze national and global health policies, frame public health research, galvanize advocacy campaigns, develop technical tools such as health indicators, and support accountability for health advancement. This movement grew out of experiences in the early years of HIV/AIDS response, which had exposed how human rights violations undermined disease prevention (Gruskin, Mills, and Tarantola 2007).

Case Study: The Birth of the "Health & Human Rights" Movement

Widespread human rights violations experienced by people with living with HIV and AIDS played a significant role in fomenting growing recognition of the relevance and importance of human rights to health. Social bias related to HIV and AIDS was central in motivating the seminal work of Jonathan Mann, as seen in Figure 4.1, who, as the Director of WHO's Global Programme on AIDS, recognized an "inextricable linkage" between human rights and health. Human rights-based principles of non-discrimination and equitable access to care became central WHO policies and programs on HIV, which came to address the rights of most vulnerable populations and the necessity of preventing

Figure 4.1 Jonathan Mann, Director of the Global Programme on AIDS, opens the 1988 World AIDS Day Youth Forum at the WHO Headquarters in Geneva (WHO/Tibor Farkas)

discrimination and stigma. Human rights-based approaches would also be advanced by activist organizations across the world, holding governments to account for providing necessary prevention and treatment and serving as a foundation for litigation and campaigns for access to antiretroviral medication. Building from this experience, social movements and civil society organizations have increasingly framed activism and advocacy for health justice under human rights. Women's organizations grounded calls for reproductive autonomy and sexual and reproductive health information and services in human rights protections under international law, highlighting issues of preventable maternal mortality and a lack of access to safe abortion as human rights violations. Human rights NGOs such as Amnesty International and Human Right Watch, which had previously advanced civil and political rights, expanded their work to address the right to health as well as other economic, social, and cultural rights. This work rapidly expanded beyond HIV to include maternal health, mental health, and access to drug dependency treatment, bringing together public health data to identify violations of international human rights law.

Building from the rights-based efforts of the Global Programme on AIDS, WHO in the 1990s created a health and human rights team; initiated interagency collaborations to advance global health through international human rights law; and created human rights focal points in particular programs, country, and regional offices (Nygren-Krug 2004). The development of this human rights capacity in the WHO Secretariat responded to the UN's human rights mainstreaming imperative as well as rising health and human rights advocacy in civil society. Engaging with women's health advocates, WHO's Special Programme on Human Reproduction established a Gender Advisory Panel in the late 1990s (later expanding its remit to the Gender and Rights Advisory Panel) to provide an institutional review of all aspects of reproductive health and research with attention to gender and rights. The Programme later appointed a Human Rights Advisor, with other such human rights advisors and technical officers also appointed to oversee human rights-based approaches to child health and mental health in WHO technical guidance and cooperation. These human rights focal points have provided expertise to progressively integrate human rights more broadly across WHO governance, through organizational policies and technical guidance, building upon a growing recognition of the contribution of human rights-based approaches to health-related policy and programming (Gruskin, Mills, and Tarantola 2007).

2. Implementing the Right to Health

International treaties codifying the right to health and health-related human rights have now been ratified by the vast majority of states. This widescale legal acceptance of the right to health has seen this right subjected to increased interpretation and oversight, formalizing the fundamental normative proposition that every person has a right to healthcare, health-related services, and underlying determinants of health—with states holding corresponding duties to realize these entitlements (Tobin 2012). These human rights norms, upheld through binding international legal obligations, have provided a universal framework for public health, and these norms have been implemented domestically, by both courts and policymakers, (Hunt et al. 2013) and at the global level by international organizations (Meier and Gostin 2018).

At the domestic level, over one hundred countries have integrated the right to health and other health-related human rights into their national constitutions, providing a legal guarantee to protect health (Heymann et al. 2013). The growing legal, political, and social force of the right to health and other health-related rights have resulted in increased instances of court cases brought by individuals and civil society organizations to challenge health-related decisions by governments and private actors (Yamin and Gloppen 2011). Such right to health-based litigation and advocacy have permitted social actors to access the potential of the normative and operational framework of the right to health, and these gains have seen human rights more prominently addressed in relation to distinct health issues, including sexual and reproductive health, disability rights, and mental health.[4]

The right to health has also come to frame global health policy. Drawing on WHO's Constitutional protection of the right to health, the 1978 Alma-Ata Declaration on Primary Health Care, which recognized that primary healthcare was essential to realizing health through underlying determinants, proclaimed the right to health as the central normative framework supporting primary health care (Meier 2010). This vision of health in the Declaration of Alma-Ata, first introduced in Chapter 3, was seen to advance underlying determinants of health, and this global health policy, in turn, was influential twenty years later in the framing of the right to health under General Comment 14. Civil society actors also drew on human rights arguments and protections to challenge the inaccessibility of antiretroviral drugs under international trade law (Forman 2014). AIDS treatment access campaigns sought to ensure that access to medicines became interpreted as a fundamental element of the right to health and a basis for global governance across the UN.

3. Mainstreaming Human Rights across the UN

Although the UN human rights system long focused on state implementation of human rights, UN agencies have come to support human rights mainstreaming in global governance. In an early advancement of human rights mainstreaming, UNICEF reframed its mission statement to advance child rights following the development of the 1989 Convention on the Rights of the Child. Following the UN's efforts in the 1990s to establish human rights as a "cross cutting" focus of all UN activities (UN Secretary General 1997), other international organizations within and beyond the UN family began to consider how human rights would impact their policies, programs, and practices. Whereas some health-related agencies, such as the United Nations Population Fund (UNFPA) and the Joint United Nations Programme on HIV/AIDS (UNAIDS) rapidly embraced human rights, WHO took limited initial steps to integrate human rights, despite its constitutional recognition of the right to health. WHO's human rights work has long been hampered by financial and political constraints, as well as lingering resistance to human rights among WHO's medical staff (Meier, Fisseha, and Bueno de Mesquita, *forthcoming*). Yet WHO has recently come to promote human rights

---

[4] For example, an NGO mounted legal action in Uganda for the deaths of two mothers during childbirth, with Uganda's Supreme Court holding in 2020 that the government's failure to provide adequate maternal health services violates human rights protected in international treaties and the Ugandan Constitution including the right to health, the right to life, the rights of women, and the prohibition on inhuman and degrading treatment.

more prominently in its global health leadership, with Director-General Tedros, as reaffirmed in the Foreword, championing calls for the right to health in global health governance.

Further, select global health partnerships between international organizations and other state and non-state actors have drawn on human rights to frame mission statements or goals—mainstreaming human rights in their activities. The Partnership on Maternal, Newborn, Child and Adolescent Health (PMNCH) developed a human rights-based accountability procedure, the Independent Expert Review Group (subsequently replaced by the Independent Accountability Panel) to review progress under the Global Strategy on Women's, Newborn, Child and Adolescent Health. Making human rights central to its global health funding, the Global Fund to Fight AIDS, Malaria and Tuberculosis (Global Fund) has developed a human rights complaints procedure, ensuring human rights protections in country programming. Despite these successful models of rights-based partnerships, the majority of such partnerships have only selectively addressed human rights and equity in reports, toolkits, or advocacy documents, with partnerships lagging in efforts to ensure human rights mainstreaming (Hawkes, Kreienkamp, and Buse 2018).

Beyond these central actors and partnerships in global health governance, the reach of international human rights law has been more limited in institutions of global economic governance—with implications for global health. These economic interests, discussed in detail in the chapters in Section III, have often looked to financial considerations over human rights imperatives, especially in the impacts of their policies and agreements in the Global South. The financing arrangements and policy guidance issued to states by the World Bank and the International Monetary Fund (IMF) have repeatedly come under scrutiny for their impact on health-related human rights; however, these institutions have long resisted calls to comply with international human rights standards (Shawar and Prah Ruger 2018). Despite the promise of international law to hold states to account for human rights and social justice, international law has stood accused of entrenching global inequalities and perpetuating neocolonial relations, with states in the Global South remaining beholden to economic interests in the Global North—at the expense of the health and human rights of their own populations (Linarelli, Salomon, and Sornarajah 2014). Extended to international trade governance, the World Trade Organization has been widely criticized, particularly in the context of the HIV/AIDS and COVID-19 pandemics, for prioritizing and protecting patents and profits of pharmaceutical corporations in the Global North over the right to essential medicines in the Global South (Sekalala et al. 2021).[5] Pharmaceutical companies, in turn, have

---

[5] As discussed in greater detail in Chapter 12, these conflicts have been exemplified during the COVID-19 pandemic by the opposition of pharmaceutical companies and their host governments in the United States and the EU to a proposal to waive intellectual property law for the duration of the pandemic.

remained resistant to calls to realize human rights at the expense of corporate profits, as discussed in Chapter 13, highlighting the limitations of international human rights law to frame duties and facilitate accountability for non-state actors in global health governance.

B. Advancing Equity and Equality in Global Health Governance

Improving the health of marginalized and disadvantaged groups, including people in poverty, rural populations, children and adolescents, women, and persons with disabilities, has become central to global health governance. This framing of inequity as an injustice is exemplified in the 2008 report of the WHO Commission on Social Determinants of Health (CSDH), as discussed in greater detail in Chapter 20, which declared that "social injustice is killing people on a grand scale" (WHO 2008, preface). The CSDH report firmly placed the achievement of global health equity in the context of ethics and social justice.[6] Proposing a bold new global agenda for health equity—to close health gaps in a generation—the CSDH framed a global health policy agenda to address systematic differences in health (within and between countries) that are avoidable by reasonable action, recognizing this effort to address dramatic differences in health across the world as a moral and ethical imperative. By situating the achievement of global health equity in the context of ethics, social justice, and human rights, the CSDH called for a range of actions to improve daily living conditions, tackle the inequitable distribution of power, money, and resources, and assess the impact of action to address determinants of health.

This focus on equity has continued to be a central focus of global health efforts. In global health governance, a social justice approach takes account of structural determinants of inequity, through, for example, international trade and development policies or the actions of states in the Global North, the problems created by a history of colonialism, and the need for low-and middle-income country autonomy and self-determination in governance. For example, the UN General Assembly has repeatedly framed efforts to advance global access to medications as a question of equity.

Other social justice issues regarding racial inequalities and accountability are still emerging or had historically received limited attention in the public health community. Racial injustice in the health context is receiving considerably greater attention in recent years as public awareness of structural racism

---

[6] Despite clear links with the right to health, the CSDH report did not embrace the concept of human rights, despite a recommendation by its Secretariat to do so, reflecting often missed opportunities to bring together complementary human rights and equity approaches (Chapman 2016).

has grown, triggered in part by social protest in the United States over police violence against racialized people, a global resurgence of white nationalism, and increasing evidence of racial disparities in COVID-19 mortality globally (Erondu et al. 2023).[7] Glaring global disparities in access to COVID-19 vaccines have reinforced claims that the COVID-19 pandemic response needs to facilitate health equity (Geng, Reid, and Abdool-Karim 2021).

C. Bringing Together Human Rights, Equity, and Social Justice under the SDGs

With sweeping efforts underway to mainstream human rights, equity, and social justice across global governance, including on health issues from social determinants of health to sustainable development, these normative foundations became central concern in the 2015 adoption of the Sustainable Development Goals (SDG). The 2030 Agenda for Sustainable Development, first introduced in Chapter 3, commits to human rights and equity as cross-cutting commitments that underpin global health efforts. While SDG 3 (ensure healthy lives and promote well-being for all at all ages) does not explicitly reference the right to health, its ambition of assuring universal health coverage has been interpreted as a "practical expression of the right to health" (Ooms et al. 2014, 1). Complementing this normative foundation of the SDGs, the 2030 Agenda has raised equity and social justice concerns relevant to global health, including a focus on the health of disadvantaged communities left behind by past efforts.

In striving for a comprehensive approach to sustainable development—built upon three core pillars "people, planet and prosperity"—the 2030 Agenda also looks to the future, with the concept of "sustainable development" centered on meeting the needs of the present without compromising the ability of future generations to meet their own needs. This approach, inspired by the challenges of climate change and ecological crises, advances emerging interpretations of equity and human rights, conceptualizing intergenerational equity and human rights of future generations (Bos and Duwell 2016). The concept of sustainable development thus brings together norms of human rights, equity, and social justice to frame the global response to past, present, and future challenges.

---

[7] As a result, racism is increasingly recognized as a structural driver of social determinants of health, and efforts to integrate anti-racism into health professional curricula and global health governance have amplified (Chandler et al. 2021).

III. Old and New Challenges to Norms in Global Health

Normative frameworks have come to shape global health governance, yet rising challenges are limiting and reframing implementation of human rights, equity, and social justice in global health law. In these uncertain times, the COVID-19 pandemic has highlighted a practical and conceptual gap in the protection of human rights during public health emergencies; global crises are reinforcing the need to define and implement extraterritorial obligations to respond to shared threats; and health inequalities between the Global North and Global South have raised calls to decolonize global health. It remains unclear whether frameworks of human rights, equity, and social justice can be brought together in confronting these future threats.

A. Human Rights amid Public Health Emergencies

Human rights-based approaches have come to frame public health to ensure individual dignity, liberty, and equality, with human rights promotion supporting public health protection. The COVID-19 pandemic has reinforced the inextricable linkages between health and human rights; yet, in echoes of the early HIV/AIDS response, pandemic control measures around the world have frequently veered into human rights violations, universal health systems in most countries have struggled to provide adequate COVID-19 care, and Black and Indigenous people of color (BIPOC) in many places have experienced greater risks of COVID-19 exposure, infection, and death—at least in part because of the health impacts of long-standing systemic racism and discrimination (Forman 2021). The pandemic has underscored the imperative for strong, integrated protections of human rights in:

- Upholding the right to health—where the right to health requires that governments take steps to prevent, treat and control epidemic, endemic, occupational, and other diseases and provide "medical service and medical attention in the event of sickness," states must assure that health goods, services, and facilities (including diagnostics, treatments, and vaccinations) are available, accessible, acceptable, and of good quality (Pūras et al. 2020).
- Enabling people to comply with disease control measures through health-related human rights—where almost every country has implemented stringent COVID-19 responses that significantly impacted on individual rights to free movement, assembly, privacy, and economic activity, these responses have also resulted in extensive and significant disruptions to human rights

that underlie public health, including rights to food, education, and an adequate standard of living (Forman 2021).
- Restricting human rights when necessary to protect public health—where international human rights law permits limitations of human rights to protect public health,[8] restrictions of human rights in the pandemic response were often taken in ways that were not necessary or proportionate to the aim of responding to the pandemic (Forman, Sekalala, and Meier 2022).
- Strengthening international assistance and cooperation—where the pandemic response exposed vast inequities across countries, states in the Global North often neglected extraterritorial human rights obligations as a foundation of global solidarity (Meier, Bueno de Mesquita, and Williams 2022).

The COVID-19 pandemic has thus underscored both a practical and conceptual gap in how human rights—especially economic, social, and cultural rights—are protected during public health emergencies (Habibi et al. 2023). Human rights violations in the pandemic response have prompted important initiatives that are redefining the human rights principles that should govern policy during public health emergencies, and it will be crucial to ensure that these evolving human rights principles are codified in ongoing reforms of global health law (Bueno de Mesquita, Kapilashrami, and Meier 2021). The ongoing drafting of global health law reforms will create opportunities to strengthen human rights promotion and protection, providing a more equitable approach in future pandemic responses; yet the protection of these values is not assured, and it remains to be seen how far such processes will embrace these normative foundations in responding to global threats.

B. Extraterritorial Obligations to Address Global Threats

The COVID-19 pandemic has illuminated the limited extent to which extraterritorial obligations have been elaborated and implemented to facilitate solidarity across a global response. Although human rights protection has often been cast within a territorial and state-centric perspective—looking to a state duty-bearer to uphold the rights of an individual rights-holder—human rights law has long recognized

---

[8] The 1984 Siracusa Principles on the Limitation and Derogation Provisions of the International Covenant on Civil and Political Rights clarify grounds to guide human rights restrictions in pandemics, setting out that such restrictions must be proportionate, necessary, non-discriminatory, of limited duration, and subject to review. However, these Principles proved difficult to apply in the COVID-19 crisis given uncertainties surrounding the public health threat and means of transmission in the early stage of the pandemic.

that economic, social, and cultural rights, such as the right to health, must be realized through both national effort and international cooperation (Langford et al. 2012). The ICESCR, for example, binds states parties to take steps "individually and through international assistance and cooperation" to realize economic social and cultural rights (UN General Assembly 1966, art. 2), requiring states to ensure these rights in other countries through development cooperation, trade policy, membership in international organizations, and regulation of multinational corporations.

The rise in focus on these extraterritorial human rights obligations aligns with increasing focus on health equity and social justice, realizing global solidarity to ensure health worldwide. In a world that is increasingly globalized yet riven by social and economic inequities (linked to power and resource imbalances and the legacies of colonialism), normative frameworks of human rights, equity, and social justice have aligned to frame calls to narrow these health-related inequalities and power imbalances. Such calls have become more prominent as the international community has responded to shared global threats, including the COVID-19 pandemic and climate change, which require (but have often lacked) a high degree of multilateral coordination, cooperation, and solidarity (Meier, Bueno de Mesquita, and Williams 2022). Since the onset of the COVID-19 pandemic, UN human rights bodies have increasingly highlighted human rights obligations of international assistance and cooperation to address the pandemic (CESCR 2020), while global civil society campaigns have called for vaccine equity as a moral imperative. Despite these normative claims, states in the Global North have continued to resist binding extraterritorial obligations, particularly insofar as they may be construed as requiring a transfer of resources. Rather than coming together in common purpose, the COVID-19 pandemic has witnessed a surge of nationalism, as countries looked inward to protect their own populations at the expense of global equity – exercising power at the expense of the most vulnerable (Sekalala et al. 2021).

C. Decolonizing Global Health

Amid these nationalist challenges, the normative framing of equity and rights in global health governance is increasingly being articulated as one based on the need to decolonize global institutions. As first introduced in Chapter 3, the language of "decolonization"—originating out of decolonization movements in the 1960s and Indigenous peoples' self-determination movements in the 1970s[9]—has become a rallying cry for a range of projects

---

[9] As decolonized states rapidly joined the UN, the UN General Assembly adopted a 1960 "Declaration on Decolonization of Granting Independence to Colonial Countries and People,"

that seek to advance equity, rights, and social justice—including in governance of both global health (Abimbola 2019) and human rights (Sekalala et al. 2021). In seeking to reform global health governance, studies have found stark and enduring racial disparities in leadership of global health, perpetuating Eurocentric worldviews that do not respond to many of the world's needs (Büyüm et al. 2020). Decolonization movements seek to redress these injustices.

Efforts to decolonize global health seek to eradicate systemic disparities and inequities in ways that are synergistic with efforts to decolonize human rights. In human rights, the charge for decolonization builds on longer-standing critiques of human rights as a Western creation that is inextricable from the colonial project (Mutua 2008). A decolonial framing of human rights in global health is thus viewed as enabling a "focus on ways in which structural or systemic issues reproduce inequalities and, we hope, can help to galvanise more effective human rights struggles from below" (Sekalala et al. 2021, 1–2). These twin efforts to decolonize global health and human rights thus provide a path to bring together normative frameworks for human rights, equity, and social justice.

D. Bringing Together Human Rights, Equity, and Social Justice

There is a recognized link between health equity, social justice, and human rights related to health, with the right to health "understood to be reflected by the standard of health enjoyed by the most socially advantaged group within a society" (Braveman and Gruskin 2003, 255). This conceptual overlap is apparent in contemporary interpretations of equality under international human rights law, which is defined not simply to require treating everyone the same (so-called formal equality), but also requires taking steps to remedy disparities—paying attention to groups experiencing historic or persistent prejudice, discrimination, and disadvantage (substantive equality) (CESCR 2009). However, these complementary approaches have sometimes been addressed in divergent ways, and as a consequence:

---

which asserted that "an end must be put to colonialism." By the 1970s, considerable scholarship on decolonization in Africa and Asia had emerged, and over the next two decades, this idea also found expression in "postcolonial" scholarship and literature focused on societies emerging from colonial rule (Betts 2012). Contemporary usage of "decolonization" also has deep roots in indigenous peoples' struggles for self-determination, land, and equal rights in the Americas and Asia-Pacific. Indeed, indigenous scholars note that the move in many human rights and social justice projects to employ the language of "decolonization" turns the term into a metaphor in ways that ignore indigenous struggles and which "[kill] the very possibility of decolonization" (Tuck and Yang 2012, 3).

- International human rights law has been insufficiently attentive to considerations of power, requiring attention to structural inequality (Mutua 2008).
- Global health has provided limited examination of issues of intersectionality, neglecting interactions across multiple bases of disadvantage or oppression that exacerbate inequalities and result in systemic exclusion (Kapilashrami and Hankivsky 2018).
- Equity and social justice have paid less attention to accountability, including monitoring, review, and remedies, which are central to institutional arrangements for human rights protection (Hunt et al. 2013).

Concepts of equity, human rights, and social justice must be recognized as mutually reinforcing in supporting global health. Equity has proved a powerful frame to highlight injustice in global health, but as demonstrated in the fight against HIV and COVID-19, human rights bring necessary binding normative standards, accountability, and the rule of law (Khosla and Gruskin 2021).

Used in combination, equity and human rights can reinforce one another to address global health inequalities. Yet all too often, the concepts have not been integrated, with global health governance often favoring equity over human rights. This neglect of human rights has been variously attributed to a lack of understanding of what human rights brings and to diplomatic pressures, with states finding equity framings in global health more politically palatable than legally binding human rights (Khosla and Gruskin 2021). To reinforce the interconnections across these normative frameworks, institutions and activists have sought to integrate norms of human rights, equity, and social justice in WHO standard setting under a proposed Framework Convention on Global Health (Gostin et al. 2020).

Case Study: Bringing Together Normative Frameworks under a Framework Convention on Global Health

The idea of a Framework Convention on Global Health (FCGH) was developed by academics and civil society in 2007 as a binding legal instrument to address health inequalities within countries and between the Global North and Global South. Centered on the right to health, as well as principles of equality and non-discrimination, this proposed treaty would serve as a mechanism to channel cooperative action to address global health. As a basis to bring the world together around common norms, the FCGH looks to various actors and institutions across the global health landscape. Bringing these actors together to realize the right to health for all, the FCGH draws on central human rights norms and principles, including participation, equality, non-discrimination, and the obligation to devote maximum available resources to health. The FCGH would build on existing right to health obligations, enhancing accountability for those obligations by establishing specific standards and mechanisms to embed the right to health within global governance for health, including specific standards on inclusive participation, right to health assessments, and health equity programs of action. An FCGH Alliance was established to maintain pressure on state and non-state actors to move toward the development of the FCGH as a way to address global health shortcomings in terms of limited accountability, cooperation, and financing and the realization of the right to health; however, this Alliance has found it difficult to gain traction with WHO Member States—given the ambitiousness of the FCGH proposal, state hesitancy to increase their own accountability, and tendencies within the global health community to focus on immediate global health challenges rather than the cross-cutting principles. The FCGH Alliance's experiences highlight the diplomatic challenges to advancing normative frameworks in global health law.

To advance interconnected norms under WHO governance, the creation of the WHO Gender, Equity and Human Rights team has presented an opportunity for WHO to align these distinct normative traditions in global health, with these normative frameworks coming together in WHO's 13th General Programme of Work (2019-23); yet even so, human rights has continued to face obstacles in global health governance under WHO (Meier, Fisseha, and Bueno de Mesquita forthcoming). Aligning these normative lenses in global health governance can provide a powerful strategy to ensure justice in global health.

Conclusion

Norms of human rights, equity, and social justice have come to provide a moral—and, in the case of human rights, a legal—foundation for realizing the highest attainable standard of health for all. The international legal framework of human rights has been developed over the past seventy-five years to bind states under international law, but these legal norms are increasingly applied together with equity and social justice in global health governance institutions—under the UN and through civil society advocacy. These normative frameworks are the justification for developing global health law and policy, providing a shared foundation to bind together actors to prevent disease and promote health. As the world has faced new and re-emerging global health challenges, these norms have aligned to develop mutually reinforcing imperatives in global health. It will be crucial to understand how these normative frameworks are binding together state and non-state actors in global health governance to support cooperative global health efforts.

Yet even as these frameworks gain importance in structuring global health efforts, these norms face new challenges in a context of wavering solidarity amid global crises. Despite repeated reminders that the COVID-19 crisis was a global threat requiring a globally coordinated responses, this crisis witnessed a return to self-defeating self-interest, with states neglecting duties of global solidarity and international cooperation in health in favor of nationalist responses, prioritizing select populations in violation of norms of equity, social justice, and human rights. Global health is at risk from rising challenges in a globalizing world, with threats disproportionately experienced in the Global South; however, necessary cooperation and solidarity from Global North countries has remained absent.

Normative frameworks must evolve to meet these challenges—through increasing emphasis on extraterritorial obligations, inter-generational equity, and global solidarity, bringing the world together under common values. Whereas some states have reneged on their post-war commitment to human rights, young activists have been resurgent in fighting for these values as a basis for a more sustainable and fairer future. Meeting these challenges will require the force of a new generation to elaborate these evolving normative frameworks, and much will depend on how future generations implement these normative frameworks under global health law and policy.

Questions for Consideration

1. What political and social precursors gave rise to norms of rights, equity, and social justice in global health? Why are there distinct normative frameworks?
2. How did the protection of human rights under international human rights treaties come to frame global governance across the UN?
3. Why did the advancement of the right to health prove politically contentious amid the international divisions of the Cold War? How did the end of the Cold War open a political space to advance human rights in global health governance?
4. What are the differences between the norms of human rights, equity, and social justice in global health? How can these normative frameworks complement each other to support global health with justice?

5. In what ways did the HIV/AIDS pandemic catalyze attention to human rights in global health—giving rise to a "health and human rights" movement and advancing human rights in global health governance?
6. What does it mean to "mainstream" rights in global health governance? How have human rights helped to bind together partnerships across the global health architecture?
7. Why have global health governance institutions come to look to equity rather than human rights as a normative foundation of global health policy?
8. How has the COVID-19 pandemic challenged human rights in global health? How can extraterritorial obligations shape global solidarity in responding to shared threats?
9. What are the differences between decolonizing approaches and rights-based approaches to global health? Why is it necessary to decolonize both global health and human rights?
10. How are the concepts of equity, human rights, and social justice being drawn together to the address health inequalities between countries? What challenges will advocates face in codifying these norms in global health law through a Framework Convention on Global Health?

Acknowledgments

The authors wish to thank Taylor Corpening and Hanna Huffstetler for their editorial support in developing this chapter.

References

Abimbola, Seye. 2019. "The Foreign Gaze: Authorship in Academic Global Health." *BMJ Global Health* 4: e002068.

Beauchamp, Dan E. 1976. "Public Health as Social Justice." *Inquiry* 13(1): 3–14.

Betts, Raymond F. 2012. "Decolonization: A Brief History of The Word." In *Beyond Empire and Nation: The Decolonization of African and Asian Societies, 1930s–1970s*, by Els Bogaerts and Remco Raben. Fink: Brill.

Bos, Gerhard and Marcus Duwell. 2016. *Human Rights and Sustainability: Moral Responsibilities for the Future*. London: Routledge.

Braveman, Paula and Sofia Gruskin. 2003. "Defining Equity in Health." *Journal of Epidemiology and Community Health* 57: 254–258.

Bueno de Mesquita, Judith, Anuj Kapilashrami, and Benjamin Mason Meier. 2021. "Strengthening Human Rights in Global Health Law: Lessons from the COVID-19 Response." *Journal of Law, Medicine & Ethics* 49: 328–331.

Büyüm, Ali Murad, Cordelia Kenney, Andrea Koris, Laura Mkumba, and Yadurshina Raveendran. 2020. "Decolonising Global Health: If Not Now, When?" *BMJ Global Health* 5: e003394.
CESCR (UN Committee on Economic, Social and Cultural Rights). 2009. General Comment 20, Non-Discrimination in Economic, Social and Cultural Rights. E/C.12/GC/20.
CESCR (UN Committee on Economic, Social and Cultural Rights). 2020. Statement on the coronavirus disease (COVID-19) pandemic and economic, social and cultural rights. E/C.12/2020/1.
Chandler, Caroline E., Caitlin R. Williams, Mallory W. Turner, and Meghan E. Shanahan. 2021. "Training Public Health Students in Racial Justice and Health Equity: A Systematic Review." *Public Health Reports* 137(2): 375–385.
Chapman, Audrey R. 2016. *Global Health, Human Rights, and the Challenge of Neoliberal Policies*. Cambridge: Cambridge University Press.
Erondu, Ngozi A., Tlaleng Mofokeng, Matthew M Kavanagh, Margareta Matache, and Sarah L Bosha. 2023. "Towards Anti-Racist Policies and Strategies to Reduce Poor Health Outcomes in Racialised Communities: Introducing the O'Neill–Lancet Commission on Racism, Structural Discrimination, and Global Health." *Lancet* 401 (10391): 1834–36.
Freeman, Michael. 2022. *Human Rights*. Cambridge: Polity Press.
Forman, Lisa. 2014. "A Rights-Based Approach to Global Health Policy." In *The Handbook of Global Health Policy*, edited by Garrett Brown, Gavin Yamey, and Sarah Wamala, 459–482. West Sussex: Wiley-Blackwell.
Forman, Lisa. 2021. "The Future of Health and Human Rights in Pandemic Societies?" In *Shocks and Transformations in Pandemic Societies*, edited by Catherine Regis, Jean Louis Denis, and Daniel Weinstock. Montreal: McGill-Queen's University Press.
Forman, Lisa, Sharifah Sekalala, and Benjamin Mason Meier. 2022. "The World Health Organization, International Health Regulations, and Human Rights Law." *International Organizations Law Review* 19: 37–62.
Geng, Elvin H., Michael J. A. Reid, and Quarraisha Abdool Karim. 2021. "COVID-19 and Global Equity for Health: The Good, the Bad and the Wicked." *PLoS Med* 18(10): e1003607.
Gostin, Lawrence, Matiangai Sirleaf, and Eric Friedman. 2020. "Global Health Law: Legal Foundations for Social Justice in Public Health." In *Foundations of Global Health and Human Rights*, edited by Lawrence O. Gostin and Benjamin Mason Meier. New York: Oxford University Press.
Gruskin, Sofia, Edward J. Mills, and Daniel Tarantola. 2007. "History, Principles, and Practice of Health and Human Rights." *Lancet* 370: 449–455.
Habibi, Sam, Luciano Bottini Filho, Judith Bueno de Mesquita, Gina Luca Burci, Luisa Cabal, Thana Cristina de Campos, Danwood Chirwa, et al. 2023. *Principles and Guidelines on Human Rights & Public Health Emergencies*. New York: Social Science Research Network. 27 May.
Hawkes, Sarah, Julia Kreienkamp, and Kent Buse. 2018. "The Future of Inter-Governmental Partnerships for Health and Human Rights." In *Human Rights in Global Health: Rights-Based Governance for a Globalizing World*, edited by Benjamin Mason Meier and Lawrence Gostin. New York: Oxford University Press.
Heymann, Jody, Adèle Cassola, Amy Raub, and Lipi Mishra. 2013. "Constitutional Rights to Health, Public Health and Medical Care: The Status of Health Protections in 191 Countries." *Global Public Health* 8(6): 639–53.

Hunt, Paul. 2017. "Configuring the UN Human Rights System in the 'Era of Implementation': Mainland and Archipelago." *Human Rights Quarterly*. 39(3): 489–538.

Hunt, Paul, Judith Bueno, Joo-Young Lee, and Sally-Anne Way. 2013. "Implementation of Economic, Social and Cultural Rights." In *Routledge Handbook of International Human Rights Law*, edited by Sir Nigel Rodley and Scott Sheeran. London: Routledge.

Hunt, Paul and Sheldon Leader. 2010. "Developing and Applying the Right to the Highest Attainable Standard of Health: The Role of the UN Special Rapporteur (2002-2008)." In *Global Health and Human Rights: Legal and Philosophical Perspectives*, edited by John Harrington and Maria Stuttaford. London: Routledge.

Kapilashrami, Anuj and Olena Hankivsky. 2018. "Intersectionality and Why It Matters to Global Health." *Lancet* 39: 2589–2591.

Khosla, Rajat and Sofia Gruskin. 2021. "Equity without Human Rights: A False COVID-19 Narrative." *BMJ Global Health* 6: e006720.

Langford, Malcolm, Wouter Vandenhole, Martin Scheinin, and Willem Van Genugten. 2012. "Introduction: An Emerging Field." In Global Justice, State Duties: The Extraterritorial Scope of Economic, Social, and Cultural Rights in International Law, 3–31. Cambridge: Cambridge University Press.

Linarelli, John, Margot Salomon, and Muthucumaraswamy Sornarajah. 2014. *The Misery of International Law*. Oxford: Oxford University Press.

Jensen, Steven. 2016. "Decolonization – Not Western Liberals – Established Human Rights on the Global Agenda." *OpenGlobalRights*. September 29.

Meier, Benjamin Mason. 2010. "Global Health Governance and the Contentious Politics of Human Rights: Mainstreaming the Right to Health for Public Health Advancement." *Stanford Journal of International Law* 46: 1–50.

Meier, Benjamin Mason, Judith Bueno de Mesquita, and Caitlin R. Williams. 2022. "Global Obligations to Ensure the Right to Health: Strengthening Global Health Governance to Realise Human Rights in Global Health." *Yearbook of International Disaster Law* 3:3–34.

Meier, Benjamin Mason, Senait Fisseha, and Judith Bueno De Mesquita. Forthcoming. "The Development and Implementation of Human Rights Law in WHO Governance." In *Elgar Companion to the Law and Practice of the World Health Organisation*, edited by Scarlett McArdle and Stephanie Switzer. Cheltenham: Elgar.

Meier, Benjamin Mason and Lawrence O. Gostin. 2018. "Framing Human Rights in Global Health Governance." In *Human Rights in Global Health: Rights-Based Governance for a Globalizing World*, 63–86. New York: Oxford University Press.

Meier, Benjamin Mason, Thérèse Murphy, and Lawrence O. Gostin. 2020. "The Birth and Development of the Human Rights to Health." In *Foundations of Global Health and Human Rights*, edited by Benjamin Mason Meier and Lawrence Gostin. New York: Oxford University Press.

Morsink, Johannes. 1999. *The Universal Declaration on Human Rights: Origins, Drafting and Intent*. Philadelphia: University of Pennsylvania Press.

Mutua, Makau. 2008. "Human Rights in Africa: The Limited Promise of liberalism." *African Studies Review* 51(1): 17–39.

Nygren-Krug, Helena. 2004. "Health and Human Rights at the World Health Organization." *Saúde e Direitos Humanos* 1: 7.

Ooms, Gorik, Laila Abdul Latif, Attiya Waris, Rachel Hammonds, Eric E. Friedman, Claire E. Brolan, and Lisa Forman. 2014. "Is 'Universal Health Coverage' the Practical Expression of the Right to Health?" *BMC International Health and Human Rights* 14(3): 1–7.

Ostlin, Piroska, Asha George, and Gita Sen. 2001. "Gender, Health, and Equity: The Intersections." In *Challenging Inequities in Health: From Ethics to Action*, edited by Timothy Evans, Margaret Whitehead, Finn Diderichsen et al. New York: Oxford University Press.
Prah Ruger, Jennifer. 2018. *Global Health Justice and Governance.* New York: Oxford University Press.
Pūras, Dainius, Judith Bueno de Mesquita, Luisa Cabal, Allan Maleche, and Benjamin Mason Meier. 2020. "The Right to Health Must Guide Responses to COVID-19." *Lancet* 395: 1888–1890.
Rawls, John. 1993. *Political Liberalism.* New York: Columbia University Press.
Sekalala, Sharifah, Lisa Forman, Timothy Fish Hodgson, Moses Mulumba, Hadijah Namyalo-Ganafa, and Benjamin Mason Meier. 2021. "Decolonising Human Rights: How Intellectual Property Laws Result in Unequal Access to the COVID-19 Vaccine." *BMJ Global Health* 6: e006169.
Shawar, Yusra Ribhi and Jennifer Prah Ruger. 2018. "The World Bank." In *Human Rights in Global Health: Rights-Based Governance for a Globalizing World*, edited by Lawrence O. Gostin and Benjamin Mason Meier, 353–373. New York: Oxford University Press.
Sim, Fiona and Martin McKee. 2011. *Issues in Public Health.* 2nd edition. New York: Oxford University Press.
Tobin, John. 2012. *The Right to Health in International Law.* New York: Oxford University Press.
Tuck, Eve and K. Wayne Yang. 2012. "Decolonization Is Not a metaphor." *Decolonization: Indigeneity, Education & Society* 1(1): 1–40.
UN Secretary General. 1997. *Renewing the United Nations: A Programme for Reform.* A/51/950.
UN General Assembly. 1948. *Universal Declaration on Human Rights.*
UN General Assembly. 1966. "International Covenant on Economic, Social and Cultural Rights." December 16. Res. 2200A (XXI).
Venkatapuram, Sridhar. 2013. *Health Justice: An Argument from the Capabilities Approach.* Hoboken: Wiley and Sons.
Whitehead, Margaret, Timothy Evans, Finn Diderichsen, Abbas Bhuiya, and Meg Wirth. 2001. *Challenging Inequities in Health: From Ethics to Action.* New York: Oxford University Press.
World Conference on Human Rights. 1993. "Vienna Declaration and Programme of Action."
WHO (World Health Organization). 2008. "Commission on Social Determinants of Health." *Closing the Gap in a Generation: Health Equity through Action on the Social Determinants of Health—Final Report of the Commission on Social Determinants of Health.* Geneva: World Health Organization.
Yamin, Alicia E. and Siri Gloppen. 2011. *Litigating Health Rights: Can Courts Bring More Justice to Health?* Cambridge: Harvard University Press.

5
Global Health Diplomacy
The Process of Developing Global Health Law and Policy

Gian Luca Burci and Björn Kümmel

Introduction

Diplomacy is an old concept, as old as the attempts to systematize the manner in which states conduct international relations. Diplomatic mechanisms have come to encompass the processes by which state and non-state actors exercise power, persuasion, bargaining, and networking in their mutual relations. These means of cooperation and coordination in global health have led to the establishment of new global governance institutions. As a technique of international relations and global negotiations, the exercise of diplomacy has a decisive importance for the rules and policies that underpin global health governance as well as for the content of global health law. At a time when the world faces compounding challenges—emerging from the COVID-19 pandemic, preparing for the next pandemic, and grappling with existential health threats such as climate change—global health diplomacy is an essential aspect of contemporary global governance that demands skilled and continued engagement from across the global health landscape.

Global health diplomacy can be characterized as the methods of negotiation, adoption, implementation, and review of legal instruments, programs, and policies related to global health. In the development of global health law and policy, global health diplomacy frames the governance of global institutions, and global health governance influences how diplomatic processes play out and which actors can influence their development. Health has become an increasingly central value in the management of international legal and policy regimes across sectors, from environment and trade to human rights and security. Given changes in health determinants and health governance, health considerations influence diplomatic processes in the institutions managing those regimes. Even as the World Health Organization (WHO) remains the central actor in global health diplomacy, global health governance is increasingly fragmented among many international organizations. With the partial retreat of the state as the sole actor in global governance, new non-state actors—including non-governmental organizations (NGOs), private philanthropic foundations, and public-private partnerships—now operate alongside states and engage directly and indirectly in diplomatic processes.

This chapter provides an overview of the processes, methods, and manifestations of diplomacy in the development of global health law and policy. Tracing the evolution of global health diplomacy, Part I frames the historical roots of multilateral cooperation in the field of health. Part II looks more broadly at how global health governance has been shaped and influenced by political developments and diplomatic engagements—within and outside the health sector. Responding to these governance shifts and new threats, Part III addresses challenges amid a crisis for multilateralism, examining the shock of COVID-19 to global health diplomacy, analyzing WHO's search for its role in an uncoordinated global health landscape, and framing ongoing diplomacy to develop a new "pandemic treaty" under global health law. This chapter concludes that global health diplomacy has undergone profound transformations and is now diffused in an uncoordinated manner across multiple actors and levels of governance; yet the growing collective action problems of the international community and the role that health plays in them will ensure the enduring relevance of global health diplomacy in global health governance.

I. International Cooperation through Global Health Diplomacy

Global health diplomacy arose out of international cooperation to prevent epidemics in the second half of the 19th century. As cooperation intensified, diplomacy became more professionalized and institutionalized, culminating in the establishment of the United Nations (UN). Through the UN system of governance, WHO became the center of global health diplomacy, but diplomatic actors and processes came to be deeply influenced by the tectonic shifts of the Cold War and decolonization.

A. Origins of Diplomacy to Prevent Disease

Diplomacy in global health finds its historical roots in the colonial and imperialistic policies of major European powers. The expansion of trade in Asia and military subjugation across Africa opened new markets, but, as introduced in Chapter 1, these forces also opened the door to the faster and more frequent spread of infectious diseases. The inability of individual states alone to prevent the spread of diseases traveling along increasingly open travel and trade routes led to the search for multilateral solutions through diplomatic processes (Fidler 2005).

A series of international sanitary conferences between 1851 and 1938, as described in Chapter 2, aimed to reach public health consensus on the etiology of "Asiatic diseases" such as cholera and plague and to harmonize quarantine and other control measures to stop their spread at national borders (Howard-Jones 1975). The diplomacy at these early conferences reflected state representation by both politicians (diplomats) and experts (epidemiologists and other scientists), leading to the formation of transboundary alliances on disciplinary rather than national lines. Yet despite this disciplinary grounding in science, there remained an enduring political tension—between protecting public health as a form of national security and protecting economic interests for major trading powers, with the latter looking to scientific uncertainty to preserve their competitive advantage (Cueto 2020).[1]

The intensification of diplomatic cooperation in public health led to a search for common rules, which would develop in the form of multilateral conventions. Negotiated across a series of international sanitary conferences, the first International Sanitary Convention was adopted in 1892, followed thereafter by an acceleration and consolidation of new international rules. Supporting these early conventions, the need to put international cooperation on a permanent footing—rather than relying on sporadic conferences between states—led to the establishment of regional and international health institutions. The establishment of the Pan-American Sanitary Bureau (now Pan-American Health Organization—PAHO) in 1902 was rapidly followed by the *Office International d'Hygiène Publique* in 1907 and, following World War I, the Health Organization of the League of Nations in 1921 (Brown, Cueto, and Fee 2006). This institutionalization of diplomacy introduced new actors as active participants in diplomatic processes, including secretariats of international organizations, NGOs, technical experts, and philanthropic foundations.[2] As detailed in Chapter 3, the experiences of these early institutions would shape the establishment of WHO, as global health diplomacy progressively evolved into a professionalized and permanent process facilitated by international institutions and shaped by organizational rules and practices.

---

[1] This latter concern was particularly evident in the disproportionate influence exercised by the United Kingdom, as cholera and plague largely moved within the confines of the British Empire but then spilled over into the rest of Europe. Despite this health risk, the United Kingdom systematically used its political and economic leverage in the international sanitary conferences to preserve its trading interests, and in the process, created long-standing public health tensions and rivalries with France, Germany, and Russia.

[2] A particularly influential philanthropic role was played throughout the first half of the 20th century by the Rockefeller Foundation, whose International Health Programme trained public health leaders in a large number of countries and colonial territories (Birn 2009).

B. Early Challenges Facing WHO

The adoption of the Constitution of the World Health Organization (WHO Constitution) in July 1946 was the start of a new era in global health diplomacy. The negotiations to develop the WHO Constitution were deeply influenced by visionary leaders who had been instrumental in the work of the Health Organization of the League of Nations.[3] The WHO Constitution thus embodied a number of structural and governance innovations that would provide policy and normative guidance to global health diplomacy, including an expansive definition of health—as a positive concept extending to mental and social well-being—and most importantly, as introduced in Chapter 4, the declaration of health as a fundamental human right (Grad 2002).

While WHO's status as a specialized agency would ensure some distance and protection from the difficult political environment prevailing at the UN, the rapidly escalating Cold War would leave WHO governance subject to ongoing conflicts in international relations (Pethybridge 1965).

The onset of the Cold War deeply influenced WHO's role and the direction of its work, with clashing ideologies across nations shaping diplomatic processes within the World Health Assembly. In its early years, WHO was politically and financially dominated by the United States, which looked to its involvement in WHO's programs of technical assistance as a tool to counter the advance of communism in the developing world and facilitate the spread of Western technologies and ideologies (Evang 1967). Under this U.S. influence, the early Cold War period saw the expansion of WHO's disease-based vertical programs and its ideological focus on disease eradication—rather than addressing underlying social and economic determinants of health (Brockington 1975). The programs and policies adopted by the World Health Assembly during these early decades thus reflected the dominance of a Western biomedical approach. This ideological competition between the United States and the Soviet Union determined the success or failure of WHO's major technical programs. While WHO's ambitious attempt to eradicate malaria ended in failure, as will be discussed further in Chapter 6, a détente between the Superpowers led to unprecedented international cooperation to eradicate smallpox. The World Health Assembly came together to give its political support to this risky and ambitious,

---

[3] It is important to note that global health diplomacy is not an impersonal and mechanical process, but that it can be deeply influenced by charismatic and powerful personalities, including in these early years by health leaders in the League of Nations and academic pioneers in the field of social medicine such as Ludwik Rajchman and Andrija Štampar. Drawing from his leadership under the League of Nations, Štampar served a crucial role in the International Health Conference that developed the WHO Constitution and would later serve as president of the first World Health Assembly in 1948.

if ultimately successful, undertaking, culminating in the eradication of smallpox in 1980 (Cueto, Brown, and Fee 2019).

C. Decolonization Struggles and the Primary Health Care Revolution

However, the complexity of global health diplomacy only increased with the rise of new nations in the Global South and the growing politicization of public health. The 1970s and 1980s were marked by a changing political balance of power within international organizations due to the progressive decolonization of vast areas of the world (Chorev 2012). Developing countries gradually became the numerical majority in the UN and its specialized agencies, as introduced in Chapter 3, and these "new" nations used their numerical advantage to push for deep changes in the structure of global governance to break the legacy of colonialism and set a new agenda for global health (Pannenborg 1979).

This period saw the diplomatic rejection by many developing countries of the Western model of health systems (heavily based on hospital care and expensive technology) and a renewed focus on "primary health care" —as a bottom-up approach that privileged prevention and health promotion as much as health care. Primary health care sought to ensure basic health needs, advancing horizontal health systems and recognizing that health must be affordable and acceptable at the community level (Litsios 2002). Arising out of pressures from developing countries, the advancement of primary health care within WHO reflected the leadership of Halfdan Mahler, the charismatic and tactically skilled WHO Director-General, who struck a close relationship with Henry Labouisse, UNICEF's Executive Director, and convinced him that strengthening basic health services was the optimal approach for children and mothers in the developing world (Cueto, Brown, and Fee 2019). Highlighting the role of international organizations as active and independent actors in global health diplomacy, especially when states are politically divided (Chorev 2012), WHO's advancement of primary health care would culminate in the WHO/UNICEF 1978 International Conference on Primary Health Care, as seen in Figure 5.1, with the resulting Alma-Ata Declaration committing the world to "health for all" by the end of the century.

Yet even as WHO appeared to have won diplomatic support for primary health care, the rise of neoliberalism would subsequently reverse global health policy in favor of more pragmatic and lower-cost vertical health interventions—dubbed "selective primary health care." The mobilization of the United States and other Western countries to advance neoliberal policies created strong tensions across global health governance and decreased the space for political compromises

Figure 5.1 WHO Director-General Halfdan Mahler and U.S. Representative Edward Kennedy at the 1978 International Conference on Primary Health Care (Alma-Ata, USSR) (WHO)

in global health diplomacy (Starrels 1985). Amid funding challenges in the UN system, the waning of primary health care as the principal tool to achieve health for all was accelerated by the 1988 election of Hiroshi Nakajima as WHO Director-General, leading to a "remedicalization" of WHO at a moment when WHO leadership would be crucial in responding to a rising pandemic that would require renewed focus on underlying determinants of health.

Case Study: HIV/AIDS as a Turning Point in Global Health Diplomacy

The international response to HIV/AIDS in the 1980s and 1990s further politicized global health governance and raised challenges to global health diplomacy under WHO leadership. Unlike previous diseases and health threats that could be addressed from a technical perspective, HIV/AIDS—spreading rapidly across vulnerable populations, threatening economic growth in the Global South, and lacking any biomedical treatment in its early years—forced WHO to move into uncharted political terrain and led to institutional tensions and competition with other UN system organizations. WHO initially provided strong global leadership in the global response to this new threat, but this unprecedented pandemic rapidly shifted to an increasingly complex interaction between public health and rising paradigms across sectors: human rights, economic governance, and international security. The initial stigmatization and criminalization of communities most affected by HIV/AIDS, first introduced in Chapter 4, caused unnecessary suffering and undermined efforts to manage the spread of the disease, leading to efforts across the UN system to advance human rights in global health policy. Economic governance would also play a crucial role in global health diplomacy, with the spread of HIV/AIDS coinciding with the dominance of neoliberal economic policies that weakened national health systems and, even once effective HIV treatments were developed, limited the affordability of these necessary treatments. With HIV causing states to look to global health as a foundation of national and international security, the proliferation of emerging and reemerging infectious diseases led many Western countries to redefine infectious diseases as threats to security, contributing to the "securitization of health."

These conflicting paradigms in the HIV/AIDS response expanded global health governance—shifting global health diplomacy beyond WHO.

II. Global Health Diplomacy and the Complexification of Global Health Governance

An expanding landscape of global health diplomacy has focused attention on the processes, actors, and institutions driving global health law and policy. Political and geopolitical interests now play a growing role in WHO governance. As global health governance has moved beyond WHO, global health diplomacy has shaped policy processes across the UN system, in political networks, and within new public-private institutions that complement and sometimes compete with the work of WHO.

A. Global Health Diplomacy within WHO: The Politics of a Global Health Agency

Global health diplomacy plays an obvious and essential role in WHO. While WHO long held itself out as a "technical" rather than "political" agency, it cannot be considered merely a technical public health body (Huang and Meltzer 2018). Diplomacy is central to WHO governance, influencing the governing bodies, Director-General, and non-state actors that structure WHO's role and functions.

1. Political Groupings in WHO Governing Bodies

The diplomatic focus on WHO has increased in recent years, with the meetings of WHO governing bodies providing a forum for political interest groups to gather and coordinate their positions. The World Health Assembly, bringing together all WHO Member States, meets for about a week every May, with a subset of states in the Executive Board holding a longer session in January and a one-day session immediately after the Assembly in May (Peterson 2009). Beyond these Assembly and Executive Board meetings in Geneva, the six WHO regional offices have played an important role in coordinating regional and subregional positions within WHO governance. Each region has its own regional committee where Member States meet in annual sessions and define regional policies.[4] Over the past seventy-five years, each region has developed its own unique dynamics and culture, and the decentralization of WHO governance has shaped WHO's history into one of constant tensions among the Geneva Secretariat and regional offices (Cueto, Brown, and Fee 2019).

Further dividing WHO Member States, numerous political "like-minded" groups coordinate their interests within WHO governing bodies, including the:

- G7, the group of most industrialized states, which coordinate their positions in World Health Assembly debates on specific agenda items.
- Western European and Other States Group (WEOG), a dialogue group of 28 countries from Western Europe and North America (as well as like-minded countries such as Israel), which share Western democratic principles that underpin their coordinated engagement.
- Geneva Group, an informal grouping of 17 states that each contribute more than 1% of the regular budget of the UN, and which focus their coordination less on technical issues than on governance improvements throughout the UN system.
- European Union (EU), a "regional economic integration organization" that provides a basis for its 27 member states to coordinate their positions and develop "common statements" for almost all WHO substantive agenda items.[5]

---

[4] Unlike other UN agencies, WHO's regions are enshrined in the WHO Constitution, thus giving the regions and regional directors legal authority and political autonomy. WHO's structure and constitutional practice therefore codifies a tension between the centralization of global functions in Geneva and the extreme decentralization of the organization, a unique feature within the UN system that has shaped WHO's history, governance, and diplomacy (Burci and Vignes 2004).

[5] Furthermore, a growing number of thematically driven groups coordinate a common position across states through joint statements. For example, Indonesia was effective and successful, as discussed in detail in Chapter 16, in mobilizing like-minded states to push for new conditions for the international sharing of pandemic influenza viruses. (Similarly, Brazil has established a cross-regional coalition concerning equitable access to medicines.) These thematic groups can be quite limited in their focus on specific issues, as seen where states came together to respond to sexual exploitation, abuse, and harassment in WHO's response to the Ebola outbreak in the Democratic Republic of the Congo (Samarasekera 2021).

Even though this coalition-building may at times be tactical and opportunistic, it can have a tremendous influence in achieving common goals despite opposition from other states. In influencing WHO's governing bodies, these coalitions and groupings influence the development of WHO programs and policies, and they have also recently come to frame the election of the WHO Director-General.

2. WHO's Director-General: The Politics of Elections

In 2017, WHO held its first open election for Director-General. This new open election process would be more politicized than in the past, involving a much longer process with public interviews, a shortlisting of three candidates, public webcast hearings, and a final election by the entire World Health Assembly (Kickbusch and Liu 2017). While past practice had the Executive Board nominate only one candidate, giving the World Health Assembly merely a confirmation vote, this new process shifted decision-making power to the Assembly. The election of the Director-General now requires the political support of the majority of WHO Member States, and this election process has considered not only the technical competencies of candidates but also political expectations for their term of office. This new diplomatic process has radically altered the kind of political support that states presenting candidates must secure, recognizing the importance of regional and other political blocks. The election process through the World Health Assembly has thus boosted public and media interest in the election and the role of the Director-General—advantaging candidates who can balance geopolitical interest groups while serving as strong communicators in a public campaign. On May 23, 2017, the World Health Assembly elected Tedros Adhanom Ghebreyesus, formerly Ethiopia's foreign minister and health minister, as its first African Director-General.

Director-General Tedros has shown keen awareness of the current geopolitical environment, and over the course of his term of office, he has engaged with foreign policy to advance global health. Compared with his predecessors, Director-General Tedros more frequently reaches out to national leaders beyond health ministers, particularly heads of state and governments and foreign ministers. Where past directors-general were criticized for maintaining a passive role in global health diplomacy, waiting for the consensus of WHO Member States before taking a clear stance on global challenges, Director-General Tedros has sought to take an active diplomatic role in leading Member States—looking to global equity and human rights as normative foundations of his leadership (Ghebreyesus 2020).[6] With the reelection of Director-General Tedros in 2022, the

---

[6] Some critics have argued that this outreach to political leaders in Member States, beyond the "technical" health arena, has added to the politicization of WHO (Yang 2022); however, in the context of the highly politicized COVID-19 response, the Director-General's leadership in opposing "vaccine apartheid," criticizing the inequity of COVID-19 vaccine access, has set the diplomatic agenda to advance vaccine equity.

WHO Secretariat continues to take a proactive position on global health issues without always seeking the approval of WHO's governing bodies, influencing the decision-making of many WHO Member States and engaging with non-state actors that look to WHO as the leading voice on global health.

3. Role of Non-State Actors and Experts in Global Health Governance

Non-state actors have come to play a growing role in the global health landscape. Academia, civil society, the private sector, and philanthropic foundations all contribute to global health, working as implementers of global health policy and actively shaping global health governance (Packard 2016). Within WHO, there has been an extensive debate on the role of non-state actors in the development of global health policy.[7] While some WHO Member States have sought to increase WHO's engagement with non-state actors, looking to these actors to support and influence complex global health negotiations, other Member States see severe risks for WHO's independence and integrity (Rached and Ventura 2017). WHO's engagement with the private sector, in particular, has generated concerns among Member States and public interest NGOs, fearing that corporate interests may seek to subvert global health policies and WHO governance. Given these conflict-of-interest concerns, states long debated WHO's engagement with non-state actors, with these negotiations culminating in the 2016 World Health Assembly adoption of the WHO Framework of Engagement with Non-State Actors (FENSA) (Buse and Hawkes 2016).

Case Study: FENSA Negotiations within WHO

FENSA is the first integrated policy in the UN system that seeks to regulate the engagement of an international organization secretariat with all non-state actors. Within WHO, this global health diplomacy reform arose out of the more general process of WHO reform that began in 2011. Public interest NGOs saw this diplomatic process as an opportunity to increase their engagement in WHO governance while differentiating themselves from non-state actors in the private sector. These reforms could also provide a path to formalize the role of philanthropic foundations such as the Gates Foundation while circumscribing their role and influence. However, FENSA negotiations

---

[7] Outside of WHO, other global health actors, such as the Global Fund to Fight AIDS, Tuberculosis and Malaria (Global Fund), the Coalition for Epidemic Preparedness Innovations (CEPI), and the Gavi Alliance have a stronger direct involvement of non-state actors—even in their governing body meetings. In these public-private partnerships, first introduced in Chapter 3, non-state actors are essential for the successful financial replenishment of these entities, as these actors play a crucial role in advocating for funding.

soon became dominated by a coalition of middle-income countries that saw FENSA as a powerful instrument to limit the influence of multinational pharmaceutical companies in the work of the WHO Secretariat. Tensions got so high at times that some high-income countries confidentially floated the possibility of stopping the negotiations entirely when it became clear that it was going against their interests. Despite these contentious debates, the perceived reputational risks of scuttling a policy with widespread support led to last-minute compromises that secured the adoption of the new policy. FENSA now provides a set of principles and a defined procedure that seeks to ensure that WHO's engagement with non-state actors is in the best interest of the organization and its functions. Distinguishing non-state actors, FENSA contains specific policies for engagement with NGOs, industry associations, philanthropic foundations, and academic institutions. To allow participation in WHO's governance bodies, FENSA has also revised the process to grant "official relations" of non-state actors with WHO, opening a new path for diplomatic engagement.

Non-state actors have thus become key diplomatic actors in WHO governance, with NGOs seeking to advance specific health negotiations and academic institutions providing technical and policy analysis. Given that many low-income states lack the human and financial resources to prepare for and participate in WHO diplomacy (Kickbusch, Silberschmidt, and Buss 2007), non-state actors play a crucial role in leveling the playing field during complex negotiations—working to brief and inform national delegations, write their statements, and even occasionally be included in national delegations. This support from non-state actors, seen repeatedly in complex global health law negotiations, has transformed NGOs and other non-state actors into indirect but powerful participants in the diplomatic process and enabled otherwise disadvantaged countries to engage more effectively in global health diplomacy—in WHO governance and throughout the global health landscape.

B. Global Health Diplomacy Beyond WHO: Influencing Global Health Law and Policy

Global health diplomacy is not exclusively within the purview of WHO, as health has become a part of policymaking across institutions of global governance. Given the absence of a central coordinating authority, global health governance lacks a distinct division of labor in addressing health issues—even among the most prominent actors (Meier and Gostin 2018). After the adoption of the Sustainable Development

Goals (SDGs) in 2015, as introduced in Chapter 3, it became clear that the world would fall short in successfully implementing health-related goals without a proper coordination of health responsibilities across the UN (Smith and Lee 2017). Under these overarching policy goals, global health diplomacy has come to include the entire UN system, powerful political networks, and new multi-stakeholder initiatives—presenting new coordination challenges in global health governance.

1. UN Engagement

Many UN programs and organizations hold responsibility for health-related issues within their respective mandates. Global health has increasingly been taken up by the UN General Assembly, which has addressed select health issues through high-level "special sessions"—notably on HIV/AIDS, non-communicable diseases, antimicrobial resistance (AMR), and universal health coverage (Rodi et al. 2022). Given the absence of health expertise in the UN secretariat, the UN General Assembly has looked to WHO in preparing for these special sessions—and thereafter implementing its decisions. Beyond these occasional special sessions, the Assembly has included an item on health and foreign policy in its regular sessions since 2007. Under this agenda item, the General Assembly has adopted a series of thematic resolutions on central global health issues, ranging from universal health coverage to protection of health workers, transforming global health into a central component of UN diplomacy rather than a "technical" issue confined to WHO governance (Kickbusch et al. 2021). The UN General Assembly has thus created an implicit division of labor within the UN system, providing a role for itself and ensuring the continuing relevance of public health among broader political considerations.

Global health actors have largely supported this UN claim of authority, calling for stronger UN involvement to provide greater political leadership. The inclusion of a health topic on the agenda of the UN General Assembly elevates political attention. While debates in WHO are often characterized by technical expertise with limited senior political participation, the attention of heads of states and governments in UN debates may support sustained political focus. However, this political attention comes with potential challenges. WHO operates within an "epistemic community" of public health actors—who share similar understandings, technical expertise, and priorities (Mukherjee and Ekanayake 2009)—but this shared expertise, language, and focus is lacking both in the UN secretariat and among General Assembly delegations, with potentially negative consequences for the interests of the public health community.[8]

---

[8] The political divide between different geopolitical groups is omnipresent in UN debates; yet, in WHO, the "Geneva spirit" is often seen to prevail, as there is a broad understanding across delegations that global health challenges can only be adequately addressed through consensus to reach a common position.

The needed "technical focus" and community support for global health governance may be lost in favor of a stronger political focus, as bringing global health issues to the UN may politicize topics that could be advanced more effectively by technical considerations.

Yet, in further expanding political consideration of global health within the UN system, the UN Security Council has sought to address issues relevant to "global health security." Having begun to discuss the HIV/AIDS epidemic in Sub-Saharan Africa in 2000, the Security Council returned to global health concerns amid the 2014–2016 Ebola outbreak in Western Africa, adopting a September 2014 resolution to recognize that the outbreak constituted a threat to international peace and security (Voss, Kump, and Bochtler 2022). That strong political message, as examined in detail in Chapter 6, was instrumental in mobilizing international support and cooperation for the most affected countries, providing the political weight that had been lacking under WHO's leadership. The Security Council continued to take action in the 2019–2021 Ebola outbreak in the Democratic Republic of the Congo—and most recently in the COVID-19 pandemic. Addressing global health challenges where its members perceive a strong nexus to security issues, this expansion of security debates in global health has attracted concern about the increasing "securitization" of health, with global health security becoming increasingly political in multilateral diplomacy outside the UN system (Burci 2014).

2. Political Networks under the G7 and G20

Although health was once neglected in political networks of powerful states such as the G7 and the G20, which historically focused on issues ranging from financial stability to peace and security, their agenda has broadened over the years and today covers a wide spectrum of global health issues. Since the establishment of the Global Fund, engineered by the G7 in 2001, a health working group of the G7 now seeks to address diverse global health challenges, including pandemic preparedness and AMR (McBride, Hawkes, and Buse 2019). Similarly, the G20 established a health working group in 2017, seeking to create a more direct link between finance and health ministers. These self-appointed networks (or "clubs") of politically and financially powerful governments now seek to address a wide range of development policies and global health issues (Slaughter 2012). The decisions emerging from their meetings, albeit without formal legal status, spill over into global health diplomacy processes in WHO and other institutions. Yet, with many questioning the legitimacy and accountability of such political networks—given the exclusion of actors affected by the decisions taken by a small group of powerful states—it is crucial to consider the diplomatic dynamics and negotiations within those networks—through which politically powerful states seek to influence global governance agendas and multi-stakeholder initiatives in global health.

3. Multi-Stakeholder Initiatives

Beyond "traditional" institutions, global health diplomacy has expanded to encompass new partnerships among states, international organizations, and non-state actors. Promoting new forms of multi-stakeholder governance, "public-private partnerships" (PPPs), first introduced in Chapter 3, encompass initiatives taken by a variety of public and private actors to bring together the comparative advantages of participants in pursuit of a common goal, ranging from resource mobilization to the development of new medicines (Andonova 2017). Such initiatives in global health—as exemplified by the Global Fund— often result in the creation of separate governance structures, whether incorporated as distinct institutions under national law or hosted by an existing international organization. Diplomacy remains crucial in managing three stages in the development and implementation of PPPs:

(1) the political and diplomatic dynamics that lead to the creation of a new PPP, often emerging from a sense of urgency in tackling neglected gaps in global health in a different way from "traditional" international organizations;
(2) the relations among participants in a PPP, influenced by the diverse motivations of actors who have come together to pursue a shared goal but may have deeply different expectations of priorities, accountability, representation, and results; and
(3) the management of the relationship between PPPs and international organizations, which can be members of PPPs (participating in their governance and policy-setting), hosts of the PPP secretariat (supporting them from an institutional and administrative perspective), and technical partners (and sometimes competitors) (Burci 2009).

Coordinating such a complex PPP architecture entails diplomatic processes, whether between the governance bodies of participants, their executive heads, or their secretariats.

4. The Challenge of Coordination

The growing number of actors and initiatives in global health reflects growing political interest, but at the same time, coordination has become one of the key challenges faced by global health diplomacy. The fragmentation of the global health landscape has concrete implications for the ability of stakeholders to take part in global health governance (Alter and Raustiala 2018). While actors with greater resources might be able to strategically engage in every diplomatic setting, ensuring that their interests are well represented, diplomatic capacity will be more challenging for small organizations and low-income countries (Kickbusch, Silberschmidt, and Buss 2007). This growing fragmentation of global health will continue to limit inclusivity in global health diplomacy amid rising uncertainty.

III. Global Health Diplomacy in an Age of Uncertainty

Global health diplomacy has become more complex as it faces new challenges from the rise of nationalist politics and new health crises. With global health crises requiring global cooperation, changing dynamics in a crowded global health landscape are forcing WHO to define its priorities in global health. Given this growing crisis of multilateralism, it will be crucial for actors across global health governance to come together to reform global health law to prepare for future challenges.

A. Defining WHO's Priorities

WHO has a unique role as the leading global health organization, with a broad mandate that provides flexibility to adapt to emerging challenges; however, the world's expectations regarding WHO are as unrealistic as its mandate—with WHO's role and authority far outweighing its abilities and resources. Amid this gap in expectations, WHO has been struggling to clarify its own priorities, seeking to identify its comparative advantage in global health. Where the WHO Constitution defines WHO's primary function as "to act as the directing and coordinating authority on international health" (WHO 1946, art. 2), this constitutional "authority" alone is insufficient without political, financial, and technical resources (Meier et al. 2020). Without such support, WHO has struggled to balance its priorities—torn between realizing its global normative and policymaking functions (to a large extent through its headquarters in Geneva) and providing individual support to countries (through six regional offices and roughly 150 country offices) (Burci and Vignes 2004).

In balancing these visions of WHO's role and priorities, WHO's emergency functions—to prevent, detect, and respond to health threats as well as provide assistance to affected countries—have been central to its leadership. However, WHO's leadership in health emergencies came under scrutiny during the Ebola outbreak in West Africa in 2014–2016, as WHO was heavily criticized for not

Figure 5.2 WHO Daily Press Conference on the COVID-19 Response (WHO/Pierre Albouy)

responding quickly and adequately enough. This criticism reflected the obvious fact that WHO lacked the structural capacity to undertake an outbreak response (Moon et al. 2015), and in assessing the Ebola response, stakeholders debated whether it would be necessary to set up an entirely new structure for this response function. Rather than looking outside WHO, however, Member States confirmed WHO's central response role in 2015 by establishing the WHO Health Emergencies Programme (Ryan 2019). Yet, the COVID-19 pandemic has tested the effectiveness of the Health Emergencies Programme while placing it at the center of WHO priorities.

Amid the COVID-19 crisis response, WHO's senior management sought to reposition WHO as the leading coordinating authority in times of health emergencies. WHO was present in the media as never before, as seen in Figure 5.2, strategically making use of regular press briefings webcast to the entire world. Unlike in past political emergencies, WHO senior management deliberately led highly controversial discussions—on issues ranging from the origins of the virus to the fair distribution of COVID-19 vaccines. This public political role gave the Director-General credibility and leverage vis-à-vis Member States as an unrivaled leader in global health diplomacy.

Defining WHO's priorities within its broad mandate has thus become a crucially important diplomatic process driven by distinct political interests, as seen in the political tensions that arose between recalcitrant Member States and the Director-General during the COVID-19 response.[9] These tensions have made it clear that while WHO Member States expect leadership and initiative from the Director-General—and give due deference to WHO secretariat priorities—states seek to maintain decision-making authority in global health governance.

The most important "mechanism" for Member States to set WHO priorities remains the Programme Budget, laying down WHO goals and allocating the resources to pursue them. Approved by the World Health Assembly for a two-year period, the Programme Budget process is one of the most decisive opportunities for states to set concrete priorities for WHO, with intense diplomatic debates regarding the split of resources between the WHO headquarters and the regional offices, as states seek adequate country support alongside WHO's global mandate. Beyond the Programme Budget, states and non-state donors have increasingly looked to influence WHO's priorities through bilateral funding for specific donor goals. This targeted "extra-budgetary" funding now makes up the majority of the WHO budget, yet these individual donor agreements have long been criticized for denying WHO the flexibility necessary to set the global health agenda (Gostin, Sridhar, and Hougendobler 2015). With voluntary contributions distorting the priorities set collectively by Member States through the Programme Budget, the dysfunction of this financing model has created mismatches between priorities and financing, chronically overfunded and underfunded programs, and internal competition over limited and earmarked resources (Daugirdas and Burci 2019). The sudden need for WHO to react to the COVID-19 pandemic and coordinate the international response confirmed the unsustainability of this funding model, and the World Health Assembly sought to redress this historic challenge in May 2022, adopting the recommendations of the WHO Working Group on Sustainable Financing. This unexpected breakthrough in global health diplomacy—through the credibility and perseverance of the chairperson of the Working Group, a negotiating technique that narrowed possible options, and the unacceptability of the status quo—convinced recalcitrant states to develop a new model for WHO funding (Kümmel 2022). This historical reform will see a progressive increase in assessed contributions through 2031, with these long-term resources supporting a stronger WHO amid an ongoing crisis of multilateralism.

---

[9] Under the Trump administration, the United States took the unprecedented decision to seek to leave WHO, arguing that WHO was subservient to Chinese interests; however, this withdrawal was reversed by the Biden administration during its first week in office.

B. COVID-19 Diplomacy and the Crisis of Multilateralism

The increased political interest in WHO leadership in global health has come at a time in which multilateralism itself is in crisis. As WHO faces threats from geopolitical divides, with states seeking to strengthen WHO authority through the development of a new pandemic treaty, global health diplomacy is facing challenges across institutions of global health governance.

1. Challenging WHO in COVID-19 Diplomacy

While WHO was long seen primarily as an organization of interest to public health experts from the health ministries and development agencies, both foreign ministries and the security sector are giving more attention to global health security—challenging WHO leadership in the global health landscape. Looking beyond WHO to advance diplomatic efforts, the United States brought together sixty states in 2014 to establish the Global Health Security Agenda (GHSA) (Ayala et al. 2022). The GHSA's main purpose, as discussed in greater detail in Chapter 6, is to support the development of outbreak response capacities across countries, but the initiative has been kept outside WHO to ensure tighter control by its main sponsors—carving out a central part of WHO governance beyond the oversight of the World Health Assembly.

Further challenging WHO leadership, increasing interest in WHO has been mirrored by a growing politicization and polarization of WHO's work—with significant implications for negotiations in WHO's governing bodies. Given a growing geopolitical divide across nations, in the COVID-19 response and beyond, recent meetings of the World Health Assembly have seen an unprecedented proliferation of majority voting because consensus was not achievable.[10] Many delegations have expressed strong concerns about the challenges to international consensus and the politicization of technical health debates, fearing that geopolitical interests may make global health diplomacy less predictable, more conflictual, and dominated by WHO's most powerful members (Gostin, Moon, and Meier 2020).

The COVID-19 pandemic struck during these changing political dynamics, raising challenges in developing a coordinated and uniform approach amid the fragmentation of global health governance. Responding to these challenges to WHO leadership, the World Health Assembly launched a number of processes aimed at drawing lessons from the international response to COVID-19, considering ways to strengthen global prevention, preparedness, and response

---

[10] Like in other international organizations, decision-making by consensus is central to WHO governance, emphasizing the importance of consultations and negotiations to achieve a generally acceptable outcome.

for future pandemics and exploring the need for new global health laws and policies. Yet, despite initial consensus support for global health law reforms, differences soon emerged between Global North and Global South countries—concerning the balance of health security obligations with guarantees of equitable access to vaccines and other countermeasures—and subsequent sessions of the World Health Assembly have launched negotiations on two new distinct reforms: amending the International Health Regulations (IHR) to increase their effectiveness and developing an entirely new legal instrument on pandemic preparedness and response (Gostin, Meier, and Stocking 2021).

Case Study: Developing the Pandemic Treaty

With limitations of global health law hindering pandemic preparedness and response, state and non-state actors have called for the development of a new WHO convention, agreement, or other international instrument, developing what has come to be known as the "pandemic treaty." The initiative to negotiate a WHO treaty on pandemic preparedness and response initially came from the European Union (EU), arguably as a strategic move to place Europe at the center of global health diplomacy at a time of international division and polarization. The EU was instrumental in building an interregional coalition of "friends of the treaty," providing a critical mass of political support from WHO Member States; however, the initial EU proposal for a pandemic treaty generated uncertainties and skepticism—in part due to EU opposition to a waiver of intellectual property rights on COVID-19 vaccines. In moving forward to develop the pandemic treaty, the World Health Assembly established an Intergovernmental Negotiating Body (INB) to consider prospective treaty provisions. Although political divisions slowed early negotiations, the INB agreed in principle in July 2022 to develop the instrument as a treaty under Article 19 of the WHO Constitution. Continuing INB debates on the content of the prospective treaty point to states' intention to complement, rather than replace, the IHR, with this new treaty detailing additional provisions to address gaps in the scope and content of the IHR as well as other legal instruments. In seeking to advance legal authorities that would be more effective, equitable, and enforceable, the INB process remains open and its outcome remains uncertain, as states work to meet a May 2024 deadline for the World Health Assembly adoption of the treaty and amendments to the IHR.

The negotiations across two parallel diplomatic processes will be very challenging, in particular to ensure complementarity and coordination between the

IHR amendments, examined in detail in Chapter 6, and a new pandemic treaty (Meier, Habibi, and Gostin 2022). Pandemic conditions may further strain diplomatic processes. The COVID-19 pandemic, characterized by social distancing measures and border closures, rendered in-person multilateral diplomacy impossible for an extended period of time and forced international negotiations and other international meetings into a fully online environment or hybrid mode.[11] Even as global health diplomacy has continued to move toward necessary reforms, the suspension of some physical meetings and limitations on in-person interactions has impoverished multilateral diplomacy and may challenge efforts to maintain commitments adopted in haste through nontraditional diplomatic processes—in WHO and beyond.

2. COVID-19 Diplomacy Beyond WHO

The COVID-19 pandemic has confirmed that global health diplomacy cannot be limited to WHO; however, the fragmentation of global governance has cast in stark relief the need for coordination and coherence through diplomatic processes to address collective action problems. As seen in the COVID-19 response, the rapid and overwhelming spread of the virus in early 2020 was accompanied by an acute scarcity of life-saving diagnostics and therapeutics and by the frantic development of effective vaccines. Global health diplomacy reacted in an unprecedented manner across institutions. A coalition of states, international organizations, PPPs, and philanthropic foundations announced in April 2020 the creation of the Access to COVID Technologies Accelerator (ACT-A)—to be organized around four pillars, including a vaccine pillar, the COVID-19 Vaccines Global Access (COVAX). COVAX, as examined in greater detail in Chapter 14, quickly developed its own multi-stakeholder governance and management, relying on leading PPPs, with global health diplomacy taking place among diverse public and private actors to ensure vaccine access. While COVAX aimed to become the global one-stop shop for COVID-19 vaccine procurement, creating a model for PPPs to achieve an equitable allocation of predictably scarce vaccines, this approach proved hard to maintain, in part because of the self-interested behavior of wealthy countries that hoarded vaccines directly from manufacturers (Danaya Usher 2021).

---

[11] This unprecedented and sudden shift online presented major implications for global health diplomacy in a time of crisis. Through what has been previously described as "netpolitik" (Lee and Smith 2011), information technology has made it possible for WHO to connect hundreds throughout the world and formally hold online sessions; however, differential capacity in technological resources and online connectivity have increased the power differential between high-income and low-income countries and drastically reduced the space for participation from non-state actors.

Beyond vaccine access, low-income states have faced continuing challenges in pandemic preparedness and response, as they search for innovative approaches to finance national preparedness, strengthen health systems, and deliver medical countermeasures. There is a consensus among key stakeholders about the need for additional and sustainable resources to prepare for new pandemics. With agreement that WHO should not take on that funding responsibility, the G20 has stepped in as a powerful but relatively unrepresentative "club" of financially significant countries (G20 2021). This G20 initiative has allowed for the retention of political control by the most powerful states; yet, this financial authority has to be balanced against critical questions of legitimacy and inclusion in the search for equitable and sustainable funding models. To alleviate some of these concerns, the political leadership and financial power of the G20 led to the 2022 establishment by the World Bank of a new "Pandemic Fund." The Fund, legitimized by the global governance authority of the World Bank, can provide for independent governance representing both financing and implementing countries (World Bank 2022), seeking to balance issues of legitimacy and inclusion against considerations of pragmatism and the need to maintain good diplomatic relations with powerful states. In learning from the COVID-19 pandemic and preparing for future pandemics, new governing institutions are being developed, but it is unclear whether the political dynamics of global health diplomacy have changed at all.

Conclusion

Global health diplomacy remains a young field of multilateral diplomacy that—amid the rise of non-state actors in the global health landscape—is still defining its principles, norms, and objectives. While the COVID-19 pandemic has accelerated the development of global health law and policy, focusing political attention on global health governance at the highest levels of political leadership, many diplomatic questions remain unanswered. Diplomacy will see further complications as the global health landscape is reshaped to reflect the challenges presented by the COVID-19 pandemic. As global health governance is increasingly recognized as a political endeavor, global health diplomacy must advance decisive normative and political values in the development of global health law.

In bringing together actors to develop global health law, global health diplomacy must take into account the polycentric nature of global health governance—across sectors and actors. Health is not only a topic of global health governance, characterized by overarching values such as equity and human rights, but also a central value in many other legal and institutional regimes, including regimes impacting the environment, security, and economics. For health advocates, it will be necessary to ensure that diplomatic processes and negotiations across sectors uphold the importance of health across global governance. Further, the plurality of actors in global governance for health, including non-state actors and multi-stakeholder platforms, will continue to interact with, and at times challenge the primacy of, states as the ultimate decision-makers in global governance. These shifting dynamics substantially complicate diplomatic processes in global health, questioning the boundaries of global health governance, but they can also enrich global health diplomacy, increasing the legitimacy of global governance through the inclusion of all relevant voices.

These considerations point to the importance of developing the diplomatic skills and expertise necessary to engage in the development of global health law and policy. The need for awareness, expertise, and training in diplomatic and substantive skills highlights the important role that academic and research institutions can play. Public health officials across institutions must understand the political, legal, and institutional aspects of issues that they will have to negotiate. Conversely, government officials, professional diplomats, and other actors responsible for non-health sectors should develop awareness of the role that health plays—as an input, output, and indicator in their respective fields of global governance. In building the diplomatic capacities of health officials and the public health capacities of diplomats, global health diplomacy can aspire to a more level playing field in global health governance, ensuring the ultimate goal of "health in all policies."

Questions for Consideration

1. What political tensions arose between nations in the early negotiations of international sanitary conferences? How did the development of international sanitary conventions and international health institutions seek to resolve these political tensions?
2. Why was WHO unable to avoid the political conflicts that undermined its institutional predecessors? How did the Cold War tensions between the United States and Soviet Union manifest itself in WHO governance?
3. How did decolonization shift global health diplomacy to support primary health care? In what ways does the Declaration of Alma-Ata reflect the independent organizational leadership of WHO and UNICEF?
4. How did the HIV/AIDS response challenge WHO leadership in global health diplomacy and complicate global health governance?
5. How do WHO Member States come together to influence the agenda of WHO governing bodies? What independent role does the WHO Director-General play in setting the WHO agenda?

6. Why does WHO policy constrain non-state actor engagement in global health governance? What are the risks and benefits of non-state actor engagement in WHO deliberations? How have FENSA negotiations sought to structure the engagement of non-state actors in the global health diplomacy?
7. Why has the UN General Assembly sought to take on a larger role in global health policy? What are the benefits and drawbacks of high-level diplomatic debates in the UN General Assembly and Security Council? How have networks and partnerships outside the UN challenged coordination in global health governance?
8. How has the COVID-19 pandemic clarified WHO priorities as a leader in global health governance? How will World Health Assembly efforts to increase the WHO Programme Budget provide flexibility to the WHO Secretariat in addressing new threats?
9. How have geopolitical conflicts among Member States constrained WHO authority in the COVID-19 response? Why have WHO Member States sought to negotiate a new pandemic treaty to strengthen WHO under global health law?

Acknowledgments

The authors are grateful to Neha Saggi and Erin Jones for their research assistance and editorial support.

References

Alter, Karen and Kal Raustiala. 2018. "The Rise of International Regime Complexity." *Annual Review of Law and Social Sciences* 14: 329–349.

Andonova, Liliana. 2017. *Governance Entrepreneurs: International Organizations and the Rise of Public-Private Partnerships*. New York: Cambridge University Press.

Ayala, Ana, Adam Brush, Shuen Chai, Jose Fernandez, Katherine Ginsbach, Katie Gottschalk, Sam Halabi et al. 2022. "Advancing Legal Preparedness through the Global Health Security Agenda." *Journal of Law, Medicine & Ethics* 50(1): 200–203.

Birn, Anne-Emanuelle. 2009. "The Stages of International (Global) Health: Histories of Success or Successes of History?" *Global Public Health* 4(1): 50–68.

Brockington, Fraser. 1975. *World Health*. London: Churchill Livingstone.

Brown, Theodore M., Marcos Cueto, and Elizabeth Fee. 2006. "The World Health Organization and the Transition From 'International' to 'Global' Public Health." *American Journal of Public Health* 96(1): 62–72.

Burci, Gian Luca. 2009. "Public/Private Partnerships in the Public Health Sector." *International Organizations Law Review* 6(2): 359–382.

Burci, Gian Luca. 2014. "Ebola, The Security Council and the Securitization of Public Health." *Questions of International Law* 10: 27–39.

Burci, Gian Luca and Claude-Henri Vignes. 2004. *World Health Organization*. Alphen aan de Rijin, Netherlands: Kluwer Law International.

Buse, Kent, and Sarah Hawkes. 2016. "Sitting on the FENSA: WHO Engagement with Industry." *Lancet* 388: 446–447.

Chorev, Nitsan. 2012. *The World Health Organization Between North and South*. Ithaca: Cornell University Press.

Cueto, Marcos. 2020. "The History of International Health: Medicine, Politics, and Two Socio-Medical Perspectives, 1851 to 2000." In *The Oxford Handbook of Global Health Politics*, edited by Colin McInnes, Kelley Lee, and Jeremy Youde, 17–36. Oxford: Oxford University Press.

Cueto, Marcos, Theodore Brown, and Elizabeth Fee. 2019. *The World Health Organization: A History*. New York: Cambridge University Press.

Danaya Usher, Ann. 2021. "A Beautiful Idea: How COVAX Has Fallen Short." *Lancet* 397: 2322–2325.

Daugirdas, Kristina and Gian Luca Burci. 2019. "Financing the World Health Organization." *International Organizations Law Review* 16(2): 299–338.

Evang, K. 1967. "Political, National and Traditional Imitations to Health Control." In *Health of Mankind*. London: J. & A. Churchill Ltd.

Fidler, David P. 2005. "From International Sanitary Conventions to Global Health Security: The New International Health Regulations." *Chinese Journal of International Law* 4(2): 325–392.

G20. 2021. *A Global Deal for Our Pandemic Age: Report of the G20 High-Level Independent Panel*. Financing the Global Commons for Pandemic Preparedness and Response.

Ghebreyesus, Tedros. 2020. "Human Rights are Foundational to Global Health." In *Foundations of Global Health and Human Rights*, edited by Lawrence O. Gostin and Benjamin Mason Meier. XIII–XIV. New York: Oxford University Press.

Gostin, Lawrence O., Benjamin Mason Meier, and Barbara Stocking. 2021. "Developing an Innovative Pandemic Treaty to Advance Global Health Security." *Journal of Law, Medicine & Ethics* 49: 503–508.

Gostin, Lawrence O., Devi Sridhar, and Daniel Hougendobler. 2015. "The Normative Authority of the World Health Organization." *Public Health* 129(7): 854–863.

Gostin, Lawrence O., Suerie Moon, and Benjamin Mason Meier. 2020. "Reimagining Global Health Governance in the Age of COVID-19." *American Journal of Public Health*. 110: 1615–1619.

Grad, Frank P. 2002 . "The Preamble of the Constitution of the World Health Organization." *Bulletin of the World Health Organization* 80(12) : 981–984.

Howard-Jones, Norman. 1975. "The scientific background of the International Sanitary Conferences, 1851-1938." World Health Organization.

Huang, Yanzhong and Gabriella Meltzer. 2018. "Reforming the World Health Organization." In *Routledge Handbook on the Politics of Global Health*, 135–149. New York: Routledge.

Kickbusch, Ilona and Austin Liu. 2017. *Global Health Leadership*. Graduate Institute of International and Development Studies.

Kickbusch, Ilona, Haik Nikogosian, Michel Kazatchkine, and Mihaly Kokeny. 2021. *A Guide to Global Health Diplomacy*. Geneva: Graduate Institute of International and Development Studies.

Kickbusch, Ilona, Gaudenz Silberschmidt, and Paulo Buss. 2007 . "Global Health Diplomacy: The Need for New Perspectives, Strategic Approaches and Skills in Global Health." *Bulletin of the World Health Organization* 85(3) : 230–232.

Kümmel, Björn. 2022. Report by Mr. Björn Kümmel, Chair of the WHO Sustainable Financing Working Group, to the Seventy-five World Health Assembly. May 26.

Lee, Kelley and Richard Smith. 2011. "What Is Global Health Diplomacy: A Conceptual Review." *Global Health Governance* 5(1): 1–12.

Litsios, Socrates. 2002. "The Long and Difficult Road to Alma-Ata: A Personal Reflection." *International Journal of Health Services* 32(4): 709–732.

McBride, Bronwyn, Sarah Hawkes, and Kent Buse. 2019. "Soft Power and Global Health: The Sustainable Development Goals Era Health Agendas of the G7, G20, and BRICs." *BMC Public Health* 19(815).

Meier, Benjamin Mason, Allyn Taylor, Mark Eccleston-Turner, Roojin Habibi, Harifah Sekalala, and Lawrence O. Gostin. 2020. "The World Health Organization in Global Health Law." *Journal of Law, Medicine & Ethics* 48: 796–799.

Meier, Benjamin Mason and Lawrence O. Gostin. 2018. "Framing Rights in Global Health Governance." In *Human Rights and Global Health: Rights-Based Governance for a Globalizing World*, edited by Benjamin Mason Meier and Lawrence O. Gostin. 63–86. New York: Oxford University Press.

Meier, Benjamin Mason, Roojin Habibi, and Lawrence O. Gostin. 2022. "A Global Health Law Trilogy: Transformational Reforms to Strengthen Pandemic Prevention, Preparedness, and Response." *Journal of Law, Medicine & Ethics* 50: 625–627.

Moon, Suerie, Devi Sridhar, Muhammed A. Pate, Ashish K. Jha, Chelsea Clinton, Sophie Delauney, Valnora Edwin et al. 2015. "Will Ebola Change the Game? Ten Essential Reforms Before the Next Pandemic. The Report of Harvard-LSHTM Independent Panel on the Global Response to Ebola." *Lancet* 386(10009): 2204–2221.

Mukherjee, Amit and E. M. Ekanayake. 2009. "Epistemic Communities and the Global Alliance Against Tobacco Marketing." *Thunderbird International Business Review* 51(3): 207–218.

Packard, Randall M. 2016. *A History of Global Health: Interventions into the Lives of Other Peoples*. Baltimore: Johns Hopkins University Press.

Pannenborg, Charles O. 1979. *A New International Health Order: An Inquiry into the International Relation of World Health and Medical Care*. Alphen aan den Rijn: Sijthoff & Noordhoff.

Peterson, Poul Erik. 2009. "Global Policy for Improvement of Oral Health in the 21st Century – Implications to Oral Health Research of World Health Assembly 2007, World Health Organization." *Community Dentistry and Oral Epidemiology* 37(1): 1–8.

Pethybridge, Roger. 1965. "The Influence of International Politics on the Activities of 'Non-Political' Specialized Agencies—a Case Study." *Political Studies* 3(2): 247–251.

Rached, Danielle Hanna and Deisy de Freitas Lima Ventura. 2017. "World Health Organization and the Search for Accountability: A Critical Analysis of the New Framework of Engagement with Non-State Actors." *Cadernos de Saúde Pública* 33: e00100716.

Rodi, Paolo, Werner Obermeyer, Ariel Pablos-Mendez, Andrea Gori, and Mario C. Raviglione. 2022. "Political Rationale, Aims, and Outcomes of Health-Related High-Level Meetings and Special Sessions at the UN General Assembly: A Policy Research Observational Study." *PLoS Medicine* 19(1): e1003873.

Ryan, Michael J. 2019. "Partnerships for Global Health Security: WHO Health Emergencies Programme and the Republic of Korea." *Journal of Global Health Science* 1(1): 1–4.

Samarasekera, Udani. 2021. "Experts Criticize WHO Response to Sex Abuse Allegations." *Lancet* 398(10308): 1291–1293.

Slaughter, Steven. 2012. "Debating the International Legitimacy of the G20: Global Policymaking and Contemporary International Society." *Global Policy* 4(1): 43–52.

Smith, Richard and Kelley Lee. 2017. "Global Health Governance: We Need Innovation Not Renovation." *BMJ Global Health* 2(2): 1–3.

Starrels, John M. 1985. *The World Health Organization: Resisting Third World Ideological Pressures*. Washington: The Heritage Foundation.

Voss, Maike, Isabell Kump, and Paul Bochtler. 2022. "Unpacking the Framing of Health in the United Nations Security Council." *Australian Journal of International Affairs* 76(1): 4–10.

Yang, Hai. 2022. "Politicizing Global Governance Institutions in Times of Crisis." *Global Governance: A Review of Multilateralism and International Organizations* 28(3): 405–431.

World Bank. 2022. "Financial Intermediary Fund for Pandemic Prevention, Preparedness and Response – Engagement and Overview." World Bank.

WHO (World Health Organization). 1946. *Constitution of the World Health Organization*. New York: WHO.

II
GLOBAL HEALTH GOVERNANCE FOR DISEASE PREVENTION & HEALTH PROMOTION

6

Infectious Disease

Preventing, Detecting, and Responding to Pandemic Threats under International Law

Pedro A. Villarreal and Lauren Tonti

Introduction

Protection against the cross-border spread of disease is the oldest and most robust area of global health law. Yet, despite numerous advances in medical sciences, a rapidly globalizing world has fostered the rise of emerging and re-emerging communicable disease threats, including Human Immunodeficiency Virus (HIV) and Severe Acute Respiratory Syndrome (SARS), as well as novel strains of Influenza, Ebola, and Coronavirus disease (COVID-19). Coinciding with the rise of new disease threats, local outbreaks can now spread more rapidly throughout an increasingly interconnected world, consequently increasing morbidity and mortality and requiring a global response. With governments increasingly viewing infectious disease as a threat to security, efforts to prevent the spread of disease can cause disruptions to international travel and trade, as well as potential violations of human rights.

In responding to these infectious disease threats, global health law has become crucial in combating the spread of disease through a rules-based international response. Establishing state obligations under law can frame measures to address disease outbreaks that are necessary to uphold public health and are proportional to restrictions on travel, trade, and rights. To this end, World Health Organization (WHO) Member States sought to balance the need for public health prevention and the protection of individuals in the 2005 revision of the International Health Regulations (IHR). Through the IHR (2005) and other instruments and mechanisms for global health security, policymakers have sought to strengthen surveillance systems across WHO Member States and foster disease control partnerships between international organizations, governmental agencies, and non-governmental organizations (NGOs). Despite these advancements under global health law, inside and outside of WHO, emerging public health threats, including the COVID-19 pandemic, have exposed weaknesses in existing frameworks, raising an imperative for IHR revisions and global health law reforms to prevent, detect, and respond to the cross-border spread of infectious disease.

This chapter examines how global health law has sought to combat the spread of communicable diseases, examining international responses to public health emergencies of international concern. Part I reviews the evolution of this international law regime to address the cross-border spread of disease, leading to the establishment of the IHR and drawing on WHO governance in coordinating the infectious disease response. Yet, with WHO facing limitations in early responses under the IHR, Part II examines the 2005 revision of the IHR and subsequent global health law reforms to respond to the changing nature of public health emergencies in a globalizing world. Despite these reforms, the COVID-19 pandemic and renewed infectious disease threats from mpox and Ebola have posed unprecedented challenges to global health law. Part III examines these legal limitations, considering how novel threats have stretched global health law beyond its limits. Reflecting on the challenges of the COVID-19 pandemic and the promise of ongoing reforms, this chapter concludes by considering future directions for global health law in responding to future pandemic threats.

I. Legal Responses to Cross-Border Health Threats: The Evolution of International Law on Infectious Disease

Infectious disease threats brought nations together in the development of international law on infectious disease, with early understanding of the spread of disease influencing the evolution of modern legal tools under WHO governance. This understanding of disease transmission led to pharmaceutical advancements, which then gave rise to biomedical optimism—the notion that scientific progress could lead to disease eradication. However, the HIV/AIDS pandemic undermined that optimism. The rise of new disease threats in a globalizing world exposed the limitations of a biomedical approach to disease prevention and catalyzed advocacy for human rights in policy responses to infectious disease.

A. From Fragmentation in Governance to Harmonization through the WHO

Given the perpetual threat posed by communicable disease, states developed specialized international law instruments to govern emerging challenges from cross-border disease spread.[1] Since the first International Sanitary Conference in

---

[1] Until the middle of the 20th century, communicable diseases were the leading cause of death throughout the world, surpassing even casualties in military conflicts.

1851, states have considered the potential of international law to protect against these cross-border challenges. These early conferences, first introduced in Chapter 2, intended to harmonize national quarantine measures against specific diseases. The first legally binding instrument developed among these states, the International Sanitary Convention, was approved more than forty years later in 1892 (Fidler 1999). This Convention was a byproduct of 19th century diplomatic processes and public health advancements, whereupon European states coordinated their efforts to protect themselves against the spread of communicable disease threats from other regions of the world. In seeking to advance national self-interests, the Convention reflected efforts to promote national security, focusing on protecting the economic and military interests of powerful nations. To maintain state power, national governments needed quick and reliable information on diseases beyond their territories, requiring cross-national systems of epidemiological surveillance that would allow states to respond rapidly when communicable diseases eventually reached their own territories (Zacher 1999).

Several tenets of 19th century international lawmaking were abandoned with the rise of international health institutions, marking a major shift in health governance beyond states through the development of international legal instruments. However, making sense of overlapping legal obligations became an increasing challenge for states. The first international sanitary conventions were European undertakings that, in contrast to contemporary instruments, did not seek to have a global reach. As parallel conventions in the Americas were approved, binding international instruments to ensure communicable disease prevention and control became fragmented across regions—as national responses to disease threats remained inconsistent throughout the world (Fidler 2005). The heightened fragmentation and the diverging membership of these sanitary conventions made it increasingly difficult to ascertain which rules applied in restrictions of travel and trade to protect public health.

The establishment of WHO helped to end this fragmentation in international health law. The passage of the 1946 Constitution of the World Health Organization (WHO Constitution) brought together twelve International Sanitary Conventions and Protocols regulating different aspects of the cross-border spread of disease. As introduced in Chapters 1 and 2, the WHO Constitution grants the World Health Assembly the authority to develop legally binding regulations in five specific areas:

1. sanitary and quarantine requirements and other procedures to prevent the international spread of disease;
2. nomenclatures of diseases, causes of death, and public health practice;
3. international standards on diagnostic procedures;

4. international standards for trade on the safety, purity, and potency of biological, pharmaceutical, and similar products; and
5. standards for advertising and labelling of biological, pharmaceutical, and similar products subjected to international trade (WHO 1946, art. 21).[2]

The first of these areas led to the adoption of the International Sanitary Regulations of 1951, which superseded a patchwork of existing conventions. In 1969, the World Health Assembly approved a revision of the instrument, naming them the "International Health Regulations."

The core objective of the IHR is to ensure the provision of information on diseases with the potential to spread across borders, aiming to support public health responses while preventing excessive restrictions on international travel and trade. Yet, states historically failed to uphold these obligations under the IHR. In the first fifty years of WHO governance over infectious disease, states often belatedly notified WHO when diseases emerged in their territories, and other states often responded to these notifications with disproportionate travel and trade restrictions. These legal limitations were recognized early in the evolution of the IHR. WHO identified a vicious cycle in which states failed to promptly report diseases because they feared excessive reactions by other states, and in turn, other states would react excessively due to the lack of sufficiently reliable information provided by the state experiencing the disease-related event (Dorolle 1968). This vicious cycle was compounded by disparities across national health systems, with many states lacking sufficient capacity to rapidly assess the emergence of a disease within their territories (Roelsgaard 1974). The enduring global divide in national health capacities would undermine the implementation of IHR obligations and shift focus to biomedical responses to infectious disease.

B. The Rise and Fall of Biomedical Optimism: The Unfulfilled Promise of the "End of Disease"

Although communicable disease control was a top priority in the early decades of WHO governance, WHO did not prioritize the implementation of the IHR and national public health capacities in disease preparedness and response—looking instead to medical advancements and disease eradication programs as

---

[2] As compared with WHO conventions and recommendations, the legal nature of WHO regulations is a subject of ongoing doctrinal debate. While they are not treaties, in the strictest sense of the term (Heath 2016), the legally binding status of regulations derives from a treaty, the WHO Constitution. Thus, there is now ample consensus that WHO Member States hold legal obligations under WHO regulations, where such regulations bind states automatically unless they formally express their rejection or reservation.

a basis to realize the promised "end of infectious disease." A sense of biomedical optimism had emerged among policymakers, viewing the administration of pharmaceutical products as the solution to communicable disease challenges throughout the world (Cueto, Brown, and Fee 2019). The discovery of these new products—including vaccines, antivirals, and antibiotics to address specific diseases—led to a growing belief that the global distribution of such pharmaceutical interventions could stop the spread of infectious disease altogether (Lee 2009). Multiple international campaigns were launched for the distribution of these specific medicines, as seen in Figure 6.1. These vertical disease eradication initiatives led to vast increases in international health funding, but they all fell short of their ultimate objective, with one exception: WHO's Smallpox Eradication Programme.

Figure 6.1 WHO Smallpox Eradication Campaign, Vaccination in Afghanistan (WHO, 1970) (WHO/Paul Almasy)

Case Study: From Failed Eradication Efforts to the Successful Eradication of Smallpox

WHO Eradication Programmes were central to international health governance efforts in the 1950s and 1960s. Malaria and smallpox were among the initial diseases targeted for eradication, each with their own distinct programs, personnel, and budget. The Malaria Eradication Programme rapidly failed to meet its expected goals, however, as (a) the continent with the highest burden of disease, Africa, was not included in the campaign and (b) there was an overreliance on the widespread use of the insecticides against this mosquito-borne disease—disregarding the underlying social contexts where malaria spread. Recognizing the limitations of this vertical initiative, the Malaria Eradication Programme was formally discontinued in 1969. This high-profile eradication failure risked derailing WHO's leadership in international health governance, undermining the central role of communicable disease control at the core of WHO's mandate. In redoubling its eradication efforts, the WHO Smallpox Eradication Campaign advanced consistently over the next decade. Even during the height of the Cold War, the active participation of the two major global rivals (the Soviet Union and the United States of America) and the Non-Aligned Movement allowed for the global deployment of healthcare workers in targeted immunization efforts. Multilateral cooperation would come to drive the success of this eradication campaign. Supported by a partnership of international organizations—including the WHO, UNICEF, and numerous non-state actors, including the Red Cross and Red Crescent Societies—smallpox eradication was a success of global governance and, in spite of geopolitical divides, a victory for international cooperation in achieving disease eradication. WHO issued the final Declaration of Smallpox Eradication in 1980, highlighting the possibility of permanently ending the threat of disease.

Despite the abandonment of several disease eradication programs, the second half of the 20th century nevertheless witnessed an epidemiological transition—a gradual decline in the burden of infectious diseases (Omran 1971). This reduction in the global disease burden was framed as a triumph of scientific progress, with smallpox eradication demonstrating the potential of new and effective medicines to conquer the diseases afflicting the world. Seeking to ensure the distribution of these medicines, international attention again turned to biomedical optimism, hopeful that medical science could bring an end to infectious disease—at least in the developed world (Cliff and Haggett 1998). Yet, amid this moment of perceived triumph in international health governance, a series of new and re-emerging communicable disease threats shook global leaders' faith that the world would achieve the end of disease.

C. The HIV/AIDS Pandemic and the Rise of the Health and Human Rights Movement

Prevailing biomedical optimism faltered at the beginning of the HIV/AIDS pandemic response. Without effective pharmaceutical drugs in the early years of the global response, the disease rapidly became a pandemic threat, resulting in millions of deaths and the loss of millions of disability-adjusted life years. The high prevalence of the disease among specific groups of persons—including homosexual men, racial minorities, controlled substance users, and impoverished individuals—gave rise to social stigmatization, discrimination, and exclusion (Condon and Sinha 2008). The initial public health response, relying on traditional public health approaches to quarantine, isolation, and reporting, furthered the challenges faced by these populations, who banded together to demand their rights. In the early years of the AIDS response, as introduced in Chapter 4, affected populations advocated for human rights to protect those who were at risk—to end discriminatory laws and policies that harmed vulnerable groups and undermined public health efforts. Beginning with the 1983 Denver Principles, "people living with AIDS" demanded human rights in the public health response, including non-discrimination in medical care, social services, privacy and confidentiality of medical records, and the right to refuse treatment. This advocacy gave rise to a "health and human rights" movement, with the evolving public health response to HIV/AIDS showing that human rights promotion could support infectious disease prevention (Amon and Friedman 2020).

Even as the pharmaceutical industry developed effective antiretroviral drugs in the 1990s, human rights challenges would remain central to the HIV/AIDS response, as these medicines remained financially inaccessible to the vast majority of infected persons throughout the world. Pharmaceutical corporations secured enormous profits, but they remained unwilling to lower prices to ensure health for all. Despite negotiations with national public health institutions, the Sub-Saharan African region, in particular, experienced a decades-long delay in providing treatment to persons affected by HIV/AIDS. This global inequity in the distribution of antiretroviral drugs led to millions of unnecessary deaths and shed light on the need to recognize health as a human right (Sekalala and Harrington 2020). Drawing from the right to health under international law, NGOs deployed strategic litigation to improve access to essential medicines, raising awareness of human rights violations and facilitating reforms in global health governance.

From this human rights movement, alongside key advances in the right to health under international law, the United Nations (UN) developed new institutions to coordinate the HIV/AIDS response. The establishment of the Joint United Nations Programme on HIV/AIDS (UNAIDS) provided global governance support for people living with HIV/AIDS. Advancing human rights in global health, UNAIDS brought together civil society with government representatives as a basis to engage with global health governance across normative frameworks, draw on scientific evidence, and realize access to medicines (Nygren-Krug 2018). Such multi-stakeholder collaborations, with financial support from the Global Fund for AIDS, Tuberculosis and Malaria (Global Fund), have operated with the understanding that global health cannot be achieved without tackling the underlying conditions of structural inequality that fuel the spread of infectious disease. However, infectious disease policy was eventually framed as a matter of "global health security," and this led to new priorities that have risked overriding human rights approaches in responding to health emergencies (Hoffman 2010).

II. Global Health Security: Countering the Threat of Novel and Re-emerging Diseases

Broadly speaking, global health security views novel and re-emerging diseases as existential dangers to a functioning society (Kamradt-Scott 2015). As threats to global health have become securitized, they are viewed in the same light as invasions, insurgencies, or terrorist attacks, resulting in the restriction of human rights and fundamental freedoms in the name of safeguarding national security (Sekalala and Harrington 2020). Securitizing health through the evolution of global health law, the current IHR was approved by the World Health Assembly in 2005. The IHR (2005) framed global governance over infectious disease in the years that followed, structuring international responses to a rapid series of public health emergencies and finding policy support through new partnerships outside of WHO.

A. Enter SARS: The First Globalized Disease of the 21st Century Catalyzes IHR Reform

The 2002 outbreak of Severe Acute Respiratory Syndrome (SARS), a novel coronavirus, raised the challenge of navigating a novel contagion in a new era of global connection. The challenges of the international response revealed gaps in legal protections, transformed WHO's role in emergency management, and paved the way for re-evaluating existing legal frameworks to confront modern health threats. SARS illustrated the legal gaps in preparing for and responding to the cross-border spread of disease, exposing the limited capabilities of IHR (1969) and triggering questions on the reach of WHO's authority. Although

SARS was first detected in China, the Chinese government's belated notification was compounded by the fact that the IHR did not strictly apply to this new coronavirus, as by then the IHR (1969) applied only to outbreaks of three specific diseases: cholera, plague, and yellow fever. In the absence of an applicable legal framework, there was uncertainty on state obligations regarding novel pathogens, particularly in obligations to notify WHO of the disease's emergence and spread (Kamradt-Scott 2016).

Left without concrete legal obligations during the 2002–2003 SARS crisis, WHO embraced a new role in emergency management, looking to its constitutional authorities to frame the international response. WHO spearheaded scientific inquiries into the outbreak in China, after learning of the potential pathogen from non-state sources, and led efforts to develop public health mitigation strategies (Fidler 2004). Facing an initial lack of cooperation from the Chinese government, which denied WHO a reliable and accurate assessment of the rising threat, the WHO Director-General issued global alerts, advisories, and recommendations, often without seeking the explicit consent of WHO Member States. WHO would lead a concerted effort throughout the world, and given the pathogen's comparatively lower transmission rate, the spread of SARS subsided, bringing the emergency threat to an end. In evaluating the response, WHO was praised for its rapid and authoritative actions, fostering coordination between state and non-state actors (Kreuder-Sonnen 2019).[3] However, these WHO actions were not ground in any legal authority and did not rely upon legal obligations of states, intergovernmental organizations, or any other actors. The limits of heavily relying upon goodwill cooperation demonstrated an imperative for global health law reform to support global health governance.

The SARS experience created the needed momentum to concretize reforms of the IHR (1969). Gaps in legal preparedness and governance, put into sharp relief by SARS, fueled the necessary impetus to reframe state obligations in responding to infectious disease, galvanizing stakeholders to bring a decade-long revision of the IHR to completion. The delay in notification from China and case underreporting across nations raised questions surrounding notification obligations, hampering other states' abilities to monitor and detect disease with their own jurisdictions (Halabi, Gostin, and Crawley 2016). Furthermore, the global response to SARS exposed a complete absence of respect for human rights, including those rights related to unwarranted restrictions on international travel and trade (Forman, Sekalala, and Meier 2022). Revisions of the IHR (1969) that had been requested by the World Health Assembly since 1995 were

---

[3] With WHO praised for acting as a source of reliable information, WHO looked to its Global Outbreak Alert and Response Network (GOARN), an international network of state and non-state institutions, to monitor, coordinate, and orchestrate technical understanding of health events.

now seen as essential in responding to the novel and re-emerging communicable diseases not regulated until then (Fidler 2005). Within a year of the SARS debacle, WHO consultations, revisions, and negotiations occurred and, with widespread support of Member States, led to the adoption of a revised IHR in 2005, establishing a reimagined governance framework for public health emergencies.

B. Framing the IHR for the 21st Century

These shared global experiences set the scene for the revisions of the IHR to meet modern challenges. Founded on both past and modern principles, the IHR (2005) included an expanded reach and scope as well as an embrace of essential human rights principles. However, infectious disease challenges have continued to test the fitness of these revisions, revealing underlying limitations in IHR obligations.

1. An Expanded Reach and Scope

The 2005 revisions of the IHR resulted in a set of regulations with an expanded reach and scope that would equip stakeholders with new authorities and mechanisms to meet modern threats to global health security:

- From a "Closed" to an "Open" List of Diseases—A core limitation of the IHR (1969) was its disease-specific approach, being only applicable to three specific disease threats. Amid new and re-emerging disease, states framed the IHR (2005) broadly to address "events" and "public health risks"—embracing an all-hazards approach (Ottersen, Hoffman, and Groux 2016). This all-hazards approach acknowledges that threats to health can arise from a variety of sources, human, animal, or environmental, as a result of numerous causes, whether natural, accidental, or intentional (Burci and Negri 2021). Such an expansion would allow for enhanced applicability across emergencies, making the IHR (2005) better suited to a globalized world facing novel health threats.
- From State-Centered to Multi-Actor Disease Surveillance—Whereas previous IHR iterations relied heavily on state reporting, the revised IHR (2005) would expand the surveillance system to encompass more actors. The SARS response highlighted the utility of acting on information from non-governmental sources (Gostin 2014), and the IHR (2005) would allow WHO to consult non-state actors and consider information from unofficial sources.[4] WHO and its Member States can thus leverage disease surveillance

---

[4] Although WHO must first take confirmatory measures with the affected state(s), surveillance information under IHR (2005) can arise from non-state actors—and beyond the official confines of governmental channels.

through both official and unofficial sources, broadening the range of tools to detect infectious disease outbreaks.
- Emergency Declarations as a Governance Tool—The IHR (2005) defines a public health emergency of international concern (PHEIC) as an "extraordinary event which is determined . . . (i) to constitute a public health risk to other States through the international spread of disease and (ii) to potentially require a coordinated international response" (WHO 2005, art. 1). These declarations by the WHO Director-General are framed as a tool of global governance, as they put stakeholders on notice about the risk of cross-border spread of a disease, acts as a call for global cooperation in addressing a health emergency, and allows the WHO Director-General to issue non-binding recommendations on national response measures (Fidler and Gostin 2006).
- Developing Core Surveillance Capacities—Assessments of IHR limitations repeatedly underscored the lack of sufficient state capacities to promptly detect communicable disease outbreaks occurring within their territories and to notify WHO of a potential public health emergency (Taylor 1997); however, the IHR (1969) lacked any obligations to develop national capacities. Under the IHR (2005), states bear responsibilities to "develop, strengthen and maintain" the capacities to "detect, assess, notify and report events" to WHO (WHO 2005, art. 5). Annex 1 of the IHR (2005), in turn, provides a detailed list of core capacities for states and include a self-assessment reporting process to determine whether states have developed and maintained core capacities.

These additions, granting novel authorities under global health law, sought to establish new governance mechanisms to match contemporary health challenges. The IHR (2005) would provide WHO with a range of legal tools to utilize in the face of threats posed by "old" and "new" pathogens, reflecting the expanding nature of global health threats in the 21st century and providing new legal principles for an internationally coordinated response.

2. Principles Framing IHR (2005)

The IHR (2005) reflect both traditional legal principles and new normative principles to guide efforts to prevent the cross-border spread of disease. In extending traditional principles of international health practice, following from long-standing norms of communicable disease control introduced in Chapter 1, public health strategies to prevent and respond to the cross-border spread of disease must be balanced against the need to maintain the continuity of international trade and travel (Fidler 2005). Yet, in comparison to predecessor legal instruments, the IHR (2005) envisaged a more prominent role for medical and public health evidence in this balancing. States seeking to address health threats must base their public health decision-making on scientific principles, methods, and information (Burci and Negri 2021). This focus on data in decision-making under the IHR (2005) provides an opening for states to pursue measures they deem to offer a higher level of health protection than those recommended by WHO (Habibi et al. 2020).

Adding to the normative frameworks structuring infectious disease control, IHR (2005) elevates key principles of respect for "the dignity, human rights and fundamental freedoms of persons" in the implementation of its provisions (WHO 2005, art. 32). Thus, respect for travelers' dignity, human rights, and fundamental freedoms are assured, with additional health measures to be applied in a "transparent and non-discriminatory manner" (ibid., art. 42). This explicit elevation of human rights in the IHR (2005) is joined by the principle of striving for "the protection of all people of the world from the international spread of disease" (ibid., art 3)—implicitly advancing the right to health under global health law (Forman, Sekalala, and Meier 2022). In viewing communicable disease control as a common responsibility across all states, this principle is reflected in state commitments to collaborate with each other in the provision of technical assistance, the mobilization of resources, and the formulation of laws and administrative provisions for implementing IHR obligations (Cinà et al. 2022). International collaboration and assistance have been central to the development of IHR core capacities across states; yet in developing these obligations to strengthen health systems, states recognized their legal limitations.

3. The Inherent Limits of the IHR (2005)

Although the scope of the IHR (2005) is broader than its predecessors, it retains inherent limitations that limit its effectiveness. Firstly, the IHR (2005) is designed to apply only to states, not non-state actors that can also play important roles in preventing, protecting against, controlling, and providing a public health response (Habibi et al. 2020). While reliance on cooperation between states is a foundational principle, this focus on state action can simultaneously limit WHO's authority in emergency response. Secondly, the IHR (2005) provides states parties significant discretion to conform with their legal obligations; however, unlike past regulations,[5] states may exercise their own discretion to restrict international travel and trade when they deem it necessary. This overreliance on the good faith fulfillment of obligations by states can create obstacles where states are unprepared or uncooperative in the face of a public health emergency.

---

[5] Both the International Sanitary Regulations of 1951 and the IHR of 1969 had established "maximum measures" related to international travel and trade that could be adopted by states when responding to disease outbreaks, and states were barred from going beyond those health measures.

In the case of non-compliance, the IHR (2005) holds limited potential to facilitate accountability across states parties, lacking mechanisms for the assessment and enforcement of obligations. Despite efforts to support states in establishing core capacities, the IHR (2005) does not expressly provide for an independent assessment of the implementation of these obligations. Initially, the evaluation of state preparedness relied on self-assessments, inherently unreliable metrics given non-uniformity and inconsistency in data collection and reporting (Gostin and Katz 2016).[6] Beyond evaluation mechanisms, the IHR (2005) lack enforcement mechanisms to ensure implementation. There are no administrative or dispute settlement mechanisms to incentivize compliance or sanction non-compliance, denying accountability for states that disregard WHO's temporary or standing recommendations, fail to report, act non-transparently, or otherwise violate the provisions of the IHR. Without the authority to sanction non-compliance, the IHR (2005) leaves states to voluntarily comply with their legal commitments.

Where such legal commitments require resource allocations, inequities in resources across countries continue to undermine the effectiveness of the IHR (2005). Implementation obligations is heavily dependent on the allocation of resources for an emergency response (Ottersen, Hoffman, and Groux 2016); yet where states lack necessary resources, there remains insufficient global financing for health emergency preparedness and response. WHO's budget has long been dependent on earmarked voluntary contributions from both states and non-state actors, as introduced in Chapter 5, and this voluntary WHO financing system has contributed to inconsistent funding streams and cycles of neglect (Daugirdas and Burci 2019). The insufficiencies of this system of WHO governance under the IHR (2005) have become increasingly clear in recent public health emergencies.

C. The Application of IHR (2005) in Public Health Emergencies

The limitations of the IHR (2005) have been exposed most clearly in emergency responses. A series of high-profile PHEICs have been declared so far—most recently in the context of COVID-19 and mpox. These experiences under the IHR illustrate the prospects and pitfalls in leadership, institutional governance, and procedural hurdles that can be decisive factors in the control of infectious diseases.

---

[6] In early annual reports on the implementation of the IHR (2005), a number of states had yet to confirm the existence of core capacities, and these self-assessments by national authorities were later supplemented by an external evaluation through specific country missions (Villarreal, Habibi, and Taylor 2022).

The first test of the IHR (2005) came from H1N1 Influenza, first detected in Mexico in March 2009. In line with IHR obligations, Mexico and the United States notified WHO of the emergence of a new strain of Influenza, likely arising from a zoonotic spillover between pigs and humans (Villarreal 2021). In April 2009, the WHO Director-General convened an Emergency Committee under the IHR (2005), and upon the advice of the Committee, declared a PHEIC for the first time.[7] Alongside this PHEIC declaration, the Director-General issued temporary recommendations to ensure that states would not impose any unnecessary restrictions on international travel or trade. Yet, these WHO actions under the IHR (2005) were subject to criticism, with some perceiving a WHO "overreaction" to what was otherwise a "mild" disease. In the aftermath of the H1N1 Influenza pandemic, WHO created an IHR Review Committee to assess the response. This review found that several aspects of the IHR (2005) functioned well—including the notification process, the Emergency Committee, and the PHEIC declaration—while identifying areas for improvement, including state disregard of WHO recommendations on travel and trade restrictions (Katz 2009). In looking ahead, the zoonotic origins of the 2009 H1N1 Influenza pandemic illustrated the need to bring together human, animal, and environmental health systems under a One Health approach (Phelan and Gostin 2017), as discussed in greater detail in Chapter 9, and this inattention to animal-human transmission would arise repeatedly amid a subsequent series of rapidly re-emerging threats.

Given this continuing inattention, WHO and national authorities wavered in the 2014–2016 Ebola crisis in West Africa. With animal-human transmission again sparking an outbreak, suboptimal national capacities, flawed information sharing, and an overall slow response by the international community facilitated the spread of Ebola across several countries, mainly Guinea, Liberia and Sierra Leone (Kamradt-Scott 2016).

Case Study: Ebola in Town

"Ebola in town" is the powerful refrain from one of many songs that brought attention to the 2014–2016 Ebola crisis that devastated West Africa. Despite animal-human transmission of Ebolavirus in December 2013, suboptimal national technical capacities allowed for the undetected spread of the virus. It was several months after the first cases—following an investigation of an unknown illness by the Guinean Ministry of Health, Médecins Sans Frontières

---

[7] As the disease spread, WHO Director-General Chan declared the event to be a "pandemic" in June 2009, looking outside the IHR to recognize the geographical spread of a disease across multiple regions.

INFECTIOUS DISEASE   161

("MSF"), and WHO personnel of an unknown illness—that Guinea notified WHO in March 2014 of an Ebola outbreak, which by then had already spread to Liberia and Sierra Leone. Following a delayed Emergency Committee assembly and eventual PHEIC declaration in August 2014, WHO saw repeated disregard of IHR recommendations by national governments. Without vocal WHO leadership, the Ebola response further entrenched the securitization of global health—at the expense of human rights. As with H1N1, states enacted trade and travel restrictions without reference to scientific evidence, failing to report these discretionary measures to WHO. The collapse of already fragile health systems in the three most affected countries triggered a risk of civil unrest, regional destabilization, and severe deterioration of national institutions. Looking outside WHO in responding to this security risk, the UN Security Council issued a September 2014 resolution to declare the Ebola outbreak a threat to international peace and security, asserting the link between infectious disease and international peace and security. Amid WHO's continuing inaction, the UN Secretary General mandated the creation of a separate UN Mission for Ebola Emergency Response (UNMEER), tasked with coordination of the humanitarian response. Such a response further entrenched the securitization of global health – at the expense of human rights.

Examining these limitations in the West African Ebola crisis, a WHO Review Committee was again commissioned to develop a post-PHEIC report, alongside a number of independent panels. They undertook to evaluate, review, and learn from the experience through understanding weaknesses in the Ebola response, including a lack of national capacities, lack of transparency, and lack of accountability (Gostin and Katz 2016). The identified limitations of the Ebola response would spur WHO to establish the Joint External Evaluation (JEE), a voluntary monitoring and evaluation tool to help states measure their progress toward optimal preparedness—providing an assessment process to gauge, track, and incentivize core capacities to prevent and respond to health threats. Beyond these WHO reforms, the limitations of the IHR in Ebola responses would give rise to new governance institutions outside WHO to support global health security.

D. Securitizing Health Beyond WHO: The Global Health Security Agenda

With other international and regional partnerships seeking a role in addressing gaps in public health emergency responses, the Global Health Security Agenda

(GHSA) has arisen as a multi-stakeholder partnership to counter novel and re-emerging diseases threats. Launched in 2014 to help strengthen countries' core health system capacities, the GHSA offers action steps, targets, and benchmarks to encourage national preparedness and IHR compliance—with implications for the development of law reforms to ensure legal preparedness (Meier et al. 2017). The GHSA Actions Package Working Groups bring together technical experts with policymakers to meet specific benchmarks to prevent, detect, and respond to public health threats.

Reflecting the importance of law reforms to global health security (in parallel with the "policy and legislation" pillar of IHR (2005)), the GHSA has launched a Legal Preparedness Action Package to support foundational legal knowledge, skills, and assets for public health emergency preparedness and response, seeking to "develop needed guidance and capacity building tools to support countries in achieving greater legal preparedness" (Ayala et al. 2022, 201). Where this focus on legal preparedness extends a focus on public health challenges as "existential threats to national and international security," the securitization of the infectious disease response continues to override other crucial areas of global health (Meier, Evans and Phelan 2020, 245). This securitization of global health law, creating an overreliance on the logic of security to tackle disease outbreaks, has resulted in counterproductive measures that fail to achieve health objectives, creating a dynamic that has tested the limits of global health law amid the COVID-19 pandemic.

III. COVID-19 and the Pandemics of Tomorrow: Stretching Global Health Law beyond Its Limits

Like no other health event before, the COVID-19 pandemic became a stress test for WHO governance and global health law. Affecting every person in the world, the pandemic led to a multitude of public health measures taken by states in violation of IHR obligations and disregarding WHO recommendations, leading to unprecedented restrictions on all aspects of life. These cataclysmic challenges exposed continuing gaps in global health law and pressing needs for legal reforms (Meier, Habibi, and Gostin 2022). Alongside the development of a novel convention or agreement on pandemic prevention, preparedness and response—the "pandemic treaty" introduced in Chapter 5—the World Health Assembly is planning targeted amendments to strengthen the IHR in facing future infectious disease threats, with the WHO Secretariat already taking a new approach to the global spread of mpox. With these reforms reshaping the global health landscape, the combination of the pandemic accord and an amended IHR will be crucial to future efforts to address infectious disease under global health law.

A. COVID-19: An Unprecedented Global Challenge to Global Health Governance

The sweeping impact of COVID-19 exposed the core limitations of both the biomedical and securitized approaches to pandemic preparedness and response enshrined in IHR (2005). Despite reforms to support prompt notification under the IHR (2005), reports on the emergence of this new coronavirus threat were again delayed, with the insufficient sharing of information hampering the PHEIC declaration. Following the declaration, states imposed unprecedented restrictions on international travel and trade—purportedly to prevent the cross-border spread of disease (Habibi et al. 2020). Human rights standards, as introduced in chapter 4, were trampled in the pandemic response, with states undertaking draconian rights limitations that were not always necessary (backed by scientific evidence), proportionate (to the threat involved), or non-arbitrary (non-discriminatory) (Sekalala et al. 2020). An initial scarcity in available vaccines against COVID-19 led to the rise of "vaccine nationalism," where high-income states stockpiled doses thereof without regard for lower-income countries, with disparate vaccination rates increasing health inequity and impeding global solidarity (Phelan et al. 2020).

In seeking to bring nations together in a common response, the World Health Assembly issued a landmark resolution on COVID-19 in May 2020, which called for respect of human rights and fundamental freedoms, renewed solidarity, and external reviews on the handling of the COVID-19 pandemic—by both WHO and its Member States (WHO 2020). These reviews questioned the one-week delay by the WHO Director-General in declaring a PHEIC, examined state disregard for WHO's initial recommendation not to impose any travel and trade restrictions, and scrutinized early deference toward the Chinese government.[8] These concerns highlight the difficult diplomatic challenges against the backdrop of the pandemic response through WHO governance.

Considering the magnitude of the COVID-19 pandemic and its global implications, a number of multilateral institutions beyond WHO issued their own resolutions, as seen in Table 6.1 through the resolutions of three UN

---

[8] Debates on the prompt and transparent notification by the Chinese government of the first detected outbreak of SARS-CoV-2 in Wuhan are still ongoing.

Table 6.1 Resolutions from Key UN Bodies Focused on COVID-19 (Villarreal and Tonti)

Institution	Resolution(s)	Content
UN General Assembly	Global solidarity to fight the coronavirus disease 2019 (COVID-19) (April 2, 2020)	Affirmed the central role the UN in the global response to the COVID-19 pandemic and called for intensified international cooperation to "contain, mitigate and defeat the pandemic . . . by exchanging information, scientific knowledge and best practices," including through guidelines developed by WHO.
	International cooperation to ensure global access to medicines, vaccines and medical equipment to face COVID-19 (April 21, 2020)	Reaffirmed the fundamental role of the UN and the leadership of WHO in coordinating the global response to the spread of COVID-19 and called upon states to take steps to prevent all stockpiling and hindering access to safe, effective, and affordable essential medicines, vaccines, personal protective equipment, and medical equipment required to effectively face COVID-19.
UN Security Council	Resolution 2532 (2020) (July 1, 2020)	Considered the COVID-19 pandemic as likely to endanger the maintenance of international peace and security and demanded a "general and immediate cessation of hostilities" across all states, calling for a 90-day ceasefire for enabling the delivery of humanitarian assistance.
UN Human Rights Council	Ensuring equitable, affordable, timely and universal access for all countries to vaccines in response to the coronavirus disease (COVID-19) pandemic (March 23, 2021) and Ensuring equitable, affordable, timely and universal access for all countries to vaccines in response to the coronavirus disease (COVID-19) pandemic (April 1, 2022)	Both resolutions called upon states and other stakeholders to take measures to guarantee "fair, transparent, equitable, efficient, universal and timely access and distribution of safe, quality, efficacious, effective, accessible, and affordable COVID-19 vaccines" through international cooperation.
	Civil society space: COVID-19: The road to recovery and the essential role of civil society (July 12, 2021)	Affirmed the need for all stakeholders to be included in responses to the COVID-19 pandemic: first, by providing access to timely and accurate information online and offline; and second, by facilitating contributions by civil society as well as the private sector to devising pandemic responses.

bodies: the General Assembly, the Security Council, and the Human Rights Council.

Given the widespread havoc wreaked by COVID-19 and the challenges faced by WHO, questions arose about whether existing rules under the IHR (2005) are fit for their purpose (Burci 2020), with the pandemic catalyzing political momentum for global health law reforms in ways not seen since the 2002–2003 SARS crisis. While the IHR Review Committee initially recommended against amending the IHR (WHO 2021), the U.S. government tabled a proposal in January 2022 to amend select IHR (2005) provisions. The World Health Assembly opened an IHR amendment process in May 2022, with reform proposals seeking to address its limitations during the COVID-19 pandemic and over past emergencies through:

- The reformulation of PHEICs to include a middle-level alert declaration, shifting from the current binary emergency/non-emergency declaration, which may not reflect the variable nature of emergencies or the diversity of disease-related events.
- The removal of procedural requirements to consult authorities from affected countries before declaring an emergency, as this may lead to undue delays in acute situations.
- The creation of a new subsidiary body within WHO to scrutinize the extent to which states comply with their obligations under the IHR (2005), particularly to notify WHO concerning the presence of events that may constitute an emergency and to justify the adoption of restrictions on international travel and trade that go beyond WHO recommendations.

Beyond these substantive issues, which may shift as negotiations advance, the procedural aspects of these reforms will change the application of global health law. Unlike the pandemic accord proposals introduced in Chapter 5, WHO regulations do not require ratification by Member States before entering into force. These amendments to the IHR (2005) will become automatically binding for WHO Member States that have not specifically rejected them within twelve months.

As reviewed initially in Chapter 2, these reforms are adopted under different authorities under the WHO Constitution. The implementation of regulations will prove more straightforward than a convention, accord, or treaty, and these procedural differences between the IHR (2005) and the pandemic accord will lead to different substantive issues being addressed in each instrument. Meanwhile, on 5 May 2023, the WHO Director-General declared that the spread of COVID-19 was no longer a PHEIC, after more than three years and an estimated twenty million deaths since the emergency declaration was first issued. Moreover, even amid the COVID-19 pandemic, WHO has continued to face new public health emergencies, leading to new interpretations in the exercise of legal authorities provided under the IHR (2005).

B. Monkeypox (mpox) Enters the Scene

With the COVID-19 pandemic still ongoing, the mpox virus,[9] a re-emerging threat previously present in the African region, acquired a cross-border dimension affecting dozens of countries. Although mpox mortality rates have remained low, particularly in comparison to those of COVID-19, the disease can lead to severe symptoms. (The long-term health consequences of this zoonotic disease are unknown.) This cross-border 2022 outbreak initially affected mostly, but not exclusively, men, particularly men who have sex with men (MSM). Given the similarities in outbreak clusters in MSM communities between mpox and HIV/AIDS, advocates rapidly campaigned against stigmatization and discrimination in approaches to treatment, community education, and public messaging. The surge of mpox posed considerable shifts in WHO's practice of declaring a PHEIC under the IHR (2005).

Case Study: Monkeypox and Governance Shifts in WHO Emergency Decision-Making

The WHO Director-General convened an Emergency Committee in June 2022 to address the rapidly evolving threat of mpox. Yet, despite the presence of the mpox virus in dozens of countries from multiple regions, the Emergency Committee advised against a PHEIC declaration. The WHO Director-General initially paid heed to this advice, but as the situation worsened in the ensuing weeks, the Emergency Committee was once again convened in July 2022 to reassess the situation. This second meeting yielded divided opinions, leading to a deadlock among experts, where the majority of Emergency Committee members (9) advised against declaring a PHEIC, with a sizable minority (6) in favor. Despite the majority opinion against a PHEIC declaration, and in a break with the practice of deferring to Emergency Committee's majority opinion, the WHO Director-General declared the multi-country spread of mpox to be a PHEIC. Where the event was deemed to fulfill the criteria of a PHEIC under IHR (2005), the Director-General issued the PHEIC declaration as a basis to promptly adopt response measures before the event evolved and became even more widespread.

In light of the diversity of approaches considered when declaring the multi-country spread of mpox a PHEIC, this event represents a substantive change

---

[9] In November 2022, WHO began using the term "mpox" to denote this disease, shifting to terminology that would be less stigmatizing and would recognize the global risk.

in WHO governance. Unlike past decision-making processes related to the input provided by Emergency Committee, the arguments for and against declaring a PHEIC were published in detailed fashion. The Emergency Committee no longer speaks in "one voice" to the public, with this new practice offering an enhanced transparency of deliberations. These changing practices in facing public health emergencies will require an alignment across global health law reforms to strengthen global health governance. Although the WHO Director-General declared on 11 May 2023 that the spread of mpox was no longer a PHEIC, challenges remain for more precisely gauging both its epidemiology and the best strategies to counter the unduly discrimination of at-risk groups, such as MSM.

C. Aligning the IHR (2005) and Pandemic Accord to Strengthen Global Health Governance

Improving the system of rules-based governance over infectious disease control requires clearer insights on how global health law has faltered in past responses. In facing COVID-19, the combination of a lack of transparency by the Chinese government and the initial indifference of multiple states led to a quickly unraveling global spread of the disease (IPPPR 2021). Despite these failures, calls for reforming existing instruments were not universal, with some reports noting the cumbersome nature of negotiations and risks of "backsliding" in global health law (WHO 2021). The process for negotiating and approving a pandemic treaty has a higher number of pitfalls—given the scope of the agreement, the disagreements among states, and the higher ratification threshold—and these reforms will be further complicated by the need to align pandemic treaty negotiations with IHR amendments (Solomon 2022).

Potential overlaps between the IHR (2005) and a new pandemic accord have been identified, reflecting the intertwined nature of both instruments under the global health security framework. For instance, enhanced data-sharing through transparency requirements could fall within the aegis of both legal instruments. The need to provide incentives to states to be more forthcoming when notifying WHO—and, by extension, the international community—of events within their territories can be addressed through either new obligations or amendments to existing ones. Similarly, envisaging stronger commitments to offer financial support for countries reporting disease outbreaks could be undertaken through the consolidation of minimum core disease surveillance and response capacities under the IHR or in future obligations within a convention on pandemic prevention, preparedness, and response.

In aligning these global health law reforms, one of the long-standing challenges holding back WHO remains its budget. The organization has been subjected to a decades-long dependency on voluntary "extrabudgetary" commitments instead of assessed contributions by Member States and other non-state donors. In the face of these financial challenges, as introduced in Chapter 5, the World Health Assembly approved a 2022 resolution adopting the recommendations from a Working Group on Sustainable Financing, committing to a gradual increase in the percentage of assessed contributions in the overall budget. These steps place the organization in a better position to support its programs for communicable disease threats with sustainability and could enhance its capacity to monitor the implementation of obligations within both the IHR (2005) and a pandemic accord (Meier, Habibi, and Gostin 2022).

Conclusion

Some events throughout the world are so sweeping and so universal that they unite states across borders, cultures, and interests in shaping a unified response. Contrary to the 20th century optimism that pharmaceutical breakthroughs would herald the "end of disease," the plight posed to the world by infectious disease is far from an afterthought. A globalizing world has brought forth a continuing stream of disease threats in the 21st century, and this new "age of pandemics" will necessitate strengthening global health law. Despite the proliferation of medical and public health research on the nature of COVID-19 and other communicable diseases, and on the effectiveness of specific interventions against them, a final verdict on which policy lessons ought to be learned from these past and ongoing outbreaks is still due. Considering that the eradication of communicable diseases in the immediate future is unlikely, their continuous spread across the globe raises questions about whether and how global health law can steer states in their responses against continuing pandemic threats.

As in the period following the SARS crisis in 2002–2003, the global community is now experiencing a moment in which interest and momentum are aligned to reshape the tools of pandemic preparedness and response. Global health law reforms amid the COVID-19 pandemic are underway to facilitate global solidarity in preparing for future pandemic threats. By entrenching new international law principles and obligations, law reforms can not only contribute to avoiding a repetition of the failures of global health governance in past and present disease outbreaks but also can better protect against future pandemic threats that may need quite different medical and public health responses. At the core of these reforms, WHO must remain a central organization in the development of global health law, and it will be necessary to ensure its active participation in decision-making and legal reforms within other institutions directly involved in pandemic preparedness and response.

It remains to be seen whether and how existing and future international law reforms will be framed and interpreted to foster enhanced solidarity within and among countries in infectious disease control. Given the momentum triggered by the COVID-19 pandemic, and in line with the ongoing parallel reform processes, the field of global health law on communicable disease control will continue to evolve in the years to come, but the trajectory remains uncertain. In these and other global health governance developments, a closer engagement by all stakeholders of the international community, including states and non-state actors, is the best means to ensure justice in global health. If the goal is to sway decision-making in the face of future communicable disease threats, it will be necessary to steer the diplomatic negotiations toward the international community's collective response in order to prevent, detect, and respond to pandemic threats on the basis of global equity and solidarity. Today's students, who bear witness to the pandemic events of their time and the evolution of modern instruments, will be well positioned to shape the trajectory of tomorrow's response to communicable disease threats.

Questions for Consideration

1. How did the rise of evolving understanding of the spread of infectious disease lead to the development of international law? What was the added value of a rules-based international order for infectious disease preparedness and response?
2. What was unique about lawmaking authorities under WHO governance? Why were these authorities thought to be crucial in responding to infectious disease under the IHR?
3. How did biomedical optimism shape WHO's early approaches to disease eradication? Why did WHO's disease eradication programs largely fail, and why did the Smallpox Eradication Programme succeed?
4. Why did traditional public health approaches to quarantine, isolation, and reporting face limitations in the early years of the HIV/AIDS response? How did these public health limitations shift global health governance to recognize the importance of human rights in global health?
5. How did infectious disease come to be seen as a threat to "global health security"? Why did the SARS response highlight the need to revise the IHR—and create political momentum for IHR revisions?

6. How does the expanded reach and scope of the IHR (2005) reflect the expansion of infectious disease threats in the 21st century? How does the IHR (2005) seek to balance public health efforts to prevent the spread of disease while preventing excessive restrictions on individual travel, international trade, and human rights?
7. Which continuing limitations of the IHR (2005) have been highlighted by subsequent PHEICs? Why did the larger UN system seek to respond to the 2014–2016 Ebola epidemic in West Africa—rather than looking to WHO leadership? How do other global health security initiatives beyond WHO, such as the GHSA, both support and hinder coordinated pandemic preparedness and response?
8. What new limitations of global health law were exposed by the COVID-19 response? How can amendments to the IHR (2005) strengthen WHO's legal authorities to address infectious disease?
9. How has the WHO altered its approach to implementing the IHR in facing mpox (monkeypox)?
10. How can ongoing reforms to develop a pandemic accord support obligations under the IHR (2005)? What steps must WHO Member States take to align their efforts across global health law reforms?

Acknowledgments

The authors would like to extend a heartfelt thanks to Benjamin Mason Meier for extensive editorial guidance and conscientious review of multiple drafts of this chapter, Sonam Shah for research and direct contributions to the text, and Rishabh Sud for additional editorial work. Gratitude is also owed to Lawrence Gostin for his tireless leadership and oversight of the publication process.

References

Amon, Joseph J. and Eric Friedman. 2020. "Human Rights Advocacy in Global Health." In *Foundations of Global Health and Human Rights*, edited by Lawrence O. Gostin and Benjamin Mason Meier, 133–153. New York: Oxford University Press

Ayala, Ana, Adam Brush, Shuen Chai, Jose Fernandez, Katherine Ginsbach, Katie Gottschalk, Sam Halabi et al. 2022. "Advancing Legal Preparedness through the Global Health Security Agenda." *Journal of Law, Medicine & Ethics* 50(1): 200–203.

Burci, Gian Luca. 2020. "The Legal Response to Pandemics." *Journal of International Humanitarian Legal Studies* 11(2): 204–217.

Burci, Gian Luca and Stefania Negri. 2021. "Governing the Global Fight against Pandemics: The WHO, the International Health Regulations, and the Fragmentation

of International Law." *New York University Journal of International Law and Politics* 53(2): 501–522.
Cinà, Margherita, Steven J. Hoffman, Gian Luca Burci, and Thana Cristina de Campos 2022. "The Stellenbosch Consensus on the International Legal Obligation to Collaborate and Assist in Addressing Pandemics: Clarifying Article 44 of the International Health Regulations." *International Organizations Law Review* 19: 158–187.
Cliff, Andrew D. and Peter Haggett. 1998. "Global Trends in Communicable Disease Control." In *Communicable Disease. Epidemiology and Control*, edited by Noah Norman and Mary O'Mahony. Chichester: John Wiley & Sons.
Condon, Bradly and Tapen Sinha. 2008. *Global Lessons from the AIDS Pandemic: Economic, Financial, Legal and Political Implications*. Heidelberg: Springer.
Cueto, Marcos, Theodore M. Brown, and Elizabeth Fee. 2019. *The World Health Organization: A History*. Cambridge: Cambridge University Press.
Daugirdas, Kristina and Gian Luca Burci. 2019. "Financing the World Health Organization. What Lessons for Multilateralism?" *International Organizations Law Review* 16(2): 299–338.
Dorolle, Pierre. 1968. "Old Plagues in the Jet Age. International Aspects of Present and Future Control of Communicable Disease." *WHO Chronicle* 23: 103–111.
Fidler, David. 1999. *International Law and Infectious Diseases*. Oxford: Oxford University Press.
Fidler, David. 2004. *SARS, Governance and the Globalization of Disease*. Heidelberg: Springer.
Fidler, David. 2005. "From International Sanitary Conventions to Global Health Security: The New International Health Regulations." *Chinese Journal of International Law* 4(2): 325–392.
Fidler, David P. and Lawrence O. Gostin. 2006. "The New International Health Regulations: An Historic Development for International Law and Public Health." *Journal of Law, Medicine & Ethics* 34(1): 85–94.
Forman, Lisa, Sharifah Sekalala, and Benjamin Mason Meier. 2022. "The World Health Organization, International Health Regulations and Human Rights Law." *International Organizations Law Review* 19(1): 37–62.
Gostin, Lawrence O. 2014. *Global Health Law*. Cambridge: Harvard University Press.
Gostin, Lawrence O., and Rebecca Katz. 2016. "The International Health Regulations: The Governing Framework for Global Health Security." *The Milbank Quarterly* 94(2): 264–313.
Habibi, Roojin, Gian Luca Burci, Thana C. de Campos, Danwood Chirwa, Margherita Cinà, Stéphanie Dagron, Mark Eccleston-Turner et al. 2020. "Do Not Violate the International Health Regulations during the COVID-19 Outbreak." *Lancet* 395(10225): 664–666.
Habibi, Roojin, Steven J. Hoffman, Gian Luca Burci, Thana Cristina De Campos, Danwood Chirwa, Margherita Cinà, Stéphanie Dagron, et al. 2020. "The Stellenbosch Consensus on Legal National Responses to Public Health Risks: Clarifying Article 43 of the International Health Regulations." *International Organizations Law Review* 19 (1): 90–157.
Halabi, Sam F., Lawrence O. Gostin, and Jeffrey S. Crowley. 2016. *Global Management of Infectious Disease after Ebola*. Oxford: Oxford University Press.
Heath, J. Benton. 2016. "Global Emergency Power in the Age of Ebola." *Harvard International Law Journal* 57: 1–47.
Hoffman, Steven. 2010. "The Evolution, Etiology and Eventualities of the Global Health Security Regime." *Health Policy and Planning* 25: 510–522.

IPPPR (Independent Panel on Pandemic Preparedness and Response). 2021. *COVID-19: Make it the Last Pandemic.*
Kamradt-Scott, Adam. 2015. *Managing Global Health Security. The World Health Organization and Disease Outbreak Control.* Basingstoke: Palgrave MacMillan.
Kamradt-Scott, Adam. 2016. "WHO's to Blame? The World Health Organization and the 2014 Ebola Outbreak in West Africa." *Third World Quarterly* 37(3): 401–418.
Katz, Rebecca. 2009. "Use of Revised International Health Regulations during Influenza A (H1N1) Epidemic, 2009." *Emerging Infectious Diseases* 15(8): 1165.
Kreuder-Sonnen, Christian. 2019. *Emergency Powers of International Organizations. Between Normalization and Containment.* Oxford: Oxford University Press.
Lee, Kelley. 2009. *The World Health Organization.* London: Routledge.
Meier, Benjamin Mason, Kara Tureski, Emily Bockh, Derek Carr, Ana Ayala, Anna Roberts, Lindsay Cloud et al. 2017. "Examining National Public Health Law to Realize the Global Health Security Agenda." *Medical Law Review* 25(2): 240–269.
Meier, Benjamin Mason, Dabney P. Evans, and Alexandra Phelan. 2020. "Rights-Based Approaches to Preventing, Detecting, and Responding to Infectious Disease." In *Infectious Diseases in the New Millennium,* by Mark Eccleston-Turner and Iain Brassington, 217–253. Cham: Springer.
Meier, Benjamin Mason, Roojin Habibi, and Lawrence O. Gostin. 2022. "A Global Health Law Trilogy: Transformational Reforms to Strengthen Pandemic Prevention, Preparedness, and Response." *Journal of Law, Medicine & Ethics* 50(3): 625–627.
Nygren-Krug, Helena. 2018. "The Joint United Nations Programme on HIV/AIDS: With Communities for Human Rights." In *Human Rights in Global Health. Rights-Based Governance for a Globalizing World,* 281–299. Oxford: Oxford University Press.
Omran, Abdel. 1971. "The Epidemiologic Transition. A Theory of the Epidemiology of Population Change." *The Milbank Memorial Fund Quarterly* 49(4): 509–538.
Ottersen, Trygve, Steven J. Hoffman, and Gaëlle Groux. 2016. "Ebola Again Shows the International Health Regulations Are Broken: What Can Be Done Differently to Prepare for the Next Epidemic?" *American Journal of Law & Medicine* 42(2): 356–392.
Phelan, Alexandra and Lawrence Gostin. 2017. "Law as a Fixture between the One Health Interfaces of Emerging Diseases." *Transactions of the Royal Society of Tropical Medicine & Hygiene* 111(6): 241–243.
Phelan, Alexandra, Mark Eccleston-Turner, Michelle Rourke, Allan Maleche, and Chenguang Wang. 2020. "Legal Agreements: Barriers and Enablers to Global Equitable COVID-19 Vaccine Access." *Lancet* 396(10254): 800–802.
Roelsgaard, E. 1974. "Health Regulations and International Travel." *WHO Chronicle* 28(6): 265–268.
Sekalala, Sharifah and John Harrington. 2020. "Communicable Diseases, Health Security, and Human Rights. From AIDS to Ebola." In *Foundations of Global Health & Human Rights,* edited by Lawrence O. Gostin and Benjamin Mason Meier, 221–242. New York: Oxford University Press.
Sekalala, Sharifah, Lisa Forman, Roojin Habibi, and Benjamin Mason Meieer. 2020. "Health and Human Rights Are Inextricably Linked in the COVID-19 Response." *BMJ Global Health* 5(9): e003359.
Solomon, Steven. 2022. "Challenges and Prospects for the Intergovernmental Negotiations to Develop a New Instrument on Pandemic Prevention, Preparedness and Response." *Journal of Law, Medicine & Ethics.* 50(4): 860–863.

Taylor, Allyn. 1997. "Controlling the Global Spread of Infectious Diseases: Towards a Reinforced Role for the International Health Regulations." *Houston Law Review* 33: 1327–1362.

Villarreal, Pedro, A. 2021. "Pandemic: Building a Legal Concept for the Future." *Washington University Global Studies Law Review* 20: 611–626.

Villarreal, Pedro A., Roojin Habibi, and Allyn Taylor. 2022. "Strengthening the Monitoring of States' Compliance with the International Health Regulations." *International Organizations Law Review* 19(1): 215–240.

WHO (World Health Organization). 1946. "Constitution of the World Health Organization."

WHO. 2005. "Revision of the International Health Regulations." WHA58.3.

WHO. 2020. *COVID-19 Response*. Resolution WHA 73.1. May 19.

WHO. 2021. *Report of the Review Committee on the Functioning of the International Health Regulations (2005) during the COVID-19 Response*. April 30. A74/9 Add.1.

Zacher, Mark. 1999. "Global Epidemiological Surveillance. International Cooperation to Monitor Infectious Diseases." In *Global Public Goods: International Cooperation in the 21st Century*, edited by Inge Kaul, Isabelle Gruberg, and Marc Stern. 266–283. New York: Oxford University Press.

7

Non-Communicable Disease

Regulating Commercial Determinants Underlying Health

Roger Magnusson and Lawrence O. Gostin

Introduction

Chronic, non-communicable diseases (NCDs) are the dominant killers of our time, responsible for around 41 million deaths each year, including 19 million people who die before the age of 70 years, mostly in low- and middle-income countries. Few people, anywhere in the world, will remain unaffected during their lifetimes by the leading NCDs: cardiovascular diseases, cancer, chronic respiratory diseases, and diabetes. In framing the risk factors underlying NCDs, the World Health Organization (WHO) has looked to a "4 × 4" framework, which emphasizes these four major NCDs, and seeks to address their shared risk factors: tobacco use, alcohol use, unhealthy diets, and physical inactivity. More recently, the scope of NCDs has widened to encompass mental health and environmental pollution. Yet despite the rising profile of NCDs in global health governance, global progress on NCDs has stagnated, largely due to a lack of resources and the slow rate of progress in implementing effective policy measures.

The social transmissibility of NCDs through their risk factors is an important focus of global health law. The global expansion of NCD risk factors is not the result of individual choices made in isolation but the product of commercial actions in a globalizing world. Globalization has led to trade liberalization, opening up new markets in low- and middle-income countries to commercial determinants of health. These shared risk factors direct attention to the law's role in controlling the commercial determinants of NCDs—regulating industries with vested interests in selling tobacco, alcohol, unhealthy foods, and sugary drinks. With these industries operating at a global level and contributing to the spread of NCDs, a focus on transmission through social environments directs policy attention to unequal patterns of NCDs and their risk factors, within and between countries. The social transmissibility of risk factors across populations explains why NCDs can be described as a pandemic that calls for international coordination through global health law.

This chapter examines how NCDs are conceptualized and governed at the global level, initially by WHO but increasingly through a broader United Nations (UN) response to the global spread of unhealthy products. Part I identifies the commercial determinants driving the global shift from communicable to non-communicable diseases, with actors recognizing these globalized NCD risk factors as an emerging priority in global health. Part II describes the mosaic of legal and policy instruments that comprise the global governance of NCDs: legally binding instruments regulating tobacco as well as soft law instruments that seek to address other underlying determinants of NCDs. Building on WHO leadership in developing global norms on NCDs, global governance has broadened to engage a larger set of UN agencies, accelerating the NCD agenda while presenting challenges in coordinating the global health landscape. Part III analyzes constraints and opportunities in the global governance of NCDs, examining new efforts under international trade law and international human rights law and rising threats posed by obesity, vaping, and alcohol. This chapter concludes that innovative global health law reforms will be needed across sectors to address commercial determinants of NCDs.

I. Rise of NCDs in a Globalizing World

The prevalence of NCDs has increased rapidly in a globalizing world—shifting the global disease burden from infectious diseases to NCDs. The globalization of commercial determinants of health, especially tobacco and alcohol use and unhealthy foods and drinks, have provided opportunities for prevention and mitigation through global health law and policy, initially under WHO but expanding across the global governance landscape.

A. Transition from Infectious Diseases to NCDs

NCDs are not new, but a predictable consequence of the sharp declines in child mortality and the global expansion of commercial determinants of health. By the 1990s, NCDs had already emerged as leading causes of death in both developed and developing regions (Murray and Lopez 1994). Yet the processes underlying this "epidemiological transition"—from communicable to non-communicable disease threats—were dynamic and complex. Declines in communicable, maternal, and young child diseases led to increasingly older populations—who bear the disproportionate burden of chronic diseases. Beyond these demographic shifts, NCDs were also influenced by underlying NCD risk factors, access to screening and treatment services, and a broad range of environmental and social variables.

With the rise of NCDs linked to poverty, NCDs are increasingly clustered in populations with lower levels of income and/or education, and indeed, the vast majority of premature NCD deaths occur in low- and middle-income countries (Niessen et al. 2018). Correspondingly, NCDs further entrench poverty, particularly in countries where out-of-pocket healthcare costs are substantial.[1] The speed of the transition from communicable to non-communicable diseases has left low- and middle-income countries struggling to adapt their health systems to chronic conditions requiring management over a significant period of time. With communicable diseases still an ongoing threat, many low-income countries now face a "double burden of disease," with the burden of disease from NCDs almost equivalent to that from communicable, maternal, and young child diseases (Gouda et al. 2019).

Globalization has accelerated the rise of NCD risk factors in countries throughout the world, drawing attention to the role of global markets and social environments in the transmission of NCD risks. The growth of the internet and mobile telecommunications, coinciding with the end of the Cold War, accelerated the global dispersion of ideas, brands, and lifestyle aspirations. At the same time, trade and investment liberalization policies in the neoliberal era, as first introduced in Chapter 3, boosted foreign direct investment, imports, and advertising—expanding global access to commercial products. Consumer preferences and patterns changed accordingly, with new consumption patterns threatening public health. The liberalization of trade and globalization of consumption have, for example, contributed to the destruction of traditional food cultures, replacing them with cheap and highly processed imports that are higher in fat, salt, and sugar (Baker, Kaye, and Walls 2014). Health throughout the life course has been threatened by the consequences of tobacco and alcohol use; sugary drinks; and foods high in fat, salt, and sugar, alongside sedentary lifestyles (Moodie et al. 2021).

Yet NCDs long remained neglected on the global health agenda. NCDs first gained traction in global health statistics through the "Global Burden of Disease Study," which formed the basis for the "World Development Report 1993" (World Bank 1993). Placing NCDs on the global governance agenda, this early World Bank report projected a terrifying expansion of tobacco-related deaths in

---

[1] NCDs have an impoverishing effect on households as risk factors for NCDs, including tobacco and alcohol, may consume a substantial proportion of household income, especially in poorer households. Further, people with NCDs may be less able or unable to work, which may push others, including children, into caring roles, interrupting schooling and perpetuating the poverty cycle. In countries that lack universal health coverage, treatment costs may also have a substantial direct and ongoing impact on household finances (UNDP 2015).

the 21st century, providing the impetus for a subsequent 1999 collaborative report between the World Bank and WHO, "Curbing the Epidemic." In uncovering the economic aspects of tobacco use, and making the economic case for tobacco taxation, this partnership helped to elevate tobacco control as a priority for WHO leadership and provided an opening to respond to rising NCD risk factors in WHO governance.

B. WHO Recognizes the Threat

By the turn of the 21st century, NCDs were causing around 60% of global deaths, with almost half caused by the four leading NCDs—cardiovascular disease, cancer, chronic respiratory disease, and diabetes (Beaglehole and Yach 2003). The foundation for WHO's early work to address this rising threat was a short, understated policy: the 2000 Global Strategy for the Prevention and Control of Noncommunicable Diseases. Noting that the four leading NCDs shared preventable risk factors—tobacco use, unhealthy diet, and physical inactivity—the Global Strategy called for an integrated approach to risk factor reduction, targeting both high-risk individuals and levels of excess risk across the population. The World Health Assembly resolution adopting the Global Strategy added the rising impact of alcohol and urged WHO member states to exercise their regulatory functions to combat NCDs and their risk factors (World Health Assembly 2000). This "4 X 4" framework, which evolved from earlier WHO strategies to control cardiovascular disease and stroke in high-income countries (Schwartz, Shaffer, and Bukhman 2021), provided the conceptual framework for WHO's response to NCDs.

In addressing NCD risk factors, WHO initially prioritized tobacco control. Tobacco use was—and remains—the leading cause of preventable death worldwide. Yet in a globalizing world—beset by cross-border advertising, illicit trade, and expanding markets—tobacco had become increasingly difficult for nations to regulate in isolation. By the mid-1990s, there was growing WHO interest in the possibility of codifying a binding convention to address smoking, creating WHO's first international treaty. Although the notion of a treaty was initially disparaged as "ambitious to a fault," the World Health Assembly in 1996 authorized the WHO Director-General to begin negotiations to develop a Framework Convention on Tobacco Control (FCTC) (Roemer, Taylor, and Lariviere 2005). After taking office in 1998, WHO Director-General Gro Harlem Brundtland made tobacco control a top priority. WHO established the Tobacco Free Initiative as a special cabinet project with the mandate to stimulate global support for evidence-based tobacco control policies (WHO 2009). Expanding negotiations among WHO Member States recognized that tobacco use was socially determined and globally promoted: an international problem that required an international response. With strong support from tobacco control NGOs throughout the world, the World Health Assembly adopted the FCTC in 2003, laying the foundation for future international legal efforts to stem the supply of and demand for tobacco.

The FCTC's stated aim is to "protect present and future generations from the devastating health, social, environmental and economic consequences of tobacco consumption and exposure to tobacco smoke...." Its "general obligations" detail broad actions to advance this aim, including multisectoral national tobacco control strategies, while acknowledging the importance of interstate cooperation. Beyond these general obligations, the FCTC details specific minimum measures, as detailed in Table 7.1, to reduce both the supply of and demand for tobacco products. While stopping short of a total ban on tobacco, the FCTC seeks to reduce tobacco supply by requiring states to eliminate illicit trade in

Table 7.1 FCTC Provisions (Magnusson and Gostin)

Objective and Guiding Principles

- To protect present and future generations from the devastating health, social, environmental and economic consequences of tobacco consumption and exposure to tobacco smoke
- All persons informed of the health consequences, addictive nature, and mortal threat posed by tobacco and protected from exposure to tobacco smoke
- Strong political commitment at all levels for comprehensive multisectoral measures
- International cooperation – particularly transfer of technology, knowledge and financial assistance—for effective tobacco control
- Civil society participation in national and international tobacco control efforts

Obligations

General	*Demand Reduction*	*Supply Reduction*
• National tobacco control strategies • Protection of policies from tobacco industry interference • Cooperation	• Price and tax measures • Protection from exposure to tobacco smoke • Regulation of contents and emissions • Tobacco packaging and labeling • Education, communication, training, and public awareness • Tobacco advertising, promotion, and sponsorship • Tobacco dependence treatment and cessation	• Elimination of illicit trade • Ban on sales to and by minors • Support for economically viable alternatives for workers, growers, and some individual sellers

tobacco, ban the sale of tobacco products to and by minors, and support viable employment alternatives for tobacco workers. The FCTC lists a far wider range of demand-reduction measures, designed to prevent tobacco initiation (especially by children and adolescents), and assist people to reduce or end their use of tobacco. These demand-reduction measures deploy both binding ("shall") and non-binding ("recognize," "should") language through recommendations on tax and price policies and requirements to: regulate the harmful contents of tobacco products; provide education, communication, and public awareness; codify measures to protect people from exposure to tobacco smoke; and implement programs to promote tobacco cessation and treatment for tobacco dependence (WHO 2003).

Although the FCTC represented an unprecedented achievement in developing binding international law, WHO's subsequent responses to NCDs in the first decade of the 21st century were built on a series of "soft law" instruments:

- Global Strategy on Diet, Physical Activity, and Health (2004)—which made the case for coordinated actions to strengthen diet and support physical activity and adopted an advocacy-based approach to bring together WHO with Member States, international partners, civil society, and the private sector.
- NCD Action Plan (2008–2013)—which acknowledged the role of evidence-based legislation and fiscal policies to reduce NCD risk factors yet provided little elaboration of these policies beyond tobacco tax and price measures.
- Global Strategy on the Harmful Use of Alcohol (2010)—which advocated a multisectoral approach to policy action and identified ten target measures, including drink-driving policies, restrictions on alcohol marketing and availability, and pricing measures.

WHO acknowledged that NCDs were becoming a "slow motion disaster" (Chan 2011); however, funding and development priorities continued to focus on communicable, maternal, and neonatal conditions (Greenberg, Leeder, and Raymond 2016). Without strong WHO action, this untenable global health situation provided the impetus for health diplomacy on NCDs to shift elsewhere in the UN system.

C. From WHO to the UN General Assembly

UN action on NCDs was galvanized by advocacy in the Caribbean Community (CARICOM), a regional intergovernmental organization representing fifteen Caribbean countries and five dependencies. CARICOM heads of state had met in 2007 in Trinidad and Tobago for a world-first regional summit on NCDs, and in May 2010, Trinidad and Tobago called for a High-Level Meeting of the UN General Assembly on the prevention and control of NCDs (Hassell and Hennis 2011).[2] With the UN General Assembly adopting this call for a High-Level Meeting, momentum was building for General Assembly action; yet for all the high hopes generated in the lead-up to the UN High-Level Meeting, the achievements of the High-Level Meeting were modest (Morrison 2011).

Case Study: Global Health Diplomacy and the First UN High-Level Meeting on NCDs

The 2011 UN High-Level Meeting comprised speeches from the UN, WHO, and national leaders during the plenary sessions, which took place alongside interactive roundtable sessions that provided opportunities for substantive input by civil society organizations. This Meeting culminated in a Political Declaration, which drew attention to the global burden of tobacco, alcohol, poor diet, and physical inactivity. The Declaration avoided referring to NCDs as an "epidemic," but admitted they were a "challenge of epidemic proportions." Further limiting implementation, the Political Declaration avoided targets to be met by states, committed to no changes in trade practices, and provided no significant resources for NCD prevention. While the High-Level Meeting provided a forum to highlight the severity and neglect of NCDs, it lacked formalized processes to mobilize resources, implement programs, and establish effective ways of framing the challenges of NCDs. (By contrast, the 2001 High-Level Meeting on HIV/AIDS was far more successful in elevating HIV/AIDS on the global agenda, as this earlier UN action was also promoted by the UN Secretary-General, by a purpose-built global institution (UNAIDS), and with spirited activism from affected communities.) Despite a credible civil society voice on NCDs through the NCD Alliance, NCDs cover a broad range of illnesses, and the voices of these divided communities were muted during the High-Level Meeting. In the absence of coordinated civil society advocacy, this UN effort was undermined by lobbying from the tobacco, alcohol, junk food, and sugary drinks industries, which had a vested interest in weak regulation and proved effective in eliminating any time-bound commitments and clear references to legally binding interventions. Given the limitations of the High-Level Meeting, it became clear that addressing NCDs would need to involve regulating the industries responsible for commercial determinants of health.

---

[2] CARICOM found broad support from the Heads of Government of the British Commonwealth, representing one-third of the world's population, whose 2009 Statement on Commonwealth Action to Combat NCDs called specifically for a 2011 UN Summit on NCDs.

Notwithstanding these limitations, the 2011 High-Level Meeting expanded global governance of NCDs beyond the World Health Assembly to become a matter of broader international concern within the UN General Assembly. In a subsequent 2012 resolution, the General Assembly recognized NCDs as "one of the major challenges for sustainable development in the twenty-first century" (UN General Assembly 2012, para. 141). While the UN Secretary-General lamented in 2013 that progress in implementing the High-Level Political Declaration's commitments remained "insufficient and highly uneven" (UN General Assembly 2013, 44), the UN General Assembly remained involved, developing a specific target on NCDs under the 2015 Sustainable Development Goals (SDGs). This SDG target—to reduce premature morality from NCDs by one-third by 2030—laid the foundation for shared global governance of NCDs between WHO and the broader UN system.

II. Shared Global Governance of NCDs

Continuing efforts to address NCDs would shift global governance toward a public health approach to NCD prevention and control. In framing NCD prevention as a public health challenge, the prioritization of NCDs on the global health agenda required policy efforts to confront dominant neoliberal norms, which had framed NCD risk factors as personal lifestyle choices, giving undue deference to markets and industry while characterizing government regulations as "nanny state" interference (Lencucha and Thow 2019). Regulating underlying commercial determinants of NCDs would push states and non-state actors to confront determined opposition from the tobacco, alcohol, junk food, and sugary drinks industries, strengthening government obligations and accountability mechanisms through shared global governance across the UN and WHO.

A. Greater Accountability under the WHO Global Action Plan

The 2011 UN High-Level Meeting recognized NCDs as a global health threat, but national implementation and international accountability were lacking. Following from this UN General Assembly action, the World Health Assembly in 2012 adopted a global target to seek a 25% reduction in NCD mortality by 2025: the "25 X 25" mortality target (World Health Assembly 2012). To operationalize the commitments made at the UN High-Level Meeting, the WHO Secretariat developed the Global Action Plan for the Prevention and Control of Noncommunicable Diseases 2013–2020, which was approved by the World

Health Assembly in 2013. This second Global Action Plan has remained the cornerstone of WHO's strategy on NCDs, setting out six objectives for global health governance, including action on modifiable risk factors and actions to prevent and treat NCDs through universal health coverage and primary health care. These objectives look to address NCDs through multisectoral action, since the determinants of NCDs—and their solutions—mostly lie outside health ministries, including ministries with responsibility for finance, agriculture, communications, education, employment, law and justice, transport, urban planning, and youth affairs (WHO 2013).

Facilitating accountability for national implementation through international monitoring, the Global Action Plan also established the Comprehensive Global Monitoring Framework. This WHO monitoring framework, highlighted in Table 7.2, comprised nine voluntary global targets: the overall 25 X 25 mortality target and eight supporting targets addressing risk factors

Table 7.2 Selected Global Targets for Reductions in NCD Mortality and Risk Factors (Magnusson and Gostin)

Comprehensive Global Monitoring Framework, including 9 voluntary global targets for prevention & control of NCDs, as updated in accordance with the WHO NCD Accountability Framework	**Overall target:** By 2030, a one-third relative reduction in overall mortality from cardiovascular disease, cancer, diabetes or chronic respiratory diseases (from 2015 baseline)
	Eight supporting targets: By 2030, at least a 20% relative reduction in harmful use of alcohol (from 2010 baseline) (adopted in 2022)
	By 2030, a 15% relative reduction in prevalence of insufficient physical activity (from 2016 baseline) (adopted in 2018)
	By 2025, a 30% relative reduction in mean population salt intake
	By 2025, a 30% relative reduction in prevalence of tobacco use
	By 2025, a 25% relative reduction in prevalence of raised blood pressure
	By 2025, 0% increase in diabetes & obesity
	By 2025, 50% coverage for drug therapy & counseling for those at risk of cardiovascular disease
	By 2025, 80% coverage of affordable technologies & essential medicines for treating NCDs in public & private facilities

and health system responses, supported by twenty-five indicators for measuring progress.[3]

Of all the targets in WHO's Comprehensive Global Monitoring Framework for NCDs, "Halt the rise of diabetes & obesity" is surely the most ambitious—and most unlikely to be met (Swinburn et al. 2015).

Case Study: Obesity: Failure of Global Health Governance?

Globally, around 650 million adults are obese, as are 39 million children under five years of age. Obesity contributes to around 5 million NCD deaths each year. A wide range of factors have contributed to this global imbalance between energy intake and expenditure, including urbanization, technological changes resulting in more sedentary forms of work and leisure, and a global "nutrition transition"—toward highly processed, energy dense but nutritionally poor foods. These dietary changes are affecting all countries and driving a global diabetes epidemic. Alarmed by rising rates of childhood obesity, former WHO Director-General Margaret Chan in 2014 established the Commission on Ending Childhood Obesity, which recommended an effective tax on sugar-sweetened beverages. However, this recommendation was omitted two years later from recommendations of the Independent High-Level Commission on NCDs—due to lack of consensus. Promoting healthier diets and preventing obesity will require confronting the food industry and its marketing and promotion of sugary beverages and foods high in saturated fats, sugar, and salt. Beyond marketing restrictions, new ways of incentivizing industry to improve commercially produced foods are needed. WHO has thus intensified its global leadership on obesity, developing recommendations for prevention and management of obesity over the life course, supported by an acceleration plan, global targets, and regular reporting. Yet, as rates of overweight and obesity continue to rise across all age groups, there remains little chance of meeting the Global Monitoring Framework's goal of a 0% increase in obesity and diabetes.

---

[3] Beyond the Comprehensive Global Monitoring Framework in the Global Action Plan, global goals and targets proliferated in the decade following the 2011 UN High-Level Meeting, mirroring the shift of NCDs as a concern within the broader UN system. Separate UN reporting frameworks were introduced to report on outcomes from the second High-Level Meeting on NCDs in 2014 and to monitor progress toward the SDG targets in 2015. In addition to SDG Target 3.4 (reducing NCD mortality by one-third by 2030, and promoting mental health and well-being), the SDGs include other targets that are linked to the larger NCD agenda: preventing harmful use of alcohol (SDG 3.5); achieving Universal Health Coverage (SDG 3.8); and reducing deaths and illness from air, water, and soil pollution (SDG 3.9).

In addition to monitoring progress to achieve global targets, the WHO Global Action Plan has supported national public health law reforms through a menu of cost-effective interventions (including "best buys") that states could employ to achieve the voluntary global targets:

- raising taxes and prices on tobacco and alcohol products;
- comprehensive bans or restrictions on tobacco and alcohol advertising, promotion, and sponsorship;
- second-hand smoke laws in indoor workplaces, public places, and transport;
- restrictions on the availability of alcohol;
- standardized packaging and large graphic health warnings on tobacco products; and
- front-of-pack labeling to reduce salt intake (WHO 2013b).

However, the Global Action Plan did not include a strategy for policy change, raising broader questions about the pathways linking global policy on NCDs to national actions (Magnusson and Patterson 2021).

The WHO Global Action Plan, as a normative instrument of global health policy, has sought to marshal evidence, inform policy, and exert normative pressures for policy change. To support accountability for the Global Action Plan in the absence of binding legal obligations, high-level political accountability mechanisms are required. These mechanisms have looked to global goals, targets, and their supporting indicators to facilitate monitoring of progress and generate political pressure on national governments to implement effective policies. Additional, purpose-built governance arrangements, such as task forces and independent commissions, can support this process.[4] In rallying the world to address NCDs, advocacy and global health diplomacy by non-state actors—including civil society organizations such as the NCD Alliance and global ambassadors such as former New York City Mayor and current philanthropist Michael Bloomberg, as seen in Figure 7.1—can generate awareness of the impact of NCDs and provide support for policy change.[5]

---

[4] Global governance arrangements have supported national policy implementation through intergovernmental task forces; time-limited independent commissions such as the WHO Independent High-Level Commission on NCDs; formal arrangements for policy dialogue, research programs, and routine surveillance; and reporting arrangements for NCD data. Global governance can further support national action through capacity building—both in global health law and in effective national laws and policies to implement evidence-based global norms—with WHO providing technical assistance to national governments on legal issues raised by NCDs (Magnusson et al. 2019).

[5] WHO established the role of Global Ambassador for NCDs and Injuries to raise awareness about the impact of leading NCDs and cost-effective prevention policies, to advocate with governments to invest in prevention, and to collaborate with local policymakers in developing plans and strategies. In 2022, Michael Bloomberg was re-appointed to a fourth two-year term as the WHO Global Ambassador for NCDs and Injuries.

Figure 7.1 Michael R. Bloomberg, WHO Global Ambassador for NCDs and Injuries, meeting with WHO Director-General Tedros Adhanom Ghebreyesus (Bloomberg Philanthropies)

B. Extending the FCTC under the Conference of the Parties

In supporting policy change, the FCTC presents a unique model of global health law to regulate the commercial threat posed by tobacco use throughout the world. The international legal strategy adopted to promote global tobacco control under the FCTC reflected a "framework convention-protocol" approach. WHO looked to this approach to encourage wider acceptance of the treaty, skirting political opposition while leaving room for political consensus to evolve over time through future international negotiations (Bodansky 1999). The framework convention-protocol approach offered states parties a degree of flexibility to decide issues at the level of specificity that was politically expedient at the time of the FCTC negotiations, securing commitment to core principles under the framework convention while leaving more substantive issues and emerging concerns for later protocols to be developed by the FCTC Conference of the Parties (COP) (Gostin 2014).

The COP is the FCTC's governing body, established under the treaty and comprised of all parties to the FCTC. Meeting every two years, the body's mandate is to review and promote FCTC implementation, which it does through the monitoring and review of state implementation efforts and the adoption of protocols, guidelines, and amendments.

Since its first meeting in 2006, the COP has adopted only one binding protocol: the Protocol to Eliminate Illicit Trade in Tobacco Products. Illicit trade—including smuggling, illicit manufacturing, and counterfeiting—undermines national tobacco control efforts, threatening the FCTC's overall objectives. Eliminating illicit trade was therefore seen as a matter of great significance to the COP. The Protocol was adopted by consensus in 2012 and entered into force in 2018. All other COP expansions of FCTC obligations have taken the form of non-binding guidelines, which, while not having the force of law, carry substantial normative weight—reflecting best practices in tobacco control and clarifying obligations under the FCTC. The FCTC looks to the COP to develop implementation guidelines on key demand-reduction measures, including protection from exposure to environmental tobacco smoke; tobacco product packaging and labeling; and tobacco advertising, promotion and sponsorship. However, the COP has gone further, developing guidelines on price and tax measures, and tobacco dependence and cessation. The FCTC and COP guidelines have presented a policy model for elaborating state approaches to tobacco control and addressing emerging areas of concern since the development of the FCTC (Zhou and Liberman 2018).

C. WHO and the UN Align Normative Instruments on NCDs

Beyond the FCTC, policy instruments—including global strategies, action plans, and regulatory recommendations—have been the backbone of WHO's response to NCDs, providing a foundation for broader UN engagement with the multisectoral determinants of NCDs. The WHO Global Action Plan for NCDs initially adopted the "4 X 4" framework, focusing on the four leading NCDs and four leading risk factors. However, since 2019, WHO has broadened its approach to NCDs to encompass mental health (as examined in detail in Chapter 8) and environmental pollution (as examined in detail in Chapter 9), creating a "5 X 5" framework. In 2019, the World Health Assembly recognized the Global Action Plan for Prevention and Control of NCDs 2013–2020 and Comprehensive Mental Health Action Plan 2013–2020 as contributions toward the NCD target under the SDGs—and extended the time frame for both plans to 2030 to align with the 2030 Agenda for Sustainable Development. The library of global health policy instruments, as illustrated by Figure 7.2, has expanded accordingly.

"Global strategies" have now been developed by WHO for each of the leading risk factors that underlie NCDs: diet, physical activity, and health (2004), alcohol (2010), and tobacco (2018). The Global Strategy to Accelerate Tobacco Control, adopted by the FCTC COP in 2018, is not legally binding but is intended to accelerate the implementation of the FCTC—to help achieve the tobacco target in

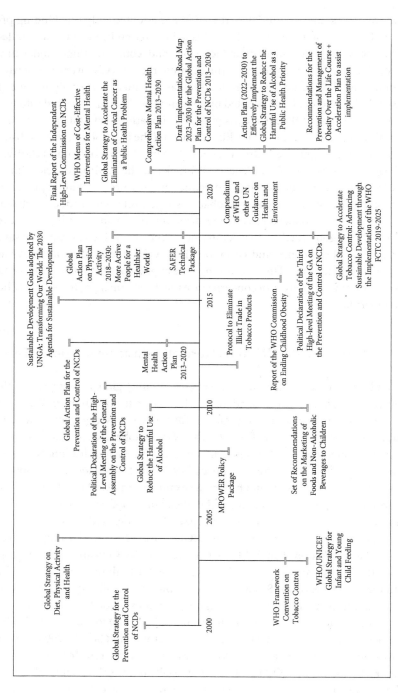

Figure 7.2 Selected WHO Normative Instruments and UN Declarations Shaping the Global Governance of NCDs (Magnusson and Gostin)

the Comprehensive Global Monitoring Framework and contribute to the SDGs (COP 2018).[6] As the slow rate of progress on NCDs has become apparent, a range of new-generation documents have emerged to strengthen guidance and support implementation, including the Implementation Road Map 2023–2030 for the Global Action Plan on NCDs and the Global Alcohol Action Plan 2022–2030. These new-generation documents seek to accelerate country-level actions, recover lost momentum, and integrate WHO recommendations for prevention and control of NCDs.

Building from these WHO policies, the broader UN system has become more heavily involved in NCD policy, developing complementary policy instruments to guide and accelerate action toward UN-wide goals. In meeting SDG 3, as discussed in greater detail in Chapter 10, the UN has brough together thirteen health, development, and humanitarian agencies under the Global Action Plan for Healthy Lives and Wellbeing for All, with this UN Global Action Plan reconceptualizing how UN agencies address NCDs (WHO 2019). This shift in global health governance is built on four key commitments by participating agencies:

- Engage: a commitment to coordinate global, regional, and in-country work to achieve "intensified, joint support" that reaches across ministries and draws on civil society, the private sector, and other development partners.
- Accelerate: an action plan built around joint actions under seven mutually reinforcing "accelerator themes" that cut across the mandates of partner agencies, including primary health care, sustainable financing, civil society engagement, gender equality, and the determinants of health.
- Align: a commitment to align and streamline internal operational and financial policies to ensure greater efficiency and reduced administrative burden on countries.
- Account: a monitoring system to facilitate implementation of the Global Action Plan through joint annual progress reports.

This conceptual footprint of the UN Global Action Plan is reflected in subsequent WHO initiatives. The Implementation Road Map 2023–2030 for the WHO Global Action Plan on NCDs is structured according to the four commitments above, while WHO's 2022 recommendations for strengthening the prevention

---

[6] Although implementing the FCTC under domestic law is already a legal obligation of parties to the FCTC, the 2018 Global Strategy is intended to accelerate progress by providing a shared vision for implementation, time-bound strategic and specific objectives, and opportunities for fundraising.

and control of NCDs in humanitarian emergencies reflect the Action Plan's accelerator theme of innovative programming in fragile and vulnerable settings, including the COVID-19 pandemic (WHO 2022).[7]

Through greater alignment of policy instruments between WHO and UN agencies, governance arrangements have evolved to facilitate multisectoral action on NCDs across the UN system. In 2013, the UN Economic and Social Council requested the UN Secretary-General to establish a UN Inter-Agency Task Force on Control and Prevention of NCDs (UNIATF) to coordinate the activities of UN funds, programs, and agencies to support the implementation of the Political Declaration of the 2011 High-Level Meeting. UNIATF has since acquired a unique role in global NCD governance, bringing together technical expertise across the UN to advance multisectoral action within countries. UNIATF initiatives include joint programming missions to countries, contributions to the UN Global Action Plan for Healthy Lives and Wellbeing for All, and advice on NCDs in COVID-19 response and recovery plans. Further, UNIATF administers the NCD and Mental Health Catalytic Fund, recommended by the WHO Independent High-Level Commission on NCDs and in Economic and Social Council resolutions and established in 2021 to provide development assistance to low- and middle-income countries to scale up actions on NCDs and mental health.

Separate from UNIATF initiatives across the UN, WHO Member States in 2013 established the WHO Global Coordination Mechanism for NCDs (GCM/NCD). The function of the GCM/NCD is to support implementation of the WHO Global Action Plan by fostering engagement across sectors and at "local, national, regional and global levels," while safeguarding WHO and public health from conflicts of interest. GCM/NCD hosts the Knowledge Action Portal on NCDs, which brings together a wide range of resources from WHO and other stakeholders. It additionally hosts multi-stakeholder dialogues and online communities of practice, including on "NCDs, Health and Law" and "NCDs and the Commercial Determinants." Despite ambiguity about the division of roles between UNIATF and the GCM/NCD, WHO has extended the terms of reference for GCM/NCD to 2030, further supporting a multisectoral approach to address expanding NCD risk factors.

---

[7] The COVID-19 pandemic has had a significant negative impact on mental health and wellbeing—exacerbating tobacco use, alcohol consumption, unhealthy diets, and other NCD risk factors—with smokers, people with obesity, and people with NCDs such as diabetes, cardiovascular disease, or respiratory disease facing a higher risk of severe illness (WHO 2022). Despite this rising NCD threat, the COVID-19 pandemic has caused delays in the diagnosis and treatment of NCDs due to overburdened health systems and workforce shortages.

III. Challenges and Opportunities for Global Governance of NCDs

The global response to NCDs is now shaped by a growing number of WHO law and policy instruments, a conceptual expansion of NCDs through the "5 X 5" framework, and an increasing involvement from UN agencies. This complex landscape faces new challenges, however, from conflicting bodies of international law, particularly international trade law and international human rights law, and rising NCD risk factors, including obesity, vaping, and alcohol.

A. The Broader Legal Environment of NCDs

The growing body of WHO and UN instruments that support global governance in the NCD response cannot be understood in isolation, as they are situated within a broader body of international law that significantly impacts national actions, with international trade law and international human rights law, in particular, carrying risks of regime conflict that can either undermine or support law and policy to prevent NCDs.

1. International Trade Law

The end of the Cold War accelerated the trend toward economic globalization, supported by the World Trade Organization (WTO) and a family of trade agreements that have liberalized trade while creating new challenges for NCD regulation. In addition to an expanding range of multilateral agreements to liberalize trade under the WTO, as discussed in greater detail in Chapter 12, the past thirty years have seen a sharp rise in bilateral investment treaties, free trade agreements, and broader regional trade and investment agreements that extend beyond WTO obligations (McNamara et al. 2021). These international trade law obligations are not inherently antagonistic to public health, and some scholars argue that well-framed public health laws and policies should survive WTO scrutiny (Thow et al. 2018). Yet, governments have often been reluctant to regulate some commercial determinants of NCDs—hesitant to restrict the sale of goods in ways that might run afoul of international trade law. The fact that international trade law obligations apply with full force to tobacco, alcohol, and unhealthy foods illustrates the broader political economy of NCD governance.

While trade and investment agreements typically include exceptions for public health protections, they may nevertheless raise additional regulatory risks—by permitting tobacco, food, or alcohol interests to challenge public health measures that impact the sale of their products and investments. The technical complexity and standard of evidence required to withstand scrutiny of good-faith public health measures is often high under trade agreements, creating risks of "regulatory chill" that limit government action to implement effective NCD policies (Thow et al. 2022). For example, New Zealand's decision to delay the implementation of tobacco "plain packaging" legislation, pending the outcome of a trade complaint against Australia's nearly identical legislation, reflects the real-world pressures (Kelsey 2017). Beyond the enforcement of trade agreements, the lack of public health input in trade negotiations (Friel et al. 2019) often leads to international trade policies that deny governments the policy space needed to regulate leading NCD risks. As global health stands to gain when global standards are developed in a forum "where public health issues predominate" (Bettcher and Shapiro 2001, 67), efforts must be taken to extend public health considerations across global governance institutions.[8] Such alignment between NCD prevention policies and international trade law will be crucial to counterbalance industry involvement and realize global NCD prevention policy.

2. International Human Rights Law

Rather than conflicting with NCD prevention policy, international human rights law provides an important conceptual and operational framework that could strengthen the governance of NCDs—as a human rights imperative. Under a wide range of international human rights treaties, a broad range of human rights support the prevention and control of NCDs: the right to health and adequate health care, the right to adequate food, to education, access to appropriate information, and freedom from discrimination.[9] Even as regulated industries have sought to co-opt human rights language—arguing for the individual "freedom" to consume harmful products (Cabrera and Constantin 2020)—scholars have recognized the potential for human rights to accelerate progress in a wide range of areas, including tobacco control, healthy diets, obesity prevention, and regulation of unhealthy food advertising (Toebes and Patterson 2020). In empowering health advocacy, a rights-based approach to addressing NCDs provides a space for civil society participation to press states to meet their human rights

---

[8] For example, the Global Action Plan on Diet, Physical Activity and Health (2004) envisaged a leading role for the Codex Alimentarius Commission (Codex), the global food standards body jointly administered by WHO and the Food and Agriculture Organization, in the development of food labeling and food composition standards. Facilitating the development of global norms under the Codex may provide benefits for public health, since Codex standards have authoritative status in setting regulations under trade and investment agreements. However, significant risks arise from the participation of the food industry in Codex standards-setting committees and their inclusion in member state delegations.

[9] As introduced in Chapter 4, relevant international human rights treaties include the 1966 International Covenant on Economic, Social and Cultural Rights (ICESCR); the 1989 Convention on the Rights of the Child (CRC); the 1979 Convention on the Elimination of All Forms of Discrimination Against Women (CEDAW); and regional agreements such as the 1982 African Charter on Human and People's Rights.

obligations and strengthens the effectiveness of multilateral bodies as they seek to hold states accountable (Patterson et al. 2019).

Human rights, including the right to health, can accelerate progress on NCDs by focusing attention on key risk factors and on state obligations to protect public health through regulation. The obligation to protect the right to health speaks to regulatory failures in NCD policy, imposing an obligation on states to take positive steps to prevent third parties, including corporations, from violating the right to health and other health-related rights through the marketing and sale of tobacco, alcohol, and unhealthy food and drink (Toebes and Patterson 2020). Similarly, obligations to fulfill the right to health require states to devote resources to implementation, adopting "legislative, administrative, budgetary, judicial, promotional and other measures" toward the full realization of the right (CESCR 2000). To realize these benefits, governments must undertake steps to assess the compliance of national NCD policies with human rights obligations.

In facilitating international accountability for human rights implementation, state compliance with human rights obligations is reviewed through UN monitoring and review mechanisms. This review process—through human rights treaty bodies and the Human Rights Council's Universal Periodic Review—provides opportunities to strengthen the alignment between global NCD governance and international human rights law (Meier and Brás Gomes 2018). Ensuring accountability through international review processes, the constructive dialogue and concluding observations steps in the periodic review cycle provide opportunities for promoting NCD policy priorities through state human rights implementation (Magnusson et al. 2019). WHO and the Office of the UN High Commissioner for Human Rights (OHCHR) have begun to consider ways of aligning the mandate of both organizations in the area of NCDs, with scholars calling for joint WHO/OHCHR guidelines on human rights and healthy diets, recognizing intersectional obligations under the right to health and the right to food (Buse et al. 2019). Such human rights accountability will be crucial in addressing rising new commercial determinants of NCDs.

B. Facing New Threats

Despite progress in preventing NCDs, threats from commercial determinants are rising, keeping the world from meeting global goals set under WHO and UN governance. The core challenge facing global governance is that the leading preventable risk factors for NCDs, including tobacco use, alcohol use, and unhealthy diets, are driven by transnational corporate interests that benefit politically-powerful high-income countries (Hoe et al. 2022). The obstacles to progress in this inequitable diplomatic landscape are reflected in the continuing challenges facing global governance in preventing obesity, addressing vaping, and regulating alcohol.

1. Continuing Obstacles to Obesity Prevention

Energy imbalance—driven by diets richer in calories, saturated fats, and sugars, alongside more sedentary lifestyles—is responsible for a remarkable rise in global rates of overweight and obesity. Addressing this challenge requires an understanding of the complexity of underlying determinants of health, including commercial determinants and economic interests (Gostin 2014). This will require an understanding of the economic impacts of underlying determinants of obesity, making the "investment case" for taxation schemes, government actions, and cost-effective policies (Shiffman and Shawar 2022). To accelerate progress, UN bodies and national governments must be willing to tackle vested economic interests and to protect policy-making processes from the pervasive influence of corporate actors that benefit from unhealthy food and drink.

Simplistic assumptions about individual causes of and solutions to obesity, over-emphasizing the role of personal responsibility amid global determinants, have continued to pose an obstacle to NCD prevention efforts. Communicating the rationale for global action, and implementing WHO recommendations, will require developing public information campaigns on global determinants of obesity. In translating global obesity plans into national action, the implementation of evidence-based regulatory measures, such as restrictions on unhealthy food advertising and taxes on sugary drinks, will require greater investment in regulatory capacity. Legal capacity-building helps to develop the skillsets that national governments need to implement national laws and policies to protect their populations (Magnusson and Patterson 2021). The enforcement of public health laws must also be a priority, as greater investment in accountability could enable governments to address obesogenic environments through the laws they have already implemented.

These national and global health law reforms to address obesity are inherently interdisciplinary and multisectoral. There are opportunities to embed action on obesity in policies across sectors—including agriculture, climate change mitigation, and economic development—but entrenched economic interests will continue to resist efforts to create healthier food systems and more active living environments. Important lessons from tobacco control under the FCTC—that economic self-interest will undermine self-regulation, that government accountability is crucial, and that policymaking processes must be protected from industry interference—apply with equal force to the determinants of healthy diets. Multisectoral action, implementing mutually reinforcing policies across all relevant government ministries, is not only a key feature of WHO's strategy on NCDs but is now reflected in complementary actions taken by different UN agencies as they engage with national ministries.

2. Health Risks from Rising Vaping

In overcoming entrenched commercial interests to change unhealthy behaviors, it will be necessary to protect the next generation from the rapidly rising commercial threat from vaping. When the FCTC was negotiated, the range of globally available tobacco products consisted almost exclusively of cigarettes, cigars, waterpipes, and smokeless tobacco. Yet, just as smoking rates began to decline, tobacco companies began aggressively marketing new nicotine products—particularly electronic nicotine delivery systems (ENDS), including e-cigarettes or "vapes." Many of these products contain high nicotine concentrations, and the rapid proliferation of these novel threats has complicated regulation. Whereas the FCTC defines tobacco products as "entirely or partly made of the leaf tobacco as raw material which are manufactured to be used for smoking, sucking, chewing or snuffing" (WHO 2003), these addictive new products skirt FCTC regulation by using nicotine, rather than leaf tobacco itself. Where the applicability of the FCTC is unclear, governments face challenges in seeking to regulate ENDS under tobacco control laws.

Although the tobacco industry has claimed that vaping is less harmful than traditional cigarettes, e-cigarette use presents several adverse health risks, including nicotine addiction, increased risk of smoking initiation in never-smokers, and relapse in former smokers (Baenziger et al. 2021). There is additional evidence that these products contain toxic chemicals that may be harmful to health, and the impact of their long-term use remains understudied (WHO 2021). Current research on these health harms has shown that ENDS are associated with increased risk of cardiovascular diseases and lung conditions in adults, vaping by children and adolescents carries risks of brain development impacts, and exposure to vape chemicals may harm fetal brain development in utero. Given these health risks, the sale and appeal of vapes to children and adolescents is of particular concern. The high prevalence is driven by aggressive marketing to minors, and this use among minors could lead to nicotine addiction by a new generation—undoing the successes of global tobacco control efforts (Yoong et al. 2021).

The FCTC COP, since its fourth session in 2010, has discussed ENDS marketing and vaping regulation. At COP5, parties sought to clarify the status of e-cigarettes under the FCTC, identifying several potentially applicable provisions (Gruszczynski 2019). In a report to the COP, WHO later identified an outright ban on ENDS as a legitimate regulatory approach, while recognizing a range of other regulatory options:

- banning promotion of ENDS to non-smokers;
- banning sale of ENDS to minors;
- banning health claims in the absence of regulatory approval;
- banning use of ENDS indoors and where smoking is banned;
- regulation of product design and a ban on fruit and candy-like flavors; and
- protection of ENDS policies from vested commercial interests (WHO 2014).

Drawing from COP governance, over thirty countries currently ban these devices, and WHO maintains its recommendation that countries strictly regulate ENDS where there is not an outright ban. Nonetheless, these novel and harmful products remain relatively elusive under the FCTC, impeding a holistic approach to global tobacco control and highlighting the challenges of regulating rising risks based upon new public health evidence.

3. Rising Threats from Alcohol

Alcohol has not received the same level of policy attention as other NCD risk factors, even ignored as a risk factor in the WHO's original Global Strategy for NCDs. Yet alcohol is responsible for around three million deaths each year—with health harms rising among younger populations. Despite this rising threat, WHO Member States have made little progress in developing effective measures to reduce alcohol-related harm, as alcohol industry lobbying, as discussed in greater detail in Chapter 13, has challenged WHO policymaking.[10] With global per capita alcohol consumption expected to increase in the coming years, advocates have repeatedly criticized the voluntary actions undertaken by the alcohol industry in the name of "corporate social responsibility," looking to WHO to develop a legally binding regulatory framework similar to the FCTC: a Framework Convention on Alcohol Control (Burci 2021).

Case Study: Diplomatic Efforts to Develop a Framework Convention on Alcohol Control

With public health research long showing the harmful effects of alcohol consumption, WHO began work in 2008 to develop a Global Strategy to Reduce the Harmful Use of Alcohol, supported by a World Health Assembly resolution that—controversially—encouraged collaboration

---

[10] While WHO does not partner directly with the alcohol industry, it relies heavily on industry estimates about levels of alcohol consumption and consults with industry representatives about how "economic operators" might contribute to the Global Strategy to reduce harmful alcohol use, the more recent Global Alcohol Action Plan (2022–2030), and commitments made in UN High-Level Meetings.

with "economic operators" to reduce the harmful use of alcohol. This Global Strategy thus encouraged voluntary self-regulation by the alcohol industry to reduce harm from alcohol use. However, as alcohol use continued to increase under this non-binding policy (without any substantial reductions in alcohol-related mortality and morbidity), advocates pressed for a legally binding framework under international law, calling on WHO Member States to codify a Framework Convention on Alcohol Control. These non-state advocates looked to WHO to develop a legally binding treaty, noting that, like tobacco, the global market for alcohol poses substantial challenges to effective regulation at a national level—given the scale of the industry (dominated by large multinationals), pervasive corporate political activity, cross-border advertising and promotion, and limitations to domestic health regulations under trade and investment agreements. Advocates argued that a Framework Convention on Alcohol Control, developed under WHO's lawmaking authorities, could successfully challenge corporate interests and trade agreements that expand alcohol markets and weaken national and local regulation. However, states have not yet acted to develop this international treaty, with many analysts finding that a legally binding international instrument is not politically feasible at present and, if developed, might formalize weak international obligations while doing little to advance evidence-based "best buys." Recognizing that progress in reducing alcohol-related harm has continued to stall, WHO developed a 2022 action plan that highlights the inherent conflict of interest among alcohol producers and recommends regulatory approaches under national law but fails to advance a binding international instrument.

There is no safe level of alcohol, yet global efforts to regulate alcohol use have faced challenges from an entrenched industry and reluctant governments. Alcohol control advocates have sought to draw from the model of tobacco control negotiations to develop the FCTC, where momentum toward a legally binding convention benefited from: leadership and direction from the WHO Director-General, a high-profile tobacco control program within the WHO Secretariat, governance structures that coordinated tobacco control work across the UN system, and a highly motivated civil society movement—the Framework Convention Alliance (WHO 2009). In matching these diplomatic forces in alcohol control, strengthened global governance to address the threat of alcohol may be needed before the tide turns in favor of a binding international agreement to regulate this rising risk factor for NCDs.

Conclusion

Through expanding global health law and policy instruments over decades, NCDs have earned their place on the global health agenda. Global governance has shifted from infectious diseases to NCDs. These threats are increasingly framed as an imperative for justice in global health; however, NCDs cover an increasingly disparate group of conditions that are difficult to frame as an existential challenge. In a world where urgency in global health governance derives from the speed of disease transmission, the pervasive threat of NCDs will continue to struggle for attention and resources while facing ongoing resistance from corporate interests that push tobacco and vaping products, sugar-sweetened beverages, ultra-processed foods, and alcohol as personal decisions rather than global health threats.

Global health law and policy are continuing to evolve in response to these rising harms. Since the first High-Level Meeting of the UN General Assembly in 2011, the global governance of NCDs has moved beyond WHO and into the broader UN system. While WHO continues to provide technical leadership, the UN General Assembly has been the catalyst for the urgency and the initiatives that now comprise the global governance framework for NCDs. Broader UN involvement in supporting political commitments is necessary, but it will be insufficient in the absence of legal obligations. Shifting from global policy to international law, the FCTC provides a model for hard law to address underlying determinants of NCDs, and in coming years, the world will likely see additional efforts to regulate these persistent threats under binding global health law reforms.

Addressing commercial determinants of health in a globalizing world will require global health law. There is growing recognition of the importance of underlying determinants of health and the need for collective action to create healthy environments. NCDs have never been an epidemic of unhealthy choices made by individuals acting in isolation, but a predictable consequence of physical, economic, and social environments that fail to support healthy lifestyles. These environments are shaped by global governance. Future efforts in global health governance, establishing new models of global regulation, will be critical in advocating for, designing, and promoting the next generation of global health law to reduce the devastating impact of NCDs and their risk factors.

Questions for Consideration

1. Why have NCDs eclipsed communicable diseases as the prevailing causes of death and disability? How do transnational corporations shape the global health threat of commercial determinants of health? Why has governance continued to neglect NCDs relative to communicable diseases?

2. What does WHO see as the advantages of pursuing "soft law" in many NCD policies? Why did WHO pursue "hard law" in the context of tobacco under the FCTC?
3. Why did the UN General Assembly seek to exert governance over NCDs? What were the strengths and weaknesses of the first UN High-Level Meeting on NCDs?
4. Why are the risk factors for NCDs framed as a public health policy issue rather than a personal lifestyle decision? How did the individual behaviors underlying NCDs come to be seen as a "global" health threat requiring global health law?
5. What were the legal and political advantages of a framework convention–protocol approach to tobacco control? Why is the COP necessary to advance tobacco control beyond the development of the FCTC?
6. How does WHO monitoring facilitate accountability for national policy changes? What domestic policies are necessary to implement WHO's Global Action Plan? What should WHO monitor to assess NCD progress?
7. Why has WHO faced challenges in halting the rise of obesity and diabetes? How have WHO and the broader UN system sought to align multisectoral strategies for the risk factors that underlie NCDs?
8. Why would human rights obligations support the development of NCD policies? How can human rights monitoring mechanisms support human rights accountability for NCD obligations?
9. What challenges have vaping products posed for tobacco control under the FCTC?
10. How could a Framework Convention on Alcohol Control advance efforts to strengthen alcohol control through global health law? What obstacles do states face in developing such a treaty under WHO governance?

Acknowledgments

The authors are grateful to Kerstan Nealy and Quintin A. Gay for their research assistance in describing the evolution of global health governance responses to NCDs and to Alexandra Finch for her thoughtful analysis of the FCTC.

References

Baenziger, Olivia Nina, Laura Ford, Amelia Yazidjoglou, Grace Joshy, and Emily Banks. 2021. "E-cigarette Use and Combustible Tobacco Cigarette Smoking Uptake Among Non-smokers, including Relapse in Former Smokers: Umbrella Review, Systematic Review and Meta-Analysis." *BMJ Open* 11: e045603.

Baker, Philip, Adrian Kay, and Helen Walls. 2014. "Trade and Investment Liberalization and Asia's Noncommunicable Disease Epidemic: A Synthesis of Data and Existing Literature." *Globalization and Health* 10: 66.

Beaglehole, Robert, and Derek Yach. 2003. "Globalisation and the Prevention and Control of Non-communicable Disease: The Neglected Chronic Diseases of Adults." *Lancet* 362: 903–908.

Bettcher, Douglas and Ira Shapiro. 2001. "Tobacco Control in an Era of Trade Liberalisation." *Tobacco Control* 10: 65–67.

Bodansky, Daniel. 1999. "The Framework Convention/Protocol Approach." WHO/NCD/TFI/99.1

Buse, Kent, David Patterson, Roger Magnusson, and Brigit Toebes. 2019. "Urgent Call for Human Rights Guidance on Diets and Food Systems." *The BMJ Opinion*. October 30. https://blogs.bmj.com/bmj/2019/10/30/urgent-call-for-human-rights-guidance-on-diets-and-food-systems/.

Burci, Gian Luca. 2021. "A Global Legal Instrument for Alcohol Control: Options, Prospects and Challenges." *European Journal of Risk Regulation* 12: 499–513.

Cabrera, Oscar, and Andrés Constantin. 2020. "Tobacco Control in International Human Rights Law." In *Human Rights and Tobacco Control*, edited by Marie Elske Gispen and Brigit Toebes, 45–62. Cheltenham: Edward Elgar Publishing.

CESCR (United Nations Committee on Economic and Social Council). 2000. "General Comment No. 14: The Right to the Highest Attainable Standard of Health (Art. 12 of the International Covenant on Economic, Social and Cultural Rights)." August 11. E/C.12/2000/4.

Chan, Margaret. 2011. "Noncommunicable Diseases Damage Health, Including Economic Health." Address to the High-level Meeting on Noncommunicable Diseases, UN General Assembly, New York, September 19.

COP (Conference of the Parties to the WHO Framework Convention on Tobacco Control). 2018. "Global Strategy to Accelerate Tobacco Control: Advancing Sustainable Development through the Implementation of the WHO FCTC 2019–2025." FCTC/COP8(16). October 16.

Friel, Sharon, Phillip Baker, Anne Marie Thow, Deborah Gleeson, Belinda Townsend, and Ashley Schram. 2019. "An Exposé of the Realpolitik of Trade Negotiations: Implications for Population Nutrition." *Public Health Nutrition* 22(16): 3083–3091.

Gostin, Lawrence O. 2014. *Global Health Law*. Cambridge: Harvard University Press.

Gouda, Hebe N., Fiona Charlson, Katherine Sorsdahl, Sanam Ahmadzada, Alize J. Ferrari, Holly Erskine, Janni Leung et al. 2019. "Burden of Non-communicable Diseases in Sub-Saharan Africa, 1990–2017: Results from the Global Burden of Disease Study 2017." *Lancet Global Health* 7: e1375–e1387.

Greenberg, Henry, Stephen R. Leeder, and Susan U. Raymond. 2016. "And Why So Great a 'No'? The Donor and Academic Communities' Failure to Confront Global Chronic Disease." *Global Heart* 11(4): 381–385.

Gruszczynski, Lukasz. 2019. "Taming Schrödinger's Cat: E-Cigarettes under the Framework Convention on Tobacco Control." In *The Regulation of E-Cigarettes*, edited by Lukasz Gruszczynski, 76–98. Cheltenham: Edward Elgar Publishing.

Hassell, T. and AJ Hennis. 2011. "The Road to the United Nations High Level Meeting on Chronic Non-communicable Diseases." *West Indian Medical Journal* 60(4): 384–386.

Hoe, Connie, Caitlin Weiger, Marela Kay R. Minosa, Fernanda Alonso, Adam D. Koon, and Joanna E. Cohen. 2022. "Strategies to Expand Corporate Autonomy by the

Tobacco, Alcohol and Sugar-sweetened Beverage Industry: A Scoping Review of Reviews." *Globalization and Health* 18: 17.
Kelsey, Jane. 2017. "Regulatory Chill: Learnings from New Zealand's Plain Packaging Law." *QUT Law Review* 17(2): 21–45.
Lencucha, Raphael and Anne Marie Thow. 2019. "How Neoliberalism Is Shaping the Supply of Unhealthy Commodities and What it Means for NCD Prevention." *International Journal of Health Policy & Management* 8(9): 514–520.
McNamara, Courtney, Ronald Labonté, Ashley Schram, and Belinda Townsend. 2021. "Glossary on Free Trade Agreements and Health Part 1: the Shift from Multilateralism and the Rise of 'WTO-Plus' Provisions." *Journal of Epidemiology & Community Health* 75: 402–406.
Magnusson, Roger, Benn McGrady, Lawrence Gostin, David Patterson, and Hala Abou Taleb. 2019. "Legal Capacities Required for Prevention and Control of Noncommunicable Diseases." *Bulletin of the World Health Organization* 97: 108–117.
Magnusson, Roger and David Patterson. 2021. "Global Action, but National Results: Strengthening Pathways Towards Better Health Outcomes for Non-communicable Diseases." *Critical Public Health* 31: 464–474.
Meier, Benjamin Mason and Virginia Brás Gomes. 2018. "Human Rights Treaty Bodies: Monitoring, Interpreting and Adjudicating Health-Related Human Rights." In *Human Rights in Global Health: Rights-Based Governance for a Globalizing World*, edited by Benjamin Mason Meier and Lawrence Gostin, 509–535. New York: Oxford University Press.
Moodie, Rob, Elizabeth Bennett, Edwin Jit Leung Kwong, Tiago M Santos, Liza Pratiwi, Joanna Williams, and Phillip Baker. 2021. "Ultra-Processed Profits: The Political Economy of Countering the Global Spread of Ultra-Processed Foods—A Synthesis Review of the Market and Political Practices of Transnational Food Corporations and Strategic Public Health Responses." *International Journal of Health Policy and Management* 10(12): 968–982.
Morrison, Stephen. 2011. "Reflections on the UN High-Level Meeting on Noncommunicable Diseases." *Centre for Strategic & International Studies*, September 26.
Murray, C.J.D. and A.D. Lopez. 1994. "Global and Regional Causes-of-Death Patterns in 1990." *Bulletin of the World Health Organization* 72(3): 447–480.
Niessen, Louis, Diwakar Mohan, Jonathan K. Akuoku, Andrew J. Mirelman, Sayem Ahmed, Tracey P. Koehlmoos, Antonio Trujillo, Jahangir Khan, and David H. Peters. 2018. "Tackling Socioeconomic Inequalities and Non-communicable Diseases in Low-income and Middle-income Countries under the Sustainable Development Agenda." *Lancet* 391: 2036–2046.
Patterson, David, Kent Buse, Roger Magnusson, and Brigit Toebes. 2019. "Identifying a Human Rights-Based Approach to Obesity for States and Civil Society." *Obesity Reviews* 20 Suppl 2: 45–56.
Roemer, Ruth, Allyn Taylor, and Jean Lariviere. 2005. "Origins of the WHO Framework Convention on Tobacco Control." *American Journal of Public Health* 95(6): 936–936.
Schwartz, Leah N., Jonathan D. Shaffer, and Gene Bukhman. 2021. "The Origins of the 4 X 4 Framework for Noncommunicable Disease at the World Health Organization." *Population Health* 13: 100731.
Shiffman, Jeremy and Yusra Ribhi Shawar. 2022. "Framing and the Formation of Global Health Priorities." *Lancet* 399: 1977–1990.

Swinburn, Boyd, Vivica Kraak, Harry Rutter, Stefanie Vandevijvere, Tim Lobstein, Gary Sacks, Fabio Gomes, Tim Marsh, and Roger Magnusson. 2015. "Strengthening of Accountability Systems to Create Healthy Food Environments and Reduce Global Obesity." *Lancet.* June 20.

Thow, Anne Marie, Alexandra Jones, Corinna Hawkes, Iqra Ali, and Roland Labonté. 2018. "Nutrition Labelling Is a Trade Policy Issue: Lessons from an Analysis of Specific Trade Concerns at the World Trade Organization." *Health Promotion International* 33(4): 561–571.

Thow, Anne Marie, Amandine Garde, L. Alan Winters, Ellen Johnson, Andi Mabhala, Paul Kingston, and Pepita Barlow. 2022. "Protecting Noncommunicable Disease Prevention Policy in Trade and Investment Agreement." *Bulletin of the World Health Organization* 100: 268–275.

Toebes, Brigit and David Patterson. 2020. "Human Rights and Non-communicable Diseases: Controlling Tobacco and Promoting Healthy Diets." In *Foundations of Global Health & Human Rights*, edited by Lawrence Gostin and Benjamin Mason Meier, 243–262. New York: Oxford University Press.

UNDP (United Nations Development Programme). 2015. "*Guidance Note on the Integration of Noncommunicable Diseases into the United Nations Development Assistance Framework.*" Geneva: WHO and UNDP.

UN General Assembly. 2012. "The Future We Want." A/RES/66/288. July 27.

World Bank. 1993. *World Development Report 1993: Investing in Health, Volume 1.* New York: Oxford University Approach.

World Health Assembly. 2000. "Prevention and Control of Noncommunicable Diseases." WHA53/17. May 20.

World Health Assembly. 2012. "Prevention and Control of Noncommunicable Diseases: Follow-up to the High-level Meeting of the General Assembly on the Prevention and Control of Non-communicable Diseases." WHA 65(8). May 26.

WHO (World Health Organization). 2003. "WHO Framework Convention on Tobacco Control." May 21. 2302 UNTS 166.

WHO. 2009. *History of the WHO Framework Convention on Tobacco Control.* Geneva: WHO.

UN General Assembly. 2013. "Note by the Secretary-General Transmitting the Report of the Director-General of the World Health Organization on the Prevention and Control of Non-communicable Diseases." A/68/650. December 10.

WHO. 2013. *Global Action Plan for the Prevention and Control of Noncommunicable Diseases 2013–2020.* Geneva: WHO.

WHO. 2014. Electronic Nicotine Delivery Systems: Report by WHO. Conference of the Parties to the WHO Framework Convention on Tobacco Control. September 1. FCTC/COP/6/10 Rev.1.

WHO. 2019. *Stronger Collaboration, Better Health: Global Action Plan for Healthy Lives and Well-Being for All.* Geneva: WHO.

WHO. 2021. *WHO Report on the Global Tobacco Epidemic: Addressing New and Emerging Products.* Geneva: WHO.

WHO. 2022. "Recommendations on How to Strengthen the Design and implementation of Policies, Including Those for Resilient Health Systems and Health Services and Infrastructure, to Treat People Living with Noncommunicable Diseases and to Prevent and Control their Risk Factors in Humanitarian Emergencies." May 27. A75/10 Add. 2.

Yoong, Sze Lin, Alix Hall, Alecia Leonard, Sam McCrabb, John Wiggers, Edouard Tursan d'Espaignet, Emily Stockings et al. 2021. "Prevalence of Electronic Nicotine Delivery Systems and Electronic Non-Nicotine Delivery Systems in Children and Adolescents: A Systematic Review and Meta-Analysis." *Lancet Public Health* 6 (9): e661–73.

Zhou, Suzanne and Jonathan Liberman. 2018. "The Global Tobacco Epidemic and the WHO Framework Convention on Tobacco Control—the Contributions of the WHO's First Convention to Global Health Law and Governance." In *Research Handbook on Global Health Law*, edited by Gian Luca Burci and Brigit Toebes, 340–388. Cheltenham: Edward Elgar Publishing.

8
Mental Health
From Institutions to Community Inclusion

Priscila Rodríguez and Eric Rosenthal

Introduction

Over the last thirty years, human rights organizations, journalists, health professionals, and others have documented human rights violations occurring whenever people with mental health diagnoses or other disabilities are segregated from society—a threat exacerbated when individuals are placed in institutions. Recognizing the historical segregation, institutionalization, and abuse of people with mental health conditions worldwide, global health policy has developed under the United Nations (UN) to respect, protect, and fulfill human rights, close institutions, and support people's mental health needs in the community. The transformation of mental health systems from large institutions to community-based care has been successful in certain countries, but remains unfinished in others. Mental health—and the challenges faced by people with mental health conditions—remains a global issue, requiring global health law and policy to support human rights in global health.

The 2006 adoption of the UN Convention on the Rights of Persons with Disabilities (CRPD) was a groundbreaking development in international law and disability rights and brought about a paradigm shift in global health law—from a medical model to a social or "human rights" model of disability. Instead of seeing human beings as "ill" or "damaged," the CRPD now recognizes disability as "an evolving concept" that results from the interaction between persons with impairments and social barriers that hinder their full and equal participation in society. The CRPD thus creates a government obligation to remove attitudinal and environmental barriers to inclusion, guaranteeing the right of all persons to live in the community. This obligation frames the operation of social welfare and mental health care systems—and the protection of all rights. To implement these rights in mental health care systems, the CRPD creates an affirmative obligation on governments to ensure access to a full range of community support services "to support independent living and inclusion in the community, and to prevent isolation or segregation from the community."

This chapter analyzes the evolution of global health law in shifting mental health policy from institutionalization to community inclusion—and from a medically based to a disability-based model of human rights protection. Part I examines the long history of segregating people with disabilities in institutions and addresses how the horrors of World War II spurred the evolution of global standards to uphold mental health and human rights. Drawing from this evolution of global mental health law and policy, Part II details the diplomatic process that led to the codification of the CRPD, shifting from a medical to a social definition of disability and framing contemporary legal obligations to uphold human rights to legal capacity and community living. Part III addresses the challenges to implementing the CRPD and its obligations to ensure deinstitutionalization and community inclusion, recognizing the impediments to continuing progress amid the COVID-19 pandemic and amid rising humanitarian crises. This chapter concludes that continuing global health law reforms will require the participation of people with disabilities, alongside transformations in policies and programs aligned with the CRPD, to realize the highest attainable standard of mental health.

I. Long-Standing Threats to Human Rights in Mental Health

Societies have long subjected people with mental health conditions to horrific abuses and rights deprivations, including institutionalization and denial of the rights and opportunities to make their own choices. The harms of this treatment influenced the development of international human rights law following global attention to Nazi crimes against people with disabilities. However, it took far longer before specialized mental health standards at the regional and international level evolved and disability rights principles gained recognition, laying a foundation for the development of the CRPD.

A. Removing Capacity and Secluding from Community

Throughout the world and across the centuries, people with disabilities have faced removal from their communities and indefinite segregation in abusive institutions. Closely linked with this segregation, individuals were long denied the right to make decisions about their lives. The denial of the right to legal capacity, as introduced in Chapter 4, has been imposed on those with disabilities through substitute decision-making regimes such as guardianship (Craigie et al. 2019). This removal of legal capacity is based on the unfounded presumption that people with disabilities, particularly people with mental health conditions, are incapable of making choices for themselves, with legal authorities appointing a "guardian" to make decisions for them.

The history of guardianship can be traced back over two thousand years, with the Greek and Roman Empires creating the first known legal systems of "guardianship," wherein men deemed incapable of managing their lives were treated by law in the same way as children (Lewis and Pathare 2020). In the 14th century, this model was codified under English law through the doctrine of *"parens patriae,"* under which the government served "as a benevolent parent with the responsibility of caring for those unable to care for themselves" (Tester et al. 2005, 12). While the concept of guardianship was framed as a charitable approach to care, the effect of guardianship on people with disabilities has been a complete denial of rights. The denial of and restrictions to the legal capacity of persons with disabilities pervades all aspects of life, leading to the loss of control over their lives and exposing people with mental health needs to high levels of violence, abuse, and neglect. This denial of rights followed the expansion of mental health laws throughout the world, permitting—without the consent of the individual—detention and forced treatment in institutions.

B. Development of Institutions and Complete Removal of Rights

People with actual or perceived "mental illness" or mental health conditions have been detained and segregated for centuries in mental health institutions. The first "hospitals" for people with "mental illness" were built in Arab countries, starting in Baghdad around 700 AD (Bellack and Hersen 1998). Such institutions rapidly spread throughout the world.[1] These "asylums"—supposedly places of safety—effectively functioned as places of detention, often for indefinite periods of time. Conditions in asylums were frequently poor, with inadequate food, lack of treatment, and crowded and unhygienic living areas. Despite the spread of these facilities, legal regulations largely overlooked them – and neglected the populations inside.

Segregating a person from society in a closed institution would prove to be inherently threatening to a person's life, health, and well-being; and put the person at risk of severe abuse, exploitation, and torture. The perception of a person's inability to take care of themself and make choices led to further impairments and further abuse: indefinite deprivation of liberty in inhumane and degrading

---

[1] Exported through colonization, the first mental health hospital in the Americas, Hospital San Hipolito, was built in Mexico in the 16th century. By the 19th century, Mexico had one of the largest psychiatric institutions in the continent, "La Castañeda," holding thousands of people with mental disabilities (Mental Health Rights 2000).

conditions; lack of basic medical care; physical and sexual abuse; denial of the right to legal capacity; lack of access to justice, including recourse to challenge detention; and practices that amount to torture, including forced treatment, forced sterilization, seclusion, and the use of physical and chemical restraints. A person placed in an institution lost the right to make even the most fundamental daily decisions of life, losing any form of independence (Rosenthal, Jehn, and Galvan 2009).

Such abuses are prevalent throughout institutions, but disproportionately burden marginalized populations facing multiple forms of discrimination. Women with disabilities experience aggravated forms of discrimination and specific violations against their right to legal capacity, including the loss of autonomy regarding their reproductive and sexual health and rights and resulting in highly discriminatory and harmful practices such as forced sterilization and abortion (Rodriguez 2015). Children are also particularly at risk, as the psychosocial deprivation inherent to institutions and the lack of opportunity to form a stable and emotional connection with a committed caregiver deeply impacted the emotional, cognitive, psychological, and physical development of a child. Children in institutions are further threatened by violence, sexual exploitation, and trafficking (Rosenthal 2019). In the 20th century, these discriminatory abuses would only worsen with the rise of eugenics in public health practice, as the threats to individuals in institutions gave rise to crimes against humanity.

C. Nazi Crimes and Birth of the United Nations

Eugenic theories became foundational principles of public health in the late 19th and early 20th centuries, with these theories promoting the "improvement of the population" by eliminating persons perceived as "inferior" or "unfit" (Petersen 2010). These theories were translated into laws and policies to control persons with disabilities and mental "illnesses," who were seen as fundamentally "unworthy" of life (Filax 2014). Psychiatrists in Germany promoted the sterilization of people with mental illnesses, and with the rise of the Nazi Party in 1933, this psychiatric foundation provided a medical basis for the Law for the Prevention of Hereditarily Diseased Offspring (Luty 2014). This "racial hygiene" law required the sterilization of people with schizophrenia, bipolar disorder, alcoholism, and other perceived mental illnesses. Over two hundred "hereditary health courts" were set up across Germany, with these courts authorizing over four hundred thousand sterilizations between 1934 and 1939, many under the judicial decision of "mentally ill" (Mottier and Gerodetti 2007).

During World War II, the Nazi regime continued to look to eugenic theory to support Nazi ideology, shifting from the sterilization to the institutionalization to the murder of those deemed "incurably ill." Between 1939 and 1941, eighty thousand to one hundred thousand "mentally ill" persons were killed across six psychiatric institutions, which had installed gas chambers to support this killing machine (Luty 2014). The murder of those with mental illness would provide the foundation for the genocidal extermination of millions. The Holocaust exposed the horrors suffered by minorities at the hand of the state, including people with disabilities, and gave rise to a new form of global governance founded upon equal dignity and rights of all persons.

At the conclusion of World War II, states came together to establish a new international legal regime under the UN. The UN would seek to ensure human rights for all people, with the 1945 Charter of the United Nations looking to "reaffirm faith in fundamental human rights, in the dignity and worth of the human person" and "to promote social progress and better standards of life in larger freedom" (UN 1945, Preamble). Given the Holocaust experience, states expanded these rights to people with disabilities – particularly those with mental health conditions (Lewis and Pathare 2020).[2] Under the UN, the 1946 Constitution of the World Health Organization (WHO) explicitly launched an international effort to ensure "complete physical, mental and social well-being" for all (WHO 1946, Preamble). This new system of global governance provided a basis to negotiate international standards to support mental health.

D. Evolution of International Standards

The nascent human rights system under the UN looked to international law to hold states accountable for human rights violations. Arising out of the 1948 Universal Declaration of Human Rights, the UN developed an evolving progression of international instruments, as seen in Figure 8.1, to guarantee the rights of persons with disabilities (Lewis and Pathare 2020).

In building from rising advocacy around "mental disability," the 1971 UN Declaration on the Rights of Mentally Retarded Persons (MR Declaration) was the first international instrument to articulate human rights principles relating specifically to people with disabilities. However, the MR Declaration reinforced a "deficit" model of mental health (Lord, Suozzi, and Taylor 2010, 566), and this paternalistic understanding limited rights for people with intellectual disabilities by providing that "the mentally retarded person has, to the maximum degree of feasibility, the same rights as other human beings"

---

[2] Despite international efforts to create an international regime that moved past Nazism, laws reflecting eugenic theory did not end after World War II and continued to influence policies in institutions in the ensuing decades (Kevles 1999).

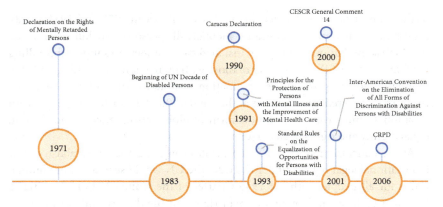

Figure 8.1 The Evolution of International Standards to Address Disability, Mental Health, and Human Rights (Rodríguez and Rosenthal)

(UN General Assembly 1971, para. 8) – with the implication that the exercise of rights for some people is not "feasible."[3] The MR Principles took for granted that institutionalization was "necessary for some" and permitted the removal of rights based upon the severity of the impairment, as determined by medical experts, for those individuals unable "to exercise all their rights in a meaningful way" (ibid., para. 7).

The advancement of rights started to take hold as disability rights principles developed in the 1983–1992 UN Decade of Disabled Persons. Declared by the UN General Assembly, this decade-long effort sought to develop minimum human rights standards for people with disabilities (Rosenthal and Rubenstein 1993). The resulting 1991 Principles for the Protection of Persons with Mental Illness and the Improvement of Mental Health Care (MI Principles) provided the UN General Assembly with an opportunity to focus specifically on people with psychosocial disabilities – even if still defining their identity under a medical model, as "patients" or "persons with mental illness."

Case Study: Advancing Rights under the MI Principles

The MI Principles reconceptualized mental health systems throughout the world, framing the call for deinstitutionalization and community

---

[3] With greater attention of the social construction of disability, the very term "mental retardation" is now considered a highly stigmatizing epithet that has been rejected by advocates and in policymaking (Nash et al. 2012).

integration as a matter of fundamental human rights. Shaping government obligations through human rights, the MI Principles established that every person with a "mental illness" shall have the right to live and work in the community. To make this possible, the MI Principles recognized that every "patient" shall have the right to be treated and cared for, as far as possible, in their own community, detailing a list of rights intended to ensure that those detained in psychiatric facilities are "treated with humanity and respect for the inherent dignity of the human person." The MI Principles continued to permit forced treatment and civil detention of people with mental illness, although this would require approval by an independent authority and include a range of procedural protections. Commentators at the time of the MI Principles observed that the balance between the provision of care and the protection of autonomy was still resolved "in a manner that favors paternalistic state coercion exercised through the actions of professionals over individual autonomy." While this resolution was consistent with mental health law trends throughout the world, the result compromised the protection of individual liberty. Despite these continuing limitations, the MI Principles gained recognition at the time as the most authoritative and comprehensive statement of human rights for people receiving mental health care.

Drawing from the MI Principles, the UN General Assembly adopted the 1993 UN Standard Rules on the Equalization of Opportunities for Persons with Disabilities. These Standard Rules represented an important step in establishing a global framework for a rights-oriented approach to disability issues, leading to the appointment of a UN Special Rapporteur for the rights of people with disabilities; however, these Rules were not binding and "did not result in the effective integration of disability issues into the mainstream UN human rights system" (Lord, Suozzi, and Taylor 2010, 567). In the absence of international human rights obligations to protect people with mental disabilities, mental health advocates would look to regional governance to uphold rights (Gostin and Gable 2004).

E. Regional Advancements

As the UN continued to develop non-binding human right standards, regional health and human rights bodies took the lead in calling for concrete legal steps to realize human rights for people with mental disabilities. In Latin America, the Pan American Health Organization (PAHO) organized a

1990 Regional Conference on the Restructuring of Psychiatric Care in Latin America, bringing together legislators, mental health professionals, human rights leaders, and disability activists to shape human rights protections in mental health care (Meier and Ayala 2014). The resulting Declaration of Caracas reflected a new consensus among health professionals, declaring that exclusive reliance on psychiatric hospitals "imperil the human and civil rights of patients" and seeking to "promote alternative services models that are community-based and integrated into social and health care networks" (PAHO 1990, paras. 2, 9). These regional standards influenced human rights in the Americas, leading to the adoption of the 2001 Inter-American Convention on the Elimination of All Forms of Discrimination Against Persons with Disabilities (Gostin 2004).

Building from these regional efforts, the UN human rights system began to consider human rights in mental health, looking to interpretations of the right to health as encompassing expansive obligations for mental health care (Gable and Gostin 2009). In interpreting the right to health, General Comment 14, adopted by the Committee on Economic, Social and Cultural Rights in 2000 and first introduced in Chapter 4, developed a broad definition of health to include mental health, allowing persons with disabilities to call on governments to provide a rights-based realization of mental health care (Gable and Gostin 2009). These international and regional efforts established a foundation for a binding UN treaty to recognize the health and human rights of persons with mental disability.

II. Convention on the Rights of Persons with Disabilities

The CRPD created a new global health law standard for people with mental health conditions and psychosocial disabilities. While many of the rights enshrined in the CRPD had been recognized in other human rights treaties, this new Convention "fundamentally enriches and modifies the content of existing rights when applied to people with disabilities, often by reformulating and extending rights" (Petersen 2010, 93). The CRPD moved away from the traditional distinction under international law between "civil and political" rights and "economic, social, and cultural" rights. By embracing a more holistic view of human rights for persons with disabilities, the CRPD shifted from a medical model to a social model of disability (Mégret 2008). The resulting treaty codified legal obligations to promote human rights essential to mental health—including legal capacity and the right to live included in the community—establishing a human rights basis for global mental health policy.

A. Participatory Processes in Developing the Convention

The participatory process that led to the CRPD shaped its inclusive obligations. Mexico launched this diplomatic effort in 2001, proposing that the UN General Assembly develop a convention on the rights of people with disabilities. In establishing rights to prevent discrimination on the basis of any disability, this proposal sought to develop a singular treaty on both mental and physical disability, codifying a holistic approach to disability health care. By unifying mental and physical disability, supporting states sought to ensure that no exclusion would be made based upon which type of disability an individual had, focusing instead on the inclusion of all. This initial proposal was adopted, with the General Assembly calling for the establishment of an Ad Hoc Committee of states to elaborate "a comprehensive and integral international convention to promote and protect the rights and dignity of persons with disabilities, based on the holistic approach of the work done in the field of social development, human rights and non-discrimination" (UN General Assembly 2001, art. 1).

Throughout the five-year development of the CRPD, the diplomatic negotiations repeatedly saw the meaningful participation of affected communities. In the months leading up to the first Ad Hoc Committee meeting in July 2002, disability organizations successfully pressed the UN for full access to and participation in the drafting process (Lord, Suozzi, and Taylor 2010). The diplomatic process of developing the CRPD came to be characterized by an unusually high degree of participation from non-state actors, particularly by representatives of disabled peoples' organizations (DPOs) (Lord 2008).[4] With the drafting process moving forward, advocacy became less divided between impairment groups (bringing together those with physical, mental, intellectual, or sensory impairments), as NGOs worked together in a cross-disability approach to human rights (Lewis and Pathare 2020). More than eight hundred representatives of DPOs and NGOs registered to participate in the Ad Hoc Committee process. Integration of NGOs and community voices became critical, as seen in Figure 8.2, and they became a driving actor in the CRPD drafting process.

The integration of various communities and stakeholders allowed for a uniform disability perspective – across impairments and throughout the world. Persons with disabilities, once relegated to institutions and out of sight of society, now had a vital role in promoting mental health in global health policy, meaningfully impacting the language and obligations enshrined in the resulting treaty.

---

[4] People with disabilities and NGOs formed the International Disability Caucus to support this participation, allowing people with disabilities to speak in a coordinated voice and work with technical experts and government representatives to draft the CRPD (Lewis and Pathare 2020).

Figure 8.2 Advocacy to Support CRPD Development (Sinn Féin)

In December 2006, the UN General Assembly adopted the CRPD, establishing "a key landmark in the emerging field of global health law and a critical milestone in the development of international law on the rights of persons with disabilities" (Petersen 2010, 109). The CRPD came to be signed and ratified by states at an unprecedented rate.[5] Reshaping global mental health policy, the CRPD rejected the medical model—which had focused on the need to care for, treat, and protect persons with mental health conditions—and instead embraced a social model of disability and human rights.

---

[5] While its swift adoption by nearly all states may point to a broad consensus on disability policy, nearly fifty states conditioned their ratifications of the CRPD with declarations, reservations, or objections.

B. Transition from Medical Model to Social and Human Rights Model

The CRPD acknowledges the interaction between impairments and barriers, recognizing that it is societal barriers (both attitudinal and environmental) that create disability. Where the medical model of disability focuses solely on the impairment of the individual, viewing disability "as a personal tragedy to be pitied, protected, or fixed on an individual level" (Rosenthal 2021, 96), the social model examines how societal structures construct the experience of disability. The social model conceptualizes the disability experience not in individual deficiency, but as the product of the interaction between a person's impairment and the socially constructed environment, examining the barriers that impede participation in society (Lord, Suozzi, and Taylor 2010). This conceptual shift offered by the social model reflects a fundamental break in mental health policy – away from focusing on the physical limitations of individuals and toward "the way the physical and social environments impose limitations on certain groups or categories of people" (Oliver and Sapey 1983, 23). The social model thus aligns with human rights, recognizing that society has the obligation to provide the supports and services necessary to ensure that the community is accessible to everyone.

The UN human rights system heralded the CRPD as a rejection of the framing of persons with disabilities as mere objects of charity in need of special care or treatment and instead as human beings equal in dignity and rights. Celebrating the adoption of the CRPD, the UN High Commissioner for Human Rights looked to the CRPD as a basis to ensure that persons with disabilities are "active members of society" – viewed as "subjects with rights, who are capable of claiming those rights and making decisions for their lives based on their free and informed consent" (UN General Assembly 2007, art. 25). As a foundation for human rights in global health governance, WHO looked to the CRPD as a basis to assist nations in building rights-based interventions, with WHO publishing guidance and providing technical assistance to Member States in reforming mental health systems to meet CRPD obligations (WHO 2021). The CRPD has played an important role in framing mental health across global governance, highlighting the importance of free will, self-determination, and inclusion within society.

By embracing a rights-based social model of disability, the CRPD signified a fundamental shift from previous international mental health policy instruments. This human rights framing provides that people with mental health conditions must be at the center of decision-making when it comes to their own treatment and the policies that affect them. As a basis for mental health policymaking, this shift toward human rights requires the full and meaningful participation of persons with disabilities in global health decision-making, and thereby "fundamentally alters the power dynamic that has prevailed in decision-making around the lives of persons with disabilities in law, policy and programming including, though not limited to, participation in the processes of global health governance" (Lord, Suozzi, and Taylor 2010, 568). This participation in the development of global health law and policy would provide a basis for the implementation of international legal obligations under the CRPD, guaranteeing the right to legal capacity and community living in mental health policy.

C. Legal Obligations

In framing mental health obligations under human rights law, the general principles of the CRPD reflect key pillars of respect for dignity, freedom to make one's own choices, independence, non-discrimination, full and effective participation, and accessibility. These CRPD general principles further seek to respect differences and ensure equality of opportunity, looking to the freedom to make one's own choices (right to legal capacity) and the right to independence (right to community living) in seeking to guarantee the right to live in the community.

1. Legal Capacity

Legal capacity encompasses the right to make decisions over your own life and to have those decisions acknowledged and recognized as valid. The ability of a person to make decisions about their own life is so fundamental that it is linked in the CRPD with "the right to recognition everywhere as persons before the law" (UN General Assembly 2007, art. 12). The CRPD thereby recognizes that "persons with disabilities enjoy legal capacity on an equal basis with others in all aspects of life" (ibid., art. 12.). While legal systems have long put people with disabilities under guardianship, conservatorship, or other "substitute decision making" regimes,[6] the CRPD is designed to allow people with disabilities—including those with mental health conditions—to maintain the maximum possible control of their lives, even if they have some limitations on their ability to understand or communicate their choices.

Under the first General Comment on the CRPD, the UN Committee on the Rights of Persons with Disabilities (CRPD Committee), the treaty body

---

[6] Under formal substitute decision-making regimes, a legal representative is appointed to make decisions on behalf of people with disabilities, or decisions are made by designated medical personnel or by a court. Beyond this *de jure* denial of legal capacity, the CRPD also seeks to limit any *de facto* loss of capacity, wherein people with disabilities who have not been formally placed under any form of substituted decision-making nevertheless face day-to-day restrictions in exercising their rights.

responsible for interpreting the obligations and monitoring the implementation of the CRPD, found that the right to legal capacity consists of two parts:

(1) the legal standing to hold rights and to be recognized as a legal person before the law; and
(2) the legal agency to act on those rights and to have those actions recognized by the law (CRPD Committee 2014, para. 14).

Through General Comment 1, the CRPD Committee has been emphatic in stating, "there are no permissible circumstances under international human rights law in which a person may be deprived of the right to recognition as a person before the law, or in which this right may be limited" (ibid., para. 5). Legal capacity is thus regarded as one of the CRPD's pillars and core values, as the ability to make decisions that have legal effect is crucial for mental health promotion and instrumental to exercising all the other rights recognized by the Convention (Rosenthal, Jehn, and Galvan 2009).

This new human rights-based model of legal capacity implies a shift from the substitute decision-making paradigm—where an individual is appointed to make decisions on behalf of a person with disabilities—to one that is based on "supported decision making." The CRPD recognizes that all persons with disabilities retain some abilities to make choices, requiring that governments take appropriate measures to provide access by persons with disabilities to the support they may require in exercising their legal capacity. The CRPD prohibits resorting to the standard of the "best interest" of the individual in relation to adults with disabilities, requiring that significant efforts be made to determine the individual's will and preferences and thereby ensuring that all possible accommodations, supports, and diverse methods of communication are made available and accessible before allowing a court to appoint a guardian to make a decision in place of the individual. These accommodations to ensure legal capacity provide a basis to realize a right to community living.

2. Community Living

One of the most important contributions of the CRPD is that it upholds the right of people with mental health conditions to full inclusion in society, establishing the right of all persons with disabilities to live in the community. Under the CRPD, no person is too impaired to enjoy and to benefit from the right to live as a full member of the community, with choices equal to others (Rosenthal 2021). In clarifying this principle, the CRPD Committee's General Comment 5 has recognized that the "level of support" needed by a person may not be "invoked to deny or limit the right to independent living," nor may the cost of care or support in the community be used to justify any limitation of the right (CRPD 2017, paras. 20–21).[7]

As a central foundation of community living, a person may never be detained in an institution solely on the basis of their disability or mental health condition. The CRPD Committee has recognized that any involuntary and/or prolonged commitment on disability grounds is unjustified, with this arbitrary detention in violation of the CRPD. Thus, the Committee has concluded that states parties should not permit mental health policies to allow for involuntary commitment of persons with disabilities in institutions based solely on actual or perceived impairments – finding that states must repeal legislation and policies that allow or perpetuate involuntary commitment (Szmukler 2020).

In responding to the continuing institutionalization of children with mental disabilities, this right to full inclusion and community living has been interpreted as prohibiting the placement of children in residential facilities outside the family (Rosenthal 2019). Where the immediate family is unable to care for a child with mental disabilities, the CRPD requires that the government take every effort to ensure that care is provided to the child by the "wider family" or "within the community in a family setting" (UN General Assembly 2007, art. 23). The CRPD Committee has clarified that "[f]or children, the core of the right to be included in the community entails a right to grow up in a family," reasoning that "there is no substitute for the need to grow up with a family" (CRPD Committee 2017, paras. 37, 16(c)). Despite this clear obligation under the CRPD, other human rights bodies continue to provide for the removal of children from families and placement into residential institutions.

Case Study: Debates on Community Living: Conflict between the CRPD and CRC

The 1989 Convention on the Rights of the Child (CRC), the first international human rights treaty to include a provision protecting the rights to children with disabilities, provided a basis for CRPD protections of family life; however, the CRC permits placement outside the family if a child does not have family or if they face abuse from the immediate family. In the context of disability, the CRC established that a child who is "temporarily or permanently deprived of his or her family environment" is entitled to "special protection" and placement in "alternative care," including institutionalization. During the decades

---

[7] To implement the right to live in the community, governments agree to take the necessary measures to facilitate the full enjoyment by persons with disabilities of this right and their full inclusion and participation in the community, including necessary community support services. For example, if people with disabilities lack a home in the community, they have a right to "a range of in-home, residential, and other community support services . . . to prevent isolation or segregation from the community" (UN General Assembly 2007, art. 19).

since the CRC was drafted, as research has continued to reveal the dangers of institutional placement for the physical and emotional development of the child, there have been a series of efforts to limit institutionalization as a violation of both children's rights and disability rights. The CRC Committee initially adopted a General Comment in 2007 to make it clear that institutional placement should be a "measure of last resort." This CRC interpretation provided human rights support for the 2010 UN Guidelines for the Alternative Care of Children, a non-binding but highly regarded set of professional standards that called for the "progressive elimination" of institutions. Yet despite seeking to eliminate large institutions, these Guidelines preserved smaller institutions, calling on governments to maintain a system of "residential care" facilities. This distinction between large and small institutions for children continues to be seen as incompatible with obligations under the CRPD, with the first UN Special Rapporteur on the rights of persons with disabilities reiterating the right of all children to grow up in a family, finding that placement of children in any residential setting outside a family is placement "in an institution."

These tensions between UN bodies highlight the evolving nature of international law—honing international standards until they are inclusive of all—with policymakers looking to these human rights standards as a basis for deinstitutionalization amid ongoing challenges in the continuing evolution of human rights to support mental health.

III. Deinstitutionalization and Community Inclusion Challenges to Mental Health

In implementing the CRPD to frame global mental health policy reforms, states must make efforts to support deinstitutionalization and community inclusion; however, amid ongoing challenges to global health and global governance, states have faced challenges in supporting health amid ongoing emergencies, including public health crises and rising humanitarian contexts. It will be necessary to ensure that CRPD implementation upholds the rights of people with disabilities, especially of those in institutions, in times of emergencies.

A. Implementing the CRPD

The CRPD recognizes the right of persons with disabilities to live independently, be included in the community, and to have choices equal to others. In supporting mental health, the CRPD thus requires that states ensure access to supports and services to enable persons with disabilities to live independently and avoid segregation and isolation from the community (OHCHR 2009). The UN High Commissioner on Human Rights has identified three key elements to ensure community integration: (1) independent living legally recognized and enforceable, (2) national policies and planning that integrate interventions, and (3) community-based support services (OHCHR 2009). With the adoption of the CRPD, the obligation to end mental health institutions and create community-based support services has become a fundamental human right.

The CRPD obligation to "prevent isolation or segregation from the community" (UN General Assembly 2007, art. 19) is incompatible with persons being detained in institutions. The CRPD Committee has repeatedly called on states to create deinstitutionalization strategies and community services in consultation with NGO partners – to ensure participation of persons with disabilities (Parker 2011). Where states are required to develop a plan for transitioning from institutions to community-based services, effective deinstitutionalization and community integration requires social supports for persons with mental disabilities (Hammarberg 2012). These supports entail an interconnected system of social services, assisted housing, education, work, as well as access to general health and mental health care.[8]

The right to live independently in the community will thus require access to services that promote mental health. Such services must be progressively realized through increasing state resources, with the CRPD obligating the state to "take measures to the maximum of its available resources ... with a view to achieving progressively the full realization of these rights" (UN General Assembly 2007, art. 4(2)). This progressive realization of underlying determinants of mental health extends to the state's obligation to provide resources, support services, and mental health care necessary to realize the right to community living for persons with disabilities. In fulfilling these obligations, the CRPD provides a framework to advance mental health in all policies, embracing both a rights-based and medicine-based framework to advance care for those with disabilities.

B. Advancing Mental Health Care

Health is not merely the absence of disease or the quality of medical care, with the right to health encompassing all aspects of mental health. WHO has thus made

---

[8] Because of the indivisible, interdependent, and interrelated nature of human rights, as introduced in Chapter 4, many civil, political, economic, social, and cultural rights recognized by the CRPD and other human rights treaties are relevant to the enjoyment of the right to live independently in the community.

it abundantly clear that an expansive human right to mental health is an essential pillar of the global health system. The human right to mental health seeks to establish medical care alongside core principles of equal dignity and well-being (Chapman et al. 2020). Despite global health movements to realize a human right to mental health—including the promotion of mental health care under the Sustainable Development Goals—large gaps remain in global health governance (OHCHR 2020). Adopting a human rights model for mental health care will call for realizing underlying determinants of mental health in communities. Improving these social determinants of health will require decreasing risks of violence and abuse, adverse childhood exposures, and environmental conditions – alongside medical care.

Yet, as global mental health frameworks slowly shift from institutionalization and community integration, there remain concerns that this shift is being accompanied by increasing medicalization of mental health. The shift toward medicalization frames mental illness solely in terms of medical and technical solutions for the individual (Clark 2014). This medical framing of mental health risks "pathologizing" normal variations in human experience, neglecting more holistic social understandings of mental wellness (Conrad and Slodden 2013). Overmedicalization of mental health may further entrench biomedical models of illness that can undermine community-centric approaches to advance public health and human rights. The continued presence of mental health hospitals introduce questions of involuntary medicalization that the CRPD frames as largely discriminatory (Szmukler, Daw, and Callard 2014). In seeking to avoid involuntary medicalization and promote mental health, WHO has developed a "World Mental Health Report" to examine how best to ensure the delivery of holistic community-based care.

This holistic care under the CRPD requires attention across social determinants of health – looking to a multisectoral approach to ensure the highest attainable standard of mental health in all policies. A multisectoral approach to mental health has long been neglected, with mental health concerns often addressed solely as a "health policy" issue – or outside of health policy altogether. These single-sector approaches fail to include psychosocial factors, determinates of mental health care delivery, and systems of discrimination (Lewis and Pathare 2020). A multisectoral approach can ensure CRPD implementation through a coordinated response across all sectors of policy. This will require bringing together a range of state and non-state actors to address mental health across the global health landscape (Lewis and Pathare 2020). Supported by human rights advocacy in developing global health policy, this multisectoral response would address social dimensions of mental health care policy in times of emergencies.

C. Public Health Emergencies

In spite of these efforts to address mental health policy under global health governance, the COVID-19 pandemic exposed just how vulnerable people with mental disabilities are to abuse and neglect during public health emergencies. From the start of the pandemic, WHO noted that people with disabilities, particularly those detained in institutions, would likely be at greater risk of contracting COVID-19 (WHO 2020). The UN Special Rapporteur on the rights of persons with disabilities expressed her concern for the rights of those in institutions, psychiatric facilities, and prisons "due to the risk of contamination and the absence of external supervision" (UN News 2020).[9] This lack of supervision would be exacerbated amid states of emergency.

As COVID-19 spread throughout the world, people in residential institutions, and particularly institutionalized people with disabilities, were at increased risk of contracting the virus and dying (Booth 2020). Looking across countries, the Disability Rights Monitor (DRM) gathered testimonies from thousands affected during the pandemic, concluding that "states have overwhelmingly failed to take sufficient measures to protect the rights of persons with disabilities in their responses to the pandemic" (DRM 2020, 7). These testimonies revealed the grave and systemic violations of the rights of persons with disabilities in large- and small-scale institutions – including the denial of access to health care, bans on visitors, and isolation of residents. The DRM report recommended that states "enact emergency deinstitutionalization plans, as informed by persons with disabilities and their representative organizations, including adopting an immediate ban on institutional admissions during and beyond the pandemic, and the transfer of funding from institutions into community supports and services" (DRM 2020, 13). This civil society advocacy during the pandemic, which evidenced the health risks in institutionalized settings, provided further support for efforts to close institutions and move people into the community.

Based on this report and its recommendations, the CRPD Committee in 2022 issued "Guidelines on Deinstitutionalization, including in Emergencies" to provide direction to states in shifting away from institutions and toward comprehensive community services during public health emergencies. These Guidelines are the first time the CRPD Committee has issued such detailed parameters for states to carry out deinstitutionalization. Providing a checklist for states to ensure that deinstitutionalization processes are done in accordance with the CRPD, the Guidelines detail measures to respect specific fundamental rights, like the right

---

[9] Similarly, the Inter-American Commission on Human Rights (IACHR) noted that people deprived of liberty in psychiatric hospitals "face a situation of special risk of contagion from COVID-19," observing that "these centers of deprivation of liberty would be characterized by overcrowding, lack of adequate hygiene, negligent medical care, and inadequate food" (IACHR 2020, para. 3).

to legal capacity, and include vulnerable groups like children with disabilities. With the pandemic emergency compounded by the invasion and occupation of Ukraine by the Russian Federation in February 2022, global health actors have been forced to move further to recognize the rights of people with disabilities amid complex humanitarian emergencies.

D. Humanitarian Contexts

Among the consequences of war, armed conflict, and other humanitarian contexts, the impact on the mental health of the civilian population is one of the most significant. Studies show an increase in the incidence and prevalence of mental disorders during and following conflicts (Murthy and Lakshminarayana 2006); yet people with disabilities, particularly those with mental health conditions, are often overlooked by humanitarian efforts. In these complex humanitarian emergencies, the UN General Assembly and Human Rights Council have repeatedly established that international human rights law applies in situations of armed conflict alongside, as discussed in greater detail in Chapter 18, international humanitarian law. The rights recognized by the CRPD remain in effect during armed conflict, including the right to community inclusion, to grow up in a family for children, and to be free from discrimination. However, these rights to protect those with mental disability have often been ignored by warring states in recent conflicts (Rosenthal et al. 2022).

Case Study: Mental Health amid Conflict: The War in Ukraine

After the Russian Federation invasion of Ukraine in February 2022, children and adults with disabilities were largely abandoned in evacuation efforts. Less impaired or non-disabled children from war zones were moved to neighboring countries while those with greater needs were transferred to institutions in western Ukraine or left behind in institutions in the east – even as the war intensified around them. In echoes of the horrors of the Holocaust, children with disabilities continued to live in atrocious conditions, with their harms exacerbated by the separation from families. However, little is being done to prevent or end the separation and ensure that children with disabilities and their families are supported. The international funding that is being provided for mental health in Ukraine is largely directed toward improving conditions within institutions—creating a risk of legitimizing such institutions and normalizing the abuses within them—as international development and humanitarian relief agencies have reported that they are unprepared to provide support for family and community integration in times of emergency. While WHO is providing support to community mental health teams, as illustrated in Figure 8.3, there has been little or no organized outreach to help children in institutions return to families. Recognizing the harm of segregating children with disabilities, the implementation of the CRPD and the UN Guidelines on Deinstitutionalization will require a commitment—on the part of Ukraine and the international community—to ensure disability rights and community inclusion as part of humanitarian relief efforts.

Figure 8.3 WHO Director-General Tedros Adhanom Ghebreyesus Inspects Destroyed Hospital in Ukraine (WHO/Andrei Krepkih)

In resolving these concerns for children's mental health care amid humanitarian conflict, the Inter-Agency Standing Committee (IASC)[10] has developed Guidelines on the Inclusion of Persons with Disabilities in Humanitarian Action (IASC Guidelines). The IASC Guidelines, first developed in 2019, call for the identification of children living in residential facilities – and the inclusion of children in family tracing and reunification when in "their best interest" (IASC 2019). However, this language is not fully compliant with CRPD requirements, leaving open the possibility of indefinite and continued institutionalization and

[10] The IASC is the highest-level humanitarian coordination forum of the UN system, which seeks to bring together all organizations to formulate policy, set strategic priorities, and mobilize resources in response to humanitarian crises.

exclusion from family tracing (DRI 2022). Where the CRPD Committee has recognized the right of children to grow up in a family (CRPD 2017), family tracing and reunification provides a means to guarantee that right for children in institutions. Children with mental disabilities should always be included in humanitarian efforts, but this will require aligning the IASC Guidelines with the CRPD to guarantee the right to grow up in a family for all children, particularly to protect children with disabilities in institutions – and reunite them with their families when the conflict has ended.

Conclusion

Global mental health policy has developed to recognize the dignity and rights of people with mental health conditions. The adoption of the CRPD was a watershed moment for people with disabilities, especially for those with mental health conditions, who had for centuries been stigmatized, institutionalized, segregated, and abused. The CRPD clearly outlines human rights violations and provides tools to ensure legal capacity and community integration. However, challenges remain, as people with mental health conditions still face segregation and abuse worldwide, with rising obstacles to deinstitutionalization amid pandemic threats and humanitarian suffering. These unprecedented challenges will need to be considered by global health policymakers to ensure that no one is left behind, particularly children with disabilities in institutions, in efforts to realize the highest attainable standard of mental health.

The task now is to implement international mental health standards fully and guarantee the rights of people with mental health conditions globally. Respecting, protecting, and fulfilling human rights throughout the world will require the development and implementation of global health law, arising out of the CRPD but expanding beyond it in the coming years. Global health policy needs to ensure the provision of accessible mental health services in the community that respect and protect human rights, including the right to full participation in decision-making for people with disabilities and organizations that represent them. This approach must be accompanied by a multisectoral approach to health that looks at other supports and services without which mental health cannot be fully realized. This approach to mental health in all policies will need to be accompanied by a comprehensive deinstitutionalization strategy that is rooted in international standards, such as the UN Guidelines on Deinstitutionalization. Such a global governance effort will need the perspectives of all relevant stakeholders, involving people with mental health conditions and disabilities, scholars, civil society, governments, international organizations, and international human rights bodies, including the CRPD Committee.

It will be crucial to further expand global health law to ensure community inclusion and support mental health in the years to come. These legal reforms will require efforts to grapple with international humanitarian situations, including public health emergencies and armed conflicts, which have created unprecedented new challenges to global mental health policies. Reforms must ensure effectiveness in humanitarian crisis, ensuring the right to community inclusion in all contexts. Protections against discrimination, inhumane and degrading treatment, and life-saving health care under international law create immediate obligations. A serious effort is long overdue to ensure that people with psychosocial disabilities are treated with dignity and that their rights and choices are respected when they seek mental health treatment. Individuals should no longer be asked to give up their right to live as part of society and yield their right to legal capacity in order to receive essential mental health treatment and care. Recognizing the long history of rights violations, the need for emergency reforms, and the challenges ahead, there is an urgent imperative to engage with policy reforms and start acting now to ensure justice in mental health.

Questions for Consideration

1. What human rights are threatened by guardianship and institutionalization approaches to mental health?
2. How did eugenic theories lay the foundation for Nazi sterilization and genocide of disabled populations? How did these Nazi horrors shape the human rights foundations of UN governance?
3. Why was the 1971 MR Declaration inadequate to protect human rights amid the continuing institutionalization of those with intellectual disabilities? How did the 1991 MI Principles seek to overcome these continuing challenges to shape mental health law?
4. Why did the CRPD bring together physical, mental, intellectual, or sensory impairments under a single treaty? How did the participation of disabled peoples organizations influence the drafting of the CRPD?
5. What did it mean for the CRPD to transition from a medical model of disability to a social model of disability? Why does the social model better reflect human rights norms and principles? How does the social model shift the practice of mental health?
6. What does it mean to be deprived of "legal recognition as a person before the law"? Why is "legal capacity" a core pillar of the CRPD and a core value of mental health policy? How can "supported decision making" overcome the limitations of "substitute decision making"?

7. Why has it proven challenging to realize a right to community living through the elimination of detention in residential institutions? Why have treaty bodies disagreed on the best way to ensure that children with mental disabilities are provided with a family life?
8. What national policies are necessary to advance deinstitutionalization strategies and community-based support services in implementing the CRPD? How can the human right to health support mental health in all policies, framing mental health care and underlying determinants of mental health?
9. How has the COVID-19 pandemic challenged mental health – inside and outside of institutions? How has the CRPD Committee's "Guidelines on Deinstitutionalization, including in Emergencies" sought to support states in long-awaited efforts to carry out the process of deinstitutionalization?
10. Why do humanitarian relief efforts neglect institutionalized populations in the context of armed conflict? What steps are being taken by WHO amid the war in Ukraine to support mental health and what further steps can be taken to overcome limitations in the international response?

Acknowledgments

The authors greatly appreciate the editorial guidance of Lawrence O. Gostin and the research assistance of Chris Burch and Kerstan Nealy.

References

Bellack, Alan S., and Michel Hersen. 1998. *Comprehensive Clinical Psychology*. 1st ed. New York: Pergamon.

Booth, Robert. 2020. "Half of Coronavirus Deaths Happen in Care Homes, Data from EU Suggests." *The Guardian*. April 13.

Chapman, Audrey, Carmel Williams, Julie Hannah, and Dainius Pūras. 2020. "Reimagining the Mental Health Paradigm for Our Collective Well-Being." *Health and Human Rights* 22(1): 1–6.

Clark, Jocalyn P. 2014. "Medicalization of Global Health 2: The Medicalization of Global Mental Health." *Global Health Action* 7(1): 24000.

Conrad, Peter and Caitlin Slodden. 2013. "The Medicalization of Mental Disorder." In *Handbook of the Sociology of Mental Health*, edited by Carol S. Aneshensel, Jo C. Phelan, and Alex Bierman, 61–73. Dordrecht: Springer Netherlands.

Craigie, Jillian, Michael Bach, Sándor Gurbai, Arlene Kanter, Scott Y.H. Kim, Oliver Lewis, and Graham Morgan. 2019. "Legal Capacity, Mental Capacity and Supported Decision-Making: Report from a Panel Event." *International Journal of Law and Psychiatry* 62: 160–68.

CRPD Committee (Committee on the Rights of Persons with Disabilities). 2014. "General Comment No. 1 (2014): Article 12: Equal Recognition Before the Law." May 19. CRPD/C/GC/1

CRPD Committee. 2017. "General Comment No. 5 (2017) on Living Independently and Being Included in the community." October 27. CRPD/C/GC/5

Disability Rights International (DRI). 2022. "Left Behind in the War: Dangers Facing Children with Disabilities in Ukraine's Orphanages." 5 May. 1-22.

DRM (Disability Rights Monitor). 2020. *Disability Rights During the Pandemic: A Global Report on Findings of the COVID-19 Disability Rights Monitor*. Washington: DRM

Filax, Gloria. 2014. *Disabled Mothers: Stories and Scholarship by and about Mother with Disabilities*. Chicago: Demeter Press.

Gable, Lance and Lawrence O. Gostin. 2009. "Mental Health as a Human Right." In *Realising the Right to Health*, edited by Andrew Clapham and Mary Robinson, 249–261. Geneva: Rüffer & Rub.

Gostin, Lawrence O. 2004. "International Human Rights law and Mental Disability." *The Hastings Center Report* 34(2): 11–12.

Gostin, Lawrence O. and Lance Gable. 2004. "The Human Rights of Persons with Mental Disabilities: A Global Perspective on the Application of Human Rights Principles to Mental Health." *Maryland Law Review* 63(1): 20–121.

Hammarberg, Thomas. 2012. *The Right of People with Disabilities to Live Independently and be Included in the Community*. France: Council of Europe.

IACHR (Inter-American Commission on Human Rights). 2020. "En el contexto de la pandemia COVID-19, la CIDH llama a los Estados a garantizar los derechos de las personas con discapacidad." April 8. No. 071/20

IASC (Inter-Agency Standing Committee). 2019. "Guidelines: Inclusion of Persons with Disabilities in Humanitarian Action." July.

Kevles, D. J. 1999. "Eugenics and Human Rights." *BMJ* 319(7207): 435–438.

Lewis, Oliver, and Soumitra Pathare. 2020. "Chronic Illness: Disability and Mental Health." In *Foundations of Global Health & Human Rights*, edited by Lawrence O. Gostin and Benjamin Mason Meier, 285–306. New York: Oxford University Press.

Lord, Janet E. 2008. "Disability Rights and the Human Rights Mainstream." In *The International Struggle for New Human Rights*, edited by Clifford Bob. 83–92. Philadelphia: University of Pennsylvania Press.

Lord, Janet E., David Suozzi, and Allyn L. Taylor. 2010. "Lessons from the Experience of U.N. Convention on the Rights of Persons with Disabilities: Addressing the Democratic Deficit in Global Health Governance." *Journal of Law, Medicine & Ethics* 38(3): 564–579.

Luty, Jason. 2014. "Psychiatry and the Dark Side: eugenics, Nazi and Soviet Psychiatry." *Advances in Psychiatric Treatment* 20(1): 52–60.

Mégret, Frédéric. 2008. "The Disabilities Convention: Human Rights of Persons with Disabilities or Disability Rights?" *Human Rights Quarterly* 30: 494–516.

Meier, Benjamin Mason and Ana S. Ayala. 2014. "The Pan American Health Organization and the Mainstreaming of Human Rights in Regional Health Governance." *Journal of Law, Medicine & Ethics* 42(3): 356–374.

Mottier, Veronique and Natalia Gerodetti. 2007. "Eugenics and Social Democracy: Or, How the European Left Tried to Eliminate the 'Weeds' from Its National Gardens." *New Formations* 60: 35–45.

Murthy, R. Srinivasa and Rashmi Lakshminarayana. 2006. "Mental Health Consequences of War: A Brief Review of Research Findings." *World Psychiatry* 5(1): 25–30.

Nash, Chris, Ann Hawkins, Janet Kawchuk, and Sarah E Shea. 2012. "What's in a Name? Attitudes Surrounding the Use of the Term 'Mental Retardation.'" *Pediatrics & Child Health* 17(2): 71–74.

OHCHR (Officer of the United Nations High Commissioner for Human Rights). 2009. "Thematic Study by the Office of the United Nations High Commissioner for Human Rights on Enhancing Awareness and Understanding of the Convention on the Rights of Persons with Disabilities." January 26. A/HRC/10/48

OHCHR 2020. "Report of the Special Rapporteur on the right of everyone to the enjoyment of the highest attainable standard of physical and mental health." June 16. A/HRC/44/48.

Oliver, Michael and Bob Sapey. 1983. *Social Work with Disabled People*. London: Basingstoke Macmillans.

PAHO (Pan American Health Organization). 1990. "The Caracas Declaration." The Conference on the Restructuring of Psychiatric Care in Latin America within the Local Health Systems.

Parker, Camilla. 2011. *A Community for All: Implementing Article 19 – A Guide for Monitoring the Implementation of Article 19 of the Convention on the Rights of Disabilities*. New York: Open Society Public Health Program.

Petersen, Carole J. 2010. "Population Policy and Eugenic Theory: Implications of China's Ratification of the United Nations Convention on the Rights of Persons with Disabilities." *China: An International Journal* 8(1): April: 85–109.

Rodriguez, Priscila. 2015. *Twice Violated: Abuse and Denial of Sexual and Reproductive Rights of Women with Psychosocial Disabilities in Mexico*. Washington: Disability Rights International.

Rosenthal, Eric. 2019. "The Rights of All Children to Grow Up with a Family under International Law: Implications for Placement in Orphanages, Residential Care, and Group Homes." *Human Rights Law Review* 65(80): 65–137.

Rosenthal, Eric. 2021. "Residential Care Controversy: The Promise of the UN Convention on the Rights of Persons with Disabilities to Protect All Children." *International Journal of Disability and Social Justice* 1(1): 95-117.

Rosenthal, Eric, Erin Jehn, and Sofia Galvan. 2009. *Abandoned & Disappeared: Mexico's Segregation and Abuse of Children and Adults with Disabilities*. Washington: Disability Rights International and the Comisión Méxicana de Defensa y Promoción de los Derechos Humanos.

Rosenthal, Eric, Halyna Kurylo, Dragana Ciric Milovanovic, Laurie Ahern, and Priscila Rodriguez. 2022. "Protection and Safety of Children with Disabilities in the Residential Institutions of War-Torn Ukraine: The UN Guidelines on Deinstitutionalization and the Role of International Donors." *International Journal of Disability and Social Justice* 2(2): 15–22.

Rosenthal, Eric, and Leonard S. Rubenstein. 1993. "International Human Rights Advocacy under the 'Principles for the Protection of Persons with Mental Illness.'" *International Journal of Law and Psychiatry* 16: 257–300.

Szmukler, George. 2020. "Involuntary Detention and Treatment: Are We Edging Toward a 'Paradigm Shift'?" *Schizophr Bull* 46(2): 231–235.

Szmukler, George, Rowena Daw, and Felicity Callard. 2014. "Mental Health Law and the UN Convention on the Rights of Persons with Disabilities." *International Journal of Law and Psychiatry* 37(3): 245–252.

Tester, Pamela, Erica Wood, Naomi Karp, Susan Lawrence, Winsor Schmidt Jr., and Marta Mendiondo. 2005. *Wards of the State: A National Study of Public Guardship*. Chicago: The Retirement Research Foundation.

UN (United Nations). 1945. *Charter of the United Nations*. New York: UN.

UN General Assembly. 1971. "Declaration on the Rights of Mentally Retarded Persons." December 20. A/RES/2856(XXVI).

UN General Assembly. 2001. "Ad Hoc Committee on a Comprehensive and Integral International Convention on the Protection and Promotion of the Rights and Dignity of Persons with Disabilities." December 20. A/RES/56/168.

UN General Assembly. 2007. "Convention on the Rights of Persons with Disabilities." January 24. A/RES/61/106.

UN News. 2020. "Las personas con discapacidad, en riesgo por el coronavirus." *UN News*. March 17.

WHO (World Health Organization). 1946. *Constitution of the World Health Organization*." New York: WHO

WHO. 2020. "Consideraciones relativas a la discapacidad durante el brote de COVID-19." April 23.

WHO. 2021. *Guidance and Technical Packages on Community Mental Health Services*. Geneva: WHO.

9

Environmental Health

Regulating Clean Air and Water as Underlying Determinants of Health

Marlies Hesselman and Benjamin Mason Meier

Introduction

Global health is dependent on environmental health. A safe environment is an underlying determinant of health, with the health of humans linked to the health of the planet, but rising environmental health threats face the planet in the coming decades, ranging from climate change, pollution of water, air, and soil, and loss of biodiversity. Humans have degraded the environmental conditions underlying global health. Despite this global threat, environmental risks are not felt equally throughout the world. Poor water quality and polluted air disproportionately impact children under five, while low- and middle-income countries bear the greatest share of environmental challenges. These global inequities implicate issues of environmental racism, social injustice, and human rights, highlighting that communities of color and in the Global South are often burdened with, or even used as "sacrifice zones" for, some of the world's most polluting and dangerous industrial activities.

Increased understanding of new and persistent environmental health threats, including the increasingly complex nature of environmental determinants of health, requires a constant evolution in global health law and policy responses. States have long developed international treaties to protect the natural environment, with several new multilateral environmental agreements currently in development through the United Nations (UN). These legal regimes have found normative support under international human rights law, with the UN human rights system interpreting human rights to protect environmental health and the UN General Assembly adopting resolutions to recognize new human rights underlying a healthy environment. With this legal foundation, global governance has brought together UN agencies to provide novel multisectoral partnerships and institutional responses to complex environmental threats—framing a "One Health" approach across human health, animal health, and environmental protection. This global health law framework provides new attention to the fundamental global health importance of water, sanitation, and hygiene (WASH), air pollution, and clean, safe, and modern energy services.

This chapter examines the importance of global efforts to address environmental risks that adversely affect human health, analyzing how global health law and policy have been employed to address environmental health threats. Part I examines the evolution of environmental health under international law, giving rise to international environmental law, global environmental governance, and a new global agenda to protect the earth. By establishing novel institutional arrangements and instruments to uphold environmental health throughout the world, Part II considers the multisectoral partnerships and human rights foundations that have framed global health law to uphold a healthy environment. Part III analyzes the imperative for environmental justice to protect environmental health, recognizing the inequities bred from environmental racism, the need for environmental protection under a "One Health" approach to global governance, and the risks to the environment amid global transitions in the climate change response. This chapter concludes that environmental agreements have developed into one of the cornerstones of the global health landscape, but new international legal models will be necessary to address rising environmental health challenges.

I. Interlinkages between Health and the Environment under International Law

Beginning in the 1960s, policymakers came to understand that the environment is crucial to health. Recognizing the need for global cooperation to address environmental health issues, the UN became involved in environmental governance, calling for international conferences to address rising threats to the human environment—and leading to the development of international environmental law to address environmental health at the global level. This attention to environmental health under international law would expand from the 1970s through the 1990s, with a focus on air and water pollution, establishing new systems of global governance for environmental protection and sustainable development.

A. Evolution of Public Health as a Major Concern under International Environmental Law

International law to protect environmental health arose out of multilateral environmental agreements to protect public health through the preservation of clean environments. Rapid urbanization had led to an early awareness of air pollution and smog in large metropolitan cities.[1] Emissions of sulfur oxides (SOx) and nitrogen oxides (NOx) would be carried over long distances, leading to "acid rain" far from polluting sources and raising an imperative for environmental protection through international cooperation. With growing understanding of the health impacts of environmental pollution in the 1960s, air and water pollution became the first environmental issues to arise on the international policy agenda. This urgency to address global environmental health emergencies led to the birth of the modern environmental movement—with an explicit focus on environmental determinants of health (Solecki and Shelley 1996). The public health impetus for international environmental law is evident from the first multilateral environmental agreements, which were shaped in 1972 by the foundational Stockholm Declaration on the Human Environment.

Case Study: Environmental Concerns Arise at the UN

Responding to the rise of an international environmental movement, Sweden in 1968 proposed an international conference in Stockholm on the problems facing the human environment. With widespread support from the UN Secretary-General and endorsements from the UN Economic and Social Council and General Assembly, a Preparatory Committee for the Conference examined a variety of issues for the conference agenda, including the need for legally binding provisions, the relationship between the environment and development, and the role of international and domestic measures. Inspired by a landmark UN environmental report, "The Limits of Growth," debates throughout the 1972 Conference primarily focused on balancing the environmental concerns of the world's rich and poor nations—with rich nations prioritizing the regulation of pollution and poorer nations seeking assurances that these pollution concerns would not limit their economic development. The resulting Stockholm Declaration and Action Plan for the Human Environment outlined 26 principles and 109 recommendations that focused on environmental issues at the international level, detailing how higher-income countries and lower-income countries could each begin to address environmental threats. While not presenting binding legal obligations, the Declaration established important principles that would come to form the foundation of international environmental law: establishing state sovereignty over natural resources, curtailed by the obligation to prevent transboundary

---

[1] As policymakers became aware of the environmental health threats of an industrialized world, Rachel Carson's "Silent Spring" (1962) and Stewart Udall's "The Quiet Crisis" (1963) incited a public urgency to address air and water pollution.

environmental harm; managing the earth's natural resources for present and future generations, including water, air, land, flora and fauna, wildlife, and ecosystems; limiting harmful toxic emissions into the environment; and protecting the health of the oceans. Significantly, the Stockholm Declaration offered one of the first international proclamations of the "right to a healthy environment," articulating in Principle 1 that "man has the fundamental right to freedom, equality and adequate conditions of life, in an environment of a quality that permits a life of dignity and well-being."

A key outcome of the Stockholm Conference was the agreement to establish international institutional arrangements to support the implementation of the Stockholm Declaration and Plan of Action, leading the UN General Assembly to establish the United Nations Environment Programme (UNEP). Although various UN specialized agencies were already engaged in environmental activities, states recognized the need for a specialized international organization to consolidate environmental efforts and expertise under the UN (Ivanova 2010). Since its inception in 1972, UNEP has been at the forefront of environmental health policy through its work to coordinate a wide range of environmental policies across the UN system (Gray 1990). Early efforts by UNEP focused on expanding existing conventions by UN agencies, for example, by bringing together nations to address pollution of the oceans.[2] These initial UNEP efforts established it as the principal agency responsible for facilitating and coordinating multinational environmental measures.

With this grounding in global governance under the UN, international environmental law's evolution to protect public health is seen across several subsequent multilateral agreements to address global environmental health threats.

Beginning at the regional level, European nations faced increasing air pollution concerns in the 1960s and 1970s, challenged by the effects of emissions of harmful substances that caused transboundary acidification of nature in other countries. The UN Economic Commission for Europe (UNECE) responded by adopting the 1979 Long-Range Transboundary Air Pollution Convention (LRTAP Convention). This binding regional treaty explicitly defined "air pollution" as introducing substances or energy into the air that can cause "deleterious effects of such a nature as to endanger human health, harm living resources and ecosystems and material property" (UNECE 1979, art. 1(a)). In strengthening air quality management systems, the agreement specifically focused on monitoring

---

[2] In its first major effort, UNEP coordinated with twenty-two state actors to enact the Mediterranean Action Plan (1975), focused on addressing rampant marine pollution by ships in the Mediterranean ocean by implementing the UN International Maritime Organization's 1973 International Convention for the Prevention of Pollution from Ships (MARPOL) (Thacher 1977).

emission rates, assessing alternative measures for attaining environmental objectives, and ensuring education on environmental impacts of pollution—with subsequent protocols to regulate specific pollutants.

Advancing environmental policy at the global level, the UN General Assembly in 1982 adopted the World Charter for Nature, proclaiming a set of conservation principles that acknowledged respect for nature and natural processes. The Charter, while not binding, recognized that while humans may use the environment for their benefit, they may not do so in a way that endangers "the integrity of those other ecosystems or species with which they coexist" (UN General Assembly 1982, sect. I.4.). With states in the Global South seeking to shift policy from an "anthropocentric" to an "ecocentric" view of environmental health protection,[3] this more holistic vision of environmental protection—viewing "mankind" as an integral part of nature—was adopted by 111 votes in favor and 18 abstentions, with the United States casting the sole dissenting vote.

In building from this non-binding Charter, binding international legal regulation would come to be seen as essential to addressing the environmental challenge posed by the depletion of the ozone layer. The ozone layer is a thin layer of Earth's atmosphere within the stratosphere that is vital to shielding the Earth from dangerous ultraviolet (UV) radiation. Due to the release of commercial chlorofluorocarbons (CFCs), especially in aerosol products, this layer was partially depleted, and the resulting "hole" in the ozone layer exposed the Earth to high levels of UV radiation, posing a severe public health threat that necessitated an international response (Caron 1990).

The rapid development of the 1985 Ozone Layer Convention and the 1987 Montreal Protocol on Ozone Depleting Substances provided this necessary international legal response by establishing:

(1) the global objective of taking "appropriate measures . . . to protect human health and the environment against adverse effects resulting or likely to result from human activities" related to the emission of ozone depleting substances; and
(2) the concrete obligations to phase out the production and consumption of specific harmful substances.

These two binding instruments were so successful in reducing the health threat of ozone depletion that younger generations may be unaware that the world

---

[3] An "anthropocentric" view places humans at the center of nature and the environment at the disposal of human beings, whereas an "ecocentric" approach accepts the intrinsic value of nature. This shift implies that environmental regulation does not only address environmental degradation when human health and interests are at threat, but when the health of the planet, nature, other species, and ecosystem are at stake (Kotzé and French 2018).

averted this cataclysmic environmental health threat through international law (Barratt-Brown 1991).

B. Advancement of International Environmental Health Law through the "Earth Charter"

To strengthen international environmental law, world leaders convened a second global environmental conference on the 20th anniversary of the Stockholm Conference. This 1992 UN Conference on Environment and Development (UNCED) in Rio de Janeiro, Brazil, also called the "Rio Conference" or "Earth Summit," would seek to codify the goals laid out in the Stockholm Declaration and create binding obligations for addressing environmental threats alongside development. Much like the preceding Stockholm Conference, concrete negotiations and preparation for the conference began well in advance of the Rio Conference. The UN World Commission on Environment and Development (WCED), under the leadership of former Norwegian Prime Minister Gro Harlem Brundtland, had long investigated the environmental threats facing the international community and the ways and means by which these threats could be addressed, leading to the 1987 publication of "Our Common Future" (WCED 1987). This "Brundtland Report" elaborated the idea of "sustainable development," calling for a better integration of global objectives for economic growth and environmental protection.[4] Drawing from the Brundtland Report in the years leading up to the UNCED, a Preparatory Committee comprised of various industrialized and developing countries divided itself into multiple working groups to frame the UNCED debates at the Earth Summit (Kovar 1993).

The Earth Summit brought together a far larger scale of actors than prior conferences—nearly 175 governmental representatives and 100 heads of states or government, along with representatives of a wide range of NGOs, as seen in Figure 9.1—to promote a multisectoral, international approach to addressing environmental issues (Freestone 1994). (NGOs were not formally included in the Earth Summit, but non-governmental stakeholders convened a parallel 1992 Global Forum, advancing their own agenda on environmental matters.)

The Earth Summit yielded a wide range of binding and non-binding instruments, including the UN Framework Convention on Climate Change,

---

[4] The integration of economic growth and environmental protection had long been a central issue in international politics, in part because of the struggles of newly independent "Third World Countries" to develop their economies and natural resources, as discussed in Chapter 3, under a "New International Economic Order."

Figure 9.1   NGOs Convening at the 1992 Earth Summit's Global Forum
(UN/Ruby Mera)

the UN Convention on Biodiversity, and the non-binding Rio Declaration on Environment and Development. Under the Rio Declaration, or "Earth Charter," states laid out twenty-seven principles—with the aim of creating a programming tool that could chart a new course for sustainable development.

These "Rio principles" reaffirmed those of the Stockholm Declaration while establishing the concept of "sustainable development." The Earth Charter defined sustainable development as integrating environmental protection into the development process and ensuring that development is realized in such a way that the developmental and environmental needs of both present and future generations can be equitably met. In seeking sustainable development, the Earth Charter explicitly declared a central focus on public health: "Human beings are at the centre of concerns for sustainable development. They are entitled to a healthy and productive life in harmony with nature" (UN 1992, Principle 1). While not restating a "right to a healthy environment" with the same priority as the Stockholm Declaration, the resulting principles in the Rio Declaration created a far wider global coalition for sustainable development, seeking to balance the need for development raised by low-income countries with the goal of establishing a more "human-centered" and intersectoral approach to addressing environmental health concerns (Kovar 1993). Drawing from this imperative to address environmental concerns across global governance, environmental health regulations would develop further in the years that followed, through hard and soft legal instruments, addressing a wide range of new and accelerating environmental health threats (Amuasi et al. 2020).

II. Normative Foundations of Environmental Protection through Global Governance

Environmental conditions have become a central focus of global health law. Such global health law advancements have supported multisectoral UN collaborations, bringing together UNEP, WHO, and other global institutions in innovative new partnerships. The normative foundations of these environmental protection partnerships have been strengthened by international human rights law, with the UN human rights system elaborating the environmental dimensions of health-related human rights while establishing new human rights that underlie a healthy environment.

A. Expanding UN Efforts to Address Environmental Risk Factors

UN efforts to address environmental health have expanded significantly, yet often in fragmented ways. UNEP is still a central leader in environmental governance, but WHO has also evolved into a crucial actor in addressing environmental health. With different organizations now seeking to collaborate on environmental health issues, it has remained a challenge to prevent fragmentation in the environmental health landscape. Acknowledging this fragmentation under the UN, the UN Secretary-General has sought to identify why international environmental law is still often piecemeal and reactive (UN Secretary-General 2018), as the UN has developed new institutional partnerships in an effort to coordinate global environmental governance.

1. UNEP Leadership in Environmental Governance

As the primary international environmental management agency, UNEP continues to be the principal global authority for setting environmental agendas and promoting coherent implementation of the environmental dimensions of sustainable development. UNEP acts as an advocate on environmental protection and has conducted environmental assessments in support of policies to protect environmental health. Since its establishment in the Stockholm Conference, UNEP has consistently worked to incorporate environmental concerns across international policies and to support the implementation of multilateral environmental agreements (Chasek, Downie, and Brown 2017).[5] UNEP now holds an expansive mandate to address three interconnected planetary crises: climate change, nature and biodiversity loss, and pollution and waste.

Incorporating international diplomacy in UNEP governance, states in 2015 established the United Nations Environment Assembly (UNEA), bringing together the universal membership of all UN Member States. Similar to the World Health Assembly that governs WHO, UNEA can adopt ministerial declaration and resolutions, with this governing body providing leadership and catalyzing global action. UNEA is currently driving several major efforts for new global health instruments, including a groundbreaking new Plastic Pollution Treaty. Drawing from UNEA's historic 2022 resolution on "End Plastic Pollution: Towards an International Legally Binding Instrument" (UNEA 2022), which examined the risks of plastic pollution for human health and well-being, UNEA has called for the prevention, reduction, and elimination of plastic pollution and established an Intergovernmental Negotiating Committee to develop international plastics regulations across the "full life cycle" of pollution.

Given the multisectoral nature of environmental health issues, UNEP has additionally engaged in frequent collaborative partnerships with other multinational organizations. In addressing the health impacts of environmental pollution, WHO has monitored the release of Persistent Organic Pollutants (POPs) since 1987 and examined the implications of these pollutants for health under the 2001 Stockholm Convention on Persistent Organic Pollutants (Colles et al. 2008). UNEP has also worked frequently with the Food and Agricultural Organization of the United Nations (FAO) to examine the linkages between human, animal, and ecosystem health—laying the foundations for expanded collaborations across institutions of global health governance (Villanueva-Cabezas 2022).

2. WHO Guidelines, Standards, and Roadmaps on Environmental Health

As a longstanding leader in global health governance, WHO has come to hold a standard-setting role in addressing several key environmental determinants of health. Based on available health science, and in collaboration with public health experts, WHO has developed a broad range of soft law guidelines, standards, and roadmaps to help states adopt appropriate national legislation and policies:

- WHO Indoor Air Quality Guidelines: Dampness and Mold (2009)
- WHO Indoor Air Quality Guidelines: Household Fuel Combustion (2014)

---

[5] Since 1992, UNEP has administered a wide range of multilateral agreements to address discrete environmental pollutants, including the Rotterdam Convention on Hazardous Chemicals (1998), the Stockholm Convention on Persistent Organic Pollutants (2001), and the Minamata Convention on Mercury (2013).

- WHO WASH Strategy (2018–2025)
- WHO Housing and Health Guidelines (2018)
- Global Strategy on Health, Environment and Climate Change (2020)
- Strategic Roadmap on Health and Energy (2021)

To consolidate WHO's work on access to clean energy as an environmental determinant of health, the High Level Coalition on Health and Energy, convened by the WHO Director-General, adopted its first "Strategic Roadmap on Health and Energy" in 2021, prioritizing access to electricity for healthcare facilities and access to "clean" cooking. This Roadmap draws attention to the need to curb the burning of solid fuels (including wood, dung, crop residues, (char)coal, diesel, and kerosene) for daily energy needs as a basis to reduce indoor and outdoor air pollution, alleviating an enduring public health risk through WHO governance (Hesselman 2022).

In framing WHO governance, the World Health Assembly has taken an increasingly active role in responding to environmental health challenges. The Assembly's 2015 resolution on "Health and the Environment: Addressing the Health Impact of Air Pollution" established an initial framework to strengthen WHO efforts to provide technical guidance and assistance to Member States in addressing indoor and outdoor air pollution. This resolution urged states to "redouble their efforts to identify, address and prevent the health impacts of air pollution," including by developing and strengthening "international multisectoral cooperation" (WHA 2015, art. 1). Supporting collaborative partnerships to frame environmental health governance, the World Health Assembly requested that the WHO Director-General work with other UN partners, programs, and agencies, with a specific focus on collaboration with UNEP. Yet despite these efforts to strengthen environmental health partnerships, organizations have continued to face a fragmentation of global governance on environmental health issues, as the UN has looked to new collaborative institutions to coordinate efforts.

3. Establishment of UN-Water and UN-Energy

Following from the global environmental conferences in Stockholm and Rio de Janeiro, the 2002 World Summit on Sustainable Development (WSSD) in Johannesburg, South Africa led to the establishment of both UN-Water and UN-Energy as "inter-agency coordination mechanisms." These mechanisms would coordinate activities on water and energy across UN agencies to aid in the implementation of the 2002 Johannesburg Plan of Implementation (JPOI).

- UN-Water coordinates action across the UN to achieve water related targets, providing coordination on technical issues and fostering multi-stakeholder partnerships among public, private, and civil society actors (Cooley

et al. 2014). In facilitating global water governance, UN-Water supports UN institutions and national policymakers in assessing environmental health risks in water, sanitation, and hygiene through the Global Analysis and Assessment of Sanitation and Drinking-Water (GLAAS) (WHO 2020).
- UN-Energy enhances coordination, coherence, and collaboration across the UN on energy, bringing together more than 30 organizations to ensure access to affordable, reliable, sustainable, and modern energy for all. Providing evidence-based information to support informed policy making, UN-Energy acts as a gateway for information, knowledge, experiences, and good practices, and reports on sustainable energy trends and management issues.

Yet despite the establishment of these coordinating institutions, both UN-Water and UN-Energy lack authorization as formal institutions under international law. With both institutions lacking secure funding and human resources, water and energy governance have remained fragmented, leading to institutional disagreements about whether these coordination mechanisms should continue behind-the-scenes or take a more public role to advance environmental health. In finding a renewed mandate with the adoption of the UN Sustainable Development Goals (SDGs) in 2015, these coordinating institutions have looked to bring together a wider range of actors under the common goals of the SDGs[6] and common norms of human rights.

B. Advancing Human Rights for Environmental Health and a Healthy Environment

Launching a movement for human rights to advance environmental health, the 1972 UN Conference on the Human Environment conceptualized the right to a healthy environment for the first time, with the resulting Stockholm Declaration recognizing that an individual's environment is "essential to his well-being and to the enjoyment of basic human rights—even the right to life itself" (UN General Assembly 1972, sect. I). In spite of this link between environmental health and human rights, the Stockholm Declaration failed to call for a specific right to a safe, clean, and healthy environment. Through continuing efforts to advance human rights under international law as a basis for environmental health—drawing from the rights to health, water, and energy—these evolving rights would culminate in a right to a healthy environment, establishing a rights-based foundation for international environmental policy.

[6] Under the 2030 Agenda for Sustainable Development, the SDGs commit all UN Member States under SDG 6 to safe drinking water, sanitation, and hygiene and under SDG 7 to universal access to modern, affordable, reliable energy services.

1. The Right to Health

The right to health has evolved to recognize state obligations for environmental health. Under the 1966 International Covenant on Economic, Social and Cultural Rights (ICESCR), states codified the "right of everyone to the enjoyment of the highest attainable standard of physical and mental health," including government responsibilities "for the improvement of all aspects of environmental and industrial hygiene" (UN General Assembly 1966, art. 12). These aspects of "environmental and industrial hygiene" would be taken up in the advancement of international human rights law, with the 1989 Convention on the Rights of the Child requiring that governments "take appropriate measures to combat disease and malnutrition through the provision of adequate nutritious foods and clean drinking water, taking into consideration the dangers and risks of environmental pollution" (UN General Assembly 1989, art. 24).

Interpreting these interconnected environmental rights as "underlying determinants of health," the UN Committee on Economic, Social and Cultural Rights (CESCR), charged with drafting official interpretations of the ICESCR, issued General Comment 14 in 2000. As described in Chapter 4, this General Comment provides authoritative interpretation of the human right to health, concluding that:

> the right to health embraces a wide range of socio-economic factors that promote conditions in which people can lead a healthy life, and extends to the underlying determinants of health, such as food and nutrition, housing, access to safe and potable water and adequate sanitation, safe and healthy working conditions, and a healthy environment (CESCR 2000, para. 4).

The CESCR clarified that in order to protect health, states shall (drawing from the Stockholm Declaration) prevent and reduce the population's "exposure to . . . detrimental environmental conditions that directly or indirectly impact upon human health" (ibid, para. 15). In meeting this responsibility for environmental conditions, states bear an obligation to implement policies aimed at reducing and eliminating pollution by regulating polluting industries (Negri 2020).

2. Right to Water

Intertwined with concern for environmental health, the right to water has long been linked to the right to health, sharing a common history and interdependent evolution. Yet growing calls to address water pollution would come to see human rights to water and sanitation develop dramatically, from implicit responsibilities to independent rights. Flowing from the CESCR's interpretation of the right to health in General Comment 14, the CESCR defined the scope and content of a right to water in General Comment 15, holding that "the human right to water is indispensable for leading a life in human dignity. It is a prerequisite for the realization of other human rights" (CESCR 2002, para.1). Although water is not mentioned in the original text of the ICESCR, the CESCR interpreted it into the ICESCR based upon existing provisions, finding that a right to water is normatively situated under the umbrella of the human right to a standard of living and the human right to health. Recognizing that "pollution and diminution of water resources affects human health" (ibid., para. 44), General Comment 15 provides that states must protect water sources against pollution. In concluding that "the human right to water entitles everyone to sufficient, safe, acceptable, physically accessible and affordable water for personal and domestic uses" (ibid., para. 2), this interpretation of the right to water by the CESCR would lead in the ensuing years to the declaration of new human rights by the UN General Assembly (Meier et al. 2013).

Case Study: Declaring Human Rights to Water and Sanitation

The evolution of rights-based water and sanitation policy found groundbreaking political support in the UN General Assembly's 2010 Resolution on the Human Right to Water and Sanitation, reflecting international political recognition of the scope and content of this independent right. Following the adoption of General Comment 15, the legal status of the right remained politically contentious, in part because it was novel to interpret new human rights into existing treaty law. It would be vital for states themselves to declare water a human right under international law. With the UN General Assembly committing to an International Decade for Action "Water for Life" (2005-2015), states directed the UN High Commissioner for Human Rights to report on the scope and content of human rights obligations related to equitable access to safe drinking water and sanitation, looking to water pollution through inadequate sanitation. The High Commissioner concluded in 2008 that the time had come for the formulation of a distinct human right to water and sanitation. The UN General Assembly took up this recommendation in July 2010, declaring safe and clean drinking water and sanitation to be a human right under international law. Under its Resolution—"The Human Right to Water and Sanitation," adopted by a vote of 122—0, with 41 abstentions—the General Assembly recognized "the right to safe and clean drinking water and sanitation as a human right that is essential for the full enjoyment of life and all human rights," calling on states and international organizations to support international assistance and cooperation to ensure this right for all.

3. Right to Energy

Since public health depends on access to modern, clean energy supplies and services, human rights bodies have increasingly affirmed state obligations to curb environmental pollution from fossil fuels and transition to new forms of clean and renewable energy. Access to safe and clean energy at the household level—including for cooking, heating, and lighting, as well as basic access to electricity—is seen as an important underlying environmental determinant of health. Yet, while the UN has included "universal access to modern affordable and reliable energy sources" as a target under the SDGs, the right to energy has not yet been recognized as a self-standing human right under international law (Hesselman 2022).

Recognizing a new human right to energy is essential to ensure access to clean energy. Under the 1979 Convention on the Elimination of All Forms of Discrimination Against Women (CEDAW), a "right to electricity" was first seen as an essential part of a woman's right to an adequate standard of living (UN General Assembly 1979, art. 14). The CEDAW Committee subsequently clarified this obligation to implicate government responsibilities to secure clean energy access in rural areas as a basis for health (Hesselman 2021a).[7] The CESCR has since accepted that the right to an adequate standard of living implies "basic access to energy," with the Committee on Rights of the Child similarly commenting that the right to health implies access to clean cooking and living spaces free from smoke and pollution (Hesselman 2022). Access to electricity and clean cooking have since been recognized as tied to other rights, including the right to health, right to housing, right to life, right to education, right to benefit from scientific progress, and right to a healthy environment (Hesselman 2023).

4. Right to a Healthy Environment

These health-related human rights all point toward the need for a healthy environment. After initial recognition of a right to a healthy environment in the 1972 Stockholm Declaration, advocates decried a lack of human rights advancements in the 1992 Rio Declaration, with an international group of experts meeting thereafter to examine the link between environmental conditions and human rights obligations. The resulting 1994 Draft Declaration on Human Rights and the Environment framed twenty-two principles to uphold human rights, most notably that: "All persons shall have the right to a secure, healthy and ecologically sound environment" (UN Commission on Human Rights 1995, Principle 1). This right was seen to underlie global health, with the Draft Declaration seeking to promote "the right to the highest attainable standard of health free

---

[7] The CEDAW Committee noted that rural women are often responsible for solid biomass collection and use, making them disproportionally vulnerable to associated environmental health and safety risks from air pollution.

from environmental harm" (ibid., Principle, 7). However, states declined to take up this call to declare human rights for a healthy environment, holding back international human rights law in environmental health debates.

Despite these limitations under international law, advocates continued to push for the declaration of a right to a healthy environment. Responding to this growing advocacy, the UN Human Rights Council in 2012 appointed a UN Special Rapporteur on human rights and the environment to study the human rights obligations related to the enjoyment of a "safe, clean, healthy, and sustainable environment" (HRC 2012). In drawing from the work of the Special Rapporteur to map best practices across nations and clarify the normative content of this right, the Human Rights Council in 2021 unanimously recognized a right to a safe and healthy environment as essential for human life and dignity, and in early 2022, states proposed a resolution before the UN General Assembly.[8] The resulting July 2022 General Assembly resolution—passed with 161 votes in favor and 8 abstentions—recognizes the right to a clean, healthy, and sustainable environment, calling on all stakeholders "to adopt policies, to enhance international cooperation, strengthen capacity-building and continue to share good practices in order to scale up efforts to ensure a clean, healthy and sustainable environment for all" (UN General Assembly 2022, 4).

These human rights advancements have established a rights-based foundation for global environmental governance. International organizations have already begun to mainstream human rights in their global policies to advance environmental health (Buse, Hesselman, and Meier 2022). With WHO's 2021 Global Air Quality Guidelines endorsing the notion of a "right to breathe clean air" and the 2022 WHO Guidelines on Drinking Water Quality explicitly referring to the "right to water," human rights have the potential to become a cornerstone of the normative foundations shaping justice in international environmental law.

III. Environmental Health through Environmental Justice

Future international legal efforts to advance environmental health will need to embrace evolving conceptions of environmental justice. Ongoing struggles of environmental racism in low-income countries and among marginalized groups continue to challenge a "just" approach to environmental health. The COVID-19 pandemic has revealed the importance of living in harmony with nature, with the danger posed by zoonotic diseases bringing a "One Health" approach to the

---

[8] In supporting this declaration of a right to a healthy environment, every single Special Rapporteur of the Human Rights Council came together to urge the UN General Assembly to recognize "that living in a clean, healthy and sustainable environment is a fundamental human right" (OHCHR 2022).

fore of international environmental policy. As global governance approaches the enormous task of rapidly, urgently, and deeply transitioning toward a new way of living that mitigates climate change, a focus on "Planetary Health" can ensure that this "just transition" does not produce or reproduce new and existing health inequities.

A. Environmental Racism

Environmental justice must overcome the continuing legacies of environmental racism. The notion of "environmental racism" was born out of the wider environmental justice movements of the 1980-1990s, with studies revealing the disproportionate exposure to and impact of environmental degradation on people of color, especially Black communities, as well as the effects of discriminatory environmental policymaking (Bullard 1993). Responding to this ongoing injustice at the global level, the UN Human Rights Council's Working Group of Experts on People of African Descent published a 2021 thematic report on "environmental justice, the climate crisis and people of African descent." This human rights analysis acknowledged that communities of color are disproportionately affected by harmful "extractivist" economic and environmental policies, with environmentally hazardous and polluting industries (landfills, waste management facilities, polluting chemicals, and fossil fuels) often situated in Black and other communities of color (HRC 2021).[9] Concluding that the rights of people of African descent continue to be inequitably harmed by environmental hazards all over the world—resulting from generations of structural racism, economic divestments, segregation, and other forms of discrimination—the Working Group recognized the human rights imperative to address the perpetuation of these historic injustices. These international analyses make clear that environmental racism cannot be addressed in isolation from systemic manifestations and structures of racism at the global level.

Although the notion of environmental racism is typically used to identify marginalized communities affected by environmental discrimination at the local level, scholars and activists have begun to use this term to examine the injustice of global governance arrangements—reflecting structural inequities between the Global North and Global South. Drawing from debates on "environmental racism," "environmental justice," and "Third World Approaches to International Law" (TWAIL), Global South advocates seek to lay bare the

---

[9] The UN Special Rapporteur on human rights and the environment thereafter published a report on human rights in these so-called "sacrifice zones," recognizing examples of environmental racism throughout the world (Boyd 2022). In highlighting environmental racism in the United States, the Special Rapporteur drew attention to a sacrifice zone called "Cancer Alley" in Louisiana: an 85-mile stretch of land along the Mississippi River that includes 150 petrochemical plants and refineries that have caused massive and deadly levels of air, soil, and water pollution, affecting predominantly Black communities.

persistence of oppressive power dynamics in global governance, discriminatory attitudes across countries, and economic policies that reflect neocolonialism (Westra and Lawson 2001). The encompassing effort to "decolonize" global health, first introduced in Chapter 3, must include the just and inclusive design and implementation of multilateral environmental agreements on hazardous waste management, climate change, and biodiversity protection (Alam et al. 2016). Where addressing environmental racism will require efforts to redress past injustices—and remedy structural violence still experienced by communities of color—this process involves fully and equitably including the voices and interests of marginalized communities in all environmental health decision-making (Van Norren and Laats 2022). Non-Western, non-White voices must be actively championed and celebrated for their contributions to environmental health stewardship and living in harmony with nature. This can be done by expanding global environmental governance to include Indigenous and non-Western concepts and knowledge involved in caring for Mother Earth such as Pachamama, Buen Vivir, Gaia, Ubuntu, and the Rights of Nature (Kelbessa 2018).

B. One Health—From Tripartite to Quadripartite Governance

In expanding the concept of environmental health itself, the initial conceptualization of One Health arose out of a recognition that the realization of global health would require cooperation across sectors. With the emergence of SARS, West Nile Virus, Avian Influenza, and other zoonotic infectious diseases, the Wildlife Conservation Society invited experts from across sectors to discuss the spread of disease between human and animal populations. This "One World, One Health" Conference—bringing together specialists from WHO; FAO; the United States National Wildlife Health Center; and other public health, animal health, and environmental health organizations—drafted the 2004 Manhattan Principles, establishing a holistic approach to epidemic prevention (Gibbs 2014). These Principles serve as a call to action for institutions to work together to maintain ecosystem integrity—to the benefit of humans, animals, and biodiversity. Drawing from the Manhattan Principles, the notion of One Health galvanized a global response.

This multisectoral focus on One Health would require new cooperative arrangements across international organizations. Establishing this cooperative global governance in 2010, WHO, FAO, and the World Organization for Animal Health (OIE, now WOAH)[10] announced their formal collaboration to address health impacts on humans, animals, and the environment, as they recognized that infectious disease control necessitates a global multisectoral response. During their

---

[10] Originally established as the *Office International des Epizooties* (OIE), it formally reconstituted itself in May 2022 under its English-language name: the World Organization for Animal Health (WOAH).

first decade of cooperation, the "Tripartite" established action plans, guidance, and tools on matters of antimicrobial resistance (AMR), rabies, and zoonotic (including avian) influenza (OIE 2010). It further made strides to ensure joint surveillance through the Global Early Warning System (GLEWS), integrating OIE, FAO, and WHO international surveillance, alert, and disease intelligence procedures (Mackenzie, Mckinnon, and Jeggo 2014). The Tripartite expanded its multisectoral leadership to facilitate collaboration between the animal and public health sectors in the implementation of International Health Regulations (IHR), as introduced in Chapter 6, including through the joint review of national capacities for the detection of and response to health events (OIE 2017). However, addressing One Health effectively would require a greater focus on environmental health.

In 2022, the Tripartite multisectoral governance partnership formally expanded with UNEP into a "Quadripartite" governance arrangement. Bringing together this inter-institutional partnership in a Joint Statement, the Quadripartite endorsed a new definition of One Health, as depicted in Figure 9.2:

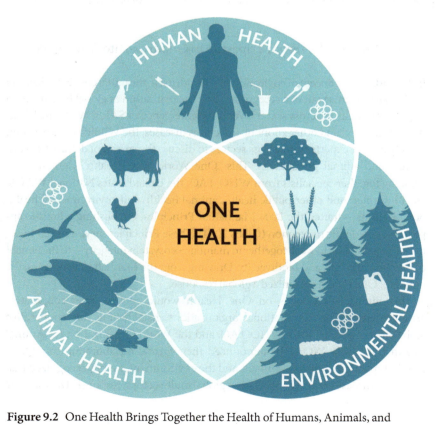

Figure 9.2 One Health Brings Together the Health of Humans, Animals, and Ecosystems (Margaret Morrison)

One Health is an integrated, unifying approach that aims to sustainably balance and optimize the health of people, animals and ecosystems. It recognizes the health of humans, domestic and wild animals, plants, and the wider environment (including ecosystems) are closely linked and inter-dependent. The approach mobilizes multiple sectors, disciplines and communities at varying levels of society to work together to foster well-being and tackle threats to health and ecosystems, while addressing the collective need for clean water, energy and air, safe and nutritious food, taking action on climate change, and contributing to sustainable development (OHHLEP 2022).

Seeing the health threats exposed by the COVID-19 pandemic, it has become clear that the environment must be addressed under One Health, bringing action to address wildlife and the environment into the global health partnerships. Looking across sectors in providing guidance and capacity-building to support global governance to uphold One Health, policymakers must look to the Quadripartite in considering human–environmental risk management under global health law (de Garine-Wichatitsky 2020).

Case Study: COVID-19 Reveals the Importance of the One Health Approach

The COVID-19 pandemic has strengthened the need for One Health policy—given the risk associated with zoonotic infectious disease and the impacts of the pandemic on communities, health systems, and economies. Pandemics due to emerging infectious diseases are increasingly caused by pressure on the environment as a result of changes in land use, international trade, and population growth. Global health law must address these connections between the health of people, animals, and the environment. With states seeking to reform global health law—developing both a pandemic treaty and targeted amendments of the IHR, as introduced in Chapters 5 and 6—it will be crucial to have all members of the Quadripartite involved so that future pandemic preparedness and response can examine the complex and multifaceted issues at the intersection of environmental conditions and infectious disease. This diplomatic moment offers a crucial opportunity for One Health to be codified in global health governance and enter the mainstream of infectious disease surveillance, response, and recovery. In particular, the pandemic treaty holds the potential to address the gaps left in IHR (2005) by facilitating greater coordinated action in human, animal, and environmental health. Facilitating necessary environmental regulations, UNEP can give substance to the environment protection dimension of the One Health approach, offering expertise on how to break transmission chains and prevent spillover of zoonotic diseases into humans. In looking outside WHO governance and beyond infectious disease threats, international environmental law must also clarify the public health impacts of environmental conditions. Future reforms of multilateral environmental agreements can provide a basis to strengthen environmental health governance across international organizations, aligning international environmental law with global health law through greater environmental collaboration to advance One Health.

This One Health approach will be crucial to future pandemic responses, but beyond these efforts to expand inter-organizational collaborations in infectious disease control, strengthening environmental health will require a new focus on Planetary Health across global governance—recognizing that humanity's very existence is dependent upon the flourishing of the natural environment.

C. Just Transitions within Planetary Boundaries

Climate change will present unprecedented complications to the global regulation of environmental health across sectors, raising an imperative to ensure environmental health alongside "Planetary Health." Anthropogenic climate change, discussed in greater detail in Chapter 19, is aggravating existing health threats—from the increase in geographical ranges of vector-borne infectious diseases like malaria, dengue, and Japanese encephalitis to the decrease in air quality through the formation of ground level ozone or smoke from forest fires (Hesselman 2021b). The response to climate change requires deep transitions to more sustainable paths of living in a very short period of time, with these transformations threatening new risks to environmental health but also providing crucial opportunities to intertwine efforts to promote sustainable development and environmental health.

Transitioning to a sustainable world will require novel, massive, disruptive changes, requiring new forms of governance and instruments of law that see the health of the planet as a crucial consideration for the future of humanity. Planetary Health, as a field of study and social movement, is advancing rapidly to reconceptualize efforts to achieve the highest attainable standard of health, well-being, and equity worldwide by means of the Earth's natural systems (Phelan 2020). Yet, global transitions to promote Planetary Health may end up strengthening the position of the rich, wealthy, and advantaged while placing disproportionate costs on marginalized communities or future generations. In the energy sector, the transition away from production and use of fossil fuel resources will mitigate the threat of climate change, but industries promoting clean renewable energy technologies are of enormous scale, developing new products that may present new risks to environmental health (Haines and Frumkin 2021). There will be major challenges ahead as new forms of energy production bring new environmental challenges, as seen in the increasing use of nuclear power (and management of nuclear waste) and the expanded mining of rare minerals (alongside mining pollution in the air and water). As these environmental health harms take shape in vulnerable communities, repeating many of the environmental injustices of past modes of production, there are unresolved questions of what will happen to the people that live in these areas—and whether new "sacrifice zones" will be left behind.

The transition to a low-carbon, sustainable, healthy future can offer new opportunities to promote both climate change mitigation and environmental health advancement, but climate change and environmental health must be considered together under global health law. The notion of a "just transition" must equitably allocate the benefits and costs of this global transition. A just transition implies that global health governance is designed in such a way that benefits are actively brought to the communities that have faced past neglect (Tigre et al. 2023). As recently stated by the UN Special Rapporteur on Human Rights and Extreme Poverty, a human rights-compliant concept of "just transition" would imply that all decision-making aims to achieve a "triple dividend"—of a cleaner planet; improved access to essential services relevant to the enjoyment of human rights, such as water, energy, or healthcare services; and the creation of decent, safe, clean jobs (UN General Assembly 2020). To avoid planetary health solutions that lead to new environmental health problems, the energy transition must be carried out in ways that realize principles of justice, equity, and human rights.

Conclusion

Environmental health threats are getting worse, becoming increasingly complex—both in their causes and consequences—and revealing the interconnectedness of the world. Given the threat to the world, global policy responses will have to become more complex, urgent, and drastic. Environmental policy in the 21st century affects the lives of billions of people and the planet itself. Due to the growing complexity of environmental health threats, environmental degradation no longer affects only human health, but the ecosystems on which all life depends. Solutions of the past may be not necessarily apply to the threats of today or tomorrow. Multilateral environmental agreements to address the major threats of this century—climate change, waste management, waterway protections—face continuing limitations in effectively protecting health. Beyond these challenges, the world faces new threats—from the impacts of plastic pollution, the risk of zoonotic diseases causing pandemics, or the pervasiveness of air pollution for vulnerable populations. Each of these challenges may not easily be addressed by existing frameworks for environmental health protection and will require novel multisectoral approaches to global governance.

Despite limitations, international environmental law has developed into one of the cornerstones of global health. Ongoing UNEP negotiations for a Plastic Pollution Treaty and WHO negotiations for the pandemic treaty provide new opportunities to strengthen environmental health under both international environmental law and global health law. To ensure that these reforms are just and effective, complementing each other to advance environmental health, they must draw from evolving normative concepts and frameworks to ensure environmental justice and human rights. Human rights continue to speak to the imagination of activists and victims, and as increasingly well-developed tools for legal action, the UN has established several new rights underlying environmental health—including the rights to water and sanitation and the right to a healthy environment. These rights-based advancements provide hope for the establishment of new rights to reflect evolving threats, from a right to clean energy to a right to a stable climate, to ensure justice through environmental health.

As scientific knowledge of global environmental health threats and environmental inequities expands, so must the global law and policy responses to them. This will require new strategic tools in global governance to advance healthier environments and to promote healthier populations amid a changing climate and energy transition. Addressing these environmental health concerns through multisectoral governance, it will be crucial to bring together international environmental law, human rights law, and global health law to respond to globalized environmental risks to public health. The urgency of these global health challenges will require rapid responses that reflect the scale of the threat, and the policies developed in years ahead will lay the foundation for environmental health in the world to come.

Questions for Consideration

1. How did public concerns about environmental health come to be seen as a global threat requiring global action under the UN? What principles from the Stockholm Convention would shape environmental protection for generations to come?

2. Why was soft law insufficient in responding to the depletion of the ozone layer? How did the Ozone Layer Convention find success in reducing ozone depleting substances throughout the world?
3. Why did the Earth Summit prove so influential in the establishment of so many legal instruments, including the UN Framework Convention on Climate Change, the UN Convention on Biodiversity, and the Rio Declaration on Environment and Development? How did the Rio Declaration shape early concern for sustainable development?
4. How does UNEP support multilateral environmental agreements? Why has UNEP sought collaborative partnerships across international organizations to promote environmental health?
5. Why is global environmental governance fragmented? Why have inter-agency coordination mechanisms (UN-Water and UN-Energy) faced challenges in coordinating the complex landscape of actors?
6. How have intersecting human rights come together to support environmental health? Why was it necessary for the right to water and the right to a healthy environment to find support from the UN General Assembly?
7. How must MEAs be reformed to redress environmental racism, ensure environmental justice, and decolonize global health?
8. Why is a One Health approach necessary to support global health? How can UNEP inclusion in Quadripartite governance strengthen the One Health approach in global health law reforms?
9. How will a changing climate compound environmental health threats? Why must Planetary Health and environmental health be seen as interconnected—ensuring policies that mitigate climate threats and protect environmental conditions?

Acknowledgments

The authors are grateful for the dedicated research assistance and editorial support of Quintin Gay.

References

Alam, Shawkat, Sumudu Atapattu, Carmen Gonzales, and Jona Razaque. 2016. *International Environmental Law and the Global South*. Cambridge: Cambridge University Press.

Amuasi, John H, Tamara Lucas, Richard Horton, and Andrea S Winkler. 2020. "Reconnecting for Our Future: The Lancet One Health Commission." *Lancet* 395(10235): 1469–1471.

Barratt-Brown, Elizabeth P. 1991. "Building a Monitoring and Compliance Regime under the Montreal Protocol." *Yale Journal of International Law* 16: 519–570.

Boyd, David R. 2022. "The Right to a Clean, Healthy and Sustainable Environment." UN Human Rights Council. January 12. A/HRC/49/53.

Bullard, Robert D. 1993. "The Threat of Environmental Racism." *Natural Resources & Environment* 7(3, Winter): 23–26, 55–56.

Buse, Kent, Marlies Hesselman, and Benjamin Mason Meier. 2022. "The Human Right to a Healthy Environment—Time for the Public Health Community to Take Urgent Action." *BMJ* 378: o2313.

Caron, David D. 1990. "Protection of the Stratospheric Ozone Layer and the Structure of International Environmental Lawmaking." *Hastings International & Comparative Law Review* 14: 755.

CESCR (Committee on Economic, Social, and Cultural Rights). 2000. "General Comment 14: The Right to the Highest Attainable Standard of Health (Art. 12)." August 11. E/C.12/2000/4.

CESCR. 2002. General comment no. 15, The right to water (arts. 11 and 12 of the International Covenant on Economic, Social and Cultural Rights). January 20. E/C.12/2002/11.

Chasek, Pamela S., David L. Downie, and Janet Welsh Brown. 2017. *Global Environmental Politics*. New York: Routledge.

Colles, Ann et al. 2008. "Fourth WHO-Coordinated Survey of Human Milk for Persistent Organic Pollutants (POPs): Belgian Results." *Chemosphere* 73(6): 907–914.

Cooley, Heather, Newsha Ajami, Mai-Lan Ha, Veena Srinivasan, Jason Morrison, Kristina Donnelly, and Juliet Christian-Smith. 2014. "Global Water Governance in the Twenty-First Century." In *The World's Water*, edited by P.H. Gleick. Washington: Island Press.

de Garine-Wichatitsky, Michel, Aurélie Binot, Serge Morand, Richard Kock, François Roger, Bruce A. Wilcox, and Alexandre Caron. 2020. "Will the COVID-19 Crisis Trigger a One Health Coming-of-Age?" *Lancet Planetary Health* 4(9): e377–e378.

Freestone, David. 1994. "The Road from Rio: International Environmental Law after the Earth Summit." *Journal of Environmental Law* 6,(2): 193–218.

Gibbs, E. Paul J. 2014. "The Evolution of One Health: A Decade of Progress and Challenges for the Future." *Veterinary Record* 174(4): 85–91.

Gray, Mark Allan. 1990. "The United Nations Environment Programme: An Assessment." *Environmental Law* 20: 291.

Haines, Andy and Howard Frumkin. 2021. *Planetary Health: Safeguarding Human Health and the Environment in the Anthropocene*. Cambridge: Cambridge University Press.

Hesselman, Marlies. 2021a. "Chapter IX.58: Energy Poverty and Household Access to Energy Services in International, Regional and National Law." In *Elgar Encyclopedia of Environmental Law*, edited by Martha Roggenkamp, Kars de Graaf, Ruven Fleming, 695–706. Cheltenham: Edward Elgar Publishing.

Hesselman, Marlies. 2021b. "Climate Change as a Global Health Threat in International Climate Law and Human Rights Law." In *Global Health Law Disrupted: COVID-19 and the Climate Crisis*, edited by Brigit Toebes et al., 87–130. The Hague: TMC Asser Press.

Hesselman, Marlies. 2022. "The Right to Energy." *Edward Elgar Encyclopedia on Human Rights Law*, edited by Christina Binder, Manfred Nowak, Jane Hofbauer and Philip Jänig, 62–69, Cheltenham: Edward Elgar Publishing.

Hesselman, Marlies. 2023. Human Rights and Access to Modern Energy Services. Groningen: PhD Dissertation.

Hesselman, Marlies, Anaïs Varo, Rachel Guyet, and Harriet Thomson. 2021. "Energy Poverty in the COVID-19 Era: Mapping Global Responses in Light of Momentum for the Right to Energy." *Energy Research & Social Science* 81(102246): 1–11.

HRC (UN Human Rights Council). 2012. "Report of the Independent Expert on the issue of human rights obligations relating to the enjoyment of a safe, clean, healthy and sustainable environment, John H. Knox." December 24. A/HRC/22/43.

HRC. 2019. "Issue of human rights obligations relating to the enjoyment of a safe, clean, healthy and sustainable environment." January 8. A/HRC/40/55.

HRC. 2021. "The human right to a clean, healthy and sustainable environment." October 18. A/HRC/RES/48/13.

Ivanova, Maria. 2010. "UNEP in Global Environmental Governance: Design, Leadership, Location." *Global Environmental Politics* 10(1): 30–59.

Kelbessa, Workineh. 2018. "Environmental Philosophy in African Traditions of Thought." *Environmental Ethics* 40(4): 309–323.

Kotzé, Louis J. and Duncan French. 2018. "A Critique of the Global Pact for the Environment: A Stillborn Initiative or the Foundation for *Lex Anthropocenae*?" *International Environmental Agreements: Politics, Law and Economics* 18(2018): 811–838.

Kovar, Jeffrey D. 1993. "A Short Guide to the Rio Declaration." *Colorado Journal of International Environmental Law and Policy* 4(119): 119–140.

Mackenzie, John S., Moira McKinnon, and Martyn Jeggo. 2014. "One Health: From Concept to Practice." *Confronting Emerging Zoonoses*: 163–189.

Meier, Benjamin Mason, Georgia Lyn Kayser, Urooj Quezon Amjad, and Jamie Bartram. 2013. "Implementing an evolving human right through water and sanitation policy." *Water Policy* 15(1): 116–133.

Negri, Stefania. 2020. "A Human Rights Approach to Environmental Health." In *Environmental Health in International and EU Law*, edited by Stefania Negri, 25–42. London: Routledge.

OHCHR (Office of the High Commissioner for Human Rights). 2022. "UN General Assembly must affirm right to healthy environment: UN experts." July 6.

OHHLEP (One Health High-Level Expert Panel). 2022. "One Health: A New Definition for a Sustainable and Healthy Future." *PLoS Pathog* 18(6): e1010537.

OIE (Office International des Epizooties). 2010. "The FAO-OIE-WHO Collaboration." April.

OIE. 2017. "The Tripartite's Commitment: Providing Multi-Sectoral, Collaborative Leadership in Addressing Health Challenges." October.

Phelan, Alexandra L. 2020. "The Environment, a Changing Climate, and Planetary Health." In *Foundations of Global Health & Human Rights*, edited by Lawrence O. Gostin and Benjamin Mason Meier, 417–438. New York: Oxford University Press.

Solecki, William D., and Fred M. Shelley. 1996. "Pollution, Political Agendas, and Policy Windows: Environmental Policy on the Eve of Silent Spring." *Environment and Planning C: Government and Policy* 14(4): 451–468.

Thacher, Peter S. 1977. "The Mediterranean Action Plan." *Ambio* 6(6): 308–312.

Tigre, Maria Antonia et al. 2023. "Just Transition Litigation in Latin America: An Initial Categorization of Climate Litigation Cases Amid the Energy Transition". *Sabin Center for Climate Change Law*, January 2023: 1–47.

UN Commission on Human Rights. 1995. "*Human Rights and the Environment*." UN Commission on Human Rights: Geneva, Switzerland.

UNECE (United Nations Economic Commission for Europe). 1979. "Convention on Long-range Transboundary Air Pollution." November 13.

UNEA (United Nations Environment Assembly). 2022. "End Plastic Pollution: Towards an International Legally Binding Instrument." March 7. UNEP/EA.5/Res.14.

UN General Assembly. 1966. "International Covenant on Economic, Social and Cultural Rights." December 16. A/RES/21/2200

UN General Assembly. 1972. "United Nations Conference on the Human Environment." June 16. A/CON.F/.48/14/Rev.1.

UN General Assembly. 1979. "Convention on the Elimination of All Forms of Discrimination against Women." December 18. A/RES/34/180.

UN General Assembly. 1982. "World Charter for Nature." October 28. A/RES/37/7

UN General Assembly. 1989. "Convention on the Rights of the Child." November 20. A/RES/44/25.

UN General Assembly. 1992. "Rio Declaration on Environment and Development." August 12. A/CONF.151/26.

UN General Assembly. 2020. "Interim report of the Special rapporteur on extreme poverty and human rights, Olivier De Schutter: The 'just transition' in the economic recovery: eradicating poverty within planetary boundaries." October 7. A/75/181/Rev.1.

UN General Assembly. 2022. "The human right to a clean, healthy and sustainable environment." August 1. A/RES/76/300.

UN Secretary-General. 2018. "Gaps in International Environmental Law and Environment-Related Instruments: Towards a Global Pact for the Environment." November 30. A/73/419.

Van Norren, Dorine and Henkjan Laats. 2022. "The Concept of Biodiversity Conservation Viewed through Philosophies of the Global South: Andean Buen Vivir, African Ubuntu and Buddhist Happiness." *Biodiversity Online* 2(2): 1–12.

Villanueva-Cabezas, Juan Pablo. 2022. "One Health: A Brief Appraisal of the Tripartite–UNEP Definition." *Transboundary and Emerging Diseases* 69(4): 1663–1665.

WCED (World Commission on Environment and Development). 1987. "Our Common Future." August 4. A/42/427.

Westra, Laura and Bill E. Lawson. 2001. *Faces of Environmental Racism: Confronting Issues of Global Justice*. Lanham: Rowman and Littlefield.

WHO (World Health Organization). 2020. *Hygiene: UN-Water GLAAS Findings on National Policies, Plans, Targets and Finance*. Geneva: WHO.

WHA (World Health Assembly). 2015. "Health and the Environment: Addressing the Health Impact of Air Pollution." May 26. WHA68.8.

III
ECONOMIC INSTITUTIONS, CORPORATE REGULATION & GLOBAL HEALTH FUNDING

10
Sustainable Development

The 2030 Agenda and Its Implications for Global Health Law

Stéphanie Dagron and Jennifer Hasselgård-Rowe

Introduction

Global health and international development strategies were not directly connected during the 20th century, with the international community simply presuming that improved health outcomes would follow from economic growth. With the United Nations (UN) declaration of the first UN Decade for the eradication of poverty (1997–2006), however, health was identified as a central cause of poverty—just as poverty was understood as an underlying determinant of health. Development policy would become central to global health. At the turn of the century, the recognition of determinants of health at the UN Millennium Summit in 2000 established specific health issues as central challenges for international development. The resulting Millennium Development Goals (MDGs) laid out a fifteen-year policy foundation to alleviate poverty and address inequality. Following the successes and limitations of the MDGs, the unanimous 2015 adoption of the 2030 Agenda for Sustainable Development (2030 Agenda) by the UN General Assembly confirmed the importance of health in development policy, laying out a broad agenda for advancing global health through international development.

The 2030 Agenda is composed of 17 Sustainable Development Goals (SDGs). While not legally binding, the SDGs are unique in framing a moral obligation for all actors across the international community to come together to address the social, economic, and environmental dimensions of sustainable development. The SDGs constitute the most ambitious global agenda adopted under the auspices of the UN, grounding all global policy under interconnected principles of social justice, equity, and human rights. As a foundation for international development policy, the SDGs in their entirety have a sweeping impact on global health, with SDG 3 (on health and well-being) strongly linked with other SDGs that constitute determinants of health. The explicit concern for health in the 2030 Agenda provides a policy strategy to advance sustainable development through public health—and public health through sustainable development. Such an approach to sustainable development requires all stakeholders to adopt policies and mobilize the necessary financial, institutional, and technological resources to advance development in an integrated manner.

This chapter examines the rise of a global development agenda that relies on health as a central goal to facilitate sustainable development. Part I frames the development agenda by reviewing the history of sustainable development, from the MDGs to the SDGs, highlighting the uniqueness of the 2030 Agenda as a global strategy adopted by all states. Reviewing the SDG targets that impact public health, Part II analyzes the institutional structures and monitoring mechanisms that have been put in place to guide state efforts and assess implementation progress. Part III analyzes the legal norms and institutions engaged in the implementation of the 2030 Agenda, exploring how international law can be used for the improvement of global health and evaluating the impact of the 2030 Agenda on global health law. This chapter concludes that the 2030 Agenda has a broad impact on global health law, confirming the central importance of global health in development policy, influencing the distribution of roles between global health actors, and inspiring the development of innovative legal instruments and institutions to ensure health for all.

I. Evolving Relationships between Health and International Development

High rates of poverty have a profoundly negative impact on the health of populations. Development policies that reduce poverty and inequality have resulted in unparalleled improvements in public health, with healthier populations leading to economic growth (Streeten et al. 1981). Given this linkage between health and wealth, states have slowly but progressively come together to develop global policies to promote economic development as a basis to promote health, implementing health initiatives as key elements of economic development strategies (Ruger 2003). At the turn of the 21st century, states developed the MDGs as a basis to alleviate poverty and address inequalities that undermine health. The fifteen-year experience of the MDGs provided a basis for the SDGs, solidifying international development as a foundation of global health.

A. Early Efforts to Promote International (Economic) Development

Eradicating poverty has been on the agenda of the UN since the end of World War II, translated into a series of plans of action to rebuild a world consumed by war. In 1941, U.S. President Roosevelt declared that a "Freedom from Want" would be central to the "Four Freedoms" that would frame the postwar world.[1] Recognizing the dangers of poverty, international organizations would advance this "Freedom from Want" amid the war, with the International Labor Organization's (ILO's) 1944 Philadelphia Declaration recognizing: "The war against want requires to be carried on with unrelenting vigour within each nation, and by continuous and concerted international effort . . ." (ILO 1944, art. I(d)). With this mission to alleviate poverty taken on by the UN, the 1948 Universal Declaration of Human Rights proclaimed the right of everyone "to a standard of living adequate for the health and well-being of himself and of his family" (UN General Assembly 1948, art. 25).

However, UN development strategies in the decades that followed did not fully integrate health considerations in economic policy. While the first UN strategy to "accelerate progress towards self-sustaining growth of the economy of the individual nations" did in fact recommend that states "accelerate the elimination of illiteracy, hunger and disease" (UN General Assembly 1961), this declaration was never followed by specific plans of actions, nor were the concepts of health and disease to be found in the strategies adopted for the UN's second, third, and fourth "development decades" (Larionova 2020). It was not until the declaration of the first decade for the eradication of poverty in 1998 that the link between economic growth and human progress was addressed—with poor health identified as a cause of poverty (Kim et al. 1999).

This radical change of approach to development—from the self-sustaining growth of the economy to the eradication of poverty—was inspired by ideological evolutions and theoretical frameworks in the economics of welfare and development. Where the objective of development had been focused on achieving high rates of economic growth, this shift toward a "capability approach" would seek to expand what people are able to do and to be (Sen 1999). This holistic, people-centered approach to development, including the capability to enjoy one's freedoms, came to be reflected in a series of UN conferences in the early 1990s, in the work of the United Nations Development Programme (UNDP), and in the establishment of a human rights-based approach (HRBA) to development—adopted

---

[1] While recognizing the challenges of the war, this "Freedom from Want" also reflected the impoverishment attendant to the "Great Depression" in the West, with the rise of poverty seen as laying the conditions that had led to World War II.

across a wide range of intergovernmental institutions (Fukuda-Parr, Yamin, and Greenstein 2014). In 1990, UNDP's first "Human Development Report" put people at the center of development, recommending economic growth to be managed as a foundation of "human development" (Hulme 2009). UNDP would examine income growth as a means, not an end, of development; human development would enable people to lead a long and healthy life, acquire knowledge, have access to resources needed for a decent standard of living, and enjoy political freedom alongside social and cultural choices (UNDP 1990).

These ideological evolutions would impact international financial institutions. The World Bank's "World Development Report 1993" considered health as a means of accelerating development – as well as a goal in itself (World Bank 1993). For the first time in economic development policy, the World Bank, as discussed in greater detail in Chapter 11, came to support global health initiatives. This expansion of global health governance furthered the idea that human rights and human development could be mutually reinforcing, with UN Conferences in the 1990s adopting a series of global goals and plans of action to strengthen development efforts to promote public health (Jolly 2004). These progressively expanding plans of action under the UN culminated at the turn of the century in the UN Millennium Declaration, through which UN Member States affirmed their commitment "to freeing the entire human race from want" (UN General Assembly 2000, para. 11).

B. The Birth of the MDGs: Focusing Global Policy on the Vicious Cycle That Links Poverty and Health

The UN Millennium Declaration would establish a fifteen-year policy foundation to alleviate poverty and address inequality under discrete development goals. In preparing for the September 2000 Millennium Summit, the UN Secretary-General launched an April 2000 preparatory report, "We the Peoples: The Role of the United Nations in the 21st Century," which recognized that: "Extreme poverty is an affront to our common humanity. It also makes many other problems worse" (UN Secretary-General 2000, 19). The Millennium Summit would seek to respond by developing a sweeping global plan of action, with the resulting Millennium Declaration serving as the first global framework to bring together all actors—from rich and poor countries—not only to address the economic, social, and environmental dimensions of poverty in a comprehensive way, but also to promote financing, implementation, and monitoring (Lee, Walt, and Haines 2004).

The eight MDGs adopted alongside the Millennium Declaration address health as central in the fight against poverty, hunger, and disease. Despite the strong focus on HIV/AIDS in the UN Secretary-General's report on MDG implementation, the MDGs looked to three separate goals to support health:

- MDG 4 – reduction of child mortality;
- MDG 5 – improvement of maternal health; and
- MDG 6 – attention to HIV, malaria, and other diseases (UN General Assembly 2000).[2]

While these MDGs were criticized for not taking a legal approach to advance development policy, the MDGs rapidly became a key policy tool linking health with development (Freedman 2005).

The adoption of the MDGs rapidly proved to be instrumental in framing state progress against poverty, hunger, and disease. In the final MDG report in 2015, the UN Secretary-General noted that this framework constituted "the most successful anti-poverty movement in history," contributing to the adoption of "wide ranging steps that have enabled people across the world to improve their lives and their future prospects" (UN 2015a, 3). Among these steps, the MDGs contributed to unprecedented health policy reforms throughout the world (Bradford 2002).

Case Study: Advancing Health Policy under the MDGs

The reduction of child mortality throughout the world, a key motivation for the development of the Millennium Declaration, provides evidence of the successful implementation of the MDGs through health policy. In framing efforts to reduce child mortality, MDG 4 looked to a key target: "reduce by two thirds, between 1990 and 2015, the under-five mortality rate." Many countries were able to meet this goal, despite facing severe poverty, by implementing evidence-based and cost-effective health interventions, including national vaccination programs, distribution of insecticide-treated bed nets, HIV controls, and treatment for childhood illness and nutritional support. States were strongly supported in these efforts by international partners, including the World Health Organization (WHO) and UNICEF, which developed guidance documents such as the 2003 "Global Strategy for Infant and Young Child Feeding." Based on the scientific evidence of the significance of nutrition for infants and young children, the Global Strategy guided states in promoting appropriate feeding for infants and young children, calling for increased public financing and collaboration across countries. The MDG period thus saw a far greater rate of reduction in child mortality than the period that preceded it. As the MDG period came to

---

[2] An additional health-related objective can be found in targets for the achievement of MDG 8 (strengthening a global partnership for development), with target 8.E looking to public-private partnerships to provide access to medicines: "in cooperation with pharmaceutical companies, provide access to affordable essential drugs in developing countries" (UN Statistics Division 2008).

a close, the global under-five mortality rate had declined by more than 50% (between 1990 and 2015)—from 12.7 million deaths globally in 1990 to 6 million in 2015. Yet despite the dramatic reduction in mortality, this success did not meet the ambitious MDG target to reduce under-five mortality by two thirds, calling into question whether states received sufficient assistance or whether the target was simply too ambitious to be realistically met.

In spite of groundbreaking advancements in health policy and improvements in public health in the first fifteen years of the 21st century, the global successes under the MDGs could not hide the limitations of this first global plan of action to combat poverty.

C. Learning from the Limitations of the MDGs

The MDGs catalyzed unprecedented health policy progress; however, the persistence of poverty and inequality reflected numerous weaknesses of the MDGs. Amid uneven progress in an increasingly unequal world, the MDGs were seen to be too limited in the number of goals and their definition at the global level, with certain goals being too ambitious for some countries or too simple for others. Given the absence of evidence concerning the feasibility of MDG implementation in low-income countries, the MDGs faced criticisms for not clarifying the roles and responsibilities of states, both individually and collectively (Fehling, Nelson, and Venkatapuram 2013). This absence of clear state responsibilities under the MDGs allowed for a lack of state ownership in meeting the MDGs, especially for many countries that were not included in the diplomatic negotiations leading up to the adoption of the MDGs.

Beyond these limitations in the identification of realistic goals and the clarification of state responsibilities, the choice of precise MDG targets and indicators to measure state progress would also lead to difficulties in advancing health systems and realizing human rights. MDG measures of state progress encouraged states to adopt vertical and technical approaches designed to achieve short-term health improvements—rather than horizontal approaches addressing the interconnectedness between economic and social goals and supporting sustainable development. As seen in the MDG focus on child mortality, the ensuing targets and indicators ignored the breadth of health issues related to child mortality as well as the human rights obligations arising out of the UN Convention on the Rights of the Child (Fukuda-Parr, Yamin, and Greenstein 2014). While the 1990s saw the emergence of holistic approaches to "human development" and "human rights-based approaches to development," the development of narrow MDG targets and indicators did not take into account human rights principles or human rights obligations under international law (Marks and Han 2020). These human rights limitations undermined equity in national progress, with the final MDG report recognizing that "although significant achievements have been made on many of the MDG targets worldwide, progress has been uneven across regions and countries, leaving significant gaps" (UN 2015a, 8).

The UN would continue to develop global goals in its ongoing efforts to realize sustainable development. Weaknesses of the MDGs did not prevent states from pursuing development efforts to meet global policy goals (Langford, Sumner, and Yamin 2013), with the final UN report on the MDGs confirming that global goals can provide a path to national progress: "with targeted interventions, sound strategies, adequate resources and political will, even the poorest countries can make dramatic and unprecedented progress" (UN 2015a, 4). Building from the MDG experience, the UN Secretary-General in 2010 launched a High-Level Panel on Global Sustainability, with the mandate of formulating a new vision for development. The 2012 UN Conference on Sustainable Development (Rio + 20) thereafter launched an intergovernmental high-level political forum to provide guidance and follow up on the implementation of recommendations for sustainable development (UN General Assembly 2012).[3] In January 2013, the UN General Assembly established a thirty-member Open Working Group to develop a proposal on the new global goals, and in early 2015, negotiations on the post-2015 development agenda began. The negotiating process was UN Member State-led, with participation from a number of UN entities, including WHO, as well as civil society stakeholders. In September 2015, the UN General Assembly unanimously adopted the 2030 Agenda, including 17 SDGs, as depicted in Figure 10.1.

II. Advancing Health under the 2030 Agenda

Health holds a central role under the 2030 Agenda, which contains a specific health goal (SDG 3) among several other health-related goals. Drawing from advancements in framing health as central to sustainable development, the 2030 Agenda proposes a comprehensive set of goals and targets—directly or indirectly related to health—as well as specific monitoring mechanisms designed to support and improve SDG implementation.

---

[3] This new vision for sustainable development, as introduced in Chapter 9, would draw from the 1987 World Commission on Environment and Development, which first popularized the concept of "sustainable development," and the 1995 World Summit for Social Development, which found that "economic development, social development and environmental development protection are interdependent and naturally reinforcing components of sustainable development which is the framework to achieve a higher quality of life for all people" (UN 1995, para. 6).

Figure 10.1 Sustainable Development Goals (UN)

A. Health as a Central Goal of the 2030 Agenda: SDG 3 on Health and Well-Being

The SDG agenda differs significantly from the MDG agenda in defining the health issues to be addressed. The three health-related MDGs arose out of the constrained scope of the concept of "international health"—an approach, as discussed in Chapter 1, that was dominant until the end of the 20th century. In accordance with this limited approach to international health, efforts to advance health in the context of international development were mostly linked to maternal and child health, as well as to the prevention of infectious diseases originating in the Global South (Dagron 2016). The progressive evolution of MDG indicators never sufficiently reflected the evolving concept of "global health" to be addressed by all states. These global health issues are no longer defined according to a limited list, but rather with regard to the following two elements: a transnational element (health can no longer be considered a purely national issue) and a cooperative element (with global health issues calling for strong cooperation across states and non-state actors) (Dagron 2022).

SDG 3 is explicitly aimed at ensuring healthy lives and promoting well-being for all—at all ages—stressing the importance of health at every stage of life. This goal encompasses a wide range of health priorities, through targets focused on traditional medicine, broader public health issues affecting populations, and financial structures and human resources necessary for their implementation. The thirteen targets corresponding to SDG 3, as examined in greater detail in Table 10.1,

Table 10.1 Targets and Indicators Related to SDG 3 (Dagron and Hasselgård-Rowe)

SDG 3 Targets	Indicators
Target 3.1: By 2030, reduce the global maternal mortality ratio to less than 70 per 100,000 live births	3.1.1: Maternal mortality ratio 3.1.2: Proportion of births attended by skilled health personnel
Target 3.2: By 2030, end preventable deaths of newborns and children under 5 years of age, with all countries aiming to reduce neonatal mortality to at least as low as 12 per 1,000 live births and under-5 mortality to at least as low as 25 per 1,000 live births	3.2.1: Under-five mortality rate 3.2.2: Neonatal mortality rate
Target 3.3: By 2030, end the epidemics of AIDS, tuberculosis, malaria and neglected tropical diseases and combat hepatitis, water-borne diseases and other communicable diseases	3.3.1: Number of new HIV infections per 1,000 uninfected population, by sex, age and key populations 3.3.2: Tuberculosis incidence per 100,000 population 3.3.3: Malaria incidence per 1,000 population 3.3.4: Hepatitis B incidence per 100,000 population 3.3.5: Number of people requiring interventions against neglected tropical diseases
Target 3.4: By 2030, reduce by one-third premature mortality from non-communicable diseases through prevention and treatment and promote mental health and well-being	3.4.1: Mortality rate attributed to cardiovascular disease, cancer, diabetes or chronic respiratory disease 3.4.2: Suicide mortality rate
Target 3.5: Strengthen the prevention and treatment of substance abuse, including narcotic drug abuse and harmful use of alcohol	3.5.1: Coverage of treatment interventions (pharmacological, psychosocial and rehabilitation and aftercare services) for substance use disorders 3.5.2: Alcohol per capita consumption (aged 15 years and older) within a calendar year in litres of pure alcohol
Target 3.6: By 2020, halve the number of global deaths and injuries from road traffic accidents	3.6.1: Death rate due to road traffic injuries
Target 3.7: By 2030, ensure universal access to sexual and reproductive health-care services, including for family planning, information and education, and the integration of reproductive health into national strategies and programmes	3.7.1: Proportion of women of reproductive age (aged 15–49 years) who have their need for family planning satisfied with modern methods 3.7.2: Adolescent birth rate (aged 10–14 years; aged 15–19 years) per 1,000 women in that age group

(*continued*)

Table 10.1 Continued

SDG 3 Targets	Indicators
Target 3.8: Achieve universal health coverage, including financial risk protection, access to quality essential health-care services and access to safe, effective, quality and affordable essential medicines and vaccines for all	3.8.1: Coverage of essential health services 3.8.2: Proportion of population with large household expenditures on health as a share of total household expenditure or income
Target 3.9: By 2030, substantially reduce the number of deaths and illnesses from hazardous chemicals and air, water and soil pollution and contamination	3.9.1: Mortality rate attributed to household and ambient air pollution 3.9.2: Mortality rate attributed to unsafe water, unsafe sanitation and lack of hygiene (exposure to unsafe Water, Sanitation and Hygiene for All (WASH) services) 3.9.3: Mortality rate attributed to unintentional poisoning
Target 3.a: Strengthen the implementation of the World Health Organization Framework Convention on Tobacco Control in all countries, as appropriate	3.a.1: Age-standardized prevalence of current tobacco use among persons aged 15 years and older
Target 3.b: Support the research and development of vaccines and medicines for the communicable and non-communicable diseases that primarily affect developing countries, provide access to affordable essential medicines and vaccines, in accordance with the Doha Declaration on the TRIPS Agreement and Public Health, which affirms the right of developing countries to use to the full the provisions in the Agreement on Trade-Related Aspects of Intellectual Property Rights regarding flexibilities to protect public health, and, in particular, provide access to medicines for all	3.b.1: Proportion of the target population covered by all vaccines included in their national programme 3.b.2: Total net official development assistance to medical research and basic health sectors 3.b.3: Proportion of health facilities that have a core set of relevant essential medicines available and affordable on a sustainable basis
Target 3.c: Substantially increase health financing and the recruitment, development, training and retention of the health workforce in developing countries, especially in least developed countries and small island developing States	3.c.1: Health worker density and distribution
Target 3.d: Strengthen the capacity of all countries, in particular developing countries, for early warning, risk reduction and management of national and global health risks	3.d.1: International Health Regulations (IHR) capacity and health emergency preparedness 3.d.2: Percentage of bloodstream infections due to selected antimicrobial-resistant organisms

reflect this broader approach to global health. Four of the targets are related to the unfinished MDG Agenda: reducing maternal mortality (target 3.1); ending preventable deaths of newborns and children under five years (target 3.2); ending the epidemics of HIV/AIDS, tuberculosis (TB), malaria, and other communicable diseases (target 3.3); and ensuring universal access to sexual and reproductive health-care services (target 3.7). Four other targets reflect the importance of new health priorities: reducing premature mortality from non-communicable diseases (target 3.4); substance abuse (target 3.5); road traffic accidents (target 3.6); and hazardous chemicals and air, water, and soil pollution and contamination (target 3.9). Four further targets have been developed to support the implementation of health targets (hence the use of letters and not numbers for these targets): strengthening the implementation of the Framework Convention on Tobacco Control (target 3.a); supporting research and development of vaccines and medicines for communicable and non-communicable diseases (target 3.b); increasing health financing and support for the recruitment, training, and retention of the health workforce (target 3.c); and strengthening the capacity for early warning, risk reduction, and management of health risks (target 3.d).

The remaining target, focused on Universal Health Coverage (UHC) (target 3.8), is considered the central target for the achievement of SDG 3 and essential to the 2030 Agenda as a whole (Dagron 2022). As discussed in detail in Chapter 20, UHC has become a principal focus in binding together global health governance. This focus on UHC has been repeatedly reaffirmed since 2015, with the UN General Assembly developing a 2019 High-Level Special Session on UHC, during which states resolved that:

> universal health coverage is fundamental for achieving the Sustainable Development Goals related not only to health and well-being, but also to eradicating poverty in all its forms and dimensions, ensuring quality education, achieving gender equality and women's empowerment, providing decent work and economic growth, reducing inequalities, ensuring just, peaceful and inclusive societies and to building and fostering partnerships (UN General Assembly 2019, para 5).

UHC has thus become both a new health priority as well as a means of implementation, laying the foundation for realizing health across the SDGs.

B. Health across the 2030 Agenda: SDGs as Social, Economic, and Environmental Determinants of Health

Where global health governance has long defined health in accordance with the 1946 WHO Constitution—as "a state of complete physical, mental and social well-being and not merely the absence of disease or infirmity" (WHO 1946, preamble)—this focus on social well-being has drawn attention to health beyond the healthcare sector. Thus, as first introduced in Chapter 1, the field of public health has structured its focus on health through an examination of underlying determinants of health—framed by political, economic, and social factors.[4] This promotion of the underlying conditions for a healthy life was extended in 2008 by the WHO Commission on Social Determinants of Health, which recognized that "together, the structural determinants and conditions of daily life constitute the social determinants of health and are responsible for a major part of health inequities between and within countries" (WHO 2008, 1).

This interconnectedness across determinants of health is mirrored by intersections across the SDGs. Looking to the SDGs as a foundation for global health governance, WHO has addressed a number of goals and targets directly related to the improvement of social determinants of health: access to safe, nutritious, and sufficient food (SDG 2.1), interventions and investments during the early years of life (SDG 4), promotion of gender equality and empowerment of women (SDG 5), fair employment and decent work (SDG 8), and many others that influence health (Pega et al. 2017). These interconnected goals and targets have thus provided a policy foundation for development partnerships to address underlying determinants of health (Brolan 2022).

Case Study: SDGs as a Basis for Development Partnerships

The 2030 Agenda was preceded by a decades-long push for increased cross-sectoral partnerships in global governance, as introduced in Chapter 3 and illustrated by the significant rise of international development initiatives and public-private partnerships in the health sector. The continuing importance of development collaboration was affirmed through SDG 17, which aims to "revitalize the global partnership for sustainable development" across interrelated areas of finance, technology, capacity building, and trade. Achieving the SDGs thereby requires engagement from a wide range of governance actors to support development initiatives that improve public health. These development partnerships have come to include financial actors (such as the World Bank and the International Monetary Fund) and specialized agencies across the UN system (such as WHO and the Food and Agriculture Organization of the

---

[4] This expansive vision of underlying determinants of health has also been embraced in the UN human rights system by the UN Committee on Economic, Social and Cultural Rights, which, as introduced in Chapter 4, defined the right to health in General Comment 14 to encompass socioeconomic factors "such as food and nutrition, housing, access to safe and potable water and adequate sanitation, safe and healthy working conditions, and a healthy environment" (CESCR 2000, para. 4).

United Nations). Since the adoption of the SDGs in 2015, a number of global governance actors have looked to the SDGs as a basis for new development partnerships to advance health, seeking to harmonize their work with the goals and targets of the 2030 Agenda. As seen in efforts to respond to environmental health challenges as a basis for sustainable development, organizations have come together under the SDGs to support the climate change response, as discussed in greater detail in Chapter 19, bringing together actors well beyond the health sector to examine the whole-of-government investments necessary to respond to sweeping changes to underlying determinants of health in the generations to come.

The SDGs thus provide a basis across intersectoral development initiatives to support health and well-being; yet, ensuring accountability for SDG implementation to advance health has required efforts to monitor progress under the SDGs.

C. Monitoring SDG Implementation to Advance Health through SDG Targets and Indicators

Monitoring and evaluation are essential parts of accountability through global governance. Across international legal regimes—in the fields of international human rights law or international labor and social security law— international treaties often contain provisions establishing committees and other mechanisms whose mission is to monitor implementation (O'Flaherty and Tsai 2012). These monitoring mechanisms, requesting states parties to submit regular reports for evaluation, seek to encourage states to implement their obligations under internationally agreed-upon treaties and thereby facilitate accountability for international law.[5] The UN had developed an initial monitoring system under the MDGs; however, the MDG monitoring framework faced challenges where the targets in some areas remained vague—as some goals, targets, and indicators were not well-aligned. When the SDGs were first negotiated, it was clear that a stronger monitoring and evaluation system would be needed to assess whether states are making progress in achieving global goals—and, in doing so, determine progress, identify challenges, and

---

[5] These monitoring mechanisms have been applied to facilitate accountability under a wide range of development initiatives, as evidenced by the Public Private Partnerships' Evaluation Methodology, and—as examined in greater detail in Chapter 14—have now become a key requirement for receiving funds from global health funding agencies such as The Global Fund; Gavi, the Vaccine Alliance; and others.

examine effects resulting from particular actions, programs, or policies. The monitoring system established under the SDGs would require the intervention of institutions as well as the clarification of specific indicators to assess government progress and analyze the complex economic, political, social, and environmental challenges.

1. Monitoring through Institutions

The 2030 Agenda establishes a system of oversight that requires governments to demonstrate whether and how they are making progress toward meeting SDG goals and targets. Presiding over this SDG monitoring system is the High-Level Political Forum on Sustainable Development (HLPF). Established in 2012, the HLPF constitutes the central UN platform for monitoring the 2030 Agenda at the global level (UN General Assembly 2015). In reporting to the HLPF, the UN Secretary-General, working with the entire UN system, produces an annual progress report on the SDGs—based on data provided by national statistical systems, information collected regionally, and the global indicator framework. This annual report aims to provide a global overview of progress on the implementation of each of the SDGs, while also pointing out areas in need of urgent action. In 2016, the UN General Assembly resolved that an additional Global Sustainable Development Report be produced every four years to inform the General Assembly's quadrennial SDG review deliberations (SDG Summit). This Global Sustainable Development Report is developed by an independent group of scientists, appointed by the Secretary-General and consisting of "15 experts representing a variety of backgrounds, scientific disciplines and institutions, ensuring geographical and gender balance" (UN Economic and Social Council 2016, para. 7).

To monitor countries in meeting SDG 3, the UN General Assembly in 2019 launched the Global Action Plan (GAP) for Healthy Lives and Well-Being for All, bringing together thirteen GAP signatory agencies—including standard-setting international organizations, public-private-partnerships, and UN funds and programs[6]—to support country implementation (Voss, Marten, and Gulati 2019). In addition to developing annual progress reports on progress achieved, the GAP signatory agencies also carry out a Joint Evaluability Assessment (JEA), the objective of which is to conduct early and rapid assessments in order to identify gaps and be able to address them before they become serious problems. This assessment

---

[6] The signatory agencies include: GAVI, the Vaccine Alliance; Global Financing Facility for Women, Children and Adolescents (GFF); International Labour Organization (ILO); The Global Fund to Fight AIDS, TB and Malaria (Global Fund); Joint United Nations Programme on HIV/AIDS (UNAIDS); United Nations Development Programme (UNDP); United Nations Population Fund (UNFPA); United Nations Children's Fund (UNICEF); Unitaid; United Nations Entity for Gender Equality and the Empowerment of Women (UN Women); World Bank Group; World Food Programme (WFP); and WHO.

mechanism set up by the GAP is important in determining the extent to which strategic and technical elements are in place and providing recommendations for actions which agencies can take to address identified health challenges.

In framing these multiple SDG assessments, the 2030 Agenda set out the need for a global indicator framework, stipulating that this framework be developed by the UN Statistical Commission. Hence, in 2015, the UN Statistical Commission created the Inter-Agency and Expert Group (IAEG), composed of UN Member States and including regional and international agencies as observers. The IAEG was tasked with developing and implementing the global indicator framework to assess the goals and targets of the 2030 Agenda (Strong et al. 2020). The result of the IAEG's work was a set of global indicators—to monitor progress toward each of the 2030 Agenda goals and targets—with these indicators adopted by the UN General Assembly in 2017.

2. Monitoring through Indicators

Identifying limitations in SDG implementation requires data reflective of SDG targets. To develop and implement a global indicator framework to monitor SDG goals and targets, the UN Statistical Commission worked with the Inter-agency and Expert Group on SDG Indicators (IAEG-SDGs) to develop an intricate global indicator framework of 230 indicators—28 of which relate directly to the health goal (UN General Assembly 2017). The SDG indicators are essential in that they specify the measurements by which the targets can be considered a success or failure. In assessing efforts to meet the SDG targets, the 2030 Agenda clearly affirms the importance of disaggregating data—by income, sex, age, race, ethnicity, migratory status, disability, geographic location, or other characteristics—and the indicators established by the IAEG-SDGs constitute an essential means to better understand, monitor, and address health inequalities (Strong et al. 2020).

Many of the indicators for SDG 3, as detailed in Table 10.1, reflect traditional public health data such as disease incidence with regard to TB, malaria, and hepatitis B (respectively indicators 3.3.2, 3.3.3, and 3.3.4); prevalence, for example, in "age-standardized prevalence of tobacco use among people over 15 years of age" (indicator 3.a.1); and mortality rates, as seen in the "maternal mortality ratio" (indicator 3.1.1), under-5 and neo-mortality (respectively indicators 3.2.1 and 3.2.2), mortality "attributed to cardiovascular disease, cancer, diabetes or chronic respiratory diseases" (indicator 3.4.1), and suicide mortality as an indicator of (the absence of) mental health and well-being (3.4.2).[7]

---

[7] Further examples of mortality rates include targets focusing on reducing: deaths and illnesses from hazardous chemicals and air, water and soil pollution, and contamination (target 3.9); mortality rates "attributed to household and ambient air pollution" (indicator 3.9.1); mortality rates "attributed to unsafe water, unsafe sanitation and lack of hygiene" (indicator 3.9.2); and mortality rates "attributed to unintentional poisoning" (indicator 3.9.3).

Beyond these traditional indicators, some indicators stand out for not using purely public health references as their basis, and in some cases refer to economic measures as well as health elements. In the context of UHC, indicator 3.8.1 measures the coverage of essential health services, and indicator 3.8.2 looks at the proportion of the population with large household expenditures on health as a share of total household expenditure or income. These efforts to monitor the implementation of SDG 3 and other health-related SDGs provide a foundation for the advancement of global health law.

III. Impact of the 2030 Agenda on the Development and Implementation of Global Health Law

Global health law, understood as a set of "legal norms, processes, and institutions that are designed primarily to attain the highest possible standard of physical and mental health for the world's population" (Gostin and Sridhar 2014, 1732), does not play an essential role in the 2030 Agenda; however, in certain areas of global health, the momentum provided by the SDGs has led to the development of norms and instruments that are moving global health law forward.

A. The Role for Global Health Law in the 2030 Agenda

There is little reference to global health law in the 2030 Agenda. For the most part, the 2030 Agenda leaves states to their own volition regarding how, from a legal point of view, they are to move toward achieving the health-related SDGs. The place of law across the 2030 Agenda may be considered questionable at best. In the elaboration of the SDG targets and indicators for health, there has been a reluctance to rely on law as an instrument for the implementation of SDG 3 (Dagron 2022). In these health-related SDG targets and indicators, only three out of the thirteen health targets refer to hard law instruments—two under WHO (the Framework Convention on Tobacco Control (FCTC) and the International Health Regulations (IHR)) and one concerning the protection of intellectual property rights under the World Trade Organization (WTO) (Agreement on Trade-Related Aspects of Intellectual Property Rights (TRIPS)). Among the health-related targets and accompanying indicators detailed in Table 10.1, there are no references to other public health "soft law" instruments or other legal instruments adopted under WHO or other UN agencies.[8]

---

[8] This absence of global health law under the health-related SDGs is seen in relation to target 3.5, which focuses on substance use, drug abuse, and the harmful use of alcohol, but lacks any reference to the international drug control conventions adopted under the auspices of the UN.

Although two global health law instruments are explicitly mentioned in the 2030 Agenda, the FCTC and IHR, the content of these legal instruments and the resulting state obligations are not part of the SDG 3 indicators. Without such indicators, efforts to monitor implementation of SDG 3 do not assess implementation of the FCTC or the IHR. Regarding the FCTC, the SDG 3 indicators only examine the realization of a specific and very limited element of tobacco control: the "age-standardized prevalence of current tobacco use among persons aged 15 years and older." Similarly for the IHR, although target 3.d seeks to "strengthen the capacity of all countries, in particular developing countries, for early warning, risk reduction and management of national and global health risks," the accompanying indicator simply refers to "IHR capacity and health emergency preparedness" without any further reference to the wide range of global health law obligations, as detailed in Chapter 6, that are enshrined in IHR (2005) (Dagron 2022).

Beyond the absence of global health law, there is no explicit reliance on international human rights law for the realization of the SDGs. While the 2030 Agenda explicitly sought to advance human rights, none of the SDG 3 targets have been formulated using clear human rights obligations (Brolan et al. 2017). The fact that it is the implementation of UHC, not the right to health, that has been specifically chosen as the central target of SDG 3 illustrates a lack of reliance upon fundamental human rights-based language, obligations, and instruments. Without efforts to align SDG indicators and human rights indicators, global health governance will not be able to benefit from synergies across SDG and human rights monitoring mechanisms (Meier, Huffstetler, and Bueno de Mesquita 2020).

Given the scarcity of international legal frameworks under the SDGs, there is only a limited role provided for institutions of global health governance, as seen in the limited influence of international standard-setting agencies in the implementation of the SDG health targets. Of the three UN agencies engaged in the implementation of the 2030 Agenda, only two (WHO and ILO) have a direct mandate in the field of health. The GAP for Healthy Lives and Well-Being for All reflects an attempt to counter difficulties that have been identified in global health governance as a result of the proliferation of global health stakeholders and, as introduced in Chapter 3, the fragmentation of the global health landscape. To reduce this fragmentation, the GAP encourages collaboration between actors active in the fields of public health, development, financing, and humanitarian activities. Yet despite this push for collaboration across sectors and institutions, the absence of key agencies such as the WTO, or of UN human rights agencies, is problematic.[9] Global health law and governance continue to

---

[9] The importance of effective cooperation between health, trade, and human rights governance is crucially important, as will be discussed in greater detail in Chapter 12, with the COVID-19 pandemic highlighting the centrality of international trade law in meeting global health goals.

have a comparatively small role in implementing the SDGs; however, the implementation of the SDGs is inspiring international organizations to develop new strategies, standards, and guidelines in order to engage more actively in the development of global health law.

B. The Impact of the 2030 Agenda on Global Health Law

The impact of the 2030 Agenda on global health law may be ascertained by observing the resulting increase in soft law to advance global health. Numerous health-related soft law instruments have been adopted in recent years to contribute to the achievement of the SDGs, particularly the achievement of health-related targets. These global health law advancements are seen in:

- Recommendations, such as the 2020 WHO Guidelines on Physical Activity and Sedentary Behavior, which seek to meet SDG target 3.4 on non-communicable disease. The Guidelines provide evidence-based public health recommendations for children, adolescents, and adults on the amount of physical activity required to offer significant health benefits and minimize health risks, offering a global health model for national policy frameworks.
- Technical standards, such as the 2018 Compendium of WHO Guidelines and Associated Standards: Ensuring Optimum Delivery of the Cascade of Care for Patients with Tuberculosis, which seeks to address SDG target 3.3 on TB. The Compendium stresses that governments have an ethical obligation to provide universal access to TB care according to international standards, going into detail about how to ensure that a patient's needs, values, preferences, and rights inform their access to and the delivery of services.
- Guidelines, such as the many guidelines on maternal health or pharmaceutical regulation developed by WHO, all of which address SDG target 3.1 on reducing the global maternal mortality ratio. The 2017 Guidelines on Maternal Health, for example, bring together all of the WHO recommendations on maternal health for policymakers, health professionals, and others working in the field.
- Strategies, such as WHO's 2021 Model List of Essential Medicines, which seeks to address SDG target 3.8 aimed at achieving UHC. Examining the availability of essential medicines in different countries and comparing them to the WHO Model List of Essential Medicines is essential to monitoring country-level progress toward UHC.
- Declarations, such as the 2018 UN General Assembly Political Declaration on the Prevention and Control of Non-Communicable Diseases, in which states

agreed to promote and implement policy, legislative, and regulatory measures to minimize the primary risk factors for NCDs; and the 2019 UN General Assembly Political Declaration on Universal Health Coverage, in which states explicitly recognized the importance of strengthening legislative and regulatory frameworks and institutions for the achievement of UHC and committed to investing in primary health care.

These soft law approaches have come together, for example, in global health efforts to address TB, which constitutes an explicit focus of SDG target 3.3. The first WHO Global Ministerial Conference on Ending Tuberculosis in the Sustainable Development Era, held in Moscow in November 2017, adopted a declaration in which states committed to key aspects such as "universal access to health care, multisectoral action and accountability, financing and research" to achieve faster progress (WHO 2017). Since then, a number of other high-level commitments to combat TB have been made, including the March 2018 Delhi End TB Summit and subsequent September 2018 UN General Assembly Political Declaration on the Fight Against Tuberculosis, with the latter confirming commitments to the SDGs and establishing new global targets and commitments to action (UN General Assembly 2018). However, despite these global health law advancements arising out of the SDGs, leading to unprecedented progress in the fight against TB,[10] challenges remain in translating the global development agenda into global health law reforms and global health progress. As noted in the 2018 Political Declaration by the UN General Assembly, although TB is the leading global cause of death for people living with HIV, states have failed to connect TB and HIV testing, "precluding treatment and resulting in preventable deaths" (ibid., para. 10). Summarizing these limitations in its recent report on progress in the field of TB, WHO notes that "high-level commitments and targets have galvanized global and national progress towards ending TB, but that urgent and more ambitious investments and actions are required to put the world on track to reach targets, especially in the context of the COVID-19 pandemic" (WHO 2020, 4).

In facilitating this investment and action, efforts are being undertaken to transform the international system for development, with the 2030 Agenda triggering new approaches to global financing for health. It was clear from the start that the realization of the 2030 Agenda would be strongly dependent on the capacities of the world community to provide adequate financing for the implementation of the SDGs. To meet this challenge, an ambitious framework

---

[10] With global action in the field of TB—under both the MDGs and SDGs—it is estimated that global commitments to TB treatment have averted more than sixty million deaths since 2000 (WHO 2020).

for financing development to reinforce the SDGs was discussed at the 2015 International Conference on Financing for Development in Addis Ababa. This Conference identified difficulties faced by many countries, particularly low-income countries facing existing inequalities, and states committed in the Addis Ababa Action Agenda to promote a "social compact" to increase public investments, bridge the global infrastructure gap in transport, energy, water and sanitation, and enable all people to benefit from growth (UN 2015b). Such public investments will be crucial to finance essential health services to meet SDG targets.

Case Study: Global Health Law Reforms to Finance the SDGs

Just as the 2002 establishment of the Global Fund to fight AIDS, Tuberculosis and Malaria created a new global health institution through global health law—authorizing a substantial increase in financing for health programs in low-income countries—the proposal to establish a new "Global Fund" for social protection seeks to overcome the financing gap for ensuring basic income security and access to health care under the SDGs. While social protection was not part of the MDG Agenda, it has taken a central position within the 2030 Agenda for the eradication of poverty and the promotion of health. This commitment is enshrined both in target 1.3 on poverty eradication, which is aimed at implementing national social protection floors, and in target 3.8, focused on the achievement of UHC. These targets are strongly linked to (and interconnected in) the improvement of underlying determinants of health. While the idea for a new Global Fund is not new, as it has already been at the center of international debates concerning the financing of development, this focus on a new fund now looks to several hundred commitments and policy actions that states agreed to take individually and collectively under the SDGs. As outlined in the UN's Financing for Sustainable Development Report 2022, it will be crucial for actors to implement their commitments through "reducing financing gaps and rising debt risks" and ensuring "financing flows are aligned with development to support a greener, more inclusive, and resilient recovery." Such reforms would greatly contribute to sustainable development and resilience in times of crisis for all.

Additional financing efforts triggered by the 2030 Agenda have also been made to better define and combat illicit financial flows, understood as constituting a main obstacle to the realization of an equitable and stable future (UN 2021). These efforts are complemented by work to create an "entire ecosystem" based on values authorizing a change in the structure and functioning of the global economy—aligning the global economy with financial integrity as well as strengthening the "social contract" between governments and people and fulfilling human rights obligations for all peoples throughout the world (ibid., 13).

Conclusion

The international community has made enormous progress in the evolution of development strategies over the last twenty-five years. The initial economics-driven vision of poverty, as limited by an economic lens, has been replaced by an understanding of poverty that allows for the lived experiences of people to be taken into account, prioritizing their needs, capacities, and aspirations to guide international development strategies and the creation of a comprehensive development policy agenda. This agenda proposes strongly interdependent targets and identifies high-income, as well as low-income, countries as being directly concerned by poverty—and needing to work together to put an end to it. It also draws a complex vision of global governance for sustainable development, recognizing the involvement of states and non-state actors as essential to addressing the multidimensional manifestations of poverty. Yet despite global efforts to implement the 2030 Agenda, progress toward the achievement of the SDGs reveals that economic, social, and environmental inequalities within and between states have worsened since the beginning of the 21st century. Financial, public health, and security crises in recent years have limited the implementation of existing development strategies and are threatening to reverse the progress that has been made across a number of fields toward greater implementation of the 2030 Agenda.

These intersecting crises highlight the importance of the fight against poverty for global health, the accuracy of sustainable development objectives, and the crucial role of global health law in promoting public health and strengthening national systems. Law can represent a powerful tool for moving forward and creating positive change in policy and practice. The 2030 Agenda itself has spurred action in global health law, manifested directly in the development of a number of global health soft law instruments, as well as indirectly in other fields—as exemplified by the evolution of the global financial system to advance global health and human rights. The 2030 Agenda is indeed a constant reminder for states (and non-state actors) of the need to envision the realization of health for all—a central goal of the Agenda—as a complex endeavor that requires the achievement of all the SDGs together. It should therefore constitute a valuable source of inspiration for the development of a new WHO "pandemic treaty" and in continuing efforts to develop global health law across determinants of health.

States have looked to social justice and solidarity as central and indispensable elements of the world order, looking to international development as a foundation for lasting peace. The complex situation of the world today, confronted with compounding challenges related to pandemics, conflict, climate change, and economic insecurity, call for the international community to renew its position on sustainable development. With the 2030 Agenda ending in less than a decade, actors are already developing new ways to ensure that development improves health. Global health law must be central to this effort, looking to actors across the global health landscape to guide actions and clarify responsibilities across sectors. The time to advance this new agenda is now.

Questions for Consideration

1. Why did early international development strategies neglect public health? How did capability theory shift development governance to focus on health as a foundation of "human development"?
2. How did the UN Millennium Declaration shape global governance to alleviate poverty? How did the MDGs succeed in linking health with development?
3. What limitations of the MDGs hindered states in meeting health-related targets? Why was progress to meet the MDGs unequal across countries? How did these limitations shape diplomacy to develop the SDGs?
4. Why is the scope of SDG 3 considered broader than the three health-related MDGs? How do the SDG 3 targets reflect the contemporary understanding of "global health"? Why is the target on UHC considered to be fundamental to realizing all of the SDGs?
5. Why is it necessary to look beyond SDG 3 to improve global health? How do the SDGs provide a basis for development partnerships across institutions of global health governance?
6. Why are monitoring mechanisms necessary to ensure accountability for implementation of the SDGs? Given the wide range of existing mechanisms, why was the High-Level Political Forum on Sustainable Development necessary to monitor progress under the SDGs? How do indicators support SDG 3 targets in assessing government progress to promote health?
7. Why do SDG 3 targets and indicators neglect hard and soft law norms of global health law? How does this neglect of global health law frameworks under the SDGs limit efforts to bring together global governance actors across sectors?

8. How have the SDGs led to global health law advancements through the development of new soft law instruments? What challenges remain in translating the global development agenda into global health law reforms?
9. Why does the 2030 Agenda raise an imperative to strengthen financing for health under global health law? How can a "global fund" for social protection support the implementation of health-related SDGs?

Acknowledgments

The authors greatly appreciate the research assistance of Neha Saggi, Ryan Doerzbacher, and Hanna E. Huffstetler.

References

Bradford, Colin. 2002. *Towards 2015: From Consensus Formation to Implementation of the MDGs – The Historical Background, 1990–2002*. Washington: Brookings Institution.

Brolan, Claire E. 2022. "Public Health and the UN Sustainable Development Goals." In *Oxford Research Encyclopedia of Global Public Health*. New York: Oxford University Press.

Brolan, Claire E., Vannarath Te, Nadia Floden, Peter S. Hill, and Lisa Forman. 2017. "Did the Right to Health Cross the Line? Examining the United Nations Resolution on the Sustainable Development Goals." *BMJ Global Health* 2(3): 1–6.

CESCR (Committee on Economic, Social, and Cultural Rights). 2000. "General Comment 14: The Right to the Highest Attainable Standard of Health (Art. 12)." August 11. E/C.12/2000/4.

Dagron, Stéphanie. 2016. "L'avenir du droit international de la santé." *Zeitschrift für schweizerisches Recht* 135(II): 5–88.

Dagron, Stéphanie. 2022. "SDG 3: Ensure healthy lives and promote well-being for all at all ages." in *Cambridge Handbook of the Sustainable Development Goals and International Law*, edited by Ellen Hey and Jonas Ebbesson. Cambridge: Cambridge University Press.

Fehling, Maya, Brett D. Nelson, and Sridhar Venkatapuram. 2013. "Limitations of the Millennium Development Goals: A Literature Review." *Global Public Health* 8(10): 1109–1122.

Freedman, Lynn P. 2005. "Achieving the MDGs: Health Systems as Core Social Institutions." *Development* 48(1): 19–24.

Fukuda-Parr, Sakiko, Alicia Ely Yamin, and Joshua Greenstein. 2014. "The Power of Numbers: A Critical Review of Millenium Development Goal Targets for Human Development and Human Rights." *Journal of Human Development and Capabilities* 15 (2–3): 105–117.

Gostin, Lawrence O., and Devi Sridhar. 2014. "Global Health and the Law." *New England Journal of Medicine* 370(18): 1732–1740.

Hulme, David. 2009. "The Millennium Development Goals (MDGs): A Short History of the World's Biggest Promise." The University of Manchester Brooks World Poverty Institute. *BWPI Working Paper No. 100*: 1–54.

ILO (International Labor Organization). 1944. *ILO Declaration of Philadelphia: Declaration concerning the aims and purposes of the International Labour Organisation.* Philadelphia: ILO.

Jolly, Richard. 2004. "Global Development Goals: The United Nations Experience." *Journal of Human Development* 5(1): 69–95.

Kim, Jim Yong, John Gershman, Joyce V. Millen, and Alec Irwin. 1999. *Dying for Growth: Global Inequality and the Health of the Poor.* Monroe: Common Courage Press.

Langford, Malcolm, Andy Sumner, and Alicia Ely Yamin. 2013. *Millennium Development Goals and Human Rights.* Cambridge: Cambridge University Press.

Larionova, Marina V. 2020. "The UN Development Decades (1961–2000): Evolution of Appraisal Systems in the Context of Development Theories." *Vestnik RUDN. International Relations* 20(1): 170–183.

Lee, Kelley, Gill Walt, and Andy Haines. 2004. "The Challenge to Improve Global Health: Financing the Millennium Development Goals." *Journal of American Medicine Association* 291: 2636–2638.

Marks, Stephen and Alice Han. 2020. "Health and Human Rights through Development: The Right to Development, Rights-Based Approach to Development, and Sustainable Development Goals." In *Foundations of Global Health and Human Rights*, edited by Lawrence O. Gostin and Benjamin Mason Meier, 155–176. New York: Oxford University Press.

Meier, Benjamin Mason, Hanna Huffstetler, and Judith Bueno de Mesquita. 2020. "Monitoring and Review to Assess Human Rights Implementation." In *Foundations of Global Health and Human Rights*, edited by Lawrence O. Gostin and Benjamin Mason Meier, 155–176. New York: Oxford University Press.

O'Flaherty, Michael, and Pei-Lun Tsai. 2012. "Periodic Reporting: The Backbone of the UN Treaty Body Review Procedures." In *New Challenges for the UN Human Rights Machinery: What Future for the UN Treaty Body System and the Human Rights Council Procedures?*, edited by M. Cherif Bassiouni and William A. Schabas. Cambridge: Intersentia.

Pega, Frank, Nicole B Valentine, Kumaan Rasanathan, Ahmad Reza Hosseinpoor, Tone P Torgerson, Veerabhadran Ramanathan, Tipicha Pasayanonda et al. 2017. "The Need to Monitor Actions on the Social Determinants of Health." *Bulletin of the World Health Organization.* 95(11): 784–787.

Ruger, Jennifer Prah. 2003. "Health and Development." *Lancet* 362(9385): 678.

Sen, Amartya. 1999. *Commodities and Capabilities.* Oxford: Oxford University Press.

Streeten, Paul, Shahid Javed Burki, Mahbub ul Haq, Norman Hicks, and Frances Stewart. 1981. *First Things First: Meeting Basic Human Needs in the Developing Countries.* Washington: Oxford University Press.

Strong, Kathleen, Abdislan Noor, John Aponte, Anshu Banerjee, Richard Cibulskis, Theresa Diaz, Peter Ghys et al. 2020. "Monitoring the Status of Selected Health Related Sustainable Development Goals: Methods and Projections to 2030." *Global Health Action* 13(1): 1–14.

UN (United Nations). 1995. "Report of the World Summit for Social Development." March 14. A/CONF.166/9.

UN. 2015a. *The Millennium Development Goals Report.* New York: UN.

UN. 2015b. *Financing for Development: Addis Ababa Action Agenda.* New York: UN.

UN. 2021. *Financial Integrity for Sustainable Development.* New York: UN.

UNDP (UN Development Programme). 1990. "Defining and measuring human development." In *Human Development Report 1990.* New York: UN.

UN Economic and Social Council. 2016. "Ministerial declaration of the high-level segment of the 2016 session of the Economic and Social Council." July 29. E/HLS/2016/1.
UN General Assembly. 1948. "Universal Declaration of Human Rights." December 10. Resolution 217A(III).
UN General Assembly. 1961. "United Nations Development Decade: A Programme for International Economic Cooperation." December 19. A/RES/1710(XVI).
UN General Assembly. 2000. "United Nations Millennium Declaration." September 18. A/RES/55/2.
UN General Assembly. 2012. "The Future We Want." September 11. A/RES/66/288.
UN General Assembly. 2015. "Transforming Our World: the 2030 Agenda for Sustainable Development." October 21. A/RES/70/1.
UN General Assembly. 2017. "Work of the Statistical Commission pertaining to the 2030 Agenda for Sustainable Development." July 10. A/RES/71/313.
UN General Assembly. 2018. "Political Declaration of the UN General-Assembly High-Level Meeting on the Fight Against Tuberculosis." October 18. A/RES/73/3.
UN General Assembly. 2019. "Political Declaration of the High-Level Meeting on Universal Health Coverage." October 18. A/RES/74/2.
UN Secretary-General. 2000. *We the Peoples: The Role of the United Nations in the 21st Century*. New York: UN.
UN Statistics Division. 2008. "Millennium Development Goals and Indicators. Official List of MDG indicators." January 15.
Voss, Maike, Robert Marten, and Daniel Gulati. 2019. "Accelerating the SDG3 Global Action Plan." *BMJ Global Health* 4(5): 1–2.
World Bank. 1993. *World Development Report 1993: Investing in Health*. Washington: Oxford University Press.
WHO (World Health Organization). 1946. *Constitution of the World Health Organization*. New York: WHO.
WHO. 2008. "Closing the Gap in a Generation: Health Equity through Action on the Social Determinants of Health." August 27. WHO/IER/CSDH/08.1.
WHO. 2017. "First WHO Global Ministerial Conference: Ending TB in the Sustainable Development Era: A Multisectoral Response." November 17. WHO/HTM/TB/2017.11.
WHO. 2020. *Overview: Progress Towards Achieving Global Tuberculosis Targets and Implementation of the UN Political Declaration on Tuberculosis*. Geneva: WHO.

11

Economic Development Policy

Poverty Alleviation for Public Health Advancement

Diane A. Desierto and Erica Patterson

Introduction

Economic development policy influences public health. Government decisions determine how public resources are allocated in ways that support or advance health outcomes. Fiscal expenditures can either subsidize, support, or incentivize public and private healthcare systems. Government decisions can also include investment projects in healthcare infrastructure and related transportation, communications, and technological facilities to ensure better access to adequate healthcare needs. Government expenditures for social security and social protection provide safety nets for occupational hazards, epidemiological events, and any other unforeseen health emergencies affecting the population. Government decisions can also shape incentives for engaging private sector partnerships in service delivery and programming that respond to community, group, local, or population-level health needs. These government decisions routinely impact social determinants of public health, such as housing, education, environment, socioeconomic status, employment, food security, water access, energy equity, and other non-medical factors that impact individual, group, community, and population health outcomes. These government decisions are shaped by global economic development policy.

Global economic development policy is a form of global health policy. Poverty alleviation strategies and development lending paradigms frame global governance under international financial institutions—including the International Monetary Fund (IMF) and the International Bank for Reconstruction and Development (World Bank)—which directly affect government agenda-setting and legislative proposals for public health, government implementation of public health programs, and evaluation of the overall effectiveness of government programs in health services delivery. These institutions have shifted economic development policy in ways that have impacted efforts to meet population health needs.

This chapter examines the critical role of economic development governance and poverty alleviation strategies in the realization of public health advancement. Part I traces the historical trajectory of economic development policy set by international organizations and international financial institutions, leading to development paradigms under the IMF and World Bank that increasingly shaped global health as a development focus. Recognizing the influence of development on global health, Part II discusses the broadening of the concept of economic development beyond economic growth, influencing global health through the promotion of social conditions, the advancement of universal health coverage, and the alignment of economic governance to achieve sustainable development. Part III examines ongoing challenges to global economic governance as a basis for global health security, with World Bank efforts challenged in the COVID-19 response and rising movements seeking to codify a right to development. The chapter concludes that it is precisely because economic development policy shapes global health policy that the global health landscape must pay closer attention to the direct and intersectional consequences of international development decisions on public health outcomes.

I. Economic Development Policy's Evolution toward a Nexus with Global Health

The emergence of global economic development governance after World War II, and the corresponding trajectory of development paradigms adopted by these international financial institutions, led to the development of lending conditionalities and structural adjustment programs. These poverty alleviation strategies, along with the turn to neoliberalism as the dominant development paradigm, yielded variable impacts on public health in the Global South, while also magnifying inequalities in public health advancement at community levels within the Global North. Responding to these health inequities, the World Bank would shift to focus on health programming, opening a space to transform economic development policy toward a more holistic vision of "human development."

A. Emergence of Economic Development Governance after World War II

Post-World War II multilateral institutions—from the United Nations (UN) to the Bretton Woods institutions—embraced development mandates since their inception. The Bretton Woods institutions arose out of the July 1944 United

Nations Monetary and Financial Conference in Bretton Woods, New Hampshire, United States (Frieden 2019). The "Bretton Woods Conference" convened forty-four states at the end of World War II to design the architecture for the new international monetary and financial system to follow the war: "a new kind of world financial order capable of withstanding the stresses that everyone expected would resume with the peace" (Lamoreaux and Shapiro 2019, 1).

This world financial order would be governed principally by two new international financial institutions, the IMF and the World Bank. The IMF would focus on exchange rate stability, balance of payments problems, and lending under Stand-By Arrangements with states that were experiencing severe temporary illiquidity. Rather than acting as a development agency engaged in long-term lending, "[i]ts intended mandate was to act as the international lender of last resort" (Reinhart and Trebesch 2016, 4). The World Bank, on the other hand, was intended to provide long-term development support. While initially developed through the Bretton Woods Conference to finance the immense reconstruction needs of the post-World War II world, the World Bank would subsequently see an expansion of its work as "its primary focus shifted early on toward economic and social development" (Marshall 2008, 23).

B. Evolving Development Paradigms

The World Bank moved almost immediately from post-World War II reconstruction in Europe to a global commitment to economic development throughout the world. This shift in development paradigms coincided with the rise of development economics as a mainstream discipline in the post-World War II period.[1] Early development paradigms contrasted approaches to economic development as either resulting from balanced growth (led by rapid mass industrialization based on the innovations of private entrepreneurs) or resulting from unbalanced growth (which focuses on development processes that result in change from one type of economy into another) (Kapur, Lewis, and Webb 2011). Operational approaches in the early years of the World Bank were largely divided as to scale and theory, debating between broad development programs more linked to balanced growth theories, and individual project loans that implemented unbalanced growth theories.

---

[1] It was during this period in which many poor countries became autonomous states through decolonization and "saw the rise of intellectual elites who had studied in metropolitan countries and had come in contact with the ideals of modernization and industrialization typical of developed countries [that] development economics moved to the edges of the so-called mainstream" (Alacevich 2009, 67).

The World Bank did not explicitly focus on poverty until the 1970s, when poverty alleviation became central to development. While the Bank's constitutional framework required that it remain apolitical and use its loans only for productive purposes, this mandate led the Bank to disperse loans for welfare considerations and infrastructure. The Bank understood development efforts as "increasing a country's development," whereas poverty alleviation involved "social and distributive considerations best left to governments" (Konkel 2014, 276).

Over time, the dominant approach to economic development for least-developed countries came to be framed through the "Washington Consensus," which used the World Bank and IMF's stabilization and structural adjustment programs to push top-down government reforms, seeking controlled inflation and the reduction of fiscal deficits to realize targets for macroeconomic stability and an accelerated pace of trade and investment liberalization. These programs further pushed the privatization and deregulation of all state enterprises and the reduction of state presence in production and service markets (Gore 2000). This approach became synonymously, albeit inaccurately, associated with neoliberalism as the path to globalization for developing countries (Williamson 2009).

C. Neoliberalism

International financial institutions widely adopted the Washington Consensus approach to "conditionality," the process of making loans to governments in exchange for substantive policy reforms (Babb 2013). Under the IMF, these imposed reforms on national governments included structural adjustment programs affecting government fiscal expenditures; assumption of foreign debt; receipt of foreign aid; and governance, especially in the areas of poverty alleviation, the delivery of basic services, legal reforms, and market-based privatization of inefficient state-owned or controlled enterprises (Owusu 2003). Given the impact of these neoliberal reforms on public health, the World Bank would come to take an active role in lending to national governments to support health programming.

1. Structural Adjustment Programs under the IMF

Structural adjustment programs, under which the IMF set fiscal parameters and a mix of liberalization and deregulation targets, have been found to contribute to health inequities within and across the developing world.[2] In the

---

[2] Researchers have found that IMF-mandated structural adjustment policy reforms in 137 developing countries between 1980 and 2014 significantly lowered health system access and increased neonatal mortality, restricting the attainment of the Millennium Development Goals (Forster et al. 2020). Other studies have found that structural adjustment programs have detrimental impacts on child and maternal health, in that they undermine access to affordable health care and limit social

African context, researchers found that IMF and World Bank structural adjustment programs, establishing conditionalities in exchange for necessary loans, were associated with both food insecurity and undernutrition, while decreasing health care access (Loewenson 1993). Because structural adjustment programs are designed to support debt repayments, fiscal balancing (and spending reductions), and export-driven growth—under the assumption that economic growth would create "trickle-down" effects for the poor—these reforms inevitably affected developing country capacities to anticipate and adapt to population health challenges, especially considering that there were few safety nets and safeguards in place to meet deteriorating social conditions (Bhutta 2001). These public health harms of IMF conditionalities prompted the UN's 1987 report, "Adjustment with a Human Face," which examined adverse findings for child welfare and health from structural adjustment programs across various country case studies. Researchers have since acknowledged that the nexus between structural adjustment programs and health outcomes indicate a significant correlative or causal relationship, which differed depending on the country context and the particular terms of a structural adjustment program as designed by the IMF or the World Bank (Breman and Shelton 2006).

Case Study: The Health Harms of Structural Adjustment Policy

The World Bank published a 1981 report, "Accelerate Development in Sub-Saharan Africa: A Plan for Action," which called for improved efficiency in public sector management to support economic development, focusing on balancing fiscal deficits as the route to achieve macroeconomic stability. With respect to healthcare systems in Africa, the report recommended a gradual contraction of African health systems on a pilot basis, mindful of the fiscal and institutional resource constraints faced by African governments, and open to the possible imposition of "user fees" for public services and private sector operation of health care systems. The same report advocated reduced public spending for social services, including health infrastructures. Based upon this shift in World Bank policy, government expenditures on health as a percentage of GDP were reduced to just around 5% for African countries. The resulting privatization of health systems through the World Bank and IMF structural adjustment policies led to ineffective health systems and inequitable health

determinants of health (Thomson et al. 2017). Child health has also been imperiled where IMF-required public sector reforms undermined the fiscal capacity of states to deliver on needed child vaccinations, while also creating harms to population health by increasing global infectious disease burdens (Nosrati et al. 2022).

outcomes into the 1990s. In Ghana, a country epitomizing the imposition of neoliberal economic policies, the main causes of death remained preventable diseases, yet only 20% of the population had access to low-cost primary health care services. Throughout Africa, there was an underinvestment in public health and primary health care services, which undermined the ability to address systemic health problems. These structural adjustments resulted in the decades that followed in the decrease of physician-to-patient ratios, scarce healthcare technologies, worsening life expectancies, and ever fewer hospitals to serve deepening long-term as well as short-term health issues—amid the rapid obsolescence of health systems throughout the African continent.

Concerns over the legitimacy of imposing neoliberal reforms in the face of persistent and widening inequalities within and across developing countries prompted many to rethink the effectiveness of structural adjustment programs in redressing inequalities throughout the development process (Piketty 2014). Intersectional impacts felt within populations (especially when rooted in race, sex, gender, language, immigration status, ethnicity, religious belief, educational attainment, among other markers of discrimination) led to calls for a reexamination of the nature of fiscal spending, the design of redistribution policies, as well as the impacts of top-down and technocratic development agenda-setting that often neglected broad community participation when deciding appropriate policy responses (Shaw 2017). These calls led development actors to become more closely attuned to the global health impacts of economic development policy.

2. Emergence of HNP Lending at the World Bank

The World Bank would come to engage with health policy through the rise of its health, nutrition, and population (HNP) programming. In 1993, the World Bank issued its World Development Report, "Investing in Health," which set a new agenda for action that focused on:

- Health policy reform in developing countries to foster enabling environments for households to improve health, to expand government investments in health, and to facilitate involvement by the private sector in health.
- International assistance for health (especially for official development assistance priorities and the development of human resources for health) as well as improving the overall effectiveness of aid in improving health outcomes.
- Addressing challenges of health policy reforms in adapting to changing demographic profiles in the developing world, new infectious diseases and epidemiological emergencies, and the need to update service delivery toward effectiveness (World Bank 1993).

Figure 11.1 World Bank Board of Executive Directors (1993) (World Bank)

The World Bank Board of Executive Directors, seen in Figure 11.1, acknowledged that policy effectiveness is not limited by one paradigm—between public and private service delivery and financing for healthcare systems—or one choice for ensuring the most effective paths for the health sectors of low-, middle-, and high-income countries.

Following from this 1993 report, the World Bank would become the world's largest external funder of health, expending $1 billion annually in lending operations to improve health in developing countries (Prah Ruger 2005). The World Bank's HNP policies, strategies, and lending targeted health reforms and health outcomes, seeking under its HNP Strategy to improve the health outcomes of the poor and protect public health from the impoverishing effects of illness, malnutrition, and high fertility by enhancing health system performance and securing sustainable health financing (Fair 2008). Examining the results of its HNP Strategy, the World Bank in 2007 noted its shift toward acknowledging the nexus between health and economic growth, recognizing the bidirectional influences of HNP and development: "Health is often thought to be an outcome of economic growth. Increasingly, however, good health and sound health system policy have also been recognized as a major, inseparable contributor to economic growth" (World Bank 2007, 12).[3] This recognized nexus between

---

[3] The World Bank would provide several examples of this nexus linking public health and economic development: "The complex HNP-development dynamic operates in both directions. Higher incomes allow capacity expansion, which, in turn, may inspire investment in better access to safe water, sanitation, cleaner indoor environments, education, housing, diet and health care . . . [thus] ensuring economic growth is also crucial to achieve HNP results" (World Bank 2007, 12).

development and health would shift development policy from economic development to "human development."

D. The Rise of Human Development and the Nexus with Global Health

The trajectory of paradigm shifts in international development policy under the IMF and the World Bank would take into account conceptual, ideological, and philosophical transformations taking place in the international system to reflect evolving notions of human development. This focus on human development, first introduced in Chapter 10, would provide a significant foothold for human rights in economic development policy, with this shift reflected in the emergence of capabilities-based approaches to development (Meier and Fox 2008). These approaches looked to development in enlarging individual freedoms—such as freedoms pertaining to well-being, agency, and autonomy—as a means for individuals and peoples to enjoy more opportunities, optimize their functioning by gaining further capabilities, and in turn, expand their choices for individual human flourishing (Sen 1999).

This conceptual focus on capabilities in development policy influenced the United Nations Development Programme (UNDP) in 1990 to frame its operations according to theories of capabilities and human development, noting that human development:

> is a process of enlarging people's choices. The most critical of these wide-ranging choices are to live a long and healthy life, to be educated and to have access to resources needed for a decent standard of living. Additional choices include political freedom, guaranteed human rights, and personal self-respect. Development enables people to have these choices ... Human development thus concerns more than the formation of human capabilities, such as improved health or knowledge. It also concerns the use of these capabilities ... (UNDP 1990, 1).

This operational shift in UNDP coincided with international political developments stemming from the 1986 UN General Assembly Declaration on the Right to Development, resolving that development "is a comprehensive, economic, social, cultural and political process, which aims at the constant improvement of the well-being of the entire population and of all individuals on the basis of their active, free and meaningful participation in development and in the fair distribution of benefits resulting therefrom" (UN General Assembly 1986, Preamble). Many civil society advocates have since pushed for different rights-based approaches to development, especially in the areas of public health and social determinants of health (Nelson and Dorsey 2018).

This conjoined approach to human development, human rights, and global health provided a path to examine the intersectional impacts of public health policies, especially when such policies were designed by states within a broader background of loan conditionalities and structural adjustment programs (Pfeiffer and Chapman 2010). When situated in public health contexts, intersectionality provokes institutional controversy for states that are routinely implementing public health policies without effectively serving vulnerable populations that have historically been excluded or underserved on the basis of race, sex, economic status, and immigration status, among other grounds of discriminatory treatment (Bowleg 2012).[4] Multilateral economic institutions have begun to incorporate this approach of examining social inclusion as part of poverty alleviation and economic development strategies (Vetterlein 2007).

II. Development Policy, Intersectionality, and Public Health

As policymakers engage with the intersectionality of health vulnerabilities and the corresponding human rights implicated by the experiences of communities that face greater or more disproportionate precarities (owing to causes such as race, gender, socioeconomic status, birth or nationality, language, religious or political belief, among other factors), global economic governance institutions such as the IMF, World Bank, and other international financial institutions have gradually recognized the need to embed social inclusion in development policies to advance public health. The public health effects of the 2008 global financial crisis would provide a further impetus to reshape global economic governance to address social determinants of health, intensifying commitments to public health outcomes in an era of enforced austerity measures. From a reactive management ethos of responding to the health impacts of protracted global economic crises, the World Bank would instead focus its development funding toward a more proactive and preventative embrace of universal health coverage to ensure a greater role in global health governance under the 2030 Agenda for Sustainable Development.

---

[4] Even in developed country contexts such as the United States, heightened attention is increasingly being directed to the intersectional effects of a state's local or internal development policies for public health, since the social determinants of health are likewise inflected by the same intersectional grounds for discrimination or unjustified exclusion (Sun et al. 2022).

A. Intersectionality of Global Health and Social Determinants of Health

Visualizing and situating the nexus of cyclical poverty, social immobility, and economic underdevelopment, experienced alongside a history of intersectional discrimination, provides the context for understanding how the effectiveness and efficacy of national public health programs and policies are assessed—particularly in terms of serving the needs of diverse communities in the developed or the developing world (Parolin and Lee 2022). In recent years, the World Bank's HNP Global Practice Division has considered the significance of social inclusion in defining and setting health policies and practices in World Bank-supported interventions to advance public health in the developing world (Das et al. 2017). The World Bank defines social inclusion as "the process of improving the terms for individuals and groups to take part in society" as well as "the process of improving the ability, opportunity, and dignity of people, disadvantaged on the basis of their identity, to take part in society" (World Bank 2013, 1).[5] By explicitly considering social inclusion in policymaking in the developing world, the World Bank has partnered with national governments and local communities to identify social inclusion needs in public health.

Before these conceptions of intersectionality were implemented at the level of global economic governance, international financial institutions struggled to recognize the importance of identifying the intersectionality of discrimination, poverty, and health experiences for multiple vulnerable communities within a population (Sun et al. 2022). Given their historically narrow focus on economic development through the path of neoliberal globalization and Washington Consensus policies, various changes had to occur within the global economic system before multilateral institutions would embrace a wider recognition of rights-based approaches to human development and public health policies in their institutional agendas and operations. The human rights impact of global economic decision-making were vividly demonstrated in the rollout of austerity measures, which led to massive cuts to social spending, public health, education, housing, and essential infrastructure (water, energy, transport, and communications), entrenching health inequalities and leading to disproportionate lived outcomes for people of color, women, children, migrants, Indigenous peoples, and other vulnerable groups.

Yet, even as the World Bank acknowledged the intersectional and asymmetric impacts of poverty within and across demographics of the most vulnerable in

---

[5] According to the World Bank, the most common identities resulting in exclusion are gender, race, caste, ethnicity, religion, sexual orientation, disability, mental health status, and addiction (World Bank 2013).

the developing world, it did not change the overall approach of Washington Consensus policies. Despite its many avowed and acknowledged weaknesses and ineffectiveness, the Washington Consensus was not eliminated as a transnational policy paradigm for global economic institutions such as the World Bank and the IMF (Babb 2013). Global economic policy continued to emphasize macroeconomic stability, fiscal discipline and management, trade and investment liberalization, reordering fiscal expenditure priorities, and mass privatization of state assets and services—as a foundation to create more private-sector led, export-oriented, industrialized economies (World Bank 2018). For example, as African nations faced new and re-emerging disease threats in the early years of the 21st century, as introduced in Chapter 6, some World Bank and IMF leaders acknowledged that Africa's resilience to serious health crises had been negatively impacted by structural adjustment programs that reduced spending on African health care systems.[6] Amid this continuing focus on the Washington Consensus, economic crises would continue to challenge global economic development governance in grappling with the intersectional impacts of poverty on health.

B. A Global Economic Crisis Reshapes Global Economic Governance

The 2008 global economic crisis, which initially began in the Eurozone, sparked intense controversy over the wisdom of continuing Washington Consensus policies, particularly in developing countries that were already mired in preexisting economic hardships—hardships exacerbated under the strict fiscal austerity measures prescribed by multilateral economic institutions (Desierto 2012). Scholars attributed the worsening of global health amid the financial crisis to decades of entrenchment of neoliberal policies, as these policies deprioritized government expenditures on health care and other social services for populations—as a basis to meet the World Bank and IMF's structural adjustment conditionalities (Benatar, Gill, and Bakker 2011). In Greece, the hardest hit European country during the 2008 crisis, the imposition of austerity measures deeply affected the Greek healthcare system, with fiscal policies affecting the direct structural components of health care, including hospitals, due to rapid understaffing, deficits, and shortages of basic medical and surgical supplies. Beyond basic health care services, cuts to public health systems constrained disease

---

[6] This dynamic continued through the 2014–2016 Ebola crisis in West Africa, as continuing underinvestment in African healthcare systems led to a cascade of problems of capacity, scale, responsiveness, technology, accessibility, and affordability for countries to expeditiously and effectively address the Ebola epidemic through their respective healthcare systems, forcing affected countries to increase their dependence on foreign aid and foreign donors.

prevention and health education initiatives and eroded social services and public protections (Ifanti et al. 2013).

These health impacts of the 2008 global economic crisis were tied to continuing austerity measures throughout the crisis, which led to significant fiscal cuts to the systems underlying health (Basu, Carney, and Kenworthy 2017). Spending cuts during the global economic crisis often focused on public sector programs, education and healthcare systems, and social services that are most needed by the poorest communities, leading to massive health declines among the most vulnerable populations throughout the world (Ifanti et al. 2013). Apart from spending cuts affecting the social determinants of health, the lived experience of austerity directly implicated psychological resilience and mental health outcomes for children, youth, and newer generations of workers (Costa et al. 2020).

While multilateral economic institutions were not ambivalent to the social costs of these austerity measures, it took time for them to act to address the public health impacts arising out of this protracted global economic crisis. The Independent Evaluation Group that assessed the World Bank's responses to the global economic crisis observed that:

> Bank responses during the financial crisis were partially relevant for raising the effectiveness of social protection, but the Bank was limited by the inadequacy of effective and flexible country programs that protect workers whose incomes were reduced during the crisis ... [T]he crisis provided an opportunity for the Bank to start to move ahead on the long-term agenda of building social protection systems (Independent Evaluation Group for the World Bank, IFC, and MIGA 2012, 130).

The Independent Evaluation Group also observed that while the World Bank undertook extensive lending activities to help mitigate the impacts of the crisis on poverty in many developing countries, this focus on maintaining public investment in infrastructure faced sustainability challenges given the ensuing rollback of fiscal stimulus, social security, pensions, and health system benefits. The World Bank and IMF failed to fully protect these critical social programs during the 2008 global financial crisis (Benatar, Gill, and Bakker 2011). In spite of these recognized failures, independent assessments overlooked the internal paradigm shifts that were already taking place across the international development landscape, with such shifts quietly transforming these core economic institutions to support global public health. Even as global economic development institutions neglected the health impacts of the 2008 global financial crisis, the World Bank was becoming one of the world's largest external funders of global health.

C. World Bank Shifts Development Funding Trajectories: From Reactive Mitigation of Health Impacts of Economic Crises toward Proactive Efforts to Realize Universal Health Coverage

The expansion of multilateral economic lending for global health, especially during the 2008 global economic crisis, indicated greater institutional consciousness about the importance of supporting healthcare systems and social health protection in times of precarity through a focus on universal health coverage. The World Bank responded to the interest of low- and middle-income countries in achieving universal health coverage through the publication of the 2010 World Health Report, "Health Systems Financing: The Path to Universal Coverage." In its subsequent 2014 report, "Universal Health Coverage for Inclusive and Sustainable Development: A Synthesis of 11 Country Case Studies," the World Bank recommended that countries invest in primary healthcare services to improve access to care and manage healthcare costs. These World Bank reports detailed how countries can enact bold policies to redistribute resources and reduce disparities in access to care through a balanced approach—between prioritizing expenditures to manage finances and expanding coverage in health programs. The World Bank has thus committed to help countries reach universal health coverage through "support [for] countries to build healthier, more equitable societies, as well as to improve their fiscal performance and country competitiveness" (World Bank 2022). Advancing this support in global economic governance, the World Bank has pushed its commitment to universal health coverage through global, regional, and country-level research, financial investments, and technical assistance.[7]

Notwithstanding this laudable attention to universal health coverage, however, it was clear that none of the multilateral economic institutions have recognized themselves as bound by international human rights law in global economic governance. This neglect of human rights norms has denied attention to key health-related human rights obligations in development policy, including the right to the highest attainable standard of physical and mental health; the prohibition against non-discrimination; the right to self-determination as the free pursuit of economic, social, and cultural development; the prohibition against deprivation of means of subsistence; and the emerging right to development (Shawar and Prah Ruger 2018). Multilateral economic institutions have publicly

---

[7] Not all multilateral economic institutions have taken the same path as the World Bank in the extensiveness and depth of its commitments to global health advancement and universal health coverage. The IMF, for example, has continued to impose conditionality requirements without exempting a state's health expenditures, at the severe price of reduced fiscal space for urgent investments in health, workforce reductions of doctors and nurses, and budgetary challenges for health systems (Forster et al. 2020).

declared their lending, financing, trading, and investing activities to be in support of "development," but without attention to human rights norms, the concept of "development" in practice has been too nebulous to enable populations to assert any legal right to participate in development decision-making or to seek accountability for any harmful impacts arising from these institutions' global development decisions (Desierto et al. 2020). Without a shared meaning of "development," it became harder to establish criteria for determining whether or not such development was indeed realized for populations in whose name decisions were taken by multilateral economic institutions. This imperative to define development consistently across the global development landscape would lead to policy shifts through the UN to shape all global efforts to achieve "sustainable development."

D. Implementing the Sustainable Development Goals

Greater convergence on the international understanding of "development," especially in the context of global health, became possible in 2015 as the UN General Assembly issued 17 Sustainable Development Goals (SDGs) and 169 targets under the 2030 Agenda for Sustainable Development. Drawing from the Millennium Development Goals that preceded them, the SDGs envisioned a world that would advance health and human rights through development:

> a world with equitable and universal access to quality education at all levels, to health care and social protection, where physical, mental and social well-being are assured. A world where we reaffirm our commitments regarding the human right to safe drinking water and sanitation and where there is improved hygiene; and where food is sufficient, safe, affordable and nutritious. A world where human habitats are safe, resilient, and sustainable and where there is universal access to affordable, reliable and sustainable energy . . . a world of universal respect for human rights and human dignity, the rule of law, justice, equality and non-discrimination; of respect for race, ethnicity and cultural diversity; and of equal opportunity permitting the full realization of human potential and contributing to shared prosperity . . . a just, equitable, tolerant, open, and socially inclusive world in which the needs of the most vulnerable are met (UN General Assembly 2015, paras. 7, 8)

Both the IMF and the World Bank have become close institutional partners in operational programming to assist in the implementation of the SDGs, especially in efforts to promote universal health coverage and other health-related goals and targets. To ensure healthy lives and promote well-being under the

SDGs, the UN set thirteen targets under SDG3, as detailed in Chapter 10, that would provide a new foundation for these economic development institutions to implement the SDGs to advance global health.

Case Study: Economic Institutions Implement the SDGs

Multilateral economic institutions intensified their cooperation with the UN to implement the global health governance agenda defined by the SDGs. The World Bank had collaborated with the UN in the implementation of the Millennium Development Goals, and has continued to partner with UN institutions in monitoring the "Health, Nutrition and Population" SDGs, producing various SDG implementation reports on child mortality, stillbirths, maternal mortality, and child malnutrition. In supporting sustainable development for global health, the World Bank has worked with states to implement the SDG target on universal health coverage, establishing priority areas to help low- and middle-income countries accelerate their progress to achieve universal health coverage by (1) ramping up investments in affordable, quality primary health care; (2) engaging the private sector and unlocking new models for health financing and delivery; (3) improving health outcomes and supporting communities by improving education, broadening social services, and creating jobs; and (4) catalyzing domestic resources to build sustainable national health systems. Partnering with WHO and other institutions to advance SDG 3, the World Bank is a co-signatory and partner to the Global Action Plan for Healthy Lives and Well-Being for All, which was established in 2019 with thirteen multilateral health, development, and humanitarian agencies to help countries reach the health-related SDG targets through coordinated institutional support and financing. The World Bank's role under the Global Action Plan has been pivotal in ensuring the flow of financing and technical expertise to advance global health under the SDGs.

The World Bank continues to find points of alignment with the UN in supporting implementation of the SDGs related to health. Under the SDGs, the World Bank's partnerships with the UN and WHO now enable the Bank to fill a significant role in global health governance and multilateral cooperation on global health issues, as seen through its voluntary commitments, operational practices, and long-term strategies around SDG targets relating to universal health coverage and social determinants of health (Clinton and Sridhar 2017). The concrete expectations flowing from the SDGs and its targets avoid the abstract conceptions of "economic development" that had previously justified prioritizing incremental public health interventions, regardless of their inequalities or disparate impacts for different sectors or vulnerable populations. The SDGs now provide a clear framework of empirically measurable data points that assist in evaluating the effectiveness of global health strategies and the adequacy of global health outcomes (Cole and Broadhurst 2021), with the World Bank implementing development decisions for global health and thus becoming increasingly relevant in the global health law response to global health security challenges.

III. Global Health Security and International Economic Cooperation through Law

Global economic governance is crucially relevant in facing global health security challenges; yet, the COVID-19 pandemic response highlights weaknesses in World Bank engagement in global health governance. In strengthening global economic governance to prevent disease and promote health, the increasing turn toward the right to development provides a normative basis to reframe economic development policy in a more holistic approach under international human rights law.

A. World Bank and WHO Partnership to Strengthen Global Health Security

Drawing from partnerships to advance universal health coverage, the World Bank joined WHO in 2018 in launching the Global Preparedness Monitoring Board, establishing a joint mechanism to strengthen global health security. This Global Preparedness Monitoring Board would provide stringent independent monitoring and regular preparedness monitoring to anticipate and respond to pandemics and other emergencies with health consequences (World Bank 2018). Building on decades of work across the two institutions,[8] this new partnership aligned with the UN General Assembly's emphasis on greater collaboration and partnership to respond to current and emerging threats against human security (UN General Assembly 2012). Despite this rising partnership, World Bank

---

[8] Historically, the World Bank and WHO built a strong partnership dating back to WHO's 1995 "Recommendations for Action for Health Development," leveraging complementary technical and financial expertise in support of health development programs in developing countries (WHO 1995). In this early effort, WHO Representatives were tasked with facilitating dialogue on health development between the World Bank and a developing country's ministries on health, finance, and planning, and to create institutional structures for external aid coordination in support of nationally identified needs in the health sector (WHO 1996).

engagement in global health security would falter amid the rising COVID-19 pandemic, as WHO Representatives lacked timely information on the real scale and impact of the pandemic across local, national, regional, and global contexts.

B. Weaknesses of Global Economic Governance in the COVID-19 Response

As the threat from the COVID-19 pandemic began to take shape, the World Bank declared that it was mounting the "fastest and largest health crisis response in its history to save lives from COVID-19" (World Bank 2020); however, the failure of pandemic bonds and limitations of vaccine support reveal continuing weaknesses of global economic governance in advancing global health.

1. Failure of "Pandemic Bonds"

The World Bank had launched specialized bonds in 2017 to provide financial support to the Pandemic Emergency Financing (PEF) Facility, which would provide emergency financing to enable expeditious surge funding to developing countries facing pandemic risks. These "pandemic bonds" sought to raise capital that was specifically earmarked for responding to pandemic outbreaks, with investors receiving coupons (just like regular bonds) that would be repaid at the maturity of the bond if there was no pandemic outbreak (World Bank 2017). (Conversely, investors would lose their capital investment in the event of a pandemic before the maturity of the investment.) Providing a form of "pandemic insurance" to developing countries, a set of predetermined criteria had to be satisfied for an outbreak to be categorized as a pandemic that would trigger a PEF payout.

Prior to the COVID-19 pandemic, the PEF had already failed initially during the 2018 Ebola outbreak in the Democratic Republic of Congo, when the earmarked capital investment to address the outbreak was not paid out. Because of the bond criteria that required a disease to spread across international borders before the affected nation could receive the payout, the failure to deliver urgently needed health financing amid mass death allowed investors to profit on their returns even as developing countries struggled with health emergencies. Critics had already dubbed pandemic bonds "a good deal for investors, not for global health" – as the pandemic bonds neglected in 2019 to pay out during a second Ebola outbreak (Jonas 2019).[9] With the outbreak of COVID-19, the pandemic

---

[9] Many who see health as a public good and a government responsibility bristled at the idea that external aid during a dire health crisis would be recast into an investment or insurance vehicle through pandemic bonds—dependent on arbitrary criteria that protected investors' high returns at a time when healthcare systems were in peril and in urgent need of surge financing.

bonds failed once again to deliver the surge funding needed by the world's poorest countries—with too little funding that came too late (Strohecker 2020). Ultimately, the PEF could not meet payout demands from bondholders after the trigger events (i.e., pandemics) arose, denying necessary support from global economic governance throughout an unprecedented global health security threat.

2. Limited Influence in Pandemic Response

The World Bank continued to have limited influence across national COVID-19 responses, focusing its influence instead on providing for reconstruction and recovery. In March 2020, the International Finance Corporation (IFC) arm of the World Bank Group extended an $8 billion facility for financial support to private sector clients to help keep businesses afloat and preserve jobs. The Multilateral Investment Guarantee Agency (MIGA) of the World Bank Group correspondingly launched a program at the same time to underwrite up to $6.5 billion in financial guarantees for investors and lenders to be able to withstand the pandemic. With global economic activity grinding to a halt, as governments rapidly instituted nationwide "lockdowns," the World Bank and IMF supported the implementation of a debt service suspension initiative; however, this initiative did not receive broad participation from public and private creditors, which mistrusted the World Bank's failure to suspend its own debt service payments while requesting private creditors to do so.[10] The World Bank's research arm continued to offer guidance to build sustainable development pathways during the pandemic, but the Bank's influence in the pandemic response was limited. While recognizing the cataclysmic development consequences of the pandemic, it was on the periphery when it came to marshaling resources for the global pandemic response and the global vaccination campaign.

Case Study: Limitations of World Bank-IMF Joint Strategies on COVID Vaccination

Soon after issuing a 2021 Joint Statement on the importance of vaccine equity in the COVID-19 response, the World Bank, IMF, WHO, and World Trade Organization (WTO) created a Task Force on Scaling COVID-19 Tools, meeting with the leading vaccine manufacturing companies to discuss operational strategies to improve vaccine access for low-and lower middle-income countries. The Task Force sought to realize a 40% vaccination coverage target for the end of 2021, seeking transparency on vaccine stocks and supply chains,

---

[10] Since private creditors were not offering debt suspension, the World Bank could not do so alone, as it would have jeopardized its credit rating and limited its future financing ability (Saldinger 2020).

the elimination of export restrictions and tariff and non-tariff barriers, and regulatory streamlining and harmonization on vaccine approval. To meet this target, the World Bank Board of Executive Directors approved a $6 Billion Global COVID-19 Response Program (also called the COVID-19 Strategic Preparedness and Response Program), with partners adding financing of $12 billion. This World Bank financing enabled the purchase of 630 million doses, with 460 million doses delivered in around 78 countries. Yet, despite the massive development resources of the World Bank, it remained subject to the demand and supply realities of the markets for COVID-19 vaccines, with intellectual property rights under the WTO sharply enforced by behemoth pharmaceutical companies that developed the vaccines and hold a monopoly over their distribution and rollout throughout the world. Given these constraints under international trade law, this vaccine distribution effort fell well short of the 40% coverage target, and certainly did not observe uniform delivery, quality, and quantity timelines—leading to a rise in vaccine inequity between the Global North and Global South.

The World Bank has not shown a demonstrably successful track record in providing the needed surge financing during pandemic outbreaks for developing countries' health resilience needs. Much of the challenge is the misalignment of the design of its proposals (e.g., pandemic bonds and vaccination programs) with the speed and efficiency required to respond to pandemic health risks and the challenge of coordinating within and across bureaucracies during public health crises. Effective and efficient coordination with governments and the private sector during an unraveling COVID-19 pandemic (with its multiple variants) has not been easy for the World Bank—despite its own mandated neutrality and apolitical programming.

Where the COVID-19 pandemic has exposed the inadequacy of the World Bank in addressing pandemic threats, especially in low- and middle-income countries, the World Bank is looking to prepare for future pandemics through the Pandemic Fund—formerly the Financial Intermediary Fund for PPR. Launched in September 2022, this Fund is exclusively dedicated to pandemic preparedness and response and seeks to strengthen these capabilities in low- and middle-income countries. The inclusion of WHO guidance in shaping the World Bank's future pandemic response seeks to redress the gaps in investments and technical support while providing essential financial support in long-term, proactive pandemic preparedness and response efforts (McDade and Yamey 2022). Establishing the World Bank as a long-term partner for ensuring global health will require that the World Bank ensure its own institutional relevance and responsiveness in proactively anticipating, addressing, and redressing global health crises, providing a path to join in reliable and equal partnerships across the global health landscape to safeguard human rights in development governance.

C. Right to Development

The World Bank long avoided discussions concerning human rights in development governance, viewing itself as an economic development institution uninvolved in the political affairs of countries. Under this apolitical presentation of its work, the World Bank largely rejected the human rights obligations associated with health and development under the 1948 Universal Declaration of Human Rights (UDHR) and the human rights treaties codified in the decades that followed. As new developing countries joined the UN, they would push global governance to recognize the importance of economic development, as introduced in Chapter 3, leading the UN General Assembly in 1986 to adopt the Declaration on the Right to Development. Under this General Assembly Declaration, the right to development was framed as an inalienable human right—tied to the enjoyment of economic, social, cultural, and political development (Fox and Meier 2009). This human right to development was reaffirmed following the Cold War in the 1993 Vienna Declaration and Programme of Action, with this larger recognition of development as a fundamental human right leading to changes in World Bank policies.

Under pressure from NGOs concerned about the social impacts of structural adjustment programs, the World Bank and its new leaders took a prominent role in global health work and began to recognize that development could not occur without the consideration of human rights (Shawar and Prah Ruger 2018). This trend toward human rights was solidified by the World Bank's 1988 publication, "Development and Human Rights: The role of the World Bank," which laid out the fulfillment of human rights as a precursor for economic development goals.

The codification of a human right to development can provide a human rights foundation in global economic governance. This human right is currently being developed into a legally binding Convention on the Right to Development, with an emphasis on the indivisibility, interrelatedness, and interdependence of all human rights with the right to development. Applying the right to development to economic development policy would further call for a reframing of how such policy enables participation, contribution, and enjoyment of development by all persons and peoples in a manner that is indivisible from and interdependent with the realization and implementation of all other human rights (Desierto 2023). Such a human rights foundation will be essential for the continuing advancement of development policy to promote global health.

Conclusion

Precisely because economic development is a fundamental and bidirectional determinant of global health, it behooves global economic actors such as the IMF, World Bank, and even regional development banks, to deliberately and intentionally participate in the broader dialogue between states, populations, vulnerable groups, the private sector, civil society, and international organizations on the rising influence of the global economic system in global health governance. However, instead of shaping the future of global health policies, internalizing human rights law in the global economic system, global economic governance actors still choose to remain in a vacuum of their own making. By operating selectively in deciding when to align programs, policies, and financing commitments with public health and human rights, multilateral economic institutions risk not just a crisis of legitimacy toward the very same populations that are the ultimate recipients of global health interventions, but also the political durability of its declared commitments to international cooperation for economic development.

By refusing to anchor economic development commitments for global public health advancement in the hard law of treaties or other sources of international law—bypassing the binding effect of international human rights law through a selective alignment with rights-based approaches to development—international financial institutions ironically lay themselves open to outworn geopolitical criticisms from new entrants in multilateral economic lending (primarily driven by China) that themselves openly decry any reference to social policies as pretextual renewals of old Western imperialisms into new colonialisms and Western hegemonies.

If global economic institutions wish to maintain their leadership and influence in global public health, serious consideration must be given to entrenching these institutions' global public health commitments in legally binding treaties or the hard law of international human rights law, rather than relying on soft and non-binding instruments that could be just as ephemeral as the political winds. If multilateral economic institutions were able to instantiate the Washington Consensus through the hard law of binding agreements with states to implement structural adjustment programs and other long-term market reforms, these institutions are more than capable of ensuring that their commitments to achieve universal health coverage and ensure global health advancement for all can, and should, also be entrenched in the binding and accountable language of law. Development governance is a public health issue and a global health paradigm on its own. How development efforts succeed will depend critically on how development paradigms, decisions, and institutions deliver global public health outcomes.

Questions for Consideration

1. Why did states develop two separate institutions—the IMF and the World Bank—to govern the world financial order after World War II? How did the mission of these institutions shift once the reconstruction following the war was complete?
2. What government reforms were sought under the "Washington Consensus"? How did the IMF and World Bank impose loan conditionalities to frame structural adjustments? What did these structural adjustment programs mean for national health policies in the Global South?
3. When did public health gain prominence among global economic institutions? How did the World Bank's HNP lending influence global health governance?
4. What distinguishes economic development from human development in development policy? How did the focus on human development provide an opening to discuss health and human rights in economic development policy?
5. How has the World Bank's focus on social inclusion provided a framework for developing global health policy? Despite this shifting attention to health and human rights, why has the Washington Consensus not been fundamentally reformed?
6. How did Washington Consensus policies precipitate public health challenges amid the 2008 global economic crisis? How did the World Bank respond to the public health challenges of the global economic crisis?
7. As the World Bank took on an expanded role in global health governance under the SDGs, how has it sought to work with WHO to advance universal health coverage? How has this focus on universal health coverage provided an opening for World Bank efforts to implement the health targets of SDG3?
8. Why has the World Bank sought to partner with WHO to strengthen global health security? Why have pandemic bonds failed repeatedly to provide rapid resources to nations facing pandemic threats?
9. Are global economic institutions most suited for global and human security challenges such as pandemics, which threaten global health security? Why did the Task Force on Scaling Covid-19 Tools fail to reach its vaccine distribution targets? How could the World Bank and IMF have been more effective in the COVID-19 pandemic response?

Acknowledgments

The authors greatly appreciate the contributions and editorial support of Rishabh Sud and Ryan Doerzbacher.

References

Alacevich, Michele. 2009. *The Political Economy of the World Bank: The Early Years.* Stanford: Stanford University Press and the World Bank.

Babb, Sarah. 2013. "The Washington Consensus as Transnational Policy Paradigm: Its Origins, Trajectory and Likely Successor." *Review of International Political Economy* 20(2): 268–297.

Basu, Sanjay, Megan A. Carney, and Nora J. Kenworthy. 2017. "Ten Years after the Financial Crisis: The Long Reach of Austerity and Its Global Impacts on Health." *Social Science & Medicine* 187: 203–207.

Benatar, Solomon R., Stephen Gill, and Isabella Bakker. 2011. "Global Health and the Global Economic Crisis." *American Journal of Public Health* 101(4): 646–653.

Bhutta, Zulfiqar Ahmed. 2001. "Structural Adjustments and Their Impact on Health and Society: A Perspective from Pakistan." *International Journal of Epidemiology* 30(4): 712–716.

Bowleg, Lisa. 2012. "The Problem with the Phrase Women and Minorities: Intersectionality—an Important Theoretical Framework for Public Health." *American Journal of Public Health* 102(7): 1267–1273.

Breman, Anna and Carolyn Shelton. 2006. "Structural Adjustment Programs and Health." *Globalization and Health* 1: 219–233.

Clinton, Chelsea, and Devi Sridhar. 2017. "Who Pays for Cooperation in Global Health? A Comparative Analysis of WHO, the World Bank, the Global Fund to Fight HIV/AIDS, Tuberculosis and Malaria, and Gavi, the Vaccine Alliance." *Lancet* 390(10091): 324–332.

Cole, Megan J. and Jennifer L. Broadhurst. 2021. "Measuring the Sustainable Development Goals (SDGs) in Mining Host Communities: A South African CaseSstudy." *The Extractive Industries and Society* 8(1): 233–243.

Costa, Diogo, Marina Cunha, Cláudia Ferreira, Augusta Gama, Aristides M. Machado-Rodrigues, Vítor Rosado-Marques, Helena Nogueira, Maria-Raquel G. Silva, and Cristina Padez. 2020. "Children Mental Health after the 2008 Global Economic Crisis: Assessing the Impact of Austerity in Portugal." *Children and Youth Services Review* 118: 105332.

Das, Maitreyi Bordia, Timothy Grant Evans, Toomas Palu, and David Wilson. 2017."Social Inclusion: What Does It Mean for Health Policy and Practice." *Health, Nutrition and Population Discussion Paper.* Washington: World Bank.

Desierto, Diane A. 2012. "Growth versus Austerity: Protecting, Respecting, and Fulfilling International Economic and Social Rights during Economic Crises." *Ateneo Law Journal* 57: 373.

Desierto, Diane A. 2023. "The Human Right to Development as a New Foundation for International Economic Law." *Tulane Journal of International Law* 31: 1–17.

Desierto, Diane, Anibal Perez-Linan, Khawla Wakkaf, Rachel Gagnon, and Belen Carriedo. 2020. "The 'New' World Bank Accountability Mechanism: Observations from the ND Reparations Design and Compliance Lab." *EJIL:Talk!*, November 11.

Fair, Mollie. 2008. "From Population Lending to HNP Results: The Evolution of the World Bank's Strategies in Health, Nutrition and Population." *IEG Independent Evaluation Group* 2008/3. 1–101. Washington: World Bank.

Fox, Ashley M. and Benjamin Mason Meier. 2009. "Health as Freedom: Addressing Social Determinants of Global Health Inequities through the Human Right to Development." *Bioethics* 23(2): 112–122.

Forster, Timon, Alexander E. Kentikelenis, Thomas H. Stubbs, and Lawrence P. King. 2020. "Globalization and Health Equity: The Impact of Structural Adjustment Programs on Developing Countries." *Social Science & Medicine* 267: 112496.

Frieden, Jeffry. 2019. "The Political Economy of the Bretton Woods Agreements." In *The Bretton Woods Agreements*, edited by Naomi R. Lamoreaux and Ian Shapiro. 21–37. New Haven: Yale University Press.

Gore, Charles. 2000. "The Rise and Fall of the Washington Consensus as a Paradigm for Developing Countries." *World Development* 28(5): 789–804.

Ifanti, Amalia A., Andreas A. Argyriou, Foteini H. Kalofonou, and Haralabos P. Kalofonos. 2013. "Financial Crisis and Austerity Measures in Greece: Their Impact on Health Promotion Policies and Public Health Care." *Health Policy* 113(1–2): 8–12.

Independent Evaluation Group for the World Bank, IFC, and MIGA. 2012. "The World Bank Group's Response to the Global Economic Crisis: Phase II."

Jonas, Olga. 2019. "Pandemic Bonds: Designed to Fail in Ebola." *Nature* 572(7769): 285–286.

Kapur, Devesh, John P. Lewis, and Richard C. Webb. 2011. *The World Bank: Its First Half Century*. Vol. 1. Washington: Brookings Institution Press.

Konkel, Rob. 2014. "The Monetization of Global Poverty: The Concept of Poverty in World Bank hHstory, 1944–90." *Journal of Global History* 9(2): 276–300.

Lamoreaux, Naomi R. and Ian Shapiro. 2019. *The Bretton Woods Agreements. Together with Scholarly Commentaries and Essential Historical Documents*. New Haven: Yale University Press.

Loewenson, Rene. 1993. "Structural Adjustment and Health Policy in Africa." *International Journal of Health Services* 23(4): 717–730.

Marshall, Katherine. 2008. *The World Bank: From Reconstruction to Development to Equity*. New York: Routledge.

McDade, Kacia Kennedy and Gavin Yamey. 2022. "Three Big Questions Facing the World Bank's New Pandemic Fund." *BMJ* 379: o2857.

Meier, Benjamin Mason, and Ashley M. Fox. 2008. "Development as Health: Employing the Collective Right to Development to Achieve the Goals of the Individual Right to Health." *Human Rights Quarterly* 30 (2): 259–355.

Nelson, Paul J. and Ellen Dorsey. 2018. "Who Practices Rights-Based Development? A Progress Report on Work at the Nexus of Human Rights and Development." *World Development* 104: 97–107.

Nosrati, Elias, Jennifer B. Dowd, Michael Marmot, and Lawrence P. King. 2022. "Structural Adjustment Programmes and Infectious Disease Mortality." *Plos One* 17(7): e0270344.

Owusu, Francis. 2003. "Pragmatism and the Gradual Shift from Dependency to Neoliberalism: The World Bank, African Leaders and Development Policy in Africa." *World Development* 3(10): 1655–1672.

Parolin, Zachary and Emma K. Lee. 2022. "The Role of Poverty and Racial Discrimination in Exacerbating the Health Consequences of COVID-19." *Lancet Regional Health-Americas* 7: 100178.

Pfeiffer, James and Rachel Chapman. 2010. "Anthropological Perspectives on Structural Adjustment and Public Health." *Annual Review of Anthropology* 39: 149–165.

Piketty, Thomas. 2014. *Capital in the Twenty-First Century*. Cambridge: Harvard University Press.

Prah Ruger, Jennifer. 2005. "The Changing Role of the World Bank in Global Health." *American Journal of Public Health* 95(1): 60–70.

Reinhart, Carmen M. and Christoph Trebesch. 2016. "The International Monetary Fund: 70 Years of Reinvention." *Journal of Economic Perspectives* 30(1): 3–28.

Saldinger, Adva. 2020. "As World Bank Pushes Others on Debt Relief, It Doesn't Participate." *Devex*. October 19.

Sen, Amartya. 1999. *Development as Freedom*. New York: Knopf.

Shaw, Mae. 2017. "Community Development: Reviving Critical Agency in Times of Crisis." In *The Routledge Handbook of Community Development*, 26–39. New York: Routledge.

Shawar, Yusra Ribhi, and Jennifer Prah Ruger. 2018. "The World Bank: Contested Institutional Progress in Rights-Based Health Discourse." In *Human Rights in Global Health: Rights-Based Governance for a Globalizing World*, edited by Benjamin Mason Meier and Lawrence O. Gostin, 353–374. New York: Oxford University Press.

Strohecker, Karin. 2020. "World Bank Pandemic Bond under Pressure as Coronavirus Spreads." *Reuters*. February 20.

Sun, Michael, Tomasz Oliwa, Monica E. Peek, and Elizabeth L. Tung. 2022. "Negative Patient Descriptors: Documenting Racial Bias in The Electronic Health Record: Study Examines Racial Bias in the Patient Descriptors Used in the Electronic Health Record." *Health Affairs* 41(2): 203–211.

Thomson, Michael, Alexander Kentikelenis, and Thomas Stubbs. 2017. "Structural Adjustment Programmes Adversely Affect Vulnerable Populations: A Systematic-Narrative Review of Their Effect on Child and Maternal Health." *Public Health Reviews* 38(1): 1–18.

UN General Assembly. 1986. "Declaration on the Right to Development." December 4. A/RES/41/128.

UN General Assembly. 2012. "Follow Up to Paragraph 143 on Human Security of the 2005 World Summit Outcome." October 25. A/RES/66/290.

UN General Assembly. 2015. "Transforming Our World: The 2030 Agenda for Sustainable Development. October 21. A/RES/70/1.

UNDP (United Nations Development Programme). 1990. *Human Development Report 1990: Concept and Measurement of Human Development*. New York: UN.

Vetterlein, Antje. 2007. "Economic Growth, Poverty Reduction, and the Role of Social Policies: The Evolution of the World Bank's Social Development Approach." *Global Governance* 13: 513.

WHO (World Health Organization). 1995. "World Health Organization/World Bank Partnership: Recommendations for Action for Health Development." November 2. WHO/INA/95.1.

WHO. 1996. "World Health Organization/World Bank Partnership: Procedural Strategies for Implementation of Recommendations for Health Development." WHO/INA/96.1.

Williamson, John. 2009 "A Short History of the Washington Consensus." *Law & Business. Review of the Americas* 15: 7.

World Bank. 1993. *Investing in Health*. New York: Oxford University Press.

World Bank. 2007. *Healthy Development: The World Bank Strategy for Health, Nutrition, and Population Results*. Washington: World Bank

World Bank. 2013. *Inclusion Matters: The Foundation for Shared Prosperity*. Washington: World Bank.

World Bank. 2017. "World Bank Launches First-Ever Pandemic Bonds to Support $500 Million Pandemic Emergency Financing Facility." *World Bank*. June 28.

World Bank. 2018. *Poverty and Shared Prosperity 2018: Piecing Together the Poverty Puzzle*. Washington: World Bank

World Bank. 2020. "The World Bank Group Mounts the Fastest and Largest Health Crisis Response in its History to Save Lives from COVID-19." *World Bank*. December 7.

World Bank. 2022. "Universal Health Coverage: Supporting Country Progress." *World Bank*. February 9.

12

International Trade Governance

Free Trade and Intellectual Property Threaten Public Health

Lisa Forman, Katrina Perehudoff, and Chuan-Feng Wu

Introduction

Global health is deeply impacted by international trade. Building from the postwar foundations of the General Agreement on Trade and Tariffs (GATT), the establishment of the World Trade Organization (WTO) in 1995 expanded global governance over the trade of goods, services, and intellectual property rights. With WTO agreements automatically binding on all WTO member states, states have often seen their national health regulations subverted to international trade imperatives. As governments have sought to regulate commercial determinants of health and ensure access to medicines, this binding trade system has constrained government public health authority to ensure underlying determinants of health—with states and corporations enforcing free trade imperatives through the WTO's binding dispute settlement system.

Drawing from these binding trade requirements, the WTO has extended its influence over global health through a range of international agreements that significantly impact state regulatory authority in relation to health and health-related policy, including through patents, agriculture, and health and safety regulations. The impact of WTO agreements on global health has been so profound that international trade law is now considered a crucial part of global health law. This impact is exemplified by the impact of the Agreement on Trade-Related Aspects of Intellectual Property Rights (TRIPS Agreement) on access to affordable medicines. Given these health impacts of intellectual property, civil society advocates have rallied for essential drugs to be seen as central to the human right to health, and international organizations have sought to balance intellectual property protections and access to affordable medications. With trade obligations and WTO authorities reinforcing existing power imbalances and undermining human rights, the challenge posed by intellectual property rights under the TRIPS Agreement was underscored by the push from low- and middle-income countries for the WTO to develop a "TRIPS waiver" during the

COVID-19 pandemic – to limit international trade law in order to protect global health.

This chapter examines how international trade governance has impacted global health and how global health advocates have challenged international trade law. Part I chronicles the history of international trade governance from the postwar development of GATT to the establishment of the WTO and the development of the TRIPS Agreement. Describing the impact of the TRIPS Agreement on access to medicines, Part II outlines TRIPS obligations and flexibilities, examining human rights challenges and global policy responses. Part III considers how trade governance has become crucial to global health, analyzing human rights in the WTO dispute settlement mechanism, nationalist challenges to WTO governance, and the TRIPS waiver during the COVID-19 pandemic. The chapter concludes that despite limited public health concessions in trade governance, trade rules within and beyond the WTO have not significantly improved. It remains to be seen if ongoing reforms in international trade governance and global health governance can effectively respond to the deleterious impacts of the international trade regime on global health.

I. Evolving International Governance to Liberalize Trade

Trade has long been a focus of international law. Connecting nations for centuries through the exchange of goods, trade agreements spread global progress while furthering colonial empires and enabling the slave trade (Eltis 1987). Trade relations long centered around a network of bilateral treaties to lower trade barriers—yet without multilateral cooperation or institutional foundations (Irwin 1995). The contemporary global governance system for international trade was first created to bring the world together after World War II, and international trade governance has evolved from the development of an initial postwar international agreement to the establishment of a permanent international institution.

A. Postwar Development of GATT

There has long been a broad consensus among economists and policymakers that economic prosperity depends upon international trade. However, trade barriers increased in number and magnitude between World Wars I and II, as nationalist governments sought "protectionist" measures to protect domestic industries against foreign competition (Irwin 1995). This protectionism became ingrained in trade relations, limiting international trade, leading to economic depressions, and fueling conflict in the years leading up to World War II (Oxley 1990). To ensure the potential of international trade for economic prosperity, policymakers agreed after the war that economic globalization had to be regulated at the international level, with initial multilateral agreements seeking to advance free trade throughout the world.

1. The Rise of International Trade Law

The 1944 Bretton Woods Conference, introduced in Chapter 11, laid the foundation of the postwar financial system, establishing the International Monetary Fund (IMF) and the International Bank for Reconstruction and Development (World Bank). However, the negotiations to develop these institutions recognized the need for separate international institutions to ensure free and fair trade. Under the United Nations (UN) Economic and Social Council, states would work together to develop a new trade system under international law (Van den Bossche and Zdouc 2022). The United States would take the lead in establishing this new multilateral trade system, with postwar trade negotiations resulting in a multilateral agreement for the reciprocal reduction of tariffs—the taxes levied by a national government on imported or exported goods.

The resulting General Agreement on Tariffs and Trade (GATT) would come into force in 1948, giving rise to an international legal framework for international trade. The first GATT agreement would include general obligations on states to refrain from trade-impeding measures, establishing a GATT panel to adjudicate trade disputes between states.[1] Alongside this agreement, nations sought to form an International Trade Organization (ITO); yet international agreement to develop this new institution was not ratified by the U.S. Congress, and the project rapidly lost international support (Van den Bossche and Zdouc 2022). Parties continued to look to GATT regulations to prevent unnecessary trade-restrictive measures while providing security and predictability to trade under domestic laws. Despite the absence of an international institution for trade, the GATT, conceived as a multilateral agreement, established free trade as a norm of the postwar world.

The architects of this postwar international economic framework believed that trade liberalization was essential to achieve the economic goal of monetary stability and full employment. This goal was supported by the major trade powers, which strived to make tariff concessions that would remove tariffs on a non-discriminatory basis (Irwin 1995). These norms of free trade across all nations were then codified into the GATT—as a multilateral foundation to prevent

---

[1] GATT panels were created to deal with disputes between individual contracting parties. These panels were made up of three or five independent experts, whose recommendations for resolving the dispute would be submitted to the GATT Council of state representatives, which could then decide whether to adopt them.

arbitrary or discriminatory trade restrictions and unilateral trade retaliation. Under a series of substantive legal rules establishing trade liberalization, the GATT was regarded as a step in the direction of free and fair trade through the harmonization of national regulations (Bronz 1949). Through principles of non-discrimination and reciprocity, the GATT enshrined these commitments in:

- the most-favored-nation (MFN) clause, which guarantees all parties equality of opportunity to preferential trade access;
- the national treatment clause, which allows tariffs on imports no greater than taxes on similar domestic products; and
- the end of quantitative restrictions on imports or exports, which forbid parties from banning imports/exports or subjecting them to quotas (Matsushita et al. 2015).

Through the GATT, free trade norms and multilateral legal commitments among states would be set out within a body of public international law, which would be revised periodically to address ongoing challenges to international trade.

2. Challenges to Realizing Free Trade through the GATT

Notwithstanding the success of this multilateral regime in setting standards for trade policies and improving market access through the systematic reduction of tariffs, the GATT suffered from inherent weaknesses, with the lack of legal identity or institutional structure leading to ambiguity in its authority and ability to regulate trade (Skeen 2004). As the primary focus of the GATT is the reduction of tariffs, it only implicated certain trade policies, leaving states with significant discretion over other domestic regulations that impacted trade. Despite further negotiating rounds over the years, these efforts to clarify and expand GATT provisions failed to eliminate tariffs for several products (such as steel), reduce non-tariff barriers to trade (such as food safety), or address emerging trade areas (such as trade in services and intellectual property) (Barton et al. 2006). The GATT structure, designed as a treaty between states rather than an institution with legal personality, limited efforts over the decades to develop a new international free trade agenda (Matsushita et al. 2015).

Yet this free trade agenda was already seen to undermine public health. Advocates recognized rapidly that international trade rules limited national authority to regulate products in order to protect public health (Cromer 1995). For example, efforts to realize the free trade of tobacco—opening domestic markets to foreign producers—led to rapid increases in smoking (Hageman 1992). The justification of trade liberalization on economic grounds alone often neglected to consider the complex correlations between trade openness, economic growth, poverty reduction, and public health (Harrison 2007).

Although the GATT set out exceptions to free trade for public health measures "necessary to protect human . . . life or health" (GATT 1990, art. XX(b)), few national health measures were adjudged to be in conformity with this exception, highlighting the GATT panel's reluctance to make exceptions to free trade (Charnovitz 1995). The failure of these cases to protect public health lies in the GATT panel's interpretation of the ambiguous term "necessary"—and the high threshold for deeming a measure necessary to protect health. As seen in efforts by Thailand to regulate cigarettes, the GATT panel found that import restrictions on tobacco could be considered "necessary" only if there were no alternative measures that could have been taken consistent with the GATT (GATT 1990). Addressing these and other limitations during the 1986–1994 "Uruguay round" of negotiations, GATT contracting parties recognized that a well-functioning global trade system required institutional mechanisms and a binding system for dispute resolution—leading to the establishment of the WTO.

B. Establishment of the WTO

The WTO was created as a basis to administer and enforce international trade agreements, to provide a forum for trade negotiations, and to support continuing trade liberalization. Proposed jointly by the European Community, Canada, and Mexico, the Uruguay round of GATT negotiations initially developed a 1993 Draft Agreement Establishing the Multilateral Trade Organization. As negotiations progressed, some countries (such as the United States) opposed the creation of a new supranational institution out of concern that sovereignty could be derogated to international law, but the United States came to reverse its position, supporting the final 1994 Marrakesh Agreement to establish the WTO with a broad and ambitious mandate (Van den Bossche and Prévost 2021). The WTO thus became the central institution of international trade governance, with the legal personality, legal capacity, and privileges and immunities to facilitate the implementation of all WTO agreements. Like the GATT, the WTO provides rules on market access, rules on unfair trade, rules on the balance between trade liberalization and societal values, and rules regarding harmonization of national regulations.[2] As a permanent institution, however, the WTO provides a forum for negotiations, administers the system of dispute settlement, and cooperates with other international institutions (WTO 1994).

---

[2] Despite a larger and more complex set of regulations under the WTO, the tenet of non-discrimination with the Most-Favored-Nation (MFN) treatment obligation and national treatment obligation provide common features with the GATT.

1. Binding Nature of WTO Agreements

WTO member states are automatically bound by all legal commitments developed under the WTO, meaning that WTO agreements are regarded as a single undertaking—with members unable to opt in or out of individual agreements. The principal source of WTO law is the Marrakesh Agreement and its Annexes, including eighteen covered agreements (Van den Bosshe and Prévost 2021). All covered agreements are binding on all WTO member states (known as the "single undertaking" rule), binding these states to ensure conformity of their laws, regulations, and administrative procedures with all WTO obligations.[3] By extending international trade rules from the trade in goods under the GATT to trade in services and technologies, these sweeping WTO agreements created harmonized standards across countries for measures affecting a wide range of international trade, with binding enforcement mechanisms under the WTO to facilitate accountability for state implementation.

2. Accountability through a Dispute Settlement Body

A trade agreement alone is insufficient to secure state compliance. To ensure the effective implementation of WTO obligations, a single integrated dispute settlement system was established to resolve disputes between member states—and thereby clarify provisions of WTO agreements. Three institutions administer the WTO dispute settlement system:

- The Dispute Settlement Body (DSB), which establishes panels, supervises the implementation of recommendations and rulings, and authorizes sanctions for failure to comply with decisions.
- Panels, which are ad hoc bodies established by the DSB for the purpose of adjudicating a particular dispute.
- The Appellate Body, which is a standing institution appointed by the DSB to hear appeals and review panel rulings.

This interconnected dispute settlement system is widely considered to be the most enforceable system under international law, allowing WTO member states to negotiate binding trade obligations and adjudicate trade disputes—facilitating accountability under international trade governance (Matsushita et al. 2015). Beyond the dispute settlement system, an accountability system of "preemptive noncompliance" has been established through the Trade Policy Review Mechanism (TPRM), wherein national trade policies are subject to periodic monitoring and review to facilitate compliance with a wide range of WTO agreements.

---

[3] The only exceptions to this single undertaking rule are found in the Agreement on Trade in Civil Aircraft and the Agreement on Government Procurement, which are binding only on members that have expressly agreed to them.

3. Range of Agreements That Impact Global Health

WTO agreements have advanced trade liberalization in ways that have imposed sweeping effects on public health. In limiting state public health authority to regulate transnational corporate interests, trade liberalization has exacerbated inequalities within and between countries, diminished government control over health, and magnified commercial determinants of health (Wu 2010). These public health effects are driven by international trade law, with key WTO agreements, outlined in Table 12.1, posing significant impacts to underlying determinants of health (Wu and Wu 2020).

Table 12.1 WTO Agreements (Forman, Perehudoff, and Wu)

Agreement	Purpose	Public Health Impacts
General Agreement on Trade in Services (GATS)	To reduce requirements that create obstacles to trade in services	Raises challenges to national health regulations on national licensing requirements for health professionals, foreign investment in health facilities, delivery of health services from abroad (including telemedicine), and provision of health services to foreigners (medical tourism)
Agreement on the Application of Sanitary and Phytosanitary Measures (SPS Agreement)	To reduce agricultural non-tariff trade barriers and to balance trade liberalization and the government's right to ensure food safety and protect human life from plant or animal diseases	Sets out rules (such as least trade restrictive) for national measures that aim to reduce hazards to animal, plant, and human health, including food safety regulations
Agreement on Technical Barriers to Trade (TBT Agreement)	To ensure that product requirements and procedures do not create unnecessary obstacles to trade	Conforms technical standards and assessments to international standards on the safety and quality of products (covering tobacco and alcohol, toxic substances and waste, pharmaceuticals, biological agents, foodstuffs, and manufactured goods)
Agreement on Agriculture (AoA)	To establish a fair and market-oriented agricultural trading system	Impacts food security by increasing low- and middle-income country dependence on food imports and favoring agricultural producers in industrialized countries
Agreement on Trade-Related Aspects of Intellectual Property Rights (TRIPS Agreement)	To establish minimum standards for protecting and enforcing intellectual property rights	Grants monopoly control over patentable pharmaceuticals, resulting in sale restriction and price elevation that restricts the accessibility of medicines

These impacts have galvanized health activism in trade governance. The 1999 WTO Ministerial Conference in Seattle was met with violent protest, as protestors decried the harms of trade agreements for public health, labor rights, and environmental protection. The ensuing riot demonstrated the importance of framing WTO objectives to ensure people's needs. Drawing from this activism, the UN human rights system came to recognize the challenges presented by trade governance, with UN treaty bodies and special rapporteurs concluding that liberalization in trade may undermine the realization of health-related human rights (Meier 2006). This human rights framing would come to challenge the public health impacts of the international trade regime under the TRIPS Agreement.

C. Development of TRIPS Agreement

As the WTO came into existence, pharmaceutical corporations were able to ensure the legal advancement of their intellectual property interests under international trade law through the 1994 TRIPS Agreement (Sell 2003). Yet, the focus of the TRIPS Agreement on corporate interests—rather than human rights or public health—has highlighted the tension between free trade policy and public health advancement in global governance.

Case Study: Diplomacy to Shift IP Governance under the WTO

The TRIPS Agreement shifted intellectual property (IP) policy under WTO governance. Prior to the TRIPS Agreement, the UN had long governed IP rights protection through the World Intellectual Property Organization (WIPO). However, powerful states criticized WIPO for its tendency to consider the objectives of developing countries, prioritizing public health protection over IP rights and lacking binding sanctions where IP rights were violated. When efforts to reform IP enforcement under WIPO collapsed, developed countries (particularly the United States) looked to shift forums for IP policy. As the WTO was coming into being, these states turned to link IP enforcement to trade liberalization, creating the notion that IP was "trade related." The resulting diplomacy on "trade related aspects" of IP was introduced as part of the Uruguay round of GATT negotiations, giving rise to the TRIPS Agreement. The adoption of the TRIPS Agreement alongside the establishment of the WTO would enrich transnational pharmaceutical corporations with extensive patents on medicines. These patents give pharmaceutical corporations an effective marketing monopoly over the manufacture and sale of medicines, supporting corporate profits while driving up prices and limiting necessary access. Developing countries showed great concern for the possibility that TRIPS may be abused, and that pharmaceutical corporations would exploit these new patent protections to charge prices far above research and development costs, impeding access to essential medicines. Yet, under pressure from developed countries, which offered a compromise on agricultural tariff concessions, states broadly supported the adoption of the TRIPS Agreement, enlisting the governance authority of the WTO in the harmonization of IP law across nations.

The TRIPS Agreement was widely seen as a diplomatic success for developed countries, as a monumental international agreement rapidly took shape to fundamentally alter international trade governance under the WTO—strengthening global IP enforcement, advantaging multinational pharmaceutical corporations, and threatening global health. Although WIPO remains crucial to IP rights protection, the WTO enforcement and dispute settlement mechanisms provided by the TRIPS Agreement have made the WTO the institutional leader in the governance and interpretation of IP standards (Gin 2004). This forum shifting under international trade law has proven devastating to public health.

II. TRIPS Agreement Reshapes Access to Medicines

The TRIPS Agreement has impacted the pricing, sale, movement, and production of medicines globally. This unprecedented influence of international trade law on access to medicines has presented sweeping impacts for global health, limiting efforts to respond to communicable and non-communicable diseases, ensure the highest attainable standard of mental health, and realize universal health coverage. With TRIPS obligations regulating IP protections under international trade governance, human rights advocates have sought to clarify flexibilities under the TRIPS Agreement to allow national governments to meet public health imperatives.

A. TRIPS Obligations

Obligations under the TRIPS Agreement have introduced a global standard for patenting new inventions and other forms of IP protection that WTO member states must implement in domestic law, and this global standard would have a significant impact on access to medicines. With IP protections delaying the production of lower-priced generics (an identical non-patented drug with the same active ingredient as its patent-protected counterpart), the TRIPS Agreement would lead to an accompanying rise in drug prices (Correa 2005). This global IP standard has limited the ability of governments to monitor and protect public health by restricting their capacity to ensure access to affordable medications. Despite flexibilities under the TRIPS Agreement to limit patent protections when necessary to protect public health, these flexibilities have proven challenging for states to exercise in practice.

1. A Global Standard

The TRIPS Agreement has ushered in a new age of uniform IP protection standards throughout the world, with patents subject to extensive domestic and international enforcement, including through the WTO's formal dispute settlement mechanisms. Under the TRIPS Agreement, WTO members must codify patent protections in national law—with a (minimum) twenty-year patent term available for products and processes in all fields of technology. Through these requirements, the TRIPS Agreement largely harmonized patent laws globally (Kapczynski 2009).

A patent is a negative right granted to the inventor, allowing it to exclude any other entity from commercializing an innovation for a period of time. Such patents give exclusive rights to patent holders, regardless of where the innovation originated, to prevent nonconsensual use. These IP protections are thought to be necessary to incentivize scientific innovation through the award of a patent to the inventor. While the need for patents to spur innovation is contested, this patent incentive is claimed to be crucial for the creation of new medical innovations (Outterson 2005).[4]

However, the establishment of stringent international standards relating to patents under the TRIPS Agreement has posed a direct conflict with efforts to ensure broad access to essential and other medicines. The extension of IP rights under the WTO has proven to delay the development of cheaper generic drugs, cause rises in drug prices, and limit the ability of developing countries to ensure access to affordable medications (Forman 2007). To ensure that such TRIPS obligations would not threaten health needs, the TRIPS Agreement included flexibilities (such as compulsory licenses, parallel importation, and government use) when necessary to protect public health.

---

[4] There are a range of product areas where the incentive of future patent protection has been insufficient to spur companies to invest in biomedical research and development, including areas related to vaccines for pandemic pathogens, conditions primarily affecting small populations (e.g., rare diseases), and populations living in poverty (e.g., neglected tropical diseases) (Swaminathan et al. 2022).

2. TRIPS Flexibilities

The TRIPS Agreement introduced several "flexibilities" to the exclusive rights of patent holders, with these flexibilities offering exceptions to patenting and limitations on exclusivity in the interests of public health and social welfare. Such flexibilities offer WTO member states the room to maneuver in implementing their obligations under the TRIPS Agreement, providing states with the ability to issue a compulsory license and public non-commercial use (also called "government use"), which allows national governments to authorize the production and/ or the importation of the raw materials necessary to make a medicine in question and/or the finished products (Forman 2007). In this way, compulsory licenses can be useful tools for governments to address the public health challenges of high medicines prices and/or low domestic supply of patented medicines while still accounting for the patent holders' interests—by paying them royalties.[5] With this need for compulsory licensing first exposed in the face of global inequities in HIV treatment, WTO member states reaffirmed the flexibility of states to ensure compulsory licensing through the 2001 Doha Declaration (Sekalala 2017).

Case Study: Doha Declaration on TRIPS and Public Health

The Doha Declaration on TRIPS and Public Health (Doha Declaration) was adopted by states at the WTO 2001 ministerial meeting to reiterate and clarify that states have the authority to utilize flexibilities under the TRIPS Agreement in service of public health. Through this statement by WTO Member States, the Doha Declaration put to rest uncertainties that certain governments had about when it is legally justifiable to use flexibilities to the TRIPS Agreement. Global inequities in access to patented HIV/AIDS medicines had raised an imperative to clarify the scope and application of TRIPS flexibilities, particularly where states lacked local capacity to manufacture their own medicines under a compulsory license. This Declaration emerged from an initiative of the African Group (African Members of WTO) as a basis to reiterate that the TRIPS Agreement should not impair WTO members from taking measures to protect public health, including through the TRIPS flexibilities. However, states were largely polarized in WTO debates on this declaration, with a large coalition of developing countries seeking guarantees that they would not be penalized for taking steps domestically to address unfolding health crises and

---

[5] Granting a compulsory license does not revoke patent rights on a product. The patent holder retains the right to exploit their own patent as they see fit; however, a compulsory license allows another entity or entities, selected by government authorities, to make or sell the patented technology under specific conditions.

developed countries seeking to promote a narrower understanding of TRIPS flexibilities. WTO negotiators finally reached an agreement between these opposing groups, declaring:

> We agree that the TRIPS Agreement does not and should not prevent Members from taking measures to protect public health. Accordingly, while reiterating our commitment to the TRIPS Agreement, we affirm that the Agreement can and should be interpreted and implemented in a manner supportive of WTO Members' right to protect public health and, in particular, to promote access to medicines for all.

The Doha Declaration thus affirmed that each WTO member state has the sovereign authority to grant compulsory licenses—and to determine the grounds on which they are granted, including the determination of what constitutes a national emergency or other situation of extreme urgency. This state flexibility to address public health emergencies would be explicitly extended beyond HIV, encompassing any public health crisis, "including those relating to HIV/AIDS, tuberculosis, malaria and other epidemics" which may represent a national emergency or other situation of extreme urgency.

Yet, even as the Doha Declaration clarified TRIPS flexibilities to protect public health, states have continued to face limitations regarding when and how a compulsory license may be invoked under national law. The TRIPS Agreement explains the conditions under which compulsory licenses may be invoked—in a national emergency or "other circumstance of extreme urgency" and for public non-commercial use (Perehudoff, 't Hoen, and Boulet 2021). Compulsory licenses can also be used by governments outside of national emergencies or cases of extreme urgency when all other efforts to negotiate reasonable commercial terms and conditions were unsuccessful "within a reasonable amount of time." This provision provides that compulsory licenses could legally be used outside of public health emergencies, such as in cases of unaffordable cancer medicines or unavailable antibiotics. However, this vague language in the TRIPS Agreement and Doha Declaration has failed to clearly define criteria for what are "reasonable" terms and conditions, and this vagueness has enabled states to contest the use of such mechanisms and constrained the application of compulsory licensing (Forman 2008).

Compounding the application of these flexibilities in practice, compulsory licensing has proven challenging in countries that lack the manufacturing capacity to develop their own medicines. The TRIPS Agreement permitted government authorities to grant compulsory licenses only for the supply of their domestic market. This provision made compulsory licenses a workable solution for countries with their own capacity to produce medicines, but states without sufficient manufacturing capacity were left without viable legal tools to respond to a health emergency ('t Hoen 2002). Where the Doha Ministerial Meeting shone a spotlight on the plight of WTO members lacking sufficient pharmaceutical manufacturing capacity, and therefore unable to make effective use of compulsory licenses amid the HIV/AIDS pandemic, the Doha Declaration instructed the TRIPS Council "to find an expeditious solution to this problem" (WTO 2001, para. 6).[6] The TRIPS Council would thereafter establish rules for using compulsory licenses for export purposes, allowing for the use of a compulsory license to support other countries with insufficient production capacity (Garrison 2020a). Yet, this clarification of TRIPS flexibilities has proven cumbersome to implement in practice, leaving countries unable to ensure compulsory licenses when necessary, limiting the realization of health and human rights.

B. Human Rights Challenges

The continuing challenges to pharmaceutical access under the TRIPS Agreement illustrate how the imperatives of international trade law have conflicted with state obligations under international human rights law. The human right to health—codified in the 1966 International Covenant on Economic, Social and Cultural Rights (ICESCR)—has paved the way for the development of obligations to ensure essential medicines (Forman 2007). In applying the right to health to ensure the provision of essential medicines, as introduced in Chapter 4, the UN Committee on Economic, Social and Cultural Rights (CESCR) in 2000 interpreted the right to health in General Comment 14. Against the backdrop of the HIV/AIDS pandemic, the CESCR found core human rights were implicated in access to medicines, holding that states bear an obligation to provide essential medicines to all, especially to people living in poverty (CESCR 2000).

The TRIPS Agreement has significantly increased the financial burden on states and individuals seeking access to medicines, limiting states from progressively realizing the right to health by restricting access to affordable medicines. Given these human rights limitations of the TRIPS Agreement, human rights activists have sought to pressure domestic governments, international donors, pharmaceutical companies, and the WTO itself to take steps to promote access to specific medicines (Moon and Balasubramaniam 2018).

Yet despite these conflicts between human rights obligations and international trade obligations, the UN human rights system lacks accountability

---

[6] The TRIPS Council is the body within the WTO that administers and monitors the implementation of the TRIPS Agreement.

mechanisms like the binding dispute settlement body under the WTO. While important steps have been made using human rights law and norms to bring previously unavailable and unaffordable medicines to people who need them, antiretroviral drugs for HIV and other essential medicines have remained out of reach for many in the world who lack access to justice.[7] Examining this injustice through global human rights governance, human rights treaty bodies have continued to monitor access to medicines and press governments to ensure affordability as a human rights obligation. In its General Comment 17 on authors' and inventors' rights, the CESCR in 2006 underscored that high medicine prices should not impair access for large segments of the population (CESCR 2006). The CESCR explained that while a patent has a social function, the private interest of the inventor does not override the public interest to access the invention. Instead, states must balance authors' rights and other rights—including the right to health—in regulating corporate activities (CESCR 2006). Revisiting this balance in General Comment 25 on the right to science, the CESCR in 2020 found that states must progressively realize all aspects of the right to science, regulating affordable access to medicines, so that people can access the applications of science "that are critical to the enjoyment of the right to health" (CESCR 2020, para 52). These human rights obligations have provided a normative foundation to seek access to medicines under the TRIPS Agreement.

C. Seeking Access to Medicines under the TRIPS Agreement

Given the tensions between international trade law and human rights law in addressing issues of access to medicines, the UN Secretary General convened a UN High-Level Panel on Access to Medicines to examine how greater coherence and equity could be brought to pharmaceutical innovation and access to medicines. The UN High-Level Panel's 2016 report proposed incremental steps aimed at preventing trade and intellectual property incentives from minimizing public health and human rights concerns (UN High-Level Panel on Access to Medicines 2016). Although these incremental steps included monitoring and enforcement strategies, one major challenge remained: a lack of a clear legal mandate and global enforcement mechanisms to ensure accountability for the actions of pharmaceutical companies, forcing advocates to rely on voluntary licensing and public-private partnerships to achieve access to medicines under the TRIPS Agreement.

---

[7] In the absence of a global adjudication mechanism, human rights advocates have looked to national litigation to access publicly financed medicines from their respective governments, revealing the potential power of human rights arguments before the courts (Forman 2008).

1. Voluntary Licensing
Patent holders (often pharmaceutical companies) play an important role in determining when, where, in what quantity, and at what price their patented technologies become available to the public. Given this authority, patent holders can support greater access to medicines simply by voluntarily licensing the IP to another manufacturer that can market generic versions of the patented medicine, often increasing supply to lower prices in defined territories (Garrison 2020b). These "voluntary licenses" have both been applauded for helping to increase access to essential medicines and criticized for failing to include those in many countries who need treatment.

Voluntary licensing, providing pharmaceutical access without violating IP protections, is an imperfect, non-legal answer to the challenge of access to medicines. Such agreements for a voluntary license are established on a case-by-case basis and tend to be highly specific to a particular medicine, to a selected generic manufacturer, and to a specific territory (Baker 2018). In relying on a private corporation's charitable decision to license patented medicines to other producers or sellers, this corporate discretion allows the private business sector to have complete control over significant public policy decisions that impact public health. Allowing voluntary licensing to be the primary strategy for improving access to medicines thus undermines government authority to regulate the private business sector and secure access to medicines to realize the right to health. Given the challenges of negotiating and implementing each voluntary license for each health threat, advocates have looked for a "more structured and predictable approach towards voluntary licensing and move away from the hand-to-hand combat that had become the mainstay of increasing access to medicines" ('t Hoen 2016, 74).

2. UNITAID and the Medicines Patent Pool
One structured approach to address IP barriers through voluntary licensing of patented medicines has been seen in the creation of a "patent pool" for medicines. A patent pool seeks to provide management of IP collectively through a public-private partnership—between a public health institution and private pharmaceutical companies (Burrone 2018). Supporting access to health products, a patent pool aims to increase the availability of a particular technology by negotiating licenses with multiple patent holders, and then licensing select patents to generic manufacturers to develop and market the product in low-income countries in exchange for royalty payments. Such patent pools have been institutionalized in global health through the 2006 establishment of UNITAID. As a new global health financing mechanism and public-private partnership, as discussed in greater detail in Chapter 14, UNITAID seeks to expand global access to patented health products, particularly in low- and middle-income countries, by providing

"sustainable, predictable, and additional funding" for drugs and diagnostics. Governed by a partnership of financing states, civil society, and WHO, UNITAID has been given a clear mandate address intellectual property licensing in the context of access to medicines, making it a fertile space for cultivating a medicines patent pool (Cox 2012).

UNITAID thus established the Medicines Patent Pool in 2010, allowing any qualified generic producer to use its pooled IP to make generic versions of needed medicines. Providing a cooperative mechanism to make essential medicines available at affordable prices in low-income countries, the Medicine Patent Pool has facilitated access to treatments for HIV/AIDS and Hepatitis C. Working within the TRIPS framework, the Medicines Patent Pool facilitates wider geographic access to patented medicines for the world most vulnerable populations while still taking account of the pharmaceutical industry's financial interests. Despite this promise, the Medicines Patent Pool remains dependent on the voluntary cooperation of patent-holding pharmaceutical companies and generic manufacturers, threatening global health where the law does not structure trade agreements and WTO governance faces new challenges.

III. Challenges to WTO Governance

WTO governance is facing new forces that have led to groundbreaking shifts in international trade law, upending trade agreements and WTO supremacy. These challenges to trade regulations have advanced health and human rights in tobacco control, presented nationalist challenges to free trade, and pressed for a waiver of the TRIPS Agreement in responding to the COVID-19 pandemic. With WHO member states now negotiating a pandemic treaty, this new international health instrument may shift the balance that long left public health considerations subservient to international trade imperatives.

A. WTO Recognizes Health and Human Rights

Through the diplomacy of low- and middle-income countries and the advocacy of human rights actors globally, the WTO has increasingly come to recognize health and human rights consideration in the implementation of its trade agreements. Tobacco control has emerged alongside access to medicines as a high-level issue at the WTO, where greater appreciation of global health has strengthened the role of human rights in regulating commercial determinants of health (Moon and Balasubramaniam 2018). This acknowledgment of public health has become apparent in WTO decision-making on tobacco plain packaging—with the dispute settlement mechanism recognizing national public health needs over corporate IP concerns (Wu and Wu 2020).

Case Study: WTO Dispute Settlement/Tobacco Plain Packaging

Seeking to implement obligations under the Framework Convention on Tobacco Control, as introduced in Chapter 7, Australia enacted the 2011 Tobacco Plain Packaging Act (TPPA), whereby tobacco corporations are required to standardize the retail packaging and appearance of tobacco products. The TPPA sought to prohibit all identifying advertisements on tobacco packaging, leaving, as seen in Figure 12.1, only the brand name, business/company name, or variant name in a standardized form. Since packaging constitutes an essential instrument for tobacco advertising, these efforts to standardize the packaging and eliminate corporate logos were seen to discourage smoking and increase the effectiveness of graphic health warnings. Tobacco corporations challenged the TPPA as a violation of their IP—infringing trademark protections of tobacco packaging.[a]

Figure 12.1 Plain Package of Tobacco (WHO)

[a] Protected under the TRIPS Agreement, trademarks refer to "any sign, or any combination of signs, capable of distinguishing the goods or services of one undertaking from those of other undertakings."

The fight against Australia's "plain packaging" scheme intensified in the international trade sphere, with Honduras and the Dominican Republic challenging Australia's public health regulation under the TRIPS Agreement and the TBT. However, the WTO Panel and Appellate Body both held that there was no violation of any WTO agreements. In reaching this conclusion under the TBT, the Panel found that the plain packaging requirements, as technical regulations, use the "least trade restrictive" means to fulfill a legitimate objective – to improve public health by reducing the use of, and exposure to, tobacco products. While the Panel and the Appellate Body agreed that plain packaging measures are inconsistent with TRIPS obligations, they found that encumbering the use of trademarks in this case was acceptable, as Australia was addressing a grave health threat involving a high level of preventable morbidity and mortality.

This WTO decision provides evidence of a shift in WTO governance, highlighting that, if public health measures are framed in a proper regulatory context and policy objectives are clear and legitimate, national public health authorities could be afforded greater flexibility to regulate commercial determinants of health.

B. Nationalist Challenges to WTO Governance

As the WTO has come to recognize national efforts to protect health and human rights, it has faced challenges to international trade governance from rising nationalism, growing isolationism, and increasing trade restrictions, with many states looking outside the WTO in developing "TRIPS-plus" measures in bilateral trade agreements. Even as low- and middle-income states have been reluctant to exercise TRIPS flexibilities, the TRIPS Agreement has increasingly been supplanted by even stricter IP rights in regional and bilateral free trade agreements (FTAs) that significantly restrict the use of TRIPS flexibilities. These TRIPS-plus rules, advanced by high-income countries that are home to transnational pharmaceutical corporations, seek to extend monopoly pricing over longer periods and limit market entry for generics, including by restricting the grounds on which compulsory license can be issued (Forman 2012).[8] Beyond the governance of the WTO, these new FTAs have also included provisions targeting national pharmaceutical coverage programs and regulation of pharmaceutical marketing—as seen in U.S. trade agreements with Australia and Korea, the Trans

---

[8] The United States has by far been the primary initiator of such agreements, signing bilateral trade agreements and negotiating regional trade agreements that enforce stricter IP protections than those found under the TRIPS Agreement (Gleeson et al. 2019).

Pacific Partnership Agreement (TPP), and the United States-Mexico-Canada Agreement (USMCA). These provisions provide an increasing number of potential intersections between trade rules and pharmaceutical policy—"going beyond the well-trod territory of IP and access to medicines with a range of implications for UHC [universal health coverage]" (Gleeson et al. 2019, 2).

Compounding this shift toward agreements outside the WTO, nationalist challenges to WTO authority and protectionist decisions from populist governments have intensified in recent years. With national governments seeking to employ protectionist measures that restrict free trade to protect domestic industries, states have increasingly sought to step back from international trade governance—and to neglect WTO Panel decisions. Taken to the extreme, the Trump administration in the United States sought to constrain the proper functioning of the WTO appeals body—an approach largely continued under the Biden administration (McBride and Siripurapu 2022). These threats to the foundations of WTO governance arrived just as the COVID-19 pandemic upended the global trade system, with nationalist governments resorting to protectionist measures during the pandemic and with pharmaceutical corporations looking to the TRIPS Agreement to restrict access to necessary medical countermeasures and essential vaccines.

C. TRIPS Waiver in the COVID-19 Pandemic

Repeating the mistakes of the HIV/AIDS response, the TRIPS Agreement would again prove unable to ensure access to essential pharmaceutical advancements in the face of a public health emergency. Pharmaceutical corporations would quickly develop innovative new technologies in the face of a rapidly escalating COVID-19 threat, but these transnational corporations retained the right to decide when, where, and at what price these medical needs were marketed (Gostin, Abdool Karim, and Meier 2020). COVID-19 vaccines were thus stockpiled by some high-income countries, leading to tremendous profits for vaccine developers while many low- and middle-income countries were denied access entirely. Such inequitable distributions of these essential COVID-19 therapies, diagnostics, and vaccines prompted India and South Africa in October 2020 to propose a temporary waiver from the implementation, application, and enforcement of key sections of the TRIPS Agreement. This "TRIPS waiver" proposal noted the institutional and legal difficulties many countries, especially low-income countries, face when seeking to exercise TRIPS flexibilities. It proposed that the TRIPS Council recommend to the WTO General Council a waiver of TRIPS provisions in relation to the prevention, containment or treatment of COVID-19 "until widespread vaccination is in place globally, and the majority of the world's population has developed immunity" (Council for Trade-Related

Aspects of Intellectual Property Rights 2022, para 13). While the TRIPS waiver proposal received broad support from over one hundred low- and middle-income countries, it was blocked from passage at the WTO by the United States and European Union, alongside other high-income countries, leading to widespread civil society protests throughout the world, as seen in Figure 12.2, in support of "vaccine equity" (Green 2021).

Figure 12.2 Vaccine Equity Protestors (Alyson Bancroft)

This movement for a TRIPS waiver has galvanized international debate about whether IP rights should be loosened or waived; whether this would negatively impact the innovation of new medicines; and whether these vaccine disparities are even about IP rights at all, as opposed to inadequate health systems and insufficient manufacturing capacity in low- and middle-income countries (Green 2021).

The resurfacing of these debates during the COVID-19 pandemic suggests that lessons learned from past pandemics—and policy reforms in facing past threats—count for little when it comes to global cooperation to face new and emerging crises. Reflecting continuing coloniality in international trade law, past lessons do not appear to factor into current efforts to avert global inequity in allocating essential medicines and vaccines during a major global health crisis, threatening health and human rights (Sekalala et al. 2021). In early May 2022, a year and a half after the original TRIPS waiver was tabled, a compromise agreement was suggested. The proposed compromise is significantly narrower in scope, applying only to COVID-19 vaccines and only for three to five years, and as a result, has received criticism from industry and civil society alike for not going far enough in protecting private interests or ensuring access to medicines ('t Hoen 2022). In June 2022, this compromise was adopted at a WTO ministerial conference; however, there is no indication at this stage that WTO members will follow through on their commitment to expand the waiver to also cover COVID-19 diagnostics and therapeutics. As the debate about the potential TRIPS waiver carries on in the WTO, global leaders are looking beyond WTO governance to consider how to ensure equitable access to medicines in future public health emergencies under a potential pandemic treaty.

D. The Potential Impact of a Prospective Pandemic Treaty

The inadequacies of international trade law to prevent or respond to global health inequities has strengthened calls for a new global health law instrument, looking to global health governance to clarify international trade law. Drawing from the recommendation of the Independent Panel for Pandemic Preparedness and Response (IPPPR) to adopt a "Pandemic Framework Convention" (IPPPR 2021), a November 2021 special session of the World Health Assembly established an Intergovernmental Negotiating Body (INB) to draft and negotiate a new WHO convention, agreement or other international instrument on pandemic preparedness and response. To the extent that this so-called pandemic treaty is able to effectively address the impact of IP on access to medicines, this global health law reform may have significant implications for international trade law and the TRIPS Agreement.

To frame the substantive elements of the pandemic treaty through global health diplomacy, as first introduced in Chapter 5, the INB is considering a range of issues to ensure access to essential medicines, including adequate investments to build vaccine and therapeutics development and manufacturing capacity and strengthening health systems capacity and universal health coverage (WHO 2022). The draft text makes multiple references to the imperative to address the impact of trade-related intellectual property rights on access to vaccines, with the preamble recognizing the tensions between IP rights and equitable access to essential pandemic treatments. Drawing from this preambular text, the draft text notes deep concern for "the gross inequities that prevailed in timely access to medical and other COVID-19 pandemic response products, notably vaccines, oxygen supplies, personal protective equipment, diagnostics and therapeutics" (WHO 2022, para 11). The pandemic treaty thus holds promise in emphasizing the importance of access to medicines and of mitigating the impact of IP protections—reaffirming the flexibilities and safeguards of the TRIPS Agreement and thereby reframing the future relationship between global health law and international trade law (Perehudoff et al. 2022).

Conclusion

International trade has a sweeping influence on public health in a globalizing world – from access to medicines, to the global movement of health-related goods and services, to a broad range of health issues at the heart of global health. Health and human rights actors over time have sought to challenge the restrictive impacts of international trade laws, especially on access to essential medicines as well as on other commercial determinants of health such as the marketing of tobacco products. The successful challenge of WTO rules in the context of tobacco has shown that public health measures can be granted greater authority to regulate unhealthy products, but continuing efforts are needed to ensure access to medicines.

The COVID-19 pandemic is continuing to reshape international trade governance. While some concessions in the formulation and interpretation of IP rights have been won, health and human rights campaigns have not significantly influenced trade rules within the WTO more broadly nor constrained the expansion of even stronger trade rules outside the multilateral trade regime. Inequitable distribution of vaccines in the COVID-19 pandemic response has underscored the complexities of these challenges under the TRIPS Agreement and the need for more effective, enduring, and equitable global health law solutions. These health challenges to international trade law are taking place amid sweeping changes to international trade governance, exemplified in the debate over the TRIPS waiver and the ongoing negotiations to establish a new pandemic treaty. Global health law reforms in the coming years will have direct impacts on international trade law.

Whatever these reforms hold for the international trade regime, international trade will continue to impact global health, raising an imperative to find new ways to align international trade law and global health law. International trade governance was born of the idea that an interconnected world, bound together by trade, can ensure mutual prosperity for all, but powerful forces have tailored international trade law to the detriment of public health. While international trade could be a force for good, trade cannot come at the expense of health. Ongoing reforms within the WTO must effectively respond to the deleterious impacts of the international trade regime on global health. The imperative is clear: there is a deep need for a better balance between global health governance and international trade governance so that free trade does not come at the expense of health and human rights. The question remains whether global health law and human rights law can offer a more appropriate balance in international trade law.

Questions for Consideration

1. What prompted the development of the international trade governance regime after World War II? How did the GATT extend free trade throughout the world? Why did this international free trade regime undermine national public health laws?
2. How did the establishment of the WTO seek to rectify limitations of the GATT agreement? Why are WTO agreements thought to be the strongest and most accountable form of international law? How did the public health impacts of WTO agreements catalyze public health and human rights activism in opposition to international trade governance?
3. What diplomatic efforts by transnational pharmaceutical corporations gave rise to the TRIPS Agreement? How did forum shifting under the TRIPS Agreement alter the balance between intellectual property protections and public health needs?
4. How have trade-related intellectual property rights under the TRIPS Agreement impacted access to medicines?
5. How did states seek to clarify the use of TRIPS flexibilities under the Doha Declaration to ensure access to medicines? Why have TRIPS flexibilities proven ineffective in practice in securing compulsory licensing to protect public health?

6. Why are intellectual property rights seen to be in conflict with health-related human rights? How have human rights institutions and activists sought to challenge the TRIPS Agreement to realize the right to health?
7. Why have voluntary licenses proven ineffective in providing access to medicines? How do public-private partnerships like UNITAID seek to develop "patent pools" without violating the TRIPS Agreement?
8. How did the WTO Panel decision on Australia's Tobacco Plain Packaging Act shift the balance between international trade imperatives and national public health protections? Could this WTO approach to health and human rights provide a model for addressing other commercial determinants of health?
9. Why have advocates been unable to secure a TRIPS waiver within the WTO amid the COVID-19 pandemic? How can the WHO pandemic treaty reframe the balance between international trade and global health?

Acknowledgments

The authors greatly appreciate the substantive contributions of Roojin Habibi and the editorial support of Rishabh Sud.

References

Barton, John H., Judith L. Goldstein, Timothy E. Josling, and Richard H. Steinberg. 2006. *The Evolution of the Trade Regime: Politics, Law, and Economics of the GATT and the WTO*. Princeton: Princeton University Press.

Baker, Brook K. 2018. "A Sliver of Hope: Analyzing Voluntary Licenses to Accelerate Affordable Access to Medicines." *Northeastern University.Law Review* 10(2): 226–315.

Bronz, George. 1949. "The International Trade Organization Charter." *Harvard Law Review* 62: 1089–1125.

Burrone, Esteban. 2018. "Patent Pooling in Public Health." In *The Cambridge Handbook on Public-Private Partnerships, Intellectual Property Governance, and Sustainable Development*. Cambridge: Cambridge University Press.

CESCR (Committee on Economic, Social, and Cultural Rights). 2000. "General Comment 14: The Right to the Highest Attainable Standard of Health (Art. 12)." August 11. E/C.12/2000/4.

CESCR. 2006. "General Comment No. 17: The Right of Everyone to Benefit from the Protection of the Moral and Material Interests Resulting from any Scientific, Literary or Artistic Production of Which He or She is the Author (Art. 15, Para. 1 (c) of the Covenant)." January 12. E/C.12/GC/17.

CESCR. 2020. "General Comment No. 25 (2020) on Science and Economic, Social and Cultural Rights (Art. 15 (1) (b), (2), (3) and (4) of the International Covenant on Economic, Social and Cultural Rights)." April 30. E/C.12/GC/25.

Charnovitz, Steve. 1995. "The Environment vs. Trade Rules: Defogging the Debate." *Environmental Law* 23: 475.

Council for Trade-Related Aspects of Intellectual Property Rights. 2022. "Minutes of Meeting." *World Trade Organization*. May 6. IP/C/M/104/Add.1.

Correa, Carlos M. 2005. "TRIPS Agreement and Access to Drugs in Developing Countries." *Sur. Revista Internacional de Direitos Humanos* 2: 26–39.

Cox, Krista L. 2012. "The Medicines Patent Pool: Promoting Access and Innovation for Life-Saving Medicines through Voluntary Licenses." *Hastings Science and Technology Law Journal* 4: 291–323.

Cromer, Julie. 1995. "Sanitary and Phytosanitary Measures: What They Could Mean for Health and Safety Regulations Under GATT." *Harvard International Law Journal* 36: 557–569.

Eltis, David. 1987. *Economic Growth and the Ending of the Transatlantic Slave Trade*. New York: Oxford University Press.

Forman, Lisa. 2007. "Trade Rules, Intellectual Property and the Right to Health." *Ethics and International Affairs* 21(3): 337–357.

Forman, Lisa. 2008. "'Rights' and Wrongs: What Utility for the Right to Health in Reforming Trade Rules on Medicines?" *Health and Human Rights: An International Journal* 10(2): 37–52.

Forman, Lisa. 2012. "From TRIPS-Plus to Rights-Plus: Exploring Right to Health Impact Assessment of Trade-Related Intellectual Property Rights through the Thai Experience." *Asian Journal of WTO and International Health Law and Policy* 7: 347–375.

Garrison, Christopher. 2020a. "Never Say Never—Why the High Income Countries That Opted-Out from the Art. 31bis WTO TRIPS System Must Urgently Reconsider Their Decision in the Face of the Covid-19 Pandemic." *Medicines Law and Policy* 16: 2020.

Garrison, Christopher. 2020b. "What Is the "Know-How Gap" Problem and How Might It Impact Scaling Up Production of Covid-19 Related Diagnostics, Therapies and Vaccines?" *Medicines Law and Policy* 16: 2020.

GATT (General Agreement on Tariffs and Trade). 1990. "Thailand – Restrictions on Importation of and Internal Taxes on Cigarettes." November 7. DS10/R.

Gin, Elaine. 2004. "International Copyright Law: Beyond the WIPO & (and) TRIPS Debate." *Journal of the Patent and Trademark Office Society* 86(10): 763–791.

Gleeson, Deborah, Joel Lexchin, Ronald Labonté, Belinda Townsend, Marc-André Gagnon, Jillian Kohler, Lisa Forman, and Kenneth C. Shadlen. 2019. "Analyzing the Impact of Trade and Investment Agreements on Pharmaceutical Policy: Provisions, Pathways and Potential Impacts." *Globalization and Health* 15(1): 1–17.

Gostin, Lawrence O., Safura Abdool Karim, and Benjamin Mason Meier. 2020. "Facilitating Access to a COVID-19 Vaccine through Global Health Law." *The Journal of Law, Medicine & Ethics* 48(3): 622–626.

Green, Andrew. 2021. "Where Are We on COVID-19 after a Year of TRIPS Waiver Negotiations?" *Devex*. October 7.

Hagerman, Andrea J. 1992. "U.S. Tobacco Exports: The Dichotomy between Trade and Health Policies." *Minnesota Journal of Global Trade* 1: 175–200.

Harrison, James. 2007. *The Human Rights Impact of the World Trade Organisation*. London: Bloomsbury Publishing.

IPPPR (Independent Panel for Pandemic Preparedness and Response). 2021. "COVID-19: Make It the Last Pandemic." *IPPPR*. May 2.

Irwin, Douglas A. 1995. "The GATT in Historical Perspective." *The American Economic Review* 85(2): 323–328.

Kapczynski, Amy. 2009. "Harmonization and its discontents: A Case Study of TRIPS Implementation in India's Pharmaceutical Sector." *California Law Review* 97(6): 1571–1649.

Matsushita, Mitsuo, Thomas J. Schoenbaum, Petros C. Mavroidis, and Michael Hahn. 2015. *The World Trade Organization: Law, Practice, and Policy*. New York: Oxford University Press.

McBride, James and Anshu Siripurapu. 2022. "What's Next for the WTO?" *Council on Foreign Relations*. June 10.

Meier, Benjamin Mason. 2006. "Employing Health Rights for Global Justice: The Promise of Public Health in Response to the Insalubrious Ramifications of Globalization." *Cornell International Law Journal* 39: 711.

Moon, Suerie and Thirukumaran Balasubramaniam. 2018. "Carving Out the Right to Health to Promote Access to Medicines and Tobacco Control in Trade Arena." In *Human Rights in Global Health: Rights-Based Governance for a Globalizing World*, edited by Benjamin Mason Meier and Lawrence O. Gostin, 375. New York: Oxford University Press.

Outterson, Kevin. 2005. "Pharmaceutical Arbitrage: Balancing Access and Innovation in International Prescription Drug Markets." *Yale Journal of Health Policy, Law, and Ethics* 5(1): 193–291.

Oxley, Alan. 1990. *The Challenge of Free Trade*. New York: Harvester Wheatsheaf.

Perehudoff, Katrina, Ellen 't Hoen, and Pascale Boulet. 2021. "Overriding Drug and Medical Technology Patents for Pandemic Recovery: A Legitimate Move for High-Income Countries, Too." *BMJ Global Health* 6(4): e005518.

Perehudoff, Katrina, Ellen 't Hoen, Kaitlin Mara, Thirukumaran Balasubramaniam, Frederick Abbott, Brook Baker, Pascale Boulet et al. 2022. "A Pandemic Treaty for Equitable Global Access to Medical Countermeasures: Seven Recommendations for Sharing Intellectual Property, Know-How and Technology." *BMJ Global Health* 7(7): e009709.

Sekalala, Sharifah. 2017. *Soft Law & Global Health Problems: Lessons from Responses to HIV/AIDS, Malaria and Tuberculosis*. Cambridge: Cambridge University Press.

Sekalala, Sharifah, Lisa Forman, Timothy Hodgson, Moses Mulumba, Hadijah Namyalo-Ganafa, and Benjamin Mason Meier. 2021. "Decolonising Human Rights: How Intellectual Property Laws Result in Unequal Access to the COVID-19 Vaccine." *BMJ Global Health* 6(7): e006169.

Sell, Susan K. 2003. *Private Power, Public Law: The Globalization of Intellectual Property Rights*. Vol. 88. Cambridge: Cambridge University Press.

Skeen, Richard. 2004. "Will the WTO Turn Green—The Implications of Injecting Environmental Issues into the Multilateral Trading System." *Georgetown International Environmental Law Review* 17: 161.

Swaminathan, Soumya, Bernard Pécoul, Hisham Abdullah, Christos Christou, Glenda Gray, Carel Jsselmuiden, Marie Paule Kieny et al. 2022. "Reboot Biomedical R&D in the Global Public Interest." *Nature* 602(7896): 207–210.

't Hoen, Ellen. 2002. "TRIPS, Pharmaceutical Patents, and Access to Essential Medicines: A Long Way From Seattle to Doha." *Chicago Journal of International Law* 3: 27–45.

't Hoen, Ellen. 2016. *Private Patents and Public Health: Changing Intellectual Property Rules for Access to Medicines*. New York: AMB Publishers.

't Hoen, Ellen. 2022. "Protection of Clinical Test Data and Public Health: A Proposal to End the Stronghold of Data Exclusivity." In *Access to Medicines and Vaccines*, edited by Carlos M. Correa and Reto M. Hitly, 183–200. New York: Springer.

UN High-Level Panel on Access to Medicines. 2016. *Promoting Innovation and Access to Health Technologies*. New York: United Nations Development Programme.

Van den Bossche, Peter and Denise Prévost. 2021. *Essentials of WTO law*. Cambridge: Cambridge University Press.

Van den Bossche, Peter and Werner Zdouc. 2022. *The Law and Policy of the World Trade Organization: Text, Cases, and Materials*. Cambridge: Cambridge University Press.

WHO. 2022. "Member States Working Group on Strengthening WHO Preparedness and Response to, 'Report of the Working Group on Strengthening WHO Preparedness and Response to Health Emergencies to the seventy-fifth World Health Assembly.'" May 23. A75/17.

WHO. 2022. "Working Draft, Presented on the Basis of Progress Achieved, for the Consideration of the Intergovernmental Negotiating Body at Its second meeting." July 13. A/INB/2/3.

WTO.1994. "Marrakesh Agreement Establishing the World Trade Organization (Art. II)." April 15, 1867, I-31874.

WTO. 2001. "Declaration on the Trips Agreement and Public Health." November 20. WT/MIN(01)/DEC/2.

Wu, Chuan-Feng. 2010. "Raising the Right to Health Concerns within the Framework of International Intellectual Property Law." *Asian Center for WTO & International Health Law and Policy* 5: 141–205.

Wu, Chuang-Feng and Chien-Huei Wu. 2020. "International Trade, Public Heath, and Human Rights." In *Foundations of Global Health and Human Rights*, edited by Lawrence O. Gostin and Benjamin Mason Meier, 351–372. New York: Oxford University Press

13
Commercial Determinants of Health
Corporate Social Responsibility as Smokescreen or Global Health Policy?

Roojin Habibi and Thana C. de Campos-Rudinsky

Introduction

Transnational corporations (TNCs) have the power to shape the physical and social environments in which people are born, grow, and live. These effects of corporate power on the health of individuals and populations are known as "commercial determinants of health" (CDoH). These commercial determinants arise and are influenced either by the sale of goods and services that impact health or through the process by which such goods and services are manufactured, marketed, regulated, distributed, and taxed. Acting beyond national regulation, TNCs operate outside national boundaries and impact health outcomes throughout the world. TNCs influence public health through a variety of pathways, including through marketing that may make unhealthy commodities more desirable, government lobbying practices that may impede public health policies, supply chain control that calibrates a company's global influence, and corporate social responsibility strategies that serve to neutralize corporate scrutiny and deflect accountability.

With national governments unable to effectively regulate TNCs in a globalizing world, health advocates have looked to corporate self-regulation to address CDoH through frameworks of "corporate social responsibility" (CSR). In its early formulations, CSR referred to a business model that integrates legal, ethical, and social accountability with economic profitability. More recently, CSR has come to encompass the responsibility of an organization for its social and environmental impacts. As a form of global health policy, CSR considers the contributions of organizations toward sustainable development, including the promotion of global health. Yet it remains uncertain what form a CSR initiative may take, and whether social responsibility can ever be ascribed to a corporate entity that arguably exists for the sole purpose of increasing profits. This poses difficulties for global health law, which must contend with the contribution, if any, of CSR initiatives to the control of harmful corporate behavior and the promotion of global health.

This chapter examines the growing influence of TNCs in global health and the promises and pitfalls of CSR doctrines in promoting accountability for global health equity. Part I frames the evolution of corporate responsibility in global health, beginning with the emergence of TNCs and the development of CSR initiatives to advance global health—establishing early voluntary codes and standards of self-regulation. In considering whether CSR is anything more than a smokescreen for corporate profit, Part II surveys the rise of efforts to control harmful corporate activity in a globalizing world through global policies. Acknowledging the limitations of CSR and other global policies in regulating TNCs, Part III looks to the future prospects for legally binding human rights obligations on corporate entities and to the prospective role of public–private partnerships in the promotion of global health equity and justice. The chapter concludes that while CSR exists as a form of global health policy, it fails to provide sufficient accountability for corporate practices, and requires stronger regulatory infrastructures—mediated by intergovernmental organizations, national authorities, and local communities—to uphold the global common good.

I. Expanding CDoH and Evolving Doctrines of CSR in Global Health

Where CDoH relates to conditions, actions, and omissions by the private sector that underlie public health, this focus on commercial determinants, as first examined in Chapter 7, points to "an inherent tension between the commercial and the public health objective" (Kosinska and Ostlin 2016, 127). These tensions reflect manifestations of corporate power and the vestiges of colonialism and exploitation (de Lacy-Vawdon, Vandenberg, and Livingstone 2022). In responding to these threats through self-regulation, corporations have looked to CSR initiatives to frame the "responsibility of an organization for the impact of its decisions and activities on society and the environment, through transparent and ethical behaviour that contributes . . . to sustainable development, including health and the welfare of society" (ISO 2010, 2.18). The rise of TNCs propelled the use of CSR strategies, staving off international legal regulation by providing industry-led standards to hold corporations accountable for their impacts across the globe. However, the voluntary nature of CSR has presented conflicts of interest and favored the profit-seeking goals of TNCs to the detriment of public health outcomes, as seen in early CSR efforts that failed to bind firms to protect health over profits.

A. The Rise of TNCs

Corporate actors hold a unique position in the global health landscape. Established under national law, a corporation holds the right to own assets, create binding legal agreements, and be held independently liable for its actions. The legal rights and obligations of corporations are distinct from the entitlements of the owners, with corporations, according to a libertarian account, existing exclusively to produce profit for the owners. In expanding corporate operations globally, TNCs (interchangeably referred to as multinational enterprises or multinational corporations—MNCs) are defined as companies that are established and operate in more than one country (OECD 2011). Yet despite variations in types of TNCs, they are a "distinct type of business enterprise," sharing several common features, including the ability to locate and exploit productive capacity in global markets, trade inputs across borders, and maintain control over their global organizational structure (Muchlinski 2021).

The rise of TNCs has long presented challenges to public health, with TNCs prioritizing business profits over the well-being of societies, and global trade has expanded these health harms across countries. As instruments of private profit and trade, the earliest TNCs took the shape of colonial trading companies such as the Dutch East India and the English East India companies (Bartley 2018). These trading companies played a vital role in colonial expansion, as companies could take risks where governments could not, and as such, corporations were often given royal "charters" over designated areas—and expected to maintain order in those areas (Amao 2011). Corporate abuses of health and human rights were pervasive in the operations of these early enterprises.[1] Supported by colonial administrations, the legacies of dominance and exploitation are felt to this day in formerly colonized communities, with repercussions for the success of global public health initiatives (Richardson 2019).

Responding to the rise of corporate power, developments following World War II irreversibly shaped the regulation of TNCs. Following the establishment of the United Nations (UN), countries adopted the 1948 Universal Declaration of Human Rights (UDHR), first introduced in Chapter 4, paving the way for the contemporary international human rights system and the recognition of state obligations to protect the human rights of their inhabitants—as well as of inhabitants in other countries—from corporate abuses (Ratner 2001). Concurrently, countries in the Global South began gaining independence and establishing their sovereign equality. Flowing from their long-standing distrust

---

[1] The transatlantic slave trade, for instance, grew alongside the expansion of European economies, as prosperous slave trading companies such as the British Royal African Company gave rise to new forms of social and economic power, investing their newfound wealth into other economic sectors (Richardson 2019).

of corporate entities in the West, decolonization led to a wave of initiatives to "nationalize" assets previously owned by foreign companies, placing private corporate assets under national government control, and gave rise to efforts to reshape global economic relations under a "New International Economic Order" (Zerk 2006).[2]

At the international level, the UN looked to rein in transnational corporate injustices through global policies. Seeking to respond to corporate efforts to ensure profits through the search for cheaper and faster labor, lower wages, and weaker regulatory frameworks, the UN Economic and Social Council initiated a study in 1972 on the "role of multinational corporations and their impact on the process of development"—leading to recommendations to develop UN guidance on the regulation, management, and oversight of TNC activities (Zerk 2006). While TNCs generally do not bear obligations under public international law, international efforts sought to articulate and codify corporate roles and responsibilities through soft law standards (OECD 2011). A series of global policy initiatives followed from the UN Economic and Social Council's study, including efforts to develop the UN Code of Conduct on Transnational Corporations in 1975, the OECD Guidelines for Multinational Enterprises in 1976, the International Labor Organization's Tripartite Declaration of Principles concerning Multinational Enterprises and Social Policy in 1977, and the WHO/UNICEF International Code of Marketing of Breast-milk Substitutes in 1981 (Sikkink 1986).

Case Study: Developing the International Code of Marketing of Breast-milk Substitutes

The International Code of Marketing of Breast-milk Substitutes was adopted in 1981 by the World Health Assembly after non-governmental organizations (NGOs) galvanized public debate on the unethical TNC promotion of breast-milk substitutes in the "developing world." Such debates focused on Nestlé's relentless yet negligent campaign to market infant formula while ignoring the widely documented harms associated with bottle feeding in certain low-income settings. In response to rising infant disease, malnutrition, and death from mixing powdered formula with unclean water, NGOs formed a transnational activist network to challenge Nestlé, as seen in Figure 13.1, generating economic, moral, and political pressure on TNCs to stop discouraging breastfeeding and pushing infant formula without considering the detrimental

---

[2] However, as discussed in Chapters 3 and 10, these efforts to transform international relations to expand development largely floundered, as Western states mounted resistance to economic development efforts in the Global South.

Figure 13.1 Protest Rallying for a Boycott of Nestlé Products (IBFAN)

health impacts. A global boycott of all Nestlé products in the 1970s was so influential in hampering corporate profits that the industry ultimately looked to the World Health Organization (WHO) to mediate between the industry and the activists. Through this WHO intervention, the major actors (industry, NGOs, and governments) came to favor the development of a corporate code as a basis to protect and promote breastfeeding and to regulate the marketing and distribution of breast-milk substitutes. The resulting Code called on manufacturers and distributors to ensure that marketing activities are aligned with the best practices related to breastfeeding and the safe use of breast-milk substitutes. Despite this seminal policy development, there remains a long-standing debate as to whether the Code, as a non-legally binding WHO recommendation, has succeeded in curtailing the aggressive marketing of breast-milk substitutes. With only a fraction of WHO Member States adopting legislation or regulation to implement the provisions of the Code, public health advocates have questioned whether this corporate self-regulation has provided an adequate basis to prevent disease and promote health.

Amid these early regulatory efforts, a neoliberal agenda was rising in global governance throughout the 1980s, with a focus on freeing corporate activities from government regulation. Global economic governance institutions such as the World Bank and the International Monetary Fund, as introduced in Chapter 11, began implementing "structural adjustment" programs that conditioned loans and other development assistance on the adoption of national policies friendly to TNCs, including trade liberalization, deregulation, privatization, and foreign investment. At the multilateral level, international trade negotiations led in 1995 to the establishment of the World Trade Organization (WTO), as discussed in Chapter 12, which catalyzed new agreements on trade in services, the protection of intellectual property rights, and the reduction of barriers to trade. This confluence of policies across the global economic governance system established a policy landscape more favorable to TNCs, often resulting in the deregulation of consumer protections, erosion of social safety nets, and privatization of health systems (Zerk 2006). In the absence of legal accountability, civil society movements began advocating for corporations to assume greater responsibility for their health impacts. Yet rather than looking to international legal regulation, these calls were met with concerted efforts by TNCs to support CSR initiatives.

B. Origins of CSR to Advance Global Health

CSR doctrines rest on the idea that corporations exist not only as commercial entities, but also as social institutions—responsive to the interests of society and the common good. The earliest CSR initiatives took shape as voluntary and charitable commitments to improve working conditions, with corporations for the first time acknowledging obligations to stakeholders beyond shareholders (Zerk 2006). The social, political, and economic changes of the 1960s, characterized by anti-war and anti-establishment protests, helped garner widespread support for curtailing the power of corporations (Agudelo, Jóhannsdóttir, and Davídsdóttir 2019). Early advocates of CSR saw corporations as major players in the changing social and economic landscape, arguing that obligations for social welfare should exist within the scope of business practices (Frederick 1960). These ideological changes broadened the scope of social responsibilities of corporations—to emphasize the relationship between corporations and society as well as the importance of CSR for a firm's social influence (Agudelo, Jóhannsdóttir, and Davídsdóttir 2019). However, libertarians continued to contend that businesses are solely responsible for generating profit and should not change their business practices for any other purpose. While recognizing the public relations justifications for engaging in the rhetoric of CSR, these skeptics saw CSR as merely a basis for marketing to customers rather than an obligation to do good for societies (Friedman 1970).

Drawing from these long-standing debates, a wide range of early CSR initiatives arose, from the development of voluntary codes of conduct by TNCs or industry associations to philanthropic global health initiatives to donate medicines. These initiatives extended across all types of TNCs, from those that produce and distribute potentially harmful CDoHs such as tobacco and alcohol to those that research and develop health-enhancing products, such as pharmaceuticals and vaccines. Such efforts to build out company- and industry-wide CSR strategies became ubiquitous across modern industries, with the motivating forces behind CSR initiatives delineated into four broad categories:

(1) an ethical category that understands the relationship between business and society;
(2) an integrative category that considers it necessary for business to integrate social demands for its survival;
(3) a political category that emphasizes the social and political power of a corporation; and
(4) an instrumental category in which the corporation holds wealth creation as its sole social responsibility (Garriga and Mele 2004).

Regardless of the type of CSR initiative, these CSR standards were understood to be voluntary, imposed by TNCs on themselves, and therefore serving as a form of self-regulation—rather than establishing legally binding obligations. However, such self-regulation has often failed in corporate contexts because it has been predicated on an individualistic, self-reliant, and ultimately self-serving approach, rather than a more desirable communal approach that emphasizes mutual dependence to uphold the global common good.[3] As a result, early CSR initiatives were criticized by public health advocates as inherently limited, failing to bind corporations to protect health over profits.

C. Limitations of Early Efforts to Promote CSR

Whether CSR initiatives contribute to tangible improvements in global health remains a subject of fierce debate. As there is little evidence of any public health benefits from CSR initiatives (Mialon and McCambridge 2018), some argue that the limited effectiveness of CSR initiatives is tied to the conflict of interest these initiatives pose for TNCs whose inherent function is to increase profits. Although profits and public health benefits need not necessarily contradict,

---

[3] This CSR emphasis on self-regulation has been detrimental to ethical, integrative, political, and instrumental values in upholding the global common good, i.e., the set of conditions, values, and reasons that justify collaboration among all global actors in the international community in a way that enables mutual flourishing – the good of each and every member of the international community, leaving no one behind (de Campos-Rudinsky and Undurraga 2021).

such conflicts of interest are particularly pronounced for companies whose CSR strategies entail public health campaigns while manufacturing products that may lead to adverse health consequences (Geiger and Cuzzocrea 2017). For example, the tobacco industry has a long history of promoting youth smoking prevention programs as a way of undermining government public health campaigns to prevent the harms of tobacco consumption (Gilmore et al. 2015).[4]

Facing conflicts of interest, the voluntary nature of CSR initiatives may serve corporate profit-seeking motives, allowing TNCs to enhance their brand and reputation – and influence public policy decision-making to the detriment of public health outcomes. Despite the harmful impacts of alcohol, the alcohol industry has often supported global health initiatives, with critics arguing that the industry, by partnering with global health actors and policymakers, gains legitimacy and credibility to pursue the aggressive marketing of their products and prevent the development of regulatory measures toward alcohol (Marten and Hawkins 2018). While the industry argues that it is seeking to benefit society, critics retort that "society" to a corporation "is nothing else but the totality of actual or potential customers—and their judgments about a company being socially responsible help to determine their choice of products" (Leisinger 2005, 592). Such self-serving CSR strategies may therefore limit efforts to ensure corporate accountability through global policy.

II. Corporate Accountability through Global Policy

With TNCs proliferating and expanding their operations in a world of increasingly porous borders and open trade relations, holding "as much or more power over individuals as governments" (Ratner 2001, 461), the search for ways to promote corporate accountability through normative standards has only accelerated. Global policymaking efforts have increasingly sought to promote accountability for the exercise of such corporate power, looking to initiatives to develop industry-wide codes of conduct written by and for TNCs; establish soft law standards through intergovernmental organizations, ranging from the UN to the WHO; and enforce accountability for transnational corporate abuses in domestic courts, bringing human rights norms into corporate practice.

---

[4] As seen in the United States, Philip Morris International worked in 1990 to take control of the industry-led "It's the Law" program, which assisted retailers in posting signs stating that they do not sell tobacco to individuals under the age of 18. By fostering a network of local retailers, however, the tobacco industry was able to detect and defeat local tobacco control measures and preserve the industry's access to youth (Landman et al. 2002).

A. Corporate Codes of Conduct and Other Self-Regulatory Norms

Since the establishment of the UN, increasing numbers of transnational business and trade associations have looked to develop industry-wide "codes of conduct," and in doing so, pre-empt the push for binding laws and regulations. These trade associations—which can operate at national, regional, and global levels—provide a platform for knowledge exchange among their constituent members, which are usually national corporations and TNCs united by their shared interest in a common industry. Trade associations also act as public relations groups for the industry, increasing the credibility of industry norms, supporting lobbying efforts to influence policymakers, and promoting self-regulation (Brownell and Warner 2009). Through trade associations, TNCs may band together to deploy a vast array of tactics to undermine evidence of the harmful nature of their products—to thwart national and international regulation.

The tactics of these "merchants of doubt" have earned these industries the names of Big Pharma, Big Tobacco, and Big Food, with these industries often employing similar strategies to block regulatory efforts (Oreskes and Conway 2011). In relation to the tobacco industry, WHO has elaborated at length on "tobacco industry tactics for resisting effective tobacco control," ranging from simple intelligence gathering to the intimidation and harassment of the tobacco industry's opponents through litigation and the exercise of political and economic power (WHO 2008, 12–13). These industry tactics often operate in hidden ways, including the funding of academic research that sows doubt about product harms, philanthropic support for consumer advocacy groups that support industry-allied policy goals, press releases and journalistic ties that secure media presence for industry-friendly messaging, and marketing of products through influencers on social media platforms. Such subversive tactics often blur the lines between deceptive industry advertising and the legitimate exercise of corporate speech.[5] As the WHO Director-General recognized following the FCTC experience: "it is not just Big Tobacco anymore. Public health must also contend with Big Food, Big Soda, and Big Alcohol. All of these industries fear regulation, and protect themselves by using the same tactics" (Chan 2013).

Beyond serving as a vehicle for interest group lobbying at the domestic and international policy level, industry trade associations are also important

---

[5] The Foundation for a Smoke Free World, for instance, purports to be an independent and non-profit organization with a mission to end smoking in this generation, through grants and support for medical, agricultural, and scientific research. However, the Foundation receives substantial annual funding from Phillip Morris International. Among other initiatives, the Foundation is a strong proponent of "tobacco harm reduction," which aims to reduce the harms caused by tobacco through the use of nicotine in ostensibly less harmful forms, such as e-cigarettes, which are largely sold by transnational tobacco companies.

gatekeepers of self-regulatory codes. These self-regulatory codes—developed by and for corporations and industry associations—seek to influence a wide range of corporate activities, from setting product development standards to espousing criteria for the ethical marketing of goods and services. In some industries, these non-binding codes may be the only form of regulation in a specific sphere of corporate activity. Insofar as they seek to promote corporate conduct that is socially responsible and aligned with the interests of the public's health, these codes reflect a form of CSR practice. Proponents of self-regulation argue that such industry-wide codes of conduct can be modified more quickly and efficiently than other international regulatory efforts, aligning standards across an entire industry; however, the self-serving motives inherent when trade associations are entrusted with self-regulating conduct pose a risk to public health and society at large (Shaw and Whitney 2016). Such associations may thus be incentivized to discharge their regulating functions, for instance, by drafting deliberately vague codes lacking in comprehensive sanctions (Ziganshina and Lexchin 2010). The reliance on weak self-regulatory frameworks through corporate codes of conduct may have contributed, at least partially, to the rise of the global opioid crisis.

Case Study: The Opioid Crisis and the Pharmaceutical Industry's Self-Regulation of Prescription Drug Marketing Activities

The transnational boycott of Nestlé and the adoption of the International Code of Marketing of Breast-milk Substitutes alerted the pharmaceutical industry to the potential for future encroachment of global policymaking efforts on its own industry activities. Shortly after the development of the 1981 Code on breast-milk substitutes, the International Federation of Pharmaceutical Manufacturers & Associations (IFPMA), representing the world's research-based pharmaceutical manufacturers, drafted its own code on pharmaceutical marketing practices in an effort to pre-empt intergovernmental initiatives. The IFPMA Code of Practice, last revised in 2019, sets out a "rules-based compliance framework" for a range of corporate marketing activities, such as physician sales visits and sponsorship of continuing medical education. While the IFPMA Code outlines minimum requirements for member companies (and provides for industry-led adjudication in cases of an alleged breach), it looks to individual corporate members to establish their own company codes to reflect the IFPMA Code. However, with a lack of incentives and enforcement mechanisms, these minimum global standards offered little resistance to the unfolding global opioid crisis, driven largely by the aggressive marketing and promotion of prescription pain relief medications by pharmaceutical manufacturers. From 1996 to 2001, Purdue Pharmaceuticals influenced physician prescribing to promote OxyContin through a wide range of marketing practices: recruiting physicians and nurses at paid pain-management symposia; providing highly lucrative incentives for sales representatives; distributing promotional items to healthcare professionals, and systemically minimizing the risk of addiction from OxyContin in spite of increasing evidence of its high risk. Even after Purdue was fined by the U.S. government for misbranding OxyContin in 2007, other drug manufacturers continued to engage in aggressive marketing of oxycodone throughout the world—funding key opinion leaders and delivering continuing medical education that downplayed the risk of addiction. In the absence of an effective international regulatory framework on pharmaceutical marketing, accountability for many opioid-related deaths may prove elusive.

Despite the clear limitations of industry codes, efforts to regulate pharmaceutical marketing at a global level have largely floundered, with WHO's Ethical Criteria for Medicinal Drug Promotion, endorsed by the World Health Assembly in 1988, all but forgotten since its development. This absence of global governance has left the pharmaceutical industry open to conflicts of interest between the goals of manufacturers and "the social, medical and economic needs of providers and the public to select and use drugs in the most rational way" (WHO 1993). Critics continue to argue that drug companies focus solely on raising profits for their shareholders, like corporations in any other industry, with industry codes of conduct serving more to profit corporations than to protect patients.[6] Yet, where WHO efforts to implement global health policy have failed to influence Big Pharma, UN policy efforts have sought to codify CSR across a spectrum of corporate landscapes.

B. The UN Global Compact

Looking to establish global policies to frame CSR, the UN Global Compact represents a global normative authority within the broader corporate sustainability movement. The Global Compact initiative was launched in 2000 under the leadership of former UN Secretary-General Kofi Annan (Kell 2005). With growing public concern over the role of market liberalization in driving social inequality, reflected in the burgeoning anti-trade and anti-globalization

---

[6] The industry may not disagree entirely—as the IFPMA Director General Thomas Cueni writes in his foreword to the 2019 Code, "doing the right thing creates a competitive advantage and therefore increases shareholder value" (IFPMA 2019).

Figure 13.2 Launch of the Global Compact Initiative (UN/Mark Garten)

movements introduced in Chapter 12, Annan challenged business leaders at the 1999 World Economic Forum in Davos to work with the UN to adopt a "global compact of shared values and principles" that would promote more sustainable and inclusive global markets (Bremer 2008). This UN engagement with the private sector was based on the conviction that businesses have a self-interest in promoting a sustainable and inclusive market, and therefore would find value in working with the UN to frame and internalize key CSR principles (Rasche, Waddock, and McIntosh 2013). The launch of the Global Compact initiative, as seen in Figure 13.2, ushered in a new era of cooperation between the UN and the global business community.[7]

The resulting Global Compact consists of ten principles across four areas—human rights, labor, environment, and anti-corruption—establishing health-related goals related to protecting human rights, abolishing child labor, prohibiting forced labor, ensuring non-discrimination in the workplace, using environmentally friendly technologies, promoting environmental responsibility, and working against extortion and bribery.

While established under global governance through the UN, the Global Compact's public–private approach to governance contributed to its adoption as

---

[7] This UN governance replaced the previously state-centered approach to dealing with transnational corporations, which was seen as "hostile" toward corporations, with a global approach seen as flexible, voluntary, and encompassing multiple actors (Rasche, Waddock, and McIntosh 2013).

the world's largest voluntary CSR initiative. Through its multi-stakeholder governance model, businesses, civil society actors, and governments are given the opportunity to engage in discussions on social and environmental issues and deliberate together on how to best apply global principles to local contexts (Rasche, Waddock, and McIntosh 2013). Corporations enter the Compact through a written commitment from the Chief Executive Officer (with support from the corporation's board) and a formal pledge to conduct business in ethical ways. With this "pledge" reflecting the voluntary nature of the initiative, some critics lament that the Global Compact remains inadequate to ensure socially responsible business practices due to its lack of regulatory enforcement mechanisms (Kell 2005).

Critics thus contend that the Global Compact provides little more than a "public relations" scheme, raising a corporation's international reputation and legitimacy while avoiding meaningful changes to corporate behavior. Where the Compact lacks binding obligations, relying on a public "honor system" for accountability, corporate participants are merely required to produce an annual report that outlines progress on efforts to operate in accordance with the goals of the Global Compact. Further limiting accountability, scholars also criticize the power imbalances among participants in the Global Compact, arguing that civil society actors largely remain excluded from the initiative, despite the Compact's goal of promoting a multi-actor global governance structure (Rasche, Waddock, and McIntosh 2013). While the "universal legitimacy" of its principles can serve to complement existing regulatory mechanisms (Kell 2005), the Global Compact's lack of regulatory oversight has limited its potential as a tool of corporate accountability for health harms.

C. Domestic Sources of Corporate Regulation and Accountability

Compounding these challenges to regulatory oversight, TNCs operate across multiple countries, with their conduct beyond territorial boundaries limiting accountability under national law. Such limitations of domestic legislation and regulation have proven especially detrimental to the health and livelihoods of people in low- and middle-income countries that "host" the subsidiaries of TNCs, as major disparities in economic power often exist between the TNC and the host country (McCorquodale and Simons 2007).[8] For instance, TNCs that operate in extractive industries such as mining, oil, and gas have often been accused of environmental damage and human rights abuses, including pollution, land expropriation, and displacement of local communities. National governments,

---

[8] The efforts of national governments to lure corporate investments to their countries has led to a "race to the bottom" in corporate regulation, with states competing against each other to establish regulatory frameworks that are friendly to foreign direct investment—at the expense of product quality control and rights-based labor and public health standards.

dependent on investments and taxes from TNCs, may be unwilling or unable to effectively regulate the activities of TNCs operating within their borders, and, by extension, may struggle to regulate corporations in ways necessary to protect the health and human rights of their peoples from violative and harmful corporate conduct (Roorda and Leader 2021). However, some national governments have looked to global models, domestic litigation, and human rights obligations to regulate TNCs operation within their country.

National governments have drawn from global models in regulating TNCs under domestic law, as seen in domestic efforts to mitigate the harms inflicted by the global food and soda industries. Following WHO's Global Action Plan for the Prevention and Control of Non-Communicable Diseases 2013–2020, as first discussed in Chapter 7, some national governments have adopted taxes that raise consumer prices of sugar-sweetened beverages by at least 20% (Roache and Gostin 2017). These domestic regulations, following recommendations set under global health policy, have reduced sugar consumption at the individual level and encouraged TNCs to reduce sugar content in their product formulations. While simply importing successful models from high-income countries has not worked well for low- and middle-income countries, certain global models have made it easier for a wider range of national governments to develop context-specific regulations to protect their populations.

Looking beyond the host countries, the home countries of TNCs have the ability to apply their own domestic law to hold TNCs accountable for health harms committed abroad. The application of domestic law and litigation to promote accountability for transnational harms offers the possibility of tangible justice for victims of corporate abuse throughout the world. These domestic courts in the home countries of TNCs are often well-placed to enforce judgments and provide remedies—including monetary compensation. When carefully considered and fought for through a dedicated network of local and global activists, journalists, and other stakeholders, landmark results can be attained. In addressing environmental harms, the Netherlands Court of Appeal found the transnational oil corporation Shell Global liable in 2021 for damages caused by its subsidiary in Nigeria, the Shell Petroleum Development Company of Nigeria (SPDC). Specifically, the Dutch Court held that the SPDC subsidiary was responsible for multiple oil spills in the Niger Delta and that the Dutch parent company had violated its duty of care in failing to prevent these threats to the livelihoods of local villagers (Roorda and Leader 2021).[9] Health and human

---

[9] The likelihood of success in such litigation against corporations for foreign damages depends largely on the legislation and jurisprudence of the home state. In the United States, for example, the U.S. Supreme Court has recently shown reluctance to finding U.S. corporations liable under the Alien Tort Claims Act, noting in its 2021 decision in *Nestlé USA, Inc. v. Doe*—in which plaintiffs sued U.S. corporations for their contribution to child slavery abroad—that the creation of new pathways for civil claims against corporations by non-U.S. citizens depended on guidance from the legislature, not judicial pronouncements.

rights activists widely welcomed the judgment as a warning for all Dutch TNCs involved in injustice worldwide.

In supporting national regulatory efforts to protect public health and human rights, international human rights law has evolved to incorporate recognition of "extraterritorial obligations," acknowledging that "States have obligations to respect, protect and fulfill human rights . . . both within their territories and extraterritorially" (International Commission of Jurists and Maastricht University 2013). Since home states often have the power to influence the conduct of TNCs through their laws, regulations, and policies, extraterritorial human rights obligations recognize that states bear a duty to ensure that the activities of TNCs based within their jurisdiction respect human rights—even if those activities take place outside the home state's borders. Drawing from these extraterritorial obligations, as initially described in Chapter 4, international and regional human rights courts and tribunals—including the UN human rights treaty bodies, the Inter-American Court of Human Rights, and the European Court of Human Rights—have begun to examine state obligations to regulate TNCs. The Inter-American Court of Human Rights has led the way in solidifying the extraterritorial duty of states to regulate, supervise, and monitor activities that may pose "significant risks to the health of individuals" in another jurisdiction (Abello-Galvis and Arevalo-Ramirez 2019). These decisions have provided some degree of accountability for corporate abuses, shifting TNCs from self-regulation under CSR frameworks to legal obligations under international law.

III. Legal Obligations of Corporate Actors in Global Health

One of the biggest challenges in global health governance is to contain the outsized influence of TNCs on the health and well-being of people around the world—as these non-state entities are neither formal members nor signatories to global health law instruments. However, progressive reforms in international human rights law may broaden the dimensions of legally enforceable corporate responsibility, potentially paving the way for more human rights compliant and accountable business practices in global health. This expanding potential of international human rights law has led to robust debates regarding the human rights obligations of the pharmaceutical industry in ensuring access to essential medicines. Where such top-down, prescriptive approaches to governing TNCs are difficult in practice, public–private partnerships (PPPs) may present a more pragmatic means of ensuring that corporations work toward a positive impact on health, leveraging their resources, expertise, and networks to achieve shared goals across the global health landscape.

A. Businesses and International Human Rights Law

Although corporate entities are not signatories to international human rights treaties, their activities may nevertheless have significant impacts on human rights, and as such, they have increasingly been found by the UN human rights system to bear human rights responsibilities for public health harms (Alston 2005). In developing human rights standards to frame the conduct of corporations, the Special Representative of the UN Secretary-General (SRSG) on the issue of human rights and transnational corporations and other business enterprises developed a 2008 "Protect, Respect and Remedy Framework" for business and human rights (Ruggie 2008). This early UN effort sought to close the "governance gaps" that historically left corporate human rights violations unchallenged—under the traditional assumption that only states have human rights responsibilities (Wettstein 2015)—framing corporate responsibilities under three pillars:

(1) the state duty to protect against human rights abuses by business enterprises;
(2) the corporate responsibility to respect human rights; and
(3) the fundamental right of victims of human rights abuses committed by businesses to access an effective remedy through both judicial and non-judicial processes.

Efforts to operationalize this Framework and provide practical recommendations on its implementation led the UN Human Rights Council to the unanimous 2011 endorsement of the United Nations Guiding Principles on Business and Human Rights (UNGPs). Seeking to apply human rights to "all States and to all business enterprises, both transnational and others, regardless of their size, sector, location, ownership and structure" (Ruggie 2011, 6), the UNGPs do not follow an exclusively voluntary nor a legal framework approach—instead, they combine both approaches to clarify obligations for all companies (Wettstein 2015).

While the UNGP approach was successful in overcoming the voluntarism that characterized previous initiatives and debates on the application of human rights to businesses, human rights scholars and practitioners fundamentally disagree on the three pillars of the UNGPs (protect, respect, and remedy) and the actors to whom such pillars are addressed. In the absence of legal obligations, critics have argued that the UNGPs fall short because they do not provide for mechanisms of independent monitoring and accountability (Parker and Howe 2011). Other scholars argue that the focus on consensus-building in developing the UNGPs has diluted the human rights obligations of companies and undermined "the normative importance attached to human rights" (Deva

2013, 103).[10] Further efforts would be needed to strengthen the effectiveness of corporate human rights obligations and accountability for human rights abuses (Wolfsteller and Li 2022).

Considering these shortcomings of the UNGPs and other CSR initiatives, the UN Human Rights Council resolved in 2014 to establish an open-ended intergovernmental working group on transnational corporations and other business enterprises with respect to human rights (the Working Group), with a mandate to "elaborate an international legally binding instrument to regulate, in international human rights law, the activities of transnational corporations and other business enterprises" (HRC 2014, para. 1).

Case Study: Proposed Treaty on Business and Human Rights

Despite the explicit opposition of the SRSG to opening international negotiations to develop a legally binding instrument on business and human rights, the decision to embark on an intergovernmental negotiation process was urged in part by the misgivings of states in the Global South, which saw such an instrument as crucial to ensuring accountability for human rights violations committed by TNCs within their territories. Since the establishment of the Working Group, three drafts of the proposed legally binding instrument have been debated, with intergovernmental negotiations continuing—both on the substance and on the need for such an instrument. In the latest draft of the instrument, states have sought to identify the basic objectives of the proposed treaty:

(1) clarifying and facilitating effective implementation of the obligation of states to respect, protect, fulfill, and promote human rights in the context of business activities, particularly those of transnational character;
(2) clarifying and ensuring respect and fulfillment of the human rights obligations of business enterprises;
(3) preventing and mitigating the occurrence of human rights abuses in the context of business activities by effective mechanisms of monitoring and enforceability;
(4) ensuring access to justice and effective, adequate, and timely remedy for victims of human rights abuses in the context of business activities; and
(5) facilitating and strengthening mutual legal assistance and international cooperation to prevent and mitigate human rights abuses in the context of business activities.

---

[10] This critique takes issue with the terminology of "responsibilities," "expectations," and "due diligence"—instead of "duties"—eroding the normative force of soft law in the business and human rights domain (Wettstein 2015).

The Working Group looks to this draft instrument to provide a legal path to articulate binding human rights obligations on states, create a new human rights treaty monitoring body, and establish an International Fund for Victims—to provide legal and financial aid to those who experience corporate harm.

While some human rights scholars and practitioners remain cautiously optimistic about the prospects of adopting an international treaty on business and human rights, progress in the Working Group has been slow, and it remains unclear whether statements made in generality in the draft instrument can be further specified and effectively applied in the context of health.

B. Pharmaceutical Corporations in Global Health

In the absence of human rights obligations for all corporations, scholars and advocates have looked to narrow obligations on pharmaceutical corporations to ensure access to essential medicines. Pharmaceutical corporations are uniquely positioned in the global health landscape—as they are often the sole producers of medications, vaccines, and other products that support and promote global health—making them indispensable actors in global health governance.[11] The intellectual property owned by pharmaceutical corporations, as introduced in Chapter 12, may make them the only distributor of medicines, effectively controlling the market for specific drugs; yet, pharmaceutical corporations often fail to assume human rights responsibilities to ensure access to these essential medicines. While pharmaceutical corporations control the ability to save lives and reduce suffering, the extent to which these corporations bear obligations to uphold human rights by promoting access to essential medicines remains a contested and evolving issue (Forman, Al-Alami, and Fajber 2022).

Advancing these corporate obligations under the right to health, the first UN Special Rapporteur on the right of everyone to the enjoyment of the highest attainable standard health incorporated in his final report to the UN General Assembly a set of Human Rights Guidelines for Pharmaceutical Companies in Relation to Access to Medicines (Hunt 2008). These Guidelines outline pharmaceutical company responsibility in "transparency, management, monitoring, accountability, pricing, ethical marketing, and against lobbying for more protection in intellectual property laws, applying for patents for trivial modifications of existing medicines, inappropriate drug promotion, and excessive pricing" (Hunt

---

[11] There are important exceptions to this general rule, where governments have been directly involved in pharmaceutical innovation and development. For instance, the U.S. federal government has long played a central role in contributing to the research and development that eventually served as the foundation for mRNA vaccines to prevent COVID-19.

and Khosla 2010, 1). Whereas the UNGPs offer a conceptual and policy framework to anchor the business and human rights debate in general, the Guidelines try to provide a practical list of policy strategies that pharmaceutical companies should address when developing and implementing their own human rights policy statements (de Campos 2017). Pharmaceutical companies thus have more far-reaching responsibilities under the Guidelines than under the UNGPs, with health responsibilities under the Guidelines that "encompass, but also look beyond, the corporate responsibility to respect" (Lee and Hunt 2012).

In practice, however, efforts to advocate human rights-oriented conduct in the pharmaceutical industry's product development and marketing practices have met with limited success. Seeking to advance these norms in the context of the COVID-19 pandemic, the UN Committee on Economic, Social and Cultural Rights has underscored the obligations of private corporations to refrain from taking actions that may prolong the harmful effects of the pandemic, such as invoking intellectual property rights "in a manner that is inconsistent with the right of every person to access a safe and effective vaccine against COVID-19" (CESCR 2021, para. 9). Given the obstacles faced in prescribing new normative instruments to govern corporate conduct, some experts argue that the most effective strategy for reining in corporate conduct is creating platforms for corporate partnerships, establishing shared objectives between the private sector and other global health stakeholders.

C. Public–Private Partnerships

Public–private partnerships (PPPs) hold the promise of lending greater corporate investment, speed, and innovation to the promotion of public health goals and realization of human rights obligations—particularly where national governments and international agencies are unable to advance such goals on their own. Scholars have posited three approaches in assessing the human rights responsibilities of pharmaceutical corporations: top-down, bottom-up, and horizontal. The top-down approach assesses if companies are working alongside states to meet the state's legal obligations to guarantee access to emergency medicines. The bottom-up approach includes the governance of public–private partnerships and their impact on human rights, as well as access to medicine. The horizontal approach includes bringing other stakeholders in to work on human rights and anti-corruption related issues that bear on health. These three approaches can work in interconnected ways to hold corporations and states to a standard that protects both health and human rights.

Advancing the bottom-up approach to human rights responsibilities of corporations, these PPPs can provide a formal collaboration between one or more actors in the public sector—such as governments, NGOs, civil society groups, and intergovernmental organizations—and private sector entities such as corporations and philanthropies. Such cross-institutional partnerships have a long history of influence in global health, as introduced in Chapter 3, and include models for public–private cooperation, as seen in Gavi, The Vaccine Alliance; the Drugs for Neglected Diseases Initiative; and the Global Fund to Fight AIDS, Tuberculosis and Malaria. The purpose of these collaborative relationships is to promote common public health objectives through the sharing of risks, responsibilities, and decision-making processes (Prah Ruger 2012).

However, where donors often drive decision-making in PPPs, TNC power creates imbalances in governing structures. Discordant values and interests between the actors involved in the partnership may inhibit relationships of trust, and more fundamentally, suggest that PPPs can be leveraged by TNCs and other powerful actors for less altruistic and more self-serving causes. For example, the Clinton Foundation, the American Heart Association, and other actors joined a partnership with Coca-Cola and PepsiCo to remove sugary sodas from schools. Even as public health experts expressed concern about the impact of this partnership, agreements within the partnership allowed for the introduction of other high-caloric, sugar-filled, nutrient-deficient "vitamin waters" and "sports drinks" in place of sodas (Ludwig and Nestle 2008). With the purported legitimacy provided by the PPP, Coca-Cola and PepsiCo leveraged the partnership to market sports drinks and other sugary beverages to a new, younger market, and with it undermined effective public health measures to remove sugar-sweetened beverages from school lunchrooms.

These concerns with PPPs extend to partnerships with the pharmaceutical industry. Amid the turbulent trajectory of global vaccine procurement and distribution in the COVID-19 response, PPPs have not yielded benefits equitably across countries. Crucial to the success of PPPs is the ability of the public sector to negotiate on behalf of the public, making decisions for how their health needs can best be met through such partnerships (Campos-Rudinsky and Canales 2022). Yet, as seen in the COVID-19 response, as discussed in greater detail in Chapter 14, these abilities were not honored within the COVAX partnership structure, which extended corporate profits without ensuring vaccine equity.

Conclusion

The human spirit has an inextinguishable thirst for knowledge, innovation, and creativity, and at their very best, businesses provide a platform for the flourishment of enterprise and ingenuity. Yet societies have benefited unevenly from business practices. Looming large over the increasing intertwinement of people and economies in a globalizing world is the corollary entanglement of TNCs with environments, ways of life, and day-to-day lives. Global health is shaped in a multitude of ways by commercial determinants, and the ubiquitous impact of corporate activities will only gain in importance with the passage of time. To prevent, mitigate, as well as redress possible harms which may arise from these commercial effects, the development of policy frameworks will be necessary—regulating TNC activities across countries through global health policies.

The concept of CSR, while broad, accommodates an evolving recognition of the responsibilities that TNCs bear for their actions throughout the world. By some accounts, such voluntary corporate initiatives constitute a form of global health policy—with the potential to provide some measure of normative guidance and restraint over the profit-seeking influence that private sector actors may have on global health. Others, however, approach any benevolent or ethical posturing from TNCs with skepticism and distrust, recognizing the inherent misalignment of interests between the self-serving motives of TNCs and the normative frameworks in global health. Irrespective of the ulterior motives behind CSR initiatives, these initiatives are largely designed and driven by and for TNCs and are often lacking in mechanisms of transparency and accountability. New policy frameworks will be necessary to regulate private sector engagement to uphold the global common good.

As global health law evolves, it must find new ways to regulate the activities of TNCs to prevent adverse health consequences and human rights violations, promoting partnerships that advance justice in global health. Acknowledging the need for greater regulatory infrastructure, the international community has sought to move beyond avenues of industry self-regulation by developing soft law mechanisms mediated under intergovernmental entities and promoting consensus-based articulations of responsibilities incumbent on both states and corporations. Further reforms will be necessary to impose obligations on states and TNCs alike under international law. While the ongoing contested negotiations on the proposed draft treaty on business and human rights may provide a novel approach to this unfolding debate, the field of global health must examine more specific health-related obligations for engagement with the private sector, structuring governance in ways that limit corporate harm from both unhealthy products and unhealthy production while encouraging partnerships that promote health and the global common good.

Questions for Consideration

1. Why are national governments unable to regulate TNCs in a globalizing world? Why was WHO necessary to ensure accountability for the harm of Nestlé marketing of breast-milk substitutes in the Global South?

2. What are the pitfalls of ascribing social responsibilities to multinational corporations? How have corporations used social responsibility as a foundation for self-regulation?
3. How do TNCs use CSR strategies to undermine regulatory efforts? Is it possible for TNCs to avoid an inherent conflict of interest between profit-seeking and social responsibility?
4. Why are trade associations poorly structured for the development and implementation of industry-wide codes of conduct? Why did the IFPMA Code of Practice fail to prevent the overuse of opioid drugs? Should the pharmaceutical industry bear greater obligations to protect patients than other industries have to protect their customers?
5. How did the UN come to be involved in developing CSR principles under the Global Compact? What challenges has the Global Compact faced in providing accountability for corporate actions that impact health?
6. Why are national governments in low- and middle-income countries often unwilling to regulate TNC subsidiaries that harm public health? How can global models support national governments in developing domestic public health legislation and litigation?
7. How did the UN human rights system come to see human rights obligations under international law as applying to non-state actors? Why do the Guiding Principles on Business and Human Rights (UNGPs) provide both voluntary responsibilities and legal obligations? What would be the costs and benefits achieved through the codification of a treaty on business and human rights?
8. How do the Human Rights Guidelines for Pharmaceutical Companies in Relation to Access to Medicines extend the UNGPs to strengthen the human rights responsibilities of pharmaceutical corporations?
9. How have TNCs leveraged PPPs to gain legitimacy for their profit-seeking motivations? How can global health partners seek to provide accountability for pharmaceutical corporations?

Acknowledgments

The authors express their gratitude to Roxana Rabet for her invaluable research assistance throughout the drafting of this chapter.

References

Abello-Galvis, Ricardo and Walter Arevalo-Ramirez. 2019. "Inter-American Court of Human Rights Advisory Opinion OC-23/17: Jurisdictional, Procedural and Substantive Implications of Human Rights Duties in the Context of Environmental

Protection." *Review of European, Comparative & International Environmental Law* 28(2): 217–222.
Agudelo, Mauricio Andrés Latapí, Lára Jóhannsdóttir, and Brynhildur Davídsdóttir. 2019. "A Literature Review of the History and Evolution of Corporate Social Responsibility." *International Journal of Corporate Social Responsibility* 4(1): 1–23.
Alston, Philip. 2005. "Non-State Actors and Human Rights." In *The 'Not-a-Cat' Syndrome: Can the International Human Rights Regime Accommodate Non-State Actors?* edited by Philip Alston, 13.3: 3–36. Collected Courses of the Academy of European Law. Oxford: Oxford University Press.
Amao, Olufemi. 2011. *Corporate Social Responsibility, Human Rights and the Law: Multinational Corporations in Developing Countries.* New York: Routledge.
Bartley, Tim. 2018. "Transnational Corporations and Global Governance." *Annual Review of Sociology* 44(1): 145–165.
Bremer, Jennifer Ann. 2008. "How Global Is the Global Compact?" *Business Ethics: A European Review* 17(3): 227–244.
Brownell, Kelly D. and Kenneth E. Warner. 2009. "The Perils of Ignoring History: Big Tobacco Played Dirty and Millions Died. How Similar Is Big Food?" *The Milbank Quarterly* 87(1): 259–94.
CESCR (Committee on Economic, Social, and Cultural Rights). 2021. "Statement on Universal Affordable Vaccination against Coronavirus Disease (COVID-19), International Cooperation and Intellectual Property." April 23. E/C.12/2021/1.
Chan, Margaret. 2013. "Opening Address at the 8th Global Conference on Health Promotion." *World Health Organization.* June 10.
de Campos, Thana Cristina. 2017. *The Global Health Crisis: Ethical Responsibilities.* Cambridge: Cambridge University Press.
de Campos-Rudinsky, Thana Cristina and Mariana Canales. 2022. "Global Health Governance and the Principle of Subsidiarity: In Defense of a Robust Decentralization Approach." *International Journal of Constitutional Law* 20(1): 177–203.
de Lacy-Vawdon, Cassandra, Brian Vandenberg, and Charles Henry Livingstone. 2022. "Recognising the Elephant in the Room: The Commercial Determinants of Health." *BMJ Global Health* 7 (2): e007156.
Deva, Surya. 2013. "Treating Human Rights Lightly: A Critique of the Consensus Rhetoric and the Language Employed by the Guiding Principles." In *Human Rights Obligations of Business: Beyond the Corporate Responsibility to Respect?*, edited by Surya Deva and David Bilchitz. Cambridge: Cambridge University Press.
Forman, Lisa, Basema Al-Alami, and Kaitlin Fajber. 2022. "An Inquiry into State Agreement and Practice on the International Law Status of the Human Right to Medicines." *Health and Human Rights Journal* 24(2): 125–140.
Frederick, William C. 1960. "The Growing Concern over Business Responsibility." *California Management Review* 2(4): 54–61.
Friedman, Milton. 1970. "The Social Responsibility of Business Is to Increase Its Profits." *The New York Times.* September 13.
Garriga, Elisabet and Domenec Mele. 2004. "Corporate Social Responsibility Theories: Mapping the Territory." *Journal of Business Ethics* 53: 51–71.
Geiger, Ben Baumberg and Valentina Cuzzocrea. 2017. "Corporate Social Responsibility and Conflicts of Interest in the Alcohol and Gambling Industries: A Post-Political Discourse?" *The British Journal of Sociology* 68(2): 254–272.
Gilmore, Anna B., Gary Fooks, Jeffrey Drope, Stella Aguinaga Bialous, and Rachel Rose Jackson. 2015. "Exposing and Addressing Tobacco Industry Conduct in Low-Income and Middle-Income Countries." *Lancet* 385(9972): 1029–1043.

HRC (UN Human Rights Council). 2014. "Elaboration of an International Legally Binding Instrument on Transnational Corporations and Other Business Enterprises with Respect to Human Rights." July 14. A/HRC/RES/26/9.

Hunt, Paul. 2008. "Report of the Special Rapporteur on the Right of Everyone to the Enjoyment of the Highest Attainable Standard of Physical and Mental Health." A/63/263.

Hunt, Paul and Rajat Khosla. 2010. "Are Drug Companies Living Up to Their Human Rights Responsibilities? The Perspective of the Former United Nations Special Rapporteur (2002–2008)." *PLOS Medicine* 7(9): e1000330.

International Commission of Jurists and Maastricht University. 2013. *Maastricht Principles on Extraterritorial Obligations of States in the Area of Economic, Social and Cultural Rights*. Heidelberg: ETO.

IFPMA (International Federation of Pharmaceutical Manufacturers and Associations). 2019. *Code of Practice: Upholding Ethical Standards and Sustaining Trust*. Geneva: IFPMA.

ISO (International Standards Organization). 2010. *ISO 26000:2010, Guidance on Social Responsibility*. Geneva: ISO.

Kell, Georg. 2005. "The Global Compact Selected Experiences and Reflections." *Journal of Business Ethics* 59(1/2): 69–79.

Kosinska, Monika and Piroska Ostlin. 2016. "Building Systematic Approaches to Intersectoral Action in the WHO European Region." *Public Health Panorama* 2(2): 124–129.

Landman, Anne, Pamela M. Ling, and Stanton A. Glantz. 2002. "Tobacco Industry Youth Smoking Prevention Programs: Protecting the Industry and Hurting Tobacco Control." *American Journal of Public Health* 92(6): 917–930.

Lee, Joo-Young and Paul Hunt. 2012. "Human Rights Responsibilities of Pharmaceutical Companies in Relation to Access to Medicines." *Journal of Law, Medicine & Ethics* 40(2): 220–233.

Leisinger, Klaus M. 2005. "The Corporate Social Responsibility of the Pharmaceutical Industry: Idealism without Illusion and Realism without Resignation." *Business Ethics Quarterly* 15(4): 577–594.

Ludwig, David S. and Marion Nestle. 2008. "Can the Food Industry Play a Constructive Role in the Obesity Epidemic?" *JAMA* 300(15): 1808.

Marten, Robert and Ben Hawkins. 2018. "Stop the Toasts: The Global Fund's Disturbing New Partnership." *Lancet* 391(10122): 735–736.

McCorquodale, Robert and Penelope Simons. 2007. "Responsibility Beyond Borders: State Responsibility for Extraterritorial Violations by Corporations of International Human Rights Law." *Modern Law Review* 70(4): 598–625.

Mialon, Melissa and Jim McCambridge. 2018. "Alcohol Industry Corporate Social Responsibility Initiatives and Harmful Drinking: A Systematic Review." *The European Journal of Public Health* 28(4): 664–673.

Muchlinski, Peter. 2021. *Multinational Enterprises and the Law*. Third edition. Oxford: Oxford University Press.

OECD. 2011. *OECD Guidelines for Multinational Enterprises, 2011 Edition*. Paris: OECD.

Oreskes, Naomi and Erik M. Conway. 2011. *Merchants of Doubt: How a Handful of Scientists Obscured the Truth on Issues from Tobacco Smoke to Climate Change*. New York: Bloomsbury Publishing.

Parker, Christine and John Howe. 2011. "Ruggie's Diplomatic Project and Its Missing Regulatory Infrastructure." In *The UN Guiding Principles on Business and Human Rights: Foundations and Implementation*, edited by Radu Mares and Brill Nijhoff. Geneva: OHCHR.

Prah Ruger, Jennifer. 2012. "Global Health Governance as a Shared Health Governance." *Journal of Epidemiology and Community Health* 66(7): 653–661.

Rasche, Andreas, Sandra Waddock, and Malcolm McIntosh. 2013. "The United Nations Global Compact: Retrospect and Prospect." *Business & Society* 52(1): 6–30.

Ratner, Steven R. 2001. "Corporations and Human Rights: A Theory of Legal Responsibility." *The Yale Law Journal* 111(3): 443–545.

Richardson, Eugene T. 2019. "On the Coloniality of Global Public Health." *Medicine Anthropology Theory* 6(4): 101–118.

Roache, Sarah A. and Lawrence O. Gostin. 2017. "The Untapped Power of Soda Taxes: Incentivizing Consumers, Generating Revenue, and Altering Corporate Behavior." *International Journal of Health Policy and Management* 6(9): 489–493.

Roorda, Lucas and Daniel Leader. 2021. "Okpabi v Shell and Four Nigerian Farmers v Shell: Parent Company Liability Back in Court." *Business and Human Rights Journal* 6(2): 368–376.

Ruggie, John. 2008. "Protect, Respect & Remedy: A Framework for Business and Human Rights." *Innovations: Technology, Governance, Globalization* 3: 189–212.

Ruggie, John. 2011. "Guiding Principles on Business and Human Rights: Implementing the United Nations 'Protect, Respect and Remedy' Framework." March 21. A/HRC/17/31.

Shaw, Brendan and Paige Whitney. 2016. "Ethics and Compliance in Global Pharmaceutical Industry Marketing and Promotion: The Role of the IFPMA and Self-Regulation." *Pharmaceuticals Policy and Law* 18(1–4): 199–206.

Sikkink, Kathryn. 1986. "Codes of Conduct for Transnational Corporations: The Case of the WHO/UNICEF Code." *International Organization* 40(4): 815–840.

Wettstein, F. 2015. "Normativity, Ethics, and the UN Guiding Principles on Business and Human Rights: A Critical Assessment." *Journal of Human Rights* 14(2): 162–182.

WHO (World Health Organization). 1993. "Clinical Pharmacological Evaluation in Drug Control." EUR/ICP/DSE 173.

WHO. 2008. *Tobacco Industry Interference with Tobacco Control*. Geneva: WHO.

Wolfsteller, René and Yingru Li. 2022. "Business and Human Rights Regulation after the UN Guiding Principles: Accountability, Governance, Effectiveness." *Human Rights Review* 23(1): 1–17.

Zerk, Jennifer A. 2006. *Multinationals and Corporate Social Responsibility: Limitations and Opportunities in International Law*. Cambridge: Cambridge University Press.

Ziganshina, Lilia and Joel Lexchin. 2010. "Regulation of Pharmaceutical Promotion: Why Does Regulation Matter?" In *Understanding and Responding to Pharmaceutical Promotion: A Practical Guide*, edited by Barbara Mintzes, Dee Mangin, and L. Hayes, 123–144. Amsterdam: Health Action International.

14
Global Health Funding Agencies
Developing New Institutions to Finance Health Needs

Sam Halabi and Lawrence O. Gostin

Introduction

The beginning of the 21st century witnessed a catastrophic increase in the toll that infectious diseases, particularly HIV, were imposing on the world's most vulnerable populations. The response to the HIV/AIDS pandemic took shape through both bilateral health assistance and the establishment of entirely new global agencies dedicated to funding global health efforts. Supporting health advancements in low-income countries, these new forms of governance included the creation of Gavi, the Vaccine Alliance (Gavi) in 2000 to continue the World Health Organization's (WHO) work to expand childhood immunization; the Global Fund to Fight AIDS, Tuberculosis and Malaria (Global Fund) in 2002; and the U.S. President's Emergency Plan for AIDS Relief (PEPFAR) in 2003. These were followed rapidly by the U.S. President's Malaria Initiative (PMI), the Coalition for Epidemic Preparedness Innovations (CEPI) to invest in the research and development of vaccines, and Unitaid to facilitate access to diagnostics, medicines, and other goods necessary for health systems' strengthening. The rise of these institutions of development assistance—both bilateral and multilateral—have resulted in a tidal wave of global funding for health—largely supporting the most vulnerable populations in the world.

These new global funding agencies have created an entirely new and complex system of laws, agreements, and understandings between governments, major international charities, private sector actors, and ground-level provider organizations. Law has become a critical aspect of these new financing agreements and governance partnerships in global health. As actors have increasingly looked to public-private partnerships (PPPs) to finance global health—bringing together a range of public, private, civil society, and other actors—these partnerships, bound together by legal agreements, have transformed the global health funding landscape. The contractual relationships between firms, governments, and health-oriented foundations serve as a new source of global health law.

This chapter traces the rise of funding agencies in global health governance, looking to these funding institutions as founded by legal agreements and as sources of new legal agreements across the global health landscape. Beginning in the establishment of early global health funding support through WHO, Part I analyzes how global health funding was long inadequate to meet major international health challenges, with subsequent bilateral efforts similarly falling short of global health needs. Part II looks to the rise of the modern and expanding landscape of global health funders, developed on the basis of contractual arrangements to meet pressing health needs, but facing criticism for their colonial foundations and current practices. Looking to the legal challenges faced by these funding agencies in the COVID-19 response, Part III identifies major new developments in PPPs and evolving efforts to improve their funding models to extend their role and influence. This chapter concludes that despite the growing number of funding institutions, the current legal framework addressing them is inadequate, raising a need to address health financing in ongoing global health law reforms.

I. The Rise of Funding Agencies in Global Health Governance

When WHO was established in 1946, its mission, as introduced in Chapter 3, was to lead global efforts to attain the highest attainable standard of mental and physical health for all people. This mission would require significant resources and support; however, WHO's budgetary limitations have never allowed it to pursue the expansive mission laid out in its Constitution (Reddy, Mazhar, and Lencucha 2018). These gaps in global health funding would lead to the rise of a robust buildup of global funding actors, including the Global Fund and Gavi, to support global health financing.

A. WHO's Early Funding

WHO has long faced constraints in its efforts to finance public health efforts across its expansive international health mandate. As WHO pursued disease eradication in its early years, as first discussed in Chapter 6, its ambitious effort to eradicate malaria demonstrated how resource scarcity constrained its hopeful ambitions. In 1955, the World Health Assembly established the Global Malaria Eradication Programme, aimed at eradicating a disease that killed hundreds of thousands per year—most of them in Africa and children living in poverty (Siddiqi 1995). Alongside this unprecedented eradication program, WHO established the Malaria Eradication Special Account to channel public and private contributions (Nájera et al. 2011). However, with this Programme premised on the wide use of insecticide, the sheer scale of the effort (along with the environmentally hazardous effects of the insecticide) caused WHO to permanently shelve the program—after fourteen years of enormous investments. Given that malaria represented only one global health challenge, it was clear that WHO could not, on its own, fund a global response to the world's major health threats necessary to meet its expansive mandate.

Nor could other international organizations play a significant role. The International Bank for Reconstruction and Development (the World Bank) was established to help European countries recover from the devastation of World War II; yet, as introduced in Chapter 11, it would become a crucial actor in health programming (Clinton and Sridhar 2017). Even as the World Bank came to play an increasing role in health funding, it was forced to use relatively blunt instruments to address public health. Under its chartering agreement, the World Bank may "guarantee, participate in, or make loans" to any member country, central bank, or "business, industrial, and agricultural enterprise in the territories of a member" under its mandate to end extreme poverty—not improve public health (Shawar and Prah Ruger 2018). Notwithstanding the relationship between health and poverty, the World Bank went long stretches investing in infrastructure having little to do with healthcare access or prevention-oriented public health investment.

With the 1980 eradication of smallpox, global health governance looked again to support vertical, disease-specific efforts to advance immunization. Global health funding—flowing largely through WHO, UNICEF, and the World Bank—shifted to focus on accelerating immunization and other basic interventions[1] against common diseases in lower-income countries, taking a "selective" approach to primary health care. This policy of "selective primary health care" attracted the support of donors, but was criticized for its narrow focus, vertical programming, and diversion of funding from comprehensive primary health care to address social determinants of health (Cueto 2004). Facing inadequate resources, efforts to expand global immunization against preventable childhood diseases stalled by the late 1980s. Amid these challenges facing global health funding, the global health landscape would be confronted with an unprecedented new threat that would require innovative new funding: HIV/AIDS.

---

[1] These basis services were later identified as GOBI: Growth monitoring, Oral rehydration techniques, Breast-feeding, and Immunization (Cueto 2004).

B. The Birth of Funding Agencies: The Global Fund

The explosion of HIV/AIDS cases worldwide, particularly in Africa, prompted an acknowledgment that a coordinated global commitment to funding in low- and middle-income countries was needed, leading to the establishment of the Global Fund to Fight AIDS, Tuberculosis and Malaria (Global Fund). The idea of a global fund dedicated to funding interventions to address the disproportionate burden of these three diseases was first discussed at the G8 Summit in Kyushu-Okinawa in 2000, with Japan's leadership fundamental to putting this discussion on the agenda. Through this G8 diplomacy, states reached a consensus that HIV/AIDS, tuberculosis, and malaria were threatening to "reverse decades of development and to rob an entire generation of hope for a better future" (Triponel 2009, 178–179). In 2001, during a special summit of the Organization of African Unity, African leaders voiced support for the creation of a global fund separate from WHO, with this support for a global health "war chest" finding strong support across the United Nations (UN).

Championed by UN Secretary General Kofi Annan, the 2001 UN General Assembly Special Session on AIDS, introduced in Chapter 2, called for the formal creation of the Global Fund. A Transitional Working Group was then created, bringing together forty representatives from international organizations, developing countries, donor countries, non-governmental organizations (NGOs), and the private sector to develop new structures and methods that could enable the Global Fund to utilize resources in the most cost-effective and productive ways (Youde 2012). As states, NGOs, and philanthropists began to pledge funding, the legal personality of the Global Fund rapidly took shape. While the Transitional Working Group initially considered an informal alliance with an existing organization, this proposal was ultimately rejected as:

(1) to enter into binding legal contracts, the Global Fund would need a separate legal personality;
(2) a separate, independent, formal organizational status would help promote public confidence; and
(3) the formal status would allow the Global Fund to receive other public and private source contributions (Triponel 2009).

The Transitional Working Group resolved to develop an independent legal entity, and the Global Fund was incorporated as a nonprofit under Swiss law and became operational in 2002.

The Global Fund's governing structure includes representatives of multiple nations and organizations, and it accepts donations and pledges from an even wider array of nations, private foundations, and private individuals. Rather than the state-led governance of international financing organizations, the Global Fund

Board is comprised of twenty voting members and eight non-voting members, with voting members including representatives from low- and middle-income countries, donors, civil society, and the private sector.[2] The eight non-voting members consist of the Board chair, the Board vice-chair, one WHO representative, one Joint United Nations Programme on HIV/AIDS (UNAIDS) representative, one representative from the Partners' constituency, one representative from the trustee of the Global Fund, one Swiss citizen authorized to act on behalf of the Global Fund to the extent required by Swiss law, and the Executive Director of the Global Fund. To give voice to these partners, the Global Fund created a Partnership Forum, with participation open to stakeholders that actively support the Fund's objectives (Jürgens et al. 2018).[3] The Global Fund became the leading funding agency in global health, administering national grants through contractual arrangements with national Country Coordinating Mechanisms (CCMs). Its diversified governance structure and CCM funding mechanism have created a model for inclusive partnerships that would be replicated as funding agencies rapidly proliferated across the global health landscape.

C. Funding Agencies Proliferate in Global Health

A proliferation of global funding agencies arose following the establishment of the Global Fund, as the PPP model of funding came to occupy much of the global health landscape. As seen in Gavi efforts to fund a revitalized focus on immunization, these new global health partnerships have taken a "vertical" or disease-specific approach to health financing, largely with a focus on access to medicines to treat or prevent targeted diseases.

1. Public-Private Funding Initiatives: Gavi, the Vaccine Alliance

PPPs work with governments—and are supported by them—but draw support from diverse streams and work with private sector actors who are often on-the-ground implementers of health support. In the last several decades, these PPP initiatives have proliferated largely because the private sector has been able to bring:

(1) funding and fundraising mechanisms,
(2) expertise and innovation, and
(3) inclusion of more diverse actors (Buse and Harmer 2007).

---

[2] Civil society and private sector representatives are further separated into one representative from each of the following: (1) an NGO from a developing country, (2) an NGO from a developed country, (3) the private sector, (4) a private foundation, and (5) an NGO representing persons living with HIV/AIDS, tuberculosis, or malaria.

[3] For example, in 2006, U2 lead singer Bono and Bobby Shriver partnered with the Global Fund to develop a campaign to fight the AIDS pandemic called "Product (RED)," which has raised hundreds of millions in corporate funds to support Global Fund efforts.

However, PPPs present challenges for global health governance, including potential conflicts of interest with private sector partners, duplication of mandates and dilution of resources among actors, and a focus on vertical programs to the exclusion of horizontal initiatives.

Emblematic of PPP governance, Gavi brings together both state and non-state actors, including manufacturers, to establish sustainable systems for vaccine procurement and distribution.

Case Study: The Development of Gavi

Supporting UNICEF efforts to prevent infant mortality, WHO established the Expanded Program on Immunization (EPI) in 1974 to deliver basic vaccines to children. By 1990, these WHO efforts, combined with UNICEF's Universal Childhood Immunization campaign, substantially raised immunization rates around the world—from 5% to 80% for the six EPI vaccines (tuberculosis, diphtheria, tetanus, pertussis, measles, and polio). However, immunization rates in low-income countries stagnated in the 1990s, as donor priorities shifted, governments struggled to maintain vaccination campaigns, and countries saw a dramatic drop-off in vaccination rates. Without funding mechanisms, pharmaceutical companies lacked the financial incentive to invest in the production and distribution of vaccines to the most vulnerable parts of the world. New vaccines were adopted widely for children in the United States and other high-income countries, but these innovations remained absent in low- and middle-income countries—with close to thirty million children in developing countries not fully immunized. In response to this global vaccine inequity, serious questions were raised about the future of international vaccination efforts. Amid these challenges, James Wolfensohn, head of the World Bank, convened the Vaccine Summit in 1998, bringing together WHO, UNICEF, independent academics, health ministers, international agencies, and the pharmaceutical industry. The agenda at the Summit was simple: to consider how to get vaccines to the children who needed them most. Later that year, Bill and Melinda Gates also hosted a gathering for scientists and scholars to discuss what could be done to overcome the barriers preventing millions of children from receiving essential vaccines. The hosts challenged their guests to come back with proposals for solutions. Led by UNICEF, and supported by the Bill & Melinda Gates Foundation, Gavi was established to complete the work commenced by EPI – to fund the delivery of basic vaccines to children.

In the rush to increase vaccine distribution, Gavi was formed in concept before a specific determination could be made about its legal personality and jurisdiction of incorporation. When Gavi was launched in 2000, it had two boards: The Board of the Global Alliance for Vaccine and Immunization and the Gavi Fund Board, which served as a fiduciary agent for the Alliance (Saul 2011). In 2008, these two boards merged to form the Gavi Alliance Board. The Gavi Alliance Board is now the supreme governing body and provides a forum for strategic decision-making, innovation, and partner collaboration. It consists of twenty-eight members, including representatives from donor and recipient states, the Bill and Melinda Gates Foundation, international organizations, vaccine manufacturers, civil society, and academia.

As with the Global Fund, low- and middle-income states identify their own needs in the context of immunization, apply for funding from Gavi, and implement approved vaccination programs (Lob-Levyt 2011). Gavi finances its programming in significant measure through international bond sales collateralized by promises of support from donor governments.[4] Donors then guarantee financing of eligible vaccines, with pharmaceutical firms guaranteeing an affordable price for the vaccines in participating countries. The relationships and responsibilities across the Gavi partnership are governed by contract, with significant influence on the firms that participate to ensure access to immunization for specific diseases.

2. Focus of Funding Agencies on Access to Medicines

Subsequent funding agencies have largely taken a "vertical" approach to global health financing, targeting specific diseases rather than health systems as a whole, with a focus on access to medicines to prevent or treat targeted diseases. This vertical funding approach is seen to allow for strong financial and operational control, focused and measurable objectives, and the ability to achieve goals within definable funding cycles (Cairncross, Periès, and Cutts 1997). Despite the importance of horizontal reforms to create sustainable health systems, the need for rapid funding results—along with the continuing allure of eradicating a disease—are often attractive to donors compared to long-term reforms to strengthen the health sector overall.

This vertical focus has prioritized access to medicines. The Global Fund, for example, invests heavily in access to antiretroviral therapies for HIV and oral antimalarials (Clinton and Sridhar 2017). Gavi brokers routine childhood immunizations with recipient governments, while only peripherally working to stockpile vaccines for emergencies. In bilateral funding, PEPFAR became the

---

[4] The bonds are issued by the International Finance Facility for Immunisation (IFFIm), legally an English charitable foundation, with the World Bank acting as IFFIm's treasury manager.

largest global health financing program devoted to a single disease, with a primary focus on access to antiretroviral treatment and pre-exposure prophylaxis (PrEP) for HIV (Schieber et al. 2007). Created by the U.S. government in 2003, PEPFAR consolidated all U.S. bilateral and multilateral funding and activities for HIV/AIDS, with several U.S. agencies, host country governments, and other public and private partners involved in implementation.

NGOs and civil society actors continued to push for this funding focus on access to medicines. This NGO advocacy was instrumental in deploying human rights litigation against the monopolistic practices of pharmaceutical corporations and raising an imperative for international funding for antiretrovirals, setting off rights-based action for greater access to essential medicines and catalyzing an unprecedented expansion of foreign assistance for access to antiretroviral therapies in the Global South (Meier and Yamin 2011). The participation of NGOs in global health policymaking has continued to shape the direction of global health law, as contracts between firms, governments, and international organizations internalize regulatory norms for global health funding (Halabi 2020).

II. The Development of Modern Funding Agencies

As WHO faced continuing resource strains, unable to address major health threats across the world, bilateral assistance and independent funding agencies would be born, including the Global Fund and Gavi. Faced with rising health emergencies, new threats would continue to give rise to new funding agencies. The current landscape of global health funding agencies would expand the purview of funding agencies in the global health landscape. However, the power wielded by these funders would highlight the lasting colonial nature of these agencies, with advocates pushing back against these agencies in an effort to decolonize global health.

A. Changes Wrought by Health Emergencies

Public health emergencies have spurred both the creation and the reform of financing mechanisms and institutions for global health. The faltering progress of international immunization programs in the late 1990s gave rise to Gavi to coordinate a public-private response to advance global health policy. Since then, the emergence of new disease threats has likewise led to the creation of additional agencies focused on preparing for and responding to new infectious diseases. Global health actors have regularly responded to health emergencies by creating new funding agencies—with narrower mandates and novel governance—rather than reforming existing agencies, leaving a loss of trust in those agencies to respond to future emergencies.

The West African Ebola epidemic, beginning in 2014, revealed gaps in preparedness, deployment time, and availability of biomedical countermeasures. Although Gavi quickly endorsed plans that would see up to $300 million committed to Ebola vaccines, this emergency funding would result in minimal stockpiles, limited research and development, and insufficient clinical data sharing (Gostin and Friedman 2015). As the epidemic worsened, a lack of timely and sufficient funds hindered the global response. By March 2015, Ebola was on track to cost $6 billion in direct expenses, which amounted to three years of funding for WHO, and over twenty times the cost of WHO's emergency response in its 2015–2016 budget (ibid.). Compounding this strain on international assistance, the affected states suffered from chronically underfunded health systems that limited their ability to respond in the absence of international assistance (Wenham 2017).[5] Subsequent studies on early funding flows for Ebola concluded that innovative financing models were needed to invest quickly to respond to infections with pandemic potential (Fitchett et al. 2016). To address this slow and inadequate funding, several financing initiatives were launched in the immediate aftermath of the Ebola epidemic, developing new financing mechanisms in WHO and the World Bank and leading to the creation of a new funding institution to invest in vaccine research.

To facilitate added funding from existing institutions, WHO rapidly developed new financing initiatives to address gaps in global health preparedness. The Contingency Fund for Emergencies (CFE) was established in 2015 by a resolution of the World Health Assembly. As an internal financing mechanism, the CFE would provide WHO with resources to rapidly respond to disease outbreaks and health emergencies—allocating up to $500,000 within 24 hours for events that constitute a significant global health threat (Ryan 2019). The WHO Director-General clarified that "The CFE has proved that a small investment at the right time can pay life-saving dividends and dramatically reduce the direct costs of controlling outbreaks and responding to emergencies" (WHO 2021). With greater capacity for investment in an emergency, the World Bank established the Pandemic Emergency Finance Facility in 2017 as an additional source of funding to help low-income countries respond to cross-border, large-scale outbreaks. This financing mechanism provides funding through either its cash or insurance window, with the cash window providing immediate financial support to

---

[5] Health systems across African states remained underfunded as a continuing impact of the structural adjustment programs of previous decades, which, as introduced in Chapter 11, placed loan conditionalities on states that required massive reductions in government expenditures (Kim 1999).

countries fighting outbreaks while the insurance window operates much like a typical insurance policy—donor countries pay premiums to provide insurance for the countries unable to, with the funds to be paid out when specific criteria are met for six covered diseases (World Bank 2019).

In developing a new PPP to prepare for future disease threats following the Ebola outbreak in West Africa, the Coalition for Epidemic Preparedness Innovations (CEPI) was launched at the 2017 World Economic Forum. States recognized that a coordinated, international, and intergovernmental plan was needed to develop and deploy new vaccines (Bernasconi et al. 2020). As reflected in Table 14.1, CEPI was designed to fill critical gaps in vaccine funding and implementation, with CEPI helping to further optimize resource allocation for vaccine development. CEPI's approach to strengthening global health security is threefold: (1) it supports early-stage vaccine development against known threats and establishes investigational vaccine stockpiles; (2) it funds and accelerates vaccine development and manufacture against unknown pathogens; and (3) it strengthens the global response to epidemics, particularly in high-risk countries, by advancing regulatory science and public policy. CEPI has dedicated nearly all of its investments to vaccine research and development; however, this mission has expanded through its early years (Gouglas et al. 2019).

Case Study: Mission Creep of CEPI

Although CEPI was initially formed to facilitate vaccine development for diseases like Ebola, for which development by the commercial market was unlikely or impossible, mission creep has seen the expansion of CEPI's work beyond its original goals. Whereas Gavi focuses on expanding access to decades-old vaccines like measles, mumps, and rubella, CEPI was established to support the development of the next generation of vaccines to address diseases that threatened to cause epidemics and pandemics. Its objectives were to build a portfolio of platform technologies to accelerate development, manufacturing, and testing of vaccines against "Disease X" (a designation given to an unknown pathogen), leading to vaccine development efforts for an expanding range of pathogens. Amid the COVID-19 pandemic, CEPI drastically expanded its collaborations to advance the development of COVID-19 vaccines. In April 2020, WHO launched the Access to COVID-19 Tools (ACT) Accelerator, a partnership to develop COVID-19 diagnostics, therapeutics, and vaccines. The ACT-Accelerator—seeking to facilitate access to COVID-19 diagnostics, therapeutics, and vaccines for low- and middle-income countries—created a forum where governments, scientists, businesses, civil society, philanthropists, and global health funding organizations could allocate

Table 14.1 Key Global Health Funding Agencies (Halabi and Gostin)

Funder	Year established	Governance including partners/actors	Priorities	Financing
Global Fund	2002	<ul><li>Board comprised of 20 voting members balanced between implementers and donors, including representatives from governments, NGOs, communities impacted by HIV/TB/malaria, foundations, the private sector, and 8 non-voting members from partner organizations including UNAIDS, WHO, and World Bank</li><li>Board provides strategy development, oversight, risk management</li><li>Marginalized populations involved in decision-making in country coordinating mechanisms (CCMs)</li></ul>	<ul><li>Fighting 3 priority diseases (AIDS, TB, and Malaria) through catalytic investments and innovation</li><li>Breaking down structural and human rights barriers to access to services for priority diseases</li><li>Has expanded into COVID-19 and Resilient and Sustainable Systems for Health</li><li>Implementing partners carry out Global Fund-supported programs</li></ul>	<ul><li>Uses results-based financing</li><li>Prioritizes lower-income countries, marginalized populations</li><li>Invests billions annually to fight 3 diseases; invests $1.5 billion annually into health systems</li><li>Private sector and non-government partners contribute funding, innovation, expertise, and advocacy</li><li>Government donors contribute funding, as well as being involved in governance</li></ul>
Gavi	2000	<ul><li>Board comprised of 28 members drawn from a range of partner organizations, as well as experts from the public sector</li><li>Partner organizations include WHO, UNICEF, World Bank, Gates Foundation, multilateral organizations, vaccine manufacturers, research and technical institutes, as well as individuals with expertise in investment and financing</li><li>Civil society engaged in service delivery, awareness-raising, outreach to remote populations</li></ul>	<ul><li>Uniting public and private sector with the shared goal of saving lives and protecting people's health by increasing equitable and sustainable use of vaccines</li><li>Supply and delivery of vaccines in lower-income countries</li><li>Health system strengthening to support immunization: health worker training, vehicles, cold chain equipment</li><li>Facilitates access to technical assistance through partners</li></ul>	<ul><li>Receives support from donors in five ways: direct funding, match funding that sustains corporate giving, long-term pledges to the International Finance Facility, long-term pledges to the Advance Market Commitment, and the loan buydown facility (a mechanism for Gavi to receive low-interest loans)</li><li>Alongside the Advanced Market Commitment (AMC) for pneumococcal vaccine, Gavi also launched the COVID-19 AMC for COVAX</li><li>International Finance Facility for Immunization (IFFIm), donor-backed vaccine bonds sold on capital markets</li></ul>

(continued)

Table 14.1 Continued

Funder	Year established	Governance including partners/actors	Priorities	Financing
CEPI	2016	• Board comprised of 12 voting members, four investors, and eight independent members representing competencies including industry, global health, science, resource mobilization, finance—also includes five non-voting observers • Diverse leadership drawing from international organizations, NGOs, academia, and the private sector; founders were Norway, India, Gates Foundation, Wellcome, World Economic Forum • Has faced criticism for lack of civil society and low- and middle-income country representation, lack of transparency in private sector contracts	• Accelerate the development of countermeasures against epidemic and pandemic threats • Focus on WHO R&D Blueprint priority diseases, which include COVID-19, Ebola, MERS-CoV, and "Disease X" • Support activities to improve pandemic response	• Investors include USAID, UN Foundation, Nestlé, European Commission, Gates Foundation, and over two dozen countries • Investors council comprised of those contributing to CEPI's funding pool; council nominates representatives to the board and has rights to approve investments over $100 million

responsibility and resources in a coordinated (if not perfectly efficient) way. Under the ACT-Accelerator, CEPI established new partnerships, funding dozens of vaccine developers and manufacturers. These collaborations have led CEPI to take increasing responsibility for regulatory approval and negotiation with manufacturers, roles previously played by its partners, investing in vaccine technology platforms at various universities and private partners and rapidly creating the world's largest portfolio of COVID-19 vaccines. These early experiences in the COVID-19 response vastly expanded CEPI's mission, leading it to become a major player in the funding and implementation of all stages of vaccine development, manufacturing, and deployment. Yet despite its expansive role, CEPI is just one of several financing agencies with increasing influence and impact on global health.

B. Proliferation of Funding Agencies

Global health challenges compel collective action across borders and organizations, leading to new types of funding partnerships involving governments, NGOs, intergovernmental organizations, and the private sector. The proliferation of such funding partnerships has dramatically increased the resources available to tackle key global health threats; however, the expanding purview of funding agencies has created further complications across an already crowded global health landscape.

The proliferation and remarkable growth of global health funding partnerships has been driven largely by the unprecedented new financing provided by philanthropic foundations such as the Gates Foundation, Rockefeller Foundation, and Wellcome Trust, which are responsible for a sizable proportion of financing for several partnerships (Hesselmann 2011). Most significant among these is the Gates Foundation, with five of the top eleven recipients of grants from the Gates Foundation (1998–2007) going to funding partnerships: Gavi Alliance, the Global Fund, the Medicines for Malaria Venture, the International AIDS Vaccine Initiative, and the Global Alliance for TB Drug Development. The Gates Foundation remains a significant funder for every major funding partnership.

While the expanding number of partnerships has led to more flexibility and innovation in addressing health issues that transcend national boundaries, this proliferation of funders has come with a lack of coordination across institutions. These funding agencies are seeing expanding missions, yet there is insufficient monitoring and evaluation to measure the effectiveness of these partnerships (Buse and Harmer 2007). In efforts to seek accountability for good governance across

PPPs, there are often information and power asymmetries between actors involved in a partnership, particularly between governments, the private sector, and civil society organizations (Ciccone 2010). As demonstrated by the creation of the Global Fund, which includes non-state actors along with states on its governing board, the Global Fund's CCMs have not always adequately involved civil society, with participatory processes often facing obstacles to purposeful engagement, such as lack of funds to travel to meetings and relevant information (Bartsch 2007).[6]

The proliferation of financing actors has presented core challenges for global health governance.

(1) Poor governance – While some global health funders like the Global Fund have pioneered equitable governance structures (by reserving seats on their governing bodies for representatives of civil society organizations and affected communities), others have reserved governing power in the hands of a few wealthy actors. Without good governance, funders face a lack of clarity in the roles and responsibilities of their partners, lack of accountability for private sector partners, and lack of transparency in decision-making (Gostin and Mok 2009).

(2) Power asymmetries – The proliferation of global health funders can obscure how power within each of them manifests, with unequal power dynamics influencing financing decisions (Kentikelenis and Rochford 2019). Bringing together powerful partners in the Global North, PPPs can pose conflict-of-interest concerns with private sector partners or entrench the charity-based model for the distribution of critical resources to low- and middle-income nations and marginalized communities.

(3) Funding duplication – Poor harmonization among global health funders can lead to a duplication of mandates, activities, and resources, including between PPPs and their own constituent partners (Buse and Tanaka 2011). Transparency within and across PPPs can seek to combat duplication, avoid redundancies, and facilitate coordination where mandates align.

(4) Resource competition – The proliferation of global health funders creates competition for resources from scarce donors, as traditional actors and new partnerships all request support from the same foundations and governments. There remains no system in place to rationalize or coordinate where funders direct their funds, leaving it to the global funding agencies to make their best case for investing in themselves without concern for funding equity, disease burden, or country demand.

---

[6] As with CEPI, this lack of coordination was exemplified during the COVID-19 pandemic, as Gavi, long established to facilitate immunizations in low- and middle-income countries, was quickly tasked with vaccine development and therapeutic identification, something for which it lacked both the mandate and expertise.

While these new funding agencies have greatly expanded the resource pool for global health priorities, their growing influence over the global health agenda, particularly in the Global South, threatens to replicate colonial structures in global health.

C. Critique of Funding Agencies as "Colonial"

Beyond concerns for the inefficiency and ineffectiveness of funding agencies, these funding approaches have been criticized for extending colonial dynamics in global health—raising calls to reform funding agencies to "decolonize" global health. Global health, as first introduced in Chapter 1, has evolved from colonial and tropical medicine, which were initially "designed to control colonized populations and make political and economic exploitation by European and North American powers easier" (Khan et al. 2021, 1). Given the power differentials in global health funding, there are rising concerns that current funding agencies serve the same role, using financing dynamics in place of formal colonial subjugation (Sirleaf 2018).[7] The overwhelming allocation of institutional funding is based in the Global North, imposing conditions on the Global South in ways that fortify control of the global health policy agenda while perpetuating reliance of low- and middle-income countries on the charity of the rich. CEPI, Gavi, and the Global Fund were all formed or funded in significant part at the World Economic Forum, an elite gathering of the world's richest governments and companies at their gatherings in Davos, a Swiss town wildly out of financial reach for almost all of the world. These agencies are supported in large part by allocations from donors within the Global North—and the wealthiest individuals in the world.

The locus of activity of funding agencies also remains in the Global North. CEPI is a Norwegian legal entity with main offices in London and Oslo and a presence in Washington, D.C. It has specifically disavowed "constituency-based" governance, although it is conscientious of its role in facilitating equitable access to vaccines, especially with respect to its Equitable Access Policy and the Equitable Access Committee (Usher 2022).[8] Gavi is similarly based in Geneva

---

[7] Where countries in the Global North are rightly concerned about global health security, this securitization of global health is often seen to replicate colonial medicine, where global health security is historically linked to the efforts of colonial powers to protect their own populations from diseases endemic to their colonial territories while expanding and securing their interests in those territories. This dynamic can impact funding allocation and response measures. The 2014 West African Ebola epidemic received international attention, in part because it threatened the health security in the Global North, whereas prior Ebola outbreaks in Africa, which were not seen as threatening global health security, garnered little international attention (Karan 2020).

[8] Correspondingly, CEPI has secured an overwhelming share of its financing from the Global North—USAID, the Gates Foundation, the European Commission, Canada, Denmark, and over a dozen other countries and private sector entities in the Global North.

and Washington, D.C., while the Global Fund operates almost exclusively out of Geneva, even as its country coordinating mechanisms are local. Compounding the inequities in the governance of funding agencies, many of the contractors and consultants used by these organizations are based in Europe and North America, leaving these organizations susceptible to the allegation that, in the name of serving the world's most vulnerable, they enrich those who already have plenty. Such an allegation is oversimplistic, but it raises an imperative for dialogue on how the movement to decolonize global health might reframe funding dynamics.

Given these ties to the Global North, funding agencies are often perceived as providing a form of charity—with affluent institutions that support the poorest countries in a donor-recipient relationship—there is a debate about whether international assistance should be considered a form of charity at all – or instead a legal obligation. The United Nations Charter includes among its goals the achievement of "international cooperation in solving international problems of an economic, social, cultural and humanitarian character" (UN 1945, art. 1). The International Covenant on Economic, Social and Cultural Rights (ICESCR), the International Health Regulations, and numerous UN treaties likewise proclaim a duty of international cooperation, with the right to health, introduced in Chapter 4, providing a moral and legal duty to support global health (Gostin and Archer 2007). Nevertheless, disagreement arises about the extent to which this obligation implies the specific provision of funding resources, prioritizing international assistance over international cooperation (Khamdamova and Tashev 2017). Even when assuming that assistance is required, as the plain language of the ICESCR indicates ("international assistance and co-operation"), there remains the question of the level of financial assistance required.

In seeking to establish new normative frameworks to guide international assistance, many global institutions began work over the past decade to "decolonize" global health. These decolonization efforts have sought to reframe global health financing models from a post-colonial perspective – promoting health equity, social justice, and human rights as guiding principles. Gavi and the Global Fund have worked to integrate greater community representation on their boards. CEPI's most recent board additions acknowledge the importance of decolonizing its governance, as it has begun to develop policies prioritizing the research and development of vaccines for diseases that disproportionately impact poor communities and underrepresented populations. Even so, colonial structures remain in funding agencies. Facing the rising challenges of COVID-19, new funding structures were rapidly created, with these novel institutions developed by a group of advisors comprised primarily of Global North philanthropists, academics, and consultants, and absent any feedback or meaningful representation from low- and middle-income countries and regional institutions (Elder 2022). Amid these continuing pandemic funding challenges, there remains a need to decolonize funding institutions and provide greater equity in the distribution of funds.

III. Continuing Challenges of Funding Institutions

Ongoing disease threats have shifted the landscape of global funding agencies such that their roles are now less distinct, the necessity for them to coordinate with one another is more pronounced, and they are increasingly central to public health emergency planning and response. Where once WHO played a convening role, PPPs have proliferated in response to COVID-19, bringing together governments, private corporations, researchers, and philanthropic organizations in ways that are no longer coordinated in global health governance. Global health law provides a path to revisit the expanding global health financing structures to ensure greater coordination of actors and actions.

A. Changes Wrought by COVID-19

COVID-19 led to fundamental changes to the global health landscape of international funding agencies. An effective response to the COVID-19 pandemic demanded a wide range of rapid actions: research and development for medical countermeasures, manufacturing capacity, regulatory approvals, market commitments, and distribution arrangements. Recognizing the shared health risk to all countries and the benefits of collective action, public, private, and philanthropic organizations started working together to establish new PPPs (Stein 2021). In framing the need for unprecedented funding and global coordination, WHO, UNICEF, the World Bank, CEPI, the Salk Institute, and the Gates Foundation came together to create a public health emergency "superagency." This superagency, or super-PPP, has sought to align multiple existing PPPs and funding agencies – working together in an alliance alongside multilateral organizations, governments, and private corporations. Creating such a superagency has been challenging, however, because the different agencies may not be perfectly adapted to this new purpose, requiring an expansion of their respective missions (Storeng, de Bengy Puyvallée, and Stein 2021).

The ACT-Accelerator is comprised of four "pillars": the Diagnostic Pillar supported by the Foundation for Innovative New Diagnostics (FIND) and the Global Fund; the Therapeutics Pillar supported by Unitaid and Wellcome Trust; the Health Systems Pillar supported by the World Bank, Global Fund, and WHO; and the Vaccine Pillar supported by Gavi, CEPI, and WHO. This

Figure 14.1 Delivery of COVID-19 Vaccine from COVAX (WHO)

vaccine pillar became known as "COVAX." While it is not strictly speaking a new global health funding agency—as it has no independent legal existence apart from the tacit agreement between its partners to work together—COVAX has brought together co-leads and implementing partners' efforts to finance the selection, procurement, and delivery, as seen in Figure 14.1, of COVID-19 vaccines throughout the world. CEPI, Gavi, and WHO serve as co-leads of COVAX, with each actor assigned its own workstream, and look to UNICEF as an implementing partner.[9]

The COVAX Advance Market Commitment (AMC), overseen by Gavi, serves as the principal financing mechanism to incentivize the manufacture of large volumes of vaccines, with the funding coming from contributions to COVAX from high-income countries and enabling equal treatment of lower-income countries to receive vaccines for free (Usher 2020). COVAX was intended to represent a bargain: high-income "self-financing" governments would contribute monetarily toward the cost of a global vaccine distribution system and enter into advanced purchase agreements with COVAX to purchase a predefined number of doses for their own populations, covering the costs of these vaccines themselves. These self-financing governments would also commit to numerous other financial and non-financial obligations, such as supporting the delivery of vaccines in AMC eligible countries, fast-track licensure of vaccines, reporting all epidemiological and virological data, and maintaining transparency about all bilateral vaccine agreements. While placing obligations on high-income countries,

---

[9] In the Americas, WHO's regional office, the Pan American Health Organization (PAHO), also serves as an implementing partner, with the PAHO Revolving Fund recognized as a procurement agent for COVAX.

COVAX also sought to benefit high-income countries, providing access to a diverse candidate vaccine portfolio (which CEPI had largely assembled through its pre-pandemic investments) and thereby seeking to create a higher probability that high-income countries would be able to access successful candidate vaccines (Kremer, Levin, and Snyder 2022). For these self-financing countries, COVAX would serve as an insurance policy, enhancing a state's probability of securing doses of effective vaccine as compared with bilateral agreements with each vaccine manufacturer.[10] For low-income countries unable to otherwise afford necessary vaccines, procurement agreements for these ninety-two "donor-supported" countries (the so-called AMC92) would be funded largely through official development assistance and contributions from the private sector and philanthropy, with vaccines allocated at a subsidized cost. These procurement agreements to pay for vaccines—across high-, middle-, and low-income countries—would seek to provide COVAX with the commitments and resources to purchase vaccines from manufacturers and distribute them equitably.

However, this elaborate architecture aimed at burden sharing and health equity fell far short of its target. Despite the unpreceded speed at which safe and efficacious vaccines were developed and authorized for emergency use, vaccination rates continued to lag in low-income countries, as wealthy governments and major vaccine manufacturers, in spite of commitments to COVAX, struck bilateral deals that undermined COVAX and denied vaccine access to most of the world. Vaccine nationalism has challenged COVAX efforts to raise funds from wealthy donors and procure vaccines for vulnerable populations (Eccleston-Turner and Upton 2021).

Case Study: Challenges for COVAX Funding in the COVID-19 Response

Despite its novel funding mechanism, COVAX has not met its aims in the COVID-19 response. COVAX was supposed to work through up-front commitments by both "self-financing" and "AMC92" governments and through voluntary commitments by wealthy donor governments. High-income countries could enter into optional purchase agreements with COVAX that would give them the option to opt in or out of certain vaccine arrangements without endangering their ability to receive other products. In spite of these contingencies, little of what was initially envisioned materialized,

---

[10] For the vast majority of the world's governments, even among high-income nations, bilateral procurement was out of reach due to the high financial burdens.

as nationalist actions undermined global health funding. Some governments, like France and Germany, agreed to financially support COVAX but would not buy vaccines through the COVAX program, rather opting to procure vaccines either through a European Union purchasing scheme or bilateral agreements. Until 2021, the United States rejected COVAX entirely, refusing to be constrained by multilateral organizations but has since sought to contribute financially to the organization—even as it has struggled to amend its agreements to donate its own excess doses to COVAX or to those countries in need. Without additional funds from high-income countries, COVAX lacked the flexibility to purchase additional vaccines. Despite concerted efforts from low-income nations and global health advocates, COVAX was ultimately prevented from acquiring the vaccines it had committed to supply due to the hoarding of vaccines and the failure of financial support. Falling billions of dollars behind expectations, COVAX has been unable to adapt to uncertainties around the coronavirus's evolution, including the need for repeated doses of booster shots and vaccines for new variants; the infrastructures to support readiness among lower-income countries to receive and deliver vaccines; and the additional costs of rollouts, such as those for syringes, transport, and no-fault compensation insurance.

Despite these continuing challenges to vaccine equity, COVAX has been an essential funding source in helping balance global inequities in vaccine allocation and distribution. Without COVAX's aid, many countries would have struggled to access COVID-19 vaccines entirely (Storeng, de Bengy Puyvallée, and Stein 2021). Among AMC countries, those with the lowest income experienced greater benefits than wealthier ones in terms of how many vaccines they received from COVAX, evincing that, for all its shortcomings, COVAX did make a significant contribution to the global distribution of COVID-19 vaccines—and will be looked at as a model for health equity in future emergencies (Vogel 2022). However, amid a rapidly changing global health funding landscape, reforms beyond COVAX will be necessary to ensure collaborative financing in facing future threats.

B. Changing Landscape

A wide range of global funding institutions came together to respond to the COVID-19 pandemic, but due to inadequate financing and other factors, the response was not what it could—or should—have been. In preparing for future funding challenges in global health emergencies, reforms will be needed to support swift and resilient collaboration between funding agencies.

1. Push for Increased Funding

There are a finite number of wealthy governments and major foundations with the ability to fund global health responses. Spurred by WHO's central role in responding to COVID-19 and the growing risks of pandemics that COVID-19 underscored, WHO Member States agreed to increased mandatory contributions to WHO. This 2022 decision by the World Health Assembly, first introduced in Chapter 5, would support an increase in assessed contributions from Member States in ways that will double WHO funding in the coming years. The decision to increase assessed contributions to WHO is significant, as it would grant the agency greater flexibility and control over its own agenda, freeing it from reliance on voluntary contributions usually earmarked to donors' priorities and enabling it to direct financing toward critically underfunded global health concerns (Finch et al. 2022). Yet these reforms within WHO are only the beginning of what is needed to ensure funding across the global health landscape.

It will be necessary to develop more sophisticated and robust global health financing instruments across institutions of global economic governance. The World Bank pandemic bonds, issued through the Pandemic Emergency Financing Facility (PEF), sought to facilitate financing in a pandemic response, but, as discussed in Chapter 11, were plagued with shortcomings and delayed payouts—exhausting funds early in the COVID-19 response. In building from these limited efforts, the World Bank in 2022 established a new financial intermediary fund (FIF) for pandemic prevention, preparedness, and response (PPR). The FIF aims to provide a committed stream of additional, long-term financing to bankroll PPR operations in low- and middle-income countries, addressing critical gaps at the national, regional, and global levels. The FIF has pooled funds in initial pledges from a range of countries, including G20 nations, as well as foundations, with the FIF looking to its Governing Board to help mobilize the fund and develop priorities leading up to the first call for proposals (Reid-Henry et al. 2022). The FIF's Governing Board will contain equal representation of governments of wealthier countries that will fund FIF and potential implementing country governments, as well as representatives from foundations and civil society organizations. With technical support from WHO,[11] this new Fund intends to avail itself of the advantages of key institutions already engaged in PPR, provide technical support, improve coordination among partners, incentivize further investments, support advocacy, and address crucial health system gaps (World Bank and WHO 2022).

---

[11] The Secretariat, while hosted at the World Bank, will include technical staff from the WHO. The Governing Board will appoint a Technical Advisory Panel, chaired by WHO and comprising leading experts, to evaluate and make recommendations on the technical merits of proposals for funding and to ensure linkages to the International Health Regulations.

Beyond state support, wealthy philanthropists and their foundations are leveraging their vast resources to fund global health initiatives, including providing significant financing for PPPs. These foundations—notably the Bill and Melinda Gates Foundation, the Rockefeller Foundation, the Wellcome Trust, and Bloomberg Philanthropies—have long played a role in funding global health, as introduced in Chapter 3; yet the increasing contributions of these foundations to global health funders has necessarily come with a degree of control over those funders' activities. The Gates Foundation, for instance, prioritizes funding for technical solutions to global health challenges, while being a vocal advocate for strong intellectual property protections over lifesaving pandemic products. While philanthropic contributions are almost always earmarked to priorities that align with the foundations' missions, these philanthropic foundations remain crucial partners in increasing financing for global health. New global health law and policy instruments present opportunities to hold those foundations to the same standards of good governance as public entities, and with the creation of new funding mechanisms to face uncertain challenges, it will be crucial to look to global health law and policy instruments to coordinate funding agencies.

2. Need for Greater Coordination

These changes amid the pandemic response may be a harbinger of an even greater competition for resources among funding agencies—as the missions of agencies expand and increasingly overlap. CEPI has already announced "2.0" and "100 day" initiatives, which seek increased contributions from stakeholders to support a supply chain and delivery infrastructure focus (Usher 2022). Gavi is making its case to governments and bondholders that increased funding is necessary for it to play a greater role in expanding access not only to routine immunizations but also to novel ones that may have a significant benefit for population health in low- and middle-income countries. Meanwhile, with the setbacks that COVID-19 has created in combating longstanding diseases like tuberculosis and malaria, the funding needs of other agencies, including the Global Fund, look to grow in the years to come. These overlapping mandates and resource competitions are continuing to unfold even as new funding agencies like FIF emerge.

The ACT-Accelerator and COVAX demonstrated what is possible through greater coordination, although it also demonstrated important limitations of inter-agency partnerships. CEPI and Gavi, for example, possess significant areas where synergies are ascertainable. CEPI has many of the most important agreements in place for new vaccines, while Gavi's infrastructure for procurement and distribution is over twenty years old and integrates important partners like WHO and UNICEF (Excler et al. 2022). Formal understandings and agreements between these international organizations, perhaps as part of the broader pandemic preparedness movement that will accompany the development of a prospective "pandemic treaty" under WHO, could cement the normative development of global health financing in order to ensure that funding for essential medicines and the healthcare systems in which they are housed is sustainable, equitable, and redistributive.

Global health law could begin to address the imperatives for coordination in global health financing. New legal instruments, from a pandemic treaty and World Health Assembly resolutions to PPP contracts, can create pathways for increased financing, establishing a "global medical war chest" (Gostin 2021). Legal instruments hold the unique power to align global health funders with a common set of norms and objectives. Global health law could lead to the creation of agencies, like an expanded permanent mechanism for equitable distribution of medical countermeasures during health emergencies, with rules that limit separate purchase agreements that hinder the mechanism's effectiveness. It could even include a framework for how countries allocate funds, with agreed principles for equity, that may at least modestly ease competition among agencies (Gostin, Moon, and Meier 2020). And critically, it could enhance monitoring and reporting, paving the way for greater accountability in global health funding.

Conclusion

The COVID-19 pandemic has highlighted the need to form multilayered and multifaceted funding frameworks for cooperation among diverse stakeholders, particularly with a new and growing number of funding agencies seeking to promote public health in a globalizing world. Just as the establishment of the Global Fund and Gavi heralded major breakthroughs against HIV/AIDS, malaria, tuberculosis, and preventable childhood diseases, CEPI, Unitaid, and coordinating mechanisms like the ACT-Accelerator will herald major strides in preparedness and response for future global health threats. The ACT-Accelerator, as a super-PPP, is a particularly powerful example of coordination, bringing together different actors in global health, themselves governed by and partnering with numerous governments and organizations, into a common cause; however, the limitations of COVAX highlight the challenges of such funding agreements that lack binding legal commitments. Funding agencies are crucially necessary in global health governance, but they are facing unprecedented challenges and will need to adapt dramatically to be as prepared and flexible as possible for new challenges.

Global health law remains inadequate to support funding institutions. Where international law is state-centric, today's global health landscape is comprised of diverse and varied partnerships of states and non-state actors, ranging from programs hosted by international organizations to distinct legal institutions such as the Global Fund. These global funding agencies require sufficient funding to achieve their critical and expanding missions, but they also require normative frameworks with binding obligations. Binding legal obligations could transform the model of global health funding from one that relies on charity to one that achieves equity. Funding agencies must work together to develop an overarching approach to responding to competing agencies and needs, to direct funds where they are most needed, to ensure that funding agencies are accountable to the people they are supposed to benefit, and to ensure adequate financing.

Reforms to funding models will continue to develop, raising an imperative to find new ways and mechanisms in global health law to ensure that funding agencies are able to continue their important work to promote global health, but with sufficient funding and greater coordination and accountability, all while prioritizing global health equity. Innovative approaches will be necessary to bind together funding partnerships under global health law. In these law reforms, funding agencies can look to embedding contract law in agreements between states and non-state actors and soft law instruments that could directly incorporate global agencies. The COVID-19 pandemic has presented a unique opportunity for truly transformative reforms to the global health financing landscape through law. Incorporating funding agencies under global health law will be crucial to ensuring sustainable global health funding.

Questions for Consideration

1. Why were states long resistant to funding disease eradication initiatives through WHO? Why was the World Bank unable to serve this funding role?
2. What were the advantages of creating a single independent funding agency to coordinate funding for AIDS, tuberculosis, and malaria? How does the Global Fund bring together state and non-state actors in funding decisions?
3. How does Gavi incentivize the pharmaceutical industry to develop vaccines for low-income countries? Why do PPPs prioritize disease-specific initiatives and respond through access to medicines?
4. How was funding inadequate to meet the needs of the West African Ebola response? Why do donors often respond to health emergencies by creating new funding agencies—rather than reforming existing institutions?
5. What did CEPI offer that existing funding agencies did not? How has the COVID-19 response led to "mission creep" in CEPI governance?

6. How has the proliferation and growth of PPPs challenged coordination in global health financing? How has the proliferation of PPPs complicated the availability of resources for global health?
7. How do funding agencies reproduce colonial dynamics in global health? What reforms of funding agencies would support efforts to decolonize global health?
8. Why was a "super-PPP" necessary to respond to COVID-19? How did COVAX seek to ensure benefits to both high-income and low-income countries in procuring vaccines? How did vaccine nationalism undermine COVAX efforts to ensure vaccine equity?
9. How will the rise of new funding agencies in the COVID-19 response further complicate global health financing? How can global health law reforms strengthen coordination across funding agencies?

Acknowledgments

The authors greatly appreciate the research assistance and editorial support of Alexandra Finch, Chris Burch, and Ryan Doerzbacher.

References

Bartsch, Sonja. 2007. "The Global Fund to Fight AIDS, Tuberculosis and Malaria." In *Global Health Governance and the Fight Against HIV/AIDS*, edited by Wolfgang Hein, Sonja Bartsch, and Lars Kohlmorgen, 146–171. London: Palgrave Macmillan UK.

Bernasconi, Valentina, Paul A. Kristiansen, Mike Whelan, Raúl Gómez Román, Alison Bettis, Solomon Abebe Yimer, Céline Gurry et al. 2020. "Developing Vaccines against Epidemic-Prone Emerging Infectious Diseases." *Bundesgesundheitsblatt - Gesundheitsforschung - Gesundheitsschutz* 63(1): 65–73.

Buse, Kent and Sonja Tanaka. 2011. "Global Public-Private Health Partnerships: Lessons Learned from Ten Years of Experience and Evaluation." *International Dental Journal* 61: 2–10.

Buse, Kent and Andrew M. Harmer. 2007. "Seven Habits of Highly Effective Global Public–Private Health Partnerships: Practice and Potential." *Social Science & Medicine* 64(2): 259–271.

Cairncross, Sandy, Hervé Periès, and Felicity Cutts. 1997. "Vertical Health Programmes." *Lancet* 349 (June): S20–21.

Ciccone, Dana Karen. 2010. "Arguing for a Centralized Coordination Solution to the Public-Private Partnership Explosion in Global Health." *Global Health Promotion* 17(2): 48–51.

Clinton, Chelsea and Devi Lalita Sridhar. 2017. *Governing Global Health: Who Runs the World and Why?* Oxford: Oxford University Press.

Cueto, Marcos. 2004. "The ORIGINS of Primary Health Care and SELECTIVE Primary Health Care." *American Journal of Public Health* 94(11): 1864–7184.

Eccleston-Turner, Mark and Harry Upton. 2021. "International Collaboration to Ensure Equitable Access to Vaccines for COVID-19: The ACT-Accelerator and the COVAX Facility." *Milbank Quarterly* 99(2): 426–449.

Elder, Kate. 2022. "COVAX: A Broken Promise for Vaccine Equity." *Doctors without Borders*, February 21.

Excler, Jean-Louis, Lois Privor-Dumm, Peter Hotez, Dame Sarah Gilbert, Didi Thompson, Salim Abdool Karim, Soumya Swaminathan, and Jerome H. Kim. 2022. *A New Era for Vaccine Innovation: Harnessing the Lessons Learned from COVID-19*. Doha: World Innovation Summit for Health.

Finch, Alexandra, Kevin A. Klock, Eric A. Friedman, and Lawrence O. Gostin. 2022. "At Long Last, WHO Member States Agree to Fix Its Financing Problem." *Think Global Health*, June 1.

Fitchett, Joseph R. A., Amos Lichtman, Damilola T Soyode, Ariel Low, Jimena Villar de Onis, Michael G. Head, and Rifat Atun. 2016. "Ebola Research Funding: A Systematic Analysis, 1997–2015." *Journal of Global Health* 6(2): 020703.

Gostin, Lawrence O. and Emily A. Mok. 2009. "Grand Challenges in Global Health Governance." *British Medical Bulletin* 90(1): 7–18.

Gostin, Lawrence O. and Eric A Friedman. 2015. "A Retrospective and Prospective Analysis of the West African Ebola Virus Disease Epidemic: Robust National Health Systems at the Foundation and an Empowered WHO at the Apex." *Lancet* 385(9980): 1902–1909.

Gostin, Lawrence O. 2021. *Global Health Security: A Blueprint for the Future*. Cambridge: Harvard University Press.

Gostin, Lawrence O. and Robert Archer. 2007. "The Duty of States to Assist Other States in Need: Ethics, Human Rights, and International Law." *Journal of Law, Medicine & Ethics* 35(4): 526–533.

Gostin, Lawrence O., Suerie Moon, and Benjamin Mason Meier. 2020. "Reimagining Global Health Governance in the Age of COVID-19." *American Journal of Public Health* 110(11): 1615–1619.

Gouglas, Dimitrios, Mario Christodoulou, Stanley A Plotkin, and Richard Hatchett. 2019. "CEPI: Driving Progress Toward Epidemic Preparedness and Response." *Epidemiologic Reviews* 41(1): 28–33.

Halabi, Sam F. 2020. "The Origins and Future of Global Health Law: Regulation, Security, and Pluralism." *Georgetown Law Journal* 108: 1607–1654.

Hesselmann, Elena. 2011. "The Limits of Control: The Accountability of Foundations and Partnerships in Global Health." In *Partnerships and Foundations in Global Health Governance*, edited by Simon Rushton and Owain David Williams, 228–252. London: Palgrave Macmillan UK.

Jürgens, Ralf, Joanne Csete, Hyeyoung Lim, Susan Timberlake, and Matthew Smith. 2018. "The Global Fund to Fight AIDS, Tuberculosis and Malaria Funding Basic Services and Meeting the Challenge of Rights-Based Programs." In *Human Rights in Global Health*, edited by Benjamin Mason Meier and Lawrence O. Gostin. 421-440. New York: Oxford University Press.

Karan, Abraar. 2020. "How Should Global Health Security Priorities Be Set in the Global North and West?" *AMA Journal of Ethics* 22(1): E50–54.

Kentikelenis, Alexander and Connor Rochford. 2019. "Power Asymmetries in Global Governance for Health: A Conceptual Framework for Analyzing the Political-Economic Determinants of Health Inequities." *Globalization and Health* 15(S1): 70.

Khan, Mishal, Seye Abimbola, Tammam Aloudat, Emanuele Capobianco, Sarah Hawkes, and Afifah Rahman-Shepherd. 2021. "Decolonising Global Health in 2021: A Roadmap to Move from Rhetoric to Reform." *BMJ Global Health* 6(3): e005604.

Khamdamova, Firuza and Farrukh Tashev. 2017. "International Cooperation and Assistance as a Legal Human Rights Obligation of States." *Journal of Law Research* 8: 3–16.

Kim, Jim Yong. 1999. *Dying for Growth: Global Inequality and the Health of the Poor*. Monroe: Common Courage Press.

Kremer, Michael, Jonathan Levin and Christopher M. Snyder. 2022. "Designing Advance Market Commitments for New Vaccines." *Management Science* 68 (7): 4786–4814.

Lob-Levyt, Julian. 2011. "Contribution of the GAVI Alliance to Improving Health and Reducing Poverty." *Philosophical Transactions of the Royal Society B: Biological Sciences* 366(1579): 2743–2747.

Meier, Benjamin Mason, and Alicia Ely Yamin. 2011. "Right to Health Litigation and HIV/AIDS Policy." *Journal of Law, Medicine & Ethics* 39(S1): 81–84.

Nájera, José A., Matiana González-Silva, and Pedro L. Alonso. 2011. "Some Lessons for the Future from the Global Malaria Eradication Programme (1955–1969)." *PLoS Medicine* 8(1): e1000412.

Reddy, Srikanth K., Sumaira Mazhar, and Raphael Lencucha. 2018. "The Financial Sustainability of the World Health Organization and the Political Economy of Global Health Governance: A Review of Funding Proposals." *Globalization and Health* 14(1): 119.

Reid-Henry, Simon, Jon Lidén, Christoph Benn, Diah Saminarsih, Olivia Herlinda, and María Fernanda Bustos Venegas. 2022. "A New Paradigm Is Needed for Financing the Pandemic Fund." *Lancet* 400(10349): 345–346.

Ryan, Michael J. 2019. "Partnerships for Global Health Security: WHO Health Emergencies Programme and the Republic of Korea." *Journal of Global Health Science* 1(1): e15.

Saul, Allen. 2011. "Vaccines for Neglected Diseases." In *Vaccine Design: Innovative Approaches and Novel Strategies*, edited by Rino Pappuoli and Fabio Bagnoli. 243–252. UK: Caister Academic Press.

Schieber, George J., Pablo Gottret, Lisa K. Fleisher, and Adam A. Leive. 2007. "Financing Global Health: Mission Unaccomplished." *Health Affairs* 26(4): 921–934.

Shawar, Yusra Ribhi, and Jennifer Prah Ruger. 2018. "The World Bank: Contested Institutional Progress in Rights-Based Health Discourse." In *Human Rights in Global Health: Rights-Based Governance for a Globalizing World*, edited by Benjamin Mason Meier and Lawrence O. Gostin, 353–374. New York: Oxford University Press.

Siddiqi, Javed. 1995. *World Health and World Politics: The World Health Organization and the UN System*. Columbus: University of South Carolina Press.

Sirleaf, Matiangai. 2018. "Responsibility for Epidemics." *Texas Law Review* 97(285): 285–354.

Stein, Felix. 2021. "Risky Business: COVAX and the Financialization of Global Vaccine Equity." *Globalization and Health* 17(1): 112.

Storeng, Katerini Tagmatarchi, Antoine de Bengy Puyvallée, and Felix Stein. 2021. "COVAX and the Rise of the 'Super Public Private Partnership' for Global Health." *Global Public Health* October 1–17.

Triponel, Anna. 2009. "Global Fund to Fight AIDS, Tuberculosis and Malaria: A New Legal and Conceptual Framework for Providing International Development Aid." *North Carolina Journal of International Law* 35(1): 173–232.

UN (United Nations). 1945. Charter of the United Nations.

Usher, Ann Danaiya. 2020. "COVID-19 Vaccines for All?" *Lancet* 395(10240): 1822–1823.

Usher, Ann Danaiya. 2022. "CEPI Launches 100-Day Vaccine 'Moonshot.'" *Lancet* 399(10330): 1107–1108.

Vogel, Gretchen. 2022. "The Global Plan for COVID-19 Vaccine Fairness Fell Short. Will next Time Be Different?" *Science*, December 13.

Wenham, Clare. 2017. "What We Have Learnt about the World Health Organization from the Ebola Outbreak." *Philosophical Transactions of the Royal Society B: Biological Sciences* 372(1721): 20160307.

WHO (World Health Organization). 2021. *2020 Annual report: Contingency Fund for Emergencies*. Geneva: WHO.

World Bank and WHO. 2022. "New Fund for Pandemic Prevention, Preparedness and Response Formally Established." September 9. 2023/014/HD.

World Bank Pandemic Emergency Financing Facility. 2019. "Pandemic Emergency Financing Facility (PEF) Operational Brief for Eligible Countries." World Bank.

Youde, Jeremy R. 2012. *Global Health Governance*. Cambridge: Polity Press.

IV
INTERNATIONAL LEGAL EFFORTS TO ADDRESS RISING HEALTH THREATS

15
Antimicrobial Resistance

Collective Action to Support Shared Global Resources

Isaac Weldon and Steven J. Hoffman

Introduction

Antimicrobial resistance (AMR) is a natural evolutionary process that gives rise to new disease variants that can evade existing treatments. As a result, antimicrobial medicines (including antibiotics, antivirals, and antifungals) stop working. Antimicrobials are widely used for vital purposes across many different sectors of human activity—including to treat and prevent infections in human health, animal health, and agricultural settings—however, the use of any antimicrobial potentially accelerates the process of AMR. Millions already die from AMR annually, and the morbidity and mortality of AMR is expected to grow rapidly in the coming decades. Resistant pathogens that arise from genetic mutations also have the potential to spread into deadly pandemics in a globalized and interconnected world. Given its high human and economic costs, and rising pandemic potential, AMR is among the most complex, urgent, and deadly health challenges. Swift global collective action is required to mitigate the transnational risks posed by AMR, adapt to its challenges, and sustain the shared global resource of effective antimicrobials for all.

Where antimicrobials have been crucial for achieving monumental global health gains over the past century, global health law will be necessary to ensure that these gains are not lost with the rise of AMR. Several United Nations (UN) organizations have already issued a series of non-binding agreements to address AMR; yet, the world still struggles to craft effective and sustainable global strategies across countries and sectors. Despite ongoing struggles and waning attention to AMR amid the COVID-19 pandemic, the UN is poised to act in advancing law and policy, and there is a unique opportunity to crystalize global action on AMR under global health law, with existing high-profile initiatives and a renewed interest in improving global health governance for future pandemics.

This chapter considers how global health law can be leveraged to address AMR throughout the world, supporting multisectoral and multilateral cooperation in global health governance. Part I outlines: the causes and effects of AMR, including its drivers across One Health sectors; its interdependent global challenges of improving access, conservation, innovation, and prevention; and its consequences for global health, food, and environmental justice. The transnational nature of AMR creates global interdependencies and shared vulnerabilities that necessitate the use of international law. Despite this legal imperative, Part II considers why existing non-binding and binding regulations through international organizations have failed to adequately address the complex challenge of AMR, with a lack of centralized governance mechanisms that can unite regulations. As nonstate actors have emerged to fill these governance gaps, they will need to be considered in any future attempt to improve global governance for AMR. Part III considers how new global health law frameworks can address AMR, either through revisions of existing laws, incorporation of AMR in a new pandemic treaty, or a new stand-alone agreement on AMR. This chapter concludes that—given the scale and intensity of the problem, the recent increase in attention to address pandemic threats, and the potential for law to improve governance—global health law provides new opportunities for collective action to address AMR.

I. The Interdependent Challenges of Rising Global AMR

Antimicrobial resistance is a complex problem that presents a series of interlinked challenges. Paradoxically, each antimicrobial pill is a private good for individual consumption, but every use potentially diminishes the global common pool of antimicrobial effectiveness. The reduced effectiveness of existing antimicrobials because of AMR undermines the shared global goal of sustained access to effective antimicrobials for all. Achieving this shared goal—where antimicrobials remain effective for everyone (non-excludable), yet their effectiveness is not unduly compromised by individual use (not very rivalrous)—will require efforts to conserve the existing stock, replenish it through innovation, and expand access to antimicrobials across sectors and countries. The rise of AMR thus presents two sets of interdependent relationships that require global coordination and collaboration, as AMR intersects human, animal, agriculture, and environmental sectors and demands a coordinated One Health response (White and Hughes 2019). AMR requires action across the four interdependent challenges of access, conservation, innovation, and prevention (Hoffman and Outterson 2015). With the rise of AMR undermining efforts to realize sustainable development, global collective action will be necessary to ensure the global public good of sustained access to antimicrobial medicines for all.

A. AMR Requires a One Health Approach

Addressing AMR across sectors requires coordination through a One Health approach (Léger et al. 2021).[1] Many societies depend upon antimicrobials as critical infrastructure to simultaneously treat and prevent infectious diseases in humans, animals, and plants, improve crop and agricultural yields, and enable many lifesaving medical procedures (Chandler 2019). Yet, every use, regardless of the setting or sector, potentially accelerates resistance. The same antimicrobials are used across settings, and improper waste practices accelerate AMR in many natural environments. The structural demand for and availability of antimicrobials across sectors, combined with poor prescribing habits, unenforced regulations in human, animal, and agricultural settings, and the accumulation of antimicrobials in ecosystems, has accelerated AMR to a point of global crisis. AMR now heightens the risk posed by zoonotic diseases (i.e., infectious diseases transmitted from animals to humans or between species) and requires coordination.

Case Study: AMR and Zoonotic Threats

Both AMR and zoonoses are accelerated by structural forces that increase the threat of disease at the human, animal, and environmental interface. For zoonoses, the continued destruction of natural habitats and urban growth into formerly uninhabited spaces increase interactions between humans and animals, and with it, the likelihood of zoonotic "spillover." Raising the risk of AMR, the use of antimicrobials in industrial feed operations increases the likelihood of a resistant pathogen emerging and transferring from animals to humans. The reduced effectiveness of antimicrobials, moreover, inhibits our ability to treat pathogens and heightens the risk of deadly infections. Meanwhile, zoonotic pandemics often increase the number of antimicrobials consumed globally, which can further hasten the rise of AMR and spillover into humans. In a globalizing world, where pathogens spread quickly and easily, zoonotic pathogens and AMR both have the potential to spread into deadly pandemics and affect human societies around the world. An emerging pathogen anywhere, whether resistant or zoonotic, poses risks everywhere. However, in responding to these interdependent transnational threats,

---

[1] A One Health perspective, first introduced in Chapter 9, draws attention to the myriad and complex ways that human health is entwined with animal and environmental health, including the ability of microbes to transfer across species, places, and from natural reservoirs (Lerner and Berg 2017). Because of these deep connections, a One Health perspective suggests that solutions should ideally intersect human, animal, and environmental spheres of activities.

governments face challenges in the absence of global commitments. The world has struggled to act in concert to address these shared vulnerabilities, as embodied by the ongoing inequitable distribution of antimicrobials and vaccines to curb emerging resistance and zoonoses. The failure to appreciate the interlinked nature of both zoonotic diseases and AMR has led to various interventions in isolation rather than through global multisectoral collaboration. There remains a crucial need to address interdependent issues together to maximize the effectiveness of global efforts and protect human health from the threat of infectious diseases emerging from both AMR and zoonoses.

To reduce the likelihood of zoonotic spillover and AMR, global commitments are needed to prioritize action across countries and sectors.

B. AMR Requires Action to Improve Access, Conservation, Innovation, and Prevention

Working across sectors to address AMR, global action must respond to four simultaneous challenges: (1) expanding access to antimicrobials; (2) bolstering conservation of the existing stock; (3) fostering innovation for new antimicrobials, diagnostic technologies, and alternative therapies; and (4) improving global infection prevention measures (Weldon et al. 2022).

1. Access

One of the most urgent challenges for AMR is ensuring that those who need effective antimicrobials can access these essential medicines (Årdal et al. 2016). However, many individuals around the world, especially in lower income and rural settings, still lack sustainable access to antimicrobials given weak healthcare systems, unstable supply chains, and a lack of market incentives (Access to Medicine Foundation 2022). This imperative to improve access to antimicrobials is especially important for low- and middle-income countries that bear a triple burden of lack of antimicrobial access, high infectious disease, and high AMR mortality and morbidity (Murray et al. 2022).[2] Several financing strategies exist to improve global access to antimicrobials—as seen in the global funding mechanisms introduced in Chapter 14—but they require global commitments to ensure their implementation.

---

[2] A lack of access also accelerates AMR by enabling infections to spread while also forcing people to use antimicrobials inappropriately—by, for example, taking smaller doses or seeking substandard drugs.

2. Conservation

Expanding access to effective antimicrobials must also be balanced against the need to conserve the effectiveness of existing antimicrobials for current and future generations. Around the world, antimicrobials are used in inappropriate and unsustainable ways that accelerate resistance (Ray et al. 2019). Antimicrobials can be acquired without prescription in some jurisdictions, leaving individuals without the proper understanding to administer these medicines (Shafiq et al. 2021). Even in places that require prescriptions, studies have found that antimicrobials are still used without appropriate therapeutic justification (Ray et al. 2019). Crucial strategies can help curb rising resistance, including creating better prescribing protocols, raising awareness of AMR among healthcare providers, and banning the manufacture and import of substandard and falsified drugs (Rogers Van Katwyk, Weldon, et al. 2020). Global conservation efforts also need to address structural drivers of antimicrobial use, in healthcare and across sectors—advancing a One Health approach to conservation in human, animal, and agricultural settings. Despite evolving recognition that antimicrobial use is shaped by deeply embedded incentives and systems of behavior, conservation efforts have long sought to change only individual behavior (Chandler 2019). Where individual action alone cannot support sustainable solutions, programs aimed at altering individual behavior must be accompanied by coordinated social efforts to change the structures of incentives and interests that lead to antimicrobial use (Weldon et al. 2022).

3. Innovation

Given failures of access and conservation, as well as the inevitable evolution of resistance, innovation is needed to develop new antimicrobials. While innovation is necessary to replenish the depleting stock of effective drugs, new drugs and technologies are not developed fast enough to keep pace with rising resistance (Outterson et al. 2015). This ongoing innovation challenge is driven by market failures, where pharmaceutical companies argue that they are poorly incentivized to discover new antimicrobials because of the high costs of research and development but low market value of prospective new drugs.[3] The importance of establishing new antimicrobial research and development models and mobilizing funds for these innovations highlights the importance of thinking about innovation beyond just scientific advancements. New innovative drug financing models will be needed to help change approaches to the challenge of AMR (Minssen et al. 2020).

---

[3] New antimicrobial development is claimed to offer high risk with low reward, as new antimicrobials must either compete against off-patent generics, which restricts potential returns; or be saved in reserve as critically important last lines of defense, which present a smaller immediate market.

4. Prevention

Overlaying these challenges, improving global infection prevention is crucial to diminish the incidence of infectious disease, thus lessening the demand for antimicrobials. However, as introduced in Chapter 6, challenges remain for global infection prevention and outbreak response. Preventing disease at a global level will require improved global AMR surveillance, as an understanding of AMR rates could enable more accurate prescribing and antimicrobial use around the world. However, the world still lacks a standardized way to measure AMR across human, animal, and environmental sectors. As it remains difficult to compare the evolution and spread of infections and AMR across the world (Wernli et al. 2020), the unchecked rise of AMR continues to undermine health, food, and environmental justice.

C. AMR Undermines Global Progress for Sustainable Development

AMR has hindered development efforts while stymieing global progress to meet the Sustainable Development Goals (SDGs) (Esiovwa et al. 2022). The far-reaching challenges of AMR affect nearly all aspects of human life, presenting multisectoral challenges to health security, human rights, food and environmental security, and economic development—threatening to deepen health inequities throughout the world. SDG 3, as reviewed in Chapter 10, seeks to improve human health and well-being, but without effective antimicrobials, even the most basic infections can be deadly.[4] If a resistant pathogen spiraled into a global pandemic, moreover, it would amount to an untreatable pathogen, straining health systems and threatening public health (World Bank 2017). Looking beyond the health sector, AMR also impacts other underlying determinants of health, including SDG 2 on ending hunger and malnutrition. Rising antimicrobial resistance already disrupts fragile food supply chains in places where populations depend upon antimicrobial usage in animal and agriculture settings to ensure food security.

These impacts of AMR, like many other human health issues, are borne disproportionately along the lines of race, gender, and income—with these inequalities undermining SDGs 1, 5, and 10 on ending poverty and reducing

---

[4] Similarly, antimicrobials are relied upon to enable lifesaving treatments, and without effective antibiotics, routine medical procedures such as cesarean sections, chemotherapies, and surgeries become more dangerous.

income and gender inequality. The inequities of AMR are already playing out through an uneven burden of infection, mortality, and morbidity in lower-income settings (Murray et al. 2022). Compounding this injustice, AMR is disproportionately affecting women and other marginalized groups, who tend to be frontline and informal workers and who face greater obstacles when accessing healthcare. The harms of AMR stand to reproduce colonial relations between high-income countries, where most antibiotic investment occurs (Simpkin et al. 2017), and low- and middle-income countries that continue to bear the greatest infectious disease burden (Institute for Health Metrics and Evaluation 2020). Yet, despite this differential health risk, microbes do not discriminate, as AMR is a transnational threat from which no person, community, nor country is immune, raising an imperative to address this global threat through global solutions.

D. AMR Requires Global Collective Solutions

Resistance can emerge anywhere antibiotics are used, and resistant microbes can spread rapidly throughout the world. The continued movement of goods, people, animals, and microbes in a globalizing world means that no country can wholly mitigate the transnational threat of AMR on their own (Hoffman and Behdinan 2016). In a globalizing world, the global response to AMR will only be as strong as the weakest response in any given setting. While some states have developed national policies to enable the appropriate use of antimicrobials—as well as the identification, containment, control, and mitigation of resistant bacteria (Rogers Van Katwyk et al. 2019)—these policies are underutilized and less likely to be effective in the absence of unified global commitments and global cooperation (WHO 2020).

The multifaceted challenge of mitigating AMR—addressing the pillars of access, conservation, innovation, and prevention—suggests that strong, coordinated, and global policies and institutions are required to alleviate AMR risk and sustainably protect antimicrobial effectiveness as a shared global resource. Yet, even though all nations collectively stand to gain from sustained access to effective antimicrobials, there remains a reluctance to act for the collective benefit (Baekkeskov et al. 2020). As a result of these collective action problems, the continued supply of effective antimicrobials remains precarious; their distribution remains inequitable; and they continue to be overused, misused, and abused in ways that accelerate resistance. Given these interdependencies, which also create shared vulnerabilities, global governance has looked to develop global regulation to address the global threat of AMR.

II. Existing Global Governance Responses to Rising AMR

The complex and multifaceted challenge of AMR requires ambitious global action to prevent, detect, mitigate, and adapt to its impacts—across all sectors and all countries. While binding treaties are rare in global health, international law has come to be seen as warranted when challenges are transnational and justify enforcement for collective action (Hoffman, Røttingen, and Frenk 2015b). Considering the transnational causes and consequences of AMR, as well as the many collective action problems that limit progress toward global AMR governance, the strongest forms of hard law, as introduced in Chapter 2, are appropriate (Hoffman, Røttingen, and Frenk 2015a). Comprehensive, binding, and enforceable international laws are needed to unite the interdependent goals of access, conservation, innovation, and prevention under a One Health approach and achieve sustainable antimicrobial use for all (Ruckert et al. 2020). International law can establish global commitments, hold actors accountable, and coordinate investments, interests, and incentives, ensuring cooperation and maximizing the likelihood of success. Harnessing international law to support global AMR governance, therefore, can strengthen the world's collective ability to respond to this global health threat. However, only non-binding and unenforceable agreements currently exist specifically for AMR. While there are existing binding and enforceable agreements relevant for some aspects of AMR governance, these international legal regimes are diffusely distributed across several institutions, which limits their effectiveness in the face of AMR's multisectoral complexity. This mix of non-binding policy agreements and uncoordinated legal regulations has contributed to the rise of non-state actors, which are pioneering new partnerships to fill governance gaps and strengthen AMR governance.

A. Non-Binding AMR Agreements

A series of important policy advancements have framed global AMR governance, but these efforts have only produced non-binding and unenforceable "soft law" agreements. Beginning in 2010, a joint concept note published by the World Health Organization (WHO), Food and Agriculture Organization of the United Nations (FAO), and World Organization for Animal Health (WOAH) formalized a "Tripartite" collaboration among the three organizations (FAO, OIE, and WHO 2010). The Tripartite agreed to unify a global AMR response under a One Health banner. An early success for the Tripartite was the adoption of a 2015 Global Action Plan for AMR (WHO 2015a). The Global Action Plan, a non-binding agreement arising out of a World Health Assembly resolution, aimed to establish coordinated mechanisms to predict, detect, and respond to AMR across all countries while promoting sustainable development. It identified five areas for global collective action to address AMR, including antimicrobial surveillance, infection prevention and control measures, global awareness campaigns, responsible use and stewardship promotion, and innovation for new antimicrobial drugs (ibid.). With states expected to create their own national plans that align with these thematic areas, the resolution acknowledges the need for a whole-of-society engagement to improve prevention, access, and sustainability across sectors (WHO 2015b).

Coinciding with the Tripartite's efforts, AMR gained traction politically and became the focus of a 2016 High Level Meeting of the UN General Assembly. The resulting political declaration recognized the urgency of AMR, its One Health drivers, and its widescale impacts (UN General Assembly 2016). In meeting this urgency, the declaration put forward a series of international commitments to support the development and implementation of national action plans in accordance with the Tripartite Global Action Plan. Specific commitments also include deepening inter-organization and multisectoral collaboration under a One Health approach, mobilizing funding for AMR, and raising awareness of the issue. The declaration tasked the UN Secretary-General with developing an Inter-Agency Coordination Group for AMR (IACG). Formed in 2017, the IACG completed its mandate in 2019 with the publication of a report that recommended further global action for AMR, largely guided by similar themes for improving global AMR governance (IACG 2019).

In expanding the AMR governance landscape, the United Nations Environmental Programme (UNEP) formally joined the WHO, FAO, and WOAH in their One Health efforts in 2022, as introduced in Chapter 9, and the Tripartite evolved into the "Quadripartite" collaboration (UNEP et al. 2022). The policy agreements that have emerged through the work of these four organizations have helped to spur collaboration on AMR, generating attention and momentum for action while establishing norms around antimicrobial stewardship and prevention (Tejpar et al. 2022). However, these policy agreements remain limited—often lacking important enforcement mechanisms to facilitate transparency, oversight, compliance, and accountability—and thus cannot compel actors to fulfill their promises (Behdinan, Hoffman, and Pearcey 2015). While non-binding agreements can often include stronger language and tend to be more flexible and adaptable than binding mechanisms, compliance is unlikely without strong enforcement mechanisms under international law (Hoffman et al. 2022). As a result, many countries have struggled to craft and implement national action plans as stipulated under the Global Action Plan, looking instead to binding legal standards across international organizations.

B. Binding International Law Standards Applicable to AMR

Binding legal mechanisms could help bridge existing gaps and facilitate accountability for state implementation (Weldon and Hoffman 2021), but in the absence of a comprehensive legal framework, existing legal regulations have evolved under the narrow sectoral scopes of several international organizations. While a wide range of international law standards apply to AMR—under global health governance and international trade governance—these regulations across organizations have yet to achieve the level of impact needed to adequately mitigate, adapt, and respond to the challenge.

1. AMR Governance through WHO: The International Health Regulations

To promote cooperation on global health security under WHO governance, the measures outlined in the International Health Regulations (IHR) include a coordinated legal system of global preparedness and response to emerging health issues. The most recent revision of the IHR in 2005, as detailed initially in Chapter 6, expanded its scope from a few targeted diseases to encompass any human health threat. This broadened scope enables its application to AMR, providing a path under international law to respond to emerging resistant pathogens, strengthen global prevention measures, and set international standards for antimicrobial surveillance and stewardship.

Resistant pathogens emerging from AMR can evade all available treatments and spiral into uncontrollable pandemics, necessitating the international coordination mechanisms offered by the IHR (Wernli et al. 2011). Although this has not yet happened, a resistant pathogen with pandemic potential can rapidly lead to a public health emergency of international concern (PHEIC), with a PHEIC declaration triggering global coordination and response when a resistant pathogen emerges. Indeed, the United Kingdom has already looked to the IHR to determine whether the spread of a drug-resistant gonorrhea warranted the declaration of PHEIC. Even though this AMR outbreak did not meet the criteria of a PHEIC at the time, the United Kingdom was able to notify the international community of the potential threat via the processes outlined in the IHR, further highlighting the instrument's relevance to AMR (Ming, Puddle, and Wilson 2019).

Beyond these coordination mechanisms, the IHR also require states to maintain the capacity to mount public health responses to potential outbreaks. This preparedness effort under the IHR must include shoring up capacities to address AMR at the national level, including prevention measures to lessen AMR and access measures to distribute effective antimicrobials.[5] Further, where AMR

---

[5] Further, the IHR requires states to uphold human rights, which could be interpreted to mean that states have an obligation under the IHR to improve access to antimicrobials, as access to essential medicines, as discussed in Chapter 12, is inextricably linked to the human right to health.

specifically requires improved surveillance, the IHR stipulate that states must maintain the capacity to investigate all disease outbreaks. In applying the IHR to AMR, WHO concluded in 2014 that "the capacity to perform antimicrobial susceptibility testing, which can inform surveillance of AMR, also falls within the scope of the IHR" (WHO 2014). Facilitating accountability for AMR surveillance under the IHR, both WHO's Global Antimicrobial Resistance and Use Surveillance System (GLASS) and its ongoing monitoring of state capacities through its Joint External Evaluation (JEE) could eventually fill the surveillance gap for AMR. GLASS, launched in 2015, already monitors gaps in AMR surveillance (WHO 2020); meanwhile, the JEE, which assesses country capacity in relation to the IHR, already monitors and evaluates important AMR-specific capacities, including the ability to detect, track, and respond to rising resistance rates (WHO 2018).

While the IHR contain promising avenues to strengthen the global response to AMR, many countries, especially low- and middle-income countries, lack the national capacity to strengthen core capacities and meet these requirements on their own, further underscoring the need for global solutions and funding mechanisms (Wernli et al. 2011). Moreover, the IHR's human-centric nature limits its scope to the human health sector only, even as AMR also requires strong mechanisms across animal health, agriculture, and environmental sectors. Without centralized AMR governance under WHO, AMR-specific revisions to the IHR would need to be pursued alongside revisions to a diverse set of applicable instruments beyond WHO (Rogers Van Katwyk, Weldon et al. 2020).

2. AMR Governance beyond WHO: FAO, WOAH, and UNEP

Like WHO, other organizational members of the Quadripartite (FAO, WOAH, and UNEP) have the authority to create international law, collect data, make recommendations, and mobilize funding. These four agencies, together and independently, are in a position to support the implementation of international law for AMR (Rogers Van Katwyk, Giubilini et al. 2020). Working together to provide collaboration and coordination around One Health issues, the Quadripartite has already begun to establish initiatives on AMR through their One Health Joint Plan of Action.

In strengthening global health governance under international law, WOAH, FAO, and UNEP could better regulate more appropriate use of antimicrobials in animal health, agriculture settings, and environmental contexts. While WHO has already indicated a need to protect special human-only classes of antimicrobials, WHO alone lacks the ability to enforce this measure across agricultural and animal health sectors (Rogers Van Katwyk, Weldon et al. 2020). Working with WHO, WOAH, and FAO could monitor and enforce a ban on the use of human-only antimicrobials in other settings, while also banning antimicrobial use for prophylactic (to prevent infection) or metaphylactic purposes (to treat entire herds). By adding environmental regulation to the Quadripartite, UNEP has the power to adopt environmental regulations, including regulations on the disposal of antimicrobial waste, which can prevent antimicrobial runoff into the environment. Such regulations across sectors will be crucial given the ways in which AMR can undermine important economic activity (World Bank 2017), and these economic implications require that international trade law also be considered in the global effort to address AMR.

3. AMR Governance under the World Trade Organization
International trade governance provides an underutilized and understudied avenue for delivering much-needed AMR action. Under the World Trade Organization (WTO), international trade agreements can be leveraged to improve access to antimicrobials and guide regulations on substandard or falsified drugs and products that use antimicrobials unnecessarily. The WTO Agreement on the Trade-Related Aspects of Intellectual Property Rights (TRIPS), for example, provides powerful tools that can support AMR regulations through intellectual property law.

Looking to intellectual property law, existing legal mechanisms pursuant to TRIPS could improve AMR access through voluntary and compulsory patent licensing agreements. Under the TRIPS agreement, first detailed in Chapter 12, governments can approach pharmaceutical companies for an agreement to voluntarily license a patent to manufacture essential medicines like antibiotics for their domestic market; however, if a voluntary agreement cannot be reached, governments have flexibilities under TRIPS to issue a compulsory license—authorizing these activities without the permission of the patent holder (WTO 2006).[6] These TRIPS flexibilities, which are already established under international law, could significantly address AMR by improving global access to antimicrobials, especially in low-resource settings, but these flexibilities have never before been employed for antimicrobials (Rogers Van Katwyk, Weldon et al. 2020). Given the institutional constraints faced by these international organizations in regulating antimicrobials, undermining efforts to coordinate governance to prevent AMR across the global health landscape, non-state actors have stepped in to advance AMR initiatives.

---

[6] In settings without the capacity to manufacture high quality antimicrobials, governments can issue a compulsory license and arrange for a third party in another country to produce the medicine for them.

C. Limitations of International Institutions: The Rise of Non-State Actors

Despite the promise of international law to address AMR, the narrow sectoral scope of existing international organizations and legal instruments limits their effectiveness. Each institution is limited to developing legal provisions that are consistent with its own institutional mandates and governing documents. As seen in the challenges of Quadripartite governance over One Health, it takes significant effort to coordinate interdependent AMR regulations across international organizations. Even where such partnerships are realized, accomplishing this coordination poses challenges in mobilizing specialized knowledge across different instruments, sectors, and academic disciplines—creating the potential for gaps, overlaps, and conflicts.

Without centralized leadership, AMR governance has seen the proliferation of new actors, as depicted in Figure 15.1, which aim to fill these governance gaps and deliver much-needed AMR initiatives.

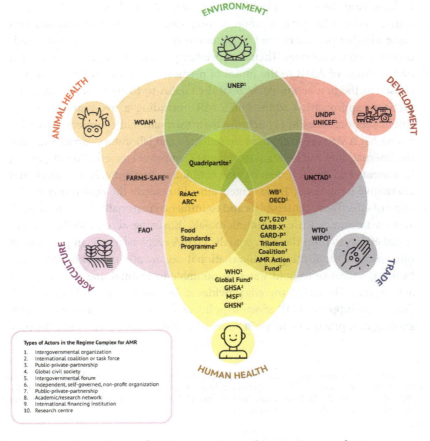

Figure 15.1 Constellation of AMR Actors Mapped Across Sectors of Activity (Weldon and Hoffman)

In the absence of a strong coordinated global response to AMR, state and non-state actors have risen to fill key gaps at the global level—mobilizing funding for antimicrobials, spurring research and innovation, and improving awareness through policy campaigns. The Global Action Plan recognizes the need to strengthen these partnerships and improve "cooperation among policy-makers, academia and the pharmaceutical industry to ensure that new technologies are available globally to prevent, diagnose and treat resistant infections" (WHO 2015a). With states looking beyond international organizations, the G7 and G20 have taken an active role to make AMR a political priority (G7 2016; G20 2017).[7] In supporting state capacity to address AMR, states have come together with non-state actors to prioritize AMR under the Global Health Security Agenda (GHSA) (Joshi et al. 2021).

Case Study: GHSA Prioritizes AMR

In launching the Global Health Security Agenda (GHSA) in 2014, as first introduced in Chapter 6, a group of forty-four countries and organizations came together outside of the UN system to create a global framework to address infectious diseases. Their first priority (Action Package 1) was focused on the threat of AMR to the future of medical countermeasures. AMR was chosen as the first action package of the GHSA to focus actors on an intersectional approach to addressing AMR, including a five-year target that would support states to (1) develop their own national comprehensive plan to combat AMR; (2) strengthen surveillance and laboratory capacity at both the international and national level; and (3) improve conservation of existing treatments and development of new antibiotics, preventative measures, and alternative treatments. These targets aimed to ensure the continuing availability of effective antimicrobials and to influence reasonable human, animal, and environmental use of antimicrobials. Ensuring accountability for national efforts to meet these targets, the GHSA emphasizes the importance of international monitoring by international organizations, looking to global health governance to hold states accountable in maintaining their national action plans. The GHSA thereby provides an "Accountability and Results Task Force" that supports AMR efforts in political spaces and provides guidance regarding best practices—to assist states in implementing their commitments.

---

[7] The G7, for example, has made AMR a priority for their activities, promising in the 2016 Ise-Shima Vision for Global Health to improve funding for antimicrobial access, conservation, and innovation (G7 2016). The G20 has similarly identified AMR as a key area for their work in promoting economic and human development (G20 2017).

Yet despite this new initiative, the GHSA AMR action package has faced limitations in implementation, with governments failing to see a connection between AMR and global health security and lacking a specific methodology to measure their policies and report their progress.

Bringing pharmaceutical corporations into these global health partnerships for AMR, new initiatives have arisen to promote drug discovery and innovation. Pharmaceutical companies have at their disposal the resources and capacity to innovate and manufacture antimicrobials but, as discussed in Chapter 13, feel poorly incentivized by market conditions to do so. The persistence of these market failures has required governmental or intergovernmental action to both reduce regulatory barriers and improve economic incentives. New public-private partnerships have sought to bridge this divide. These partnerships, including the Combating Antibiotic-Resistant Bacteria Biopharmaceutical Accelerator (CARB-X) and the Global Antibiotic Research and Development Partnership (GARD-P), work with pharmaceutical corporations to craft financial incentives that make it economically desirable to pursue research and development for new antimicrobials. They seek to create these incentives by, among other things, mobilizing funding and creating new ways of funding drug development and bringing new drugs to market. Such innovative drug financing models, including subscription models (or "Netflix models") and prizes, offer promising avenues to overcome some of these private sector challenges and spur innovation (Outterson et al. 2016).

Supported by civil society engagement on antimicrobial access, new nongovernmental organizations (NGOs) have also emerged to raise awareness on the issue while articulating the urgency of AMR as a complex global problem. These NGOs, such as the Antibiotic Resistance Coalition (ARC) and ReAct—Action on Antimicrobial Resistance, aim to promote antimicrobial stewardship, raise awareness of AMR, and strengthen the scientific and social scientific evidence base for global efforts. As global political attention to AMR has shifted in unpredictable waves, with no formalized mechanism to maintain the place of AMR on the global political agenda, civil societies groups have emerged as key actors to ensure continuing AMR work, sustaining pressure on governments, intergovernmental organizations, and private firms (Tejpar et al. 2022). Simultaneously, these groups also work to provide key recommendations for policy solutions for AMR. While many policy solutions have been developed for this complex issue, many more still need to be generated, and it will be necessary to push law and policy in new directions—to leverage existing efforts and initiatives, achieve a coordinated global response, and deliver AMR regulations.

III. Achieving a Global AMR Response: Future Directions for Global Health Law

Given the scale and intensity of the AMR threat, the codification of AMR-specific policies and regulations, and the increasing number of international organizations focused on the issue, there is significant potential for global health law to crystalize policies and provisions to improve global AMR governance. Amid a rising series of pressing global health challenges, AMR is uniquely suited to an international law solution. International law provides a powerful tool that can sustain cooperation, distribute responsibilities and burdens, and craft a system that actively engages states' ongoing efforts to address AMR—establishing the commitment, coordination, enforcement, and accountability mechanisms that the transnational challenge of AMR demands (Weldon et al. 2022). The codification of such AMR regulations under international law could be delivered through ongoing global health law reforms: revising the IHR (and complementary regulations across international organizations) to be more applicable to AMR; including AMR in a broader treaty on pandemics; or crafting a new AMR treaty (Wilson et al. 2021).

A. Addressing AMR through Regulations across Organizations

AMR could feasibly be addressed through the coordinated revision of existing legal institutions. As outlined in Table 15.1, several relevant regulations fall under the scope of existing institutions and legal instruments (Rogers Van Katwyk, Weldon et al. 2020).

WHO reforms, in particular, provide key opportunities to feasibly address AMR under global health law, including through revisions to the IHR. With IHR amendments currently underway, the IHR could be revised to better address the human health impacts of AMR—strengthening coordination across One Health sectors, addressing the root causes of AMR, and improving the global system of surveillance and notification for AMR events. However, WHO's constitutional mandate is limited to human health only, and thus revising the IHR alone is unlikely to yield the comprehensive regulatory focus that AMR requires.

Across the Quadripartite, a suite of existing agricultural, animal health, trade, and environmental laws would also need to be revised alongside the IHR, ensuring coordination to advance One Health. For example, global AMR efforts could ban the manufacture, trade, and sale of substandard and falsified drugs while also reducing unnecessary prophylactic use of antimicrobials in animal agriculture. Moreover, antimicrobial pollution accelerates the risk of AMR (by increasing wild reservoirs of resistant genes in the environment),

Table 15.1 Relevant Institutions for AMR Regulations (Weldon and Hoffman)

Existing International Law	Description	Potential Application to AMR
International Health Regulations (IHR) (2005)	An international legal agreement through WHO that promotes global health security by building capacity to detect, assess, report, and respond to public health risks.	Improve access, surveillance, and global IPC measures to strengthen core capacities. Reporting and responding to potential public health emergencies of international importance (PHEIC). Together with FAO and WOAH, enforce a class of human-only antimicrobials.
Agreement on the Application of Sanitary and Phytosanitary Measures (SPS Agreement) (1995)	An international legal agreement under the WTO to support the right of governments to protect food safety, plant and animal health, and prevent these sanitary and phytosanitary measures from being unjustified trade barriers.	Ban the routine use of antimicrobials for prophylactic and metaphylactic purposes.
Agreement on Technical Barriers to Trade (TBT Agreement) (1995)	An international legal agreement through the WTO that aims to ensure that technical regulations and standards are non-discriminatory and do not create unnecessary obstacles to trade.	Ban the manufacturing, sale, import, and export of falsified and substandard drugs.
Agreement on Trade-Related Aspects of Intellectual Property Rights (TRIPS Agreement) (1995)	An international legal agreement under the WTO that sets minimum standards for the regulation of intellectual property by national governments.	Leverage voluntary and compulsory licenses to improve access. Reserve any newly discovered antimicrobial for human use only.
Basel Convention on the Control of Transboundary Movements of Hazardous Wastes and Their Disposal (Basel Convention) (1989)	An international legal agreement that limits harmful waste pollution, promotes environmentally sound management of hazardous wastes, and restricts the transboundary movements of hazardous wastes.	Set, monitor, and enforce guidelines for antimicrobial disposal and waste management.

(continued)

Table 15.1 Continued

Existing International Law	Description	Potential Application to AMR
Rotterdam Convention on the Prior Informed Consent Procedure for Certain Hazardous Chemicals and Pesticides in International Trade (Rotterdam Convention) (1998)	An international legal agreement to protect human health and the environment from chemicals that remain intact in the environment, become widely distributed geographically, accumulate in the fatty tissue of humans and wildlife, and have harmful impacts on human health or on the environment.	(Same as Basel).
Stockholm Convention on Persistent Organic Pollutants (Stockholm Convention) (2001)	An international legal agreement designed to protect human health and the environment by eliminating or restricting the production and use of persistent organic pollutants.	(Same as Basel).

making it both a major concern and an opportune site for intervention. In the vast constellation of multilateral environmental agreements, three already govern the use, trade, and disposal of hazardous chemicals, products, and wastes—as seen in Table 15.1 in the Stockholm, Basel, and Rotterdam accords—and these three accords could be leveraged to help set, monitor, and enforce guidelines for antimicrobial disposal and waste management (Rogers Van Katwyk, Weldon et al. 2020). Curbing antimicrobial pollution (by setting standards and guidelines for antimicrobial waste disposal in places like pharmaceutical plants, farms, and hospitals) will be necessary to address AMR as a One Health challenge. To meet this One Health challenge, the FAO, WOAH, and UNEP must strengthen legal measures to ensure coherence across existing legal instruments, leveraging their respective lawmaking authorities to help enforce human-only classes of antimicrobials. Such collaborative measures will require coordination of the Quadripartite lawmaking powers, with impacts on the international trade of antimicrobials and other products that use antimicrobials.

These multisectoral, One Health measures would thus need to be weighed against existing trade laws (WHO, WTO, and WIPO 2016). As surveyed in Chapter 12, the WTO Agreement on Technical Barriers to Trade (TBT) protects the authority of states to enforce technical and quality requirements on goods. Correspondingly, the WTO Agreement on the Application Sanitary and Phytosanitary Measures (SPS) supports the authority of states to take measures to protect food safety and plant and animal health. Both agreements permit WTO member states to restrict trade to protect human health and the environment—so long as they are justified by available scientific evidence, are no more restrictive to trade than necessary, and are non-discriminatory (WTO Committee on Sanitary and Phytosanitary Measures 2020). These WTO agreements could therefore permit and support the implementation of AMR standards across countries to govern the appropriate manufacturing, use, and disposal of antimicrobials.[8]

The relevance of these existing legal instruments presents significant advantages in reforming global health law. Pursuing a coordinated suite of targeted revisions could be more diplomatically efficient than undergoing the difficult process of negotiating a new instrument, which could take years. Moreover, revisions to the IHR have the unique advantage of being automatically binding on all WHO member states, unless a state proactively rejects them within a specified time frame. Thus, pursuing this avenue may be the most efficient path, and could have a higher likelihood of successfully realizing binding and enforceable AMR regulations. However, the revision of several instruments across different institutions would present coordination challenges, considering the level of expertise needed for negotiating both AMR issues and the unique qualities of each instrument. As this strategy may struggle to deliver comprehensive AMR regulations, with the possibility of either gaps or redundancies across institutions, a more solid legal foundation may be found in new global AMR laws, with the development of a novel pandemic treaty offering the opportunity reshape the regulatory landscape for AMR.

B. Addressing AMR through a Pandemic Treaty

The many overlaps between needed regulation for pandemic threats and AMR present significant opportunity to address AMR through the proposed pandemic treaty, both in its core text and in subsequent protocols. Specifically, both AMR and zoonotic disease threats require international law in three

---

[8] In further preventing the rise of AMR under the WTO, TRIPS could be further leveraged to automatically limit any new class of antimicrobials to human-uses only until a relevant technical agency deems their use safe in animals and agriculture (Rogers Van Katwyk, Weldon et al. 2020).

crucial areas: global intersectoral cooperation, equitable resource allocation, and strengthened accountability mechanisms.

- Global intersectoral cooperation – Like zoonotic disease, addressing AMR requires intersectoral coordination through a One Health approach. While interconnectedness between human, animal, and agriculture sectors allows pathogens to spread easily, it also means there are opportunities for deeper intersectoral collaboration. A well-designed pandemic treaty, alongside revisions to the IHR, could incentivize knowledge generation and sharing across sectors and countries.
- Equitable resource allocation – Addressing both AMR and zoonotic disease will require global funding mechanisms to improve core capacities at the national level. The same core capacities that are needed for zoonoses are also needed to address AMR, including better sanitation and hygiene measures for infection prevention; procurement of personal protective equipment; and access to essential medicines and diagnostics—complemented by a global pooled fund to shore up investments in national level capacities.
- Strengthened accountability mechanisms – Where global health law suffers from a lack of accountability, strong accountability mechanism under a pandemic treaty can help facilitate implementation, track progress, and incentivize action to address AMR. Strengthened accountability and support mechanisms—including transparency, oversight, dispute resolution enforcement, and other support mechanisms—are key to ensuring that measures are implemented fairly and effectively (Hoffman and Ottersen 2015).

Considering these similarities, the core text of a pandemic instrument could begin to address AMR, especially since AMR also represents a mechanism by which new pandemic threats may emerge. Yet, given the shallow reference to AMR in the pandemic treaty negotiations, the problem is unlikely to be fully addressed by a new pandemic treaty, leaving AMR well suited as a focus for future protocols. To the extent that neither the revisions of the IHR, the adoption of a new pandemic treaty, nor the negotiation of subsequent protocols succeed in addressing AMR sufficiently, a new AMR-specific instrument could deliver much-needed AMR regulation under a stand-alone treaty.

C. Addressing AMR through a Stand-Alone Treaty

A new treaty focused on AMR could stimulate and sustain efforts to mobilize collective action, unite One Health sectors, and engage states in an ongoing effort to mitigate and adapt to the impacts of AMR. Achieving a treaty on AMR would be a monumental diplomatic task and would require great political will, but other areas of international law offer many lessons that can help deliver regulations via new treaty designed for AMR, including the importance of:

- a unifying global goal to mobilize, guide, and track global progress;
- a commitment to addressing the social structures that drive antimicrobial use—to begin transforming practices away from antimicrobial dependence;
- a combination of universal, differentiated, and individualized commitments to enable an equitable distribution of burdens and benefits according to needs, capacity to respond, and responsibility for the threat;
- a mechanism to increase the ambition of country commitments to continue accelerating global momentum and delivery of needed AMR action;
- a permanent multistakeholder forum to ensure fair and continuing deliberation, representation, and stewardship of AMR priorities and policies, and
- a science-policy evidence panel to ensure that evolving policy efforts are continually supported by the best available evidence (Weldon et al. 2022).

State and non-state actors have looked to a new AMR treaty as a basis to establish a coordinated global response to AMR, but these efforts have faced diplomatic obstacles that have thus far prevented the adoption of an AMR treaty.

Case Study: Diplomatic Push for an AMR Treaty

Calls for greater global efforts to address AMR have been mounting for decades—with WHO recognizing AMR as a global threat since the 1950s. However, past attempts to address AMR at the global level have failed given the diplomatic challenges, including the inability to generate sufficient political will and internal fragmentation due to the narrow sectoral scopes of key actors. For example, past initiatives that have focused on only human health or agricultural practices have raised conflicting perspectives, interpretations, and uncertainties about the causes of AMR—and consequently the most appropriate sites for intervention. As a result, past declarations calling for global action on AMR have not included the kinds of policies, regulations, and activities that can achieve their stated goals. Yet, leading public health officials and civil society organizations are now advocating for global and intersectoral approaches to AMR. Leveraging a wide range of political platforms, diplomatic efforts for greater AMR stewardship have increased pressure on governments to establish more effective global governance. These initiatives have yielded influential international reports, high-level meetings in governing bodies, global action plans, and political commitments to uphold and deliver AMR regulations. WHO has looked to these efforts in forming a WHO Collaborating Centre on Global Governance of AMR. In developing global health law, the diplomatic work of these past efforts has elevated the place of AMR on the global political agenda such that many opportunities could now feasibly deliver comprehensive, binding, and enforceable regulations. This political momentum has led to calls for international negotiations to develop an AMR treaty.

Whether through revisions to the IHR, a pandemic treaty, or a new treaty, international law provides a powerful tool that can support global cooperation on AMR. Greater coordination and enshrined mechanisms to support collaboration are now needed—aligning incentives and interests across sectors and guiding states in the interrelated goals of access, conservation, innovation, and prevention. Despite the diplomatic challenges of global health law reforms,[9] AMR action, both national and global, continues to progress, with many now recognizing AMR as urgent and important issue. Given the rise of existing and emerging pandemic threats, there will continue to be opportunities on the horizon to strengthen global AMR governance, especially with growing recognition of how important international law is for supporting global cooperation, and how important global cooperation is for addressing the global health threat of AMR.

Conclusion

AMR is among the greatest threats to global health, yet global health governance remains incommensurate to this rising threat. Without swift action, the cataclysmic global threat of AMR—a threat from which no country or individual is immune—will become increasingly uncontrollable. Left unaddressed, mortality and morbidity from AMR will continue to rise, placing more and more stress on health systems, national economies, and public health. The widespread and intense threat of AMR heightens the need for collective action to respond to this common challenge. Beyond this common threat to all, AMR will deepen many global health inequities, with governance efforts to address AMR advancing global justice, supporting development goals, and protecting global health

---

[9] Adding another treaty to the growing list of global health reforms could pose challenges, as some states may already be experiencing "treaty fatigue" amid a series of new international negotiations. Further, the ongoing development of many simultaneous negotiations—including a pandemic treaty, IHR, and a new AMR treaty—creates equity challenges in global health diplomacy, as examined in Chapter 5, as not all states have resources to send delegations to multiple negotiation forums.

achievements. Addressing AMR will require a One Health approach to global health law, uniting sectors to improve access, conservation, innovation, and prevention measures around the world to support sustained access to antimicrobials as a global public good.

Achieving cooperation to address the social forces that accelerate AMR will depend upon global health law as a foundation to craft institutions, align incentives, and shape interests across countries and sectors while sustaining global initiatives on AMR into the future. Many effective policy interventions to address AMR have been developed over the years, but governments are poorly incentivized to act unless others act as well, highlighting the important role that global health law can play in coordinating action. While important steps are being taken across the global health landscape to reform global health law and craft AMR regulations, collective action is urgently needed to curb the mounting threat of drug-resistant infections—effectively, sustainably, and globally.

The ongoing COVID-19 pandemic has simultaneously proven that microbes care little for national borders and that the world's ability to cooperate around emerging health threats will require law reforms. In building a legal foundation for global solidarity, many political leaders now recognize the need to strengthen global health governance, and governance reforms amid the COVID-19 pandemic present an opportunity for bold action on infectious disease threats. International law provides a powerful tool to coordinate global regulations on AMR across sectors, preserving the effectiveness of antimicrobial medicines and curbing the rising threat of resistance. Comprehensive, binding, and enforceable AMR regulations could be delivered in ongoing global health law reforms, whether through revision of the IHR and other existing instruments, inclusion of AMR into the core text or as a protocol to a pandemic treaty, or development of a new agreement specific to AMR. Looking to international law reforms in the coming years, it is possible to develop new responses to ensure that global efforts can succeed in preventing, detecting, and responding to AMR.

Questions for Consideration

1. Why does AMR require global cooperation for collective action?
2. How does the rising threat of zoonotic AMR reinforce the imperative for a One Health approach?
3. How can policies guide the distribution of antimicrobials across countries and sectors—expanding access while conserving effectiveness?
4. Why have the Global Action Plan for AMR and the UN General Assembly High Level Meeting on AMR proven ineffective in leading to national action plans to address AMR?

5. Why has the development of international law across the Quadripartite been unable to regulate antimicrobials effectively and prevent AMR? How could international trade law under the WTO improve access to antimicrobials?
6. Does the rise of new state and non-state actors in AMR governance signal a shift away from states and international organizations as the primary actors in global AMR governance? How can non-state actors, including pharmaceutical companies, support global AMR efforts?
7. How can global health law reforms across the global health governance landscape help to address AMR? Why is the revision of the IHR insufficient—requiring coordination of the revision of instruments across the Quadripartite and through the WTO?
8. In developing new AMR laws, what are the advantages of addressing AMR through a new stand-alone AMR agreement? What has held back diplomatic efforts to develop a multisectoral AMR treaty?

Acknowledgments

The authors thank Safaa Yaseen, Taylor Corpening, Ashley Lim, and Erin Jones for their research assistance, Sofía Gutiérrez for her graphic design support on Figure 15.1, and the peer-reviewers and editors for their helpful and constructive feedback on earlier versions of this chapter. The authors acknowledge funding from the Canadian Institutes of Health Research (CIHR).

Disclosures

SJH serves as Vice-President for Data & Surveillance at the Public Health Agency of Canada (PHAC). The academic views and opinions expressed in this chapter are those of the authors and do not necessarily reflect those of PHAC, CIHR, or the Government of Canada.

References

Access to Medicine Foundation. 2022. *Lack of Access to Medicine Is a Major Driver of Drug Resistance. How Can Pharma Take Action*? Amsterdam: Access to Medicine Foundation.

Årdal, Christine, Kevin Outterson, Steven J Hoffman, Abdul Ghafur, Mike Sharland, Nisha Ranganathan, Richard Smith et al. 2016. "International Cooperation to Improve Access to and Sustain Effectiveness of Antimicrobials." *Lancet* 387(10015): 296–307.

Baekkeskov, Erik, Olivier Rubin, Louise Munkholm, and Wesal Zaman. 2020. "Antimicrobial Resistance as a Global Health Crisis." In *Oxford Research Encyclopedia of Politics*, by Erik Baekkeskov, Olivier Rubin, Louise Munkholm, and Wesal Zaman. New York: Oxford University Press.

Behdinan, Asha, Steven J. Hoffman, and Mark Pearcey. 2015. "Some Global Policies for Antibiotic Resistance Depend on Legally Binding and Enforceable Commitments." *Journal of Law, Medicine & Ethics* 43(S3): 68–73.

Chandler, Clare I. R. 2019. "Current Accounts of Antimicrobial Resistance: Stabilisation, Individualisation and Antibiotics as Infrastructure." *Palgrave Communications* 5(1): 53.

Esiovwa, Regina, John Connolly, Andrew Hursthouse, Soumyo Mukherji, Suparna Mukherji, Anjali Parasnis, Kavita Sachwani, and Fiona Henriquez. 2022. "Bridging the Gaps in the Global Governance of Antimicrobial Resistance: The UN Sustainable Development Goals and Global Health Security Agenda." *Routledge Open Research* 1(April): 8.

FAO, OIE, and WHO. 2010. *The FAO-OIE-WHO Collaboration: Sharing Responsibilities and Coordinating Global Activities to Address Health Risks at the Animal-Human-Ecosystems Interface*. Geneva: FAO, OIE, WHO.

G7. 2016. "Ise-Shima Vision for Global Health."

G20. 2017. "Berlin Declaration of the G20 Health Ministers."

Hoffman, Steven J., Prativa Baral, Susan Rogers Van Katwyk, Lathika Sritharan, Matthew Hughsam, Harkanwal Randhawa, Gigi Lin et al. 2022. "International Treaties Have Mostly Failed to Produce Their Intended Effects." *Proceedings of the National Academy of Sciences* 119(32): e2122854119.

Hoffman, Steven J. and Asha Behdinan. 2016. "Towards an International Treaty on Antimicrobial Resistance." *Ottawa Law Review* 47(2): 503–534.

Hoffman, Steven J. and Trygve Ottersen. 2015. "Addressing Antibiotic Resistance Requires Robust International Accountability Mechanisms." *The Journal of Law, Medicine & Ethics* 43(S3): 53–64.

Hoffman, Steven J. and Kevin Outterson. 2015. "What Will It Take to Address the Global Threat of Antibiotic Resistance?" *Journal of Law, Medicine & Ethics* 43(2): 363–338.

Hoffman, Steven J., John-Arne Røttingen, and Julio Frenk. 2015a. "International Law Has a Role to Play in Addressing Antibiotic Resistance." *Journal of Law, Medicine & Ethics* 43(S3): 65–67.

Hoffman, Steven J., John-Arne Røttingen, and Julio Frenk. 2015b. "Assessing Proposals for New Global Health Treaties: An Analytic Framework." *American Journal of Public Health* 105(8): 1523–1530.

IACG (Inter-Agency Coordination Group for AMR). 2019. "No Time to Wait: Securing the Future from Drug-Resistant Infections." *The Interagency Coordination Group on Antimicrobial Resistance*.

Institute for Health Metrics and Evaluation. 2020. *GBD Compare Data Visualization*. Seattle: IHME, University of Washington.

Joshi, Mohan P., Tamara Hafner, Gloria Twesigye, Antoine Ndiaye, Reuben Kiggundu, Negussu Mekonnen, Ndinda Kusu et al. 2021. "Strengthening Multisectoral Coordination on Antimicrobial Resistance: A Landscape Analysis of Efforts in 11 Countries." *Journal of Pharmaceutical Policy and Practice* 14(1): 27.

Léger, Anaïs, Irene Lambraki, Tiscar Graells, Melanie Cousins, Patrik J. G. Henriksson, Stephan Harbarth, Carolee Carson et al. 2021. "AMR-Intervene: A Social–Ecological Framework to Capture the Diversity of Actions to Tackle Antimicrobial Resistance from a One Health Perspective." *Journal of Antimicrobial Chemotherapy* 76(1): 1–21.

Lerner, Henrik and Charlotte Berg. 2017. "A Comparison of Three Holistic Approaches to Health: One Health, EcoHealth, and Planetary Health." *Frontiers in Veterinary Science* 4(September): 163.

Ming, Alexandra, Jacob Puddle, and Henry Wilson. 2019. *Antimicrobial Resistance: The Role of Regulation*. Brussels: Global Governance Institute.

Minssen, Timo, Kevin Outterson, Susan Rogers Van Katwyk, Pedro Henrique D Batista, Clare I. R. Chandler, Francesco Ciabuschi, Stephan Harbarth et al. 2020. "Social, Cultural and Economic Aspects of Antimicrobial Resistance." *Bulletin of the World Health Organization* 98(12): 823–823A.

Murray, Christopher J. L., Kevin Shunji Ikuta, Fablina Sharara, Lucien Swetschinski, Gisela Robles Aguilar, Authia Gray, Chieh Han et al. 2022. "Global Burden of Bacterial Antimicrobial Resistance in 2019: A Systematic Analysis." *Lancet* 399: 629–655.

Outterson, Kevin, Unni Gopinathan, Charles Clift, Anthony D. So, Chantal M. Morel, and John-Arne Røttingen. 2016. "Delinking Investment in Antibiotic Research and Development from Sales Revenues: The Challenges of Transforming a Promising Idea into Reality." *PLOS Medicine* 13(6): e1002043.

Outterson, Kevin, John H. Powers, Gregory W. Daniel, and Mark B. McClellan. 2015. "Repairing the Broken Market For Antibiotic Innovation." *Health Affairs* 34(2): 277–285.

Ray, Michael J., Gregory B. Tallman, David T. Bearden, Miriam R. Elman, and Jessina C. McGregor. 2019. "Antibiotic Prescribing without Documented Indication in Ambulatory Care Clinics: National Cross Sectional Study." *BMJ Global Health* 367: l6461.

Rogers Van Katwyk, Susan, Alberto Giubilini, Claas Kirchhelle, Isaac Weldon, Mark Harrison, Angela McLean, Julian Savulescu, and Steven J. Hoffman. 2023. "Exploring Models for an International Legal Agreement on the Global Antimicrobial Commons: Lessons from Climate Agreements." *Health Care Analysis* 31: 25–46.

Rogers Van Katwyk, Susan, Jeremy M. Grimshaw, Miriam Nkangu, Ranjana Nagi, Marc Mendelson, Monica Taljaard, and Steven J. Hoffman. 2019. "Government Policy Interventions to Reduce Human Antimicrobial Use: A Systematic Review and Evidence Map." *PLOS Medicine* 16(6): e1002819.

Rogers Van Katwyk, Susan, Isaac Weldon, Alberto Giubilini, Claas Kirchhelle, Mark Harrison, Angela McLean, Julian Savulescu, and Steven J. Hoffman. 2020. "Making Use of Existing International Legal Mechanisms to Manage the Global Antimicrobial Commons: Identifying Legal Hooks and Institutional Mandates." *Health Care Analysis*. March.

Ruckert, Arne, Patrick Fafard, Suzanne Hindmarch, Andrew Morris, Corinne Packer, David Patrick, Scott Weese, Kumanan Wilson, Alex Wong, and Ronald Labonté. 2020. "Governing Antimicrobial Resistance: A Narrative Review of Global Governance Mechanisms." *Journal of Public Policy* 41: 515–528.

Shafiq, Nusrat, Avaneesh Kumar Pandey, Samir Malhotra, Alison Holmes, Marc Mendelson, Rohit Malpani, Manica Balasegaram, and Esmita Charani. 2021. "Shortage of Essential Antimicrobials: A Major Challenge to Global Health Security." *BMJ Global Health* 6(11): e006961.

Simpkin, Victoria L, Matthew J. Renwick, Ruth Kelly, and Elias Mossialos. 2017. "Incentivising Innovation in Antibiotic Drug Discovery and Development: Progress, Challenges and next Steps." *The Journal of Antibiotics* 70(12): 1087–1096.

Tejpar, Serena, Susan Rogers Van Katwyk, Lindsay Wilson, and Steven J. Hoffman. 2022. "Taking Stock of Global Commitments on Antimicrobial Resistance." *BMJ Global Health* 7(5): e008159.

UNEP, WHO, FAO, and WOAH. 2022. "Quadripartite Memorandum of Understanding (MoU) Signed for a New Era of One Health Collaboration." *United Nations Environmental Programme.* April 29.

UN General Assembly. 2016. "Political Declaration of the High-Level Meeting of the General Assembly on Antimicrobial Resistance." September 22. A/71/L.2.

Weldon, Isaac and Steven J. Hoffman. 2021. "Bridging the Commitment-Compliance Gap in Global Health Politics: Lessons from International Relations for the Global Action Plan on Antimicrobial Resistance." *Global Public Health* 16(1): 60–74.

Weldon, Isaac, Kathy Liddell, Susan Rogers Van Katwyk, Steven J. Hoffman, Timo Minssen, Kevin Outterson, Stephanie Palmer, A.M. Viens, and Jorge Viñuales. 2022. "A Pandemic Instrument Can Start Turning Collective Problems into Collective Solutions by Governing the Common-Pool Resource of Antimicrobial Effectiveness." *Journal of Law, Medicine & Ethics* 50 (S2): 17–25.

Weldon, Isaac, Susan Rogers Van Katwyk, Gian Luca Burci, Dr Giur, Thana C. de Campos, Mark Eccleston-Turner, Helen R. Fryer et al. 2022. "Governing Global Antimicrobial Resistance: 6 Key Lessons from the Paris Climate Agreement." *American Journal of Public Health* 112(4): 553–557.

Wernli, Didier, Thomas Haustein, John Conly, Yehuda Carmeli, Ilona Kickbusch, and Stephan Harbarth. 2011. "A Call for Action: The Application of the International Health Regulations to the Global Threat of Antimicrobial Resistance." *PLoS Medicine* 8(4): e1001022.

Wernli, Didier, Peter S. Jørgensen, E. Jane Parmley, Max Troell, Shannon Majowicz, Stephan Harbarth, Anaïs Léger et al. 2020. "Evidence for Action: A One Health Learning Platform on Interventions to Tackle Antimicrobial Resistance." *Lancet Infectious Diseases* 20(12): e307–311.

White, Allison and James M. Hughes. 2019. "Critical Importance of a One Health Approach to Antimicrobial Resistance." *EcoHealth* 16(3): 404–409.

Wilson, Lindsay A., Susan Rogers Van Katwyk, Isaac Weldon, and Steven J. Hoffman. 2021. "A Global Pandemic Treaty Must Address Antimicrobial Resistance." *Journal of Law, Medicine & Ethics* 49(4): 688–691.

World Bank. 2017. "Drug-Resistant Infections: A Threat to Our Economic Future." 114679. Washington: World Bank.

WHO (World Health Organization). 2014. *Antimicrobial Resistance: Global Report on Surveillance.* Geneva: WHO.

WHO. 2015a. *Global Action Plan on Antimicrobial Resistance.* Geneva: WHO.

WHO. 2015b. "Sixty-Eighth World Health Assembly Resolutions and Decisions." May 26. WHA68/2015/REC/1.

WHO. 2018. *Joint External Evaluation Tool: International Health Regulations (2005).* 2nd ed. Geneva: WHO.

WHO. 2020. *Global Antimicrobial Resistance Surveillance System (GLASS) Report: Early Implementation 2020.* Geneva: WHO.

WHO, WTO (World Trade Organization), and WIPO (World Intellectual Property Organization). 2016. "Antimicrobial Resistance—a Global Epidemic." *WTO.*

WTO. 2006. "Pharmaceutical Patents and the TRIPS Agreement." *WTO.*

WTO Committee on Sanitary and Phytosanitary Measures. 2020. "Review of the Operation and Implementation of the SPS Agreement." August 3. G/SPS/64/Add.1.

16
Pathogen Sharing
Balancing Access to Pathogen Samples with Equitable Access to Medicines

Mark Eccleston-Turner and Michelle Rourke

Introduction

Human pathogens, such as bacteria and viruses that cause human disease, are continuously evolving, and scientists require new samples of pathogens from different hosts and different countries to monitor the changes in genetic mutations and the geographic distribution of particular strains. Effectively combating emerging and re-emerging infectious diseases requires a coordinated international response, working across nations to facilitate diagnostic testing, disease surveillance, risk assessments, and the development of strain-specific vaccines and medical countermeasures. It is vitally important that public health researchers have rapid and ongoing access to pathogen samples and associated genetic sequence data to develop evidence-based pandemic preparedness and response measures. Low-and-middle-income countries—often the site of pathogen emergence and re-emergence—have long been expected to provide pathogen samples to the international public health community, often without the opportunity to purchase the resulting medical countermeasures. This dynamic has led to vast inequities in access to vaccines and essential medicines to protect marginalized populations.

Global health law must balance prompt access to pathogen samples for the scientific community with equitable access to essential medicines, and since 2011, these issues have been linked together through the access and benefit sharing (ABS) transaction. The ABS transaction arises out of the United Nations Environment Programme (UNEP) Convention on Biological Diversity (CBD), which holds that states have sovereign rights over their genetic resources. States can therefore regulate access to genetic resources that originate in their territories, and require that users of their genetic resources provide benefits in return. These sovereign rights over genetic resources in international environmental law later came to dominate discussions about access to pathogen samples in global health law, and the issue of pathogen sharing is now seemingly inseparable from the issue of equitable access to essential medicines. Yet, the advancement of global health objectives through the ABS transaction does not appear to have provided prompt access to pathogen samples, nor ensured equitable access to essential medicines.

This chapter evaluates the role of ABS transactions as a basis to facilitate pathogen sharing and ensure fair and equitable access to medicines under global health law. Part I outlines the evolving attention to pathogen sharing under international law, with emphasis on how pathogens came to be interpreted as sovereign genetic resources under the CBD. Proponents have argued that linking access to genetic resources with the sharing of associated benefits such as vaccines and antiviral medications is a way to facilitate sharing and promote fairness and equity. However, Part II demonstrates that, in numerous instances, the ABS transaction has had the unintended consequence of inhibiting prompt pathogen sharing, potentially endangering public health. There has been little evidence that ABS transactions support access to medicines for low- and middle-income countries, and Part III examines potential reform proposals to enhance global health justice in equitable access to medical countermeasures. This chapter concludes that global health law could provide the tools to facilitate access to pathogen samples and, separately, provide medicines, but reforms should delink these issues in global health law.

I. The Evolution of Pathogen Sharing for Global Health Security

Given the centrality of infectious diseases to global health security, biological resources—from the plants used in traditional medicines to the genetic sequence of samples—have long been shared between public health researchers and pharmaceutical scientists to advance global health. The arrangements for sharing these pathogen samples were largely informal, with scientists sharing samples within their professional networks, often without written agreement.[1] Low- and middle-income countries came to see this extraction of their nations' genetic wealth, without any sharing of the resulting benefits with the country of origin, as "biopiracy." As a result, transfers of genetic resources have become increasingly formalized. Since the introduction of the international ABS regime under the 1992 Convention on Biological Diversity, states have implemented a variety of domestic ABS laws that apply to the transfer of their genetic resources, including pathogen samples. Transfer arrangements are now often formally documented in agreements, access permits, internationally recognized certificates of compliance, and/or material transfer agreements. The world has since developed

---

[1] While these sharing arrangements have largely been informal, there have arisen various rules about import and export of pathogen samples, safe storage and transport, and patient privacy.

a complex patchwork of different ABS laws that apply to different genetic resources, including pathogen samples.

A. From Colonialism and Common Heritage of Mankind to Permanent Sovereignty over Natural Resources

The continuing legacies of colonialism in the pursuit of scientific knowledge and innovation tends to devalue non-Western sources of raw materials and knowledge (Rourke 2022). Historically, botanists and natural scientists from the Global North traveled across the Global South collecting local biological resources—including plants, animals, and microorganisms—without the permission of the countries of origin. These biological resources were transferred to the Global North, where they were used for a range of applications: some were stored in private collections of wealthy science enthusiasts, some went to public collections in museums and universities, and some were used in biological research and development (Smith 2012). When these biological resources were found in nature, they were considered to be common goods (Rhot-Arriaza 1996). However, once transferred to the Global North, these biological resources, and any products made from them, were treated as private goods that could be owned and traded. The local communities and governments that were stewards of the land and local biodiversity were rarely consulted about the extraction of their biological wealth—a practice that often continued well beyond the colonial period.

In the decades after World War II, colonized states began to assert their independence, looking to doctrines of international law as a means to regain control of their natural resources (Anghie 2005). Throughout the 1960s, newly sovereign nations of the Global South asserted permanent sovereignty over their natural resources as a means of self-determination and financial development, as first introduced in Chapter 3, resulting in a series of UN resolutions advocating for a "New International Economic Order" (NIEO) (Anghie 2005). These resolutions argued that the existing international economic order "was established at a time when most of the developing countries did not even exist as independent states," with these "developing countries" proposing the "establishment of a new international economic order based on equity, sovereignty, equality, interdependence, common interest and cooperation" in an effort to "correct inequalities and redress social injustices" (UN General Assembly 1974, 3). Central to the NIEO was the idea that all states, including newly independent states, had permanent sovereignty over their respective territory and the natural resources within it, and that states could (and should) use these natural resources to trade their way to economic prosperity—creating the so-called trade not aid agenda (Zacker 1993).

These claims of sovereignty over natural resources eventually came to encompass pathogens. By the late 1980s, scientists had developed the ability to read and interpret the genetic code, and biological resources were becoming more valuable as "genetic resources" (Schei and Tvedt 2010). This meant that even minute quantities of biological material could have major value in the agricultural sciences, therapeutics, and cosmetic industries in countries rich enough to conduct the required research and development. The potential for "green gold" meant that low- and middle-income countries became even more wary of the extraction of their biological wealth, with increasing claims of "biopiracy" (Prip and Rosendal 2015). These states sought to develop international legal instruments to support them to sustainably capitalize on biological material while at the same time conserving it for future generations.

The 1992 United Nations (UN) Conference for Environment and Development in Rio de Janeiro, Brazil, provided an opportunity to develop global policies to facilitate environmental protection and, at the same time, sustainable development. This so-called Rio Earth Summit, first introduced in Chapter 9, sought to allow states to collectively address many of the world's environmental problems and provide a path toward sustainable development: "development which would provide a better life now but not at the expense of the future survival of human beings and other species" (Panjabi 1993, 201). Three environmental treaties came out of the Rio Earth Summit: the UN Framework Convention on Climate Change, the UN Convention to Combat Desertification, and the Convention on Biological Diversity (CBD).

The CBD has three key objectives: "[1] the conservation of biological diversity, [2] the sustainable use of its components and [3] the fair and equitable sharing of the benefits arising out of the utilization of genetic resources" (CBD 1992, art. 1). The third objective gave rise to the term "access and benefit sharing," with this mechanism in the CBD designed to generate money and other benefits that could be channeled into achieving the other two objectives on conservation and sustainable development. While the UN General Assembly had previously developed resolutions about the permanent sovereignty of states over their natural resources, the notion of sovereign rights over the genetic resources within a nation's jurisdiction had now been reaffirmed in a widely adopted and binding international treaty (CBD 1992, art. 3).[2]

While states retain the ability to implement whatever ABS rules they see fit, the CBD outlines various minimum requirements for accessing genetic resources, including that users of genetic resources in research and development must obtain the prior informed consent of the country of origin, or other suitably authorized provider party. The user and provider parties should come to mutually agreed terms about how the genetic resources are to be used and what benefits will be shared with the providers of genetic resources. The aim of the ABS transaction—providing access to genetic resources in exchange for benefits such as money, intellectual property rights, shared credit or authorship of research publications, capacity-building projects such as training courses—is to ensure the benefits of scientific research and

---

[2] The CBD defines genetic resources as "genetic material of actual or potential value" and genetic material as "any material of plant, animal, microbial or other origin containing functional units of heredity" (CBD 1992, art. 2).

development on genetic resources are going back to the countries that provided the raw materials for the research, viewing pathogens as sovereign assets.

B. Pathogens Become Sovereign Assets

Despite pathogens being genetic resources and the introduction of the widely adopted international ABS minimum standards under the CBD, the exchange of pathogen samples for scientific research and development continued in a largely informal manner for more than a decade, including at the World Health Organization (WHO) (Reichman, Uhlir, and Dedeurwaerdere 2016). This was until late 2006 when the Indonesian Health Minister, Dr. Siti Fadilah Supari, seen in Figure 16.1, declared that Indonesia would no longer share influenza virus samples with WHO, arguing that such informal pathogen sample sharing was not in line with the CBD and was unfair for developing countries (Irwin 2010).

Figure 16.1 Indonesian Health Minister, Dr. Siti Fadilah Supari, Demands Action from the World Health Assembly on Pathogen Sharing (2006) (Reuters/Denis Balibouse)

Case Study: The Indonesian Virus Sharing Incident

Since the early 1950s, WHO had coordinated a network of influenza laboratories around the world that informally shared influenza samples with other laboratories in the network and with parties outside of it—including pharmaceutical companies. Indonesia's refusal to share influenza samples went against decades of customary sample sharing that had helped to monitor the spread of seasonal influenza, determine which strains of influenza should be included in the annual seasonal vaccines, and detect the emergence of strains of influenza with pandemic potential. In response to the threat posed in 2006 by H5N1 avian influenza, which had struck Indonesia harder than any other state, the World Health Assembly passed a resolution that called upon WHO member states to "[d]isseminate to the WHO collaborating centres information and relevant biological materials related to highly pathogenic avian influenza and other novel influenza strains in a timely and consistent manner." Indonesia, however, argued that developing countries were being expected to provide the raw materials of research and development for free but often lacked access to the resulting medications, which were snapped up by high-income countries. Minister Supari made the case that Indonesian virus samples were not public goods but were sovereign genetic resources under the CBD, and thereby the access and use of those samples are subject to "prior informed consent" and "mutually agreed terms."[a] In accordance with their sovereign rights over their genetic resources, as reaffirmed in the CBD, Indonesia claimed that it could negotiate a bilateral ABS agreement directly with an influenza vaccine manufacturer—providing access to their highly pathogenic novel H5N1 samples in exchange for resources that could be used to address the worsening avian influenza situation in their territories.

[a] The 1992 CBD had not been negotiated with human pathogens in mind, and the applicability of the CBD to pathogen sharing was not immediately obvious until the Indonesian government brought attention to the issue.

By refusing to share samples, Indonesia highlighted the inequity of being expected to freely share virus samples with WHO but being denied fair access to the vaccines and antivirals developed using those samples. However, this pattern of what developing countries saw as exploitation would continue as the world faced an escalating series of public health emergencies of international concern.

During the 2014–2016 West African Ebola crisis, some of the Western researchers that helped set up temporary diagnostic laboratories in Guinea,

Liberia, and Sierra Leone took patient Ebola virus samples back to their own nations' laboratories without the consent of the countries of origin (Abayomi et al. 2016). Through this unauthorized transfer of biological material, European researchers isolated a strain of the Ebola virus from a Guinean patient, sequenced the strain, and published the genetic sequence data to GenBank, an open-access online repository of genetic sequences maintained by the U.S. National Institutes of Health (Hammond 2019). These genetic sequence data were then used by the U.S. pharmaceutical corporation Regeneron Pharmaceuticals to develop an experimental Ebola drug, which has now been approved for use by the U.S. Food and Drug Administration (Bagley 2022). This Ebola drug has since attracted lucrative U.S. government contracts worth hundreds of millions of dollars (Hammond 2019), with more than one hundred patent applications filed around the world (Bagley 2022). While the Guinean patient provided the raw materials and genetic resources that were essential to developing this medical product, no ABS agreements were in place to ensure that Guinea received any share of the benefits.

These practices highlight how research relations between the Global North and Global South continue to be extractive. Pathogen samples, the raw materials necessary to facilitate pharmaceutical advancements, are still seen by high-income countries as free for the taking—even as the resulting medicines are protected by intellectual property regimes and available only to the wealthy. In these situations, many of the medical countermeasures required by low- and middle-income countries to protect their populations from infectious disease threats are shared only through coercive international trade arrangements and/or when branded as aid or charity. Yet these medical countermeasures would not exist without the raw materials provided by low- and middle-income countries. Advocates looked to global health law to address these two resource allocation issues—ensuring prompt access to pathogens for research in a health emergency and ensuring prompt access to vaccines and medical countermeasures—with WHO linking these two issues using the ABS transaction.

II. ABS under Global Health Law

Despite having been designed as a mechanism to generate benefits for environmental conservation and the sustainable use of biological diversity under the CBD, the ABS paradigm has come to dominate the discussion about access to pathogen samples and equitable access to medical countermeasures under global health law. At the height of the H5N1 influenza sharing issue in 2006, WHO accepted Indonesia's framing of pathogen samples as "genetic resources" under the

CBD, and the solution to the standoff therefore took the form of the ABS transaction: an exchange of access for benefits. With pathogens covered under the CBD and its subsequent protocols, the World Health Assembly sought to establish a non-binding framework for the sharing of influenza viruses and access to vaccines and other benefits.

A. Pathogen Access under the Nagoya Protocol

As WHO was negotiating with Indonesia and other member states about how to deal with H5N1 influenza sample sharing, the states parties to the CBD were already negotiating a supplementary protocol to the CBD that would expand on the minimum standards of the ABS transaction. The resulting 2010 Nagoya Protocol on Access to Genetic Resources and the Fair and Equitable Sharing of Benefits Arising from their Utilization to the Convention on Biological Diversity (Nagoya Protocol) provided additional details to the CBD to increase legal clarity for providers and users of genetic resources, enhance the rights of Indigenous Peoples and local communities, enhance implementation, and strengthen compliance measures.

The negotiators of the Nagoya Protocol were aware of the ongoing negotiations to resolve access to influenza viruses and the sharing of benefits associated with their use at WHO, and there were intense debates about whether to explicitly include pathogens in the scope of the Nagoya Protocol (Tvedt 2013). In the end, the Nagoya Protocol did not explicitly include pathogens within its scope, but it did include the following special consideration:

> In the development and implementation of its access and benefit-sharing legislation or regulatory requirements, each Party shall: ... (b) Pay due regard to cases of present or imminent emergencies that threaten or damage human, animal or plant health, as determined nationally or internationally. Parties may take into consideration the need for expeditious access to genetic resources and expeditious fair and equitable sharing of benefits arising out of the use of such genetic resources, including access to affordable treatments by those in need, especially in developing countries (CBD 2011, art. 8(b)).

The Nagoya Protocol thereby created "the regulatory space for Parties to ensure that general ABS rules and procedures do not interfere with public health efforts" (Morgera, Tsioumani & Buck 2014, 185). This special consideration does not exempt countries from exercising their sovereign authority over their pathogen samples, but it requires that both the access and the benefit sharing sides of the ABS transaction be carried out expeditiously in the event of a public health emergency.

WHO could no longer continue to share influenza virus samples without regard to the principles of the CBD and its newly negotiated Nagoya Protocol; yet, it could not practically engage in bilateral contract negotiations with every provider nation for every single influenza virus sample that was to be shared with WHO's global network of influenza laboratories. WHO Member States would need to come up with a new arrangement. During the negotiations for a new virus sharing arrangement that recognized sovereign rights over pathogen samples, Indonesia submitted a World Health Assembly proposal in line with the ABS requirements of the CBD:

> [A] framework of benefit sharing is to be developed through agreed terms and conditions to ensure a global stockpile of pre-pandemic and pandemic vaccines, accessibility of vaccine at an affordable price, access to and transfer of technology and know-how for production of vaccines and empowerment and capacity building of vaccine manufacturing in developing countries (WHO 2007, 9).

Four years of negotiations on this proposal among WHO Member States resulted in the adoption of the 2011 Pandemic Influenza Preparedness Framework for the Sharing of Influenza Viruses and Access to Vaccines and Other Benefits (PIP Framework). Adopted as a non-binding resolution of the World Health Assembly, the PIP Framework outlines ABS arrangements for the subset of influenza viruses that have human pandemic potential (Eccleston-Turner 2018), and thus excludes seasonal influenza viruses. The PIP Framework "recognize[s] the sovereign right of States over their biological resources and the importance of collective action to mitigate public health risks" (WHO 2011, art. 1.11). The PIP Framework seeks to encourage the sharing of influenza viruses with human pandemic potential and resulting vaccines and other benefits "on an equal footing" and "as equally important parts of the collective action for global public health" (ibid., arts. 1.3 and 2). The PIP Framework thus codified the use of the ABS transaction in the public health space—albeit multilaterally, rather than bilaterally—with the "WHO mediating a constellation of transactions between member state providers and third-party users of influenza viruses with human pandemic potential" (Eccleston-Turner and Rourke 2021, 827).

Case Study: Multilateralism and the PIP Framework

The PIP Framework is a multilateral ABS framework governing access to influenza viruses with human pandemic potential in exchange for the benefits arising from their use in research and development. It was developed by

WHO member states to (a) facilitate the timely sharing of influenza samples with human pandemic potential between member states and WHO-affiliated laboratories of the Global Influenza Surveillance and Response System (GISRS); and (b) provide access to virus samples to third-party entities that operate outside of the GISRS, such as universities, pharmaceutical companies, and vaccine manufacturers. While non-binding, the PIP Framework contains "Standard Material Transfer Agreements" (SMTAs) to facilitate these ABS transactions.[a] The shared influenza vaccines, diagnostics, and other pharmaceuticals collected by WHO under "The PIP Benefit Sharing System" are to be distributed to member states based on "public health risk and need." The PIP Framework is an ABS mechanism that puts WHO at the center of multiple transactions between providers and users of influenza viruses with human pandemic potential, creating a multilateral ABS framework for a highly specific subset of genetic resources. Given the mediator role to be played by WHO, the PIP Framework was seen as an appealing option for low- and middle-income countries, which, in a pandemic, may not be able to secure vaccines through bilateral commercial arrangements with pharmaceutical companies. By incorporating the CBD's language of sovereign rights and benefit sharing under WHO governance, the PIP Framework put formal rules around the previous informal virus sharing practices of WHO-affiliated influenza laboratories and sought to ensure compliance with those rules through WHO involvement.

[a] SMTA1 is a form contract that is used to transfer influenza viruses with human pandemic potential from a Member State's National Influenza Centers (national laboratories) to other laboratories in the WHO's influenza surveillance network. SMTA2 is a form contract entered into between the WHO and third-party entities outside of the WHO. SMTA2 commits third-party entities receiving material from the GISRS to sharing associated benefits with WHO for distribution to member states in the event of an influenza pandemic.

The PIP Framework was praised as a novel and innovative international instrument that employed standardized contracts to commit third parties to the provisions of an otherwise non-binding resolution (Fidler and Gostin 2011). However, there remain doubts as to whether the PIP Framework will be able to deliver the promised benefits to low- and middle-income countries in an influenza pandemic (Eccleston-Turner and Rourke 2021).[3]

[3] The PIP Framework has not yet been used in an influenza pandemic, so it remains unclear if it will be able to deliver the promised benefits (Eccleston-Turner and Rourke 2021). During a pandemic, there are concerns that countries with vaccine manufacturing capacity may not allow vaccine doses to leave their country until all of their own citizens are protected. These concerns have been bolstered amid the COVID-19 pandemic—by the rampant vaccine nationalism of high-income countries and the use of export controls on essential goods, including vaccines. Even if WHO has

Further, the PIP Framework has formalized ABS only for influenza viruses with human pandemic potential shared through the WHO-affiliated laboratories. All other human pathogens remain subject to the CBD and Nagoya Protocol—and the ABS laws that individual nations have developed to implement the provisions of these international agreements. The default ABS transaction envisioned by the CBD and Nagoya Protocol occurs bilaterally between the provider party and user party. The Nagoya Protocol creates a carveout for "specialized international access and benefit sharing instrument[s]" providing they are "consistent with, and do not run counter to the objectives of the [CBD]" (CBD 2011, art. 4.4). This means that the specific provisions of the CBD and Nagoya Protocol would not apply to the specific genetic resources covered by a specialized ABS instrument like the PIP Framework. This means that if the PIP Framework were recognized as a specialized international ABS instrument under the Nagoya Protocol, then all influenza viruses with human pandemic potential shared through the PIP Framework would not then be subject to the provisions of the CBD and Nagoya Protocol. It is unclear, however, whether the PIP Framework would qualify as a specialized international ABS instrument under the Nagoya Protocol (Rourke and Eccleston-Turner 2021), and there is no mechanism under international law to have it recognized as such (CBD 2018). As a result, there remains a significant degree of uncertainty within global health law about how these international instruments—the CBD, Nagoya Protocol, and the PIP Framework—interact with one another in creating an ABS system for treating influenza pathogens with human pandemic potential.

B. Pathogens as Tradable Commodities

Whether under the international ABS regime created by the CBD and Nagoya Protocol, or under the PIP Framework, ABS remains a transaction—a quid pro quo. In the case of the PIP Framework, it is giving access to sovereign influenza virus samples in exchange for a chance – not a guarantee – to obtain benefits during a pandemic response. However, there are several key conceptual problems with applying the ABS transaction to pathogens, which may make it an inappropriate mechanism in global health governance (Eccleston-Turner and Rourke 2021).

---

commitments from pharmaceutical companies to provide a portion of their vaccine doses to WHO for distribution to low- and middle-income countries, as discussed under the COVAX mechanism in Chapter 14, most high-income countries have nevertheless acted in a way that benefits their own citizens—no matter the public health need in other countries.

Global health should be seen as a shared goal for all, but the international ABS regime pits parties against each other in a buyer-seller relationship. The commodification of pathogen samples creates opposing incentives for the user and provider parties. Thus, in an ABS transaction, each stakeholder is looking to maximize their gains and minimize their costs: providers of sovereign pathogen samples want to maximize benefit-sharing and users of those pathogen samples want to minimize the benefits to be shared with the providing nations.

Creating a market for human pathogens has thus introduced the dynamics of supply and demand into pathogen "sharing." Some pathogens are common and readily available (and their value in the ABS transaction will therefore be minimal), whereas some are scarce, difficult to access, or challenging to amplify in the laboratory (and their value will be comparatively large). A pathogen sample is most "valuable" in ABS terms if the pathogen is contained within the sovereign territory of a small number of nations—and thus in high demand. In such circumstances, users of pathogen samples (e.g., pharmaceutical companies) will need to negotiate an ABS agreement with the nation (or nations) that have the pathogen contained within their territorial borders (Rourke 2017). The provider nation in such circumstances may be able to negotiate favorable benefit sharing terms through a bilateral ABS contract, securing benefits for their populations, including the supply of resulting vaccines or other medical countermeasures. However, diseases do not respect international boundaries, and the moment a rare pathogen begins to spread internationally, the negotiation position of the nation seeking to close a beneficial ABS agreement is eroded. Thus, the ABS system, when applied to human pathogens, has created a perverse situation where the most "valuable" pathogens are the ones that are both rare and stand to threaten the lives of many people. In the wake of recent public health emergencies, it is necessary to consider the suitability of framing access to lifesaving medicines as something that is purchased with the provision of sovereign pathogen samples.

C. All of the Access, None of the Benefits

There have been limited efforts to apply the CBD, Nagoya Protocol, and PIP Framework to public health emergencies of international concern. It would seem there are few scenarios in which ABS could provide a path to achieve public health goals. Since the adoption of the PIP Framework, subsequent public health responses have highlighted the confusion and legal uncertainty in the ABS system for pathogen sharing.

1. MERS

Shortly after the adoption of the Nagoya Protocol and PIP Framework, a novel coronavirus emerged in Saudi Arabia in 2012. To identify the pathogen that was causing pneumonia-like symptoms in a patient, a doctor sent a clinical specimen from Saudi Arabia to the Erasmus Medical Centre (EMC) in the Netherlands for analysis. The Dutch laboratory identified the novel coronavirus (Zaki et al. 2012), later termed Middle East Respiratory Syndrome coronavirus (MERS-CoV). The EMC then transferred isolates of MERS-CoV to other research institutions around the world under the terms of their own institutional Material Transfer Agreement (MTA), without permission of Saudi Arabia. The government of Saudi Arabia viewed this as a violation of its sovereign rights—sovereign rights over biological resources that were reaffirmed in the CBD, and that WHO had just recognized the year before with the PIP Framework (Rourke 2020). The WHO sought to mediate the tension, with then WHO Director-General Margaret Chan urging WHO member states to share "viruses and specimens with WHO collaborating centres . . . not in a bilateral manner" (BBC 2013).

However, as the PIP Framework is limited to samples of influenza virus with human pandemic potential, nothing in that instrument could compel Saudi Arabia to share samples with WHO, as MERS falls outside the scope of the PIP Framework. Indeed, the PIP Framework cannot even compel the sharing of influenza samples with human pandemic potential, as the instrument itself recognizes that these samples are the sovereign genetic resource of the country of origin, and that country is free to share, or not share the sample, as they choose.

The Saudi Arabian experience with MERS-CoV demonstrated that, even if a country has sovereign rights over a genetic resource under a widely adopted and binding international treaty (the CBD), and even if those sovereign rights are notionally recognized by WHO member states (under the PIP Framework), states could still face challenges in exercising those rights (Eccleston-Turner and Rourke 2021). As soon as the sample left Saudi Arabia without an ABS agreement in place, the Saudi Arabian government was unable to enforce its sovereign rights over the samples extraterritorially. The samples continued to be shared by EMC throughout the public health emergency, despite the continuing objections of the Saudi Arabian government, revealing the ongoing limitations of the ABS regime.

2. Zika

These limitations continued during the major outbreak of Zika in Brazil in 2015. Due to the uncertainties surrounding this novel strain of Zika and its link to negative health outcomes in infants, it was declared a Public Health Emergency of International Concern (PHEIC) by the WHO Director-General. Yet, despite this triggering of international concern under the International Health Regulations, public health and pharmaceutical researchers outside Brazil only had access to Zika samples from earlier, less severe, outbreaks. When researchers attempted to obtain new samples from Brazil in the early days of the outbreak, they faced resistance from the Brazilian government (Cheng 2016). Brazil wanted to negotiate favorable terms for the country through an ABS agreement, claiming that, in accordance with the CBD and Nagoya Protocol, the samples could not be accessed without prior informed consent of the Brazilian government.

This appeared to put Brazil in a strong negotiating position, as the outbreak was attracting international attention and the Zika virus causing more severe symptoms were found only within the territory of Brazil. However, as Brazilian lawyers negotiated terms for the access and use of their virus samples with the U.S. government, the disease spread into Puerto Rico, a U.S. territory. Researchers working for the U.S. Centers for Disease Control and Prevention (CDC) were then able to access samples of the new strain of Zika virus samples directly from Puerto Rico, without having to negotiate an ABS agreement with Brazil (Marinissen et al. 2020). Ultimately, Brazil did not manage to conclude an ABS agreement for the transfer of Zika samples. The Brazilian government's bargaining position had disappeared once the disease spread beyond its borders, and Brazil's efforts to access medical countermeasures through the ABS transaction were rendered wholly ineffective, exposing the risk that "the desire of provider governments to secure benefits to protect their populations by leveraging one of the few bargaining chips they have can backfire, leaving vulnerable populations even more vulnerable" (Eccleston-Turner and Rourke 2021, 846).

3. Ebola

Unauthorized collection and use of pathogens continued during the international response to the West African Ebola outbreak in 2014–2016. Many patient samples containing the Ebola virus were extracted from Guinea, Liberia, and Sierra Leone without the prior informed consent of the countries of origin (Abayomi et al. 2016). The CBD requires scientific research based on genetic resources "with the full participation of, and where possible in, such [states]" (CBD 1992, art. 15.6), but critics contend that "West Africa became a playground for researchers allegedly appropriating and transporting specimens and data to their home laboratories, sometimes without the knowledge or permission of the countries in which they were collected" (Heymann, Liu, and Lillywhite 2016).[4]

---

[4] Beyond the loss of pharmaceutical benefits, there was also a loss of capacity building, as researchers from high-income countries build their careers by publishing research and entering in commercial arrangements with pharmaceutical companies while researchers in the provider countries were left behind (Ranjan 2023).

These practices exhibited a complete disregard for a fundamental principle of international law that was reaffirmed in the CBD: that states have "the sovereign right to exploit their own resources" (CBD 1992, art. 3), giving them "the authority to determine access to genetic resources" (ibid., art. 15.1).

The current framing of access to vaccines and other medical countermeasures as a benefit made available through the ABS transaction makes equitable access to medicines something that can be traded, bargained, or bartered in exchange for sovereign genetic resources. However, under various international resolutions and charters, equitable access to vaccines and other medicines is a fundamental human right—a legal entitlement regardless of government engagement in trading pathogen samples (Eccleston-Turner and Rourke 2021). The ABS model, taken from international environmental law, connects once previously disconnected public health issues: facilitating access to pathogen samples for scientists and ensuring justice and equity in the distribution of medical interventions. It is questionable that the ABS transaction is the optimal model for remedying these issues. Global health law, developed under WHO governance, could deliver an alternative model to regulate access to pathogen samples, and separately, access to medical countermeasures – without reliance on an ABS transaction that was not designed to address health issues.

III. WHO Seeks to Reclaim Authority over ABS

The issue of human pathogen sharing is an active field of work for WHO that will require additional reforms in global health law. Beyond considering the current ABS arrangements for pathogens with pandemic potential, reforms must also consider whether ABS is even the appropriate tool to achieve global health goals. In many cases, the ABS transaction has not been able to adequately and fairly ensure that medical countermeasures have been provided to countries in need. Bilateral pathogen ABS arrangements can only ever benefit the country of origin of the pathogen. While multilateral pathogen ABS models, like the PIP Framework, are considered a better solution for health equity, the operation of any multilateral pathogen-sharing mechanism under WHO will always be threatened by the ability of provider countries to engage in direct bilateral talks—without using WHO as an intermediary. Yet, there is the potential for another option altogether: to delink the act of providing access to sovereign pathogen samples from the provision of essential medicines. The two issues now appear to be inextricably linked within the WHO system through the ABS transaction—and alternative options for solving these two problems have never made it to the table (Eccleston-Turner and Rourke 2021)—but if WHO wants to maintain its authority in international pathogen sharing, it must find a solution that satisfies countries that are often providers of valuable pathogen samples and the high-income countries that have the capacity to use those pathogen samples in scientific research and product development. As WHO seeks an evolving approach to pathogen data, countries will continue to implement national pathogen ABS laws that are not necessarily in line with global health goals, with WHO seeking to align the PIP Framework and Nagoya Protocol in addressing genetic data and Pandemic Treaty debates seeking to frame ABS in future emergencies.

A. WHO's Evolving Approach to Pathogen Data

In response to claims that the PIP Framework had led to instances where virus samples were made more difficult to access, the World Health Assembly in 2019 adopted decisions to examine the issue of virus sharing under both the PIP Framework and Nagoya Protocol regimes. Despite the management of infectious diseases being within the mandate of WHO, the transfer of pathogens remains largely regulated by the CBD and Nagoya Protocol, instruments that sit under UNEP governance.[5] Correspondingly, the PIP Framework falls under WHO's exclusive authority, but it covers only the subset of influenza viruses that have the potential to cause a pandemic—with continuing legal confusion around whether the CBD and Nagoya Protocol apply to pandemic influenza virus samples. WHO must chart a path forward that is consistent with existing international law, that respects the sovereign rights of countries over their genetic resources, and that can genuinely ensure "transparency, equity, clarity and consistency in pathogen-sharing practices globally" (WHO 2021, 11). Meeting these imperatives will be necessary to ensure justice in global health. The ABS transactional mechanism, which was designed to fund environmental conservation and the sustainable use of biodiversity, may not be an appropriate mechanism to deal with public health emergencies. WHO and its member states must consider other solutions to these two problems (access to pathogen samples for research and access to medicines) outside the confines of the ABS framing. As seen in the international response to

---

[5] This conflict across legal regimes is made even more difficult to navigate because some countries are party to the CBD, some are party to both the CBD and Nagoya Protocol, and others (e.g., the United States) are party to neither the CBD nor the Nagoya Protocol. This means that when a pharmaceutical company requires a sample of a pathogen to make a vaccine, it can be unclear who the authorized provider of that sample may be, and what international, national, and even subnational laws should be followed.

COVID-19, where the ABS transaction was not employed as a legal mechanism, it is unlikely that the ABS transaction could have addressed the significant disparities arising in the equitable distribution of essential vaccines (Eccleston-Turner and Upton 2021).

Case Study: Pathogen Sharing amid COVID-19

On January 10, 2020, scientists in China publicly uploaded the first genetic sequence of the then unnamed Severe Acute Respiratory Syndrome Coronavirus 2 (SARS-CoV-2) to the internet. China officially shared the genetic sequence with WHO two days later, although it did not share physical samples of the virus.[a] The first physical samples of SARS-CoV-2 were made available to the WHO and clinical researchers around the world by Australian researchers at the end of January. As SARS-CoV-2 spread rapidly across the world, almost every country was able to obtain samples of the virus directly from their own citizens. The virus became ubiquitous, and thus there was no scarcity or demand that would produce the conditions that would be conducive to negotiating access arrangements for virus samples in exchange for valuable medical countermeasures through the ABS transaction. In effect, the entire international legal system of pathogen ABS was rendered redundant by the speed at which SARS-CoV-2 spread. The circumstances in which the ABS system was designed to work are so limited that the rules could not be applied to this pandemic threat. As a result, WHO did not broach the topic of ABS in relation to COVID-19, and its legal position on access to SARS-CoV-2 samples and the sharing of associated benefits was unclear—as WHO often referred to both SARS-CoV-2 samples and COVID-19 vaccines as global public goods.

[a] While some research and development can be conducted using the genetic sequence of the virus, it is still necessary to access and use the physical samples to validate diagnostic tests and new vaccines.

The avoidance of the ABS regime in the COVID-19 response demonstrates the inherent limits of this mechanism during a public health emergency. The ABS mechanism—whether looking to bilateral negotiations under the auspices of the CBD and Nagoya Protocol or multilateral systems like that under the PIP Framework—is applicable only in specific conditions. This limited applicability raises an imperative to consider new ways to manage sample sharing, and separately, the fair and equitable distribution of vaccines and other medical countermeasures during infectious disease emergencies. Transposing a mechanism that was designed to achieve very different (environmental conservation and sustainable use) aims is clearly not fit for the purpose of advancing global health. This is especially seen in the context of sharing pathogen data.

B. Genetic Sequence Data

In looking ahead to the next challenges of pathogen ABS, both WHO and the CBD are currently dealing with questions of access to genetic sequence data. For some third-party actors, such as pharmaceutical companies, accessing genetic sequence data (also referred to as "digital sequence information") is sometimes sufficient for pathogen sharing purposes (Lawson, Rourke, and Humphries 2020). Genetic sequence data is often openly available on the internet on genetic sequence repositories such as GenBank. This means that some user parties can avoid any need to (a) enter into an ABS agreement with a government for the bilateral transfer of physical pathogen samples or (b) sign an SMTA2 for multilateral ABS concerning pandemic influenza pathogens under the PIP Framework. They can therefore "use" the genetic resource for research and development without having a physical sample of the genetic resource, and without obtaining prior informed consent of the provider party. Where the CBD and PIP Framework apply only to genetic "materials," genetic sequence data undermines the ABS transaction that was intended to compensate countries for contributing their pathogen samples for analysis.[6] This digital loophole provides a path for companies to access the genetic resources they need online—and free of charge—without the corresponding obligation to provide benefits to WHO for use in an influenza pandemic (WHO 2016).

WHO has stated that it "expects" any third party (e.g., pharmaceutical company) using genetic data generated by GISRS to contribute a voluntary Partnership Contribution to WHO, but the fact that it is usually possible to access sequence data free of charge on any number of publicly accessible databases, often without any way of determining who has accessed that data, undermines any WHO efforts to ensure fairness in ABS (Lawson, Humphries, and Rourke 2019). In seeking to address this gap in ABS coverage, the 15th Conference of Parties to the CBD agreed in December 2022 to develop a multilateral benefit

---

[6] Compounding this challenge, existing obligations under the PIP Framework encourage the publishing of genetic sequence data on "public-domain or public-access databases such as GenBank and GISAID respectively" (WHO 2011, art. 5.2.2).

sharing system for the use of digital sequence information. It will be crucial for WHO to resolve these similar concerns—alongside CBD negotiations and in the development of a prospective Pandemic Treaty.

C. Pandemic Treaty Negotiations

At a November 2021 Special Session of the World Health Assembly, WHO member states agreed by consensus to establish an intergovernmental negotiating body (INB) to draft a convention, agreement, or other international instrument for pandemic preparedness and response under the WHO Constitution. In developing this so-called Pandemic Treaty, as first introduced in Chapter 5, Member States have pressed for novel legal obligations to structure the sharing of pathogen samples, genetic sequence data, and access to medicines (INB 2022). However, these Pandemic Treaty negotiations again see these issues framed within the context of the ABS transaction—rather than in the public health need for prompt access to pathogen samples and in the human rights need for universal access to essential medicines.

The Pandemic Treaty presents a unique opportunity to delink access to pathogens from the sharing of medicines. It should provide access to vital medicines, not because a country happens to have engaged in the bilateral or multilateral trading of pathogens, but because access to medicines is a universal human right to which all people have claim. Human rights obligations to access medical countermeasures should guide future approaches to these issues, ensuring that any new solutions are fit for purpose. There are ways to recognize countries' sovereign rights over their pathogen samples as "genetic resources" and share benefits such as capacity building and technology transfer, but it will be crucial to ensure that access to medicines is not linked specifically to the sharing of pathogen samples or genetic sequence data. National governments should not have to purchase fairness and equity with their sovereign genetic resources; to require them to do so presupposes that global health justice can be achieved by market-based solutions, even as decades of evidence on the impact of ABS agreements suggest otherwise.

Conclusion

Prompt and timely access to pathogen samples for research and development is of vital importance to global health, and so too is fair and equitable access to vaccines and medicines, especially for the most marginalized and vulnerable populations in the world. The ABS transaction has come to dominate the legal and policy responses to both of these issues, linking them together, and seeking to formulate one solution to what are two, distinct resource allocation problems. Doing so has placed access to medicines at the whims of yet another type of market. Even amid global health law reforms, the ABS mechanism has such a stronghold on present policy discussions in global health governance that it may yet constrain future policy developments under global health law. If member states continue to pursue this policy option, they must reflect on serious concerns about the extent to which ABS offers an effective, fair, and equitable way to ensure that the health is safeguarded.

It is important to recognize that, while the rhetoric of equality and fairness surrounding ABS may make it sound appealing—where researchers get the samples they need and, in return, provide benefits back to the people that provide them—its ability to actually deliver equity and fairness in the public health space is questionable at best. The stated goals of the CBD, Nagoya Protocol, and PIP Framework are important, but their ability to ensure equity to those most marginalized communities is even more important. There remains a severe disconnect between the rhetoric of CBD, Nagoya Protocol, and PIP, and their utility for ensuring equitable access to vaccines in a health emergency. Indeed, the underlying logic of these instruments is that equity should be bargained for in an open market, with these market forces leading to sweeping injustice in global health. It is imperative that global health law reforms undo this injustice.

In reforming global health law, the international community should be looking to develop tailored solutions to these two problems in parallel, not directly linking them together through the ABS transaction. There was, until very recently, an established norm that pathogen samples should be shared openly with the international community for the sake of global health security. This led to exploitation of genetic resources in low- and middle-income countries, and the CBD/Nagoya Protocol and PIP Framework were employed to stop this exploitation. Yet, the previous norm of open access could be strengthened if low- and middle-income countries were not in a situation where ABS agreements are essentially their only opportunity to obtain access to vaccines and antivirals during an infectious disease emergency. States cannot return to the open trade of pathogens while medicines and vaccines continue to be treated as private goods to be purchased by the highest bidder. Global health law could address both of these issues, reviewing them in parallel, and coming up with separate solutions. Continuing to link them will likely mean that neither access to pathogens nor the sharing of the benefits associated with their use will occur in a fair and equitable manner.

Questions for Consideration

1. How does the scientific collection of biological resources throughout the world reflect the continuing legacies of colonialism? Why was sovereignty over natural resources a key focus of newly decolonized states in seeking to establish a New International Economic Order?
2. How did the Convention on Biological Diversity shift genetic resources from the "common heritage of humankind" to the sovereign resources of the provider nation? Should human pathogens have been included within the definition of "genetic resources" under the Convention on Biological Diversity?
3. Why did Indonesia refuse to share influenza virus samples with WHO amid the H5N1 avian influenza outbreak? What did Indonesia hope to gain from an ABS agreement?
4. How did the Nagoya Protocol reshape pathogen ABS agreements? Why is it important for the WHO to have a governance role in mediating ABS agreements between the provider state and third parties?
5. Are market-based solutions the most effective way to ensure access to genetic resources and/or access to essential medicines? Why do such negotiated ABS agreements often disadvantage low- and middle-income countries?
6. What limitations of the transactional ABS approach were exposed by the global response to the outbreaks of MERS, Zika, and Ebola? What are the factors that undermine equitable access to medicines and the human right to health?
7. Why did WHO not look to ABS transactions to share SARS-CoV-2 samples amid a rapidly escalating COVID-19 pandemic? Would ABS transactions have been able to ensure vaccine equity during the COVID-19 response?
8. Should pathogen sharing governance be expanded to encompass genetic sequence data?
9. How can global health law reforms under the Pandemic Treaty delink access to pathogens from access to medicines for vulnerable populations?

Acknowledgments

The authors appreciate the thoughtful editorial support of Chris Burch and Ashley Lim.

References

Abayomi, Akin, Rebecca Katz, Scott Spence, Brian Conton, and Sahr M. Gevao. 2016. "Managing Dangerous Pathogens: Challenges in the Wake of the Recent West African Ebola Outbreak." *Global Security: Health, Science and Policy* 1(1): 51–57.

Anghie, Antony. 2005. *Imperialism, Sovereignty, and the Making of International Law*. Cambridge: Cambridge University Press.

Bagley, Margo A. 2022. "'Just' Sharing: The Virtues of Digital Sequence Information Benefit-Sharing for the Common Good." *Harvard International Law Journal* 63(1): 1–62.

BBC. 2013. "WHO Urges Information Sharing over novel Coronavirus." *BBC News*, May 23.

CBD (Convention on Biological Diversity). 1992. *Convention on Biological Diversity*. Montreal: UN Convention on Biological Diversity.

CBD. 2011. *Nagoya Protocol on Access to Genetic Resources and the Fair and Equitable Sharing of Benefits Arising from Their Utilization to the Convention on Biological Diversity*. Montreal: UN Convention on Biological Diversity

CBD. 2018. *Study into Criteria to Identify a Specialized International Access and Benefit Sharing Instrument, and a Possible Process for its Recognition*. Montreal: UN Convention on Biological Diversity. CBD/SBI/2/INF/17.

Cheng, Maria. 2016. "Few Zika samples Are Being Shared by Brazil, Worrying International Researchers." STATNews. February 3.

Eccleston-Turner, Mark R. 2018. "Operationalizing the Right to Health through the Pandemic Influenza Preparedness Framework." *Global Health Governance* XII (1): 22–34.

Eccleston-Turner, Mark and Harry Upton. 2021. "International Collaboration to Ensure Equitable Access to Vaccines for COVID-19 The ACT-Accelerator and the COVAX Facility." *Milbank Quarterly* 99(2): 426–449.

Eccleston-Turner, Mark and Michelle Rourke. 2021. "Arguments against the Inequitable Distribution of Vaccines Using the Access and Benefit sharing Transaction." *International and Comparative Law Quarterly* 70(4): 825–858.

Fidler, David P. and Lawrence O. Gostin. 2011. "The WHO Pandemic Influenza Preparedness Framework: A Milestone in Global Governance for Health." *Journal of the American Medical Association* 306(2): 200–201.

Hammond, Edward. 2019. "Ebola: Company Avoids Benefit-Sharing Obligations by Using Sequences." *Third World Network* Briefing Paper 99 (May).

Heymann, David L., Joanne Liu, and Louis Lillywhite. 2016. "Partnerships, Not Parachutists, for Zika Research." *New England Journal of Medicine* 374(16): 1504–1505.

INB (Intergovernmental Negotiating Body to Draft and Negotiate a WHO Convention, Agreement or Other International Instrument on Pandemic Prevention, Preparedness and Response). 2022. "Working Draft, presented on the basis of progress achieved, for the consideration of the Intergovernmental Negotiating Body at its second meeting." July 13. A/INB/2/3.

Irwin, Rachel. 2010. "Indonesia, H5N1, and Global Health Diplomacy." *Global Health Governance* 3(2): 1–21.

Lawson, Charles, Fran Humphries, and Michelle Rourke. 2019. "The Future of Information under the CBD, Nagoya Protocol, Plant Treaty, and PIP Framework." *The Journal of World Intellectual Property* 22(3–4): 103–119.

Lawson, Charles, Michelle Rourke, and Fran Humphries. 2020. "Information as the Latest Site of Conflict in the Ongoing Contests about Access to and Sharing the Benefits from Exploiting Genetic Resources." *Queen Mary Journal of Intellectual Property* 10(1): 7–33.

Marinissen, Maria Julia, Ruvani Chandrasekera, John Simpson, Theodore Kuschak, and Lauren Barna. 2020. "Sharing of Biological Samples during Public Health Emergencies: Challenges and Opportunities for National and International Action." In *Viral Sovereignty and Technology Transfer*, edited by Sam F. Halabi and Rebecca Katz, 1st ed., 155–173. Cambridge: Cambridge University Press.

Morgera, Elisa, Elsa Tsioumani, and Matthias Buck. 2014. *Unraveling the Nagoya Protocol – A Commentary on Access and Benefit-sharing to the Convention on Biological Diversity*. Leiden: Brill.

Panjabi, Ranee K. L. 1993. "International Law and the Preservation of Species: An Analysis of the Convention on Biological Diversity Signed at the Rio Earth Summit in 1992." *Dickinson Journal of International Law* 11(2): 187–280.

Prip, Christian, and Kristin Rosendal. 2015. *Access to Genetic Resources and Benefit-Sharing from Their Use (ABS)—State of Implementation and Research Gaps*. Norway: Ridtjof Nansen Institute. FNI 5/2015.

Ranjan, Mukul. 2023. "ABS from the Perspective of an Intellectual Property Professional at a Public Research Institution." In *Access and Benefit Sharing of Genetic Resources, Information and Traditional Knowledge*, edited by Charles Lawson, Michelle Rourke, and Fran Humphries, 1st ed., 26. London: Routledge.

Reichman, Jerome H., Paul F. Uhlir, and Tom Dedeurwaerdere. 2016. *Governing Digitally Integrated Genetic Resources, Data, and Literature: Global Intellectual Property Strategies for a Redesigned Microbial Research Commons*, 1st ed. 1–7. Cambridge: Cambridge University Press.

Rhot-Arriaza, Naomi. 1996. "Of Seeds and Shamans: The Appropriation of the Scientific and Technical Knowledge of Indigenous and Local Communities." *Michigan Journal of International Law* 17(4): 919–965.

Rourke, Michelle F. 2017. "Viruses for Sale—All Viruses Are Subject to Access and Benefit Sharing Obligations Under the Convention on Biological Diversity." *European Intellectual Property Review* 39(2): 77–89.

Rourke, Michelle F. 2020. "Restricting Access to Pathogen Samples and Epidemiological Data: A Not-So-Brief History of 'Viral Sovereignty' and the Mark It Left on the World." In *Infectious Diseases in the New Millennium*, edited by Mark Eccleston-Turner and Iain Brassington. 178–179. New York: Springer International Publishing.

Rourke, Michelle. 2022. "Value Judgements and the Management of Digital Sequence Information under the International Access and Benefit Sharing Regime." In *Access and Benefit Sharing of Genetic Resources, Information and Traditional Knowledge*, edited by Charles Lawson, Michelle Rourke and Fran Humphries, , 1st ed., 112–121. London: Routledge.

Rourke, Michelle and Mark Eccleston-Turner. 2021. "The Pandemic Influenza Preparedness Framework as a 'Specialized International Access and Benefit-Sharing Instrument' under the Nagoya Protocol." *Northern Ireland Legal Quarterly* 72(3): 411–447.

Smith, Linda Tuhiwai. 2012. *Decolonizing Methodologies: Research and Indigenous Peoples*, 2nd ed. London: Zed Books.

Schei, Peter and Morten Walløe Tvedt. 2010. *'Genetic Resources' in the CBD: The Wording, the Past, the Present and the Future*. Norway: Fridtjof Nansen Institute. FNI Report 4/2010.

Tvedt, Morten Walløe. 2013. "Beyond Nagoya: Towards a Legally Functional System of Access and Benefit Sharing." In *Global Governance of Genetic Resources: Access and Benefit Sharing after the Nagoya Protocol*, edited by Sebastian Oberthür, and G. Rosendal, 1st ed., 20. London: Routledge.

UN General Assembly. 1974. "Declaration on the Establishment of a New International Economic Order." A/9559 (GAOR, 6th special sess. Suppl. no. 1).

WHA (World Health Assembly). 2007. *Pandemic Influenza Preparedness: Sharing of Influenza Viruses and Access to Vaccines and Other Benefits*. Geneva: WHA. Resolution WHA 60.28.

WHO (World Health Organization). 2007. "Sharing of Influenza Viruses and Access to Vaccines and Other Benefits: Interdisciplinary Working Group on Pandemic Influenza Preparedness." May 5. A64/8.

WHO. 2011. *Pandemic Influenza Preparedness Framework for the Sharing of Influenza Viruses and Access to Vaccines and Other Benefits*. Geneva: WHO.

WHO. 2016. "Review of the Pandemic Influenza Preparedness Framework: Report by the Director-General." December 29. EB140/16.

WHO. 2021. "The Public Health Implications of Implementation of the Nagoya Protocol; Report by the Director-General." January 16. EB148/21.

Zacker, Mark W. 1993. *The International Political Economy of Natural Resources*. Cheltenham: Edward Elgar.

Zaki, Ali M., Sander van Boheemen, Theo M. Bestebroer, Albert D.M.E. Osterhaus, and Ron A. M. Fouchier. 2012. "Isolation of a Novel Coronavirus from a Man with Pneumonia in Saudi Arabia." *New England Journal of Medicine* 367(19): 1814–1820.

17

Sexual and Reproductive Health and Rights

Advancing Human Rights to Protect Bodily Autonomy and Sexuality

Aziza Ahmed and Terry McGovern

Introduction

The realization of sexual and reproductive health and rights (SRHR) is essential for global health equity. International mechanisms and bodies—from treaty bodies to funders—have recognized the importance of SRHR in accomplishing a broader set of development goals. Human rights institutions have addressed sexual and reproductive health as central to the realization of a broader set of human rights, and sexual and reproductive rights have become central to global health governance. SRHR is seen to encompass a broad set of human rights guarantees related to sexual and reproductive health, including those in connection with pregnancy and childbirth, contraception and family planning, abortion and post-abortion care, comprehensive sexuality education, and sexual health and well-being. This expansive vision of SRHR has developed through decades of activism focused on advancing sexual and reproductive health guarantees under human rights law and global health law.

Advocates have long looked to human rights to advance recognition of the centrality of SRHR in meeting a broader set of global health law and international development goals. The first "UN Decade for Women" (1975–1985) ushered in a series of UN conferences on women, providing new opportunities for grassroots feminist groups from across the world to share strategies, shape priorities, and negotiate a global women's health and human rights agenda. Through these conferences and parallel forums, stakeholders grappled with common barriers to women's rights under international law, linking feminism to other human rights movements. Feminists sought to respond to the ongoing neglect of human rights violations faced by women and the need to reframe existing international discussions of family planning and reproductive health as human rights issues. Women's rights advocates challenged the prevailing population control paradigm—predicated on controlling fertility for developmental gains—and established an expanded vision of sexual and reproductive health grounded in fundamental human rights guarantees. These guarantees would come to frame global health governance, advancing global health policies to overcome gender discrimination and inequality, harmful practices and norms, and neglect of sexual and reproductive health services throughout the world.

This chapter examines the evolution of global health law and policy to advance sexual and reproductive health. Part I looks back on the historical struggle of women's rights advocacy and international commitments that defined reproductive health and created international governance institutions to develop global reproductive health policy. Given the rise of human rights law in global sexual and reproductive health policy, Part II analyzes how SRHR has come to be advanced by global health policy, incorporated into development agendas, and expanded to uphold abortion rights and protect sexual minorities. Part III reflects on new uncertainties for this progression of rights amid the rise of right-wing populism, including the criminalization of sexual and reproductive health services; the pushback against lesbian, gay, bisexual, and transgender (LGBT) rights; and the imperative to decolonize SRHR. This chapter concludes that SRHR remains crucial to advancing equity under global health law, with human rights advocacy central to facing rising opposition to sexual rights, safe abortion, and sexuality education.

I. From Population Control to Reproductive Rights

Governments long sought to develop policies to control fertility, but under the United Nations (UN), global governance saw an ideological shift in the 1970s – from population control to reproductive rights. This transformation in international institutions represented a victory for feminist advocates, who had long pushed for women's bodily autonomy in the context of family planning programs.

A. Early Population Control Policies and Reproductive Health Programming

Racial "science" emerging in the 18th century enabled slavery, justified colonialism, and shaped the relationship between states and their populations. From its inception, the eugenics movement, drawing from the erroneous belief that race is a biological construct, sought to promote specific characteristics across the population as a means of developing a "better" race (Levine 2010). Supporters of the eugenics movement believed that some European populations were of a superior race, as assumptions about race and class were intertwined with ideas about inherent intelligence and social standing (Roberts 2011). The qualities seen as most desirable matched those who governed much of the world through imperialism and colonialism (Levine 2010). Advancing racist ideology through public health policy, eugenics was deployed to advance population control—often through coercive means. The social hygiene and birth control movements of the early 20th century, which sought to end the spread of venereal disease and limit the number of children, often enabled and supported methods of population control, including forced sterilization (Parmet 2009).

This eugenic logic of racial superiority was mobilized during World War II and played a central role in Nazi persecution —beginning in racial hygiene laws and leading to the genocide of millions in the Holocaust. In the wake of these atrocities, as discussed in greater detail in Chapter 18, scientific theories of biological racism, like that promoted by the eugenics movement, lost explicit support, but concerns about racial and class demographics did not disappear. No longer justified explicitly by eugenics, the idea of population control maintained popularity as a means to control poverty and address growing environmental concerns. Amid the rising population control agenda, growing support for women's rights in the UN helped focus attention on the centrality of questions related to women and gender. An early example was the birth of the UN Commission on the Status of Women (CSW) in 1947, which allowed some feminists and women's rights advocates to have a formal role in UN processes, which they would use to advocate for gender equality.

The UN worked alongside non-state actors, which were growing in strength and expanding their advocacy for women's rights. Leading up to World War II, private philanthropic organizations, including the Rockefeller Foundation, were already spending money internationally to advance population control measures (Birn 1999). Advances in contraceptive methods and technologies provided additional tools to help limit population growth. Following the war, the Rockefeller Foundation worked with state and non-state actors in 1952 to establish the Population Council, which played a key role in rationalizing, designing, and implementing population control measures globally (Birn 2014). In the early years of the Population Council's existence, for example, it opened offices in Chile, India, and Egypt to assist governments with issues related to population growth, seeking to address illegal abortions and increase access to family planning (Notestein 1968). Within the UN, the United Nations Population Fund (UNFPA) would become the lead agency addressing issues related to population and development (Filmer-Wilson and Mora 2018).

Case Study: Birth of UNFPA

As conversations around the world expanded on issues of population and development, the UN would look to examine population growth, women's rights, and reproductive rights, responding to growing interest in advancing public health programming focused on family planning. In 1967, the UN Secretary General proposed creating a fund that would support population-related research, training, and advising across countries. States acted on this proposal and rapidly established the United Nations Fund for Population Activities (UNFPA). Instead of creating a program out of existing UN structures, this new multilateral body was initially developed as a trust fund to facilitate voluntary support for countries in their population control programming. The fund was transferred in 1969 to the UN Development Programme, which managed funds donated by member states. Within several years of becoming operational, the UN General Assembly passed a resolution in 1972 that institutionalized the UNFPA as a subsidiary body of the UN General Assembly. This transition reflected the expanding resources and scope of UNFPA, which had grown rapidly since its inception. As UNFPA's operating budget increased significantly through its early work, these funds were used to support a range of reproductive health, family planning, and demographic census activities across low-income countries. UNFPA today stands for the United Nations Population Fund and works in more than 150 countries to strengthen systems of sexual and reproductive health care.

This early focus on family planning through UNFPA would provide a foundation to address reproductive health in global health governance (Robinson 2010).

B. Recognizing Women's Reproductive Health in Global Health Governance

The population control paradigm operated on the principle that population growth jeopardizes development and sustainability, and that demographic targets were needed in family planning policy to control population size; however, the push for population control under the UN would eventually be challenged by feminists within and outside of international institutions, placing new focus on the need to see reproductive health as a matter of human rights. Drawing from twenty years of CSW advocacy, the UN General Assembly in 1967 adopted the Declaration on the Elimination of Discrimination against Women, detailing rights to equality in civil, political, social, and economic affairs, yet failed to address rights related to reproduction or reproductive health (UN General Assembly 1967).

When the UN General Assembly in 1968 convened the first International Conference on Human Rights in Tehran, Iran, it brought together representatives from states alongside observers from UN bodies, including the CSW; intergovernmental organizations; and non-governmental organizations (NGOs). This groundbreaking Conference would adopt resolutions that reshaped women's rights as well as the human rights dimensions of family planning (UN 1968). Based on previous UN declarations recognizing the importance of slowing reproduction to improve living conditions, this human rights consensus proclaimed the right of "parents . . . to determine freely and responsibly the number and spacing of their children" (ibid., part II, art. 16). This invocation of family planning as an individual human right, ensuring that individuals have access to information along with the benefits of advances in science and technology, would frame women's rights to reproductive health services (Grimes 1998).

Feminist organizations continued to advocate for the expansion of birth control to achieve women's equality (Ahmed 2017). Five years following the International Conference on Human Rights, the global community gathered in Bucharest, Romania for the 1974 World Population Conference, where delegates reconsidered concerns around global population growth (Freedman and Isaacs 1993).

Soon after, at the suggestion of the CSW, the UN General Assembly declared 1975 to be the "International Women's Year" and resolved to organize a World Conference on Women—the first of its kind (UN 2000). Drawing together thousands from across the world, this conference in Mexico City was a milestone for the promotion of women's rights. In contrast to the outputs from Tehran and Bucharest, the resulting document—the Declaration of Mexico on the Equality of Women and Their Contribution to Development and Peace—grounded the right to reproductive choice on a notion of bodily integrity and control (UN 1975, art. 11).

Supported by the 1975 World Conference on Women, which would begin the UN Decade for Women, many women's rights NGOs throughout the world began to network with each another. Feminists communicated with one another through newsletters, for example, helping women from across the world unite around the common project of women's rights (Hosken 1981). Organizations, including Our Bodies Ourselves Collective, founded in Boston in 1969, sent copies of their now famous book on women's health to activists and health practitioners across the world. Transnational organizing by feminist leaders in the Global North and Global South had a profound impact during this time in shaping a global women's movement on sexual and reproductive health rights (Antrobus 2004).

C. Advancing Women's Rights under International Law

Following two decades of deliberation, research, and negotiation by women's rights advocates around the world, the UN codified these rights in the 1979 Convention on the Elimination of All Forms of Discrimination against Women (CEDAW). In reaffirming equality in dignity and rights, CEDAW, as first introduced in Chapter 4, seeks to uphold the political participation of women, affirming women's right to suffrage, political representation, education, vocational training free from gender discrimination, formal employment with equal pay, social security benefits, and protection from sexual harassment and workplace discrimination. Extended to reproductive rights, CEDAW affirmed that women's health and reproductive rights are central to women's equality, extending the 1978 Declaration of Alma-Ata, which, as introduced in Chapter 3, included maternal health care, family planning, and midwives as foundational components of primary health care.

The Convention opens by recognizing that "the role of women in procreation should not be a basis for discrimination" and advocates for "a proper understanding of maternity as a social function" (UN General Assembly 1979, preamble). As a foundation for equality, CEDAW provided specific attention to shared responsibility in marriage and family relations, including property and inheritance, and proclaimed maternity protections and childcare as essential social services. Through CEDAW, autonomous control over one's own body was seen as the key to participation and development:

> 12.1 States Parties shall take all appropriate measures to eliminate discrimination against women in the field of health care in order to ensure, on a basis of equality of men and women, access to health care services, including those related to family planning.
>
> 12.2 Notwithstanding the provisions of paragraph I of this article, States Parties shall ensure to women appropriate services in connection with pregnancy, confinement and the post-natal period, granting free services where necessary, as well as adequate nutrition during pregnancy and lactation (ibid., art. 12).

Under these maternity protections, CEDAW explicitly addressed family planning and reproductive health services, obligating states to implement family planning education and guarantee women's right "to decide freely and responsibly on the spacing of their children and to have access to the information, education and means to enable them to exercise these rights" (ibid., art. 16(6)). In implementing these rights for reproductive choice, CEDAW required states to take "all appropriate measures, including legislation, to ensure the full development and advancement of women, for the purpose of guaranteeing them the exercise and enjoyment of human rights and fundamental freedoms on a basis of equality with men" (ibid., art. 3). The adoption of CEDAW, reflecting the global strength of the women's rights movement, would offer a new human rights foundation for reproductive health given the treaty's focus on ending discrimination against women.[1]

II. From Population Control to Reproductive Rights

Despite the recognition of women's rights as human rights in CEDAW, population control remained the primary normative framework for development programs related to family planning. Yet new political dynamics in the 1980s began to reshape international family planning policy. The United States had become the largest bilateral donor to family planning assistance and subsequently accrued significant influence in shaping how countries could deliver necessary services, using its funding and influence in the 1980s to stifle abortion access and limit women's rights (Hartmann 1987). Despite this bilateral interference, international momentum and organizing efforts arising out of the UN Decade for Women continued to build in the 1990s—shifting global policy from population control to reproductive rights through international conferences on human rights, population, and development and establishing new global development goals to shape global health in the 21st century.

A. Paradigm Shift: Women's Rights Advancements in Cairo and Beijing

With a firm underpinning in international law, feminists began to advocate for a new paradigm. Responding to conservative forces in the United States, the Holy See,[2] and religious countries, this feminist mobilization across nations arose out of decades of global feminist activism and extended across international

---

[1] While a large number of states have ratified CEDAW, placing women's equality at the center of global governance, it remains the UN core convention for which the highest number of nations have entered into reservations—particularly on provisions related to discrimination in marriage and family life (CEDAW 2010). As introduced in Chapter 2, international law permits states to ratify treaties with reservations, allowing states parties to opt out of certain aspects of a treaty while remaining bound by the rest.

[2] The Holy See is the sovereign body that governs the universal Catholic Church and the Vatican City State. It has non-member permanent observer status at the UN, which allows it to participate in UN General Assembly proceedings (Coates et al. 2014).

conferences in Cairo and Beijing to advance reproductive health as a human rights imperative.

1. Vienna Declaration and Programme of Action

The 1993 UN World Conference on Human Rights in Vienna formalized the notion that women's rights are human rights. The final declaration emerging from the conference, the Vienna Declaration and Programme of Action (VDPA), affirmed that "the human rights of women and of the girl child are an inalienable, integral and indivisible part of universal human rights" (UN General Assembly 1993, art. 18). During preparatory meetings for the Conference, advocates demanded that women's rights be included and recognized as human rights (Bunch and Carrillo 2015). They were successful. The VDPA affirmed the fundamental human rights of women, conceptualizing women's health, reproduction, and sexuality as matters of human rights. More specifically, the VDPA extended the guarantees of the right to health to women, recognizing "the importance of the enjoyment by women of the highest standard of physical and mental health throughout their life span" and reaffirming "on the basis of equality between women and men, a woman's right to accessible and adequate health care and the widest range of family planning services, as well as equal access to education at all levels" (UN General Assembly 1993, art. 41). Advancing the necessity of protections for women in the private sphere, the VDPA recognized as a human rights obligation the elimination of "violence against women in public and private life" (ibid., art. 38).[3] The focus on the private sphere was especially important given that feminists had identified a range of abuses to sexual and reproductive health and rights that occurred in the home – outside of the "public" domain. This challenged the view that the private sphere was a separate realm guided by personal morality rather than human rights.

2. Cairo Conference

The 1994 International Conference on Population and Development (ICPD) in Cairo drew upon the VDPA to establish an expanded vision of reproductive health and rights. The ICPD, as seen in Figure 17.1, was the product of activism by a diverse set of reproductive rights and women's rights advocates, academics, activists, and donors.

This global health diplomacy, as first introduced in Chapter 5, challenged population advocates and experts, who wanted to retain a focus on population control at the expense of women's rights (Roseman and Reichenbach 2011). The

---

[3] Where only a handful of countries had addressed gender-based violence before the VDPA, the next decade saw almost every UN member state formulate programs or pass legislation to address violence against women as a matter of universal rights.

Figure 17.1 ICPD (Cairo, 1994) (UN)

primary agenda for women's rights organizations was to ensure that women's empowerment and education were the central mechanisms through which population programs would be channeled, transforming them into reproductive health and rights interventions. These activists worked collectively to develop the "Women's Platform for ICPD," which provided minimum standards for negotiating issues of health, sexuality, and reproductive rights (Corrêa and Petchesky 2007).

Alongside support for health programming and data collection in low- and middle-income countries, UNFPA played an influential role in preparing for the ICPD in Cairo—embracing human rights for reproductive health. Drawing on the UN's normative mandate and technical expertise, UNFPA was uniquely placed to galvanize a wide range of UN, governmental, and civil society actors to advance the global reproductive rights agenda—with a strong field presence in countries to mainstream women's rights and gender equality across its organizational activities, including research, training, and advising. At the conference itself, the International Women's Health Coalition and the Women's Environment and Development Organization (WEDO) led a five-hundred person-strong Women's Caucus (Ahmed 2017). Advocates attended the NGO forum occurring in parallel with the Cairo conference, advocating with government delegations for the inclusion of women's empowerment through the ICPD negotiations (Neidell 1998).

The resulting ICPD Programme of Action (ICPD POA) departed from the population control paradigm that dominated family planning policy. Instead, the ICPD POA explicitly linked existing human rights obligations to evolving sexual and reproductive rights, stating:

> [t]hat reproductive rights embrace certain human rights that are already recognized in national laws and international human rights documents... and that these rights rest on the recognition of the basic right of all couples and individuals to decide freely and responsibly the number, spacing and timing of their children (UNFPA 1994, para. 7.3).

The ICPD defined reproductive health as including family planning, sexually transmitted disease control, and maternal health, bringing together issues that were previously considered distinct. The adoption of this language created a paradigmatic shift that moved away from a limited focus on population control to a larger agenda that addresses a range of reproductive health issues (McGovern and Ahmed 2020).

Yet, while the Cairo Conference delivered most of the elements of the "Women's Platform" to advance reproductive health, it was unable to secure language on "sexual rights" and achieved limited success in developing human rights surrounding abortion (Garcia-Morena 1994).[4] This absence of sexual rights could be read to indicate a lack of commitment to protecting bodily autonomy, ending violence against women, and supporting LGBT rights amid a surging AIDS pandemic. Although the ICPD provided that women should have access to quality services for the management of abortion complications in all nations (UNFPA 1994), the Cairo Conference did not call for the decriminalization of abortion—or explicitly state that access to abortion is a woman's right. The ICPD POA did, however, address the public health impact of unsafe abortion, advocate reducing the need for abortion by expanding family planning services, and include a right to receive reliable information, compassionate counseling, and safe abortion in places where abortion is not against the law.

3. Beijing Platform for Action

The 1995 Beijing Conference on Women extended the ICPD consensus. The resulting Beijing Platform for Action (BPFA) reaffirmed women's rights to sexual and reproductive health services and information. The BPFA recommended specific policy changes for sexual and reproductive health care, affordable healthcare

---

[4] While commonly used interchangeably, sexual rights and reproductive rights are conceptually distinct. Sexual rights refer to the human rights related to sexuality and sexual health, including rights related to sexual orientation and sexual pleasure. Reproductive rights refer to the human rights related to reproduction and reproductive health, including rights related to family planning.

services and information, and initiatives to improve women's care and education concerning sexually transmitted infections and HIV (UN 1995). Building on the ICPD POA and Vienna Declaration, the BPFA also spoke to the issue of sexual rights. Although fierce ideological battles kept the term "sexual rights" out of the text, the content of sexual rights was included, with the BPFA recognizing:

> The human rights of women include their right to have control over and decide freely and responsibly on matters related to their sexuality, including sexual and reproductive health, free of coercion, discrimination and violence. Equal relationships between women and men in matters of sexual relations and reproduction, including full respect for the integrity of the person, require mutual respect, consent and shared responsibility for sexual behaviour and its consequences (ibid., art. 96).

The BPFA thus recognized the centrality of sexuality in questions of gender and health.

B. MDGs to SDGs: From Maternal Mortality to Gender Equality

Drawing from these advancements in articulating SRHR in global health policy, the current SRHR landscape has been defined through international development agendas. These international development agendas, as outlined initially in Chapter 3 and expanded upon in Chapter 10, provided a foundation to expand SRHR programming during the transition from the Millennium Development Goals (MDGs) to the Sustainable Development Goals (SDGs).

1. MDGs

The UN General Assembly's Millennium Declaration in 2000 reflected a consensus on the part of governments to commit to a series of global goals: ending poverty, improving health, and stopping the spread of HIV. Yet, within the eight MDGs, complex interrelated areas of SRHR—including HIV, maternal health, and child health—were separated under discrete goals and monitored by different goals and indicators. As a result, intersectional issues of SRHR were neglected in government efforts to meet the MDGs (Chesler and McGovern 2015). MDG 3 focused on gender equality and women's empowerment, measured by gains in girls' education and the numbers of women in elected office, but it did not measure violence against women or address discriminatory laws. MDG 5 focused on maternal mortality, but it was not until 2007 that the UN added a target on reproductive health—with this focus on reproductive health continuing to neglect issues of sexual health.[5] The MDGs were also critiqued for lacking a clear connection to human rights (Kuruvilla et al. 2012). As the MDGs were seen to limit accountability for gender equality and SRHR advances, the international community sought to adopt a more comprehensive set of goals as the MDGs approached their completion in 2015.

2. SDGs

Developing this post-2015 development agenda, the UN General Assembly held a September 2015 summit, Transforming Our World: The 2030 Agenda for Sustainable Development. The final resolution of this summit set out 17 SDGs and 169 targets to achieve sustainable development over the next 15 years (UN General Assembly 2015). Unlike the MDGs, the 2030 Agenda's vision of sustainable development, and the actions required to achieve the SDGs, are grounded in universal respect for international law, human rights, the rule of law, justice, gender equality, and the empowerment of women and girls (Marks and Han 2020).

The 2030 Agenda specifically emphasizes the responsibilities of states for human rights, in conformity with the UN charter, recognizing that gender equality and the empowerment of women and girls will make a crucial contribution to progress across all the SDGs. SRHR issues are specifically advanced through SDG targets on health, education, and gender equality:

- Applied to health systems and services, SDG 3 focuses on health and well-being, and in seeking to ensure universal access to sexual and reproductive healthcare services—including for family planning, information, and education—target 3.7 requires the integration of reproductive health into national strategies and programs, and target 3.3 addresses specific SRHR issues related to maternal mortality, HIV/AIDS, and harmful practices such as genital mutilation and child, early, and forced marriage.
- Complemented by education efforts, SDG 4 requires that education promotes gender equality, that all girls complete primary and secondary education, that women have equal access to tertiary and vocational education, and that states eliminate gender disparities in education.
- Extending this focus on inequality and discrimination, SDG 5 obligates states to achieve gender equality and empower all women and girls, with target 5.1 seeking to "end all forms of discrimination against all women and

---

[5] At the twentieth anniversary of ICPD (ICPD + 20) in 2014, states reviewed progress on SRHR, including the 2013 Montevideo consensus in Latin America, which explicitly recognized "sexual rights" and defined these rights for the first time in an intergovernmental process—to encompass protection from discrimination and violence based on sexual orientation and gender identity (UN and ECLAC 2013).

girls everywhere," including indicators to track the implementation of this target through legal frameworks: "whether or not legal frameworks are in place to promote, enforce and monitor equality and non-discrimination on the basis of sex" and "to increase the number of countries with laws and regulations that guarantee full and equal access to women and men aged 15 and older to sexual and reproductive healthcare, information, and education" (UN General Assembly 2017).

Beyond these discrete goals, targets, and indicators, SRHR is essential to the fulfillment and success of all of the SDGs, as it is impossible to eradicate poverty, for example, without ensuring that women can control their own fertility. In expanding the SRHR agenda to a broader population, the SDGs were notable for their focus on adolescents, which recognized the critical need for investments in the health of young people across the globe (Chandra-Mouli et al. 2015).

Case Study: Adolescent Sexual and Reproductive Health and Rights

While women, children, and adolescents have historically been grouped together under international law, these groups are conceptually distinct and bear individual rights that are not contingent upon one another. SRHR is distinctly experienced across the life course, and adolescents face unique barriers in realizing SRHR. This includes social norms that hinder young people's abilities to seek information about sexuality, sexual health, and reproductive health, as well as laws that place age restrictions on SRHR-related health information, goods, and services. The 1994 ICPD Programme of Action explicitly recognized adolescent reproductive rights and urged states to meet the sexual and reproductive health needs of young people. When the MDGs were established, adolescent SRHR was reflected under MDG 5 (improve maternal health) and MDG 6 (combat HIV/AIDS, malaria, and other diseases), which incorporated adolescent-inclusive measures as indicators of progress (e.g., adolescent birth rate). Building upon the MDGs, the 2030 Agenda uses an even broader set of indicators that reflect progress toward adolescent SRHR under SDG 3 (ensure healthy lives) and SDG 5 (achieve gender equality). These SDG efforts have been supported in global health governance through the 2016 launch of the Every Woman Every Child Global Strategy for Women's, Children's and Adolescents' Health. This Strategy seeks to promote (1) early childhood development; (2) adolescent health and well-being; (3) quality, equity, and dignity in services; (4) sexual and reproductive health and rights; (5) empowerment of women, girls, and communities; (6) and engagement in humanitarian and fragile settings. The Strategy's framework for advancing health across these areas is underpinned by a commitment to core human rights principles for realizing adolescent SRHR under global health law.

These efforts to expand the populations empowered by SRHR has provided a foundation for continuing advancements in the SRHR agenda.

C. Pushing the SRHR Agenda Forward

In pushing this SRHR agenda forward to address sexual rights, activists have sought to advance human rights specifically related to sexual orientation and gender identity (SO/GI), demanding an end to the pathologization of lesbian, gay, bisexual, and transgender (LGBT) identities; removal of discriminatory laws and policies; and protections against the structural violence faced by the community (Corrêa and Jolly 2008). Where activists lamented the absence of sexual rights at Cairo and Beijing, the growing HIV/AIDS crisis underscored the importance of addressing sexuality and strengthening protections of LGBT people under international law.

Responding to this advocacy, the human rights system has supported advancements in health-related SO/GI protections, notably those related to sexual orientation, under international law. These protections have been taken up by various human rights bodies. The 21st century has seen enormous progress on rights related to SO/GI through the interpretive guidance issued by the UN Committee on the Elimination of Discrimination Against Women, the Committee on the Rights of the Child, and the Human Rights Committee (O'Flaherty 2006). Drawing from these advancements under international law, a coalition of human rights NGOs developed the 2006 Yogyakarta Principles on the application of international human rights law in relation to SO/GI, seeking to map the experiences of human rights violations by sexual minorities; the application of international human rights law to LGBT people; and the obligations of governments to respect, protect, and fulfill rights (O'Flaherty and Fisher 2008). These Principles have provided a foundation for a burgeoning set of human rights claims in national courts. For example, during the course of litigation that would eventually overturn the law criminalizing unnatural sexual offenses in India, the Delhi High Court relied on the Yogyakarta Principles to explicate international commitments to LGBT rights.

Despite the widespread influence of the Yogyakarta Principles, the advancement of SO/GI resolutions within multilateral fora, particularly those with provisions related to gender identity, has proven difficult—leaving the SRHR agenda incomplete. The first UN SO/GI resolution was not adopted until 2011, and the vote to do so was split across states (UN Human Rights Council 2011). Three years later, a follow-up resolution reiterated concerns over SO/GI-based violence and discrimination, with the resolution seeing a marginal increase in support from member states (UN Human Rights Council 2014). In 2016, the UN Human Rights Council appointed the first Independent Expert to further examine issues of SO/GI-based violence and discrimination. The Independent Expert has now presented a series of reports to the Human Rights Council, highlighting the heightened risk of physical and sexual violence experienced by LGBT and gender non-conforming individuals and calling on states to take measures to improve health and well-being (UN Human Rights Council 2017). While these initial advancements reflect a growing recognition of and conversation around SO/GI issues within the international human rights space—reflecting the success of organizing and advocacy by organizations working on sexuality—the rise of right-wing governance poses a continuing threat to these advancements.

III. New Arenas of Contestation in SRHR

New dynamics continue to challenge the global SRHR landscape under global health law and policy. The growing threat of right-wing populism that has long been associated with undermining people's rights around bodily autonomy, reproduction, and sexuality, and the rise of right-wing governance has led to regressive measures in opposition to SRHR. Amid these challenges, the SRHR movement has pressed on, looking beyond the gender binary to acknowledge human rights to gender-affirming care and seeking to decolonize SRHR to acknowledge the structural barriers to SRHR born of colonization and racism.

A. Threats of Right-Wing Populism

Deep political shifts around the world, resulting in new right-wing populist leadership, impact the ability of SRHR advocates to uphold rights established in international law and policy. Although each right-wing government takes specific form in the national context, many have targeted women's rights and the rights of sexual minorities, elevating "traditional" roles for women and stoking hatred towards LGBT people. In doing so, populist leaders have sought to portray SRHR as threats to the values of a presumed majority (Pugh 2019; Mostov 2021). Countries with conservative leadership often attempt to alter the current forward-moving consensus on SRHR at the global level. These nationalistic attacks on SRHR are often couched in religious discourse, framing SRHR as a threat to religious values and conservative social institutions (Gostin, Constantin, and Meier 2020). As a result, these countries have committed and encouraged SRHR violations and abandoned global health collaboration for SRHR by withdrawing leadership and resources from multilateral partnerships and international organizations, such as UNFPA, which support LGBT populations, family planning, access to contraception, and HIV/AIDS treatment and prevention (ibid).

Such setbacks are clear in the context of service provision on abortion. The 2016 election of Donald Trump as president of the United States, for example, immediately altered the landscape of SRHR throughout the world with the immediate reinstatement and broadening of the Global Gag Rule, which prevents any entity receiving U.S. global healthcare assistance from providing referrals for abortion services and advocating for legal abortion reform.[6] While the reinstatement of the Global Gag Rule by the Trump administration was somewhat expected, the restrictions were applied much more broadly than under past administrations and, in turn, undermined a wide range of sexual and reproductive health services throughout the world (McGovern and Ahmed 2020).

While this threat has been lessened by Trump's loss in the 2020 election, with President Biden immediately reversing the Global Gag Rule, global abortion funding remains politically contested in the United States, as the U.S. Supreme Court has since reversed fifty years of precedent upholding a right to abortion under the U.S. Constitution. Seeking to lessen the health risk posed at the national level, the World Health Organization (WHO)—supported by the UN human rights system—has called for the decriminalization of abortion services in order to improve maternal health outcomes.

These continuing attacks from right-wing populist leaders threaten to subvert sexual and reproductive rights under international law and undermine progress to realize gender equality and LGBT rights in global health governance (McGovern and Ahmed 2020; O'Connor et al. 2022).

Case Study: Conservative Backlash to SRHR in Global Health Governance

Right-wing populist governments are seeking to reverse SRHR gains through the strategic erosion of common international norms. Although the work of

---

[6] Over the past thirty years, the Global Gag Rule policy has been reinstated (sometimes with slight modifications) at the start of each Republican administration in the United States. The language used by the Trump administration, however, stated that it would be applied to any "global health assistance furnished by all departments or agencies" (Trump 2017).

the UN General Assembly has long been hampered by ideological polarization, opposition to SRHR in recent years has manifested through "anti-gender" backlash leveraged by conservative actors at the UN. This backlash reflects resistance to the advancement of "gender ideology," which is claimed to undermine "traditional" ideas of family and culture under international law. This retrogressive argument has found voice through right-wing populist leaders, religious fundamentalists, and conservative nationalists, who have used these anti-feminist and anti-gender ideas in international forums to rhetorically position gender equality and LGBT rights as a threat to the values of an imagined past. Some actors, such as the Holy See, have adapted strategies previously employed by human rights advocates (including by appropriating UN language into their arguments) to gain influence in international debates and undermine progress on SRHR-related issues. Other actors, such as right-wing governments, have adopted objections to SRHR as part of their national political strategies, using this to curb SRHR domestically and limit progress within multilateral forums. Under this right-wing vision of international affairs, populist leaders have specifically targeted the work of UN specialized agencies, NGOs, and public health policies that support LGBT populations, family planning, access to contraception, and HIV/AIDS.

Amid these challenges to SRHR in global health policy, the rise of right-wing governance marked a step backward in both recognizing and realizing LGBT rights, where anti-LGBT organizations, religious and not, have been empowered to press for regressive policies (Coates et al. 2014; Gostin, Constantin, and Meier 2020).

B. Advancing a Gender-Expansive Framework for Human Rights

The rise of conservative politics has fueled anti-LGBT bigotry around the world. This was exemplified in Uganda with the passage of the Uganda Anti-Homosexuality Bill, which in an early iteration called for the death penalty for LGBT people living with HIV who had sex (Tamale 2009). This national opposition to LGBT rights has come to influence global health policy, where opposition to LGBT rights has derailed the implementation of best practice programs on harm-reduction in the context of HIV prevention.

There has also been a conservative backlash to gender affirming health care, in reproductive justice and in public accommodations law (O'Connor et al.

2022).⁷ While responding to this backlash, global governance has remained constrained by restrictive approaches to gender under human rights law, with historical efforts to protect women's rights serving to reify a male/female binary under international law (Madrigal-Borloz 2021). These restrictive approaches to the gender binary have facilitated the human rights harms faced by people based on their sexual orientation and/or gender identity and expression, and health and human rights actors have responded to these threats by calling for a non-binary approach to human rights in global health (Mofokeng 2022a). Such a non-binary approach would explicitly name the intersectional violence and human rights violations experienced by gender diverse populations on the basis of their real or perceived sexual orientation, gender identity, or sex characteristics (O'Connor et al. 2022).

These attacks against SRHR have spurred a groundswell of progressive support. Global health and human rights actors provide the opportunity and space to advance SO/GI protections even when foreclosed by the political environment. Human rights treaty bodies, especially the Committee on the Elimination of Discrimination against Women, have highlighted the importance of integrating sexual and reproductive health services in their broader realization of the right to health, affirming that goods and services pertaining to reproductive health must be economically accessible. From treaty bodies to interstate forums, the LGBT community has continued to make gains in the Human Rights Council in calling on states to respect, protect, and fulfill the human rights of LGBT populations. For example, in 2021 the Independent Expert on Protection Against Violence and Discrimination Based on Sexual Orientation and Gender Identity released a report that underlines the need for a non-binary approach under international human rights law to advance the health and human rights of LGBT and gender non-conforming persons (Madrigal-Borloz 2021). This approach was emphasized by the UN Special Rapporteur on the right to health, who issued a report in 2022 that examined the continued violence faced by people based on their real or perceived sexual orientation and/or gender identity (Mofokeng 2022a). This report would seek to name and inclusively address the structural causes of this violence, including patriarchy and global legacies of colonialism.

---

⁷ While the Indian Supreme Court, for example, drew on core human rights treaties and texts, as well as the Indian constitution and case law, to find the "third gender" to be constitutionally protected and recognized in Indian jurisprudence and government service delivery, the Indian Government has since attempted to pass the deceptively named "Transgender Persons (Protection of Rights) Bill," which the trans* community fears will be a setback for human rights, due to an inaccurate definition of transgender person and requirements for proof of gender transformation (Dharmadhikari and Gopinathan 2018).

C. Imperative to Decolonize SRHR

As a part of the broader global health landscape, the emergence and development of SRHR is historically intertwined with colonialism and the violence of colonial rule (ICRW 2021). This includes the harms of population control efforts—from the beliefs and practices of eugenics, to research on vulnerable groups, to coercive methods, including forced sterilization—through which Western countries sought to manage populations across the Global South. Existing inequalities in SRHR reflect this history. Where the status quo within global health fails to reckon with and address the structural impacts of colonialism on health systems and outcomes, advocates have pushed for the decolonization of SRHR. In a 2022 report to the UN Human Rights Council, the UN Special Rapporteur on the right to health, as seen in Figure 17.2, leveraged the human right to health to argue for decolonizing SRHR and other health-related human rights. In her analysis, the Special Rapporteur articulates racism—which is rooted in the institutions of colonialism and slavery—as a key social determinant of health and a driver of health inequities and identifies global health aid as a key site for decolonization efforts (Mofokeng 2022b).

Efforts to decolonize SRHR seek to alleviate the structural forces that continue to impede progress toward SRHR. This could require many types of responses to ensure that the management of resources on SRHR are held by communities; that the racism and hierarchies present in knowledge production around SRHR and the delivery of SRHR services are recognized; that communities who are

Figure 17.2 Dr. Tlaleng Mofokeng Presenting Report to the UN General Assembly (Tlaleng Mofokeng)

subject to research participate in the research itself and benefit from the research; and that there should be a redistribution of SRHR resources from the Global North to the Global South (Idriss-Wheeler et al. 2021).

There is also a need to recognize how the Global South can offer a model on SRHR for the Global North. Despite implicit assumptions that the opposite is necessarily true, there is much that the Global North can and must learn from the Global South (Jain 2020). For example, if abortion is re-criminalized in the United States, feminist actors will need to rely on feminist strategies outside the United States, including in Central and South America, where advocates have engaged numerous domestic and international strategies—including engaging regional and international human rights bodies and health governance institutions in decriminalizing abortion. Centering the leadership and vision of advocates in the Global South can provide a path forward for advancing SRHR through the uncertain years to come.

Conclusion

SRHR has developed dramatically but is now facing unprecedented challenges. Despite cultural shifts over the last century that have made society more tolerant toward women, LGBT people, and others, conservative backlash against SRHR grows. With the rise of right-wing and conservative populism, SRHR is often the first attacked: abortion, gay marriage, and sexuality. These issues, which invite debates about religion and morality, speak to the heart of what it means to define culture and community nationally, regionally, and internationally. Despite this pushback, it is necessary to recognize SRHR as central to the realization of a broader range of human rights. Losing ground on SRHR threatens the realization of myriad outcomes that depend upon respect for human rights, including the ability for children to go to school and for people to live healthy and fulfilling lives.

Respecting, protecting, and fulfilling SRHR requires a commitment by governments to crafting international standards that move in the direction of better health and to having a system of global health rules that embodies the values and ideals of human rights. This will require the support of global, multinational, and transnational institutions committed to human rights and cross-sectoral support to develop a robust public health infrastructure that can effectively provide SRHR services.

National-level legal reforms to advance a human rights agenda are also a key and necessary component of moving toward respecting, protecting, and fulfilling human rights. International legal frameworks, especially those informed by progressive advocates on the ground, can further advocacy in the national context: providing supportive language for advocacy and legislation. Advocacy at the global, regional, and national level can also help advocates share strategies across borders and jurisdictions. This will be especially important in the abortion context, as abortion is recriminalized in countries like the United States and decriminalized in other jurisdictions including Ireland and Argentina. Despite setbacks, advocates continue to organize, recognizing that nearly all aspects of SRHR—at every level of governance—have only come to fruition after a long struggle.

Questions for Consideration

1. How did eugenics theories distort early population control efforts? How did the birth of the UN and establishment of UNFPA reframe population control as a women's rights issue?
2. What role did feminist advocacy play in UN efforts to advance women's equality? How did women's reproductive health come to be seen as a matter of human rights?
3. Why was CEDAW central to advancing women's equality, bodily autonomy, and human rights? What limitations kept CEDAW from advancing women's reproductive health?
4. How did the end of the Cold War provide new opportunities to advance sexual and reproductive rights? What diplomatic strategies were undertaken by reproductive rights and women's rights actors to influence the ICPD in Cairo and Conference on Women in Beijing?
5. How did the Cairo ICPD POA and Beijing Platform shift the reproductive health policy paradigm from population control to reproductive rights? Why did these conferences and instruments face limitations in advancing sexual rights?
6. How do the SDGs seek to alleviate the SRHR limitations of the MDGs? How is global health governance seeking to meet SRHR targets and indicators for adolescent SRHR under the SDGs?
7. Why have right-wing governments challenged SRHR in global health governance? How have SRHR advocates sought to respond to these challenges?
8. How has the historical progression of women's rights reified the gender binary in ways that now create obstacles to gender-affirming care? What would it mean to take a non-binary approach to human rights in global health?
9. Why is it necessary to decolonize SRHR? What can decolonial models offer for the continuing advancement of SRHR?

Acknowledgments

The authors greatly appreciate the research and editing assistance of Hanna Huffstetler and Taylor Corpening. These inspiring students contributed to the development of the main text and authored the case studies that highlight crucial successes and limitations in the evolution of SRHR in global health policy.

Disclosures

Portions of this chapter are based upon two publications by the contributing authors that examine the evolution of SRHR in greater detail: (1) McGovern, Terry and Aziza Ahmed. 2020. "Equity in Health: Sexual and Reproductive Health and Rights," in *Foundations of Global Health & Human Rights* edited by Lawrence O. Gostin and Benjamin Mason Meier. New York: Oxford University Press; and (2) Ahmed, Aziza. 2017. "Bandung's Legacy: Solidarity and Contestation in Global Women's Rights," in *Bandung, Global History, and International Law: Critical Pasts and Pending Futures*, edited by Luis Eslava, Michael Fakhri, and Vasuki Nesiah. Cambridge: Cambridge University Press.

References

Ahmed, Aziza. 2017. "Bandung's Legacy: Solidarity and Contestation in Global Women's Rights." In *Bandung, Global History, and International Law: Critical Pasts and Pending Futures*, edited by Luis Eslava, Michael Fakhri, and Vasuki Nesiah. 450–464. Cambridge: Cambridge University Press.

Antrobus, Peggy. 2004. *Global Women's Movements: Origins, Issues and Challenges*. London: Zed Books.

Birn, Anne-Emanuelle. 1999. "Skirting the Issue: Women and International Health in Historical Perspective." *American Journal of Public Health* 89(3): 399–407.

Birn, Anne- Emanuelle. 2014. "Backstage: The Relationship between the Rockefeller Foundation and the World Health Organization, Part I: 1940s–1960s." *Public Health* 128(2): 129–140.

Bunch, Charlotte and Roxanne Carrillo. 2015. "Women's Rights Are Human Rights: A Concept in the Making." In *Women and Girls Rising: Progress and Resistance Around the World*, edited by Ellen Chesler and Terry McGovern. 32–50. London: Routledge.

Dharmadhikari, Sanyukta, and Sharanya Gopinathan. 2018. "'Equal to Killing Us': Why India's Transgender Community Is Rejecting the Trans Bill." *The News Minute*. December 18.

CEDAW (UN Committee on the Elimination of Discrimination against Women). 2010. "Declarations, Reservations, Objections and Notifications of Withdrawal of Reservations Relating to the Convention on the Elimination of All Forms of Discrimination against Women." March 1. CEDAW/SP/2010/2.

Chandra-Mouli, Venkatraman, Joar Svanemyr, Avni Amin, Helga Fogstad, Lale Say, Françoise Girard, and Marleen Temmerman. 2015. "Twenty Years after International Conference on Population and Development: Where Are We with Adolescent Sexual and Reproductive Health and Rights?" *The Journal of Adolescent Health* 56(1 Suppl): S1–S6.

Chesler, Ellen and Terry McGovern. 2015. *Women and Girls Rising: Progress and Resistance Around the world*. London: Routledge.

Coates, Amy L., Peter S. Hill, Simon Rushton, and Julie Balen. 2014. "The Holy See on Sexual and Reproductive Health Rights: Conservative in Position, Dynamic in Response." *Reproductive Health Matters* 22(44): 114–124.

Corrêa, Sonia and Rosalind Petchesky. 2007. "Reproductive and Sexual Rights: A Feminist Perspective." In *Culture, Society and Sexuality*, edited by Richard Parker and Peter Aggleton. 298–315. London: Routledge.

Corrêa, Sonia and Susie Jolly. 2008. "Development's Encounter with Sexuality: Essentialism and Beyond." In *Development with a Body: Sexuality, Human Rights and Development*, edited by Andrea Cornwall, Sonia Corrêa, and Susie Jolly. 22–42. London: Zed Books Ltd.

Filmer-Wilson, Emilie, and Luis Mora. 2018. "The United Nations Population Fund: An Evolving Human Rights Mission and Approach to Sexual and Reproductive Health and Reproductive Rights." In *Human Rights in Global Health: Rights-Based Governance for a Globalizing World*, edited by Benjamin Mason Meier and Lawrence O. Gostin. 243–260. New York: Oxford University Press.

Freedman, Lynn P and Stephen L. Isaacs. 1993. "Human Rights and Reproductive Choice." *Studies in Family Planning* 24: 20–21.

Gostin, Lawrence O., Andrés Constantin, and Benjamin Mason Meier. 2020. "Global Health and Human Rights in the Age of Populism." In *Foundations of Global Health and Human Rights*, edited by Lawrence O. Gostin and Benjamin Mason Meier. 439–457. New York: Oxford University Press.

Grimes, Seamus. 1998. "From Population Control to 'Reproductive Rights': Ideological Influences in Population Policy." *Third World Quarterly* 19: 375.

Garcia-Morena, Claudia. 1994. *Reproductive Health and Justice: International Women's Conference for Cairo '94*. New York: International Women's Health Coalition and Citizenship, Studies, Information and Action.

Hartmann, Betsy. 1987. *Reproductive Rights and Wrongs: The Global Politics of Population Control and Contraceptive Choice*. New York: Harper and Row.

Hosken, Fran P. 1981. "Toward a Definition of Women's Human Rights." *Human Rights Quarterly* 3(2): 1–10.

ICRW (International Center for Research on Women). 2021. *Sexual and Reproductive Health, Rights, and Justice: A Closer Look at the Historical Impacts of Racism & Colonialism*. Washington: International Center for Research on Women.

Idriss-Wheeler, Dina, Ieman M. El-Mowaf, Karine Coen-Sanchez, Abdiasis Yalahow, and Sanni Yaya. 2021. "Looking through the Lens of Reproductive Justice: The Need for a Paradigm Shift in Sexual and Reproductive Health and Rights Research in Canada." *Reproductive Health* 18(129): 1–7.

Jain, Sagaree. 2020. "Two Eyed Seeing: Decolonizing Methodologies for Reproductive Justice" *Amplify*. May 19.

Kuruvilla, Shyama, Flavia Bustreo, Paul Hunt, Amarjit Singh, Eric Friedman, and Thaigo Luchesi. 2012. "The Millennium Development Goals and Human Rights: Realizing Shared Commitments." *Human Rights Quarterly* 34: 141–177.

Levine, Philippa. 2010. "Anthropology, Colonialism, and Eugenics." In *The Oxford Handbook on the History of Eugenics*, edited by Alison Bashford and Philippa Levine. 43–61. New York: Oxford University Press.

Madrigal-Borloz, Victor. 2021. *Reports on Gender: The Law of Inclusion and Practices of Exclusion*. Geneva: (OHCHR) Office of the High Commissioner for Human Rights.

Marks, Stephen P. and Alice Han. 2020. "Health and Human Rights through Development: The Right to Development, Rights-Based Approach to Development, and Sustainable Development Goals." In *Foundations of Global Health and Human Rights*, edited by Lawrence O. Gostin and Benjamin Mason Meier. 329–350. New York: Oxford University Press.

McGovern, Terry and Aziza Ahmed. 2020. "Equity in Health: Sexual and Reproductive Health and Rights." In *Foundations of Global Health and Human Rights*, edited by Lawrence O. Gostin and Benjamin Mason Meier. 307–326. New York: Oxford University Press.

Mofokeng, Tlaleng. 2022a. "Violence and Its Impact on the Right to Health—Report of the Special Rapporteur on the Right of Everyone to the Enjoyment of the Highest Attainable Standard of Physical and Mental Health." May 25. A/HRC/50/28.

Mofokeng, Tlaleng. 2022b. "Racism and the Right to Health—Report of the Special Rapporteur on the Right of Everyone to the Enjoyment of the Highest Attainable Standard of Physical and Mental Health." July 20. A/77/197.

Mostov, Julie. 2021. "Populism Is Always Gendered and Dangerous." *Frontiers in Sociology* 5(625385): 1–3.

Neidell, Shara. 1998. "Women's Empowerment as a Public Problem: A Case Study of the 1994 International Conference on Population and Development." *Population Research and Policy Review* 17(3): 247–260.

Notestein, Frank W. 1968. "The Population Council and the Demographic Crisis of the Less Developed World." *Demography* 5(2): 553–560.

O'Connor, Aoife, Maximillian Seunik, Blas Radi, Liberty Matthyse, Lance Gable, Hanna E. Huffstetler, and Benjamin Mason Meier. 2022. "Transcending the Gender Binary under International Law: Advancing Health-Related Human Rights for Trans* Populations." *Journal of Law, Medicine and Ethics* 50(3): 409–424.

O'Flaherty, Michael. 2006. "The Concluding Observations of United Nations Human Rights Treaty Bodies." *Human Rights Law Review* 6(1): 27–52.

O'Flaherty, Michael and John Fisher. 2008. "Sexual Orientation, Gender Identity and International Human Rights Law: Contextualising the Yogyakarta Principles." *Human Rights Law Review* 8(2): 207–248.

Parmet, Wendy E. 2009. *Populations, Public Health, and the Law*. Washington: Georgetown University Press.

Pugh, Sarah. 2019. "Politics, Power, and Sexual and Reproductive Health and Rights: Impacts and Opportunities." *Sexual and Reproductive Health Matters* 27(2): 1662616.

Roberts, Dorothy. 2011. *Fatal Invention How Science, Politics, and Big Business Re-create Race in the Twenty-first Century*. New York: The New Press.

Robinson, Rachel S. 2010. *UNFPA in Context: An Institutional History*. Washington: The Center for Global Development.

Roseman, Laura and Mindy Jane Reichenbach. 2011. *Reproductive Health and Human Rights: The Way Forward*. Philadelphia: University of Pennsylvania Press.

Tamale, Sylvia. 2009. "A Human Rights Impact Assessment of the Ugandan Anti-Homosexuality Bill 2009." *The Equal Rights Review* 4: 49–57.

Trump, Donald. 2017. "Presidential Memorandum Regarding the Mexico City Policy." White House.

UN (United Nations). 1968. "Final Act of the International Conference on Human Rights (including the Proclamation of Teheran)." A/Conf.32/41.

UN. 1975. "Declaration of Mexico on the Equality of Women and Their Contribution to Development and Peace." July 2. E/CONF.66/34.

UN. 1995. "Beijing Declaration and Platform of Action, adopted at the Fourth World Conference on Women." October 17. A/CONF.177/20.

UN. 2000. "The Four Global Women's Conferences 1975–1995: Historical Perspective." *United Nations Department of Public Information.*

UN and ECLAC (United Nations and the Economic Commission for Latin America and the Caribbean). 2013. *Montevideo Consensus on Population and Development.* Montevideo: UN.

UN General Assembly. 1993. "Vienna Declaration and Programme of Action." June 25. A/CONF.157/23.

UN General Assembly. 1967. "Declaration on the Elimination of Discrimination against Women." November 7. A/RES/22/2263.

UN General Assembly. 1979. "Convention on the Elimination of All Forms of Discrimination Against Women." December 18. G.A. Res. 24/180.

UN General Assembly. 2015. "Transforming Our World: The 2030 Agenda for Sustainable Development. October 21. A/RES/70/1.

UN General Assembly. 2017. "Work of the Statistical Commission pertaining to the 2030 Agenda for Sustainable Development." July 10. A/RES/71/313.

UN Human Rights Council. 2011. "Human Rights, Sexual Orientation and Gender Identity: Resolution Adopted by the Human Rights Council." June 17. A/HRC/RES/17/19.

UN Human Rights Council. 2014. "Human Rights, Sexual Orientation and Gender Identity: Resolution Adopted by the Human Rights Council." October 2. A/HRC/RES/27/32.

UN Human Rights Council. 2017. Report of the Independent Expert on Protection against Violence and Discrimination Based on Sexual Orientation and Gender Identity. April 19. A/HRC/35/36.

UNFPA (UN Population Fund). 1994. Report of the International Conference on Population and Development, Cairo, September 5–13. A/CONF.171/13.

18
Health in Conflict
International Humanitarian Law as Global Health Policy

Jocelyn Getgen Kestenbaum and Benjamin Mason Meier

Introduction

In addressing complex humanitarian emergencies, armed conflicts strain health systems and challenge efforts to ensure public health and human rights. Recent conflicts demonstrate that civilians bear a disproportionate burden of war's negative consequences and that, increasingly, parties to conflict deliberately target civilians to gain military advantage. Civilians continue to suffer from atrocity crimes—including genocide, enslavement, slave trading, and torture—amid conflict. Protecting civilians in such conflicts extends to protecting humanitarian and health care professionals – as well as protecting civilians from abuses by health care workers. In all circumstances, in times of peace and in conflict, states must maintain functioning health systems, which includes ensuring civilians equal access to essential primary health care, food, shelter, water, sanitation, and essential medicines. During times of armed conflict, states and non-state actors alike must protect the sick and wounded against attacks and provide protection and care without discrimination. For this reason, humanitarian workers must understand what rights civilians have—and what obligations parties to the conflict bear for public health—under international humanitarian law.

Given that conflicts overwhelm and even destroy domestic health resources, capacity, and infrastructure, these crises demand multilateral health responses under international law. To buttress the global health law framework, and to limit the negative consequences of conflict, international humanitarian law—also known as the "law of war" or the "law of armed conflict"—enumerates protections of health-related rights and access to health care during armed conflict. International humanitarian obligations mandate that state and non-state actors alike respect and protect health-related rights and healthcare providers in conflict-affected settings. These obligations under international humanitarian law frame global health law in times of armed conflict, providing for expectations, standards, and legal obligations to limit the negative public health and humanitarian consequences of war. Protecting the health and human rights of civilians and those outside of combat (*hors de combat*), meaning persons not actively engaging in hostilities, requires that all parties to conflict comply with obligations under international humanitarian law at all times.

This chapter addresses the relationship between international humanitarian law and global health law in both safeguarding public health and protecting human rights in conflict-affected settings. Examining the birth of international humanitarian law, Part I traces the path from the moral condemnation of war to the development of international obligations in war under the first Geneva Conventions. With World War II challenging efforts to protect noncombatants, Part II examines how these unprecedented harms led to the development and implementation of international humanitarian law protections for all individuals, especially civilians and humanitarian professionals, through the contemporary Geneva Conventions. Yet, the changing nature of conflicts has required the development of new institutions to address new health threats. Given the continuing and emerging challenges of conflicts for global health, Part III analyzes the current legal regime to protect health workers, deliver health care, prevent human rights abuses, and provide redress to victims in conflict-affected areas. This chapter concludes with a call to humanitarian assistance professionals to understand the changing nature of conflict, the health needs of conflict-affected populations, and the gaps in international humanitarian law frameworks—all while looking to global health law reforms to strengthen the protection of public health in conflict-affected settings.

I. Birth of International Humanitarian Law

Beginning in the 19th century, violence against noncombatants became formally proscribed under international humanitarian law, with condemnation of wartime attacks against medical professionals laying a legal foundation for modern efforts to protect health care personnel in conflict. International humanitarian law—shaped by advances in ethical norms, the Geneva Conferences, and two world wars—would evolve to solidify health protections in conflict settings.

A. Moral Condemnation of War

Principles of *jus in bello*, or "justice in war," have long regulated parties' ethical conduct during armed conflict, developing normative frameworks that form the "rules of engagement" to guide wartime decision-making. Before conducting hostilities, soldiers must consider the proportionality of the belligerent act and recognize the "reach of battle," understanding the critical distinction between combatants and noncombatants (Walzer 1992). While soldiers actively contribute to war and thereby relinquish their rights not to be killed in combat, noncombatants do not. Thus, the targeting of a noncombatant is prohibited – whether inside or outside of the conduct of hostilities.

These ethical norms came to shape an international movement. After attending to wounded soldiers in the 1859 Battle of Solferino,[1] Swiss businessman Henri Dunant pressured the international community to provide greater protections for health care workers and the wounded on the battlefield. Dunant's firsthand account in *A Memory of Solferino* gained widespread recognition, including from Gustave Moynier, the founder of the Geneva Public Welfare Society, who worked with Dunant to draft the first proposals to protect health care and health care workers in wartime (Bugnion 2012).

B. First Geneva Convention

Dunant and Moynier joined forces with other military, legal, and medical leaders in Europe to form the "International Relief Committee for Injured Combatants." Advancing the legal recognition of health care workers' neutrality in conflict, the International Relief Committee convened the 1863 Geneva Conference with the Geneva Public Welfare Society, hosting representatives from sixteen states and four philanthropic institutions to develop what would become international humanitarian law.

The 1863 Geneva Conference led to the Convention for the Amelioration of the Condition of the Wounded in Armies in the Field, which delineated the protections granted to wounded soldiers and medical personnel during wartime. During a subsequent Conference the following year, the Geneva Committee codified in much greater detail the key protections for health care systems, including the neutrality of military medical personnel and hospitals. These recommendations in the Geneva Convention served in the decades that followed as the impetus for a broader movement to concretize international humanitarian law norms.

The first Geneva Convention provided specific protections for healthcare operations, including military medical personnel and hospitals, which would be designated by the red cross emblem. This groundwork established the International Committee of the Red Cross (ICRC), a neutral and independent

---

[1] The Battle of Solferino was crucial in Italian unification and independence, engaging approximately 300,000 soldiers across the French and Austrian armies. Although Dunant was not present for the height of the battle, he witnessed the aftermath. About 40,000 men laid wounded and abandoned. Appalled by the condition of men left on the battlefield, Dunant, with several nurses, treated the wounded for three full days.

international organization that would operate to ensure humanitarian assistance and protection during armed conflict (Palmieri 2012).

Case Study: ICRC Establishment as a Humanitarian Institution

Where previous "international organizations" had only overseen relationships between nations, the first Geneva Convention established the ICRC to account for belligerent states and non-state actors' treatment of private individuals in conflict. Originally known as the "Permanent International Committee for the Relief of Wounded Soldiers," this Committee would seek to recruit, train, and deploy volunteer nurses during wartime. Collaborating with governments, the group promoted norms for health care provision in advance of conflicts—rather than negotiating protections after war had begun. Yet the Committee recognized that providing medical services would not be sufficient without offering medical professionals adequate protections on the battlefield. The Committee worked to plead the case for states to offer neutrality to health care workers. Drawing from the 1863 Geneva Conference, Belgium, Prussia, and Italy established National Societies dedicated to working within their own countries to protect health care workers in war. (Upon his return to France, Dunant himself supported the establishment of the French Red Cross.) This coalition of national organizations began to concretize ideals of humanitarian law, recognizing legal protections for health care workers in conflict. While the 1863 and 1864 Geneva Conferences sought to promote neutrality for health care workers, the ICRC's efforts institutionalized these principles in practice, supporting respect for international humanitarian law and providing essential medical care in conflict settings.

Health care worker protections afforded under international humanitarian law soon broadened to include other voluntary aid societies and those providing care for prisoners of war. These protections for health care personnel would become crucially important as unprecedented wars challenged the world order.

C. World War II Reframes Humanitarian Responsibilities

Two world wars challenged international norms and reframed humanitarian responsibilities. With forty million casualties, including ten million civilian casualties, the end of the "Great War," as World War I was then called, brought the need for international governance to maintain world peace. States at the Paris Peace Conference in 1919 developed the League of Nations as a basis to protect "collective security" (League of Nations 1919). Following the establishment of the League of Nations, the 1929 Geneva Convention provided more robust protections in wartime, including explicit rules safeguarding medical operations in combat and recognizing the humanitarian role of the ICRC. Before World War II, states had already promulgated three Geneva Conventions, each covering different classes of protected persons, but none covering civilians. By the end of World War II, fifteen million soldiers had been killed in battle, twenty-five million had been wounded, and forty-five million civilians had perished.

1. Health Challenges amid Wartime Atrocities

World War II caused unprecedented death and suffering, dividing the world into a wartime Axis (Germany, Italy, and Japan) and Allied nations (Great Britain, the United States, and the Soviet Union). Nazi atrocities during World War II resulted in a "Holocaust" that killed six million Jews and ten million other civilians (USHMM 2020). Nazi military occupation across Europe led to the systematic imprisonment, enslavement, and execution of Jews, Roma, and other minorities in concentration camps. This "Final Solution" made visible genocide and other mass atrocity as state policy.[2] With public health theories legitimizing eugenics and Nazi "racial hygiene" programs, German physicians, nurses, and scientists sterilized hundreds of thousands of individuals, as introduced in Chapter 8, and aided in theorizing, planning, and operating Nazi killing programs, which expanded from German state hospitals to Nazi concentration camps (Annas and Grodin 1992).

The War in the Pacific also caused extraordinary casualties and suffering. Japanese conquest of east and southeast Asia resulted in sweeping atrocities committed against civilian populations (Sutton 1946), non-consensual human experimentation on prisoners of war (Brody et al. 2014), and the large-scale use of so-called "comfort women," sexually and otherwise enslaved women and girls in service to the Japanese imperial army (Tanaka 2002).[3] The War in the Pacific ended with Allied bombings of civilian targets across Japan and the American use of nuclear weapons against the Japanese cities of Hiroshima and Nagasaki.

---

[2] Beyond the targets of the Nazi killing machine, these events contributed to extreme food shortages across the continent, increasing displacement, suffering, disease, and death for civilians and military personnel alike (Kesternich et al. 2014).

[3] In addition to the harms directly caused by the conflict, the War in the Pacific also saw epidemics of infectious diseases affecting both local and military populations. Imperial Japan faced outbreaks of typhoid and smallpox, while still grappling with tuberculosis, venereal diseases, and parasitic infections which spread before the start of World War II. The rapid mobilization of military personnel and displacement of populations across east and southeast Asia greatly increased the rates of infectious diseases across the Asian-Pacific theater and placed an increased burden on already strained, and often undeveloped, public health systems (Condon-Rall and Cowdrey 1998).

These two nuclear explosions alone killed over 100,000 people and resulted in the death of at least another 100,000 from radiation exposure (Condon-Rall and Cowdrey 1998).

Recognizing that international efforts to prevent wartime atrocities were insufficient, states came together in 1943 to create the United Nations Relief and Rehabilitation Administration (UNRRA). While the ICRC continued to conduct humanitarian relief missions during World War II, providing aid and resources to displaced civilians and combating famine, insufficient resources and support kept the ICRC from providing humanitarian relief in German-occupied areas and to those deported to concentration camps (ICRC 2010). Member states created UNRRA to provide global relief during the war—to "help people help themselves" by delivering aid through a "two R policy," requiring "more than Relief and less than Reconstruction" (Guins 1945, 128). Working across the European and Pacific theaters, UNRRA expanded public health infrastructure, focusing on building robust health systems, increasing the health care workforce, and providing medical supplies (Sze 1945).

2. Nuremberg Trials to Prosecute Crimes Against Humanity

After the war, the International Military Tribunal at Nuremberg (Nuremberg Trials) sought justice against those who had taken part in Nazi crimes, giving rise to modern international criminal law.[4] For the first time, these trials sought to define "crimes against humanity," reflecting "[a]trocities and offences, including but not limited to murder, extermination, enslavement, deportation, imprisonment, torture, rape, or other inhumane acts committed against any civilian population, or persecutions on political, racial or religious grounds whether or not in violation of the domestic laws of the country where perpetrated" (Bassiouni 1992, 590). As part of these Nuremberg Trials, the Doctors' Trial of 1946–1947 prosecuted Nazi health personnel, as seen in Figure 18.1, in the first international trial of health workers for patient and research subject harms (Annas and Grodin 1992).

In the Doctors' Trial, twenty-three defendants faced charges of conspiracy, war crimes, crimes against humanity, and membership in a criminal organization. In its August 1947 judgment in the case of *United States v. Karl Brandt*, the Nuremberg Military Tribunal found that "criminal medical experiments on non-German nationals, both prisoners of war and civilians, including Jews and 'asocial' persons, were carried out on a large scale" (International Military

---

[4] Five months after the opening of the Nuremberg Trials, the International Military Tribunal for the Far East (IMTFE) conducted the Tokyo Trials, wherein Allied prosecutions sought to hold Japanese officials accountable for atrocities committed during World War II—setting further precedents for international law. With eleven judges selected from each state that signed the peace agreement with Japan, the IMTFE found all twenty-five accused Japanese officials guilty and sentenced seven to death (Sedgwick 2011).

Figure 18.1 Nazi Physician Karl Brandt before the International Military Tribunal at Nuremberg (United States Holocaust Museum)

Tribunal 1949, 181). The Tribunal found that "these experiments involving brutalities, tortures, disabling injury, and death were performed in complete disregard of international conventions, the laws and customs of war, [and] the general principles of criminal law as derived from the criminal laws of all civilized nations..." (International Military Tribunal 1949, 183). This international criminal prosecution—for war crimes and crimes against humanity—would provide the normative underpinnings for health-related human rights.

The egregious humanitarian abuses of World War II led directly to the development of human rights under international law. Widespread revulsion toward Nazism and genocide across Europe led to an international focus on common human dignity (Meier, Murphy, and Gostin 2020). How a state treated those within its nation would now be a matter of international concern, and under the newly constituted United Nations (UN), the Commission on Human Rights proposed an "international bill of rights," which the UN General Assembly adopted as the Universal Declaration of Human Rights (UDHR) on December 10, 1948. The UDHR, first introduced in Chapter 4, would seek to advance "a standard of living adequate for health," encompassing both medical care and underlying determinants of health, such as food safety, nutrition, sanitation, infectious disease prevention, and social security. In addition, states would look to the development of the 1949 Geneva Conventions to protect human rights in conflict. With these two cornerstones of human rights law and international humanitarian law, the Geneva Conventions provided an accountability framework for human rights violations in armed conflict that was lacking in previous international instruments (Kolb 1998).

II. International Humanitarian Law and the Changing Nature of Contemporary Conflict

The post-World War II development of the United Nations Charter sought to provide an international institutional basis "to save succeeding generations from the scourge of war" (UN 1945, preamble). As part of this institutional peacekeeping mandate, UN member states oversee international human rights and international humanitarian law. The core aims of international humanitarian law seek to limit the negative effects of war while mitigating human suffering. International humanitarian law has thus codified universal rules to protect those no longer taking part in hostilities (*hors de combat*, which includes prisoners of war and civilians) and to limit the means and methods of warfare. These rules are based on the balance of two main principles:

- Military necessity—the notion that parties to a conflict may only resort to means and methods of warfare that are necessary to achieve a legitimate military purpose and to safeguard national interests.
- Humanity—the principle that prohibits parties to a conflict from causing suffering or destruction above and beyond what is required to meet their legitimate military purposes (Schmitt 2010).

Through core treaties and customary law, international humanitarian law sets out to resolve humanitarian issues arising from armed conflict, whether international or non-international in nature, and independent of the reasons for either party waging war. Accepted by all states, these core treaties are the 1949 Geneva Conventions (I–IV) and their Additional Protocols of 1977 and 2005. Given that the rules of international humanitarian law apply to both state and non-state actors, all parties to a conflict must respect the laws of war at all times, protecting civilians and humanitarian aid workers during conflict.

A. Postwar Geneva Conventions

In continuing international efforts to realize humanitarian law in conflicts after World War II, the 1949 Geneva Conventions and subsequent Protocols, as detailed in Table 18.1, along with customary international law, establish the principal contemporary system of international humanitarian law.

Table 18.1 The Geneva Conventions of 1949 and Their Additional Protocols (Kestenbaum and Meier)

Treaty	Year	Description
First Geneva Convention for the Amelioration of the Condition of the Wounded and Sick in Armed Forces in the Field (GC I)	1949	Expands upon the 1864 Convention to protect soldiers who are *hors de combat*. Specifically, provisions protect: • wounded and sick soldiers; • medical personnel, facilities, and equipment; • wounded and sick civilian support personnel accompanying the armed forces; • military chaplains; and • civilians who spontaneously take up arms to repel an invasion.
Second Geneva Convention for the Amelioration of the Condition of Wounded, Sick and Shipwrecked Members of Armed Forces at Sea (GC II)	1949	Adapts protections of the First Geneva Convention to protect wounded and sick combatants while on board a ship or at sea. Specifically, provisions protect: • armed forces members who are wounded, sick or shipwrecked; • hospital ships and medical personnel; and • civilians who accompany the armed forces.
Third Geneva Convention relative to the Treatment of Prisoners of War (GC III)	1949	Establishes rules for the treatment of prisoners of war (POWs), requiring that POWs be treated humanely, are adequately housed, and receive sufficient food, clothing and medical care. POWs may include: • members of the armed forces; • volunteer militia, including resistance movements; and • civilians accompanying the armed forces.
Fourth Geneva Convention relative to the Protection of Civilian Persons in Time of War (GC IV)	1949	Protects civilians in areas of armed conflict and occupied territories.
Protocol I relating to the Protection of Victims of International Armed Conflicts (AP I)	1977	Expands protections for civilians as well as military and civilian medical workers in international armed conflicts (IACs).

(*continued*)

Table 18.1 Continued

Treaty	Year	Description
Protocol II relating to the Protection of Victims of Non-International Armed Conflicts (AP II)	1977	Expands protections for victims of armed conflicts not of an international character (NIACs) (i.e., civil wars).
Protocol III relating to the Adoption of an Additional Distinctive Emblem (AP III)	2005	Designates three distinctive emblems of the red cross, red crescent, and red crystal to identify and protect medical and relief workers, military and civilian medical facilities, mobile units, and hospital ships during armed conflict.

These four Conventions and their Additional Protocols helped solidify prior efforts and general principles of conduct in war, while enacting new rules to address weaknesses highlighted by the atrocities that persisted during armed conflict in the wake of World War II. These treaties provide specific obligations for protecting combatants (i.e., members of the armed forces) who are wounded, sick or shipwrecked, and prisoners of war, as well as civilians, medical personnel, and others providing humanitarian services during conflict (American Red Cross 2011).

1. General Principles of Civilian Protection—Distinction, Proportionality, and Precaution

As the battlefield of contemporary conflicts came to involve more civilians and civilian objects (i.e., cultural property, places of worship, hospitals), additional principles emerged in international humanitarian law to limit the effects of modern warfare. In addition to the fundamental notions of military necessity and humanity that guide the conduct of hostilities toward combatants, three principles of international humanitarian law—distinction, proportionality, and precaution—evolved to guide the protection of civilians and civilian objects during armed conflict. The principle of distinction obligates parties to an armed conflict to distinguish between, on the one hand, the civilian population and civilian objects, and, on the other hand, military objectives, including combatants. Attacks must be directed only at military objectives to avoid collateral damage. Relatedly, the principle of proportionality mandates that parties to a conflict limit injury to civilians and loss of civilian life and property to what is necessary to achieve a military advantage. Finally, the principle of precaution obligates parties to a conflict to avoid unnecessary loss of civilian life or objects during military operations by checking that targets are indeed military targets and warning civilian populations of impending attacks (Melzer 2008).

These principles derive from international humanitarian law treaties—mainly in the four Geneva Conventions of 1949 and their Additional Protocols of 1977—alongside custom and general principles of law. Often, the Martens Clause, found first in the Preamble to the 1899 Hague Convention II and considered customary international law, is cited as a source of international humanitarian law principles. The Martens Clause states that, even when not expressly enumerated in international humanitarian law instruments, both combatants and civilians are entitled to minimum levels of protection, including that hostilities should be regulated by the principles of the law of nations as they result from the usages of international law, from the laws of humanity, and from the dictates of public conscience. Further, under treaty law, Additional Protocol I (API) obligates belligerents to distinguish between legitimate targets and civilians, and between military objectives and civilian objects, while Geneva Convention III (GCIII) and API require combatants to distinguish themselves from civilians. Under certain circumstances, willful civilian killings or attacks against sick and wounded individuals can constitute war crimes as grave breaches of the Geneva Conventions, triggering obligations to search for and try or extradite perpetrators.

2. Civilian Protections—Maintaining Health Systems

The Fourth Geneva Convention (GCIV) and its Additional Protocols provide specific protections for civilians during armed conflict. Specifically, enemy forces must always treat civilians under their control humanely – without any adverse distinction. Civilians under the power of enemy forces must be protected against all violence and degrading treatment, including murder and torture. In protecting civilians, certain groups—including women, children, the aged, the sick, and forcibly displaced persons (IDPs and refugees)—are highly vulnerable in conflict and thus receive explicit protections under international humanitarian law. These additional protections prohibit forced displacement by intimidation, violence, or starvation and require states to take all appropriate steps to prevent family separation and to re-establish family contact when family separation occurs in conflict-affected settings.

To ensure these protections, states must maintain functioning healthcare systems, ensuring civilian access to essential primary health care, food, shelter, sanitation, water, and essential medicines. States bear an obligation to provide health care during times of armed conflict, protecting the sick and wounded against attacks—equally and without discrimination. The Fourth Geneva Convention and Additional Protocol I prohibit attacks against ICRC personnel or facilities and require parties to the conflict to facilitate the ICRC's humanitarian health care work. Beyond the work of the ICRC, the Geneva Conventions and their Additional Protocols protect all medical personnel in order to provide impartial care to the sick and wounded, and parties to armed conflict may not impede impartial medical care or ethical medical practice.[5] To that end, parties to armed conflict also must respect and protect hospitals, ambulances, and other facilities and transport serving to provide medical care. Parties to armed conflict must therefore allow and facilitate safe passage of humanitarian assistance when civilian populations lack access to these essential supplies.

Yet, despite these robust protections under the Geneva Conventions and Additional Protocols, violations of the laws of war reveal continuing limitations of international humanitarian law. These limitations are especially true regarding accountability for individuals who commit grave breaches of international humanitarian law, given that the framework of the Geneva Conventions depends upon domestic courts to try war criminals. While states have sought to resolve this "impunity gap" by prosecuting individual perpetrators under international criminal law—drawing from the post-World War II Nuremberg prosecutions and continuing today under the International Criminal Court (ICC)—challenges to holding individual perpetrators accountable for conflict-related crimes have raised an imperative to redress evolving gaps in international humanitarian law.

B. Redressing Gaps in International Humanitarian Law

Beyond providing limited individual accountability for perpetrators of international crimes, international humanitarian law offers fewer protections in non-international armed conflicts. As noted in Table 18.1, international humanitarian law distinguishes between international armed conflicts (IACs) and non-international armed conflicts (NIACs). Armed conflicts of an international character are those involving two or more opposing sovereign states as parties to the conflict, while conflicts of a non-international character are those involving a sovereign state against a non-state armed group, or non-state groups opposing each other, whether or not sovereign states are involved in providing aid to either the state or non-state actors.

Thus, the four Geneva Conventions and First Additional Protocol apply in IACs, while Common Article 3 to the four Geneva Conventions and the Second Additional Protocol apply in NIACs. These distinctions are important for global health and humanitarian workers to understand because international humanitarian law protections are much more robust for IACs than for NIACs—given

---

[5] Such health care personnel, however, must not commit acts that are harmful to the enemy or are outside of their humanitarian functions. If a party to an armed conflict uses medical facilities or transport to trick enemy forces (while launching attacks or carrying out acts harmful to the enemy), that party has committed "perfidy," which is a war crime if it results in death or serious injury to enemy forces.

that states are much more reluctant to give up sovereign power to international scrutiny in internal, civil, or other non-international war. Consequently, healthcare workers must understand the nature of the armed conflict in which they operate to understand what protections they have and what obligations belligerents have to protect them from harm.

The Geneva Conventions more robustly regulate IACs, where sovereign states are more inclined to submit to international scrutiny over the conduct of interstate hostilities—given their mutual interests in respecting humanitarian principles. While drafters of the Geneva Conventions did not anticipate the changing nature of war following World War II, and therefore did not push for stronger protections in NIACs, many contemporary conflicts occur entirely within state borders or transnationally with non-state actors (Sarkees and Wayman 2010). In addressing these rising NIACs, customary international humanitarian law, Common Article 3 of the four Geneva Conventions, and Additional Protocol II (where non-state forces hold territory) provide protections under international humanitarian law for conflicts not of an international character.

From a humanitarian perspective, the distinction between IACs and NIACs may seem arbitrary, as victims of all conflicts experience similar harms and have similar needs; however, international humanitarian law, based on consent among equal sovereigns, does not treat international and non-international armed conflicts equally. As a result, states' monopoly on the legitimate use of force within their respective borders is considered inherent to sovereign power, and, with limited exceptions, states consider citizens waging war against their own state as a matter of internal, domestic law—limiting efforts to protect health under international humanitarian law. Similarly, international legal protections for forcibly displaced persons differ depending on whether individuals have crossed international borders (Getgen Kestenbaum 2021).

Case Study: Health of IDPs in Conflict-Affected Settings

According to international law, individuals who cross international borders and cannot return home because their lives are in danger are refugees and entitled to international protection, especially regarding the customary international law principle of *nonrefoulement* – protecting refugees with credible fears of persecution from forced return. Yet not all individuals forced to migrate are refugees. There are increasing numbers of individuals forced to flee their homes but relocating within their countries of origin as internally displaced persons (IDPs), and, consequently, unable to avail themselves of international refugee law protections. As citizens and civilians, however, IDPs retain the rights and protections under their state afforded by human rights and international humanitarian law. Importantly, international humanitarian law contains several provisions to prevent the displacement of civilians and consequent suffering. For instance, the four Geneva Conventions, their Additional Protocols, and customary rules of international humanitarian law expressly prohibit parties to an armed conflict from forcibly displacing civilians in both IACs and NIACs, unless civilian security or military necessity require displacement. Internally displaced persons are civilians and, as such, receive the same international humanitarian law protections as all persons who are not or are no longer taking part in hostilities. Thus, neither IDPs nor their places of shelter, unless turned into a military objective, can be directly attacked. Should internal displacement occur, IDPs must be provided adequate shelter, hygiene, health, safety (including protection from sexual and gender-based violence), and nutrition – equally and without discrimination. Further, international humanitarian law prohibits parties to armed conflict from attacking objects required for civilian population survival, such as crops, livestock, and drinking water supplies. Beyond these international humanitarian law treaties, the UN Guiding Principles on Internal Displacement, while not binding, contain important guidelines for states and humanitarian workers in conflict settings working with IDPs that are part of existing human rights and international humanitarian law. Without greater respect for international humanitarian law and more vigorous efforts to protect civilian populations during armed conflict, global displacement figures will continue to grow. Health care workers, therefore, must hold states and non-state actors accountable to their international humanitarian law obligations.

Conflict-related internal displacement indicates massive state failures to protect populations and ensure fundamental human rights obligations, including the right to health. In the absence of health protections for civilians under international humanitarian law, humanitarian health efforts have expanded to rely on non-state actors, including international organizations and non-governmental organizations (NGOs), to fill gaps in humanitarian assistance where government institutions are unwilling or unable to meet population needs.

C. Rise of Non-State Public Health Actors in the Humanitarian Response

NGOs at the international, regional, and local levels have proliferated in recent decades, delivering essential humanitarian assistance to civilian populations in conflict-affected settings. Given their increasingly important roles, global policy standards have become necessary to regulate these non-state humanitarian responses (Evans, Queen, and Martin 2020). Such policies across NGOs have been developed to facilitate and encourage evidence- and rights-based assistance, service delivery, and recovery in times of conflict and other complex humanitarian emergency settings.

In guiding NGOs, the Sphere Standards are based on the principles of the Humanitarian Charter, the ethical and legal agreed-upon standards to address humanitarian needs and alleviate human suffering in conflict and other complex emergencies. The Humanitarian Charter proclaimed the rights of all individuals to humanitarian assistance, equally and without discrimination of any kind, with humanitarian organizations agreeing under the Charter to meet the Minimum Standards to assist and protect affected populations (Sphere Project 2000). Drawing from the Humanitarian Charter, the Sphere Standards have sought to operationalize and coordinate humanitarian responses while holding NGOs to account for providing quality services in accordance with the minimum standards for realizing the human rights of individuals in conflict-affected settings (Evans, Queen, and Martin 2020). Revised in 2018, the Sphere Handbook guides humanitarian responses in four critical technical areas:

- water, sanitation, and hygiene promotion;
- food security and nutrition;
- shelter and settlement; and
- health (Sphere Association 2018).

Notably, these standards for humanitarian response focus on providing adequate public health services. In addition, the Handbook provides guidance on holistic humanitarian service delivery for meeting people's essential health needs in conflict and crisis.

Providing guidance for NGO humanitarian service delivery and accountability, the Sphere Standards advance the fundamental importance of human dignity and the right of individuals to participate fully in all decisions affecting them (Sphere Association 2018). While significant challenges remain in implementation and full realization of the Sphere Standards—including adequate service delivery to all in need and facing resource allocation deficits—the Sphere Handbook is an important guide for public health professionals working in conflict-affected settings, often with scarce resources and under difficult circumstances. These standards will become crucial in aligning non-state actors with rising UN efforts to address public health amid armed conflict.

D. Security Council Moves to Address Health in Conflict

The 1945 establishment of the UN Security Council opened a crucial UN effort to ensure international peace and security. Bringing together five permanent member states (Republic of China, France, Russian Federation, United

Kingdom, and United States of America) alongside ten non-permanent member states (elected to serve two-year, rotating terms), early Security Council debates on international peace and security were primarily confined to resolutions addressing "traditional threats" of armed conflict (Luck 2006). By the turn of the century, however, the UN Security Council sought to widen the scope of what could be considered a threat to international peace and security, passing multiple resolutions related to "non-traditional" security threats, including on civilian protection in armed conflict and gender in the context of post-conflict peacebuilding (Malone, von Einsiedel, and Stagno 2015). Addressing health directly, the Security Council first recognized HIV's potential to promote economic, social, and political instability and violence, passing a 2000 resolution on "HIV/AIDS and international peacekeeping operations" (UN Security Council 2000).[6] This Security Council resolution would herald a rapid transition in the coming decades to address health as a security concern (Rushton and Voss 2022).

Since 2000, the UN Security Council has increasingly involved itself in global health governance—as public health threats came to be increasingly framed as implicating "global health security" (Rushton and Youde 2014). This "securitization" of health, as introduced in Chapter 6, has addressed health challenges as threats to the state, requiring extraordinary measures through an expanded set of actors, including military forces (Wenham 2019). With the Security Council focused on terrorism after the Al-Qaeda attacks of September 11, 2001, members nevertheless ensured that health remained a part of these terrorism concerns— focusing on national public health capabilities to respond to biological, chemical, and radiological attacks (UN Security Council 2003). This securitization of health has endured, with the Security Council becoming involved in global health during the 2014–2016 Ebola epidemic, determining that "the unprecedented extent of the Ebola outbreak in Africa constituted a threat to international peace and security" (UN Security Council 2014). When faced again with an Ebola outbreak in 2018, the UN Security Council condemned the negative impact that armed groups in the Democratic Republic of Congo were having on the success of the Ebola response while recognizing gendered inequities in the Ebola outbreak—drawing on WHO policies and human rights protections (UN Security Council 2018). This narrow view of health securitization would expand to include human rights and humanitarian protections of health systems amid conflict (Sekalala, Williams, and Meier 2022). With warring parties increasingly targeting health systems, leaving populations without access to care (Fast and

---

[6] Despite several states finding HIV to be outside the mandate of the Security Council, the resolution was adopted unanimously (Rushton 2010). In 2011, the Security Council would again reflect "on the impacts of HIV/AIDS epidemic in conflict and post-conflict situations," this time focusing on HIV/AIDS vulnerability in the context of conflict (UN Security Council 2011).

Read 2022), the Security Council in 2016 condemned violence against health care systems as a violation of human rights law and international humanitarian law – stressing the importance of respecting international humanitarian law and demanding "safe and unimpeded passage for medical personnel and humanitarian personnel" (UN Security Council 2016). This focus on the protection of health systems would extend into the COVID-19 pandemic, with UN Secretary-General António Guterres calling in March 2020 for a "global ceasefire" (UN 2020). Supported by the Security Council, members called on all parties to armed conflicts to effectively cease engagement in conflict for ninety days to facilitate the pandemic response (UN Security Council 2020), thereafter looking beyond conflict to call for COVID-19 vaccine equity (UN Security Council 2021). This Security Council effort to center fair and equitable distribution of health resources may reflect a move out of the health securitization framework that began over two decades ago—reframing the relationship between conflict prevention and global health.

III. Rising Legal Responses to Advance Accountability for Health in Humanitarian Contexts

Amid increasing public health threats, human rights violations, and international crimes committed in humanitarian settings, international institutions have sought to advance accountability for health and human rights in rising conflicts. This accountability has taken wide-ranging forms across institutions, as seen in: WHO's development of international monitoring systems for attacks on health care systems; national litigation to provide accountability for health care professionals' continuing perpetration of torture and other war crimes; UN efforts to provide reparations to victims-survivors of sexual exploitation and abuse at the hands of peacekeepers; and ICC adjudication to provide redress for health-related crimes under international criminal law.

A. Monitoring for Accountability: Protecting Health Systems amid Rising Conflicts

Despite the evolution of global standards to protect health workers and ensure the delivery of health care in conflict, attacks against health systems have continued throughout the world—violating humanitarian law, undermining human rights, and threatening public health. From the targeted killing of health workers in Afghanistan to the aerial bombing of hospitals in Syria and Ukraine, health care is under attack in conflict zones. The persistence of such violence

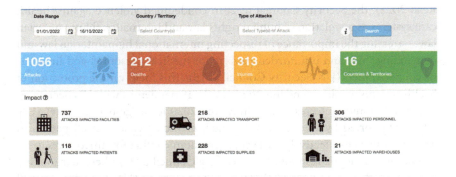

Figure 18.2 Surveillance System for Attacks on Health Care (SSA) Dashboard Interface (WHO)

against health care, especially in humanitarian crises related to armed conflict, has prompted global institutions to develop systematic monitoring mechanisms to facilitate accountability for these harms (Rubenstein 2021). Seeking to document the nature and the extent of attacks on health care, WHO has developed the Surveillance System for Attacks on Healthcare (SSA), as seen in Figure 18.2, to monitor attacks against health care in complex humanitarian emergencies, collecting and disseminating needed data as a basis to facilitate accountability for harms and alleviate violence against health care systems (Meier, Rice, and Bandara 2021).

Case Study: WHO Surveillance System for Attacks on Health Care

Established under a 2012 World Health Assembly resolution, the SSA seeks to institutionalize WHO monitoring in humanitarian crises related to armed conflict, using WHO's geographic reach and technical legitimacy to collect and disseminate data on attacks against health care systems. Pushed forward by growing demands from NGO advocates, civil society organizations came together in 2011 to request that WHO create a platform to monitor attacks against health care workers. In buttressing WHO efforts later that year, the ICRC's 2011 report, *Health Care in Danger*, examined specific attacks against health care systems across sixteen countries, seeking to determine the types of violence against health facilities, medical vehicles, and health personnel in countries experiencing armed conflict and other situations of widespread violence. While the ICRC report concluded that responding to these threats would require reforms of international humanitarian law, there remained no systematic data across countries to understand the nature of the threat and frame these proposed reforms. With growing demands on WHO to collect data on these harms against health systems, proponents saw WHO as uniquely positioned at the forefront of global health governance, with the health governance leadership, international political legitimacy, and cross-national data that would allow it to play a leading role in monitoring attacks against health care systems. The UN Security Council added further pressure for WHO action through its 2016 resolution condemning attacks on health care and reaffirming the protection of healthcare systems and workers under international humanitarian law. The 2017 launch of the SSA, drawing from methodologies developed in previous NGO monitoring efforts, has provided a new institutional mechanism for WHO to collect, analyze, and publicize data, looking to this systematic monitoring mechanism to comprehend the nature, scope, and magnitude of attacks and facilitate accountability to end attacks on health care in conflict settings.

The SSA has created a system to address attacks on health care workers, but additional mechanisms would be necessary in response to continuing harm done to civilians from healthcare and other humanitarian workers.

B. Litigation for Accountability: Litigation Against U.S. "Enhanced Interrogation" Torture Program in Guantanamo Bay, Cuba

Despite the prosecution of Nazi physicians in Nuremberg, international law violations, including human rights abuses and international crimes perpetrated by health care personnel, have continued. Medical professionals continue to ignore ethical imperatives to do no harm, perpetrating international crimes in the name of science, medicine, and public health. Such abuses continue globally in violation of international law, as states have duties under international humanitarian law and human rights law to protect civilians and others outside of combat – regardless of who perpetrates the harm.

Advocates have looked to litigation in national courts to bring justice for these violations of international humanitarian law. In the United States, for example, advocates have sought to challenge psychologists for their role in designing, implementing, and overseeing the U.S. Central Intelligence Agency's (CIA's) "enhanced interrogation" program during the "War on Terror." Working with the U.S. military prison at Guantanamo Bay, Cuba, these healthcare professionals convinced CIA officials to adopt such torture techniques, including "waterboarding," as government policy in its detention and interrogation program after the 9/11 attacks on the United States (U.S. Senate Select Committee on Intelligence 2014).[7] On behalf of three victims, the American Civil Liberties Union (ACLU) brought claims against the healthcare workers for torture; cruel, inhuman, and degrading treatment; non-consensual human experimentation; and war crimes (ACLU 2017). When the courts did not dismiss the case, the defendants settled, putting government officials on notice that torture is a violation of human rights and will not go unpunished, even in the name of national security.

C. Reparations for Accountability: UN Peacekeepers and Sexual Exploitation and Abuse

Such violations must be punished—even if the harm was caused by the very personnel deployed to protect populations and keep the peace. UN peacekeepers are tasked with the difficult mission of maintaining peace and order in conflict-affected settings. Yet given the position of power and trust that this response work necessitates in some of the world's most vulnerable communities, systemic abuse of power can arise, leading to breakdowns in trust and crises in humanitarian response systems that undermine peacekeeping goals (van Leeuwen 2019). In recent years, reports have repeatedly exposed UN peacekeepers' perpetration or complicity in sexual exploitation and abuse (SEA) of the civilians they are charged with protecting (Burke 2016). Despite the grave and pervasive nature of these abuses, the UN and deploying states have often failed to address systemic sexual abuse and resulting impunity for these crimes, denying accountability to the victims (van Leeuwen 2019).

Accountability is essential for institutional legitimacy and for rebuilding trust in UN peacekeeping missions. Where individuals have alleged SEA perpetration, the UN Office of Internal Oversight Services (OIOS) can investigate allegations of abuse and repatriate offenders; however, most peacekeepers are immune from prosecution in the host country (Hovell 2016). The home country of the peacekeepers retains exclusive jurisdiction to prosecute crimes committed by its nationals, creating a significant barrier to legal accountability for SEA crimes,

---

[7] In 2002, the U.S. Justice Department approved and paid James Mitchell and Bruce Jessen to employ protocols that used "enhanced interrogation" techniques to induce "learned helplessness" among detained prisoners. Mitchell and Jessen designed the abusive procedures, invented torture instruments, tortured detainees, and trained CIA officers to employ torture techniques on prisoners. These two health practitioners also later evaluated the program's effectiveness—in violation of ethical conflicts of interest.

even when the home country gives "formal assurances" to prosecute and punish SEA perpetrators (Hovell 2016).

In the absence of effective legal accountability, in either the host or home countries, the UN has assisted victims in recovery—to provide redress for these harms. Beyond financial compensation, the UN General Assembly in 2008 adopted the Comprehensive Strategy on Assistance and Support to Victims of Sexual Exploitation and Abuse by United Nations Staff and Associated Personnel, which provides minimum standards for medical care, legal services, and psychosocial support for victims following SEA allegations (UN 2008). Expanded in 2016, the UN Secretary-General instituted a Trust Fund in Support of Victims of Sexual Exploitation and Abuse to provide financial assistance to SEA victims in support of their recovery (UN Trust Fund 2022). While financial support and other assistance is necessary to redress victims of violence in conflict-affected settings, the international community must also commit to institutions that provide accountability and justice for victims of international crimes perpetrated in conflict.

D. Institutions for Accountability: ICC Adjudication for Crimes Against Humanity and War Crimes

International institutions continue to evolve and develop as human rights advocates bring to light gaps in international accountability for grave violations of human rights and the laws of war in conflict-affected settings. As a complement to national courts, the ICC investigates, prosecutes, and punishes individuals for the gravest crimes of international concern: war crimes, crimes against humanity, genocide, and crimes of aggression. Since the Rome Statute— the treaty establishing the ICC, its mandate, and its jurisdiction—came into force in 2002, the Court has examined grave breaches of international humanitarian law under its jurisdiction over war crimes in international criminal law. These international prosecutions of individual perpetrators of war crimes can provide an additional avenue for accountability for grave human rights violations, including health harms.

Where sexual and gender-based violence—including, but not limited to, rape as a tactical weapon of war—has always been and continues to be pervasive in conflict-affected settings, only recently has the ICC criminalized, investigated, and prosecuted such violence. Systematic gender violence perpetrated during the conflicts and genocides of the former Yugoslavia and Rwanda brought international visibility and outrage to this violative practice in war (Stephens 1999). These wartime violations galvanized activism to recognize gender-based violence as a violation of human rights. Characterizing rape as torture, this activism brought renewed attention to international humanitarian and criminal law protections for survivors—with an international coalition of women's human rights groups advocating for the codification of sexual and gender-based violence as war crimes and crimes against humanity (Spees 2003). The ICC now investigates and prosecutes crimes of rape, sexual slavery, enforced prostitution, forced pregnancy, enforced sterilization, or any other form of sexual violence of comparative gravity under its mandate (Office of the Prosecutor of the International Criminal Court 2014). To date, the ICC has convicted several perpetrators of sexual and gender-based war crimes and crimes against humanity committed in conflict-affected settings, including the Democratic Republic of Congo and Uganda, providing successful prosecutions under international criminal law and accountability for violations of international humanitarian law.

Conclusion

Throughout the world, conflict is again on the rise, bringing with it serious threats to global health and human security. At the same time, the face of conflict is evolving, with increased targeting of civilians and civilian objects and continued violations of international humanitarian and human rights law. Humanitarian and healthcare workers must understand the obligations that all parties to conflict undertake to protect civilians and other noncombatants and maximize the humanity and dignity of all individuals in times of war. Healthcare workers must also protect civilians from health harms through their responsibilities to ensure health care services and through their obligations to do no harm.

Global health law will continue to be crucial to protecting health amid conflict. In addition to the changing nature of conflict and the increased targeting of civilians, new methods of warfare—including cyberwarfare—will inflict human suffering and attack health care and other essential infrastructure. Thus, global health law must conceptualize these evolving wartime contexts and the governing law that protects them and the populations they serve. States and international institutions implement and enforce international humanitarian law, international human rights law, and international criminal law to uphold public health in times of conflict. While international law has expanded since World War II to respond to civilian deaths and human suffering in conflict-affected settings, these evolving legal frameworks remain inadequate in the face of current humanitarian challenges. In complex emergencies caused by armed conflict, humanitarian professionals must call on international law to protect those beyond the conflict and to mitigate the associated harms.

New reforms will be necessary to recognize the connections across legal regimes that are necessary to protect public health and human rights from the ongoing scourge of war and its consequences. International institutions and their leaders must better align international humanitarian law and global health law to ensure the sustainability of health services during conflict while mitigating health harms that befall civilian populations as a consequence of war. Reforms must push the limits of state sovereignty even in internal conflict settings, as civilians bear the brunt of these harms and require additional protections to secure access to health services and other basic needs. Humanitarian professionals on the front lines will be essential in these diplomatic efforts to develop international law to protect health and human rights in conflict-affected settings.

Questions for Consideration

1. Why is it thought to be morally wrong to kill noncombatants in the context of war? How did health care workers on the battlefield come to be seen as "neutral" noncombatants?
2. How did the first Geneva Conventions in the 19th century differ from previous international agreements? Why was it necessary to establish the ICRC to uphold international humanitarian law?
3. How were the atrocities of World War II enabled by health practitioners? Why was it necessary to hold individual Nazi health practitioners accountable under international criminal law?
4. Why are principles of military necessary and humanity central to the establishment of international humanitarian law? How did the 1949 Geneva Conventions codify humanitarian principles of distinction, proportionality, and precaution under international law? What obligations do states bear under the Geneva Conventions to ensure access to health care?
5. Why is international humanitarian law essential to global health law?
6. Why do the Geneva Conventions fail to address rising health threats presented by non-international armed conflicts (NIACs)? How have other institutions sought to respond to these non-international conflicts?
7. How does international law address forced migration of populations as a result of conflict? Why is it important for humanitarian professionals to know whether forced migrants have crossed an international border?
8. Where states are unable or unwilling to protect health, how can NGOs address public health challenges in conflict-affected settings? How have the Sphere Standards sought to guide NGO efforts to address humanitarian health needs?

9. Why has the UN Security Council increasingly examined global health issues? How has this securitization of health expanded international efforts to address health amid conflict?
10. How does WHO monitoring of attacks against health care facilitate accountability for the violation of international humanitarian law and the prevention of these attacks? Why have attacks against health care continued—despite UN condemnation of these attacks under international law and WHO publication of these attacks in the SSA?
11. How can ICC prosecutions facilitate accountability for public health attacks amid conflict? How have advocates reframed sexual and gender-based violence in war as war crimes and crimes against humanity?

Acknowledgments

The authors are grateful for the research assistance and editorial support of Ryan Doerzbacher, who brought his military experience and public health training to examine the evolution of international humanitarian law; and to Professor Gabor Rona, who reviewed a final draft.

References

American Civil Liberties Union (ACLU). 2017. Press Release: "On Eve of Trial, Psychologists Agree to Historic Settlement in ACLU Case on Behalf of Three Torture Victims."

American Red Cross. 2011. "Summary of the Geneva Conventions of 1949 and Their Additional Protocols." American Red Cross.

Annas, George and Michael Grodin. 1992. *The Nazi Doctors and the Nuremberg Code: Human Rights in Human Experimentation*. Oxford: Oxford University Press.

Bassiouni, M. Cherif. 1992. *Crimes Against Humanity in International Criminal Law*. Leiden: Martinus Nijhoff Publishers.

Brody, Howard, Sarah E. Leonard, Jing-Bao Nie, and Paul Weindling. 2014. "United States Responses to Japanese Wartime Inhuman Experimentation after World War II: National Security and Wartime Exigency." *Cambridge Quarterly of Healthcare Ethics: CQ: The International Journal of Healthcare Ethics Committees* 23(2): 220–230.

Bugnion, François. 2012. "Birth of an Idea: The Founding of the International Committee of the Red Cross and of the International Red Cross and Red Crescent Movement: From Solferino to the original Geneva Convention (1859–1864)." *International Review of the Red Cross* 94 (888): 1299–1338.

Burke, Roisin. 2016. "Central African Republic Peacekeeper Sexual Crimes, Institutional Failings: Addressing the Accountability Gap International Organisations and the Rule of Law." *New Zealand Journal of Public and International Law* 14(1): 97–128.

Condon-Rall, Mary Ellen and Albert E Cowdrey. 1998. *The Medical Department: Medical Service in the War Against Japan (The U.S. Army in World War II: The Technical Services)*. Washington: U.S. Army Center of Military History.

Evans, Dabney P., Edward L. Queen, and Lara S. Martin. 2020. "Health and Human Rights in Conflict and Emergencies." In *Foundations of Global Health & Human Rights*, edited by Lawrence O. Gostin and Benjamin Mason Meier. 373–394. Oxford: Oxford University Press.

Fast, Larissa, and Róisín Read. 2022. "Using Data to Create Change? Interrogating the Role of Data in Ending Attacks on Healthcare." *International Studies Review* 24(3).

Getgen Kestenbaum, Jocelyn. 2021. *Public Health, Mental Health and Mass Atrocity Prevention*. New York: Routledge.

Guins, G. "Basic Principles of U.N.R.R.A.'s Policy." *Southwestern Social Science Quarterly* 26/2 (1945): 127–134.

Hovell, Devika. 2016. "Due Process in the United Nations." *The American Journal of International Law* 110(1): 1–48.

ICRC. 2010. "1939–1945: Descent into Hell." International Committee of the Red Cross. May 11.

International Military Tribunal. 1949. *Trials of War Criminals Before the Nurenberg Military Tribunals Under Control Council Law No. 10, Nurenberg, October 1946–April 1949*. Vol. II. Washington: U.S. Government Printing Office.

Kesternich, Iris, Bettina Siflinger, James P. Smith, and Joachim K. Winter. 2014. "The Effects of World War II on Economic and Health Outcomes across Europe." *The Review of Economics and Statistics* 96(1): 103–118.

Kolb, Robert. 1998. "The Relationship between International Humanitarian Law and Human Rights Law: A Brief History of the 1948 Universal Declaration of Human Rights and the 1949 Geneva Conventions." *International Review of the Red Cross* 324(September): 409–419.

League of Nations. 1919. Covenant of the League of Nations of 1919.

Leeuwen, Jayden van. 2019. "Addressing the Gap: Accountability Mechanisms for Peacekeepers Accused of Sexual Exploitation and Abuse." *Victoria University of Wellington Law Review* 50(1): 135–156.

Luck, Edward C. 2006. *U.N. Security Council: Practice and Promise*. Abingdon: Routledge.

Malone, David M., Sebastian von Einsiedel, and Bruno Ugarte Stagno, eds. 2015. *The UN Security Council in the 21st Century*. Boulder: Lynne Rienner Publishers. ProQuest Ebook Central.

Meier, Benjamin Mason, Hannah Rice, and Shashika Bandara. 2021. "Monitoring Attacks on Health Care as a Basis to Facilitate Accountability for Human Rights Violations." *Health and Human Rights* 23(1): 55–70.

Meier, Benjamin Mason, Thérèse Murphy, and Lawrence O. Gostin. 2020. "The Birth and Development of Human Rights for Health." In *Foundations of Global Health & Human Rights*, edited by Lawrence O. Gostin and Benjamin Mason Meier. 23-44. New York: Oxford University Press.

Melzer, Nils. 2008. XI. The Principle of Distinction under International Humanitarian Law. In *Targeted Killing in International Law*, 300–366. Oxford: Oxford University Press.

Office of the Prosecutor of the International Criminal Court. 2014. "Policy Paper on Sexual and Gender-Based Crimes."

Palmieri. 2012. "An Institution Standing the Test of Time? A Review of 150 Years of the History of the International Committee of the Red Cross." *International Review of the Red Cross* 94 (888): 1273-1298.

Rubenstein, Leonard. 2021. *Perilous Medicine: The Struggle to Protect Health Care from the Violence of War.* New York: Columbia University Press.

Rushton, Simon and Jeremy Youde, eds. 2014. *Routledge Handbook of Global Health Security.* London: Routledge.

Rushton, Simon, and Maike Voss. 2022. "The United Nations Security Council and Health Emergencies: Introduction." *Australian Journal of International Affairs* 76(1): 1-3.

Rushton, Simon. 2010. "AIDS and International Security in the United Nations System." *Health Policy and Planning* 25(6): 495-504.

Sarkees, Meredith Reid and Frank Whelon Wayman. 2010. *Resort to War: 1816–2007.* Washington: CQ Press.

Schmitt, Michael N. 2010. "Military Necessity and Humanity in International Law: Preserving the Delicate Balance." *Virginia Journal of International Law* 50(4): 796–837.

Sedgwick, James Burnham. 2011. "A People's Court: Emotion, Participant Experiences, and the Shaping of Postwar Justice at the International Military Tribunal for the Far East, 1946–1948." *Diplomacy & Statecraft* 22(3): 480–499.

Sekalala, Sharifah, Caitlin R. Williams, and Benjamin Mason Meier. 2022. "Global Health Governance through the UN Security Council: Health Security vs. Human Rights?" *Australian Journal of International Affairs* 76(1): 27–34..

Spees, Pam. 2003. "Women's Advocacy in the Creation of the International Criminal Court: Changing the Landscapes of Justice and Power." *Signs: Journal of Women in Culture and Society* 28(4): 1233–1254.

Sphere Association. 2018. "The Sphere Handbook: Humanitarian Charter and Minimum Standards in Humanitarian Response." Sphere Association.

Sphere Project. 2000. *Humanitarian Charter and Minimum Standards in Disaster Response.* Geneva: Sphere Project.

Stephens, Beth. 1999. "Humanitarian Law and Gender Violence: An End to Centuries of Neglect." *Hofstra Law and Policy Symposium* 3: 87.

Sutton, David Nelson. 1946. "Brief of Atrocities—Class C Offenses: Crimes Against Humanity Committed by Japanese Troops in China, 1937–1945." Virginia Historical Society.

Sze, Szeming. 1945. "Today's Global Frontiers in Public Health." *American Journal of Public Health* 35(February): 96–99.

Tanaka, Toshiyuki. 2002. *Japan's Comfort Women: Sexual Slavery and Prostitution During World War II and the US Occupation.* New York: Routledge.

UN (United Nations) General Assembly. 2008. "United Nations Comprehensive Strategy on Assistance and Support to Victims of Sexual Exploitation and Abuse by United Nations Staff and Related Personnel." 7 March. A/RES/62/214

UN Security Council. 2000. "Resolution 1308 (2000)." 17 July. S/RES/1308 (2000).

UN Security Council. 2003. "Resolution 1456 (2003)." 20 January. S/RES/1456 (2003).

UN Security Council. 2011. "Resolution 1983 (2011)." 7 June. S/RES/1983 (2011).

UN Security Council. 2014. "Resolution 2176 (2014)." 15 September. S/RES/2176 (2014)

UN Security Council. 2016. "Resolution 2286 (2016)." 3 May. S/ RES/ 2286 (2016).

UN Security Council. 2018. "Resolution 2439 (2018)." 30 October. S/RES/2439 (2018).

UN Security Council. 2021. "Resolution 2565(2021)." 26 February. S/RES/2565 (2021).

United Nations Trust Fund in Support of Victims of Sexual Exploitation and Abuse (UN Trust Fund). 2022. "Fourth Annual Report of the Trust Fund in Support of Victims of Sexual Exploitation and Abuse."

UN General Assembly. 1945. Charter of United Nations.

UN. 2020. "UN Secretary-General Calls for Global Ceasefire to Focus on Ending the COVID-19 Pandemic."

US Senate Select Committee on Intelligence. 2014. "Committee Study of the Central Intelligence Agency's Detention and Interrogation Program."

USHMM. 2020. "Documenting Numbers of Victims of the Holocaust and Nazi Persecution." United States Holocaust Memorial Museum. December 8.

Walzer, Michael. 1992. *Just and Unjust Wars: A Moral Argument with Historical Illustrations*. 2nd ed. New York: Basic Books.

Wenham, Clare. 2019. "The Oversecuritization of Global Health: Changing the Terms of Debate." *International Affairs* 95 (5): 1093–1110.

19

Climate Change

A Cataclysmic Health Threat Requiring Global Action

Alexandra Phelan and Kim van Daalen

Introduction

Climate change is the greatest threat to health faced by humanity. Impacting every health issue, climate change exacerbates existing health threats and creates new ones – from extreme weather and food insecurity to zoonotic spillovers that could cause future pandemics. Despite the broad impacts on global health, global health law has been largely siloed away from international legal efforts to address climate change. However, this is increasingly changing, with growing awareness and understanding of the ways in which climate change is already impacting public health, health equity, and social justice. Greater attention to global health will be necessary to address climate change and to both mitigate the climate threat and adapt to the health consequences. Greater synthesis between international law and policy for climate and health is critical, as the steps needed to mitigate and adapt to climate change have co-benefits across global health.

Global cooperation is needed to address this global challenge. The transboundary nature of greenhouse gas emissions and the global climate means that mitigating climate change requires global emissions reductions. National commitments to these reductions must be part of a global collaborative effort, recognizing that any bad actor can have disastrous consequences for all. International law can support this necessary cooperation to mitigate climate change. However, the global community has failed to act swiftly enough to avoid all the likely health impacts of a changing climate. As a result, adaptation is a necessary element in addressing climate change, requiring global cooperation to develop shared public health responses. The negotiation, adoption, and implementation of international law and global policy can facilitate the cooperation necessary for climate mitigation and adaptation.

This chapter examines the myriad impacts of climate change on global health and the role of international law and policy in addressing this global health challenge. Part I sets out how humanity's activities have impacted determinants of public health resulting in cataclysmic impacts on planetary health and global health. These rising harms have provided the scientific basis for global governance, leading to core international instruments addressing climate change, including the United Nations (UN) Framework Convention on Climate Change and its protocols. Part II analyzes the global health policy response to climate change, considering how health has, or has not sufficiently, been advanced in international climate law. Through the compounding vulnerabilities of climate change, the emergence of human rights in climate change debates, and the governance lessons in light of COVID-19, Part III highlights the interconnection between global health law and international climate law, exploring key areas where climate law may be advanced to protect global health, including taking a planetary health approach, establishing loss and damage obligations, ensuring technology transfer, and pursuing the proposed crime of ecocide. This chapter concludes that climate change governance must better integrate global health considerations, with future international law and global policies presenting new opportunities to facilitate this integration.

I. Creating the Anthropocene

Humanity has created a new geological age—the Anthropocene. The effects of this epoch will be catastrophic, creating sweeping consequences on global public health through rapid global climate change. Rising temperatures, extreme weather and climate events, increasing infectious diseases, water and food insecurity, mental health challenges, and poor air quality threaten millions. Early scientific and political cooperation throughout the world has looked to respond to the Anthropocene, giving rise to global climate governance.

A. The Public Health Impacts of Global Climate Change

Since preindustrial times, global average surface temperatures have risen by roughly 1°C as a result of anthropogenic greenhouse gas (GHG) emissions, and temperatures are expected to increase further until at least the mid-21st century (IPCC 2021). The impacts of this warming on the planet have been profound for the Earth's climate, including an increase in the number of warm days and nights, accelerated sea level rise, increased (extreme) heat events, shrinking sea ice, acidification of ocean water, contraction of mountain glaciers, and increased evaporation. Left unabated, climate change could result in many severe and potentially irreversible negative impacts on natural systems and human societies, for which humanity may be ill-equipped to respond. While long neglected in climate change debates, these impacts

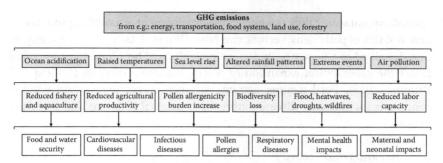

Figure 19.1 Climate Change as a "Health Threat Multiplier," Impacting Several Health Outcomes Simultaneously (Phelan and van Daalen)

include catastrophically negative effects on human health. Through a multifactorial framework of indirect and direct mechanisms, climate change acts as a so-called "health threat multiplier," as seen in Figure 19.1, influencing a wide range of health outcomes and determinants of good health for both current and future generations, including extreme weather and climate events, infectious disease, water and food security, mental health, and air quality (Romanello et al. 2021).

1. Extreme Weather and Climate Events

Extreme weather and climate events refer to weather or climate variables that are significantly different from usual weather or climate patterns (e.g., heat waves, heavy precipitation, droughts, and storms) (IPPC 2021). As a result of the warming planet, these extreme events are changing in intensity, frequency, timing, duration, and spatial extent. Beyond damage to infrastructure, livelihoods, and the economy, extreme events can have significant impacts on human health, well-being, and health systems. People can suffer a wide range of impacts on physical health (e.g., heat-related illnesses, respiratory health outcomes related to wildfire smoke, injuries, drowning, and death), mental health (e.g., post-traumatic stress disorder, depression), and community and interpersonal violence (e.g., physical abuse, sexual assault, and emotional abuse) – all of which are influenced by extreme events (Ebi et al. 2021).

2. Infectious Diseases

Together with increased urbanization and global mobility, climate change is likewise a major factor influencing the rising incidence, distribution, and transmission of vector-borne (e.g., malaria, dengue, chikungunya, leishmaniasis), water-borne (e.g., vibriosis, cholera), and food-borne (e.g., campylobacteriosis) infectious diseases. When climate and weather conditions change on a spatiotemporal scale,[1] they can impact the development, survival, reproduction, and livability of pathogens, vectors, and hosts (Wu et al. 2016). Consequently, as first described in Chapter 6, studies have highlighted how long-term warming favors the geographical expansion of several infectious diseases (Ostfeld and Brunner 2015). Furthermore, extreme weather events may create optimal conditions for clustered disease outbreaks at unusual locations and moments in time.

3. Water and Food Security

Water and food security are among the major challenges imposed by climate change. Rising temperatures are projected to increase droughts, increase floodings, and alter rainfall, snowmelt, river flows, and groundwater availability—exacerbating water scarcity. Compounded by industrial threats of water pollution, as discussed in Chapter 9, the vulnerability of freshwater resources is rising, undermining natural ecosystems. Without adequate climate action, estimates suggest that more than half of the world's population may be at water stress risk by 2050 (UNESCO 2019). Similarly for food security, negative impacts on food systems are found globally, impacting the incidence of undernutrition and hunger (Mbow et al. 2017). Without adaptation, climate change will result in 10.1 million more cases of stunted children by 2050 (impairing the growth and development of children due to poor nutrition or repeated infection), resulting in severe functional consequences on cognition, increased risk of nutrition related chronic diseases, or even death (Hales et al. 2014).

4. Mental Health

In addition to the physical health impacts of a warming planet, climate change is negatively impacting psychological well-being and mental health (Berry, Bowen, and Kjellstrom 2010). Extreme events such as prolonged drought or floods may disrupt people's livelihoods, resulting in food insecurity and other hardships that negatively impact family relationships, stress, and worry (Vins et al. 2015). Furthermore, climate change can result in conditions that lead to forced population displacement, armed conflict, and multiple forms of violence (including gender-based violence) (Koubi 2019; Theisen 2017; van Daalen et al. 2022). Displacement, conflict, and violence are further associated with mental health risks such as depression or post-traumatic stress disorder (PTSD) (Murthy 2007).

---

[1] Spatiotemporal change refers to the variation of a variable (e.g., temperature, precipitation) in location and/or time. Illustratively, land surface temperature may be higher at a specific location (such as a desert) and time in a year (such as summer), but lower in other locations (such as mountain areas) and time of the year (such as winter).

5. Air Quality

Furthermore, as introduced in Chapter 9, many of the main drivers of increased GHG emissions are simultaneously sources of air pollution, with compounding effects on climate change and environmental health. The combined impact of ambient and household air pollution is associated with millions of premature deaths each year, with almost all of the global population (99%) exposed to air quality outside of safe levels (WHO 2021).[2] These short- and long-term exposures to various air pollutants can result in acute and chronic respiratory diseases, lung cancer, cardiovascular diseases, and adverse pregnancy outcomes (Mannucci et al. 2015). Moreover, many of these air pollutants contribute to climate change by impacting sunlight reflected or absorbed in the atmosphere, with black carbon and methane among the main drivers of global warming after carbon dioxide (CO_2) (Kinney 2008).

Taken together, climate change does not pose one singular health risk. Rather, it results in a myriad of compounding, interacting, and sometimes unpredictable risks to human health and the natural systems upon which public health depends. Yet, while climate change is often cited as the "biggest global health threat of the 21st century" (Costello et al. 2009, 1693), climate action could likewise be "the biggest opportunity for global health" (Romanello et al. 2021, 1621). Well-planned mitigation and adaptation strategies can result in significant health co-benefits, supporting clean air, active transport, and healthy diets. Where health and the environment remain intimately connected, public health must be central to the global climate change response.

B. The Origins of Global Governance for Climate and Health

In responding to the public health challenges of a changing climate, there has been emerging recognition of the need for global climate governance. Shortly after the establishment of global governance under the UN, scientists began to understand more fully the role of carbon dioxide concentrations in the Earth's atmosphere, influencing surface temperatures and climate conditions.[3] Scientists identified increasing concentrations of carbon dioxide in the 1960s, and by the 1970s, a clear trend had emerged—with GHG producing activities as the suspected cause (McMichael 2017). These scientific developments paralleled the emergence of global governance for environmental issues, including, as

---

[2] Key air pollutants that drive premature mortality and health problems include fine particulate matter, ozone (O_3), carbon monoxide (CO), sulfur dioxide (SO_2), and nitrogen dioxide (NO_2).

[3] Over the course of the 20th century, scientists went from recognizing the role of the atmosphere in the Earth's surface temperature to understanding how increasing carbon dioxide concentrations in the atmosphere increased the Earth's temperature (McMichael 2017).

examined in Chapter 9, the first major international conference dedicated to the environment – the UN Conference on the Human Environment, which led to the 1972 Stockholm Declaration (UN Conference of the Environment 1972). International environmental law advancements reflected the development of increasing public consciousness surrounding the environment, but despite this, climate scientists had limited influence in national policy spaces (Nolin 1999). However, international forums provided an opportunity for scientists to collaborate and share their concerns about how human activities were causing global changes to the Earth's climate, leading the UN's World Meteorological Organization (WMO)[4] in 1979 to host the first World Climate Conference (WMO 1979).

Drawing from this initial Conference, the WMO, the United Nations Environment Program (UNEP), and the International Council of Scientific Unions would begin the following year to bring together leading scientists annually to assess the climate risk. By 1985, this conference reached a critical turning point, recognizing that climate science should no longer be just a matter of scientific interest but that "the rate and degree of future warming could be profoundly affected by governmental policies" (WMO 1985, 1). Climate change was seen as a matter requiring global governance. Yet, even as scientists recognized the potential impacts of climate change on health and well-being, this international concern was focused on the likelihood of climatic extremes in tropical regions, underestimating the global inequities of compounding health vulnerabilities (Fleurbaey et al. 2014).

Case Study: Climate Change and Inequities

Different populations have historically contributed to and currently experience the impacts of climate change inequitably—with within-country (between individuals), international (between countries), and intergenerational (between generations) dimensions. Those that have benefited the most from industrialization, capitalism, and colonialism—and thus have historically contributed the most GHG emissions—bear the least immediate and long-term adverse impacts. Instead, the worst impacts fall upon those least responsible for the climate crisis, predominantly low-income countries and populations. Further asymmetries exist in the ability to shape climate strategies and in the capacity to move toward low-carbon economies.

---

[4] The WMO is a specialized agency of the UN with the objective of facilitating worldwide cooperation in atmospheric science and climatology, as well as water resources and geophysics. Drawing from its work to address ozone depletion and international atmospheric pollution, the WMO has been central to the development of international governance for climate change.

Amplifying these asymmetries, climate change is characterized by a vicious cycle that compounds existing inequities and vulnerabilities among populations. Within countries, marginalized and socio-economically disadvantaged groups tend to experience climate-sensitive health risks disproportionately, resulting from differential exposure, sensitivity, and adaptive capacity. These groups include low-income communities, migrants and displaced people, ethnic minorities and Indigenous people, women and girls, those with chronic health conditions, and children. Illustratively, in communities dependent on the use of indoor stoves for heating and cooking, traditional gender roles mean that women and children spend greater amounts of time indoors and experience higher amounts of fine particulate matter (PM2.5) compared to men. Climate injustice refers to the unfair, inequitable distribution of damages and benefits related to climate change and its causes. Climate justice refers to the movement that acknowledges the deep entanglement between climate change and social issues, and aims to address the disproportionate adverse impacts felt by those least responsible for the climate crisis, recognizing the responsibility of countries that accumulated wealth through unrestricted carbon emissions. Global climate policymaking has the capacity to replicate and perpetuate these injustices – the composition of national delegations to international climate negotiations have historically excluded the voices of the most affected from international discussions, exacerbating climate inequity and injustice.

Scientific consensus continued to support global governance efforts, and in 1988, the WMO and UNEP established the Intergovernmental Panel on Climate Change (IPCC): a hybrid science and policy entity tasked with independently analyzing and evaluating the available information on the science and impacts of climate change and considering policy responses (IPCC 2000). Within two years, the IPCC produced its First Assessment Report, finding that it was certain that emissions from human activities were contributing to increasing atmospheric concentrations of GHG and that those emissions would lead to additional warming of the Earth. This Assessment Report arrived just prior to the second World Climate Conference in 1990, with this Conference calling for negotiations to develop an international agreement to address global warming (UN General Assembly 1990). Over the next two years, an intergovernmental negotiating committee under the UN held five sessions to negotiate and draft the proposed treaty (Sands 1992). The finalized text was opened for signature at the 1992 UN Conference on Environment and Development in Rio de Janeiro, with this so-called "Earth Summit" galvanizing the adoption of the first international legal instrument to specifically address climate change: the United Nations Framework Convention on Climate Change (UNFCCC).

II. A Global Health Disaster: Mitigation, Adaptation, and Reducing Vulnerabilities

The adverse impacts of climate change on human and natural systems give a stark warning of the consequences that further temperature increases may have, illustrating the urgent need to respond to climate change through international law. Under the UNFCCC, states have sought over the past thirty years to mitigate the threat of a changing climate (intervening to reduce GHG emissions or to enhance GHG sinks) and adapt to the health impacts of a changing climate (adjusting human or natural systems to reduce harm).

A. Responding to Climate Change under International Law

This international legal framework to respond to climate change—through the UNFCCC and its protocols, the Kyoto Protocol and the Paris Agreement—could have profound effects on global health if fully implemented by states. However, mitigation and adaptation progress under these international instruments have not yet been sufficient, leaving the world especially vulnerable to the health impacts of a changing climate.

1. UNFCCC

The UNFCCC seeks to stabilize greenhouse gas concentrations in the atmosphere at levels that prevent dangerous human interference with the Earth's climate by setting out a basic legal framework and principles for international climate cooperation. During negotiations leading to the 1992 Earth Summit, however, states disagreed on the balance between reducing GHG emissions and limiting the social and economic development of certain states, particularly given the unequal contributions to, and benefits obtained from, GHG emissions. The resulting treaty reflected a compromise—between states that wanted a high-level treaty with general obligations and states that wanted specific and binding emissions reduction targets (Sands 1992). While the treaty was opened for signature at the 1992 Earth Conference, the UNFCCC did not enter into force until 1994, after the required fifty states ratified the treaty, establishing a foundation for the international legal regime to respond to global climate change.

The resulting UNFCCC contains a suite of general commitments for states to take measures to address climate change. While bringing together all states, the UNFCCC is underpinned by the principle of "common but differentiated responsibilities," separating countries' obligations on the basis of their economic development. This principle acknowledges that high-income countries have disproportionately benefited from the development that has contributed to GHG emissions and global warming. The UNFCCC thus lists "Parties" in separate annexes, delineating their economic status and thus determining their national obligations—to reduce emissions and to provide financial and technological resources to other nations.[5] To facilitate accountability for these differentiated responsibilities, the UNFCCC requires countries to report on implementation, including an accounting of their anthropogenic emissions by source and a description of the measures taken to implement treaty obligations.

With this general agreement in the UNFCCC, many specific obligations would need to be set out in subsequent protocols. As a framework convention, a form of international law first introduced in Chapter 2, the UNFCCC sets out the high-level objectives, principles, and obligations for addressing climate change, enabling the negotiation of subsequent protocols on specific issues and measures to mitigate or adapt to climate change. The UNFCCC thus establishes: a Conference of the Parties (COP) that meets each year to discuss and negotiate interpretations of the treaty, its protocols and its mechanisms; a secretariat; a financing mechanism; a subsidiary body for scientific and technological advice (informed by the independent IPCC); and a subsidiary body for implementation.[6] The framework convention–protocol model allows for the subsequent negotiation of protocols on specific issues, with the COP thus far adopting two legally binding protocols to the UNFCCC: the Kyoto Protocol and the Paris Agreement.

2. Protocols

These UNFCCC protocols have supported the general obligations of the UNFCCC through the establishment of specific emissions reduction obligations.

---

[5] Annex I Parties are industrialized countries that were members of the Organization for Economic Co-operation and Development (OECD) (at the time when the UNFCCC was adopted), as well as countries then considered "economies in transition" (EIT), including the Russian Federation, the Baltic States, and several Central and Eastern European States. Annex II Parties are the OECD members of Annex I, but not EIT parties. Under the Convention, Annex II Parties have a range of legal obligations to provide financial and technological resources to developing countries—categorized as "Non-Annex I" Parties, including 49 Least Developed Countries, which are given special consideration due to their limited adaptive capacity—to support emission reduction and adaption to the negative impacts of climate change. Non-Annex I countries are required to report GHG emissions but are not legally required to reduce GHG emissions unless Annex II countries supply funding and technology.

[6] The framework convention–protocol format of the UNFCCC is an especially informative model for global health law, and has informed treaties like the WHO Framework Convention on Tobacco Control (as examined in Chapter 7) and the negotiations for a new international instrument for pandemic preparedness and response (as first discussed in Chapter 5).

Adopted at COP3 in 1997 (and going into effect in 2005—when parties equivalent to 55% of global emissions ratified it), the Kyoto Protocol aimed to operationalize the UNFCCC's goal of avoiding dangerous levels of GHG emissions by setting legally binding emissions reduction targets over an initial five-year period (2008–2012). However, the Kyoto Protocol provided limited obligations under international law, as (1) it only set targets at an average of 5.2% emissions reductions below 1990s levels; (2) it excluded non-Annex I countries; and (3) key states chose not to become parties, including the United States and major developing countries with large emissions. In spite of this binding obligation, global emissions increased by 50% over the initial commitment period of the Kyoto Protocol. While setting targets had appeared to be an ambitious step, the reality was that targets alone were insufficient for the Kyoto Protocol to realize the goals of the UNFCCC. In 2012, the COP amended the Kyoto Protocol for a second commitment period (2013–2020), requiring that parties to the Kyoto Protocol agree to reduce GHG emissions by at least 18% below 1990 emissions levels while also adjusting the parties subject to the protocol. However, this amendment for the second commitment period did not reach the minimum number of states parties until the end of 2020, by which time attention had already turned to a new climate protocol: the Paris Agreement.

The Paris Agreement, adopted in 2015 in the final hours of COP21 in Paris, ended a decade-long stalemate in climate negotiations. In 2011, states agreed at COP17 in Durban to develop a new "universal" GHG reduction protocol, legal instrument, or other outcome. This broad mandate reflected a compromise between a broad coalition of states seeking legally binding climate action (including the European Union, the United States, small island states, and low-income countries) and states that wanted a non-binding platform for national efforts. Over the next four years, negotiations developed draft text – as political momentum for a new agreement grew. In the lead-up to COP21 in Paris, there were a number of high-profile national commitments to address climate change, and the NGO community was heavily engaged in building momentum toward the adoption of a new legal agreement.

This landmark Paris Agreement provides greater specificity to the UNFCCC's overarching aim of preventing dangerous anthropogenic climate change—seeking to keep warming below 2°C, or ideally 1.5°C—while developing a different path for global mitigation efforts and laying a legal foundation for adaptation. Unlike previous mitigation efforts, the Paris Agreement does not set country specific legally binding emissions reduction targets. Instead, all state parties, beginning in 2020 and regardless of income status, are required to take increasingly ambitious climate mitigation measures. Setting "nationally determined contributions" (NDCs), these non-binding, self-determined emissions reduction targets are aimed at reducing emissions to meet temperature limits. Yet despite this new agreement, NDCs under the Paris Agreement have proven insufficient to decrease GHG emissions to limit temperature increases below 2°C—let alone the ideal goal of 1.5°C.

An assessment of NDCs has found that it is likely that a sizable increase in global GHG emissions will occur by 2030, 16% more than 2010 levels, leading to a catastrophic temperature rise of 2.7°C (UNFCCC 2021). These failures to meet climate change obligations—across all major GHG emitter countries—call into question governance efforts to achieve global consensus for specific obligations.

Case Study: Good Governance for Climate Justice – Expansive Participation or Specific Obligations?

The different approaches between the two UNFCCC protocols reflect a governance challenge similarly faced across many areas of international law – the use of binding obligations narrowed the scope of climate action, and ultimately, has been seen as deeply unsuccessful. However, the use of non-binding obligations has enabled a broader set of states to participate, but is still insufficient to address the scale of climate action needed. In drafting international laws, negotiators are often faced with a core tension: less-stringent obligations will lead to potentially faster agreement and a greater number of states parties, while stricter obligations may lead to protracted negotiations and more countries deciding not to join as a state party. Negotiations invariably involve compromises, but an effective treaty may need to carefully balance these considerations between binding and non-binding obligations, recognizing that simply having more parties does not necessarily make a treaty more effective. In navigating this tradeoff, the Paris Agreement has created a forum and accountability framework to build the norms of action for the global cooperation necessary to address a global challenge like climate change. Future COPs provide further opportunities to continue to build norms and to keep laws up-to-date by addressing technological changes and scientific developments. Similarly, the framework convention and protocols approach of the UNFCCC demonstrates the use of adaptable governance procedures to build action on technical and political issues. By incorporating reporting and monitoring mechanisms, the UNFCCC seeks to build state accountability for taking progressive measures toward their binding and non-binding obligations.

Recognizing the limitations of mitigation policy under the UNFCCC, the Paris Agreement for the first time examined the need for global policy to begin to address adaptation. In focusing on adaptation, international climate change law has turned toward public health, with the preamble of the Paris Agreement expressly acknowledging that climate change is a common concern of humankind, and that parties should consider the right to health when taking steps to mitigate and adapt to climate change – an inclusion that highlighted the inextricable link between the condition of one's environment and health and well-being. The WHO Director-General described this agreement as "potentially the strongest health agreement of this century" (WHO 2018). Ensuring these health benefits in climate change policy will require attention to global health policy in climate change mitigation and adaptation debates.

B. The Global Health Policy Response

Global climate policy is interconnected with global health policy, with the benefits of climate change mitigation policies advancing global health, and global health policy supporting climate change adaptation. While reducing the worst climate-induced health impacts, well-targeted climate mitigation and adaptation strategies across sectors can simultaneously have positive health benefits that are independent of those related to modifying climate risk.[7] Health researchers thus argue that framing climate mitigation and adaptation around human health may result in greater public and political support for transformative policy change, as:

(1) people across the political spectrum care about human health, thus a health framing could lend further support for climate action;
(2) a health framing may make climate change more near-term and personal, instead of an abstract problem in the future;
(3) health professionals are among the most trusted members of society, and as a result, their involvement could increase the uptake of climate-friendly behavior; and
(4) a health framing is integrative with other framings across equity, social justice, and human rights issues.

Therefore, calls to integrate health into global climate policy—and climate into health policy—are increasingly growing in mitigation and adaptation policy efforts.

1. Mitigation

Climate mitigation aims to prevent or reduce climate change by reducing the emissions of heat-trapping GHG into the atmosphere. This is achieved by either reducing the sources of GHG (e.g., increasing the share of renewable energy) or by enhancing the storage of GHG in so-called carbon sinks (e.g., increasing

---

[7] For example, reducing fossil fuel use to limit global temperature rise to 1.5C° could simultaneously improve air quality (preventing millions of premature deaths annually), and improved active transport infrastructure to reduce GHG emissions from transportation can likewise simultaneously reduce non-communicable disease.

forests). Successful mitigation makes the impacts of climate change less severe—reducing the increase in temperatures, altered rainfall patterns, extreme events, air pollution, and ocean acidification—which in turn reduces climate-related health risks. Influencing a wide range of determinants of health, climate mitigation simultaneously results in health co-benefits through the phaseout of fossil fuels (reducing health impacts related to air pollution), the reduction of GHG emissions from agriculture (by the promotion of healthier plant-forward dietary choices), and the reductions of GHG emissions from transportation (by stimulating active transport such as walking or cycling, which increases overall health and reduces risk of non-communicable diseases) (Romanello et al. 2021).

Since the 1990s, WHO has actively engaged with the UNFCCC processes as a UN Observer organization; published a series of reports on climate and health; provided public health data to support the public health justification for mitigating the risks of climate change; and participated in joint advocacy with NGOs, UN, academia, and private sector partners on key health and climate issues. One of the foundations of WHO monitoring is accomplished through the WHO UNFCCC Health and Climate Change Country Profile Project, which promotes actions to improve health while reducing GHG emissions. An important milestone for bringing human health and climate change together was reached during COP26, setting out key health ambitions for countries: (1) building climate-resilient health systems and (2) developing low-carbon sustainable health systems. Where health systems account for around 4.6% of GHG emissions, health systems are a significant source of emissions. Drawing from global commitments, the UK's National Health Service (NHS) in 2020 became the first national health service to commit to a carbon "net zero" health system, supported by the first piece of health legislation that directly addresses the health profession's response to climate change. At the COP26 Health Programme, an additional fifty countries committed to creating low-carbon, sustainable, and climate resilient health systems, with fourteen countries (e.g., Spain, Jordan, Nigeria) setting targets of net zero emissions by 2050 (Wise et al. 2021).

2. Adaptation

Yet, where mitigation efforts fail, climate change adaptation focuses on minimizing the potential public health impacts of climate change. Well-designed transformative climate adaptation measures across different sectors can simultaneously decrease negative short- and long-term health risks from climate hazards and minimize exposure and vulnerabilities. For example, the increase of green space to reduce urban heat positively influences people's mental health, provides space for physical activity, and reduces risks of health-related illnesses (Romanello et al. 2021). Given that the worst impacts of climate change are disproportionally impacting populations that historically contributed least to anthropogenic climate change, the implementation of appropriate adaptation measures is of particular relevance in ensuring social justice and health equity.

In combination with other public health risks, health systems across the world are increasingly experiencing pressure to respond to the impacts of climate change by increasing adaptive capacity and climate resilience in health system-specific adaptation measures (ibid.). Within the global health community, this has resulted in a growing recognition of the impacts of climate change on health and the role of the healthcare system in responding to climate change. Illustratively, healthcare organizations, such as the American Medical Association in 2022, have adopted policies recognizing climate change as a global public health crisis, and a growing number of healthcare professionals have started to engage with climate activism and advocacy.[8]

In adaptation efforts, WHO has provided technical support to national governments in developing the health component of National Adaptation Plans, strengthening national capacities, and improving the resilience of health systems (Campbell-Lendrum et al. 2007). A special initiative on Climate Change and Health in small island developing states (SIDS) run by the WHO and UNFCC, aims to specifically support SIDS health systems to adapt to and become resilient to climate change. At a regional level, initiatives such as the European Climate and Health Observatory (ECHO) have provided key resources to inform evidence-based, efficient, and inclusive adaptation solutions for public health.

This growing recognition of the importance of global health governance in climate change policy will force a reexamination of climate change law as central to global health law.

III. The Arc of Justice: Rethinking Climate Law for Health

The world faces a critical moment at the intersection of international climate law and global health law. Where the UN Secretary General has found that international environmental governance remains fragmented, with a lack of coherence around international environmental law principles (UN General Assembly 2018), new efforts are necessary to see the interconnections between environmental conditions and climate change. These challenges at the intersection of global governance over climate change and global health provide new opportunities to advance health justice under international climate law. In the

---

[8] For example, medical and health students from the International Federation of Medical Students' Associations (IFMSA) have been organizing efforts to enable young professionals to understand and act upon climate change using a health narrative; formally engaging with the UNFCCC and WHO to advocate for the inclusion of health in the climate discourse; and developing core competencies and learning objectives for planetary health within medical education.

face of the cataclysmic public health threats of climate change, global health law must expand: taking a planetary health approach; embracing human rights; ensuring global access to critical technologies, including technology transfer; and creating greater accountability against those who engage in ecocide.

A. Planetary Health

Planetary health has arisen as a new field of study to reframe thinking about the relationship between human health and natural systems. As climate change demonstrates, public health is deeply interlinked with and dependent upon the natural environment, and major negative impacts on human health occur as a result of humanity's disruption of natural systems (Whitmee et al. 2015). Yet climate change is not the only planetary-level disruption to human health, with planetary health also looking across issues of biodiversity loss, chemical pollution, ozone layer depletion, air pollution, land conversion, and a range of other factors (McMichael 2017). Unsustainable development can contribute to the very factors that cause ill health, with the recognition that "we have been mortgaging the health of future generations to realize economic and development gains in the present" (Whitmee et al. 2015, 1973). Although high-income countries have disproportionately obtained the benefits of development, the harms of unsustainable development are inequitably borne by low- and middle-income countries. This injustice remains a complex "mega-problem" for humanity, global health, and international law—particularly as countries not yet afforded opportunities to lift their populations out of poverty seek equitable development. In providing equitable development in ways that do not threaten the planet, a focus on planetary health can help to strengthen the climate change response by providing a systems approach to interconnected global challenges requiring global cooperation.

International law remains challenged by fragmented responses to climate change, with a lack of cross-cutting principles across global health law, international human rights, and international environmental law. The planetary health perspective seeks to overcome these challenges while supporting a "One Health" approach to global health.[9] A planetary health approach to international law thus provides a path to embed public health considerations within laws made to address planetary health issues such as climate change and biodiversity loss, while

---

[9] Planetary Health differs slightly from a One Health approach in the way they are most often conceptualized. Whereas a One Health approach primarily operates at the interfaces between human, animal, and environmental health—largely at the local level—a Planetary Health approach operates at the planetary level, complementing the One Health approach to uphold the health of the planet itself.

also recognizing under global health law the role played by climate change, biodiversity loss, and environmental damage across a suite of health hazards. Taking into account the interconnection between human health and natural systems, a planetary health approach to global health law provides new opportunities to expressly address this complexity while centering health equity and human rights in the climate change response (Phelan 2022).

B. Human Rights

Human rights law is a critical tool in seeking accountability from governments for their duty to protect health, including where health is impacted by climate change. Despite not being expressly included in the founding human rights documents, the human right to a healthy environment, as first introduced in Chapter 9, has rapidly evolved under international law. The 1972 Stockholm Declaration expressly recognized the fundamental human right to "an environment of a quality that permits a life of dignity and well-being" (UN Conference of the Environment 1972, Principle 1). While being deeply connected to other human rights like the right to health, the right to a healthy environment provides procedural obligations on states "to assess environmental impacts on human rights [and] provide access to remedies for environmental harm," as well as substantive obligations "to adopt legal and institutional frameworks that protect against environmental harm that interferes with the enjoyment of human rights" (UN Human Rights Council 2013, 13).

Until recently, there was no express recognition of a right to a safe, clean, and healthy environment under international human rights law. Instead, redress for environmental damage that impacted health relied upon the interconnection between the environment and other human rights articulated in legally binding international human rights treaties, such as the right to life, right to an adequate standard of living, right to health, and right to food (Phelan 2020). For example, the right to health under the 1966 International Covenant on Economic, Social and Cultural Rights (ICESCR), as elaborated in Chapter 4, codifies state obligations to take steps to improve all aspects of environmental hygiene. In 2000, the UN Committee on Economic, Social and Cultural Rights expanded its interpretation of the right to health in the ICESCR, with the interpretive guidance in General Comment 14 recognizing that the right to health includes a right to a healthy environment. This right to a healthy environment has provided a basis for advancing environmental health in climate change policy (Meier, Bustreo, and Gostin 2022).

Building on these foundations, the UN Human Rights Council adopted for the first time a 2021 resolution expressly recognizing the human right to a clean, healthy, and sustainable environment. The resolution called upon states to protect the environment as a basis to fulfill their human rights obligations. At the same session, the Council established a new Special Rapporteur dedicated specifically to the human rights impacts of climate change, providing new bases for human rights accountability for the health impacts of a changing climate. This was followed by UN General Assembly action, adopting a 2022 resolution recognizing the right to a clean, healthy, and sustainable environment as a human right (UN General Assembly 2022). With political momentum building on the human rights implications of a changing climate, the Human Rights Council adopted a 2022 resolution on human rights and climate change that recognized the impact of climate change on the full enjoyment of all human rights, called upon states to consider human rights in UNFCCC debates, and recognized the importance of addressing loss and damage associated with the adverse effects of climate change – seeking to hold states accountable for climate-induced loss and damage.

Case Study: Compensating for Loss and Damage

Given the reality that current efforts to reduce emissions and adapt to climate change are insufficient to curb the effects of climate change on health and livelihoods, it is inevitable that countries and people will experience losses and damages from climate change. While the UNFCCC does not expressly define "loss and damage," this concept has come to be understood as encapsulating harms from sudden onset events, like extreme weather events and disasters, as well as slow-onset processes, like sea-level rise. At present, there is no international legal instrument that expressly protects people displaced by climate change. Recognizing this legal gap in 2013, the COP established the Warsaw International Mechanism for Loss and Damage, which aims to enhance knowledge, understanding, coordination, and support to address loss and damage—including finance, technology transfer, and capacity building. This accountability mechanism was then incorporated into the text of the Paris Agreement; however, the Agreement expressly notes that the mechanism does not provide a basis for liability or compensation—an omission that reflects high-income countries' unwillingness to embrace a financing mechanism, even one that does not directly hold individual countries accountable. In 2015, the COP requested that the Warsaw Mechanism establish the Fiji Clearing House for Risk Transfer as a repository of information on insurance and risk transfer and established a Task Force on Displacement. Efforts remained unsuccessful in codifying a financing mechanism to redress developing countries' losses and damages, predominantly resisted by the twenty-seven-nation EU and the United States with fears of potential legal liability for historical emissions. Yet, a momentous victory came at COP27, where a Loss and Damage fund for the most vulnerable nations to the climate crisis was agreed upon, creating a model for international legal remedies to facilitate accountability for climate justice.

In building from new mechanisms for achieving accountability, climate justice demands the equitable distribution of, and access to, technologies necessary to mitigate and adapt to climate change.

C. Equitable Access to Technology

Beyond financing, policies to mitigate and adapt to climate change will require the development, dissemination, and implementation of new environmentally sound technologies throughout the world. These include technologies to mitigate GHG emissions (for renewable energy and carbon capture) as well as to adapt to a rapidly warming world (through more efficient cooling systems and building materials, seeds that are drought tolerant and nutrient dense, medical countermeasures, and water-source protection and treatment processes). However, there is no guarantee that such unproven technologies will be developed, and if they are, there is no reason to believe that access to these prospective technologies will be equitably distributed—without political and legal reform.

To address this need for equity, international legal obligations will be necessary to ensure "technology transfer," facilitating the sharing of physical equipment, processes, knowledge, and experience of how to use new technologies. Technology transfer is an explicit priority under the UNFCCC, and imposes obligations on high-income countries to promote, facilitate, and finance access to technologies – particularly to low-income countries. The Paris Agreement extends this obligation for technology transfer, noting it as a crucial part of sustainable development, poverty alleviation, and resilience to climate change. Beyond climate change law, it will be necessary for international intellectual property law, as introduced in Chapter 12, to provide flexibilities under the TRIPS Agreement; however, where these flexibilities have been insufficient to guarantee access to even life-saving drugs, it remains unclear whether they could be applied to environmentally sound technologies for climate change (Phelan 2018).[10] These international inequities between states will require attention to

---

[10] As seen in the COVID-19 pandemic, attempts to waive TRIPS Agreement obligations to deal with inequities in access to medicines have been subject to significant opposition from high-income

extraterritorial obligations for assistance and cooperation under international law. With the scale of health crisis faced by climate change, and the urgency of both innovation and dissemination of technologies, assessing and overcoming the barriers to climate action under existing international legal institutions must be central to efforts to ensure justice in global health.

D. Crime of Ecocide

Facilitating accountability for the climate change response will require consequences for responsible parties. Yet even in its strongest obligations, international climate law has struggled to provide a source of accountability for climate destruction that will increasingly cause death, ill health, and suffering. While human rights law provides some routes of accountability for states, it may be necessary to look beyond state obligations and monitoring mechanisms to ensure criminal repercussions. Criminal law has long provided legal tools to facilitate accountability, where specific individuals are punished for specific crimes. As introduced in Chapter 18, there are currently four crimes detailed under international law to support individual responsibility before the International Criminal Court (ICC): genocide, crimes against humanity, war crimes, and the crime of aggression. In 2021, an independent panel of lawyers proposed adding a fifth crime to this list: ecocide (Independent Expert Panel for the Legal Definition of Ecocide 2021).

While the momentum for this crime is new, ecocide is not a new concept under international environmental law. As early as the 1972 UN Conference of the Environment, the term "ecocide" was used to describe indiscriminate ecological warfare. However, the international crime of ecocide would not be focused on warfare, and despite the human health impacts of ecological destruction, it would deviate from the anthropocentricism of the four codified international crimes – to focus on attacks against the well-being of the environment itself. Over the last few decades, countries have increasingly incorporated ecocide in their domestic legislation, and in 2016, the policy of the ICC prosecutor was amended to incorporate the impact of environmental damage in assessing the gravity of international crimes.

Ongoing proposals seek to criminalize ecocide under international law. While seeking to proscribe "unlawful or wanton acts committed with knowledge that

---

countries, in particular European nations, which continue to block access to life saving technologies in emergencies and crises. Continuing from the fight for access to medicines, human rights law may support efforts to guarantee access to technology in the climate change response, whether under the right to health or the right to enjoy the benefits of scientific progress and its applications (Chapman 2009).

there is a substantial likelihood of severe and either widespread or long-term damage to the environment being caused by those acts" (Independent Expert Panel for the Legal Definition of Ecocide 2021), scholars and states have raised a number of legal issues with the theoretical scope of the definition—concerned that the *mens rea* (fault element) components of the current definition are not workable and the definition is still largely anthropocentric in its focus (Greene 2021).[11] While legal debates continue on the scope and content of this prospective criminal violation, the momentum building in relation to a crime of ecocide reflects growing commitment to accountability for environmentally destructive acts. This focus on the most egregious threats to climate change may thus provide some tailored accountability, even as states increasingly recognize that global accountability for climate action will require far more systemic reform measures for climate change mitigation and adaptation.

Conclusion

Global climate laws have increasingly recognized the impacts of climate change on global health, but these legal advancements have not yet translated into sufficient action to mitigate climate change. The Earth is continuing to warm, as the health implications of climate change continue to unfold. Global temperatures can only stabilize after GHG emissions reach a net of zero, but the world remains far from reaching this necessary goal—with many of the health repercussions continuing far into the future. Efforts to halt global warming at 1.5°C (2.7°F) will require achieving net zero emissions by the early 2050s; however, according to the latest climate data, this would require global greenhouse gas emissions to peak *before* 2025 at the very latest and reduced by a quarter within five years thereafter. The climate is changing faster than states are acting. The world is on a path that will be hotter, sicker, and more unjust.

The COVID-19 pandemic response, in its successes and failures, has demonstrated how global health is interconnected with global coordination—whether for climate or pandemics. Across global governance, the push to "build back better" recognizes that the conditions that led to the pandemic are not those the world should return to, including climate inaction. The pandemic has also

---

[11] Beyond theoretical concerns, there are also a range of practical considerations. While "aggression" has been a recognized crime in international customary law for some time, amendments to the Rome Statute (governing the ICC) to incorporate the crime of aggression only went into effect in 2018. The challenges with those amendments, namely that the amendments will only apply to states that separately ratify them, are perhaps a likely preview of how amendments for a crime of ecocide may be received (Heller 2021).

demonstrated the potential risks of relying on public health as a motivator for action on climate change. Prior to the pandemic, a range of research examined how health was a compelling framing device for individuals to seek action on climate change. However, at the policymaking level, action to protect public health, even during a pandemic, was left wanting in many countries. Pushing for good governance for climate health justice must therefore consider this potential intransigence in taking action to protect health, particularly the health of vulnerable populations.

International climate law, in all of its manifestations, is only one tool for achieving accountability for climate action. Global health law must also take up the mantle of responding to climate change. This includes embedding climate obligations in any new international instrument for pandemic preparedness and response and taking a climate-informed approach to new policies to protect global health. Unfortunately, the lessons of COVID-19 appear to be that equitable access to technologies, the protection of the right to health, and global cooperation are all too easily ignored by readily nationalistic and neocolonial governance. Global health law has long fought for equity and justice: international climate law must incorporate global health governance. This includes an incorporation of global health actors – not just advocates for law reform to mitigate climate change, but in adapting our societies to the impacts we are already experiencing. By taking a planetary health approach to international law, young advocates provide hope for incorporating public health in adaptation measures, while urgently mitigating climate change, for a more just and healthy world.

Questions for Consideration

1. How has climate change served as a "health threat multiplier" for global health? Why must the health impacts of climate change be considered together—and across all countries?
2. What inequities are faced by a changing climate—across individuals, countries, and generations? Why is it unjust that different populations have contributed climate change and experience its impacts?
3. How did scientific consensus on GHGs lead to international action through the UN? How did the IPCC strengthen the call for international law?
4. Why should the international climate law regime be considered global health law?
5. What compromises were necessary to ensure global consensus in developing the UNFCCC? How does the principle of "common but differentiated responsibilities" provide a path to advance justice in the climate change response?

6. Why have many states opposed the adoption of legally binding obligations in UNFCCC protocols? How have efforts to enlist more states parties through non-binding obligations led these protocols to be less effective in reducing GHG emissions?
7. Why should climate change policy debates be reframed to focus on the global health impacts? How does the incorporation of adaptation debates in climate change governance provide greater opportunities for global health governance engagement in the UNFCCC COP?
8. What does a focus on planetary health bring to climate change debates? How can planetary health resolve the fragmented governance landscape and embed public health considerations in climate change law?
9. How would human rights obligations reframe the climate change response to ensure a healthy environment? Why should the COP develop new mechanisms to ensure accountability for loss and damage?
10. What would it mean to define the crime of "ecocide" under international criminal law? How would international criminal prosecution provide accountability for individual acts of environmental damage?

Acknowledgments

The authors appreciate the thoughtful editorial support of Chris Burch and Mercy Adekola.

References

Berry, Helen Louise, Kathryn Bowen, and Tord Kjellstrom. 2010. "Climate Change and Mental Health: A Causal Pathways Framework." *International Journal of Public Health* 55(2): 123–132.

Campbell-Lendrum, Diarmid. 2007. "Global Climate Change: Implications for International Public Health Policy." *Bulletin of the World Health Organization* 85(3): 235–237.

Chapman, Audrey R. 2009. "Towards an Understanding of the Right to Enjoy the Benefits of Scientific Progress and Its Applications." *Journal of Human Rights* 8(1): 1–36.

Costello, Anthony, Mustafa Abbas, Adriana Allen, Sarah Ball, , Richard Bellamy, et al. 2009. "Managing the Health Effects of Climate Change: Lancet and University College London Institute for Global Health Commission." *Lancet* 37 (9676): 1693–1733.

Ebi, Kristie L., Jennifer Vanos, Jane W. Baldwin, Jesse E. Bell, David M. Hondula, Nicole A. Errett, Katie Hayes et al. 2021. "Extreme Weather and Climate Change: Population Health and Health System Implications." *Annual Review of Public Health* 42(April): 293–315.

Fleurbaey Mark, Sivan Kartha, Simon Bolwig, Yoke Ling Chee, Ying Chen, Esteve Corbera, Frank Lecocq et al. 2014. "Sustainable Development and Equity." In *Climate Change 2014: Mitigation of Climate Change. Contribution of Working Group*

III to the Fifth Assessment Report of the Intergovernmental Panel on Climate Change. Cambridge: Cambridge University Press.

Greene, Anastacia. 2021. "Mens Rea and the Proposed Legal Definition of Ecocide." *Voelkerrechtsblog*. July 7.

Hales, Simon, Sari Kovats, Simon Lloyd, and Diarmid Campbell-Lendrum. 2014. *Quantitative Risk Assessment of the Effects of Climate Change on Selected Causes of Death, 2030s and 2050s*. Geneva: WHO.

Heller, Kevin Jon. 2021. "Skeptical Thoughts on the Proposed Crime of 'Ecocide' (That Isn't)." *Opinio Juris*. June 23.

Independent Expert Panel for the Legal Definition of Ecocide. 2021. "Ecocide: Commentary and Core Text." June.

IPCC (Intergovernmental Panel on Climate Change). 2000. *IPCC Special Report. Methodological and Technological Issues in Technology Transfer. Summary for Policy Makers*. Cambridge: Cambridge University Press.

IPCC. 2021. *Climate Change 2021: The Physical Science Basis*. Geneva: IPCC.

Kinney, Patrick L. 2008. "Climate Change, Air Quality, and Human Health." *American Journal of Preventive Medicine* 35(5): 459–467.

Koubi, Vally. 2019. "Climate Change and Conflict." *Annual Review of Political Science* 22(1): 343–360.

Mannucci, Pier Mannuccio, Sergio Harari, Ida Martinelli, and Massimo Franchini. 2015. "Effects on Health of Air Pollution: A Narrative Review." *Internal and Emergency Medicine* 10(6): 657–662.

Mbow, Cheikh, Andy Reisinger, Josep Canadell, and Phillip O'Brien. 2018. *Special Report on Climate Change, Desertification, Land Degradation, Sustainable Land Management, Food Security, and Greenhouse Gas Fluxes in Terrestrial Ecosystems*. Geneva: IPCC.

McMichael, Anthony. 2017. *Climate Change and the Health of Nations: Famines, Fevers, and the Fate of Populations*. New York: Oxford University Press.

Meier, Benjamin Mason, Flavia Bustreo, and Lawrence O. Gostin. 2022. "Climate Change, Public Health and Human Rights." *International Journal of Environmental Research and Public Health* 19(21): 13744.

Murthy, R. Srinivasa. 2007. "Mass Violence and Mental Health -- Recent Epidemiological Findings." *International Review of Psychiatry* 3: 183–192.

Nolin, Jan. 1999. "Global Policy and National Research: The International Shaping of Climate Research in Four European Union Countries." *Minerva* 37(2): 125–40.

Ostfeld, Richard S., and Jesse L. Brunner. 2015. "Climate Change and Ixodes Tick-Borne Diseases of Humans." *Philosophical Transactions of the Royal Society of London. Series B, Biological Sciences* 370 (1665): 417–438.

Phelan, Alexandra. 2018. "Climate Change and Human Rights: Intellectual Property Challenges and Opportunities." In *Intellectual Property and Clean Energy: The Paris Agreement and Climate Justice*, edited by Matthew Rimmer. New York: Springer.

Phelan, Alexandra L. 2020. "The Environment, a Changing Climate, and Planetary Health." In *Foundations of Global Health & Human Rights*, edited by Lawrence O. Gostin and Benjamin Mason Meier, 417–438. Oxford: Oxford University Press.

Phelan, Alexandra. 2022. "How Climate Law Can Help to Prevent the next Pandemic." *Nature* 605(7910): 397–397.

Robinson, Mary, and Tara Shine. 2018. "Achieving a Climate Justice Pathway to 1.5°C." *Nature Climate Change* 8(7): 564–569.

Romanello, Marina, Alice McGushin, Claudia Di Napoli, Paul Drummond, Nick Hughes, Louis Jamart Harry Kennard, et al. 2021. "The 2021 Report of the Lancet

Countdown on Health and Climate Change: Code Red for a Healthy Future." *Lancet* 398(10311): 1619–1662.

Sands, Philippe. 1992. "The United Nations Framework Convention on Climate Change." *Review of European Community & International Environmental Law* 1(3): 270–277.

Theisen, Ole Magnus. 2017. "Climate Change and Violence: Insights from Political Science." *Current Climate Change Reports* 3(4): 210–221.

UN Conference of the Environment. 1972. "Declaration of the United Nations Conference on the Environment."

UN Human Rights Council. 2013. "Report of the Independent Expert on the Issue of Human Rights Obligations Relating to the Enjoyment of a Safe, Clean, Healthy and Sustainable Environment, John H. Knox." December 30. A/HRC/25/53.

UNESCO (United Nations Educational, Scientific and Cultural Organization). 2019. *Leaving No One Behind*. The United Nations World Water Development Report 2019. Paris: UNESCO.

UNFCCC (UN Framework Convention on Climate Change). 2021. 'Nationally Determined Contributions under the Paris Agreement: Synthesis Report by the Secretariat." September 17. FCCC/PA/CMA/2021/8.

UN General Assembly. 1990. "Protection of Global Climate for Present and Future Generations of Mankind." December 21. A/RES/45/212.

UN General Assembly. 2018. "Gaps in International Environmental Law and Environment-Related Instruments: Towards a Global Pact for the Environment." November 30. A/73/419.

UN General Assembly. 2022. "The Human Right to a Clean, Healthy and Sustainable Environment." July 26. A/76/L.75.

van Daalen, Kim Robin, Sarah Savić Kallesøe, Fiona Davey, Sara Dada, Laura Jung, Lucy Singh, Rita Issa et al. 2022. "Extreme Events and Gender-Based Violence: A Mixed-Methods Systematic Review." *Lancet Planetary Health* 6(6): e504–e523.

van Daalen, Kim Robin, Laura Jung, Roopa Dhatt, and Alexandra L. Phelan. 2020. "Climate Change and Gender-Based Health Disparities." *Lancet Planetary Health*.

Vins, Holly, Jesse Bell, Shubhayu Saha, and Jeremy J. Hess. 2015. "The Mental Health Outcomes of Drought: A Systematic Review and Causal Process Diagram." *International Journal of Environmental Research and Public Health* 12(10): 13251–13275.

Whitmee, Sarah, Andy Haines, Chris Beyrer, Frederick Boltz, Anthony G. Capon, Braulio Ferreira de Souza Dias, Alex Ezeh et al. 2015. "Safeguarding Human Health in the Anthropocene Epoch: Report of The Rockefeller Foundation–Lancet Commission on Planetary Health." *Lancet* 386(10007): 1973–2028.

WHO (World Health Organization). 2018. "Health Benefits Far Outweigh the Costs of Meeting Climate Change Goals." December 5. https://www.who.int/news/item/05-12-2018-health-benefits-far-outweigh-the-costs-of-meeting-climate-change-goals.

WHO. 2021. *WHO Global Air Quality Guidelines: Particulate Matter (PM2.5 and PM10), Ozone, Nitrogen Dioxide, Sulfur Dioxide and Carbon Monoxide*. Geneva: WHO.

Wise, Jacqui. 2021. "COP26: Fifty Countries Commit to Climate Resilient and Low Carbon Health Systems." *BMJ* November, 375 (no. 2734).

WMO (World Meteorological Organization). 1979. "Declaration of the World Climate Conference." Geneva: WMO.

WMO. 1985. "Report of the International Conference of the Assessment of the Role of Carbon Dioxide and of Other Greenhouse Gases in Climate Variations and Associated Impacts." WMO No 661.

Wu, Xiaoxu, Yongmei Lu, Sen Zhou, Lifan Chen, and Bing Xu. 2016. "Impact of Climate Change on Human Infectious Diseases: Empirical Evidence and Human Adaptation." *Environment International* 86(January): 14–23.

20
Universal Health Coverage
Whole of Government Approaches to Determinants of Health

Lawrence O. Gostin and Benjamin Mason Meier

Introduction

Looking across health issues, efforts to understand interconnections across determinants of health have sparked calls to translate social justice into public policy through Universal Health Coverage (UHC). In bringing together all health efforts under a single framework, UHC encompasses the full spectrum of essential health services—prevention, treatment, rehabilitation, and palliative care, with equitable access to primary healthcare services. UHC thus includes not only health care, but also public health measures and underlying determinants of health, including nutritious food, clean water, and adequate sanitation. Holding to the promise of advancing health equity, both within and across countries, UHC looks to law and policy to implement structures and standards, processes and rights, and budgetary frameworks and allocations across sectors. To establish standards for the laws and policies that shape UHC, global health governance has proven necessary for cooperation and implementation of best practices to reach those furthest behind and achieve the highest attainable standard of health.

While global health governance has long sought to ensure coverage for pressing health needs, UHC has come to be seen as the overarching goal of global health law and policy. The World Health Organization (WHO) originally framed progress toward UHC as an increase in health coverage across three dimensions—financial protections, populations, and services covered—yet contemporary interpretations and applications of UHC have sought to extend health coverage to all populations through insurance models, public-private partnership mechanisms, and increased healthcare financing and provision. As a sweeping agenda cutting across global health governance, UHC requires global health law in developing a common understanding of UHC obligations, enabling global monitoring to enhance accountability, and establishing global financing mechanisms to enable UHC in even the lowest income countries. UHC policy thus provides a set of norms and standards for states to follow in the implementation of their own national laws and policies, facilitating solidarity in achieving UHC.

This final chapter examines how global health law has sought to alleviate health inequities within and between nations through UHC. With UHC arising out of longstanding efforts to advance horizontal health systems, Part I examines the path that reshaped primary health care through a larger focus on health promotion and social determinants of health. Part II analyzes how UHC has been advanced in global policy under the United Nations (UN), drawing from WHO initiatives to become a central focus of sustainable development and human rights in global governance. As UHC has become a central focus of global governance, WHO has sought to champion UHC in global health governance, but Part III considers how this focus on UHC has been challenged by the COVID-19 pandemic, raising an imperative to codify UHC in ongoing global health law reforms. This chapter concludes that UHC can provide a foundation for justice in global health, with global health law necessary to ensure health for all.

I. Addressing Determinants of Health through Global Health Policy

The notion of an overarching global health policy agenda to frame health in all policies evolved in global governance from primary health care to universal health coverage. Early advocacy for universal coverage far predates the modern system of global governance, with early efforts for "universal adoption of sickness insurance" arising out of the social medicine revolutions in the 19th century, first introduced in Chapter 1, and seeking to operationalize universal healthcare systems. Drawing from social medicine, the focus on the social conditions impacting health would become a foundation of national efforts to rebuild welfare states after World War II (Meier and Gable 2013). This notion of universal access to health would become central to the Constitution of the World Health Organization, which defined health as "a state of complete physical, mental and social well-being," declared health to be "one of the fundamental rights of every human being," and recognized that "governments have a responsibility for the health of their peoples which can be fulfilled only by the provision of adequate health and social measures" (WHO 1946, preamble). Under WHO governance, global health policy to realize the highest attainable level of health for all would take shape through a focus on primary health care, an international agenda on health promotion, and a commission on social determinants of health.

A. Declaration of Alma-Ata

WHO's Health for All strategy would frame policy efforts to advance primary health care through the 1978 Declaration of Alma-Ata. This "Health for All" strategy, officially defined by the World Health Assembly in 1977, would seek "the attainment by all peoples of the world by the year 2000 of a level of health that would permit them to lead a socially and economically productive life" (WHO 1978, art. V). With the World Health Assembly approving WHO's socioeconomic direction in addressing underlying determinants of health, WHO considered its Health for All strategy to be linked to rising efforts among "developing nations" in the Global South to create a New International Economic Order – seeking a WHO framework to establish a "New International Health Order" (Pannenborg 1979). WHO would support other UN agencies in transitioning from a growth-based approach to a needs-based approach to development, the latter to be founded upon human rights and driven by a concern for deteriorating underlying determinants of health (Djukanovic and Mach 1975). With a renewed imperative for health equity, the WHO Director-General recognized that "this movement toward justice in health will require concerted action by the international community through the adoption of a global strategy for primary health care" (Mahler 1978, 3).

The Declaration of Alma-Ata would provide international political consensus for national primary health care systems consistent with WHO's vision of Health for All. Bringing together representatives from 134 states, the 1978 International Conference on Primary Health Care adopted the Declaration on Primary Health Care, with this Declaration of Alma-Ata memorializing agreement that primary health care was essential to realizing underlying determinants of health. The Declaration of Alma-Ata, first introduced in Chapter 3, recognized disparities in health outcomes between developed and developing nations, setting a goal that, by the year 2000, the world would reach a level of health care to permit all people "to lead a socially and economically productive life" (WHO 1978, art. V). Reaffirming the preambular language of the WHO Constitution, the Declaration opened by outlining that:

> health, which is a state of complete physical, mental and social well-being, and not merely the absence of disease or infirmity, is a fundamental human right and that the attainment of the highest level of health is a most important worldwide social goal whose realization requires the action of many other social and economic sectors in addition to the health sector (ibid, art. I).

The Declaration thus framed primary health care to include both health care and determinants of health across sectors.

The Declaration of Alma-Ata was successful in affirming international political commitment to primary health care—bringing together WHO, UNICEF, and other global health actors to lay out a programmatic vision for achieving Health for All—however, this comprehensive view of primary health care faced setbacks in the years that followed. By the end of the 1970s, the push for primary health care was challenged by escalating foreign debt, global economic recession, and, as discussed in Chapter 11, the introduction of structural adjustment programs by development banks that brought reductions to health and social sector spending. The comprehensive primary health care slogan, "Health for All by 2000," was perceived as unattainable given the financial and human resource costs.[1] Driven by the rise of neoliberalism, global health governance shifted from the comprehensive vision of primary health care to a narrower approach to "selective primary health care" (Rifkin and Walt 1986).

Case Study: The Limitations of Primary Health Care – Comprehensive vs. Selective Care

The Selective Primary Health Care agenda, arising out of a 1979 Rockefeller Foundation meeting on "Health and Population in Development," would create a parallel focus on cost-effective vertical disease prevention and medical treatment services, pressing for selective medical care rather than comprehensive primary health care. This selective focus sought to frame packages of low-cost interventions (known as "GOBI"—Growth monitoring, Oral rehydration, Breastfeeding, and Immunizations) that could address the main disease challenges in low-income countries. Global health actors came to adopt this selective approach in global health governance. Recognizing the high costs of fulfilling comprehensive primary health care, UNICEF in the 1980s began to prioritize select aspects of the GOBI approach, principally immunizations and oral rehydration. The World Bank similarly recognized financial constraints on a comprehensive approach to health, suggesting in 1981 that contracting out services to the private sector, staff lay-offs in the public sector, and liberalization in pharmaceutical trade could "cost effectively" promote health. With the abandonment of primary health care, WHO retreated back to the technical development of medical care services, implemented through a narrower focus on selective primary health care. The

---

[1] As global health actors were meeting in Alma-Ata to frame primary health care, the World Bank was estimating that it would cost billions of dollars to provide rudimentary, not even comprehensive, health services to underprivileged and poor people in developing countries by the year 2000.

emergence of HIV/AIDS, rise in malaria, and growing concern about tuberculosis further shifted the focus of international public health from the comprehensive public health approach of Alma-Ata to the selective management of health emergencies. While selective primary health care was thought to be a necessary trade-off amid financial constraints and health emergencies, this step back from the primary health care agenda would set back global health policy to promote public health.

In the absence of global health governance to promote the Declaration of Alma-Ata, international health cooperation was sharply curtailed in the early 1980s, with many states moving away from their non-binding commitments under WHO's Health for All strategy and toward a vertical disease-focused agenda (Nakajima 1989). Yet despite these challenges to the Declaration of Alma-Ata, the primary health care approach endured as a focus of global health policy, with WHO retaining its global strategy, "Health for All by the Year 2000," and providing a space in global policy to advance health promotion.

B. International Conferences on Health Promotion

Health promotion—the notion of undertaking social and environmental interventions to increase people's ability to improve their health—became an international movement in the 1980s and ultimately a series of international conferences. Beginning in 1981, European states began to focus on a "lifestyle" approach to health education, prompting a new program in the WHO Regional Office for Europe that would adopt regional targets for lifestyles conducive to health (Saan 2007). WHO called a special meeting in 1984 to clarify and direct this evolving health promotion debate, leading to its first focus on "Concepts and Principles of Health Promotion." In 1985, a WHO workshop among European states developed a policy framework on the practical aspects of implementing health promotion (Catford 2011). Such early European debates expanded across WHO regions—drawing from the larger framework established in Alma-Ata—and would frame the agenda for the First International Conference on Health Promotion.

This 1986 International Conference on Health Promotion, bringing together state representatives in Ottawa, Canada, furthered the prominence and development of health promotion in global health policy. Through the resulting Ottawa Charter for Health Promotion, delegates recommended five unprecedented actions:

1. building healthy public policies—which directed policymakers to "accept their responsibilities for health" and advance health promotion in legislation, fiscal measures, taxation, and organizational changes;
2. creating supportive environments—considering the interrelation between people, their environment, and their communities;
3. strengthening community action—to focus on empowering communities through new resources and access to information;
4. developing personal skills—highlighting the improvement of health literacy and education; and
5. reorienting health services—which advocated for health systems to go beyond clinical services and embrace social and cultural needs (WHO 1986).

The Ottawa Charter advanced health promotion through a focus on "the prerequisites of health," including "peace, shelter, education, food, income, a stable eco-system, sustainable resources, social justice and equity" (ibid., art. 1). Establishing a synergy between public policy, community empowerment, and public health, the Ottawa Charter launched a focus on determinants of health (Kickbusch 2007).

Expanding the agenda arising out of the Declaration of Alma-Ata, the Ottawa Charter framed health promotion to extend beyond selective health interventions—and even beyond the health sector—requiring a whole-of-government approach to health. In addressing the health threats of a globalizing world, the Ottawa Charter sought to "counteract the pressures" of everything from harmful products and resource depletion to poor nutrition, pollution, and occupational hazards—responsibilities reaching practically all sectors of government. Opportunities following the Ottawa Conference prompted various global and regional health initiatives to advance health promotion across sectors (Thompson, Watson, and Tilford 2018). States would hold a series of additional international conferences on health promotion in the ensuing years, providing a recurring basis to strengthen global policy efforts to address determinants of health.

C. WHO Commission on Social Determinants of Health

With an evolving understanding that health inequity is driven by underlying determinants of health, and thus cannot be redressed by the health sector alone, WHO looked to develop multisectoral policy approaches to frame social determinants of health. The WHO Director-General launched the Commission on Social Determinants of Health in 2005, assembling a global network of policymakers, researchers, and organizations dedicated to strengthening health

Figure 20.1 Commission Chair Michael Marmot Launches "Closing the Gap in a Generation" with WHO Director-General Margaret Chan (Michael Marmot)

equity (Irwin et al. 2006).² This WHO Commission examined the causes of health inequities in the underlying circumstances in which people live, with its research addressing how these underlying circumstances are structured by global, national, and local forces (Marmot et al. 2008). In this research on the health impacts of disparities in status, resources, and power, the Commission's research studied how public policies shape health inequities (Irwin et al 2006). The Commission sought to apply the normative imperative for health equity to policy development, employing its reports and political consultations to recommend policy reforms and monitoring systems to strengthen health equity.

The Commission concluded its research in a foundational 2008 report on health inequities, "Closing the Gap in a Generation: Health Equity through Action on the Social Determinants of Health." Launching this report with WHO leadership, as seen in Figure 20.1, the Commission recognized that inequities in social determinants of health are a global injustice, concluding that "[s]ocial injustice is

---

² Chaired by Professor Michael Marmot, WHO brought together twenty commissioners—distinguished individuals in their fields of expertise, including politics, academia, and advocacy—to carry out research in various countries working to reduce health inequities (Irwin et al. 2006).

killing people on a grand scale" (WHO 2008, 1). This final report described the social determinants of health holistically to include the circumstances in which people live, grow, work, and age. Where these determinants are shaped by political, social, and economic forces, the Commission recommended policy reforms to incorporate health equity into all policies, systems, and programs (Marmot et al. 2008).

The Commission on Social Determinants of Health provided three overarching recommendations for WHO and all governments:

(1) improve daily living conditions, particularly the well-being of women, children, and the elderly, through early childhood development, education, working conditions, and social protection policies;
(2) address the systemic distribution of power, money, and resources; and
(3) create metrics and routine monitoring to measure health inequity and evaluate actions, in addition to increasing research and raising public awareness of the social determinants of health (WHO 2008).

This first Commission recommendation on improving daily living conditions highlighted health inequities across countries—involving systemic disparities in the provision, access, and use of health care and underlying determinants of health—with the Commission recommending policies to ensure access to health care for all. Looking beyond the health sector, the Commission additionally recommended that governments invest in living conditions: the natural environment, land rights, and urban conditions, fair employment and decent work, and universal social protection systems.

Following the final report of the Commission on Social Determinants of Health, the World Health Assembly passed a series of resolutions to reduce health inequities by acting on social determinants of health. In 2011, more than one hundred states adopted the Rio Political Declaration on Social Determinants of Health. The Rio Political Declaration pledged to "[s]trengthen health systems towards the provision of equitable universal coverage and promote access to high quality, promotive, preventive, curative and rehabilitative health services throughout the life-cycle" (WHO 2011, art. 13). From this connection to "universal coverage," global health governance began shifting from social determinants of health to UHC, as advocates called for UHC as a means to address social determinants of health (Sanders et al. 2019).

II. Calls for Universal Health Coverage

WHO increasingly looked to UHC to advance policy efforts to ensure primary health care and address social determinants of health. UHC and primary health care came to be seen as inextricably linked, with primary care serving as the foundation of UHC. More broadly, the encompassing nature of UHC provided a foundation to advance a wide range of global health goals under a single overarching global policy. Early advocacy to advance UHC grew in the early 2000s alongside an evolving agenda for "health in all policies"—providing a means of addressing health coverage across sectors. With the UN declaring UHC as one of the targets for the Sustainable Development Goals (SDGs) in 2015, UHC has found a central place in global health policy, as advocates have looked to UHC as a basis to realize the right to health.

A. Early Advocacy

The World Health Assembly officially defined UHC for the first time in global health policy in 2005. This early resolution focused on sustainable financing for health services, with an emphasis on ensuring equitable access to a UHC benefits package. Following from this resolution, WHO published a landmark 2008 World Health Report—three decades after Alma-Ata—on "Primary Health Care: Now More Than Ever," examining primary health care as a foundation of UHC (Garrett, Chowdhury, and Pablos-Méndez 2009). WHO continued to support efforts to advance UHC. Following a subsequent 2010 World Health Report on Health Systems Financing, WHO Director-General Margaret Chan proclaimed that "universal health coverage is the single most powerful concept that public health has to offer" (Ooms, Marten et al. 2014).

The 2011 Rio Political Declaration on Social Determinants of Health provided a strong international expression of support for UHC, linking social determinants to UHC and building political momentum for broader UHC engagement beyond WHO. With representatives of 125 governments attending the Rio Conference on Social Determinants of Health, this Rio Declaration represented the first major intergovernmental commitment to act on social determinants of health, including both a normative commitment to reduce inequities and a programmatic commitment to strengthen health systems to ensure UHC (Rasanathan 2018). The World Health Assembly endorsed the Rio Declaration the following year.

The UN General Assembly thereafter focused on UHC in 2012 as a means to provide health care for all, urging member states to establish universal coverage systems. Advocates had been pressing for General Assembly action to bring UHC to the highest levels of political leadership, beyond WHO forums of health ministers, as UN action would prove crucial given the whole-of-government approach that UHC would require. The resulting UN General Assembly resolution adopted the World Health Assembly's 2005 definition of UHC—expanding political support for UHC as a means to provide health care for all (O'Connell, Rasanathan, and Chopra 2014). This resolution, urging states to accelerate progress toward UHC as a priority for international development, solidified the UN's commitment to UHC as the leading health target in a post-2015 development agenda and strengthened WHO's work to advance health in all policies.

B. Health in All Policies

The WHO focus on Health in All Policies (HiAP) came to serve as a precursor to UHC. While HiAP had long served as a focus of multisectoral policymaking at the national level,[3] international organizations began to recognize that all sectors must play a role in supporting global health. As a systemic approach to considering the impacts of all public policies on health, HiAP was seen as a basis to address social determinants of health—by developing policies across sectors to achieve universal coverage. HiAP thus recognized that many barriers to health and health services lie outside the health sector, laying a foundation for progress toward UHC through intersectoral action to address determinants of health (WHO 2013a). States came to appreciate that partnerships at all levels and sectors of government can promote health in all policies and create environments for optimal health system performance.

Drawing from efforts showing that health is largely determined by policies and actions beyond the health sector—including transportation, housing and urban planning, the environment, education, agriculture, finance, taxation, and economic development—WHO looked to frame a whole-of-government response to health. WHO's focus on HiAP was seen as a natural progression from its Commission on Social Determinants of Health, requiring a cross-cutting approach to health—across sectors and policies, as well as levels of government and stakeholders (Kickbusch 2010). WHO saw HiAP as an "approach to public policies across sectors that systemically takes into account the health and health systems implications of decisions, seeks synergies and avoids harmful health impacts, in order to improve population health and health equity" (WHO 2014, 2). Such attention to HiAP became the central focus of the 2013 Global Conference on Health Promotion in Helsinki, Finland, supporting WHO efforts to consider HiAP in global health governance (Leppo et al. 2013). This Conference led to both the Helsinki Statement on Health in All Policies,

---

[3] Prior to the Declartation of Alma-Ata in 1978, Health in All Policies had already found traction in Finland, with the Economic Council of Finland recommending in 1972 that health policy span across all sectors—from economic policy to agricultural policy. This early domestic effort set in motion the development of HiAP, in Finnish policy and throughout the world (Ståhl 2018).

calling on governments to prioritize health equity and develop the structures and capacities for a HiAP approach, as well as a Framework for Country Action. The Framework—with six components, including framing a plan of action and identifying support structures and processes—was developed to facilitate state action in applying the HiAP approach in national and subnational decision-making and policy implementation.

WHO thereby came to play a key role in coordinating multisectoral efforts to advance HiAP. Given the barriers to implementing HiAP at the country level—where states lacked a legal mandate to facilitate health governance across sectors—WHO sought to support Member States. WHO assisted country implementation of HiAP through a variety of programs, including by creating training resources and tools for capacity building; setting standards for transforming education on social determinants of health; promoting links with other WHO governance programs; supporting government policymakers, program leaders, and health providers to improve intersectoral action; and providing advice through the Global Network for Health in All Policies (WHO 2013a).[4] These efforts to assess health impacts across sectors provided a basis to examine UHC under the 2030 Agenda for Sustainable Development.

C. SDGs

The UN has sought to bind the world together to advance sustainable development, with UHC serving as a political platform for health policy under the SDGs. The Millennium Development Goals (MDGs), passed in 2000, were designed with a narrow focus on health—through efforts to reduce child mortality; improve maternal health; and combat HIV/AIDS, malaria, and other diseases. In expanding from the limited health focus of the MDGs, the UN began negotiating a more holistic post-2015 development agenda, as introduced in Chapter 10, which culminated in the adoption of the 2030 Agenda for Sustainable Development, accompanied by 17 SDGs to be achieved by 2030 (UN 2015).

Under the sweeping expanse of the SDGs, including a far greater focus on underlying determinants of health and a heightened focus on equity, the 17 goals and their 169 targets touch upon virtually every major aspect of society. Given the influence of almost all sectors on health, a point captured by the global focus on social determinants of health and HiAP, achieving the SDGs would have a significant impact on public health and health inequities. This new agenda laid

---

[4] The Global Network for Health in All Policies, launched in 2017 as a country-led initiative, seeks to work with governments and institutions across sectors to address determinants of health, embedding a whole-of-government approach to health.

a much broader foundation for global health governance, articulating goals focused not only on health (SDG 3) but also on the social determinants of health, including economic status (SDG 1), education (SDG 4), employment (SDG 8), and affordable housing and transportation (SDG 11), among others. This expansive vision created an imperative for cross-sectoral investments in supporting population health and well-being, bringing together actors both within and beyond the health sphere.

The specific attention to health under the SDGs would be focused on UHC. SDG 3 aims to "[e]nsure healthy lives and promote well-being for all at all ages" (UN 2015), with this goal seeking to reduce financial barriers to accessing health care. UHC was a natural choice for one of the SDG 3 targets, and from the beginning, UHC was viewed as the centerpiece of SDG 3. WHO had already prioritized UHC, the UN General Assembly had urged the inclusion of UHC in the international development agenda, and UHC's cross-cutting nature allowed it to contribute to numerous health and development priorities (O'Connell, Rasanathan, and Chopra 2014). UHC thus became central to the focus on health under the SDGs, leading it to become the overarching approach to advancing quality care and bringing together global health efforts to achieve sustainable development.

Case Study: Advancing UHC to Achieve the SDGs

Under the 2030 Agenda, UHC has been leveraged as a framework for addressing the systemic drivers of health inequity—notably financial barriers to accessing healthcare services and supports. Explicitly framed as the key target under SDG 3, UHC under the 2030 Agenda is defined to include "financial risk protection, access to quality essential health-care services and access to safe, effective, quality and affordable essential medicines and vaccines for all." The achievement of this target is assessed based on two indicators, evaluating (1) the coverage of "essential health services" and (2) the number of households that spend a significant proportion of their income (greater than 10%–25%) on health. While the path to achieving UHC is dependent upon a given country context, meaningful advancement of UHC requires robust and resilient systems that remove any political, sociocultural, geographic, financial, or organizational barriers to realizing health. Such health systems would not only provide supports for strengthening healthcare services, but also account for and provide the social and economic supports necessary to improve access to care—especially for those who are most disadvantaged. To advance UHC as a basis for achieving the SDGs, the UN has partnered with other organizations to monitor and provide technical recommendations on accelerating progress toward UHC. Following the adoption of the SDGs,

WHO and the World Bank worked with the International Health Partnership (IHP+) to establish the International Health Partnership for UHC 2030, which has become a key platform for facilitating multi-stakeholder dialogue around health systems strengthening for UHC.

Although UHC is only one of thirteen targets under SDG 3, it is considered integral to the achievement of all other health-related targets under the 2030 Agenda—from reducing mortality from non-communicable diseases to cutting maternal and child mortality and through to universal access to clean water and adequate sanitation (Chapman 2016). In situating the improvement of health systems as a cornerstone of sustainable development, this focus on UHC under the SDGs has provided a basis in global governance to realize the right to health (Sridhar et al. 2015).

D. UHC as a Human Rights Imperative

UHC has become a unifying policy platform to advance human rights in global health governance, with the right to health serving as a foundational normative framework for achieving UHC goals. Under the International Covenant on Economic, Social and Cultural Rights (ICESCR), first introduced in Chapter 4, states commit to "take steps, individually and through international assistance and co-operation, especially economic and technical, to the maximum of its available resources, with a view to achieving progressively the full realization of the rights recognized in the present covenant by all appropriate means" (UN General Assembly 1966, art. 12). UHC focuses on essential services in accordance with the core human rights obligation to realize essential primary health care—framing the development of health facilities that provide these essential services and supporting the progressive realization of underlying determinants of health. Anchoring UHC in the right to health under international law has raised expectations for improving health in a comprehensive way and strengthened obligations to remove barriers to accessing health care (Ooms et al. 2013).[5]

Looking to the right to health to define UHC is thereby valuable to developing measurable and achievable indicators to review the progressive realization of the right to health. Under General Comment 14, the Committee on Economic, Social and Cultural Rights (with an international legal mandate to monitor state

---

[5] Lowering barriers to accessing care, including financial and other socioeconomic barriers, is necessary to the progressive realization of the right to health, and UHC redresses these barriers by assessing (1) the extent of the population covered under UHC, (2) the financial contributions covered, and (3) the health benefits included (Ooms, Latif et al. 2014).

compliance with the ICESCR) clarified that the obligations arising from the right to health include state efforts to ensure the availability, accessibility, acceptability, and quality of health facilities, goods, and services (CESCR 2000). However, in considering the health benefits under UHC, a state's obligation toward the right to health is limited by the availability of resources (including financial and human resources), and in progressing toward UHC, countries with limited resources must set priorities surrounding health services and expenditure. While the right to health is cognizant of these resource constraints, states commit under the ICESCR to using the "maximum of [their] available resources" in progressively realizing the right to health, with human rights monitoring providing a path to review the pace of this progress (Meier and Brás Gomes 2018).[6] Where more resources do not always translate into better health outcomes, the manner in which funds are raised and spent will affect whether the resources themselves are "maximized" to realize UHC, requiring transparency in both raising funds (e.g., progressive taxation) and spending funds (e.g., insurance subsidies). Yet, even when fulfilling obligations to direct the maximum available resources to UHC, lower-income states may lack the financing needed for core UHC components, raising an imperative for global governance and international assistance (Watkins et al. 2018).

For UHC to be achieved throughout the world, states must embrace the human rights principle of shared responsibility through global governance. General Comment 14 on the right to health makes clear that "it is particularly incumbent on States parties and other actors in a position to assist, to provide 'international assistance and cooperation, especially economic and technical' which enable developing countries to fulfil their core and other obligations" (CESCR 2000, art. 12). This international assistance to ensure the progressive realization of the right to health provides a clearer path to UHC through a shared commitment to health in global governance (Nygren-Krug 2019). With a shared responsibility to the right to health, states require global solidarity through global governance to ensure UHC. WHO and other international organizations now view UHC as a practical expression of the right to health, with WHO recognizing that "support for the goal of universal health coverage is also to express concern for equity and for honoring everyone's right to health" (WHO 2013b). The 2017 election of Tedros Adhanom Ghebreyesus as WHO Director-General has provided renewed leadership in advancing human rights in global health, with Dr. Tedros advocating tirelessly during his campaign that "universal health coverage is our best path to live up to WHO's constitutional commitment to the right to health" (Meier

---

[6] International human rights law does not delineate what this maximum of states' available resources includes, although estimates suggest a target of government spending on health of at least 5–7% of GDP for progressing toward UHC (McIntyre & Meheus 2014).

2017)—and, since his election, repeatedly invoking human rights as a foundation for WHO's flagship UHC initiative in global health governance.

III. UHC as a Framework for Global Health Governance

Global governance has looked to UHC as a common framework to advance global health. WHO has long provided global leadership to advance UHC across the global governance landscape, but that leadership has been tested in the COVID-19 response, challenging UHC and threatening global health security. As states look to strengthen global health law to prepare for future threats, it will be necessary to codify UHC as a foundation of pandemic preparedness and global solidarity.

A. WHO Leadership to Advance UHC

With UHC requiring coordination and collaboration across global health actors and multiple sectors, WHO has sought to lead a global movement for UHC—ensuring that quality health services can be accessed equitably and without financial hardship. Drawing from its longstanding advocacy to frame "Health for All"—from the WHO Constitution to the Declaration of Alma-Ata and beyond—WHO initially framed priority-setting for UHC under three guiding principles:

(1) fair distribution: coverage on the basis of need, prioritizing the needs of the underprivileged;
(2) cost effectiveness: priorities to generate the greatest total improvement in health; and
(3) fair contributions: contributions based on ability to pay rather than need (WHO 2014).[7]

UHC became a central focal point for WHO's agenda in 2014, with progress toward UHC repeatedly reaffirmed that year in the Bangkok Statement on Universal Health Coverage and the Mexico City Political Declaration on Universal Health Coverage (WHO 2014). As the UN General Assembly made UHC a principal target of the SDGs in 2015, it positioned WHO as the global

---

[7] This initial WHO consideration also established unacceptable trade-offs in establishing UHC, discouraging the expansion of coverage for low- or medium-priority services before there is near-universal coverage for high-priority services (WHO 2014).

leader in meeting this SDG target, looking to WHO to build the foundations necessary to bring countries together to achieve SDG 3 (Reddy, Mazhar, and Lencucha 2018). WHO, along with the UN and the World Bank, initially stressed financial risk protection as a central element of UHC, with affordability of care essential for ensuring the right to health. Since then, WHO has adopted UHC as an overarching framework to advance promotive, preventive, curative, rehabilitative, and palliative health services (Ghebreyesus 2017).

Case Study: WHO Takes Up UHC as the Overarching Focus of Global Health Governance

Following his initial election in 2017, WHO Director-General Tedros proclaimed that "all roads lead to universal health coverage," reiterating that achieving this goal was a reflection of the right to health and the top priority for WHO at the highest political levels. WHO pledged thereafter to develop a measurement system in order to benchmark countries on their attainment of UHC, tracking progress under the SDGs. In supporting Member States, WHO has provided technical assistance to governments—upon request and based on their specific UHC needs. Through reporting and collaboration between Member States, governments can learn from and work with other nations with similar political and economic contexts to achieve UHC. Since prioritizing UHC as a goal in health policy, WHO has taken steps to assist countries in realizing UHC, through reporting requirements, frameworks to track the progress of UHC, and partnerships with different partners and sectors to advance UHC around the world. The World Health Assembly in 2017 agreed to a strategic plan to ensure that one billion more people benefit from UHC by 2023. This goal of achieving one billion more people benefitting from UHC by 2023 became a central pillar of WHO's "triple billion" targets, which also include one billion more people protected from health emergencies and one billion more people enjoying better health and well-being. Member States noted that in order to achieve these goals, WHO would need to create reliable public health leadership, focus on impact in countries, and ensure that people can access authoritative and strategic information on matters that affect their health. These steps would seek to build a solid foundation to realize UHC and meet WHO's goal to have more people benefit from UHC.

Drawing from this renewed WHO leadership for UHC, the advancement of UHC became the principal focus of the 2018 Global Conference on Primary Health Care, celebrating the 40th anniversary of the Alma-Ata Conference and

Figure 20.2 WHO Director-General Tedros Adhanom Ghebreyesus and UNICEF Executive Director Henrietta Fore, 2018 (UNICEF)

charting a path forward for UHC. In renewing pledges from the Declaration of Alma-Ata, as seen in Figure 20.2, the 2018 Astana Declaration recommitted governments to primary health care as an essential step to achieve UHC, emphasizing that "political choices for health" need to be implemented across all sectors, considering economic, environmental, and social health determinants of health (WHO 2018).

Building on this WHO effort the following year, the UN General Assembly held a special session devoted to UHC, as political leaders reaffirmed their commitment to achieving UHC by 2030. This 2019 high-level special session was the culmination of steady advancements in the General Assembly—from its 2012 resolution on UHC to its focus on UHC under the SDGs—while seeking to transform previous aspirations into wide-ranging commitments (Hammonds et al. 2019). In committing governments to UHC, the resulting declaration recognized that all people should have access to nationally determined preventive, promotive, curative, rehabilitative, and palliative care services, including essential, affordable, and effective medicines and vaccines, at no risk of financial hardship (UN General Assembly 2019). The declaration committed states to taking tangible steps toward achieving UHC, from addressing health worker shortages to addressing the needs of migrants, refugees, and Indigenous peoples. The world had come together at last to advance UHC, extending beyond health care and considering determinants of health, but this holistic focus on health across sectors would be tested by the security threat of COVID-19 across countries.

B. UHC as a Basis for Global Health Security

The COVID-19 pandemic has challenged global progress to realize UHC, with billions lacking access to quality health care when they needed it most. Undermining public health throughout the world, the COVID-19 pandemic threatened UHC in its impact on both the continued delivery of essential health services (with health systems overwhelmed and supply chains interrupted) and the socioeconomic impacts that made health goods and services increasingly inaccessible. Yet despite the ways in which COVID-19 hampered progress toward UHC, with WHO releasing a 2021 position paper recognizing the pandemic's effects on UHC (WHO 2021), the goal of UHC was not lost amid the ongoing pandemic response. Throughout this unprecedented challenge, global governance pressed for the realization of UHC. Actors called for strengthening UHC as a basis for global health security, looking to primary health care as underpinning infectious disease prevention, detection, and response. Where public health systems were necessary in disease control, UHC could provide a basis for testing and tracing, and when the time came, delivering vaccines and health services (Colombo, Jakab, and Uribe 2021).

The increasing linkages between UHC and global health security have provided a foundation to strengthen prevention, treatment, countermeasures, and future resilience to diseases—seeing UHC and global health security as "two sides of the same coin" (Ghebreyesus 2017). As first introduced in Chapter 6, global health security involves mitigating public health threats, particularly the risk of disease outbreaks with cross-border potential, focusing on disease surveillance, risk communication, and coordination. Yet, where this securitization of public health addresses outbreaks with cross-border potential, UHC instead involves increasing healthcare access, quality, and affordability, supporting primary healthcare systems and ensuring quality health services without financial burdens (Wenham et al. 2019).[8] Despite these seemingly conflicting paradigms, actors looked to UHC in the COVID-19 pandemic as a basis for improving core public health capacities and strengthening global health security.

---

[8] Global health security can pose a threat to UHC where the conceptual relationship between them is misunderstood, leading to fragmented governance, policies, and investments. The consequences of this fragmentation were seen earlier in the West African Ebola epidemic (2014–2016), during which far more people died from malaria than Ebola virus—owing to a prioritization of global health security over UHC (Lal et al. 2021).

UHC has thus been seen to strengthen global health security through the:

(1) prevention and early mitigation of disease – integrating surveillance systems for detection and tracking of disease, improving national coordination in a pandemic response, increasing demand for preventive health services, and ensuring equity in access to care and underlying determinants of health;
(2) increase in health system capacity for disease treatment and response – through greater equipment, staff protections, and population resilience to health threats;[9]
(3) facilitation of global cooperation – providing equitable access despite economic inequalities, finances, and other factors; and
(4) resilience to other threats – including related pandemic threats, as discussed in Chapter 15, from antimicrobial resistance (Lal et al. 2021).

The COVID-19 pandemic has revealed that countries with strong primary healthcare systems are better able to respond to emergencies—while also maintaining essential public health services—with the COVID-19 response highlighting the necessity of global health law to codify UHC obligations in responding to future threats.

C. Advancing UHC under Global Health Law

Both the UN and WHO have committed to making UHC a top global health priority; however, global health policy to advance UHC has remained substantively imprecise, as seen in broad indicators of UHC under the SDGs, leaving states with unclear expectations of what UHC entails. Without specific direction in global health policy, states have developed various interpretations of UHC in national policies—diverging from each other in terms of health coverage, monitoring protocols, and government financing. Yet, even if national interpretations and policies are streamlined, UHC will be meaningless if spending is inadequate, care is ineffective, or governments are corrupt—undermining UHC's goals of equity and quality.[10] To overcome these limitations, global health law reforms will be necessary.

---

[9] Where global emergencies often lead to severe global shortages in critical resources, such as personal protective equipment (PPE) and medicines, core public health functions should be properly integrated into health services before, during, and after outbreaks—with UHC ensuring that governments control outbreaks while continuing routine health services and addressing social determinants of health (Adejumo and Adejumo 2021).

[10] Corruption, often seen where states face challenges to the rule of law, has the potential to undermine UHC, with corruption resulting from poor regulatory regimes and leading to neglect among policymakers, bribes for medical resources, and poor-quality services and medicines.

Global health law is essential to achieving UHC, with legal obligations providing a basis to:

(1) translate vision into action on sustainable development, setting standards to evaluate compliance with UHC and establishing a framework under the right to health;
(2) strengthen governance under national and global health institutions;
(3) implement fair, evidence-based health interventions; and
(4) build legal capacity for health (Gostin et al. 2020).

Codifying UHC under global health law can provide a basis for global health with justice. Global health justice requires not only improved population health, but fair distribution of the benefits of health—within and between countries. Thus, realizing the goals of equity in line with UHC cannot be done by creating only health-specific policies in a single country; the entire global health landscape must address a host of issues outside the health sector, including poverty, gender and racial inequality, and widespread lack of access to education, housing, and social support. In these challenging times for global health, UHC can foster global solidarity by keeping populations healthy and safe while ensuring no one is left behind (Gostin 2021).

States have sought to take up this need for global health law to codify UHC in ongoing reforms, with global health governance advancing UHC under reform proposals in the global health security agenda (GHSA), the amendments of the International Health Regulations (IHR), and the new pandemic treaty. Under the GHSA, UHC has become linked to health system strengthening under the new Legal Preparedness Action Package, focusing specifically on the role of law in developing systems and infrastructures that will allow countries to rapidly and effectively respond to public health emergencies (Ayala et al. 2022). As states approach revisions of the IHR, states already must invest in core health system capacities that are fundamental to protecting and promoting health (UN 2020), and amendments to the IHR must seek to advance pandemic preparedness and response through resilient health systems. Ongoing efforts to develop a new pandemic treaty, complemented by new financing mechanisms for health system strengthening, provide the greatest opportunity for the World Health Assembly to codify obligations to strengthen health system resilience with a view to achieving UHC. Proposals to strengthen UHC through this novel pandemic instrument will entail strengthening public health capacities to ensure continuity of health services and UHC during a pandemic response, ensuring recovery of national health systems through UHC, and enhancing domestic financing and international financial assistance for UHC—with UHC serving as a guiding principle for the instrument's implementation (WHO 2022). Taken together, these reforms across the global health landscape provide a path to advance UHC under law to realize global health with justice.

Conclusion

UHC is the future of global health governance, framing all action to advance health. Drawing from a long history of overarching global health agendas, WHO now seeks to align all global health action under the mantle of UHC. This is a daunting task. For this effort to succeed, global health governance must expand the global health landscape to encompass all the sectors and institutions that underlie health. Global health law can provide a foundation for these partnerships to address health holistically. For laws to positively impact health, they must shape more than health care, but also health determinants across sectors. Through UHC, these laws can ensure equity, accessibility, affordability, and quality.

Such a sweeping agenda will require reforms of global health law. Through these law reforms, global health leaders can ensure that health benefits provided under UHC are comprehensive and available to everyone throughout the world. Where UHC cannot be achieved by countries acting in isolation, UHC does not just require law, but global law that encompasses real commitments by state and non-state actors across the global community. Global health law can bring necessary governance and funding to bear: strengthening national health systems, providing international assistance, and creating a process through which wealthy countries can provide assistance to low- and middle-income countries. Ensuring that law reforms bring health improvements, such global reforms can also provide mechanisms for ensuring quality of coverage and accountability under law. This encompassing agenda can promote equity in global health, pooling resources among countries and targeting those resources to low-income areas. Developing these reforms under law can offer stability in the global health system that only the rule of law can provide.

Progress to advance UHC will continue to be impeded in the absence of global health law reforms, but ongoing law reforms provide hope for the advancement of UHC. Where UHC promises to deliver on a wide range of global health priorities—disease prevention, health promotion, and treatment for communicable and non-communicable diseases, as well as the capacity to prevent, detect, and respond to health emergencies—it offers that greatest promise to advance global health in the years to come. However, meeting this global health imperative demands strong health systems supported by strong legal foundations. Achieving UHC will thus be the greatest challenge facing global health leaders, but, in learning from past successes in the development of global health law, it is a challenge that can be met.

Questions for Consideration

1. What led to the imperative for WHO to codify primary healthcare obligations in the Declaration of Alma-Ata? How did the shift to "selective primary health care" undermine the comprehensive vision laid out in Alma-Ata?
2. How does health promotion relate to primary health care? How have international conferences on health promotion served to advance whole-of-government approaches to public health?
3. Why was it necessary for WHO to establish a Commission on Social Determinants of Health? How did the Commission seek to ensure that its recommendations would strengthen policy?
4. How did UHC become the focus of efforts to ensure a whole of government response to health? How have the UN and WHO differed in their approach to addressing UHC in global health governance?
5. What does it mean in practice to examine health in all policies? How did HiAP help to shape policy approaches to achieving UHC?
6. Why is UHC the principal target for advancing health under the SDGs? How is the UHC target assessed in global health governance?
7. Why is UHC central to the right to health? How does the right to health provide support for UHC implementation?
8. How has WHO leadership strengthened UHC efforts? What were the benefits of a UN General Assembly special session devoted to UHC?
9. How did limitations of UHC implementation undermine efforts to prevent, detect, and respond to the COVID-19 pandemic? Why should UHC be thought of as part of efforts to advance global health security?
10. How can ongoing global health law reforms codify obligations to implement UHC—at national and global levels? How would this codification of UHC in global health law provide a path to global health with justice?

Acknowledgments

The authors are grateful to Eric Friedman, Sarah Wetter, and Alexandra Finch for their editorial assistance; and to Sonam Shah, Erin Jones, Hanna Huffstetler, and Oliver Redsten for their research assistance in developing this final chapter.

References

Adejumo, Oludamilola Adebola and Oluseyi Ademola Adejumo. 2021."Recalling the Universal Health Coverage Vision and Equity in the COVID-19 Vaccine Distribution Plan." *Pan African Medical Journal* 39(1).

Ayala, Ana, Adam Brush, Shuen Chai, Jose Fernandez, Katherine Ginsbach, Katie Gottschalk, Sam Halabi et al. 2022. "Advancing Legal Preparedness Through the Global Health Security Agenda" *Journal of Law, Medicine & Ethics* 50: 200.

Catford, John. 2011. "Ottawa 1986: Back to the Future" *Health Promotion International* 26(2): ii163–ii167.

CESCR (Committee on Economic, Social, and Cultural Rights). 2000. "General Comment 14: The Right to the Highest Attainable Standard of Health (Art. 12)." August 11. E/C.12/2000/4.

Chapman, Audrey R. 2016. *Global Health, Human Rights, and the Challenge of Neoliberal Policies*. Cambridge: Cambridge University Press.

Colombo, Francesca, Zsuzsanna Jakab, and Juan Pablo Uribe. 2021. "Pathway to UHC: Three Priorities for Stronger, More Resilient, More Inclusive Health Systems." *World Bank Blogs*. December 10.

Djukanovic, Vojo, Edward Paul Mach, and WHO (World Health Organization). 1975. *Alternative Approaches to Meeting Basic Health Needs in Developing Countries: A Joint UNICEF/WHO Study*. Geneva: WHO.

Garrett, Laurie, A. Mushtaque, R. Chowdhury, and Ariel Pablos-Méndez. 2009. "All for universal health coverage" *Lancet* 374(9697): 1294–1299.

Ghebreyesus T. A. 2017. "All Roads Lead to Universal Health Coverage." *Lancet Global Health* 5(9): e839–e840.

Gostin, Lawrence O., Aleksandra Blagojevic, Simon Bland, Mandeep Dhaliwal, Ranieri Guerra, John T. Monahan. 2020. "Launching the Universal Health Coverage Legal Solutions Network." *Lancet* 395(10218): 112–113

Gostin, Lawrence O. 2021. "The Legal Determinants of Health: How Can We Achieve Universal Health Coverage and What Does it Mean?" *International Journal for Health Policy Management* 10(1): 1–4.

Hammonds, Rachel, Gorik Ooms, Moses Mulumba, and Allan Maleche. 2019. "UHC2030's Contributions to Global Health Governance that Advance the Right to Health Care: A Preliminary Assessment." *Health and Human Rights Journal* 21(2): 235–249.

Irwin, Alec, Nicole Valentine, Chris Brown, Rene Loewenson, Orielle Solar, Hilary Brown, Theadora Koller, and Jeanette Vega. 2006. "The Commission on Social Determinants of Health: Tackling the Social Roots of Health Inequities." *PLoS medicine* 3(6): e106.

Kickbusch, Ilona. 2007. "The Move Towards a New Public Health." *Promotion and Education* 14(2): 9.

Kickbusch, Ilona. 2010. "Health in All Policies: Where Do We Go from Here?" *Health Promotion International* 25(3): 261–264.

Lal, Arush, Ngozi A. Erondu, David L. Heymann, Githinji Gitahi, and Robert Yates. 2021. "Fragmented Health Systems in COVID-19: Rectifying the Misalignment between Global Health Security and Universal Health Coverage." *Lancet* 397(10268): 61–67.

Leppo, Kimmo, Eeva Ollila, Sebastián Peña, Matthias Wismar, and Sarah Cook . 2013. *Health in All Policies: Seizing Opportunities, Implementing Policies*. Helsinki: Ministry of Social Affairs and Health.

Mahler, Halfdan. 1978. "Justice in Health." *WHO Magazine*. May: 1.
Marmot, Michael, Sharon Friel, Ruth Bell, Tanja AJ Houweling, Sebastian Taylor, and Commission on Social Determinants of Health. 2008. "Closing the Gap in a Generation: Health Equity through Action on the Social Determinants of Health." *Lancet* 372(9650): 1661–1669.
McIntyre, Di and Filip Meheus. 2014. "Fiscal Space for Domestic fFunding of Health and Other Social Services." *Health, Economics, Policy, and Law* 12(2): 159–177.
Meier, Benjamin Mason. 2017. "Human Rights in the World Health Organization: Views of the Director-General Candidates." *Health and Human Rights* 19 (1): 293.
Meier, Benjamin Mason and Virginia Brás Gomes. 2018. "Human Rights Treaty Bodies: Monitoring, Interpreting and Adjudicating Health-Related Human Rights." In *Human Rights in Global Health: Rights-Based Governance for a Globalizing World*, edited by Benjamin Mason Meier and Lawrence Gostin, 509–535. New York: Oxford University Press.
Meier, Benjamin Mason and Lance Gable. 2013."US Efforts to Realise the Right to Health Through the Patient Protection and Affordable Care Act." *Human Rights Law Review* 13(1): 167–190.
Nakajima H. 1989. "Priorities and Opportunities for International Cooperation: Experiences in the WHO Wester Pacific Region." In *International Cooperation for Health: Problems, Prospects, and Priorities*, edited by Micheal R. Reich and Eiji Marui, 317–331. Dover: Auburn House.
Nygren-Krug H. 2019. "The Right(s) Road to Universal Health Coverage." *Health and Human Rights* 21(2): 215–228.
O'Connell, Thomas, Kumanan Rasanathan, and Mickey Chopra. 2014. "What Does Universal Health Coverage Mean?" *Lancet* 383: 277–279.
Ooms, Gorik, Claire Brolan, Natalie Eggermont, Asbjørn Eide, Walter Flores, Lisa Forman, Eric A. Friedman et al. 2013. "Univresal Health Coverage Anchored in the Right to Health." *Bulletin World Health Organization* 91(2): 2–2A.
Ooms, Gorik, Robert Marten, Attiya Waris, and Rachel Mary Hammonds. 2014. "Great Expectations for the World Health Organization: A Framework Convention on Global Health to Achieve Universal Health Coverage." *Public Health* 128(2): 173–178.
Ooms, Gorik, Laila A. Latif, Attiya Waris, Claire E. Brolan, Rachel Hammonds, Eric A. Friedman, Moses Mulumba, and Lisa Forman. 2014. "Is Universal Health Coverage the Practical Expression of the Right to Health Care?" *BMC International Health and Human Rights* 14(3): 1–7.
Pannenborg CO. 1979. *A New International Health Order: An Inquiry into the International Relations of World Health and Medical Care*. Alphen aan den Rijn: Sijthoff & Noordhoff.
Rasanathan, Kumanan. 2018. "10 Years After the Commission on Social Determinants of Health: Social Injustice Is Still Killing on a Grand Scale." *Lancet* 392(10154): 1176–1178.
Reddy, Srikanth K., Sumaira Mazhar, and Raphael Lencucha. 2018. "The Financial Sustainability of the World Health Organization and the Political Economy of Global Health Governance: A Review of Funding Proposals." *Globalization and Health* 14(119): 1–11.
Rifkin, Susan B. and Gill Walt. 1986. "Why Health Improves: Defining the Issues Concerning 'Comprehensive Primary Health Care'and 'Selective Primary Health Care.'" *Social Science and Medicine* 23(6): 559–566.
Saan, Hans. 2007. "Ottawa 1986 revisited." *Promotion and Education* 14(2): 11.
Sanders, David, Sulakshana Nandi, Ronald Labonté, Carina Vance, and Wim Van Damme. 2019. "From Primary Health Care to Universal Health Coverage—One Step Forward and Two Steps Back." *Lancet* 394(10199): 619–621.

Sridhar, Devi, Martin McKee, Gorik Ooms, Claudia Beiersmann, Eric Friedman, Hebe Gouda, Peter Hill, and Albrecht Jahn. 2015. "Universal Health Coverage and the Right to Health: From Legal Principle to Post-2015 Indicators." *International Journal of Health Services* 45(3): 495–506.

Ståhl, Timo. 2018. "Health in All Policies: From Rhetoric to Implementation and Evaluation—the Finnish experience." *Scandinavian Journal of Public Health* 46(20): 38–46.

Thompson, S. R., M. C. Watson, and S. Tilford. 2018."The Ottawa Charter 30 years On: Still an Important Standard for Health Promotion." *International Journal of Health Promotion and Education* 56, no. 2: 73–84.

UN (United Nations) General Assembly. 1966. "International Covenant on Economic, Social and Cultural Rights." December 16. Resolution 2200A(XXI).

UN General Assembly. 2019. "Political Declaration of the High-Level Meeting on Universal Health Coverage." October 18. A/RES/74/2.

UN. 2015. "Sustainable Development Goals." New York: UN.

UN. 2020. *Policy Brief: COVID-19 and Universal Health Coverage*. New York: UN.

Watkins, David A., Dean T. Jamison, T. Mills, T. Atun, Kristen Danforth, Amanda Glassman, In *Disease Control Priorities: Improving Health and Reducing B*, edited by Dean T. Jamison, Hellen Gelband, Susan Horton, Prabhat Jha, Ramanan Laxminarayan, Charles N. Mock, and Rachel Nugent. 1108–1120. Washington: The International Bank for Reconstruction and Development.

Wenham, Clare, Rebecca Katz, Charles Birungi, Lisa Boden, Mark Eccleston-Turner, Lawrence Gostin, Renzo Guinto et al. 2019. "Global Health Security and Universal Health Coverage: From a Marriage of Convenience to a Strategic, Effective Partnership." *BMJ Global Health* 4(1).

WHO (World Health Organization). 1946. *Constitution of the World Health Organization*. New York: WHO.

WHO. 1978. *Primary Health Care: Report of the International Conference of Primary Health Care Alma-Ata, USSR, September 6–12*. Geneva: WHO.

WHO. 1986. *Ottowa Charter for Health Promotion*. Geneva: WHO.

WHO. 2008. *Closing the Gap in a Generation: Health Equity through Action on the Social Determinants of Health*. Geneva: WHO.

WHO. 2011. *Rio Political Declaration on Social Determinants of Health*. Rio de Janeiro: WHO.

WHO. 2013a. *Practising a Health in All Policies Approach—Lessons for Universal Health Coverage and Health Equity*. Geneva: WHO.

WHO. 2013b. *World Health Report 2013*. Geneva: WHO.

WHO. 2014. *Making Fair Choices on the Path to Universal Health Coverage: Final Report of the WHO Consultative Group on Equity and Universal Health Coverage*. Geneva: WHO.

WHO. 2018. "Declaration of Astana: Global Conference on Primary Health Care: Astana, Kazakhstan." October 26. WHO/HIS/SDS/2018.61.

WHO. 2021. "Building Health Systems Resilience for Universal Health Coverage and Health Security during the COVID-19 Pandemic and Beyond: WHO Position Paper." WHO/UHL/PHCSP/2021.01.

WHO. 2022. "Conceptual Zero Draft for the Consideration of the Intergovernmental Negotiating Body at Its Third Meeting: Third Meeting of the Intergovernmental Negotiating Body to Draft and Negotiate a WHO Convention, Agreement or other International Instrument on Pandemic Prevention, Preparedness and Response." November 25. A/INB/3/3.

Afterword

Foundational Information for a New Generation

Steven Solomon

Thanks to the work of scholars like Professors Gostin and Meier, and the distinguished contributors to this foundational book, there is growing academic awareness of global health law as a defined and influential area of international law and global health. Bringing this awareness into a new generation, *Global Health Law & Policy* has broadened and deepened knowledge of this vitally important field. In doing so, this book will advance a key principle laid out in the Constitution of the World Health Organization, that "informed opinion and active co-operation on the part of the public are of the utmost importance in the improvement of the health of the people."

This principle of informed opinion and active cooperation is of growing importance in the field of global health, as revealed by the rise of misinformation during the COVID-19 pandemic.

Scientifically derived, evidence-based knowledge is critical to public health improvement. Public health depends upon the use of reliable information to safeguard the health of individuals within their communities and countries. This was true in September 1854, when John Snow, after careful investigation of cholera cases on a map, identified a single water pump as the source of a disease outbreak. With the removal of the pump handle, cases of cholera quickly diminished. This same principle remained true in January 2020, when WHO declared a public health emergency of international concern, identifying a novel strain of coronavirus as a global disease threat. Before the year ended, the first vaccine countermeasures were approved by regulatory authorities—a time frame for vaccine creation that had previously been considered impossible.

However, such scientific- and evidence-based approaches to global health governance face new challenges. While misinformation in public health has a long history—with uninformed opinion long presented as alternative opinion—the megaphone of social media has given unprecedented force to misinformation in global health debates.

Informed opinion will be crucial in framing the future of global health law.

The field of global health law is, first and foremost, a body of law and policy that is extraordinarily dynamic through its evolution. Empowered by principles of human rights, inherent dignity, and equality, states adopted the WHO Constitution, which reflected a revolutionary new approach to international public health: a binding international instrument, identifying health as a fundamental human right, and aimed at improving health outcomes for all people without distinction. Unlike predecessor institutions, the WHO Constitution is largely devoid of technical and epidemiological terminology, instead employing language of a legal, institutional, and legislative nature.

The Constitution establishes the legal principle of health as a fundamental right; it sets forth a definition of health itself ("a state of complete physical, mental and social well-being"); it establishes a "democratic" global governance mechanism (every country has the same voting power); and it provides powerful legal tools to allow countries to create additional normative instruments—both legally binding and non-binding. It has laid a foundation for seventy-five years of global health law.

In the decades since the end of World War II and the beginnings of WHO, global health law has moved from a theoretical concept to a defined and concrete body of international law.

Through its evolution, global health law has come to be concerned with the intersection of health and other areas of international law, such as trade regulation, intellectual property, and environmental law. The right to health has come to be recognized in a number of human rights instruments, including the International Covenant on Economic, Social and Cultural Rights and the Convention on the Rights of the Child. An encompassing set of international organizations—including the Food and Agriculture Organization of the United Nations (FAO), the United Nations Environment Programme (UNEP), and the World Organization for Animal Health (WOAH)—now seek to advance "One Health" under their respective mandates. Global economic governance institutions frequently make development, trade, and funding decisions that impact on global health.

These institutions are now engaged in an array of law and policy reforms to address lessons learned in the COVID-19 pandemic. Within WHO, these efforts include elaborating a possible new international treaty to better prepare for, and respond to, future pandemics; amendments to further strengthen the 2005 International Health Regulations; and reforms to strengthen global governance mechanisms, making them more transparent and inclusive, in order to improve management and accountability in global health emergencies. These reforms across the global governance landscape will reshape global health law. Taken together, these initiatives can advance global health law to ensure the foundational principle of health for all.

Information will be necessary to ensure the success of these law reforms. Reliable and broadly disseminated knowledge about what global health law is, and how global health law and policy works, has never been more important. Given recent efforts aimed at broadening engagement in global health governance, this information will be useful to individuals, public and private sector organizations, health practitioners, and governments.

With growing recognition of the multifaceted and dynamic nature of this body of law, global health law now forms part of the curricula in a rapidly increasing number of law, public policy, and public health schools; it is being "practiced" in legal offices in national health ministries and public and private sector organizations around the world; and, amid reforms, it is of direct and growing relevance to the health of every human being.

Empowered by the knowledge this book provides, future reforms will see more expansive more informed, and more effective engagement in the development, implementation, and application of global health law. The foundational information in this book will provide crucial information to support the next generation. As a new generation takes its seat at the policy table, this informed engagement will be, as identified by the WHO Constitution, "of the utmost importance in the improvement of the health of the people."

Index

For the benefit of digital users, indexed terms that span two pages (e.g., 52–53) may, on occasion, appear on only one of those pages.
Note: Tables, figures, and boxes are indicated by t, f, and b following the page number

access and benefit sharing (ABS) transactions, 423–24, 441–42
  ABS under global health law, 429–30
  all of the access, none of the benefits, 434–37
  pathogen access under Nagoya Protocol, 430–33
  pathogens as tradable commodities, 433–34
  evolution of pathogen sharing for global health security, 424–25
  from colonialism and common heritage of mankind to permanent sovereignty over natural resources, 425–27
  pathogens become sovereign assets, 427–29
  PIP Framework and, 431, 431b–32, 433, 434, 437–38, 440
  WHO seeks to reclaim authority over ABS, 437–38
  genetic sequence data, 439b, 440–41
  Pandemic Treaty negotiations, 441
  WHO's evolving approach to pathogen data, 438–40
Access to COVID-19 Tools (ACT) Accelerator (ACT-A), 138, 374b–77, 381–82, 386–87
accountability. *See also under* WHO Global Action Plan
  corporate, 346–53
  of World Trade Organization (WTO), 316
accountability for health in humanitarian contexts, rising legal responses to advance, 489
  legal institutional development for accountability, 493–94
  litigation for accountability, 491–92
  monitoring for accountability: protecting health systems amid rising conflicts, 489–91
  reparations for accountability, 492–93

2030 Agenda for Sustainable Development (2030 Agenda), 459b–60, 535. *See also* Sustainable Development Goals
  adoption of, 81–82, 259, 265, 535
  advancing health under, 265–74
  and development and implementation of global health law, 274–79
  health across, 269–71
  health as a central goal of, 266–69
  overview, 81–83, 106, 259–60, 279–80, 458
  role for global health law in, 274–76
  universal health coverage (UHC) and, 536b–37, 537
air pollution
  climate change and, 505
  defined, 234–35
alcohol, 180, 196b–97
  rising threats from, 196–97
Alma-Ata Declaration, 84–85
  Health for All and, 70b, 123, 527–29
  overview and nature of, 527–29
  vision of health, 103
  and WHO as global health leader, 70b, 70
animal health. *See* World Organisation for Animal Health
Anthropocene, creating the, 502–8
antimicrobial resistance (AMR), 395–96, 416–17
  achieving a global AMR response, 410
  addressing AMR through a pandemic treaty, 413–14
  addressing AMR through a stand-alone treaty, 414–16, 415b–16
  addressing AMR through regulations across organizations, 410–13
  AMR governance beyond WHO, 405–6
  AMR governance through WHO, 404–5
  global governance responses to rising, 402
  binding international law standards applicable to, 404–6

antimicrobial resistance (AMR), (cont.)
  limitations of international institutions: rise of non-state actors, 407–9
  non-binding AMR agreements, 402–3
  interdependent challenges of rising global, 396–401
  International Health Regulations (IHR) and, 404–5, 410–14
  One Health and, 396, 397, 399, 402–3, 405, 407, 410–13, 414–15
  requires action to improve access, conservation, innovation, and prevention, 398–400
  requires global collective solutions, 401
  undermines global progress for sustainable development, 400–1
antimicrobial resistance (AMR) actors, 407–9
  constellation of, 407f
antimicrobial resistance (AMR) regulations. *See also* antimicrobial resistance
  across organizations, 410–13
  relevant institutions for, 411t
antiretroviral therapy (ART), 78b
armed conflict, law of. *See* international humanitarian law

Beijing Platform for Action (BPFA), 456–57
Bill and Melinda Gates Foundation, 351–52, 370b, 377, 386
Biodiversity Convention. *See* Convention on Biological Diversity
biopiracy, 424–26
Bloomberg, Michael R., 185, 186f
breast-milk substitutes. *See* International Code of Marketing of Breast-milk Substitutes
Bretton Woods Conference (1944), 286–87, 313
Broad Street cholera outbreak, 551
Brundtland Report, 236

Cairo Conference. *See* International Conference on Population and Development (ICPD) in Cairo
Caracas Declaration, 211–12
Caribbean Community (CARICOM), 180–81
Chan, Margaret, 55–56, 184b, 347, 435, 531f, 533
Charter of the United Nations (UN Charter), 29–30
  human rights and, 209
  purposes and functions, 28, 29, 42, 43, 93–94, 377–78, 480

WHO and, xv, 29–30
children's rights. *See* Convention on the Rights of the Child
China
  COVID-19 and, 56–57, 439b
  2002–2004 SARS outbreak and, 55–56, 154–55
climate change, 501–2, 503, 520–21. *See also* United Nations Framework Convention on Climate Change
  adaptation, 513–14
  creating the Anthropocene, 502–5
    origins of global governance for climate and health, 505–8
  crime of ecocide, 519–20
  equitable access to technology, 518–19
  global health disaster: mitigation, adaptation, and reducing vulnerabilities, 508
  global health policy response, 512–14
  responding to climate change under international law, 508–12
  human rights, 516–18
  and inequities, 506b–7
  mitigation, 512–13
  planetary health, 514–16
  public health impacts, 502–5, 503f
  weather events, extreme, 503
climate events, extreme, 503
climate justice, good governance for, 511b
Coalition for Epidemic Preparedness Innovations (CEPI)
  Ebola and, 374, 374b–77
  mission creep, 374b–77
  overview and nature of, 375t
codes of conduct. *See* corporate codes of conduct
Cold War, 66–67
  decolonization and rise of Non-Aligned Movement, 68–70
  superpower rivalry in global health, 67–68
commercial determinants of health (CDoH), 339–40
  expanding CDoH and evolving doctrines of CSR in global health, 340–46
Commission on the Status of Women (CSW), 449
community inclusion. *See* deinstitutionalization and community inclusion challenges to mental health
community living
  Convention on the Rights of Persons with Disabilities (CRPD) and, 217–19, 218b–19

INDEX   557

debates on, 218b–19
Comprehensive Global Monitoring Framework, 183–84, 183t
compulsory license, 320–23, 321b–22, 406
Constitution of the World Health Organization. See WHO Constitution
constructivist legal theories, 39, 47–48
Convention on Biological Diversity (CBD)
  ABS and, 423–24, 426–27, 429–30, 431, 433, 434, 439–41
  Ebola and, 436–37
  genetic resources and, 426–27, 428b
  Indonesian virus sharing incident and, 428b
  Nagoya Protocol and, 430, 431, 433, 438–39, 442
  objectives, 426
  PIP Framework and, 431b–32, 433, 434, 438–40
  WHO and, 429–30, 431
Convention on the Elimination of All Forms of Discrimination against Women (CEDAW), 96t, 244, 452–53
Convention on the Rights of Persons with Disabilities (CRPD), 205, 214f, 219, 221
  Advocacy to Support CRPD Development, 213, 214f
  conflict with Convention on the Rights of the Child (CRC), 218b–19
  CRPD Committee, 217–18, 220, 222–23
  implementing, 219–20
  Inter-Agency Standing Committee (IASC) Guidelines and, 224–25
  legal obligations, 216
    community living, 217–19, 218b–19
    legal capacity, 216–17
  overview, 96t, 212
  participatory processes in developing, 213–14
  transition from medical model to social and human rights model, 215–16
Convention on the Rights of the Child (CRC), 96t, 218b–19, 242
corporate accountability through global policy, 346–53
corporate actors in global health, legal obligations of, 353–58
corporate codes of conduct, 347–49
corporate regulation and accountability, domestic sources of, 351–53
corporate self-regulation, 339–40, 347, 348b–49
  self-regulatory codes, 347–48
corporate social responsibility (CSR), 339–40, 359
  limitations of early efforts to promote, 341–42
  origins of CSR to advance public health, 344–45
country coordinating mechanisms (CCMs), 77, 368–69
COVAX (COVID-19 Vaccines Global Access), 138, 381–84, 382f
  challenges for COVAX funding in the COVID-19 response, 383b–84
  COVAX Advance Market Commitment (AMC), 382–83, 383b–84, 384
COVID-19, xii, 551
  changes wrought by, 381–84
  China and, 56–57, 439b
  a global threat to global health governance, 163–65
  human rights and, 107–9
  International Health Regulations (IHR) and, xii, 55–57, 57b–58, 136–38, 147–48, 249b–50
  and the pandemics of tomorrow, 162–68
  pathogen sharing amid, 439b, 439–40
  public health emergencies of international concern (PHEICs) and, 55–57, 159, 163–65 (see also public health emergencies of international concern)
  resolutions from UN bodies focused on, 163–65, 164t
  as revealing the importance of One Health, 249b–50
  universal health coverage (UHC) and, 539, 541–42, 543
  World Health Assembly and, 53–56, 135, 136–37, 163, 165
COVID-19 diplomacy
  challenging WHO in, 136–38
  and the crisis of multilateralism, 136–39
COVID-19 response. See also COVID-19
  hard law in, 55–58, 57b–58
  soft law in, 53–55, 57b–58
  weaknesses of global economic governance in, 301
    failure of "pandemic bonds," 301–2
    limited influence of pandemic response, 302–4
    WHO daily press conference on, 134f, 134
COVID-19 vaccination, 54–55
  limitations of World Bank-IMF joint strategies on, 302b–3
COVID-19 Vaccines Global Access. See COVAX

crimes against humanity, 27n.8
  defined, 478
  ICC adjudication for, 493–94, 519
  Nuremberg Trials to prosecute, 209–10, 210f
Declaration of Caracas, 211–12
Declaration of the United Nations Conference on the Human Environment. *See* Stockholm Declaration of 1972
Declaration on the Rights of Mentally Retarded Persons (MR Declaration), 209–10
Declaration on the Right to Development, 292–93, 304
decolonization
  decolonization and rise of Non-Aligned Movement, 68–69
  decolonization struggles and primary health care revolution, 123–25
  of global health, 109–10, 246–47, 379–81
  rising imperative of, 83–85
  of human rights, 110
deinstitutionalization and community inclusion
  challenges to mental health, 219
  advancing mental health care, 220–21
  humanitarian contexts, 223–25
  implementing CRPD, 219–20
  public health emergencies, 222–23
demand reduction, 178–80, 179t
development, 297–98. *See also* economic development policy; international development
  right to, 292–93, 304
2030 Development Agenda. *See* 2030 Agenda for Sustainable Development
diplomacy. *See also* global health diplomacy
  concept of, 119
disabilities. *See* Convention on the Rights of Persons with Disabilities; mental disabilities
disabled peoples' organizations (DPOs), 213
Disabled Rights Monitor (DRM), 222
disease surveillance
  developing core surveillance capacities, 157
  from a state-centered to a multi-actor, 156–57
Dispute Settlement Body (DSB). *See also under* WTO
  accountability through a, 316
Doctors' Trial, 478–79. *See also* Nuremburg trials
Doha Declaration on TRIPS and Public Health, 52b, 321, 321b–22, 322–23
Dunant, Henri, 475

Earth Charter, advancement of international environmental law through, 236–38

Earth Summit (1992), 236–37, 426
  Global Forum, 236, 237f
Ebola. *See* Western African Ebola virus epidemic
ecocide, the crime of, 519–20
economic crises, mitigation of health impacts of, 297–98
2007–2008 economic crisis reshaping global economic governance, 295–96
economic development policy, 285–86, 305. *See also* international development
  development policy, intersectionality, and public health, 293–300
  evolution toward a nexus with global health, 286
  emergence of economic development governance after World War II, 286–87
  evolving development paradigms, 287–88
  neoliberalism, 288–92
  rise of human development and the nexus with global health, 291–93
economic institutions. *See also* World Bank
  implementing SDGs, 299b
electronic nicotine delivery systems (ENDS), 195–96. *See also* vaping
emergency declarations. *See also* public health emergencies of international concern
  as a governance tool, 157
energy
  establishment of UN-energy, 240–41
  right to, 244
environmental governance, UNEP leadership in, 238–39
environmental health, 231–32, 251–52
  advancing human rights for a healthy environment and, 241–45
  through environmental justice, 245–50
  just transitions within planetary boundaries, 250–51
  WHO guidelines, standards, and roadmaps on, 239–40
environmental justice. *See under* environmental health
environmental law, international
  advancement through "Earth Charter," 236–38
  evolution of public health as concern under, 232–36
  interlinkages between health and the environment under international law, 232–38
  normative foundations of environmental protection through global governance, 238–45
environmental racism, 246–47

INDEX   559

environmental risk factors, expanding UN efforts to address, 238–41
equity and equality in global health governance. *See also* human rights, equity, and social justice
  advancing, 105–6
  emergence of, 98–99
eugenics, 27–28, 208–9, 448–49
European Union (EU), 126
extraterritorial obligations to address global threats, 108–9, 353

feminism, 447–48, 451, 453–54. *See also* sexual and reproductive health and rights
2007–2008 financial crisis reshaping global economic governance, 295–96
Financial Intermediary Fund (FIF), 139, 385
Food and Agriculture Organization of the United Nations (FAO), 402–3, 405–6. *See also* Quadripartite collaboration
food security, climate change and, 504
Fore, Henrietta, 541*f*
Foundation for a Smoke Free World, 347n.5
Framework Convention on Alcohol Control, diplomatic efforts to develop, 196*b*–97
Framework Convention on Global Health (FCGH), 111, 111*b*–12
Framework Convention on Tobacco Control (FCTC), xii, 186
  adoption of, 178–79
  Conference of the Parties (COP), 186–87, 195–96
  objectives, general obligations, and provisions, 179–80, 179*t*
  SDG 3 and, 275
  WHO and, 178–79, 186, 196–97, 274
Framework of Engagement with Non-State Actors (FENSA), 128
"freedom from want," 261
free trade, GATT and, 314–15. *See also* General Agreement on Trade and Tariffs
free trade agreements (FTAs), 328–29
funding agencies in global health governance, 365–66, 375*t*, 387–88
  as "colonial," 379–81
  development of modern, 372–81
  proliferation of, 369–71
    focus of funding agencies on access to medicines, 371–72
    rise of, 366–72
funding institutions, continuing challenges of, 381
  changes wrought by COVID-19, 381–84
  changing landscape, 384
    need for greater coordination, 386–87
    push for increased funding, 385–86

G7 (Group of Seven), 126, 408
  political networks under, 131–32
G20 (Group of 20), 139, 408
  political networks under, 131–32
Gates, Bill and Melinda, 370*b*, *See also* Bill and Melinda Gates Foundation
Gavi, the Vaccine Alliance, 371–73
  development of, 370*b*, 371
  overview and nature of, 78–79, 370, 375*t*
Gender, Equity and Human Rights team (WHO), 112
gender equality, 457–59. *See also* sexual orientation and gender identity (SO/GI) issues
gender-expansive framework for human rights, advancing a, 463–64
General Agreement on Trade and Tariffs (GATT), 311
  challenges to realizing free trade through, 314–15
  postwar development of, 312–15
genetic resources, 426–27, 428*b*
genetic sequence data, 439*b*, 440–41
Geneva Conventions
  Additional Protocols, 480, 481*t*, 483–85, 498
  civilian protections--maintaining health systems, 482–83
  First Geneva Convention, 475–76, 480–95
  Fourth Geneva Convention (1949), 479–80, 481*t*, 482–85, 498
  general principles, 482–83
  Geneva Convention of 1864 (*see* First Geneva Convention)
  Geneva Convention on the Wounded and Sick (1929), 476–77
  Geneva Conventions of 1949 (*see* Fourth Geneva Convention)
Geneva Group (United Nations), 126
Germany, 27–28, 208–9
Ghebreyesus, Tedros Adhanom, xiii, 127–28, 542
  elected WHO Director-General, 127–28, 538–39
  photographs of, 186*f*, 224*f*, 541*f*
Global Action Plan (GAP), 272–73, 275–76
  for Healthy Lives and Well-Being for All, 272–73, 275–76, 299*b*
Global Alliance on Vaccines and Immunizations, 78–79. *See also* Gavi
Global Compact. *See* United Nations Global Compact
Global Conference on Primary Health Care (Astana, 2018), 540–41

2007–2008 global financial crisis reshaping global economic governance, 295–96
Global Fund to Fight AIDS, Tuberculosis and Malaria, 377–78
and the birth of funding agencies, 93–99
creation, 93–94
grants, 77
overview, 368, 375t
Transitional Working Group, 368
Global Gag Rule (Mexico City policy), 462
global governance
bringing together hard and soft law across, 58–59
global health requires, 21–28
requires global law, 28–34
global health
a common agenda for, 80
establishing a development agenda for new millennium, 80–81
new agenda for sustainable development, 81–84
concept of, 16–21, 266
decolonization of, 246–47, 379–81
defined, 274
global health diplomacy, 119–20, 139–40
in an age of uncertainty, 133–39
and the complexification of global health governance, 125–33
and first UN High-Level Meeting on NCDs, 180–81, 181b, 182–83
HIV/AIDS as turning point in, 124b–25
international cooperation through, 120–25
origins of diplomacy to prevent disease, 120–21
within WHO, 125–29
global health governance, 72–73
contemporary global health landscape, 73
international governments, 74–75
national governments, 73–74
non-government initiatives, 75–76 (*see also* non-governmental organizations)
transnational corporations, 76–77
partnerships among state and non-state actors, 77–79
role of non-state actors and experts in, 128–29
global health landscape
contemporary, 73
expanding, 66–72
global health law
as an evolving field, 5–7
definition, 4–5, 274
future directions, 410–16

global health law and policy
addressing determinants of health through, 526–32
global health diplomacy influencing, 129–33 (*see also* global health diplomacy)
the challenge of coordination, 132–33
multi-stakeholder initiatives, 132
(*see also* public–private partnerships)
UN engagement, 130–31
as means to advance norms in global health, 99–106
Global Health Law Consortium, xi
global health policy. *See* global health law and policy
global health security, 73–74, 131
countering the threat of novel and re-emerging diseases, 154–62
and international cooperation through law, 300–4
Global Health Security Agenda (GHSA), 136, 161–62
International Health Regulations (IHR) and, 161–62
prioritizing AMR, 408, 408b–9
purpose, 136
universal health coverage (UHC) and, 544–45
globalization, 1
neoliberal, 80–81, 294
Global Malaria Eradication Programme, 152b, 366–67
Global Network for Health in All Policies, 535. *See also* Health in All Policies
Global North and Global South, structural inequities between, 246–47
Global Preparedness Monitoring Board, 300–1
Global Smallpox Eradication Programme, 150–51
Global Strategy for Infant and Young Child Feeding (UNICEF), 263b–64
Global Strategy for the Prevention and Control of Noncommunicable Diseases, 178
Global Strategy on Diet, Physical Activity, and Health, 180
Global Strategy to Reduce the Harmful Use of Alcohol, 180, 196b–97
governance institutions, new, 25–27
greenhouse gas (GHG) emissions, 502–3, 503f, 512–13. *See also* climate change
Group of 20. *See* G20
Group of Seven. *See* G7
Guantanamo Bay detention camp, 491–92

INDEX 561

Guidelines on the Inclusion of Persons with Disabilities in Humanitarian Action (IASC Guidelines), 224–25

hard law. *See* soft law: hard law and
health. *See also specific topics*
   definitions, 16–17, 212
      WHO definition, 43, 70*b*, 122, 269–70
      scope of the term, 122, 212
   health, nutrition, and population (HNP) programming, World Bank, 290–92
   HNP Strategy, 291–92
"Health, Nutrition and Population" SDGs, 299*b*
health emergencies. *See* public health emergencies
Health for All strategy (WHO), 366
   Alma Ata Declaration and, 70*b*, 123, 527–29
   primary health care and, 69, 70*b*, 123–24
   Sustainable Development Goals (SDGs) and, 83*b*, 279
   universal health coverage (UHC) and, 539
Health in All Policies (HiAP), 140, 526
   universal health coverage (UHC) and, 532–34
   WHO focus on, 533–35
health promotion, 526, 529
   international conferences on, 529–30
healthy environment. *See also* environmental health
   right to a, 244–45
Healthy Lives and Well-Being for All, 272–73, 275–76, 299. *See also* Sustainable Development Goal 3
High-Level Political Forum on Sustainable Development (HLPF), 272
HIV/AIDS, 78*b*, 80–81. *See also* Global Fund to Fight AIDS, Tuberculosis and Malaria; UNAIDS
   and rise of health and human rights movement, 153–54
   and the soft law response, 51–52, 52*b*, 53
   as turning point in global health diplomacy, 124*b*–25
   WHO and, 50–51
Holocaust, 27–28, 208–9
horizontal vs. vertical health interventions, 2–3
human development, 261–62, 286
   rise of, 291–93
Humanitarian Charter, 487

humanitarian response, rise of non-state public health actors in the, 486–87. *See also* international humanitarian law (IHL)
human rights. *See also* "health and human rights" movement; Universal Declaration of Human Rights
   amid public health emergencies, 107–8
   climate change and, 516–18
   COVID-19 and, 107–9
   in global health law, 100–5
   "health and human rights" movement, 100–2
      birth of, 100*b*–1
      HIV/AIDS pandemic and the rise of, 153–54
human rights law, international
   businesses and, 354–56
      proposed treaty on, 355, 355*b*
   non-communicable diseases (NCDs) and, 192–93
human rights mainstreaming in global health governance, 98
human rights norms, 102
   codifying under international law, 93–98
   framing global health policy, 103
   neglect of, 297–98
human rights treaties, 464, 516. *See also* human rights law; specific treaties
   core international, 95, 96*t*
   under international law, as basis for public health, 94–98
   mainstreaming human rights across the UN, 103–5
   right to, 70*b*, 107, 110, 242
      birth of a, 94*b*–95
      definition and scope of the term, 270n.4
      ICESCR and, 94, 98, 108–9, 242, 323, 516, 537–38
      implementing the, 102–3
   to water and sanitation, 242–43
   WTO recognizes health and, 326–28
human rights, equity, and social justice
   bringing together, 110–13
   under the SDGs, 106
   origin in global health, 92–99
   philosophical foundations, 92–93
Human Rights Guidelines for Pharmaceutical Companies in Relation to Access to Medicines, 356–57

Indonesian virus sharing incident, 428*b*
industry self-regulation. *See* corporate self-regulation

562 INDEX

infectious disease, 147–48, 168–69. *See also specific topics*
   climate change and, 503–4
   evolution of international law on, 148–54
   prevention of, and antimicrobial resistance (AMR), 400 (*see also* antimicrobial resistance)
intellectual property (IP) protection, 319–20, 325–26
intellectual property (IP) rights, 318b–19, 319, 320. *See also* compulsory license, TRIPS
Inter-Agency Coordination Group for AMR (IACG), 403
Intergovernmental Negotiating Body (INB), 137b, 331–32, 441
Intergovernmental Panel on Climate Change (IPCC), 507–8
internally displaced persons (IDPs) in conflict-affected settings, health of, 485b–86
international armed conflicts (IACs), 484–85
International Code of Marketing of Breast-milk Substitutes, 50
   adoption of, 342b–43, 348b–49
   developing, 342b–43
International Committee of the Red Cross (ICRC), 478, 483–84
   establishment as humanitarian institution, 475–76, 476b
International Conference on Health Promotion, 529
International Conference on Population and Development (ICPD) in Cairo, 454–56, 455f
   Programme of Action (POA), 456–57
International Conference on Primary Health Care (Alma-Ata, 1978), 69, 69f, 70b, 123, 124f, 527
International Court of Justice, 42–43
International Covenant on Economic, Social, and Cultural Rights (ICESCR), 94, 98, 108–9, 242, 378
   right to health and, 94, 98, 108–9, 242, 323, 516, 537–38
   right to water and, 242–43
International Criminal Court (ICC), 493–94, 519
international development
   early efforts to promote (economic), 261–62
   evolving relationships between health and, 260–65
international governance. *See also* global governance
   from sanitary conferences to permanent institutions, 23–25.*See also* International Sanitary Conferences

international health
   concept of, 2, 266
   origins, 21–23
international health law
   birth of law across nations to prevent disease and promote health, 40–46
   origins, 40–42
international health order, rise of an, 23–25
International Health Partnership for UHC 2030, 536
International Health Regulations (IHR). *See also* International Sanitary Regulations of 1951
   2030 Agenda and, 274–75
   aligning IHR and pandemic treaty to strengthen global health governance, 167–68
   amendments/revisions to, 55–56, 59, 136–38, 147–48, 155–57, 405, 410, 413–14
   antimicrobial resistance (AMR) and, 404–5, 410–14
   application in responding to public health emergencies, 159–61
   core objective, 150
   COVID-19 and, xii, 55–57, 57b–58, 136–38, 147–48, 249b–50
   framing IHR for 21st century, 156
   an expanded reach and scope, 156–57
   Global Health Security Agenda (GHSA) and, 161–62
   limitations, 156, 157, 158–59
   One Health and, 247–48, 249b–50, 410–12
   overview and nature of, xii, 404–5, 411t
   PHEICs and, 55–57, 157, 159–61, 163, 165, 166, 166b, 404
   Review Committee, 160
   SARS as catalyzing IHR reform, 154–57
   WHO and, xii, 55–57, 57b–58, 147–48, 150–51, 154–55, 156–59, 404–5, 410, 413
   World Health Assembly and, xii, 55–56, 57b–58, 59, 136–37, 150, 154, 155–56, 162–63, 165
international humanitarian law (IHL), 473–74, 494–95
   birth of, 474–89
   and changing nature of contemporary conflict, 480–89
   combatants vs. noncombatants, 474–75
   distinction, principle of, 482
   evolving gaps in, 484–86
International Labor Organization, 45–46, 261
International Military Tribunal at Nuremberg (Nuremberg Trials), 209–10, 210f
International Military Tribunal for the Far East (IMTFE), 478n.4

INDEX   563

International Monetary Fund (IMF)
 functions, 287
 structural adjustment programs under, 288–90
International Sanitary Conferences, 121
 first conference (Paris, 1851), 23–24, 41b
International Sanitary Conventions, 149
 first (Venice, 1892), 41b, 121, 148–49
 preamble, 24b
International Sanitary Regulations of 1951, CP633 n.5, 44–45, 150. *See also* International Health Regulations

Joint United Nations Programme on HIV/AIDS (UNAIDS), 51–52, 75, 153–54
jus in bello, 474–75. *See also* international humanitarian law

Karl Brandt, United States v., 478–79, 479f
Kennedy, Edward, 124f
Kyoto Protocol, 509–10

law. *See also specific topics*
 as a foundation of global health, 2–4
 vs. policy, 47
League of Nations, 26–27, 476–77
 Health Organization of the League of Nations, 26f, 26–27, 121, 122
League of Nations Health Organization (LNHO), 26–27, 26f, 121, 122
Legal Preparedness Action Package (GHSA), 162, 544–45
lesbian, gay, bisexual, and transgender (LGBT). *See* sexual orientation and gender identity (SO/GI) issues
loss and damage (climate change)
 compensating for, 516–17, 517b–18
 concept of, 517b–18

Mahler, Halfdan, 123, 124f, 527
malaria, 26f. *See also* Global Fund to Fight AIDS, Tuberculosis and Malaria
Malaria Eradication Programme (WHO), 152b, 366–67
Mann, Jonathan, 100b–1, 101f
Marmot, Michael G., 316, 531f
maternal mortality, 457–58
Medicines Patent Pool, 325–26
mental disabilities, 209–12, 218. *See also* mental health
 evolution of international standards to address, 209–11, 210f
mental health, 205–6, 207, 225–26. *See also specific topics*
 amid conflict, 223b–24
 climate change and, 504
 longstanding threats to human rights in, 206
 development of institutions and complete removal of rights, 207–8
 evolution of international standards, 209–11
 Nazi crimes, 208–9
 regional advancements, 211–12
 removing capacity and secluding from community, 206–7
mental health in all policies, 220, 221, 225
mental illness, 207, 208–9, 210, 210b–11, *See also* mental health
"merchants of doubt," 347
MERS-CoV (Middle East Respiratory Syndrome coronavirus), 435
Mexico City policy. *See* Global Gag Rule
Millennium Declaration, 81, 262, 263b–64, 457–58
Millennium Development Goals (MDGs), 266–69
 advancing health policy under, 263b–64
 birth of, 81, 260, 262–64
 establishing a development agenda for new millennium, 81
 learning from the limitations of, 264–65
 MDG 3, 457–58
 MDG 4, 263, 263b–64
 MDG 5, 263, 457–58
 MDG 6, 263
 Millennium Declaration and, 81, 259, 262, 263b–64
 overview and nature of, 81, 259, 262–63, 457–58, 535
 SDGs and, 80, 81–84, 266–69, 271–72, 298, 299b, 457–58, 459b–60, 535
 sexual and reproductive health and rights (SRHR) and, 459b–60
Millennium Summit, 81, 259, 262
Mofokeng, Tlaleng, 465f
monkeypox (mpox), 166–67
 and governance shifts in WHO's emergency decision-making, 166b
multilateralism
 COVID-19 diplomacy and the crisis of, 136–39
 PIP Framework and, 431, 431b–32, 437–40
multinational corporations (MNCs)/multinational enterprises. *See* transnational corporations

Nagoya Protocol
 Convention on Biological Diversity (CBD) and, 430, 431, 433, 438–39, 442
 pathogen access under, 430–33
 PIP Framework and, 433, 434, 437–40
"naming and shaming" tactics, 47

564 INDEX

nationally determined contributions (NDCs), 510–11
Nazi Germany, 27–28, 208–9
neoliberalism, 71, 123–24, 288–92, 289b–90
    neoliberal globalization, 80–81, 294
    neoliberal reforms, 71, 80–81, 288–90. *See also* neoliberalism
Nestlé, boycott of, 342b–43, 343f, 348b–49
New International Economic Order (NIEO), 425
Non-Aligned Movement, rise of the, 68–69
non-communicable diseases (NCDs), 175–76, 198
    broader legal environment of, 191–92
    challenges and opportunities for global governance of, 191–93
    facing new threats, 193–97
    global targets for reductions in NCD mortality and risk factors, 183t
    NCD Action Plan (2008–2013), 180
    rise of NCDs in a globalizing world, 176–82
    shared global governance of, 182–90
    WHO and UN align normative instruments on, 187–90
    WHO normative instruments and UN declarations shaping governance of, 187, 188f
    World Health Assembly and, 178–79, 182–83, 187
non-governmental organizations (NGOs), 75–76
    and access to medicines, 372
    antimicrobial resistance (AMR) and, 409
    FENSA, WHO, and, 128, 128b–29, 129
non-international armed conflicts (NIACs), 484–85
norms. *See also* human rights norms
    in global health, 112–13
    global health law and policy as means to advance, 99–106
    old and new challenges to, 107–12
    norm setting beyond treaty law, 33–34
Nuremberg Trials to prosecute crimes against humanity, 209–10, 210f
nutrition. *See* health, nutrition, and population (HNP) programming

obesity, 184
    failure of global health governance, 184b
obesity prevention, continuing obstacles to, 194–95
Office International des Epizooties (OIE), 126, 247–48. *See also* World Organisation for Animal Health (WOAH)

Office International d'Hygiene Publique (OIHP), 25, 41b
One Health, 231–32, 245–46
    antimicrobial resistance (AMR) and, 396, 397, 399, 402–3, 405, 407, 410–13, 414–15
    COVID-19 as revealing the importance of, 249b–50
    defined, 248, 248f
    origin, 247
    overview and nature of, 249
    planetary health and, 245–46, 250, 515–16
    from Tripartite to Quadripartite governance, 247–50
opioid crisis and pharmaceutical industry's self-regulation of drug marketing activities, 348b–49
Ottawa Charter for Health Promotion, 529–30
"Our Common Future" (Brundtland Report), 236
ozone depletion, 235–36

Pan American Health Organization (PAHO), 121, 211–12
Pan American Sanitary Bureau, 25, 121
pandemic bonds, 385
    failure of, 301–2
Pandemic Emergency Financing (PEF) Facility, 301–2
Pandemic Fund, 303–4
Pandemic Influenza Preparedness Framework (PIP Framework), 432
    ABS and, 431, 431b–32, 433, 434, 437–38, 440
    adoption, 431
    Convention on Biological Diversity (CBD) and, 431b–32, 433, 434, 438–40
    MERS and, 435
    multilateralism and, 431, 431b–32, 437–40
    Nagoya Protocol and, 433, 434, 437–40
    overview and nature of, 431
    WHO and, 431, 431b–32, 432, 435, 437–39
pandemic treaty
    addressing AMR through a, 413–14
    International Treaty on Pandemic Prevention, Preparedness and Response (Pandemic Treaty), 162–63, 165, 249b–50, 386–87
    aligning IHR and pandemic treaty to strengthen global health governance, 167–68
    developing the, 136, 137b
    potential impact, 331–32
Paris Agreement, 509–12, 511b–18b, 518–19

INDEX 565

partnerships. *See also* public–private partnerships
developing partnerships under global health law, 79–80
global health, 78b, 78–79
patent pool for medicines, 325–26
pathogen sharing. *See* access and benefit sharing (ABS) transactions
pharmaceutical industry/pharmaceutical corporations, 76–77. *See also* transnational corporations
in global health, 356–57
self-regulation of prescription drug marketing activities, 348b–49
plain tobacco packaging, 326–27, 327b, 327f
planetary health, 245–46, 250–51, 514–16
One Health and, 245–46, 250, 515–16
population control, 450–51, 450b
programming
population control policies, early, 448–50, 450b
populism, right-wing, 461–63
positivists and soft vs. hard law, 39, 47
poverty
focusing global policy on vicious cycle linking health and, 262–64
World Bank and, 288
precautionary principle, 482
President's Emergency Plan for AIDS Relief (PEPFAR), 365, 371–72
primary health care. *See also* International Conference on Primary Health Care
Health for All strategy (WHO) and, 69, 70b, 123–24
limitations, 528b–29
primary health care revolution, decolonization struggles and the, 123–25
selective, 71, 123–24, 367, 528, 528b–29
Principles for the Protection of Persons with Mental Illness (MI Principles), 210
advancing rights under, 210b–11
private international law, 40n.1
proportionality, principle of, 482
public health, 73. *See also specific topics*
government authority for, 19–21
from individual health to, 16–19
nature of, 16–17, 19
public health emergencies
application of IHR in responding to, 159–61
changes wrought by, 381–86
and deinstitutionalization and community inclusion challenges to mental health, 222–23
human rights amid, 107–8

public health emergencies of international concern (PHEICs)
antimicrobial resistance (AMR) and, 404
COVID-19 and, 55–57, 159, 163–65
defined, 157
Ebola and, 160b–61, 161
International Health Regulations (IHR) and, 55–57, 157, 159–61, 163, 165, 166, 166b, 404
WHO and, 157, 160, 160b–61, 161, 163, 166–67, 166b
public international law, 40n.1
public–private partnerships (PPPs), 132
and legal obligations of corporate actors, 357–58
public–private funding initiatives, 365, 369–70, 378
stages in development and implementation of, 132
vaccines and, 78–79, 138, 358, 369–71, 370b

Quadripartite collaboration (WHO, FAO, WOAH, and UNEP), 403, 405–6, 407, 410–12
Quadripartite governance, 249b–50
from Tripartite governance to, 247–50
quarantine, 21–22, 23, 24b, 41b

racial hygiene laws (Nazi Germany), 208, 449, 477
racism, environmental, 246–47
Red Cross. *See* International Committee of the Red Cross
reproductive health. *See also* sexual and reproductive health and rights
defined, 456
right-wing populism, threats of, 461–63
Rio Declaration on Environment and Development, 236–38
Rio Earth Summit. *See* Earth Summit
Roosevelt, Franklin D., 261
Russian invasion of Ukraine, 223b–24, 224f

SARS-CoV-2 (severe acute respiratory syndrome coronavirus 2), 439b, *See also* COVID-19
2002–2004 SARS outbreak, 55–56, 154–55
catalyzing IHR reform, 154–56
China and, 55–56, 154–55
Saudi Arabia, MERS and, 435
securitizing health, 123–24, 131, 154, 160b–61, 378, 488–89. *See also* global health security
beyond WHO, 161–62

selective primary health care, 71, 123–24, 367
  vs. comprehensive care, 528, 528b–29
Selective Primary Health Care agenda, 528b–29
self-regulation. See corporate self-regulation
severe acute respiratory syndrome. See 2002–2004 SARS outbreak
severe acute respiratory syndrome coronavirus 2 (SARS-CoV-2), 439b, See also COVID-19
sexual and reproductive health and rights (SRHR), 447–48, 466–67. See also women's rights
  adolescent, 459, 459b–60
  anti-LGBT bigotry, 463
  conservative backlash to SRHR in global health governance, 462b–63 (see also right-wing populism)
  imperative to decolonize, 465–66
  new arenas of contestation in, 461–66
  from population control to reproductive rights, 448
    advancing women's rights under international law, 452–53
    early population control policies and reproductive health programming, 448–50, 450b
    recognizing women's reproductive health in global health governance, 450–51
  pushing the SRHR agenda forward, 460–61
sexual exploitation and abuse (SEA), UN peacekeepers and, 492–93
sexual orientation and gender identity (SO/GI) issues, 460–61, 462b–63, 464
sexual rights, 456–57. See also sexual and reproductive health and rights
  defined, 456n.4, 458n.5
smallpox, from failed eradication efforts to successful eradication of, 152b
Smallpox Eradication Programme (WHO), 150–51
Snow, John, 551
social determinants of health, intersectionality of global health and, 294–95
Social Determinants of Health, WHO Commission on, 530–32
social inclusion, 293–94
  defined, 294
social justice in global health governance. See also human rights, equity, and social justice
  emergence of, 98–99
soft law, 1, 4–5, 6–7, 34–35, 39
  as basis for global health policy, 47–48
  constructivist legal theories and, 39, 47–48
  contributions to global health law, 46–53
  definition and nature of, 46
  hard law and, 39, 47–49
    bringing hard and soft law together across global governance, 57b–58, 58–60
  in COVID-19 response, 53–58, 57b–58
  HIV/AIDS and, 51–52, 52b, 53
  harnessing soft law beyond WHO, 51–53
  human rights and, 93–94, 94b–95, 95–98
  International Health Regulations (IHR) and, 56–57, 57b–58
  necessity of, in global health governance, 48–49
  non-binding AMR agreements, 402–3
  positivists and, 39, 47
  Sustainable Development Goals (SDGs) and, 276–77
  and WHO's responses to NCDs, 180
  WHO's use of, 33, 34, 46, 49–51, 56–57, 57b–58
soft power, 73, 74
Solferino, Battle of, 475
Soviet Union, 67–68. See also Cold War
Sphere Handbook, 487
Standard Material Transfer Agreements (SMTAs), 431b–32
Stockholm Declaration of 1972, 232–33, 233b–34, 234, 236, 237–38, 241, 411t
structural adjustment policy, health harms of, 289b–90
Supari, Siti Fadilah, 427, 428b
Surveillance System for Attacks on Health Care (SSA), 485b–86, 489–91, 490f
sustainable development, 259–60, 279–80, 297–98
  AMR undermines global progress for, 400–1
  defined, 237–38
Sustainable Development Goal 3 (SDG 3), 265–69
  targets and indicators related to, 266–69, 267t
Sustainable Development Goals (SDGs), 82f, See also 2030 Agenda for Sustainable Development
  advancing UHC to achieve, 536b–37
  as basis for development partnerships, 270b–71
  bringing together human rights, equity, and social justice under, 106
  and calls for UHC, 535–37, 536b–37
  global health law reforms to finance, 278b
  implementing, 298–300

INDEX 567

Millennium Development Goals (MDGs)
and, 80, 81–84, 266–69, 271–72, 298,
299*b*, 457–58, 459*b*–60, 535
monitoring SDG implementation to advance
health through SDG targets and
indicators, 271–72
monitoring through indicators, 273–74
monitoring through institutions, 272–73
overview, 266*f*
as social, economic, and environmental
determinants of health, 269–71
universal health coverage (UHC) and, 532–
33, 535–37, 536*b*–37, 539–40, 540*b*

technology, equitable access to, 518–19
technology transfer, 518–19
Tedros Adhanom Ghebreyesus. *See*
Ghebreyesus, Tedros Adhanom
tobacco, 347. *See also* Framework Convention
on Tobacco Control; vaping
tobacco products. *See also* plain tobacco
packaging
defined, 195
Tokyo Trials, 478n.4
torture program at Guantanamo Bay, litigation
against, 491–92
trade governance, international. *See* WTO
trade law, international, 311–12, 317*t*, 332–33.
See also WTO
evolving international governance to
liberalize trade, 312–19
non-communicable diseases (NCDs)
and, 191–92
rise of, 313–14
Trade-Related Aspects of Intellectual Property
Rights, Agreement on. *See* TRIPS
Agreement
transnational corporations (TNCs)
defined, 345
rise of, 341–44
Triangle Shirtwaist Factory fire, 20
Tripartite collaboration between FAO, OIE, and
WHO, 126
TRIPS Agreement
development of, 318–19
flexibilities, 321–23
human rights challenges, 323–24
obligations under, 319–20
a global standard, 320
overview and nature of, 411*t*
reshapes access to medicines, 319–26
seeking access to medicines under, 324–26
TRIPS waiver in COVID-19 pandemic, 329–31

tropical disease, 22
tropical medicine, 22, 68, 84
tuberculosis (TB), 276, 277. *See also* Global
Fund to Fight AIDS, Tuberculosis and
Malaria

Ukraine
destroyed hospital in, 224*f*
Russian invasion of, 223*b*–24
Unitaid, 325–26
United Nations (UN). *See also specific topics*
birth of, and governance under international
law, 29–30
engagement, 130–31
environmental concerns at, 233*b*–34
establishment of UN-water and UN-
energy, 240–41
first High-Level Meeting on NCDs,
181*b*, 182–83
High-Level Panel on Access to
Medicines, 324
international lawmaking under, 42–45
mainstreaming human rights across
the, 103–5
2010 Resolution on the Human Right to
Water and Sanitation, 242–43
United Nations Charter. *See* Charter of the
United Nations
United Nations Commission on the Status of
Women (CSW), 449
United Nations Conference on Environment
and Development (UNCED), 236
United Nations Development Programme
(UNDP), 261–62, 292
United Nations Economic Commission for
Europe (UNECE), 234–35
United Nations Environment Assembly
(UNEA), 239
United Nations Environment Programme
(UNEP), 234. *See also*
Convention on Biological Diversity;
Quadripartite collaboration
AMR governance and, 405–6
UNEP leadership in environmental
governance, 238–39
United Nations Framework Convention on
Climate Change (UNFCCC), 509–12
Conference of the Parties (COP), 509–10,
511*b*, 513, 517*b*–18
overview and nature of, 507–9
protocols, 509, 510–11, 511*b*, *See also* Kyoto
Protocol; Paris Agreement
WHO and, 513

568 INDEX

United Nations Fund for Population Activities (UNFPA), 449, 450, 455
  birth of, 449, 450, 450*b*
United Nations General Assembly, 82*f*
  resolutions focused on COVID-19, 164*t*
United Nations General Assembly Special Session (UNGASS), 74, 269, 541–42
United Nations Global Compact, 349–51, 350*f*
United Nations Human Rights Council
  resolutions focused on COVID-19, 164*t*
United Nations Interagency Task Force on Prevention and Control of NCDs (UNIATF), 190
United Nations Millennium Declaration, 81, 262, 263*b*–64, 457–58
United Nations Mission for Ebola Emergency Response (UNMEER), 160*b*–61
United Nations peacekeepers and sexual exploitation and abuse, 492–93
United Nations Relief and Rehabilitation Administration (UNRRA), 28, 209
United Nations Security Council (UNSC)
  addressing health in conflict, 487–89
  Ebola and, 74n.4, 131, 160*b*–61, 488–89
  resolutions focused on COVID-19, 164*t*
Universal Declaration of Human Rights (UDHR), 94, 94*b*–95, 304, 341–42, 479–80
universal health coverage (UHC), 525–26, 545–46
  advancing under global health law, 543–45
  as basis for global health security, 542–43
  calls for, 532–33
    early advocacy, 533–34
    Health in All Policies (HiAP), 532–35
    SDGs, 535–37, 536*b*–37
    UHC as human rights imperative, 537–39
  COVID-19 and, 539, 541–42, 543
  defined, 536*b*–37
  as framework for global health governance, 539–45
  SDG 3 and, 269
  SDGs and, 532–33, 535–37, 536*b*–37, 539–40, 540*b*
  2019 UN General Assembly High-Level Special Session on, 269, 541–42
  WHO leadership to advance, 539–42, 540*b*
  WHO takes up UHC as key focus of global health governance, 540*b*
  World Bank's proactive efforts to realize, 297–98
UN-water and UN-energy, establishment of, 240–41

vaccine equity, 329–30, 330*f*
vaccines. *See also* COVID-19 vaccination

public–private partnerships (PPPs) and, 78–79, 138, 358, 369–71, 370*b*
vaping. *See also* electronic nicotine delivery systems
  health risks from rising, 195–96
vertical vs. horizontal health interventions, 2–3
Vienna Declaration and Programme of Action (VDPA), 454
voluntary licenses (medicines), 325

war, 484–85
  law of (*see* international humanitarian law)
  moral condemnation of, 474–75
war crimes. *See also* crimes against humanity
  ICC adjudication for, 493–94, 519
War in the Pacific, 477–78
water
  declaring human rights to, 242–43
  establishment of UN-water, 240–41
  right to, 242–43
    definition and scope of the term, 242–43
water security, climate change and, 504
weather events, extreme, 503. *See also* climate change
Western African Ebola virus epidemic (2013–2016), 295n.6, 378
  changes brought about by, 373
  Coalition for Epidemic Preparedness Innovations (CEPI) and, 374, 374*b*–77
  Convention on Biological Diversity (CBD) and, 436–37
  COVID-19 and, 301–2
  funding and, 373
  International Health Regulations (IHR) and, 160, 160*b*–61
  Pandemic Emergency Financing (PEF) and, 301–2
  pathogen sharing and, 428–29, 436–37
  UN Security Council and, 74n.4, 131, 160*b*–61, 488–89
  WHO and, 133–34, 160–61, 160*b*–61, 373
WHO (World Health Organization), 66.
  See also specific topics
  defining WHO's priorities, 133–35
  Director-General, 30–31, 30*f*, 134–35
    (*see also specific individuals*)
    politics of election and diplomatic role, 127–28
  early challenges facing, 122–23
  early funding, 366–67
  establishment of, 30–33
  from fragmentation in governance to harmonization through, 148–50

and fragmentation of international law in global health, 45–46
functions, 133
Gender, Equity and Human Rights team, 112
global health diplomacy beyond, 129–33
global health diplomacy within, 125–29
as global health leader, 70*b*
governing structure, 30–31, 30*f*
legal authorities: conventions, regulations, and resolutions, 32, 32*b*–33, 33
mission and core functions, 31–32
partnership with World Bank to strengthen global health security, 300–1
political groupings in WHO governing bodies, 126–27
Programme Budget, 135
securitizing health beyond, 161–62
seeks to maintain leadership over chaotic global health landscape, 71–72
use of soft law, 49–51
WHO Commission on Social Determinants of Health, 530–32
WHO Constitution (1946), xi–xii, 30–35, 32*b*–33, 43, 70*b*, 551
adoption of, 30, 43, 122, 149, 552
powers granted to World Health Assembly by, 31, 32, 32*b*–33, 43–44, 149–50
Preamble, xi, 43, 94*b*–95, 209
on WHO's primary function, 133
and WHO's use of soft law, 49–50
WHO Eradication Programmes, 150–53, 152*b*, 366–67
WHO Framework of Engagement with Non-State Actors (FENSA), 128
FENSA Negotiations within WHO, 128*b*–29
women's rights, 447–48. *See also* Convention on the Elimination
of All Forms of Discrimination against Women; sexual and reproductive health and rights
advancements of
in Cairo and Beijing, 453–57
under international law, 452–53
World Bank
Board of Executive Directors, 291*f*, 291
emergence of health, nutrition, and population (HNP) lending at, 290–92
history, 287–88
partnership with WHO to strengthen global health security, 300–1
shifting development funding trajectories, 297–98
World Development Report, 177–78, 262, 290
World Charter for Nature, 235

World Commission on Environment and Development (WCED), 236
World Development Report (World Bank), 177–78, 262, 290
World Health Assembly, 58–59, 127, 135. *See also specific topics*
COVID-19 and, 53–56, 135, 136–37, 163, 165
environmental health and, 240
Intergovernmental Negotiating Body (INB), 137*b*, 331–32, 441
International Health Regulations (IHR) and, xii, 55–56, 57*b*–58, 59, 136–37, 150, 154, 155–56, 162–63, 165
non-communicable diseases (NCDs) and, 178–79, 182–83, 187
overview and nature of, 30–31
powers that WHO Constitution grants to, 31, 32, 32*b*–33, 43–44, 149–50
Soviet Union and, 67–68, 122–23
World Health Organization. *See* WHO
World Meteorological Organization (WMO), 505–8
World Organisation for Animal Health (WOAH), 405–6. *See also Office International des Epizooties*; Quadripartite collaboration
World Trade Organization. *See* WTO
Agreement on Agriculture (AoA), 317*t*
Agreement on Technical Barriers to Trade (TBT), 317*t*, 327*f*, 411*t*, 412–13
Agreement on the Application Sanitary and Phytosanitary Measures (SPS), 317*t*, 411*t*, 412–13
Agreement on Trade-Related Aspects of Intellectual Property Rights. *See* TRIPS Agreement
Agriculture, Agreement on, 317*t*
General Agreement on Trade in Services (GATS), 317*t*
SPS Agreement, 317*t*, 411*t*, 412–13
WTO governance, challenges to, 326–33
World War I, 26, 476–77
World War II. *See also* Holocaust
challenges governance regimes, 27–28
humanitarian responsibilities reframed by, 476–77
health challenges amid wartime atrocities, 477–78
WTO (World Trade Organization), 311–12
accountability, 316

WTO (World Trade Organization), (cont.)
   AMR governance under, 406
   binding nature of WTO agreements, 316
   diplomacy to shift IP governance under, 318b–19
   dispute settlement, 316, 326–27, 327b
      (see also plain tobacco packaging)
   establishment of, 315–18
   range of agreements that impact global health, 317–18
   nationalism and, 328–29

Xi Jinping, 57f

Zika, 435–36
zoonotic threats, antimicrobial resistance (AMR) and, 397b–98